Music
from the Middle Ages
to the Renaissance

PRAEGER HISTORY OF WESTERN MUSIC

GENERAL EDITOR: F. W. STERNFELD

MUSIC
FROM
THE MIDDLE AGES
TO
THE RENAISSANCE

EDITED BY F. W. STERNFELD

PRAEGER PUBLISHERS NEW YORK WASHINGTON

BOOKS THAT MATTER

Published in the United States of America in 1973
by Praeger Publishers, Inc., 111 Fourth Avenue,
New York, N.Y. 10003

Library of Congress Catalog Card Number: 78–190596

Printed in Great Britain

49565

Music Examples

The jacket photograph shows the interior of King's College Chapel, Cambridge (photo: A. F. Kersting).

Contributors

F.W.STERNFELD is Reader in the History of Music at Oxford University where he has been since 1956, and a fellow of Exeter College. He has held teaching and research appointments at various American institutions, including the Wesleyan University, Folger Shakespeare Library, and Princeton Institute for Advanced Study. His books include *Music in Shakespearean Tragedy, Goethe and Music* and *English Madrigal Verse* (jointly with David Greer).

He is Vice-President, and Chairman of the Proceedings Committee, of the Royal Musical Association. He has served as editor of *Renaissance Quarterly*, *New Oxford History of Music* and *English Lute Songs*, and as a contributor to the *New Cambridge Modern History*.

WILLIAM LICHTENWANGER is the Head of the Reference Section of the Music Division at the Library of Congress, Washington DC, and was for a long time editor of *Notes*.

GERALD ABRAHAM is President of the Royal Musical Association and has served as Professor of Music at Liverpool University and at the University of California at Berkeley. His editorial and administrative positions have included: Secretary of the editorial board of the *New Oxford History of Music*, Chairman, *Grove's Dictionary of Music and Musicians*, Chairman, *Early English Church Music*, Assistant Controller of Music, BBC, 1962–7. He has published many books, notably on Slavonic music and has edited a series of books, 'Music of the Masters'.

WOLFGANG BOETTICHER is Professor of Music at the University of Göttingen. He is best known for his work on lute music and on Lassus. His books include *Lasso und seine Zeit* (1958), *Von Palestrina zu Bach* (1959) and *Aus Lassos Wirkungskreis* (1963). He is general editor of two new complete editions now in progress of the works of Lassus and of Schumann.

NANIE BRIDGMAN is Curator of the Music Department of the Bibliothèque Nationale and Vice-President of the *Société Française de musicologie*. Her published works include *La Vie Musicale au Quattrocento* (1962) and *La Musique italienne* (1972).

JOHN CALDWELL is Lecturer in Music at Oxford University. His publications include *Early Tudor Organ Music* (1966) which is volume vi in the series *Early English Church Music* and *English Keyboard Music Before the Nineteenth Century* (to be published in Spring 1973).

SOLANGE CORBIN has been Director of Studies at L'Ecole Pratique des Hautes Etudes at the Sorbonne University since 1958. She has served as Professor of Musicology at the University of Poitiers and has written several books on early medieval music, among them *L'Eglise à la conquête de sa musique* (1960).

DANIEL DEVOTO, who was born in Buenos Aires, has held professorships at the University of Cuyo (Argentina), the Sorbonne, and the Institute of Musicology at the University of Poitiers. He is now *Directeur de Recherche* at the Centre National de la Recherche Scientifique at Paris. His publications about Spanish music and literature include several books and numerous articles.

FEDERICO GHISI was born in Shanghai, but moved to Italy to study at the Turin Conservatoire of Music, and has been living in Florence since 1932. He is Professor of Music History at the Universities of Florence and Pisa. He is known as an authority on Italian Renaissance music and as a composer. His books include *Alle fonti della monodia* (1940) and *Studi e testi di musica italiana* (1971).

ISOBEL HENDERSON was, until her death in 1969, Fellow and Tutor at Somerville College, Oxford. Her many publications are based on her research on Ancient Greece, its culture and its music.

JOSEPH KERMAN is Heather Professor of Music at the University of Oxford. He was formerly Professor of Music at the University of California at Berkeley, also a visiting fellow at several English and American colleges. His books include *Opera as Drama* (1956), *The Elizabethan Madrigal* (1962), a study of William Byrd (in preparation), and *The Beethoven Quartets* (1967).

FRANÇOIS LESURE is head of the Music Department of the Bibliothèque Nationale, Paris; also Professor of Musicology at the University of Brussels. He is a well-known authority on French music of the Sixteenth Century and has edited *Anthologie de la chanson parisienne* (1953), *La Renaissance dans les provinces du Nord* (1956). As Secretary General of the *Répertoire International des Sources Musicales* (RISM), he has published three volumes, and he is now chief editor of the *Revue de musicologie* and President of the *Société française de musicologie*.

PHILIP L. MILLER has served as Chief of the Music Division of the New York Public Library. He has been a member of many committees, American and international, concerned with libraries and *phonothèques*, i.e. repositories of sound recordings. Among his books is the volume on *Vocal Music* in the series *Guide to Long-Playing Records*.

JACK SAGE is Senior Lecturer in Spanish at King's College, London. His publications reflect his research in the history of Spanish song, opera and theatre music, and include *La Música de Juan Hidalgo* (in an edition of *Los Celos Hacen Estrellas by Juan Vélez de Guevara* edited by J.E.Varey and N.D.Shergold), and an article 'Calderón y la música teatral'.

ERNEST H.SANDERS is Professor of Music at Columbia University, where he has taught since 1954. He is an authority on medieval polyphony, with particular reference to English polyphony, about which he has published numerous articles. Several volumes of his editions of medieval music are now in preparation.

DIMITRIJE STEFANOVIĆ received his doctorate at the University of Oxford and is now a member of the Institute of Musicology at Belgrade.

ROBERT STEVENSON is Professor of Music at the University of California at Los Angeles. He is the author of many articles and several books on Spanish and South American Music, including *Spanish Music in the Age of Columbus* (1960).

CHRISTOPHER SWAIN studied at Oxford with Edmund Rubbra and F.W.Sternfeld. He is now Director of Music at Manchester College, Oxford.

PETER WARD JONES is the Music Librarian at the Bodleian Library, Oxford. He has taught at both the Royal College of Music, London, and at Oxford, and his publications include the bibliographies for *New Oxford History*, volume vii, and for Professor Westrup's *Festschrift*.

DAVID WULSTAN is Lecturer in the History of Music at Magdalen College, Oxford. Among his many musical activities he directs the *Clerkes of Oxenford*, a choir which specialises in early music. His publications include volumes in the series *Early English Church Music* and he is the general editor of the series *English Church Music* published by J. and W.Chester.

Abbreviations

The following is a list of bibliographical abbreviations used throughout this book, including footnotes and chapter bibliographies:

Acta: *Acta Musicologica*
AfMF: *Archiv für Musikforschung*
AfMW: *Archiv für Musikwissenschaft*
CMM: *Corpus Mensurabilis Musicae*
Congress: see bibliography, section on Congresses (p. 441)
DDT: *Denkmäler deutscher Tonkunst*
DTB: *Denkmäler der Tonkunst in Bayern*
DTO: *Denkmäler der Tonkunst in Österreich*
Festschrift: see bibliography, section on *Festschriften* (pp. 441–2)
Grove: *Grove's Dictionary of Music*
HAM: *Historical Anthology of Music*
JAMS: *Journal of the American Musicological Society*
LU: *Liber Usualis*
MGG: *Musik in Geschichte und Gegenwart*
ML: *Music and Letters*
MQ: *Musical Quarterly*
Mus. Disc.: *Musica Disciplina*
NOHM: *New Oxford History of Music*
PRMA: *Proceedings of the Royal Musical Association*
SIMG: *Sammelbände der internationalen Musikgesellschaft*
ZfMW: *Zeitschrift für Musikwissenschaft*

Preface

Yet another history of music? But, then, how to make reading *about* music worth while is a problem for which each decade must find a fresh solution. In the beginning was the musical experience. But as these experiences of creating, performing and listening accumulate; as a bewildering variety of styles is offered in concert halls, opera houses and through modern mass media, the moment for reflection arrives – for ruminating about music, for fathoming how music grew to its present state. Armchair analysis, or 'music appreciation', is a possible and, at its best, illuminating approach; but, of necessity, it always remains patchy. It is my belief that to understand the miracle of Western music one must see it as a continuous development from antiquity to the present, to relate it to the civilizations from which it has grown. It is an ambitious undertaking, and he who ventures to succeed the pioneer works of Burney and of Hawkins in the eighteenth century, of Ambros in the nineteenth, of Hadow and Riemann in the early twentieth, is foolhardy indeed. In the Anglo Saxon world the three attempts in recent decades are still incomplete: the 'Norton' history, inaugurated in 1940 with a volume on the Middle Ages by Gustave Reese; the New Oxford History of Music, which began with a volume on ancient and oriental music edited by Egon Wellesz (published in 1957), and the 'Prentice Hall' History (more concise than the others), of which Albert Seay's volume of the Medieval World appeared in 1965.

The invitation to edit a history of music in five volumes, to appear in the 1970s, presented a challenge both frightening and exhilarating. The endeavour has been to produce a work more concise than the Norton and Oxford histories, and to make up for this brevity by homogeneity and various pedagogical devices, learned from one's students over the years. One condition was clear: where experts were willing and available, their voices must be heard. Tempting as it was to write oneself the chapters on, say, Stravinsky or Gregorian chant, such an indulgence would have passed by the magisterial expositions of Eric White and Solange Corbin, to name but two instances. But the total vision which binds these chapters (and volumes) together is mine. It is a view of the growth of music where great composers of various ages and countries are seen as representative of larger developments: Perotin and the Gothic cathedral; Palestrina and the Council of Trent; Cavalli and the establishment of the operatic tradition; Mozart and the Enlightenment; Berlioz and the Romantic sensibility; Stravinsky and Neo-Classicism. These cultural cross-connections are neither forced nor lengthy, nor are they permitted to interfere with the stuff of which music is made, the discussion of 'sharps and flats'. A history of music which loses sight of the music itself must be a failure, and there, one hopes, musical illustrations, bibliographies and discographies will play their role. A good deal of time and thought has been devoted to presenting comprehensive and suggestive bibliographies with a minimum of fuss.

The present volume is a book about major currents in the main stream of music; it is not a dictionary of names. We felt it was the panorama that mattered rather than an exhaustive account of any single composer. For this reason it was inevitable that a few figures, no matter how glorious, would be incompletely covered in a volume primarily concerned with the Middle Ages and Renaissance. Monteverdi is a case in point: it was obvious that his madrigal collections had to be discussed in connection with the golden age of the madrigal in Italy, but the operas, extending to his Venetian period in the 1640s, are of another order. After mature reflection it was decided to leave the prehistory of opera (*intermedi* and other genres) as well as early opera entirely to Volume II. As in Volume V, it was not a question of chronology but one of stylistic affinities.

Again, as in later volumes, the careers of certain composers are so international that it is well-nigh impossible to restrict discussion of their work to a single country. The peregrinations of Stravinsky, Schoenberg and Boulez have their counterparts in the Middle Ages and Renaissance. Indeed, it is one of the fascinating aspects of musical history to note the extreme speed with which innovations and fashions were transferred and copied across the Alps and the Channel centuries before modern transportation was developed. It is equally fascinating to observe the migration of composers from one country to another through the ages, with the consequent changes in the cultural surroundings within which much of their influence was felt. The education of Lassus in Italy (where he became Orlando di Lasso) and his life-long residence in Germany are analogous to the naturalization of Händel (as Handel) in England or to Schönberg's permanent move to America (where he called himself Schoenberg). The result of all this is an abundance of variant spellings which has been a source of confusion to lexicographers and indexers. In the present volume the wanderings of the great composers of Burgundy (or the Low Countries) to Italy and Germany presented considerable problems. Josquin is, for the most part, discussed in Chapter 4.3 on the Low Countries, and Lassus chiefly in Chapter 7 on Germany. But, in the case of Isaac, a split seemed inevitable between the Italian and German chapters. It is hoped that cross-referencing and indexing will assist the reader in a story that is so delightfully

complex that it would remain puzzling whether told in regional or in biographical terms. Ultimately, it seemed that major trends and developments
would be best accommodated in regional terms. This was not exclusively
a question of patronage or the use of the vernacular in secular works. The
importance of certain institutions and particular styles of music-making
and teaching in certain regions created major areas of musical culture
around which most of the chapters have been constructed.

Chapter 3, which deals with the beginnings of polyphony and secular
monophony, proved an exception and called for an international perspective,
but all subsequent chapters have been arranged according to region. A
word should be said about the chronological divisions within these regions.
At times the material permitted an uninterrupted narrative from *c.* 1300
to 1600, for instance in the Italian and German chapters (though for the
sake of expedience the German bibliography is subdivided chronologically).
In other cases (Spain, England) it was felt advisable to separate the material
into sub-chapters which covered earlier and later developments in sequence.
The case of France and Burgundy was more complex. To arrive at a
reasonably true exposition of musical developments in these regions it
was decided to treat the two areas together for the fourteenth and fifteenth
centuries (Chapter 4.1) but to discuss them in separate sub-chapters for
the sixteenth century (Chapters 4.2 and 4.3). Thus, the arrangement is in
accordance with the musical and historical materials available without
doctrinaire preconceptions.

The musical illustrations have not been distributed in a pre-arranged
proportion of music examples to letter-press. Where the music can be
readily located in a reasonable time no examples have been given. But
where an author bases his discussion on unpublished transcriptions of his
own making, or where the discussion of a particular text becomes obscure
to the point of incomprehensibility without the graph of musical notation,
in these cases ample illustrations have been provided. This is particularly
true of early polyphony and of English music. We have taken for granted
the accessibility of the following collections of music:

1. standard anthologies such as Apel-Davison *Historical Anthology* and
the older Schering *Geschichte . . . in Beispielen*, etc.;

2. complete works of composers such as Machaut, Dufay, Josquin,
Palestrina;

3. scholarly collections such as *Musica Britannica*, *Denkmäler deutscher
Tonkunst*, etc.

Music in the perspective of general civilization is an aspect which should
not be overlooked in the thicket of sharps and flats. While facile verbalization
without recourse to the experiences of music itself is pretentious, to gain
an understanding of the music that was composed and performed within a
particular period it becomes necessary to consider its relation to the cultural

and historical setting in which it flourished. Several instances have already been cited; of interest to this volume is the discussion of the Gothic cathedral and Gothic polyphony where contemplation of the architectural proportions illuminate what seems at first sight a bewildering complexity of musical construction. In the twentieth century as well, the search for a new grammar of music is best explained by references to developments in contemporary literature, psychology and philosophy. For this reason a certain amount of space has been allocated to the historical and cultural background of each period, and it is hoped that, with the aid of bibliographical references, the interested student will be led to do further reading. Greek music, Gregorian chant, the Gothic motet, the music of the Reformation and Counter-Reformation, the flowering of secular music at the courts of the Italian Renaissance will thus be seen in their proper context.

The bulk of the bibliography consists of a single alphabetical sequence in which scores, books and articles are listed with complete information about date and place of publication, also about the series to which an item may belong. In addition, each chapter has its separate bibliography, where an effort has been made to have the list of relevant publications brief and easy to skim through. For this reason, in these chapter bibliographies as well as in the footnotes, short 'catch' titles have been given in the case of publications that appear in the complete alphabetical bibliography. These abbreviated titles usually give the author, followed by a noun or adjective descriptive of the title. Einstein's *Italian Madrigal*, 3 vols., Princeton, 1946 (reprinted 1971) is abbreviated as Einstein, *Madrigal*; H.E.Wooldridge's *Early English Harmony*, 2 vols., London, 1897–1913, as Wooldridge, *Early English*; and H.Besseler, ed., *Dufay: Opera omnia* (Corpus Mensurabilis Musicae, i) 6 vols., Rome, 1947–66 as Besseler, *Dufay*. Further details will be found preceding the bibliography (pp. 439–40), but suffice it to say that no effort has been spared to make these abbreviated titles as simple and as lucid as possible. Authors' names and catch words are *not* abbreviated, and alphabetical abbreviations (listed on p. 19 and again on p. 439) have been reduced to a minimum.

Finally, it is a pleasant duty to acknowledge the immense help I have received from others. Several of my former students have helped to pull the material into shape, notably, Peter Ward-Jones (Bodleian Library), Susan Wollenberg (Lady Margaret Hall, Oxford), Richard Kershaw (Aberdeen University), Frank Dobbins (London University) and John Whenham (Birmingham University).

It was a great privilege to have received from so eminent authority as the late Isobel Henderson a draft of her chapter on the music of ancient Greece. David Wulstan of Magdalen College, Oxford, kindly stepped in, completed the draft, brought research up to date, and has added musical illustrations as well as other materials.

William Lichtenwanger of the Library of Congress was always a source of authoritative advice, with particular regard to North and South America. I consulted him, as well, on many other matters, historical and lexicographical. In regard to the music of the Slav countries, I have profited from the advice of Dr Gerald Abraham. As in all my publications, this one, too, has profited from my wife's insistence on plain English and lucid exposition. Such imperfections as remain are entirely due to the rash optimism with which I undertook the task.

F. W. Sternfeld
Oxford, 1972

ISOBEL HENDERSON AND DAVID WULSTAN

1 Introduction: Ancient Greece

INTRODUCTION

HARMONIC SCIENCE

ELEMENTS OF MUSIC IN THE FOURTH CENTURY BC

  THE NOTES

  THE SYSTEMS

  THE TONOI

MUSICAL DOCUMENTS

NOTATION

RHYTHM AND METRE

THE HISTORY OF GREEK MUSIC

INTRODUCTION

Not so long ago the music of Ancient Greece seemed very remote; but because it was thought to be a direct ancestor of our own music, scholars were confident that it would eventually become accessible. Nowadays our view is different. We know of far remoter music. Genuine notation,[1] dating from about 1300 BC, has been found at Ugarit, now Ras-ash-Shamra in Syria. This is not an isolated find: other tablets show that a knowledge of musical theory (including the notation) based on seven diatonic tunings, was probably quite widespread some thousand years before Homer. Research into Jewish chant has shown that one or two surviving pieces may date back as far as the Exodus. A number of features, religious and musical, were borrowed from the Egyptians: Tutankhamun's trumpets are found thinly disguised in the Book of Numbers, and the great hymn of the heretic Akhenaten reappears in the Book of Psalms. Even the names of Moses and

---

1. See Wulstan, 'The Earliest Musical Notation', *Music and Letters*, lii (1971), 365–82, and Wulstan, 'The Tuning of the Babylonian Harp', *Iraq*, xxx (1968), 215–28.

Miriam seem to be Egyptian. What became the national instruments of the Jews, the *kinnor* and *nevel*, have been found mentioned in early Canaanitic texts; and the influence of the Hittites, Sumerians and Babylonians upon the music of Israel is now well attested. In turn, it is today clear that Christian chant was profoundly influenced by Synagogue chant, causing the old assumptions of the predominant (let alone exclusive) influence of the music of Ancient Greece to be weakened.

European archaeology is now showing that not all of the north-western cultural achievements were pale reflections from the Mediterranean. An ancient work dealing with Pythagoras mentions that some of his mathematical and astronomical ideas (those that did not come from the Near East) were borrowed from north-western peoples, a story that has hardly been credited until now; but the detailed examination of megalithic sites has revealed an astronomical and mathematical competence which can hardly be called primitive. The historian Diodorus Siculus described singing and dancing to the sun at the time of the vernal equinox taking place at what he called an 'astronomical temple' whose location is almost certainly Stonehenge. The 'carol' of the Middle Ages is plausibly descended from such ring-dances to the sun; certainly the celtic word *côr* (circle) is a more likely origin of the word (still called *coraule* in the Celtic district of Switzerland) than the Greek word *chōraulēs*.

The influence of Greek theory upon the west, which at first sight seems to be a solid certainty, must also be reassessed. The modal system was inherited (via the Byzantines) from the Near East, not the Greeks. The idea that the modes were scales dies hard, but its logic is rather difficult to maintain: eight modes (the number had a magical, not musical, significance) could only be wrested from the seven possible scales by a series of equi-vocations.[2] By naming these bastard mode-scales after the Greek *tonoi*, they were purportedly given a respectable parentage; but the confusion was increased because the *tonoi* were *tunings* not scales, and their names were applied in an upside-down order.

If the influence of Greek music upon that of the west is not as great as was once supposed, it has been by no means negligible. Through theory the influence has been primarily philosophical; but the practical inheritance is evident in at least one important field, that of metre. Even were this not so, a study of the voluminous literature of such a civilized people, enlivened by some precious musical fragments, would be fascinating enough for its own sake; but, perhaps more important, such a study provides a window on the music of the ancient world in general.

The chronological relationship between the literary, philosophical and musical sources is shown in the following table:

2. See Wulstan, 'The Origin of the Modes', *Studies in Eastern Chant* ii (1971), 5–20.

	Poets and dramatists	Historians, philosophers and theorists
Before 700 BC	Homer Hesiod	
Seventh century BC	Archilochus Alcaeus Sappho Stesichorus	
Sixth century BC	Anacreon	Pythagoras
Fifth century BC	Pindar Aeschylus Sophocles Euripides Aristophanes	Herodotus
Fourth century BC	Philoxenus Timotheus	Plato Aristotle Aristoxenus
Third century BC	Callimachus	Euclid
Second century BC		Dionysius of Halicarnassus
First century BC		Pseudo-Plutarch Aristeides Quintilianus
First century AD		
Second century AD		Ptolemy Pseudo-Aristotle
Third century AD and later		Alypius Hephaestion

The Greeks kept their literature as a possession, often diminished, but never out of living memory, from Homer to the fall of Constantinople. Their music had not the same fortune. Twice at least within the period of antiquity the tradition was interrupted and the past forgotten. As a rough and ready guide, four stages in its history can be distinguished:

1. Of archaic music, from the eighth century BC to the late sixth, much was no doubt superseded and discarded, but some survived into stage 2.

2. The classical period proper, which may be schematically concluded at the fall of Athens in 404 BC. Between these two stages, in spite of great changes and innovations, there was no breach of continuity. The true classical tradition, exactly mirrored by Aristophanes in his *Frogs* of 405 BC, comprehended both brand-new music and the best of the old in perpetual rivalry and interplay.

3. From the later fifth century a new movement challenged the classical conventions and idioms, culminating in the musical revolution of Philoxenus and Timotheus. Talented and intolerant, they repudiated the past and, as Plato saw, swept away the old standards of judgement. Aristoxenus, the great professor of music, observed about 320 BC that few musicians now had ever heard the classical styles or could master their tonality. The two revolutionaries became classics in their turn, unrivalled in popular taste until, during the second century BC, their influence receded and died out.

Some diluted flavour of their style may perhaps linger in the two extant paeans of the later second century, from Delphi.

4. Of the music of later antiquity we know little except that it had ceased to be a fine art and became a background concomitant of shows, mimes, ceremonies, processions and banquets. Only Mesomedes, exploiting the Greek fashions of Hadrian's court, made any pretension to classic calibre. Music was a mere manual skill, a low occupation in the social order, no longer a matter for serious discussion. Consequently we are told almost nothing of its nature during this long period. From the extant musical fragments, however, it can be inferred that a diatonic note-series had superseded the chromatic of stage 3, interposing another break with past tradition.

For this decline of music the prime cause lies in the history of education. In the first two stages poetry and music were twins of one birth; the poet was also the composer. Big compositions of the classical period were normally given only one public performance; therefore, though composers may have used some cipher to write their music down, they had no particular need to keep the record. In fact their vocal music was transmitted first by the chorus of citizens, who learned it by ear and by heart, then by private singing of favourite works at parties, at home and at school. Plato, in the fourth century, still advocates the classical method of teaching as follows:

. . . The lyre should be used together with the voices, for the clearness of its strings, the player and the pupil producing note for note in unison. Heterophony and embroidery by the lyre – the strings throwing out melodic lines different from the *melodia* which the poet composed; crowded notes where his are sparse, quick time to his slow, high pitch to his low, whether in concert or antiphony, and similarly all sorts of rhythmic complications of the lyre against the voices – none of this should be imposed upon pupils who have to snatch out a working knowledge of music rapidly in three years.[3]

There are two points to be considered here:

1. The lesson is entirely oral. On Greek vases instrumental players never read music; and if a singer holds a scroll (which is rare), there is no evidence that it contained notation as well as words.[4] While words or names are often written on vases, a tune coming out of a singer's mouth is represented not by notational signs but by little bubbles.[5] We first hear of notation in the fourth century BC, and then only for harmonic theory, not for practical performance.[6]

---

3. *Laws*, 812 d. (In citations of Greek authors, the numbers refer to the numbered sections of standard editions.)

4. Vase of *c.* 457 BC (Fitzwilliam G 73).

5. British Museum hydria E 171 (*Corpus Vasorum* pl. 76, 2).

6. Aristoxenus, *Harmonics*, 39. In late antiquity Alypius gives descriptions of the cipher as if it were unfamiliar.

2. The instrumental accompaniment is not the composer's own, but the teacher's, free and heterophonic (i.e. not structurally polyphonic but the simultaneous use of slightly modified versions of the same melody by two performers, e.g. a melody accompanied by its own decorated variant). Plato fears that it will distract the beginner from the composer's vocal line. Some classical works (e.g. Pindar's odes) were elaborately orchestrated for strings, wind and dancers; but once the unique public performance was over, the instrumental parts expired. The classics consisted of vocal melodies, remembered and repeated by the citizen's voice to his private lyre or with a hired wind-player. The accompaniment was a decorative improvisation, not a stable element of the work; and the effect of instruments on musical practice (often exaggerated in modern treatments) was subordinate, except for a brief moment of the revolution. Instrumental music therefore was even less in need of notation than vocal. Theorists of late antiquity, indeed, distinguished the two Greek notations as 'vocal' and 'instrumental'; but they are not so used in the Delphic paeans, and the distinction is so senseless that its basis may be doubted. Archaeological evidence, at any rate, is solidly against the idea that players used written parts.[7] This is one of the weakest points in the hypothesis that the notations were tablatures.[8]

In the fifth century books were relatively scarce; educated Greeks could not only read but learned by ear, often helped by the link between poetry and music. But from the fourth century the literary inheritance of Greece was industriously collected and stored in writing. Its bulk was outgrowing oral memory, and new classes in a wider Greek world were aspiring to culture – or to the social status which it conferred. A public repertoire was created, in which revived classical tragedies were performed not once, but many times. Then, if ever, we should have expected the transcription of music to become common practice. In fact, it did not. In the early part of this century it seemed possible that quantities of Greek music might be recovered from papyri. On the contrary, the accumulation of more and more papyri has only proved that music was seldom written down and was not included in the staple Alexandrian editions which preserved and diffused the poetry.

We possess some forty written pieces of which only just over half can be regarded as being genuinely old. Three are engraved on stone for special occasions – as prize-winning compositions at Delphi or as an epitaph on a tombstone. In manuscript, there are some pieces and a few brief excerpts transmitted from ancient and Byzantine theoretical treatises; and of the papyri which are more than scraps, it is striking that they often contain

7. Representations on vases are very numerous. See also Antiphanes in Athenaeus 618 b, for a duet played by ear (if the text is rightly read).

8. Against C. Sachs, *ZfMW* (1924/5), 289 ff., see the convincing arguments of R. P. Winnington-Ingram in 'Tuning'.

short extracts, not whole works. This suggests that they were collected in some theoretical textbook as examples or illustrations, and strengthens the impression that when music was written at all it was for some more special purpose than simply to preserve it. Certainly the ancient scholars who saved the classical Greek literature from perishing took no interest in the music.

Here one curious problem should be mentioned. A papyrus of the third century BC contains a few lines from the *Orestes* of Euripides (408 BC), with notation. Is this music the original or a later setting?[9] Three lines of the text are given by the papyrus in a different order from the manuscripts, which represent ancient editions. As the text stands, the order of the papyrus seems to be corrupt, and the setting unlikely to be the original. But a recent and plausible emendation seems to vindicate the papyrus order against the ancient editors.[10] It would now seem possible – rather than probable – that the music was the original. Supposing that it was, however, we could only conclude that it was a freak survival, too little known to establish the order of lines (as familiar music should do) and ignored by editors as a factor in their textual reconstruction. Ancient scholarship, in fact, betrays no concern with musical notation; the learned Isidore of Seville writes as though it had never been invented;[11] and the assumption that it was taught in Hellenistic schools has no basis.[12] The purpose of Alexandrian editors was to produce books for reading; and reading in antiquity meant reading aloud, which was physically incompatible with singing and acting.

Notation is neither necessary nor, without practice, adequate for preserving music; yet classical music would no doubt have been written down if notation had been known and studied in this period of book-learning. Instead we find a sharp and significant contrast. Ancient writers are full of quotations and minute discussions of the words of classical poets, but they have left us only one allusion to a musical text.[13] For post-classical music the silence is no less striking. An early papyrus of Timotheus' *Persae*, the most famous musical work of two centuries, transcribes the words alone. The causes of this situation can be traced. In fifth-century Athens music was essential to a gentleman's education, and the theatre had been the school of the illiterate poor; composers new or old were brilliantly criticized on the comic stage. But Athens had fallen in 404 BC. Defeat was followed by revolution and impoverishment; in Aristophanes' post-war comedies the chorus is cut down to a minimum and plays down to the popular taste for

9. E.G.Turner, 'Papyri'. Dionysius of Halicarnassus (*De compositione verborum*, 11 and 19) refers to a setting of this play but could not know its date. It is unlikely that he had seen it himself; he did not look up documents.

10. Longman, 'Papyrus' (but he perhaps assumes too easily that the music is Euripidean).

11. *Etymologiae* III, 15, 2 (seventh century AD): though he may have been referring to the fact that music, when written down, cannot express every nuance of vocal inflexion.

12. See Marrou, 'Melographia'.

13. See above, fn. 9.

vulgar songs and rhythms. The masses were captured by the showmanship of the new virtuosi, Philoxenus and Timotheus. Military and political failure was widely blamed on wrong education, especially in music. In victorious Sparta (it was argued) gentlemen listen but do not perform; the same was true in Macedon. A rising middle class now associated practical music with professionals, who were normally not citizens but aliens.

During the fourth century a new academic ladder was constructed for the citizen. Aristotle, arguing the current question whether music, like cookery, could be judged by the consumer, or needed practice, pleaded that a little practice was not vulgarizing unless citizens learned the 'professional instruments'; but he too thought that fifth-century Athenians had overdone it.[14] Music was reduced to three (and later to two) years of the child's elementary lessons. The adult musical criticism of Aristophanes' Athens never returned; the citizen dropped out of the chorus; presently the poet stopped composing his own music. On the other hand, the professional musician, once capable of great poetry, wrote bad verse or none. His technique was high and drew enthusiastic crowds, but he was not of a social class to receive the new education, and sank to the level of a mere entertainer, despised for living on 'manual work'. The revolutionary composers had deliberately aimed at easy sensation without mental effort, and their big, noisy audiences enjoyed it, but concluded that music (as they knew it) was not a matter to be taken seriously. As a modern scholar puts it, music became a 'recessive characteristic' in Greek culture;[15] and only for brief periods has it regained its social prestige in western civilization. This was the parting of the ways between music and letters.

HARMONIC SCIENCE

The main subjects of the higher education were rhetoric, philosophy and the four mathematical sciences, of which one was *harmonics*. When practical music ceased to count among the liberal arts, harmonics was often called by the name of *mousikē* or *musica*, but it was a different subject, taught at a later stage of the student's curriculum. It had no connection with harmonics or harmony in the modern sense; it meant tuning, but the implications were wider. It had begun with Pythagoras in the sixth century BC, not as a theory of musical art but as an inquiry into the nature of the universe. In experimental science the Greeks, somewhat like modern physicists, attempted to translate material data into mathematical terms. They were not able to measure light or heat, but they discovered that musical sound could be expressed by the numerical ratios of intervals on a stretched string. Here the ideal relation between matter and numbers seemed attainable, and they took

14. Aristotle, *Politics*, 1339a–1342b.
15. Marrou, *Education*, p. 194.

harmonics as a clue to the general structure of the cosmos. '*L'on comprend que toute la pensée antique en soit demeurée fascinée. . . . Comment douter après cela que le nombre ne soit l'armature secrète du cosmos, que tout dans l'univers ne soit nombre?*'[16]

The original purpose of harmonics was to explain the astronomical world on principles supposed to be revealed in acoustic facts, and this was still Ptolemy's aim when he revived Alexandrian theory in the second century AD, ending like most complete harmonic treatises with an astronomical section. The Music of the Spheres, picturing the astronomical firmament as a scale of tetrachords, was an early expression of this hypothesis. It set the problem of attaining a theoretically satisfying scale, not for musical performance but as a principle of nature. The independent value of harmonic science was unquestioned. It was enshrined in the *quadrivium* of mathematical arts; it acquired a mystical significance in woolly minds and its bare terminology was repeated with pious veneration. Yet it inspired some fine mathematical work as well as an intolerable amount of nonsense. By its own criteria it could be good or bad, but, with one exception, its concern was not the art of music.

The exception was Aristoxenus, son of a professional musician of Tarentum. He knew the musical classics, and in fourth-century Athens he learned from Aristotle's inductive method to analyse music from real experience. But no authorized canon of his works was kept; of the 453 books ascribed to him not all were his.[17] Nor did his method survive. He had started from the realistic principle of the voice in free melodic motion, irreducible to fixed numerical terms, but known by 'ear and understanding' of intervals and their melodic functions. His successors, awed by the prestige of numbers, reverted to the theoretical harmonist's cult of equations calculated on the fixed tuning of the strings – in particular, a linear measurement by units, which Aristoxenus himself had rejected. The doctrine known as 'Aristoxenian' to Ptolemy, six centuries later, is much corrupted by such accretions, and cannot be accepted uncritically.[18] The *Harmonics*, however, though it has reached us in a jumbled and fragmentary state, does represent his authentic teaching. For the abstract ratios of the harmonist's laboratory[19] he substitutes the practical assumptions of the musician's ear. 'Consonances', i.e. the melodic progressions to the fourth, fifth and octave, could be judged by the ear exactly, or within a hair's breadth; other intervals were 'dissonant' or

16. Marrou, *Education*, p. 250; cf. Marrou, *Augustin*, pp. 197 ff.

17. Wehrli, *Aristoxenes*, attempts no historical criticism (e.g. fragment 124, among many, is obviously anachronistic).

18. See Düring, *Ptolemaios*. Fake manuals on technical subjects were common, especially in the Aristotelian school.

19. A *kitharoid* apparatus was used to measure intervals. To suppose that harmonists were observing tonalities in musical practice is to mistake their purpose.

variable, and lesser variations could be defined (so far as the ear demanded) by recognized 'shades' (*chroai*).[20] These principles can best be understood in their application to the basic figures of fourth-century Greek music, clearly expounded by Aristoxenus.

ELEMENTS OF MUSIC IN THE FOURTH CENTURY BC

THE NOTES. The melodic unit, and the basic scheme of analysis, was the tetrachord, *a—e* read downwards. (Letters of the alphabet in italics indicate pitch. Throughout this chapter relative, not absolute, pitch values are to be understood.) It could be paired with an upper tetrachord, either disjunct (*diazeugmenōn*), as in *e'—b//a—e*, or conjunct (*synēmmenōn*) as in *d'—a—e*. These are the elementary fourths and fifths pivoting on the 'fixed notes'. In the disjunct figure the fixed notes are called, in the descending order given, *nētē*, *paramesē*, *mesē*, *hypatē*; in the conjunct, *nētē*, *mesē*, *hypatē* (the function *nētē* being lowered by a tone, while *paramesē* drops out with the disjunctive tone).

The tetrachord was filled in with two 'movable notes', whose variety was classified into three *genera*. In the *enharmonic genus* of the original tetrachord the higher movable note, *lichanos*, lay about two tones below *mesē*, in the region of *f*, and the remaining interval *f—e* was split into two microtones (collectively called the *pyknon*) by the lower movable note *parypatē*. In the *chromatic*, *lichanos* lay round about *f* sharp and the *pyknon*, split by *parypatē*, was therefore larger. In the *diatonic*, *lichanos* lay round about *g* and *parypatē* about *f*. In the upper tetrachord, the corresponding movable notes were called *paranētē* and *tritē*. The names are mostly adjectives of the implied noun *chordē* (a string or simply a note) and also refer to the action of the hand playing: e.g., *lichanos* means 'forefinger'; *hypatē* means 'highest' to the hand on the tilted *kithara*, and *nētē* 'lowest' (although in pitch *hypatē* is the bottom note and *nētē* the top).

This double tetrachord is only a skeleton; in our written melodies, other notes can also be inserted. An essential principle of the music lay in the contrast of the fixed notes, bounding firmly consonant progressions, with the flexibility of the intervals between. Nothing could be further from the modern principle of tuning. Even in the diatonic genus the notes within the tetrachord are still movable or (in the Pythagorean version of the scale) transgress just intonation by using two full $9:8$ notes – e.g. *a—g* plus *g—f*, with what is left of the perfect fourth of the tetrachord (e.g. an interval appräaching *f—e*). This small 'remnant' of the tetrachord is called a *leimma* or *limma*.[21] Of the fixed notes, *mesē* had a certain priority in works of

20. E.g. Aristoxenus recognizes two 'shades' of *lichanos* in each *genus* (see below, p. 56).
21. See Winnington-Ingram, 'Aristoxenus', pp. 195 ff.

theory, but in practice it seems that a balance was maintained between the oscillating fourths and fifths; certainly no note seems to have assumed the function of the 'tonic' in our system. Indeed, the uniform octave was not an element in Greek music since two tetrachords might be of different *genera*. The unit was, and remained, the tetrachord.[22]

THE SYSTEMS. The extended note-systems drawn up in the fourth century were diagrams of harmonic theory, not elements of music, but they were partly based on musical experience. The Greater Perfect System (see example 1a) comprised two conjunct tetrachords separated by a disjunctive tone, with a bottom note (*proslambanomenos*) added to complete the double octave. It provided a convenient nomenclature for academic reference (e.g. the top note was *nētē hyperbolaiōn*; the *genus* could be specified). The Lesser Perfect System (see example 1b) exhibited three conjunct tetrachords to illustrate the mechanisms of a modulation to the fourth above.

Example 1a. The Greater Perfect System

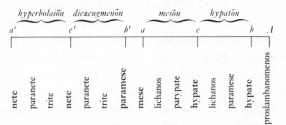

Example 1b. The Lesser Perfect System

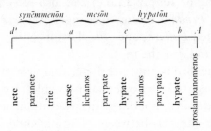

These Systems were abstractions, having no real pitch, employed to map out the degrees of harmonic and acoustic space, not the sounds of melody. No extant piece of Greek music comes near a range of two octaves. Yet the scale-form is a schematized extension of the note-series used in fourth-century music, as we see from Aristoxenus. It was called the Dorian form. There is some reason to believe that it was descended from the classical

22. E.g. in late Greek solmization, *a g e f* (relative pitch) is rendered by *te to te ta*.

tuning known as Dorian, with the difference that the classical tuning was enharmonic, while the fourth-century version was chromatic.[23]

The Lesser Perfect System was a rationalization of the use of *metabolai*, or modulations of various kinds, which was a novel and notorious feature of the post-classical revolution. Again, a diagram for cosmological speculation must not be confused with the act of modulation by performers. The point is simply that the Systems incorporate some elements which, though schematized and turned to non-musical purposes, are derived from musical practice of the fourth century, continuing probably until the end of the second. Even in this period harmonic theory deviates from music in opting for a diatonic sequence, which has become the standard and changeless scale-form of harmonic theory. For later times we have no clear evidence to determine whether this form still bears any relation to contemporary music.

Although the different natures of mathematical harmonics and practical music were demonstrated thirty years ago, scholars are not yet agreed as to which terms and concepts belong to which subject. The greatest difficulty is that, with the ejection of music from higher education in the fourth century, many ancient writers themselves confused their terms, or used them without a glimmer of musical understanding. They can be sorted out only by careful attention to the usage of archaic and classical poets, who were musicians, and musically intelligent prose-writers in the fourth century – Plato and Aristoxenus, and, to some degree, Aristotle; thereafter, hardly any.

THE TONOI. The musical fact of modulation was translated into harmonic theory by transposing the scale-form of the System to other degrees of the System's own register. The transposed scales were called *tonoi* (tunings). The term is never found in an unequivocally musical sense; e.g. musicians are not said to compose in a *tonos*, as though in a key or 'mode'.[24] Since the System itself is pitchless, one can assume that the *tonoi* transposing it have no real pitch; and, as far as concerns the *tonoi* reconstructed by Ptolemy from much earlier Alexandrian theory, this is generally agreed (example 2).

The basic scale of the System is set up vertically on the left; the double tetrachord $e'-e$, which is its core, is printed in capitals, with its *mesē* (*a*) in italics. Seven *tonoi* then transpose the same scale to the seven diatonic degrees. The core of each, printed in capitals, has the same sequence of tones and semitones TTSTTTS. (T is used here as an abbreviation for 'tone', S for 'semitone'.) The System is treated:

1. as a moving scale-form;
2. as a static register around which this scale is borne by the revolving *tonoi*.

23. See below, p. 57.
24. Except where *tonos* is obviously misused for *harmonia* or *tropos* (e.g. pseudo-Plutarch, *De musica*, 8 and 11).

Accordingly, the System's nomenclature is used in a double sense:

1. like our *tonic sol-fa*, to describe notes by their function (*dynamis*) in the uniform basic scale, whatever its *tonos*;

2. as a term of reference to notes by their position (*thesis*) on the System's static register.

Example 2. The basic scale of the System

		Mixolydian	Lydian	Phrygian	Dorian	Hypolydian	Hypophrygian	Hypodorian
a		A	a	a	a	a♯	a	a
g		G	G♯	g	g	g♯	g♯	g
f		F	F♯	F♯	f	f♯	f♯	f♯
E		E	E	E	E	e	e	e
D		D^T	$D♯^s$	D^T	D^T	$D♯^s$	d^T	d^T
C		C^T	$C♯^T$	$C♯^s$	C^T	$C♯^T$	$C♯^s$	c^T
B		$B♭^T$	B^T	B^T	B^s	B^T	B^T	B^s
A		A^s	A^T	A^T	A^T	$A♯^s$	A^T	A^T
G		g^T	$G♯^s$	G^T	G^T	$G♯^T$	$G♯^s$	G^T
F		f^T	$f♯^T$	$F♯^s$	F^T	$F♯^T$	$F♯^T$	$F♯^s$
E		e^s	e^T	e^T	E^s	E^T	E^T	E^T
d		d	d♯	d	d	D♯	D	D
c		c	c♯	c♯	c	c♯	C♯	C
b		b♭	b	b	b	b	b	B
a		a	a	a	a	a	a	a
mese		D	C♯	B	A	G♯	F♯	E

In the Dorian *tonos* the *A* in italics is *mesē* both by *dynamis* and by *thesis*. In the Phrygian, the *B* in italics is *mesē* by *dynamis*, but by *thesis* it stands at *paramesē* of the static System. But the diatonic System has neither place nor name for the Phrygian *paramesē* at *C sharp*. It can only be described as '*paramesē* in this *tonos*'. Each *tonos* therefore had to be named for reference, and defined in its relative position to other *tonoi*.

Our keys are designated A, B, C etc. by their tonics in the note-series of the musical usage to which they belong, although it is not necessarily true that music written in the *key* of C is higher or lower than that written in A, for two tunes in A and C may use the same register. Ptolemy's *tonoi* belonged to no musical usage and had no pitch. Being abstract figures of a mathematical discipline, they had to be related by inherent and independent logic. They were related by reference to the central octave *e′ −e* (by *thesis*), in which they meet and are logically comparable. Within this octave, set between horizontal lines, each *tonos* casts a different segment or *species* of the octave. The first casts the sequence TTTSTTS. This sequence, and the *tonos* which it presupposes, were named the Mixolydian. Most of these names had belonged to musical idioms which were obsolete in the fourth century, and musically ignorant harmonists confused these idioms with the octave-species.[25] It is, however, obvious that the species are artificial sections of the one standard scale and are produced inevitably by the projection of the *tonoi* on the System. Their nature is mathematically self-evident and self-sufficient. It requires more faith than most scholars nowadays possess to believe that they also happened to coincide with the 'modes' of historical music.

Since there are seven species, the logical number of *tonoi* is seven – correctly projected at the sequence of *mesai* equivalent to *d*, *c sharp*, *b*, *a*, *g sharp*, *f sharp*, *e*. If extra *tonoi* are inserted at the intermediate semitones, they will fail by a semitone to touch the central octave's terminals *e′* and *e*. Some theorists did place *tonoi* on consecutive semitones, where they wear a superficial likeness to the scales of modern pitch-keys; and on this analogy it has been supposed that they represented an agreed convention of pitch-values in music. But Ptolemy argues against them on grounds of pure logic, which would be irrelevant if their purpose was the practical expression of pitches.[26] No ancient author suggests that there were two types of *tonoi*, one abstract and the other practical. The existence of practical pitch-keys has been inferred from the statement of a late metaphysical speculator, Aristides Quintilianus, that the Dorian *tonos* serves for the lower activities of the voice, the Phrygian for the middle, and the Lydian for the higher; but as the three lie only one tonal degree apart from one another, the remark makes no more sense than if it were said of the keys of C, D and E.[27] There are other formidable objections to the hypothesis that *tonoi* were ever pitch-keys. Aristoxenus gives lists of *tonoi* from two schools of contemporary theory, as shown in example 3.

Example 3. The ascending order of relative pitch

I Hypophrygian	II Hypophrygian
(no interval stated)	3/4 tone
Hypodorian	Hypodorian
1/2 tone	3/4 tone
Mixolydian	Dorian
1/2 tone	1 tone
Dorian	Phrygian
1 tone	3/4 tone
Phrygian	Lydian
1 tone	3/4 tone
Lydian	Mixolydian

25. E.g. the ponderous polymath Heraclides Ponticus (mid-fourth century BC), cited by Athenaeus, *Deipnosophistae*, ed. C.B.Gulick (Loeb Library), 324e–5c. Aristoxenus briefly refers to the confusion in *Harmonics*, 36. To avoid it he calls the Phrygian *harmonia* a 'melos' (*canto*).

26. *Harmonics*, II, 11.

27. *Ptolemy*, ed. Jahn, p. 16; Winnington-Ingram, *Mode*, p. 23.

It is obvious that no common pitch-standard existed, at least among the theorists. If the two Dorians were the same, the two Mixolydians would differ by three tones. Besides, Aristoxenus says that the second school took their intervals from the bored stops of pipes.[28] Alternative and anomalous nomenclatures of *tonoi* persist throughout antiquity. The pitch-standard cannot be maintained without consistent terms of reference to the pitches of notes or keys; but neither the names nor the numbers of the *tonoi* were ever agreed. Placed on semitones, they were sometimes capped with an illogical thirteenth at the octave[29] and sometimes increased to fifteen for the mere pleasure of arranging *tonos*-names in triads (e.g. Hypodorian, Dorian, Hyperdorian).

One argument for a common pitch-standard is based on the notational sequences in extant pieces. If the notation implied no fixed pitches, we might have expected to find all our pieces written:

1. within the same range of signs, for use at any pitch required;

2. as far as possible in those Greek signs which we render as 'naturals', with a minimum of 'sharps'.

As to (1), all our pieces, with one inconclusive exception,[30] do lie within a central nucleus of signs covering a thirteenth (as contrasted with three octaves and one note covered by the complete notation). But as to (2), three pieces could have been written with a slight economy of 'sharps' in a different sequence; and it is argued that the choice of sequence was determined by the pitch-value of the signs. Yet the point is weakened by a modern preconception. Our sharps are harder to read than naturals. In Greek notation this was not so; for instance, the 'natural' sign M is no easier to read than its 'sharp' sign K. There was no contrast between a simple natural series and complicating sharps. A transcriber need not therefore take particular pains to avoid 'sharp' signs. It was perhaps more desirable for him to stay within the central nucleus of signs made familiar by common use.

A priori, it would be surprising if a convention of pitch-values existed in Greek music which lacked the conditions that have lately developed the animal perception of absolute pitch into a conscious standard – harmony and part-writing, extensive registers and keyboards recording a wide and stable gamut. In fact no unequivocal reference to such a standard is found in ancient sources; on the contrary, pitch is discussed in relative terms.[31] Some of the archaic and classical idioms of music (*harmoniai*), for instance,

28. Aristoxenus, *Harmonics*, 37.

29. This system was later, and incredibly, imputed to Aristoxenus, whose authentic treatment of *tonoi* has not survived.

30. The five notes of the Ajax fragment in the Berlin papyrus lie in the fifth above this nucleus, but may have been a short high passage within some work of wider compass than others now surviving.

31. It is possible, however, that in practice at least local pitch-standards existed, through the use of instruments of relatively stable pitch such as the *aulos*.

were associated with high or low pitches; but since the high Mixolydian could be sung by men as well as women, its pitch was relative to the voice. Attempts to read modern pitch-keys into the *tonoi* have not been corroborated by the evidence. The *tonoi* had no place in practical music; it is only through ignorance that some textbooks of late antiquity call them *tropoi* – a term properly meaning a musical style.[32]

Even on the assumption that the *tonoi* were pitch-keys, the modern habit of describing a written piece of Greek music as 'in the X *tonos*' has nothing to recommend it. By chance, our knowledge of Greek notation is derived from textbooks which use it to transcribe. the *tonoi*. To say that a piece is 'in the Hypolydian *tonos*' means no more than that the notes preserved occur in some segment of that *tonos*.

MUSICAL DOCUMENTS

Forty musical fragments have by now been discovered; they are collected in E. Pöhlmann's *Denkmäler Altgriechischer Musik* (1970).[33] Of these, some are of the last two or three centuries BC, others belong to the early centuries of this era, while at least a third must be suspected of being forgeries.

Three of these pieces are engraved on stone (for extracts, see the discussion on notation in the next section):

1. The 'First Delphic Hymn' or paean to Apollo, our longest piece, was composed almost certainly in the later second century BC and written on stone at Delphi, where it had presumably won a prize at the Pythian festival (see example 6). The paean celebrates Apollo and the Dragon (or Python), a theme which went back to the archaic 'Pythian Nome' and was revived by sixteenth-century precursors of Italian opera. The words and the occasion are academic; the music, too, seems archaic. A decorative tremolo or flourish of notes on one syllable was parodied by Aristophanes as a modernism of Euripides; here it is a cliché. It is used in particular to suggest the flickering of flames and the wavering flourishes of woodwind (see the translation of example 6). Timotheus, in his *Persae*, had featured sound-effects of the Battle of Salamis and set a fashion for programme music. Possibly this paean retains some faint echo of his style, which had lately lost its long influence over Greek music. (It is written in vocal notation.)

2. The 'Second Delphic Hymn', composed by one Limenius of Athens in 128-7 BC, is a very similar vocal piece (though written in the 'instrumental' notation). One passage refers to its performers, the Athenian musicians' union of (as they here call themselves) 'the great enraptured holy hive of artists of Bacchus, dwelling in the city of Cecrops'.

32. Aristoxenus uses the term *tropos* in its proper musical sense.
33. There are extensive discussions with the transcriptions of each piece; although several criticisms might be levelled against it on matters of detail, it is an excellent book with a good bibliography.

3. The 'Epitaph of Seikilos', from Aidin in Turkey, was engraved on a tombstone which has been dated on epigraphical grounds as of the first century AD.

Of almost equal fame to these inscribed pieces is:

4. The famous 'Hymns of Mesomedes' to the Muse, to the Sun and to Nemesis were first published by Vincenzo Galilei in 1581, from some Byzantine treatise of musical theory. A related source transmits the words of two of these hymns and of some metrically similar poems without music but with Byzantine annotations about the musical settings.[34] In one case the annotation so misfits the poem that the setting cannot have belonged to it in antiquity. The question arises whether the settings of the hymns were composed by Hadrian's court musician Mesomedes in the second century AD or by some Byzantine scholar. For the hymn to the Muse, at least, an ancient origin has been argued from the relation of musical pitch to speech-accent; yet it is not consistent enough to decide the question. The Byzantine annotator shows enough knowledge of ancient *tonoi* and notation to try the experiment. The figure of Mesomedes interested Byzantium; these hymns are certainly not his published 'nomes'.[35] The other pieces found in late sources (such as the settings of Pindar and a Homeric hymn published by Kircher and Marcello) attract even graver doubt as to their authenticity.

The genuine papyri can be briefly catalogued:[36]

5. P. Zenon (*c*. 250 BC): a few words, perhaps from a tragedy.

6. P. Vienna (250–150 BC): lines 338–44 of Euripides' *Orestes* (see example 8, p. 50).

7. Another P. Vienna of the same date: two extracts from a tragedy, one from a comedy; four minor fragments, same date or slightly later.

8. The Oslo papyrus, of the second century AD: two extracts from tragedies or dramatic monologues, one Hellenistic, the other perhaps a classical work redecorated with later music.

9. P. Oxyrhynchus (second century AD): lines perhaps from a satyr-play.

10. P. Michiganensis (second century AD): one or two fragmentary texts.

11. P. Berlin (after AD 156): five short heterogeneous extracts.

NOTATION

The two Greek notations are set forth in late antiquity by a certain Alypius, in the form of fifteen *tonoi* on consecutive semitones. The continuous series of signs is here abstracted from the *tonoi* and shown with the corresponding diatonic note-series, written in our staff for convenience, but with no implication of pitch (see example 4). The letters follow in continuous descent,

34. 'Codex Ottobonianus 59' (thirteenth century).
35. Dio Cassius LXXVII, 12 (through the Byzantine excerptor Xiphilinus).
36. For extensive references, see Pöhlmann's *Denkmäler*, cited above p. 41.

Example 4. The 'Alypian' notation (I 'vocal', II 'instrumental')

I   3   A' Δ' H' K' N'   ⊥ ★   A Δ H K   N Π T X   V ∇ ᴴ ⊠ И   Ц ⊣
    2   B' E' Θ' Λ' Ξ'   ⅃ ♁   B E Θ Λ   Ξ P Υ Ψ   P F ᴔ V ⊔   ⌀ ⅃
    1 ℧   Γ' Z' I' M' O'   Θ ℧   Γ Z I M   O C Φ Ω   T Ⴑ — W φ   Ⴈ ᴗ

II 1 Z' N' ⊏' <' ⅂' K'   ᴎ Z   N ⊏ < ⅂   K C F ⅄   Γ ⊢ E ᴴ H   E ᴄ
    2   ⅃' Ц' V' X' ⩊'   ⟋ ⅄   ⅃ Ц V X   ⊠ Ⴖ ⊩ ⅄   L ⊥ ⊔ ⩣ d   ᴟ ⊣
    3   ⩔' ⊐' ⊳' ʏ' Ж'   ⩘ ⅄   ⩔ ⊐ ⊳ Y   ⴎ C K   Ⴑ ⅂ Ǝ ᴴ P   ⧢ T

A and B being the sharps of Γ and so on. As the lines inserted into example
4 show, several stages of addition and modification can be detected; some
shifting of the signs must have taken place, probably at several different
times. A transcription according to Alypius suits the material roughly
contemporary with him, such as the Seikilos Epitaph and the Oxyrhynchus
hymn; this would be expected. But the earliest fragments do not come out
so well.

The Alypian explanation of the notation signs is of very much later date
than the earliest pieces; and a still wider gap between their origin and
exposition must be assumed. All these factors engender the suspicion that
there was a break in the tradition between antiquity and the time of Alypius.
Apart from the shifting signs already mentioned, there is other internal
evidence which strengthens this suspicion. The Delphic Hymns more than
once break an Aristoxenian rule that a *pyknon* (chromatic progression) should
not be followed by an interval of less than a tone. Another statement by
Aristoxenus excites curiosity, for he describes the 'Pythagorean' major third
as *dissonant*, implying a preference for another type of third. Then there is
the phrase 'disjunctive tone'; its value in Pythagorean intonation is the
same as any other tone: but in another intonation it might not be. None
of these tiny cracks in the otherwise solid façade of Greek theory is significant
in itself; but taken together they hint that this façade could be made to
crumble and reveal what lies behind.

Looking more closely at example 4 on p. 43, the obvious facts are:
  1. the highest signs (with superscript dashes) were added later;
  2. two more of the upper triads of the 'vocal' notation are also additions
(but earlier) to the original sequence; probably up to six triads of the
'instrumental' signs were similar additions;
  3. the lowest seven triads of the 'vocal' signs are later, because, as at (2),
they are not normal alphabetic signs (but archaic letters such as *san* and
qoph); the lowest three triads of the 'instrumental' signs also break the
integrity of the system: it is clear that the basic octave consisted of ranks of:
    a. upright characters;
    b. the same rotated through 90°;
    c. mirror images of (a).

It is reasonable to suppose that the central octave of the 'instrumental' notation originally commenced at **K**, which is striking. On the assumption that the 'instrumental' signs are pre-Ionic Greek letters, one would expect that the original sequence would have included the letter **A**, which was roughly the same in all pre-Ionic alphabets. Instead the sequence begins with **K**, which although it could be a Greek *kappa*, is more likely to be a Byblo-Phoenician *ālep*. The basic sequence of the 'instrumental' notation could therefore have come from the Near East, presumably imported some time after the turn of the fourth century BC, when the Ionic alphabet was gaining ground; an earlier date, when the Byblo-Phoenician signs would have looked like Greek letters, is unlikely.

The Alypian distinction between 'vocal' and 'instrumental' notations is belied by the use of 'instrumental' signs in vocal music, although some such distinction seems to have arisen by the time of the *Orestes* fragment (see below, p. 51). The idea that the 'vocal' signs were an Ionic rationalization of the archaic 'instrumental' signs probably contains an element of truth, although the exact relationship between the two systems cannot be described as simply as that. The upright signs of the earlier notation presumably denoted a scale proceeding diatonically downwards. The second and third ranks represented sharp and still sharper versions of this scale. The 'vocal' notation is vastly different. Here the order of symbols is not that of three differentiated ranks running horizontally, but a series of triads vertically ordered; furthermore the order of signs within each triad denotes progressive flattening, not sharpening. It is likely, therefore, that the two systems originated in different ways. It is possible that the 'instrumental' notation was kitharistic or *kitharoedic*; the modifications to the basic scale (whether by tuning or stopping) were indicated to the player by modified signs. The 'vocal' notation might have originated as an auletic or aulodic system: a device called a *syrinx*, placed in one or more holes of the *aulos* could have provided a whole system of different tunings. Such a use of the notation signs to indicate a series of modified *tonoi* is what Alypius conveys; but the tunings he achieves have not the subtlety expected of such an elaborate array of signs. In contrast, the early fragments of notation seem to select now one sign, now the other, precisely in order to achieve such subtlety.

The most curious feature of the early fragments is the way in which intervals of a third are delineated by mixing signs of different ranks. This seems pointless according to the tuning implied by Alypius, which is the Pythagorean scale of major tones and *limmas* or *leimmas* (204 and 90 cents) modified by a *limma* (+90 cents) in the second rank and an *apotomē* (+114 cents) in the third. But if the basic Pythagorean scale were instead sharpened by a first addition of, say, 112 cents (a perfect diatonic semitone) and a second of 182 cents (a perfect minor tone), all perfect intervals, particularly thirds, would be accessible; there would also be some point in talking about a 'disjunct' tone, for the value of the tone would be either 204 or 182 cents, depending on its position. Some sense would also be attributable to the otherwise extraordinary statement in Pseudo-Aristotle's *Problems* (xix, 20) where he talks about the necessity for tuning from the *mesē* and not altering it in a subsequent intonation.

The remaining problem is to locate the basic scale. In the following table (example 5), the traditional **E**=*c* for the 'instrumental' notation has been retained, but with **Ⅰ**=*c* taken (somewhat arbitrarily) as the basis for the 'vocal' notation.

Example 5. Proposed reinterpretation of the 'Alypian' notation

The most considerable fragment of the 'First Delphic Hymn' is shown in example 6, transcribed according to the above interpretation of the vocal notation. It may be compared with the versions in *NOHM*, i, 364 ff. Note the apparent use of 'perfect thirds'. Small notes and bracketed words are restorations; also, the majority of repeated notes are not given separate signs in the inscription. The conjectural rhythm follows the metre of the words. The differentiated natural signs (♮) indicate that the note, together with the sharpened notes, belongs to the third rank; all other accidentals imply the second rank.

Example 6. The 'First Delphic Hymn'

me - le - sin oi - da - an kre - kei: Chry - se - a'd   ha - dy - throus

ki - tha - ris hym - noi - sin a - na - mel - pe - tai.

[Listen, fair-fleshed daughters of thundering Zeus, who dwell in the deep forests
of Helicon! Hasten to sing praise to your brother Phoebus, golden locked, who,
high above the rock-dwellings of double-peaked Parnassus, encompassed by the
worthy daughters of Delphi, comes to the waters of limpid Kastalis to visit the
oracle's niche at Delphi. Famous Attica! Its great city, because of the prayer of
the warlike Triton, is impregnable. Hephaistos, on the flickering flames of holy
altars, burns loins of bullocks whose savour, mingled with Arabian incense,
floats towards Olympus. Shrill *auloi* play wavering flourishes while the golden
kithara thrums out a mellow sound.]

Comparing this extract with the 'Second Delphic Hymn' (parts of which
are given with the traditional rendering in *NOHM* i 369) it is interesting to
note that a transcription according to example 5 again shows a striking use
of 'perfect thirds'. If these interpretations are near the truth, then Safī
al-Dīn's ingenious fretting of the lute in the thirteenth century AD was not
the first solution to the problem of reconciling perfect thirds with fourths
in more than one 'key'.

The location of the basic 'vocal' scale must be changed for each of the
fragments found in the early papyri. This might seem to vitiate the tuning
theory already put forward, particularly since the Zenon and Vienna papyri
are all probably earlier than the Delphic Hymns. For the later sources of
notation, both the basic scales and the relationships of the accidentals must
be changed; again, this looks damaging. But these phenomena actually
confirm rather than disprove the idea that the Alypian readings are invalid.
Three distinct stages in the corruption of the notation are quite discernible.
The first stage is represented by the Delphic Hymns. The 'vocal' and 'instrumental' notations were still both used for the same purposes, although
the signs must already have been modified. The early papyri, however,
contrast vocal passages with non-vocal passages (using the so-called 'instrumental' notation) often introduced by a special sign called a *diastolē*.
It is clear they belong to a different tradition in this respect. Also, if different
basic tunings for each piece are assumed, the Alypian and revised readings
virtually correspond. This suggests that here is a transitional stage between
a so-called 'tablature' use of the notation and a usage which assumed differing
tunings of a hypothetical instrument. Such changes of tuning may be implied
by the *tonos* names found in some of the music of the Vienna papyri. The
transcription of the *Orestes* fragment (example 10, p. 51) is representative

of this transitional stage. The rendering is in conformity with Alypian theory, though a transcription according to example 5, p. 45 (now taking $M=c$) would not look greatly different. But such a transcription of the Seikilos Epitaph (example 8, p. 50) would not work. By now, the notational system has been re-arranged and the choice of symbols reflects not a special temperament, but an assortment which appears to have become traditional.

RHYTHM AND METRE

It is well known that Greek metre was quantitative, that is, based on the device of ordering long and short syllables into patterns. But, in addition to these patterns, was there a regular beat? If so, was there also a regular pulse? In the face of what seem to be ordinary questions, metrical scholars are extraordinarily evasive. They point out that Greek was a language with a tonic (i.e. pitch), rather than a stress accent; a stress-beat is not, therefore, implicit in the accents of the words. They further point to the difficulties that follow from ascribing an 'agogic' beat to the 'compulsory long' syllables of verse. In Latin, whose metre was based on Greek, and where there was a stress accent in speech, this accent would often clash with such an 'agogic' beat. In spite of the fact that various words for beat (e.g. *ictus*) are discussed by authors of (late) antiquity, scholars tend to dismiss the modern reliance on a metrical *ictus* as an anachronism unknown to the ancients whose ears, they say, were more finely attuned than ours to subtlety. There are other difficulties: once the concept of a 'beat' is admitted, regularity of metrical units becomes a necessity. This means abandoning the engagingly simple equation: 1 long$=$2 shorts ($- = \cup\cup$).

The fragments of musical notation that are now known, together with the gradual unearthing of more of Aristoxenus' treatise on *The Elements of Rhythm*[37] make a revision of opinion essential. There is now enough evidence to show that music regulated metre rather than *vice versa*. The 'metrists' such as Hephaestion (upon whom most of our terminology rests) were concerned only with the *lexis* of lyrics – how the longs and shorts looked on paper; it was the 'rhythmicists', such as Aristeides Quintilianus (of the Aristoxenian school), who were concerned with relationships between longs and shorts in performance. Because the terminology of the rhythmicists differs so sharply from that of the metrists it has usually been ignored. The interesting fact is, however, that these differences can be reconciled once it is seen how they arose. Take, for example, the figure $- \cup -$. The metrists called this a 'cretic', the rhythmicists a 'paeon'. But to the rhythmicists a cretic was the rhythm $- \cup - \cup$, while to the metrists paeon was $\cup\cup\cup -$. This apparently hopeless confusion is explained when we assume (using

37. See Ingrams, Kingston, Parsons and Rea *Oxyrhynchus Papyri* xxxiv (1968), 15–25.

Aristoxenus as our guide) a rhythmic kernel as the basis of the terminology, from which might stem forth two greatly differing systems of nomenclature. In example 7 below the sign ⏝ (or ‿) indicates a 'long' whose duration is equal to three 'shorts', a distinction ignored by the metrists:

Example 7. Rhythm and *lexis*

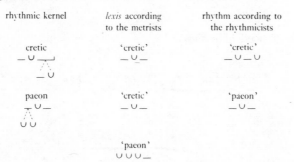

| rhythmic kernel | *lexis* according to the metrists | rhythm according to the rhythmicists |

In this way the distinction between the quintuple time of the paeon and the sextuple time of the cretic was confused under the *lexis* ‗ ∪ ‗. The majority of the other conflicts between *lexis* and rhythm can also be explained in this way.

Because the metrists' nomenclature is current today, the rhythm ‗ ∪ ‗ ∪ must be described, with Hephaestion, as trochaic. It can be seen how this rhythm is based on the kernel ‗ ∪ ⏝; the *trisēmē* ⏝ could be split into shorter values at will, with a tendency towards ‗ ∪. Hephaestion, however, regarded trochaic rhythm as consisting of smaller units, 'feet', of the form ‗ ∪. This was a particularly dangerous simplification, since trochaic metre always proceeded by two-foot lengths, called metra, and the two halves of each metron behaved differently. (Concerning the chronological position of Hephaestion see p. 29.)

As if these difficulties were not enough, a further complication arose: the words *thesis* (down-beat) and *arsis* (upbeat) were misunderstood by many later theorists. So, taking iambic rhythm as another example (rhythm ∪ ‗ ∪ ‗, kernel ⏝ ∪ ‗), the *thesis* was given by these theorists to the long syllables, the *arsis* to the short. But, was iambic rhythm really equivalent to ⅜ ♪♩ ♪♩ ? Or was it ⅝ |♪♩ ♪♩ | as we should expect from its kernel?

Fortunately, the 'Seikilos Epitaph', written in iambics, cuts away all the confusion due to the metrists. It includes, in addition to the rhythmic signs of length, a dot, or *stigme*, shown here thus: ◟. This sign is known from a theorist (referred to as Bellerman's Anonymous) to show *arsis*. Since here it always appears at the second half of the metron, i.e. on the second duple beat of the ⅝ bar |♪♩ ♪̇♩ | , the *thesis* must come at the beginning of the bar. The notion that iambic rhythm was ♪|♩ ♪|♩ is thus shown to be untenable, and with it the theory of 'feet'.

In the notation of the Epitaph, the rhythmic values of the syllables is indicated as follows: *protos chronos* (a 'short') is unmarked, while values of two and three 'shorts' are marked by the *disēmē* (—) and *trisēmē* (‿) respectively. Division of notes within a *disēmē* and *trisēmē* is marked by a slur (*hyphen*, transcribed as ⌒) joining two notes of the same value. How different is the *lexis* from the real rhythm may be seen from the prosody signs given above the notes.

Example 8. The 'Epitaph of Seikilos'

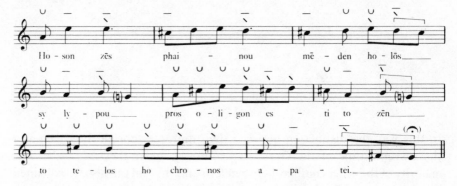

[While you live, be cheerful and grieve about nothing; life is short anyway, for Time has staked his claim.]

Here (and in other fragments) it can be seen what iambic metre was really like. The basic pattern ∪ — could be modified by treating this rhythm as one note; or by subdivision which in example 9 is called 'resolution'; or by a cross-rhythm called *anceps* ('doubtful'). The subdivisions could become quite complex as the following scheme for the iambic metron (in tragedy) shows (see example 9).

Example 9. The tragic iambic metron

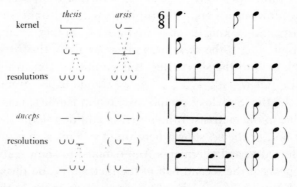

The resolutions of the *anceps* look like dactyls and anapaests in the *lexis*, but the time values must have corresponded to ⅜ time in the manner shown;

such dactyls and anapaests are often called 'cyclic' after Dionysius of Halicarnassus. It can be seen the 'free' part of the metron is at the *thesis* and corresponds with the *trisēmē* of the kernel (the trochaic metron had a 'free' *arsis*). In this way, by having a clear framework of 'up' and 'down' beats (though not necessarily accented, any more than in more recent music) audience and performer alike were able to find their way through what otherwise would be an impenetrable jungle of longs and shorts. Thus iambic and trochaic rhythms, because they behaved differently on the down-beat *sounded* dissimilar; but to the metrists they often *looked* embarrassingly similar.

For other metres there is less information. The Delphic Hymns are in paeans or 'paeons' (although according to the metrists this was known as 'cretic' metre), and seem to be in $\frac{5}{8}$ time, as shown in the transcriptions. No rhythmic signs are present. The *Orestes* fragment is in Dochmiac metre. As in many of the papyri, the rhythmic marks are sparse, although the *stigmē* and *disēmē* are occasionally found. So, too, is a dot *after* some of the pitch signs. This seems to indicate *thesis* (marked ⸌ in the transcription). The *Orestes* piece (see example 10) serves to show (although some details of the rhythmic rendering are necessarily editorial) how instrumental considerations might greatly modify the metre, as one old commentary upon this text mentions. (The first syllable of *materos* seems to be shortened *metri causa*.)

Example 10. Fragment from *Orestes*

[I bewail the shedding of your mother's blood, the cause of your frenzy. Great fortune does not endure among mortals; but a god batters it like the sail of a swift ship, and inundates it with terrible anguish as though cast among the furiously destructive waves of the sea.]

Ionic metres are not found in the musical fragments. They were based on a metron ∪∪ _ _, but there seem to have been many cross-rhythms. If it were an up-beat rhythm (that this is a possibility is shown by some up-beat rhythms in the papyri) it is tempting to suppose that Ionics (they were apparently characteristic of 'music-hall' songs) went something like this:

The 'Aeolic' metres characteristic of Sappho and Alcaeus are virtually inaccessible to us. Their base was a rhythm _ ∪ ∪ _, extended by various segments before and after. How far they used cross-rhythms and how far the *lexis* was modified is a difficult question.

Dactylic and anapaestic verse, where the simple equation, 1 long=2 shorts, seems to prevail, might be thought to be the simplest group of metres from the rhythmic point of view. But this is not so. According to Dionysius of Halicarnassus the rhapsodes recited epics in such a way that the long syllable of the dactyl (_ ∪ ∪) was somewhat shorter than the sum of the two short syllables. It might be supposed that Dionysius was trying to reconcile this rhythm with the 'cyclic dactyl' were it not for the undoubted fact that while a long was often substituted for the two short syllables in a dactylic metre, the reverse substitution is not found. Some of the vagaries of the Ajax fragment in the Berlin papyrus may point to this phenomenon.

Example 11. The 'Oxyrhynchus Hymn'

Hym - noun - tòn d'ē - mōn pa - te - ra ch'hui -
on — -ch'ha - gi - on — pneu - ma pa - sai dyn - a - meis
e - pi - phō - noun — tōn, A - mēn A - mēn. etc.

★ *e* in papyrus

[While we praise the Father, the Son, and the Holy Ghost, let the whole creation sing Amen.]

Anapaestic verse seems to have had at least two main types, that which moved *kata metron* (in two-foot units), and that which moved *kata poda* (foot by foot). Only the latter class is evident in the musical fragments. The excerpt ('Oxyrhynchus Hymn', example 11), although late, is a good example. Dactylic, anapaestic and spondaic feet ($\_ \cup \cup$, $\cup \cup \_$ and $\_ \_$) are all found mixed together. The *stigmē* clearly marks the *arsis*, showing that anapaestic rhythm was not an up-beat rhythm as is often supposed (though some dactylic rhythms with up-beat may have existed). A sign for a rest (*leimma* or *limma*) appears here, though in other papyri it is used to indicate extra length. A *colon* is also found. It seems to indicate *thesis*.

This short survey of Greek rhythms will serve to show how little is known about the subject, particularly in connection with some of the more complex rhythms such as the Aeolics or the dactylo-epitrites. We do not know how far cross-rhythms are implied by the metre and how many rhythmic modifications to the *lexis* are required. Nor is it clear how many Greek metres involved an up-beat. But it is evident that both iambic and anapaestic metres were normally down-beat metres. This is of some interest in connection with later music.

Since the *ictus* of Greek (and Latin) metre was independent of length in the iambic and anapaestic metres; independent of the tonic accent in Greek; and (to a lesser extent) independent of the stress accent in Latin, how was it marked? A number of ancient writers mention that it was an audible stress, but it is likely that the *ictus* was, in effect, more akin to the way the bar-line regulates more recent music: a regular series of beats is *felt*, but not necessarily heard; so long as accents (but these can be length- and pitch-accents as well as stresses) reinforce these beats from time to time, many conflicting cross-rhythms can be accommodated within the metrical scheme without the pulse being entirely disrupted. A strikingly parallel example to the accentual complexities which can be assumed for the settings of Greek lyrics is to be found in the English school of lutenist songwriters. Although in the lutenist settings the underlying rhythm is regular, the words often seem to be set contrary to the beat; but by substituting tonic and agogic accents for the natural stresses of the words, and other devices, the composers achieved a convincing yet wonderfully varied setting. Later critics did not understand these principles and so thought the treatment of the words to be uncouth. Without a knowledge of these same principles, similar misunderstandings of Greek metre are almost inevitable.

It would be going too far to point to Dowland's word-setting techniques as a lineal descendant of the Greek concept of the lyric. But with medieval song, the assertion is defensible. The idea of iambic motion, inherited through Latin, is a prominent feature both of monody and polyphony. The ambiguity of the rhythm ♪♩, in which there is a possibility of a stress on the short note, or of an agogic accent on the long, is a major point in medieval rhythmic theory. This, and other features stemming eventually from Greek metre, had an undoubted influence on the formulation of the rhythmic modes.[38] In addition, the collision between metres of the Germanic types (where equidistant strongly accented syllables were separated by an extremely varied number of subsidiary syllables) and of the sophisticated Graeco-Latin style of subtle *ictus* and syllable regulation, resulted in the completely different accentual-syllabic system which has dominated poetry ever since.

THE HISTORY OF GREEK MUSIC

Of the various influences which may be detected upon the music of Ancient Greece, the most obvious (but not necessarily the strongest) is from Near Eastern sources. The seven diatonic tunings now known from the Old Babylonian period may have influenced Pythagoras, but it is too early to be dogmatic. The Akkadian term *mihir zamari* ('counter-sound', *gišgigal* in Sumerian) is obviously the source of the word 'antiphon' which comes to us from Greek. The mysterious 'nomes' (*nomoi*) mentioned by Plato and other writers almost certainly had nothing to do with the Greek word for 'law'; the most likely etymology derives from the Semitic root meaning 'music' from which, by another root, came our word 'neume'. The Phoenicians (as also for the instrumental notation) are the most likely source for the ancient cry *Ai-linon* (which the Greeks took to mean 'Alas for Linus', but is really the *Ai-lānū* of the Semites). But the solid stuff of Greek musical history must rest neither on these vague clues, nor in the snippets of music that survive; our best information lies in the writings of the archaic and classical composers. If their music must be accounted lost, their words hold some of its forms and rhythms; they reflect or criticize its fashions and they show us its context in the life and thought of a whole civilization.

Homer's world, in the eighth century BC, was steeped in music at all levels of society. Not only professional bards but gods and heroes sing epics to their own lyres. Paris, the prince, plays his stringed *kitharis*, while the noise of pipes rises from the rank and file around the watch-fires of Troy.[39] The bard accompanies banquets, athletic events, and especially dances. The beat is marked by the feet of the girls and boys or by *crotala*, and two acrobats begin each verse with a somersault. There is a song for every occasion – the *Hymen Ō Hymenaiē* for wedding-feasts, the ancient and mournful *Ai-linon* sung at the vintage. Circe sings at her loom, shepherds pipe their flocks home on the *syrinx* of Pan. Over the body of Hector, bards begin the traditional form of dirge; then Hecuba, Andromache and Helen lament in turn, and after each one the household women keen in shrill chorus.[40]

38. See Waite, *The Rhythm of 12th Century Polyphony*, New Haven, 1954.
39. Homer, *Iliad*, I, 472, 601 ff.; III, 54; IX, 186 ff.; X, 13; XXII, 391.
40. Homer, *Odyssey*, VIII, 261 ff., 370 ff., *Iliad*, 491–590; XXIV, 720 ff.

Already a high and sophisticated art of music existed beside the rustic or popular kinds and was to continue thus for the next four centuries or more. Aristocracies practised it and honoured the professional poet-composer whom they paid. New music was in perpetual demand, though the old was remembered too. Competition was incessant and fierce. While certain religious and literary conventions were observed through the classical era, Greek music was not liturgical; nor is there much evidence for the view that it used groups of melodic formulas on precisely the Indian, Jewish or Byzantine analogies. Classical composers were individualists whose styles were parodied on the comic stage, and their art was quick to reflect changes of human character, mood or outlook.

In archaic Sparta lyrics ranged from the military marching-songs of Tyrtaeus to Alcman's 'maiden-song' of lovely girls. Besides such songs of daily or private life, larger genres began to emerge at the musical competitions of the various Greek festivals – for instance, the dithyramb, celebrating the birth of Dionysus, danced and sung by a circular chorus of fifty. All these developments are obscure and uncertainly dated. Later Greeks, at any rate, ascribed the invention or improvement of their main instruments, the *kithara* and the *aulos*, to the seventh century.

The *kithara* (for which Homer has the words *kitharis* and *phorminx*) was a lyre with a wooden body and a sound-box shaped like a tortoise's shell, with oxhide stretched over its face and two carved horns joined by a bar carrying the pegs, from which strings of gut were set over a bridge. They were usually plucked with the fingers of one hand and an ivory plectrum in the other. Terpander, a hazy figure of the seventh century, was supposed to have raised the strings to the symbolic number of seven; but archaeological evidence shows varying numbers (from four to eleven or twelve) in concurrent use at later dates, and the importance of the number of strings was fancifully exaggerated. Whether the notes were played by stopping strings is a more serious question. While the hypothesis of a fixed pentatonic tuning is unconfirmed and unnecessary, a gapped *accordatura*, with stopping, would best explain the attested complexity of some *kithara*-playing. But the *kithara* has no neck or fingerboard, and the possibility of effective stopping is doubtful.[41] Instruments of the lute family with a fingerboard did not appear before the fourth century BC, and never rivalled the *kithara*.

The *aulos* was a pipe of wood, bone or ivory, with a reed in the double bulb of the mouthpiece. It was made in five registers covering three octaves. Ascribed to the mythical Olympus, it was improved in the seventh century by Sacadas and in the fifth by Pronomus of Thebes, who taught Alcibiades to play it. The holes vary between six and fifteen and could be closed or half-closed with metal rings to modify notes. The player normally used a

41. See Winnington-Ingram, 'Tuning'; Higgins, 'Lute Players'.

pair of *auloi* and was able to alter the pitch by drawing them together or apart. In spite of attempts to stabilize the intonation by 'undercutting', it was erratic and wobbly;[42] *auloi* were always used to accompany the emotional frenzies of the dithyramb.

The fifth century still knew various musical idioms and tunings called *harmoniai* and labelled by the different regional dialects of Greece. By the end of that century only two, the Dorian and Phrygian, were still heard in serious music; and Plato's Socrates expelled the rest from the education of boys specially trained to see truth. During the fourth century the *harmoniai* were so far forgotten that musically uneducated theorists confused them with the mechanical segments (or species) of a uniform octave, or even with the *tonoi*.[43] Some of them were associated with old genres of song – the Mixolydian with the dreadful shrieked dirges which were legally banned from some ancient cities; the 'low Lydian' or Ionian with drinking-songs or (in a sample from Aristophanes) dirty ditties of prostitutes.[44]

The 'ethical' reasons for keeping such music away from schoolboys are not as mysterious as some ancient and modern comments suggest. To classical Greeks music was no less expressive than language, and some music was immoral or barbarous.[45]

Socrates admits the Phrygian *harmonia*, used with the *aulos* for the classical dithyramb. Its flexible or tremulous tuning contrasted with the firm intonation of the Dorian. In the early classical work of Pindar the difference between the Dorian and Aeolian idioms is not clear, but the Dorian name prevailed. A passage of Aristoxenus seems to imply that the classical Dorian tuning was associated with the enharmonic *genus* (the only *genus* analysed by theorists before him), which he and Plato call simply '*the harmonia*'.

That there is a style of composition which demands a ditonal *lichanos* – and no mean style, but about the finest of all – is far from evident to most musicians nowadays, although it could be shown to them by induction from examples. But what I say will be clear enough to those familiar with the first and second of the old styles (*tropoi*). Those accustomed only to the present style of composition will, of course, reject a ditonal *lichanos*, since the great majority nowadays use a higher tuning. The reason is a hankering for more and more sweetness: that this is their aim is shown by the fact that they practise chiefly and almost always the chromatic – or if they ever do touch the enharmonic, they approximate its tuning to the chromatic, and its stylistic character (ethos) is deranged accordingly.[46]

42. Schlesinger, *Aulos*; Landels, 'Brauron'.

43. Athenaeus, *Deipnosophistae*, ed. C.B. Gulick (Loeb Library), 324e–5c. See also p. 37, fn. 24.

44. Plato, *Republic* 398d–9a; Aristophanes, *Ecclesiazusae*, 893 ff. (in 918–19 'Ionic *tropos*' is used with a pun on the musical sense in 883).

45. E.g. the 'Adoniasm' (cf. Aristophanes, *Lysistrata*, 393 ff.), though it was later smoothed into a polite piece (Theocritus XV).

46. Aristoxenus, *Harmonics*, 23. The term translated as 'induction' is from Aristotelian logic, and shows that the tonal change was not felt as a minor matter.

This progression of a full ditone from *mesē* to *lichanos* was characteristic of the best classical styles (the enharmonic microtones were a mere decorative detail), and it was felt as a major distortion of musical syntax when fourth-century composers, who were mostly unacquainted with the classics, raised *lichanos* to a chromatic pitch – perhaps a perfect 5:4 third from *mesē* – within a note-series which was still named the Dorian.

Early amateurs of the upper class, such as Sappho and Alcaeus, had composed only small monodic songs, leaving more complex works to professionals like Pindar. In fifth-century Athens free-born citizens could compass tragedy with its chorus accompanied by the *aulos* alone. We learn more, however, from comedy, and especially from Aristophanes, the greatest musical critic of Greece and perhaps its greatest composer. He wrote for a public which talked music as it talked politics or horse-racing. He shows us music at school, at family meal-times and at night-long drinking-parties, where men sang *scolia*, improvising verse after verse in turns. He makes music which we can recognize by its various metric forms – simple chants, sophisticated versions of folksong or brilliant novelties like his Hoopoe's *aria*.[47] The Greek countryside was full of sound – the hymns of cults or festivals, the 'practical songs' sung at work by reapers, spinners or millers – and this fund of popular music often inspired high art. Aeschylus brings the old harvesting cry *Ai-linon* (see p. 54) into the refrain of a tragic chorus and is teased for using antiquated 'water drawers'' ditties in the most famous of all Aristophanes' parodies.[48] In this scene (a competition in Hades between Aeschylus and Euripides, only just dead) broad sweeping rhythms to the *kithara*'s steady *tophlattothrat tophlattothrat*, are contrasted with a subtle modern lyric involving spiders. Aeschylus wins, and the play ends with an appeal for the chorus and the arts of music – in the year before Athens fell.

Aristophanes also parodies the precursors of the musical revolution. A school of dithyrambists was exploiting the unstable intonation of the *aulos* and imitating it in their *kitharoedic* pieces. The new music, no longer clearly tuned and unwavering, was flexible and full of 'bends' (*kampai*); it wobbled like the zigzagging of ants, or eddied like snowflakes and feathers.[49] From later evidence we can infer that Aristophanes was describing the chromatic tuning and modulations which caused the breakdown of the classical tonality. Modulations and *chrōmata* are cited as features of the style of Philoxenus, and a comedian stages a protest by the Muse herself against the new dithy-

47. Aristophanes, *Peace*, 1267 ff.; *Knights*, 277, 985 ff.; *Acharnians*, 1000; *Wasps*, 1212 ff.; *Clouds*, 563–74, 1355 ff.; *Birds*, 904 ff., 745 ff.

48. Athenaeus, *Deipnosophistae*, 618e–20a; Aeschylus, *Agamemnon*, 121; Aristophanes, *Frogs*, 830 to end.

49. Aristophanes, *Clouds*, 332 ff., 967 ff.; *Thesmophoriazusae*, 66–192; *Peace*, 830 ff.; *Birds*, 1372–1409. Cf. *Frogs*, 1348.

rambists, who torture her by forcing a dozen different tunings out of five strings.[50] Timotheus defied all tradition in the blatant manifesto:

> I do not sing the old things
> Because the new are the winners.
> Zeus the young is king today;
> Once it was Cronos ruling.
> Get out, old dame Music.

The course of the movement is best described by Plato:

Our music was once divided into its proper forms. Prayers were one form of ode, surnamed hymns; opposed to this was another form, dirges; another called paeans and another dithyrambs. ... It was not permitted to exchange the melodic styles of these established forms and others. Knowledge and informed judgement penalized disobedience. ... But later, an unmusical anarchy was led by composers who had natural talent but were ignorant of the laws of music. Over-intoxicated with love of pleasure, they mixed their drinks – dirges with hymns, paeans with dithyrambs – and imitated *aulos*-music in their *kitharoedic* song. Through foolishness they deceived themselves into thinking that there was no right or wrong way in music – that it was to be judged good or bad by the pleasure it gave. ... The criterion was not music, but a reputation for promiscuous cleverness and a spirit of law-breaking.[51]

Timotheus died about 360 BC. In 207 Philopoemen came into the theatre victorious from the field of Mantinea, and the kitharists struck up the opening line of the *Persae*:

He who fashioned for Hellas the glorious adornment of Freedom.[52]

A few years later, however, a visiting musician in Crete was thanked for playing not only Timotheus but Cretan folksongs; and by the middle of the second century the two revolutionaries, Timotheus and Philoxenus, survived only in the country schoolrooms of remote arcadia.[53] The diatonic music which superseded them may have been less sophisticated, but we have too little evidence to judge it. By this time music was a topic of curious table-talk or crazy metaphysical speculation, not of intelligent comment. The virtuoso performer – especially the *kitharoedic* soloist – was highly paid but deeply despised. For entertainment, ceremony and ritual the noises were lavishly laid on; but the name of music, to an educated man, meant the 'unheard music' of an abstract mathematic science.[54]

---

50. Pseudo-Pherecrates in pseudo-Plutarch, *De musica*, 30, 3; cf. Düring, 'Terminology', 176–97.
51. *Laws*, 700a–701a (abbreviated).
52. Plutarch, *Philopoemen*, ii.
53. Polybius IV, 20–21.
54. Plutarch, *De animae procreatione in Timaeo*, 26 (the proverb: 'Unheard music is better than heard').

SOLANGE CORBIN

2 The Early Christian Period

GREGORIAN CHANT

RELIGIOUS CHANT. It is customary to look on Gregorian chant,* the patri-
mony of the Roman Church, sung until the 1960s in most Roman Catholic
churches in the west, as something unique. Before examining it here I
propose to consider its nature and its close connection with other varieties
of chant still in use and much alive. These, when compared with the
Gregorian, explain certain aspects of the latter that may surprise us.

---

* The examples cited in this chapter are Roman chants for Mass and Office and are quoted from the
well-known compendium, the *Liber usualis* (abbreviated as LU). Recently a new edition of the *Liber
usualis* (No. 801 of the books of chants prepared by the Benedictine monks of Solesmes) has appeared
(copyright 1961); but all page references given in this chapter apply equally to the 1934 and the 1961
editions. The reader should have a copy at hand so as to have access to more substantial examples than
can be accommodated in this text.

In the first place, what is the function of Gregorian chant? It accompanies and comments on the Latin prose text of the Roman service. Even if we have no examples of the original melodies of these chants – as clearly we have not – it is quite evident that the institution itself is ancient and that the principle on which it is based dates from the earliest stages of Christianity. As for the actual liturgical material – psalms, gospel readings and prayers – the requirements for the services were more or less the same throughout Christendom; consequently it is hardly surprising to find that in all Christian, and even non-Christian, cults in the Near East the basic principles of the ritual are the same. Everywhere it will be found that, despite fundamental differences in the actual musical dialects, the relation between words and the singing voice remains the same. The salient features of these different forms of liturgical music are dictated by the same requirements, namely, that the music be: (1) vocal (2) traditional (3) monophonic and (4) devoid of any instrumental accompaniment.[1]

The chant has its regular place in the liturgy, and the interpreter of this music enjoys more freedom than a western musician does. There is less difference between the Buddhist and Gregorian types of ritualistic reading or *cantillation* than there is between Gregorian and contemporary secular music.

This leads to the conclusion that for all ch
precedence over the sung text, that vocal emb
favour of meditative chant, and that certain rites
may possess features not unlike the Gregorian
are concerned with prayer and an immutable
heard in its entirety.

SOURCES. Gregorian chant may be considered as a near relation of other western Latin chants, such as the Milanese, the Mozarabic and Eastern Christian chants. Within the Latin repertoire several main categories can be distinguished, for *cantillation* of excerpts from the gospels, psalms, anthems and responds each have their own laws. These sacred texts are undeviating. Another category contains texts in verse, such as hymns, sequences and certain prose texts known as 'ecclesiastical composition'. These are generally late additions which were only gradually incorporated into the liturgy, clearly contrary to the practice of eastern churches which admitted versified prayers at a very early date, whereas Rome, for reasons of unification and from fear of heresy, continually eliminated many items from its repertoire.

In an examination of the extant manuscripts of early Gregorian plain-song we run into the difficulty that no exact neumatic notation exists earlier than the tenth century, and we often have to have recourse to liturgical books

1. See McKinnon, 'Polemic'.

without notation. As in the case of the first centuries of the Christian era, the writings of the early Church Fathers, as well as the apocryphal texts, are major sources.[2] These documents are useful only when considered in their context, and in relation to the environment of the time.

THEORETICAL AND PRACTICAL MUSIC. Theoretical music was one of the sciences taught at university level, and one of the four which constituted the *quadrivium*, the others being geometry, astronomy and arithmetic. Within this learned speculation no account was taken of the practical and aesthetic aspects of music. On the contrary, the practice of ritual chanting (the term used in the treatises is *cantus*) was regarded as something hardly worthy of mention; consequently the information available is extremely scanty and vague. While the early treatises looked upon *musica* as the hand-maiden of philosophy, the authors of the liturgy never bothered to theorize about *cantus*; and it was not until St Augustine, the first Christian philosopher to write a treatise *De musica*, that the gap between these divergent points of view was bridged. It is true that this work is concerned only with the rhythm of language, but the very fact that Augustine, the most eminent thinker of his day, included speculative music as one of the ecclesiastical disciplines enabled lesser scholars to imitate him. Gradually the theoreticians became musicians, while the ecclesiastical cantores dared to study theory. It is to this association above all that we owe our knowledge of the theory of Gregorian chant and its notation and even the evolution of western music.

CANTILLATION. We know nothing about plainsong in the first centuries of the Christian era, since there was no accepted system of notation at that time. Moreover this musical adornment of the ritual was not considered to be genuine 'art' that deserved to be studied and preserved. The sources mention 'psalms, hymns and canticles'. From what we know today it may be assumed that there were, in addition, brief responds which were probably ornamented at the discretion of the performer. We do know that gospel readings and prayers were always performed in a manner of heightened speech, known as *cantillation*, which invests the words with a rare solemnity and intensity of expression.[3] This may be one of the springs of our repertoire, for *cantillation* is the most elementary form of sacred song; i.e. the chanting of a phrase on a reciting note with cadences to mark the punctuation; a type of chanting suitable for prose. When the verbal text is in verse form, practices such as psalmody require a regular recurrence of cadences. Our

2. See again McKinnon's article, also his thesis, *The Church Fathers and Musical Instruments*, Columbia University, 1965. Concerning the relevant passages quoted in M. Gerbert's *De cantu et musica sacra*, 1774, and T. Gérold's *Les Pères de l'église et la musique*, 1931, see the new interpretations in Corbin, *Eglise*.

3. See Apel, *Gregorian*; E. Werner, *Bridge*; Corbin, *Eglise*.

sources show that the congregation responded to these chants with brief acclamations such as 'Amen' or 'Alleluia'.[4] Most of these procedures were probably Hebrew in origin, as the whole Christian scriptural apparatus was modelled on the Bible; but having spread through the Byzantine world it had absorbed some formal procedures.

MORE ELABORATE CHANTS. It is just possible to discover a few examples of more elaborate types. In 1962 Dom J. Claire began a study of the origins of certain pieces of great simplicity, principally to be found in the three great repertoires, Beneventine, Milanese and Gregorian chants.[5] The items in question were short antiphons in the Divine Office (canonical hours) and brief responds that today are rarely heard. According to Dom Claire these chants can be divided into three types, depending on the recitation tones from which they are derived, namely, those beginning on C, D and E. Their compass is small, and the so-called moveable note (that is a semitone below C) is never used. (This is clearly why Dom Claire bases his recitation on C and not on F, which, on the basis of the extant sources, would seem to be the natural choice.)

Other types (the Gradual-respond and the Tract) are known to have been sung at an early date. But while there is evidence of their antiquity, we know little of their actual melodic garb, which may have undergone profound transformation in subsequent centuries.

ORIGIN OF THE MODES. In considering the formation of the repertoire and the emergence of certain notes as pivotal points, we can assume an evolution as follows. Primitive *cantillation* of liturgical texts proceeded on a simple, melodic line, a single reciting note (called tenor). To this simple line were added formulaic, ornamental phrases to mark punctuation and cadences. The natural consequence of the introduction of these ornaments was the creation of a secondary melodic line which, with its secondary reciting note (or tenor) complemented the primary line. The resulting vocal line oscillated between the primary (lower) and secondary (upper) reciting notes. The various ornamental formulae tended to camouflage the interval between the two, the leap being difficult for the voice to perform. The ancient and primary reciting note (or root note) eventually became the 'final' of the modes; the second note became what we now call the 'dominant' (or tenor). These are the basic elements of medieval modality (described in more detail below) which the student meets on countless occasions in almost the entire Gregorian repertoire. In this stratification and evolution the ornaments became the melodic repertoire which has come down to us.

4. See E. Werner, *Bridge*, pp. 263 ff.; and Corbin, *Eglise*.
5. See Claire, 'Evolution'.

THE MODES.[6] At no time did Gregorian chant, either in its primitive or in its later fully developed form, make use of note sequences based on pre-ordained scale patterns; composers preferred to use simple melodic formulae already in existence.

Western logic soon re-formed these elements into a regular diatonic succession, though theoreticians did not accomplish this until the ninth century and later. The cantors were certainly more familiar with the melodic formulae than with scholastic scales.

The modern theory of modes is simple and logical (see example 1). It is based on so-called pentachords: that is, groups of five adjacent notes. These pentachords can start on any of the following four root notes: D, E, F and G. Each pentachord is the core of a mode which, if extended upwards by a fourth, becomes an 'authentic' mode, and, if extended downwards by a fourth, a 'plagal' mode. Since each of the four root notes gives rise to two modes, the authentic and the plagal, the result is a total of eight modes. Each of these note-sequences (which today we are inclined to look on as a kind of scale, but which was in reality an aggregate of melodic formulae) has only one 'preferential' note, namely, the lowest note of the pentachord, known as the 'final'. The degrees of the scale have no harmonic function. As regards their melodic function, it is clear that a certain importance was attached later on to a second note in each mode whose position varied according to the mode and which, in practice, was used mainly in psalmody. In modern textbooks on chant this note is usually labelled the dominant; in medieval treatises it is often called 'tenor' or 'tuba'. Whatever its name, it must be remembered that its function is melodic, not harmonic. As will be seen, it is not invariably situated a fifth above the final. True, this 'dominant' easily found its place at the fifth degree in upper modes starting on D, F and G; but in the case of the authentic mode based on E the fifth would fall on B, which was considered an unstable note since it was sometimes intoned as B natural, sometimes as B flat. For this reason the dominant was raised to C. As for the plagal modes, they would require a lower dominant, since their range and melodic centre were lower. In the plagal modes on D, E and F the dominant was placed a third lower than in the corresponding authentic modes, namely, F, A and once more A. In the plagal mode on G (to avoid the instability of B natural) it became C. In the classic modes, not only was the 'reciting tone' on a fixed dominant, but the 'finals' in psalmody were highly ornamented and varied, whereas in the old primitive system there was no 'reciting tone' as distinct from the 'final'.

6. For a clear exposition see Apel, *Gregorian*, pp. 133 ff.; concerning the Hebrew background, see E. Werner, *Bridge*, pp. 373 ff. The ancient testimony of Hucbald emphasizes melodic formulae and not rigid scales, see M. Gerbert, *Scriptores ... de musica*, 3 vols., 1784, i, 214.

Example 1. Table of Gregorian modes

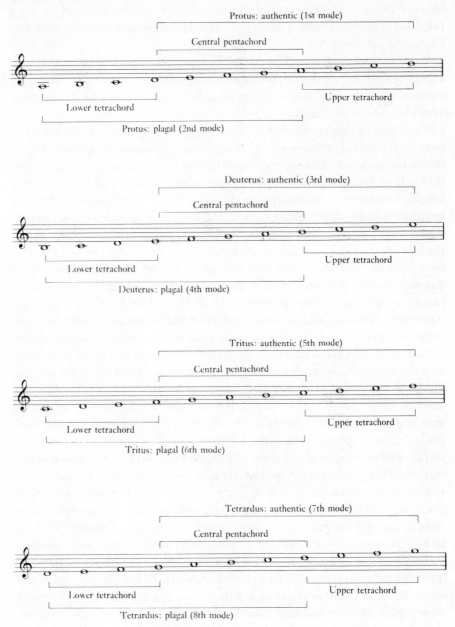

This system of eight musical modes originated in Byzantium and was probably adopted in the west towards the end of the seventh century AD. The Greek name, *Octoechos*, was retained, and the modes themselves were designated by Greek numerals in accordance with the ascending order of their finals:

I.	*Protus*	(authentic and plagal) Final – D		Dominant – A & F
II.	*Deuterus*	,,	,, E	,, C & A
III.	*Tritus*	,,	,, F	,, C & A
IV.	*Tetrardus*	,,	,, G	,, D & C

THE ORIGIN OF GREGORIAN MELODY. Before the Emperor Constantine accepted Christianity as the official religion of the Roman Empire (AD 313), the role of music as a conscious exercise in the organization of Christian worship was obscure. The needs of a clandestine and relatively simple ritual seemed to be met by a practice of *cantillation* which was instinctive and could fall back on ancient customs as models. It was not until the decrees of the Council of Laodicea (341–63) that the clerical (and professional) status of the cantor was formally sanctioned by the Church: hitherto the cantor had been a member of the laity, although the ecclesiastically appointed *scholar lectorum* had replaced the earlier lay lector from around the middle of the third century AD. Moreover the Laodicean canons expressly forbade the singing in church of 'popular' psalms (i.e. personal compositions). This leads one to believe that the afflux of conversions had given rise to certain irregularities under cover of a more elaborate ritual. As the ceremonies had become more frequent and less closely supervised, the number of musical forms had increased.

As time went on this trend became more marked, and in the next three or four centuries, a repertoire, known as Gregorian, came into being. Our knowledge of this repertoire is based on the form handed down in manuscripts of the tenth to the twelfth centuries. Was St Gregory in fact responsible in any way for the chant which bears his name? It would seem that he was not; there is nothing to show that this pope, whose influence exercised an intellectual force in the west for several centuries, was by temperament musically inclined. Indeed, his only utterance relating to music was distinctly hostile to musicians, whom he excluded from the cult.[7] We shall see, too, that Gregorian song is not 'composed' in the sense in which we speak of a modern 'composer'; and it is an historical error to look upon it as the work of one particular man.

THE COMPOSITION OF THE GREGORIAN REPERTOIRE. The question then arises: How was the repertoire made up? It certainly seems highly improbable that so many masterpieces were very much earlier than the oldest known copy and that they could have been reproduced in innumerable manuscripts with the scrupulous accuracy we can observe today. While we know of no composer, the cantor had become an important personage by the fifth century, because it was he who was responsible for handing

7. Corbin, *Eglise*, p. 178; A. Burda, 'Gregor', *Musikforschung*, xvii (1964), 388–93; *Kirchenmusikalisches Jahrbuch*, L (1966), 3; Ferretti, *Esthétique*, p. 106.

down and enlarging the repertoire by means of formulae which he had studied long and carefully, adapting and combining them so that they could be used again. He used two methods, both of which are equally well known to us: that of melody types (or melodic prototypes) and that of the melodic *cento* (or patchwork). Both these principles still form the basis of teaching in the rites of the Near East, having been handed down from remote antiquity. They are also to be found in popular song.

The 'melody type' was a pre-existing melodic motive which may or may not have been previously adapted to a verbal text. These motives must have enjoyed widespread popularity if not fame and were thus liable to be adapted indiscriminately to other words. But since the change would be from one prose text to another it is obvious that differences in length might be a problem; and so in certain sections of the melody – generally the recitative passages – the interpreter was at liberty to lengthen or shorten it by omitting or adding certain notes which might affect reciting notes or ornamental points in the melody.[8] The same melody could thus be used for all sorts of texts, sometimes even contradictory in meaning. The most typical of these interchangeable melodies was the Gradual, *Justus ut palma* (sung today for the anniversary of a non-papal confessor, LU p. 1201) which was adapted to some fifteen different Graduals in the liturgical year.

The melodic *cento* is another story.[9] The interpreter had to become thoroughly familiar with a series of short and widely used phrases, usually containing some characteristic intervals. These fragments have their allotted place in the melody: some at the beginning of a piece, others in the middle, others again in a central or final cadence. Some pieces are entirely composed of such fragments, skilfully and even artistically linked; if the piece is well put together there is no sense of effort. Each modal group has its own series of short preferential phrases which often occur in pieces sometimes put together skilfully and sometimes awkwardly. Finally, singers memorized lists of pieces classified according to their genre (Introit, Gradual, etc.), their mode or their use of the aforementioned formulae. The principle was simple, and its application delicate: there is evidence that the system was already in use by the eighth century AD. The collection in which these lists were preserved is called the *Tonarium* (*Tonale*).[10] As a result of this compilation, which must have required skills of analysis and organization, the repertoire increased quite rapidly. The items that have been preserved were clearly those that gave pleasure, especially for their musical qualities. It is in this sense that one can speak of a Gregorian composition, bearing in mind the part played by the interpreter in reproducing and skilfully adapting the

8. Ferretti, *Esthétique*, pp. 165 ff.

9. Concerning *centos* and centonization see Ferretti, *Esthétique*, p. 109. Concerning centonisation in the responds see Frere, *Sarisburiense* and Holman, 'Tropes'.

10. See Huglo, 'Tonaire'; also supplement to bibliography for this chapter, p. 444.

elements constituting a masterpiece. This was a great and difficult art, for the 'composer' was much less free than he is today; his aim was not to produce something new at all costs, but to reproduce and embellish.

FEATURES OF THE REPERTOIRE. What did the Gregorian repertoire consist of when we first encounter it – that is to say, towards the ninth century? The interpreter has to deal with three types of repertoire, that of the schola, that of the soloist and that of the congregation, this last being the simplest.

The schola's function was to sing the responses to the deacon or soloist. Its first duty was therefore to provide the antiphons interspersed between the verses of the psalms; the same practice was extended to the Mass with the Introit accompanying the opening psalm, the Offertory and the Communion. The Introit contains a psalm verse to this day, but in the Offertory and Communion the psalm verses have become suppressed in the course of centuries (except in the Mass for the Dead) and only the antiphons framing the psalm verses survive, their full names being *antiphona ad offerendum* and *antiphona ad communionem*. But in early times the schola performed these pieces, often very brief, to accompany psalms. The schola also replied to the cantor when he sang the Gradual and the Alleluia vocalizations.

Finally, the congregation, too, had a role to play; it was never passive, as is sometimes wrongly thought. It was expected to provide brief responds, in the form of an acclamation; this was all that could be expected of a congregation which could not be supplied with prayer-books, as printing did not then exist. These acclamations were the 'Kyrie', the 'Gloria', the 'Sanctus' and the 'Agnus Dei', to which the 'Credo' was added in the ninth century. The pieces that have been preserved reveal their antiquity by a simple melodic language suitable to the congregation; but they have certainly undergone alterations since which have made them more elaborate.[11]

The evening service (Vespers) was divided in the same way as the Mass: the cantors sang the responds, the schola the antiphons, while the congregation supplied the few acclamations which found a place in the evening service.

THE CHARACTER OF GREGORIAN MELODY.[12] The individual chants exhibit different styles. They may be syllabic (one note to each syllable and occasionally two or three notes); or ornamented (several notes to each syllable); or melismatic (a long vocalise on a single syllable with frequent and extended ornamentation). As might be expected, the syllabic chants are those of the congregation (the ferial 'Sanctus' which was formerly used in the Requiem Mass is of this type). The schola, too, sang certain antiphons

11. See Burne, 'Mass Cycles'.
12. For a full exposition see Apel, *Gregorian*, pp. 201–420.

of great simplicity. But the schola also had to perform ornamented chants (e.g. the Introit and the Offertory). As for the melismatic chants, they were the preserve of the cantor soloist. There were naturally some exceptions to these rules.

In addition to these categories, however, Gregorian melody has its own characteristics which are unmistakeable. Chief among these is the fact that it almost always uses conjunct or very small intervals (thirds). Its movement is therefore somewhat restricted, and even in fairly extensive melodic progressions (whether upwards or downwards) it continually falls back on itself, thus slowing down the enunciation of the melody. In pieces in the 'authentic' mode, the intervals are often larger and the movement more decisive than in 'plagal' pieces, which are generally more reserved and meditative in character.

As stated, the normal melodic procedure was to employ conjunct motion, supplemented by major or minor thirds, the latter often used to by-pass the mode's semitonal intervals. Fourths occur less frequently; fifths are even more seldom heard. The ascending fifth, however, is used as a commonplace opening formula for pieces in the first mode (D–A–B–A) and is also found in pieces in the seventh mode when the ascending fifth (G–D) is used to link the final to the dominant of the mode. The descending fifth is rare: it is found in the mode on G, for instance, the Gradual *Qui sedes* (LU p. 335) with its repeated role of taking the melody back to the lower regions; and in the Introit *Populus Sion* (LU p. 327) where it again performs a balancing role. An ascending fifth in the mode on F is frequent, as in the Communion *Exsultavit* (LU p. 352). But such examples are exceptional. As for the interval of the sixth, it is not found in the oldest pieces at all; the one that occurs in the *Alleluia multifarie* for the feast of the Circumcision (LU p. 441) is a misleading case, because this Alleluia is of a later period.[13] The ascending seventh in the Offertory *Domine Deus* is not confirmed by the surviving manuscripts.[14] Not only are the intervals deliberately restricted, but the melody itself is organized so that the whole composition remains confined within a narrow range (*ambitus*). In some cases this restricted *ambitus* is extended by an occasional higher or lower note. These extensions are exceptional, however, particularly if they are the result of ornamentation. A few examples will help to clarify this. The Introit *Dominus dixit* (LU p. 392) is recited within the compass of a fifth (C–G). The G, however, is rarely reached, so that the piece could be said to be contained within the interval of a fourth; this is characteristic of the 'meditative' type of antiphon. Another example is to be found in the Alleluia verse *Crastina die* for Christmas Eve

---

13. Husmann, 'Alleluia'; this piece is later than the old Graduals examined in Hesbert, *Sextuplex*.
14. See Steiner, *JAMS* (1966), 171.

(LU p. 361). Here the piece is in the eighth mode and lies largely within the span of a fourth (G–C); the high D is seldom touched upon.

In other instances, the highest and lowest notes are part of the overall *ambitus*; compare, for example, the above-mentioned pieces with the Gradual *Qui sedes* (LU p. 335) where the compass is deliberately and persistently extended to include a low D at one extreme and a high G at the other. This range of an eleventh is covered several times in a remarkably smooth and well-balanced fashion. Similarly, in the Offertory *Jubilate* (LU p. 487) we find an eleventh spanned within a single melisma, characterized by long repeated notes.

Finally, mention must be made of the melodic movement itself. Here again, we must make a distinction between pieces of a contemplative nature and those which have an expansive melodic curve. A good example of the contemplative type can be seen in the Offertory *Reges Tharsis* for the Epiphany (LU p. 461), where the core of the music revolves constantly around the dominant of the mode (here the 5th mode on F with C as dominant) with ornamental figurations surrounding this dominant. Such pieces could be described as 'static'. Apel (*Gregorian Chant* p. 309) sees them as derived from psalmody, which may well be the case. In any event this method of surrounding one note of the scale with various figurations (which create the impression of hovering freely) occurs frequently in the repertoire of eastern chant; thus it is not surprising that traces of it should still survive.

The 'curved' type of melody is naturally more animated. It is in general use throughout the repertoire but especially in the Gradual, the Alleluia and the Offertory. The curve usually starts from the lowest note, to which it returns at the end; very few pieces begin in the higher register to finish in the lower. The melodic shape is rarely of the simple type like that of popular song (an example is to be found in the Communion *Jerusalem* [LU p. 563] in the section on the words *Participatio ejus in idipsum*, A–C–G–A–F–G–E). As a rule the melodic movement is concealed behind a veil of ornamentation, examples of which can often be found in the oldest manuscripts. Thus the melodic curve remains unobtrusive even where the span is considerable.

Finally, throughout the repertoire we find special ways of ending the pieces and preparing their cadences, which themselves do not resemble major or minor tonal cadences. This point has only been touched upon by Ferretti (pp. 66 ff.); but there now exists a full study on this subject.[15] In these cadential formulae the musician brought up in the classical tradition is surprised to find that there is hardly ever an equivalent of the modern leading note. In such formulae the final is reached from above, and it is the first three degrees of the mode which are primarily used. Generally speaking, these

---

15. See Homan, *JAMS* (1964), 66.

degrees are sufficient to characterize the mode; to go below the final would mean going outside the confines of the central fifth; moreover, in the modes on F the interval of the semitone would thereby be introduced and this was preferably to be avoided.

To sum up, the storehouse of chant is considerably removed from that of the modern music student who is primarily familiar with current popular song or the art song of the concert hall. Gregorian chant, in fact, uses very small melodic cells moving within narrow confines, commenting on and embroidering these cells *ad infinitum*. This is the characteristic which the principal Gregorian repertoire shares with eastern chants; moreover, there is no place in it for a clearly defined melody proceeding by disjunctive intervals, the hall-mark of our popular song. It represents the antithesis of our contemporary style, and yet, few forms of music are so clear and so evocative.

THE HISTORY AND FORM OF THE REPERTOIRE.[16] Chants can be divided into three groups: those of the schola, those of the people and those of the cantor. In analysing these groups it is appropriate to begin with those of the schola, which was responsible in the first place for the antiphons alternating with the psalms and, incidentally, for the responses to the cantor in his melismatic pieces. The antiphons for which the schola was responsible were, as we have seen, the Introit, the Offertory and the Communion. In the case of the Introit only a single verse of the psalm has been retained; in the cases of the Offertory and Communion the psalm has disappeared altogether.

The Introit,[17] sung during the entry of the clergy, was originally much longer than the short piece printed in the modern *Liber usualis*: the processional entry, with lighted candles, was a slow one. Of the psalm that used to be sung, the doxology has survived, in addition to the single remaining verse (sometimes two in the oldest manuscripts). Apparently before the sixth century the entry was also accompanied by the chanting of a litany, but this was subsequently discontinued. (It is thought that, having to choose between two kinds of text, one ecclesiastical and the other based on the Biblical psalms, St Gregory chose the latter text.) The Introit exhibits the narrow compass and 'hovering' melody described above (see p. 68). That the Introits are of considerable antiquity is attested by the fact that they appear in the oldest lists as well as in early extant collections of chants for the Mass.[18]

The history of the Offertory antiphon is quite different. Here the ancient psalm verses have disappeared altogether, although vestiges survive in the

---

16. Concerning chants in the Mass in the pre-Carolingian period see Froger, 'Chants'. See also Jungmann, *Missarum*.

17. See Apel, *Gregorian*, pp. 305–10; Ferretti, *Esthétique*, pp. 260–8; Froger, 'Chants', pp. 8–13.

18. Several early manuscript versions of these collections entitled *Antiphonale missarum* have been published in the series *Paléographie musicale*. See also Hesbert, *Sextuplex*.

traditional manuscripts and even in later ones, since after the ninth century we find traces of the verses which were sung during the procession of the faithful bearing their offerings.[19] The music of the Offertory, however, is rather unusual: it is probably not as old as that of the Introit. Although it freely exploits the *cento* principle there is no close integration between the formulae, and the freedom of the melody suggests that the pieces are, in fact, newly composed, although they observe the old limitations of compass, modality and ornamentation. One of their most characteristic features is the frequent repetition of key phrases – usually the first verbal and musical section – which invests the whole piece with an atmosphere of intensity and urgency which we do not meet elsewhere. We have already referred to the formal peculiarities of the Offertory *Jubilate*, which also affords an example of the repetition of the opening section (LU p. 486). The list of Offertories given in Hesbert's *Antiphonale missarum sextuplex* includes the majority of the *incipits* in our modern collections of music for the Mass, so that one is inclined to assume some antiquity for these musical forms. But although we know that the Offertory already existed in Carthage in the time of St Augustine, it is doubtful whether even this fact provides us with irrevocable proof of a history for which a venerable length has been claimed.

There is evidence, too, of the Communion chant[20] as early as the fourth century, but in the form of a psalm obviously accompanied by an antiphon. Here, again, the antiphon has lost its psalm and the 'Gloria patri' which was sung at the end of the distribution of the Communion. It remained shorter and simpler than other parts of the Mass and bore some resemblance to certain antiphons in the Office hours.

The first category of chant in which the soloist (cantor) played an important role was the Gradual,[21] divided between cantor and schola – a division which is called 'responsorial'. The antiquity of the Gradual follows from the fact that a responsorial chant had always been sung after the first lesson. Formally, the Gradual consists of two sections: the respond, the bulk of which is sung by the chorus, and the psalm verse, sung by the soloist. In ancient practice this was followed by a repeat of the choral respond. But in modern practice, as represented by the *Liber usualis*, the repeat of the respond has become optional. The opening of the respond is sung by the cantor, the choir continuing at the point indicated by an asterisk in the *Liber usualis*. This is followed by the verse sung by the cantor, at the end of which

19. For Offertories and their verses see Ott, *Offertoriale*, primarily a practical edition. Also Ferretti, *Esthétique*, pp. 191–203; Froger, 'Chants', pp. 25–30; Apel, *Gregorian*, pp. 363–75; Hesbert, 'Offertoire'; Barroffio, 'Offertorien'; Steiner, *JAMS* (1966), 162–81.

20. See Ferretti, *Esthétique*, pp. 266–78; Froger, 'Chants', pp. 37–9; Jungmann, *Missarum* iii, p. 325 ff.; Apel, *Gregorian*, pp. 311–12.

21. Ferretti, *Esthétique*, pp. 159–74; Froger, 'Chants', p. 17; Hucke, 'Gradualweise'; Jungmann, *Missarum* ii, p. 188; Haberl, 'Gradualien'.

(again indicated in the *Liber* by an asterisk) the choir rounds off the verse. Although we have proof of the antiquity of the responsorial Gradual, the extant melodies appear to be of a later date, following the revision of the liturgy which took place between the fourth and the seventh centuries.

The music of the Gradual is characterized by its melodic animation. Some of these chants, indeed, can be termed bravura pieces: witness the unusually long melismas in the Gradual *Clamaverunt* (LU p. 1170). Often, however, the composition of the Gradual is based on melody types; thus, the Easter Gradual *Haec dies* (LU p. 778) and the Gradual *Justus ut palma*, used in the Mass of a Confessor (LU p. 1201) consist of melodic units which recur in other Graduals throughout the repertoire (Apel, *Gregorian Chant*, pp. 346–58).

The soloist is particularly prominent in the singing of the Alleluia[22] which, like the Gradual, is a responsorial form in which two sections alternate, namely, the Alleluia and the verse (or verses). The Alleluia section consists of the word 'Alleluia', sung by the soloist to a highly ornamented melody; this is repeated by the choir which (after the asterisk in the *Liber*) proceeds to a melisma over the last vowel; the so-called *Jubilus*. Now follows the second section, the verse sung by the soloist up to a certain point (again indicated by an asterisk in the *Liber*), where the choir completes the verse.

In ancient practice the Alleluia section was repeated after the verse, and the entire procedure applied to successive verses (producing something like modern rondo form). This procedure was to be found in some form or other in Roman, Oriental and Hebrew rituals. St Hippolytus (third century) arranged the Alleluia to be read during the *Agape*; it then took the form of the congregation singing the word Alleluia as a refrain after the psalm verses. Unfortunately the precise details of the early performance of the Alleluia are obscure, and one assumes that a congregational refrain must have been of great simplicity. At the time of St Jerome (*c*. 340–420) the chant became more melismatic, and as the refrain became more elaborate the psalm tended to disappear; in the west, in any event, the Alleluia was sung only at Eastertide. It was probably St Gregory who re-instated its use throughout the year, except for Lent. The number of verses was mostly reduced to one, though there are a few cases of two.

Musically these chants appear to be of more recent composition. Like the Offertory, the Alleluia introduces the repetition of musical sections, frequently the concluding portion of the Alleluia at the end of the verse, e.g. *HAM* i, No. 13. These chants often contain a series of descending diatonic passages which are not to be found in the more ancient type of compositions, namely Graduals and Tracts. The Alleluias are unusually long and ornate.

22. A comprehensive bibliography is given in *MGG*, i, 350. Note particularly Ferretti, *Esthétique*, pp. 175–91 (excellent); Jungmann, *Missarum* ii, 189–93; Apel, *Gregorian*, pp. 375–92; Wellesz, 'Alleluia'.

Even in our oldest manuscripts the span of an eleventh is found, as in the Alleluia *Veni Domine* for the Fourth Sunday in Advent (LU p. 354); but in general the compass is more restrained. Many of the Alleluia melodies are adaptations used to accommodate different texts throughout the liturgical year (Apel, *Gregorian Chant*, pp. 381–3).

In early times the Tract was the preserve of the soloist and was sung after the Gradual in Lent, instead of the Alleluia. There are reasons for believing that it was nothing but a one-time Gradual transformed, and this may account for certain of its peculiarities. Its surviving form is not at all that of a responsorial chant, like the Gradual; it is, rather, a highly ornamented form of direct psalmody, composed of verses of a psalm sung consecutively without an intervening choral refrain. The Tract can be very long: *Qui habitat*, for the First Sunday in Lent (LU p. 533) consists of thirteen out of the sixteen verses of the psalm of the same *incipit*. Tracts invariably use only two modes, the second and the eighth, and the oldest specimens nearly always employ the eighth mode (Hesbert's *Antiphonale missarum sextuplex*). The *cento* method abounds in these compositions which have been subjected to fastidious melodic analysis[23]; those in the eighth mode, however, use fewer formulae than those in the second. It is clear that in these pieces the cantor had free rein to display his talents, which he did by embroidering the melodic cells formed from the same initial formula and adapting these cells to the text of the verses. (In more recent practice the tracts are no longer chanted by a soloist but frequently by half-choruses or, at least, by a group of soloists.) In regard to compass, it is a consequence of the employment of plagal modes (second and eighth) that *ambitus* is restricted and rarely exceeds the span of a seventh. Nevertheless the melody, infinitely revolving around itself, as it were, is not monotonous, and the regular recurrence of its 'finals' has not unreasonably been considered as a form of *ostinato*, of which it exhibits the essential characteristics.[24]

It remains now to describe the chants allotted to the congregation. These are the chants whose texts do not change and which are called the 'Ordinary' of the Mass. There are five of them: 'Kyrie', 'Gloria', 'Credo', 'Sanctus' and 'Agnus Dei'. A sixth is the dismissal at the end of the Mass, namely, the 'Ite missa est' (sometimes replaced by 'Benedicamus Domino'). This chant for dismissal is often melodically related to the 'Kyrie' that has been sung earlier. All these chants are to be found at the beginning of the *Liber usualis*, and their arrangement in 'cycles' gives rise to the mistaken impression that we have inherited from the past a collection of cycles of the Ordinary. In the *Liber usualis* there is printed a collective title (*Orbis factor, Kyrie fons bonitatis*, etc.) and an approximate date appears at the head of the 'Kyrie',

23. See Ferretti, *Esthétique*, pp. 135-55; Apel, *Gregorian*, pp. 312-30; H. Schmidt, 'Tractus'.
24. See Apel, *Gregorian*, pp. 324-5.

where the century is given in Roman numerals. The historical facts in no
way suggest cyclic composition at so early a date. On examining the manuscripts the first thing one notices is that the cycles of the Ordinary do not
appear until very late (thirteenth century at least) and before then in an unexpected form: first the 'Kyries', then the 'Glorias' and so on; none of them
is named. The names later added and re-printed in the *Liber usualis*, such as
Kyrie fons bonitatis (LU p. 19), are derived from a medieval practice called
'troping', namely, the fitting of additional words to a melismatic melody;
e.g. *Kyrie eleison* is expanded to *Kyrie fons bonitatis eleison*, and leads to
the designation *Kyrie fons bonitatis*, etc. But this troping is seldom to be
found in the manuscripts where the texts are usually shown without any
verbal interpolations. The date appearing at the head of each Mass cycle in
the *Liber usualis* indicates the oldest manuscript source in which the verbal
interpolation (trope) has been found. It does not imply that the music
belongs to the same epoch, and we shall see that several pieces in the
Ordinary are very much older.

Does this mean that these 'cycles' of the Mass were unknown in the past?
On the contrary, it would seem that, in practice, a certain 'Kyrie' had always
been associated with a certain 'Sanctus'; but the results of current research
merely point to the possibility that this practice may have been an old one.
The organized polyphonic cycles which we first find in Machaut must have
had a precedent, but their origin is obscure.[25]

The cycle begins with the 'Kyrie'. This is a ninefold invocation to the Deity
in three sections: *Kyrie eleison, Christe eleison, Kyrie eleison* (each presented
three times). These invocations are remarkable for the utmost brevity of
the verbal text; even the acclamations of the 'Sanctus' are more extensive.
This is because the 'Kyrie', in the form presented by the surviving manuscripts, is only a relic of an ancient litany which was discontinued when it
became customary to sing an antiphonal psalm before the Mass (the psalm
accompanied by the Introit antiphon). The original addresses intoned by
the priest disappeared, and only the congregation's acclamations were
retained. It is therefore reasonable to suppose that they were chanted in a
simple manner suitable for an uneducated congregation. Little evidence of
this simplicity remains; only four of the formulae appear to be old, namely
those found in the Requiem Mass (LU p. 1807), the *Kyrie cunctipotens*
(LU p. 25) and the ferial 'Kyries' (LU 56, 59, 62). The other melodies are not
only very elaborate, but bear every sign of being of a later date. The *ambitus*
is often very wide, more so than would be necessary in a popular acclamation
(e.g. a span of an eleventh in the *Kyrie rex genitor* [LU p. 31]); the elaborate
vocalises would be too difficult for a large congregation (e.g. *Kyrie clemens
rector* [LU p. 74]). The intervals are larger and more disjunct than in standard

25. See Schrade, 'Cycle'; Burne, 'Mass Cycles'.

Gregorian chant (e.g. the *Kyrie stelliferi* [LU p. 51]) where the octave is covered in two leaps with scarcely any intervening notes. Other features are long diatonic descents and occasionally the lack of symmetry – all this suggests a consciously elaborate creative process.[26]

The 'Gloria in excelsis' and the 'Credo' have different histories, but they share a feature which does not apply to the other chants in the Ordinary: on account of their solemn character they are intoned by the celebrant and, in fact, according to the *Ordo Romanus* of the eighth century (analysed by Dom Froger) the 'Gloria' was reserved for the bishop. When it was included in the repertoire of the congregation it was with extremely simple melodies. We have this on the authority of Raoul (Radulph) de Rivo in the fifteenth century.[27] Most of the 'Glorias' were, in fact, strictly syllabic; and if some of them were ornamented, they never attained the same melodic diversity as the 'Kyrie', or even any other piece of ornamented Gregorian chant. Two of them were strict psalmodies: that of the Mass for Simple Feasts (LU p. 57) and the 'Ambrosian Gloria' (LU p. 88). Both these are in the fourth mode, the reciting note being the dominant A, in accordance with custom. The former, an example of a Roman chant of extreme sobriety, ascended to B for the tonic accents, whereas the more reticent Ambrosian piece merely ornaments certain finals with brief and standard vocalization. The *Gloria de angelis*, though of a later date (LU p. 37) was also distinguished by a remarkable simplicity. These features accord well with an ancient text which, though not taken directly from the Bible, was in the tradition of the *psalmi idiotici* (that is, new texts fashioned after the model of the Biblical Psalms and including various forms of acclamation).

The 'Credo' was a solemn profession of Christian faith, and for that reason was only sung at solemn Masses and intoned by the priest himself. It entered the liturgy of the Mass in Spain in the sixth century, at the time of the conversion of the Visigoths. At the end of the eighth century Charlemagne introduced it to Gaul, and in the course of the ninth century it is found in association with the 'Gloria', and thereby intended for the Mass, in a manuscript originating at Fleury. Rome did not adopt it until the eleventh century.[28] The Gregorian repertoire has preserved six melodies (LU 64–73, 90–4), the first of which (LU p. 64) is called 'authentic'. It is a simple *cantillation* of perfect and striking beauty, which unfolds within the compass of a sixth. Research has shown that it is, if not 'authentic', at least one of the oldest forms that have come down to us. Four of the six chants are in the fourth mode,

26. See Jungmann, *Missarum* ii, 87–102; Corbin, *Eglise*, pp. 108 ff.; Melnicki, *Kyrie*.

27. C. Mohlberg, *Radulph de Rivo*, 2 vols., Louvain, 1911–15, ii, 135; Bosse, *Untersuchung*; Jungmann, *Missarum* ii, 103–18; Apel, *Gregorian*, pp. 409–15; Froger, 'Chants', pp. 15–16; Huglo, 'Gloria'; Rönnau, *Tropen*.

28. See Haberl, 'Choralcredo'; Huglo, 'Credo'; Jungmann, *Missarum* ii, 233–47; Apel, *Gregorian*, pp. 412–15. The bilingual 'Credo' of AD 877 has been edited in facsimile by H. M. Bannister in *Monumenti Vaticani*, 2 vols., Leipzig, 1913, i, 29 (No. 108), ii, pl. 10 from MS Vatic. Regin. 215.

'Credo III' in the fifth mode, and 'Credo IV' in the first mode. All the melodies, except the very late 'Credo III' (LU p. 68), are related to 'Credo I'; this is true even of 'Credo IV' (LU p. 71), though the latter is in a different mode and more animated.

The 'Sanctus' is a series of three acclamations, followed by two sentences of commentary and a 'Hosanna'. The commentary, *Pleni sunt coeli*, is based on a text from the Vision of Isaiah, 6:3. This chant dates from the early Christian era and has never ceased to be in use.[29] The priest introduces it with the prefatory text (LU p. 3, tone LU p. 109) after which it is sung in unison by the priest and the whole congregation. One would expect, therefore, to find traces of music which by its simplicity suggests a folk origin. Indeed, the ferial 'Sanctus' (Mass XVIII, Preface LU p. 109, Sanctus LU p. 63) also used for the Requiem Mass, is melodically derived from the preface and suggests a popular origin by its syllabic nature, limited range, sectional organization, and manifold repetition on the four lines beginning 'Sanctus', 'Pleni', 'Hosanna' and 'Benedictus'. The popularity of this melody is further attested by the fact that it gave rise to parodies in the French vernacular. If, then, this was a typical example of popular acclamation it would be reasonable to look for paraphrases derived from it among the other 'Sanctus' chants; in fact, fragmentary but clear traces are to be found in the 'Sanctus' for Masses X, XIII, XV, XVI, XVII and *ad libitum*. On the other hand, the 'Sanctus' of Masses XI, XII, XIV and XVII are highly ornamented, are not as closely linked with the Preface and bear obvious signs of being deliberate 'compositions'.

The history of 'Agnus Dei' has been less thoroughly examined[30] than the other pieces in the Ordinary, and this is all the more surprising since these three characteristic invocations ought to have aroused the same curiosity as the 'Kyrie'. It was introduced into the Latin ritual by Pope Sergius I (687–701) and has had a place in all rituals ever since. Here again we find a very varied repertoire: while the 'Agnus' of Mass XVIII is extremely simple, the other 'Agnus' chants are highly complex. In those in Masses III, V and IX the prayer is imbued with lyrical fervour. The psalmody in the 'Agnus' of Mass XVIII is clearly archaic in tone, and its melodic restraint and the narrowness of its compass speak quite another language. We are confronted here with a repertoire that has been modified throughout the ages, allowing the singers every opportunity of displaying their talents.

This observation could well serve as a conclusion to our whole study of the Ordinary. The centuries indicated in the *Liber usualis* refer only to the date of the most ancient extant manuscripts, and we have no idea how these texts were transmitted before that. But we can say, without hesitation, that on the

29. Thannabaur, *Sanctus*; Jungmann, *Missarum* iii, 37–47; Apel, *Gregorian*, pp. 415–17.
30. See the article by B. Stäblein in *MGG*.

one hand we find texts of great antiquity and extreme simplicity, and on the other compositions that are highly ornamented. Certainly a more recent provenance is reflected by the extension of *ambitus*: we now reach the octave, the seventh having been the largest span in more ancient pieces. Also, the manner of spanning the octave is novel – sometimes, within comparatively short passages ('Agnus' of Mass III, on the words *Qui tollis peccata*), at other times in longer periods in conjunct motion ('Kyrie' of Mass II), and sometimes in triadic sequences ('Sanctus' of Mass IX, arpeggio on third invocation). This really represents the introduction of a new language, even if some of these pieces are of a lesser musical value.

LITURGICAL DRAMA

This is the name given to verbal and musical interpolations inserted into certain liturgical texts. Sometimes they are relatively brief insertions in processional chants, as, for instance, the 'tropes' attached to Introits for Christmas and Easter.[31] At other times these interpolations are more elaborately structured and are in effect theatrical in nature. Some idea of the character of both species can be gained from a study of the collections of texts assembled by Young (words only, without music) and Coussemaker (with music).[32] The Latin equivalent for the word 'drama' is never found among the titles given in the manuscripts. As regards the processional tropes they may be called *ordo*, *processio*, *officium* etc., and in the case of more highly developed pieces, *ludus*, *ad similitudinem* etc. Sometimes there is no title at all.

The purpose of these liturgical interpolations was to enhance the solemnity of the liturgy of religious feast-days. Had these presentations been intended to give the congregation spiritual guidance we would expect to find liturgical drama on days of mourning or penitence; but this is not the case. These manifestations were reserved for joyful feasts, such as Easter, Christmas and the birthdays of certain popular saints, for example, St Nicholas. Their place

31. Concerning 'tropes' and the process of 'troping' see the discussion of the troped Kyrie above, p. 74; also the comments of Handschin (*NOHM*, ii, 128 and 176) and Apel (*Gregorian*, pp. 429–42). Tropes are verbal or musical additions to the liturgy, or both. Sometimes words are added to a melisma, supplying syllables for each note. At other times the new words of a trope are fitted with new melodies. Thus, in certain chants, or sections of chants, verbal or musical substitutions were made. The relationship between these new extensions and the original chants varied considerably: the tropes ranged from brief additions clearly related to the original to independent and lengthy creations connected with the original only subtly, if not obscurely. Moreover, the general principle of 'troping' was by no means restricted to pieces technically labelled as such. Quasi-tropes and trope-like creations abound in medieval music, as one would expect in a period when a tendency towards extension and ornamentation is encountered in all the arts. Among the more important results of the troping process are not only liturgical drama, but also early instances of polyphony (*versus, organum, clausula*) as will be seen in chapter 3.

32. K. Young, *Drama* is the more complete collection; Coussemaker, *Drames*, gives only the principal texts. See also supplement to bibliography for this chapter, p. 444.

in the liturgy varied considerably according to the occasion, depending on whether the shorter *ordo* or the more elaborate *ludus* was employed. At a given moment the liturgy was interrupted and the 'actors' (clerics or nuns as the case might be) made their entry and sang their dialogue, which was never spoken, though often reduced to a few phrases. The liturgical service was then resumed and continued to the end. The timing varied according to the feast: at Christmas the play took place before Matins, and the actors, when they had finished, played an important part in the liturgy. The interpolation sometimes occurred between the Masses sung at midnight and at dawn. At Easter there would be a procession to the Sepulchre (the *Visitatio sepulchri*) towards the end of Matins, following the last lesson, after which the last canticle of Matins, the *Te Deum*, would be sung. Other 'dramas' were performed after Vespers, while some accompanied the procession that took place in the cloisters between Terce and conventual High Mass.[33] This procession was obligatory in all the rites (monastic and secular) but the liturgical books rarely give the texts used in these processions. Consequently a small repertoire was compiled for use at certain important feasts. After the procession the service continued with the Introit appropriate to the day, but the 'dramas' were never enacted during Mass, which was never interfered with.

The question of the antiquity of these liturgical 'dramas' is often discussed. The idea of a dramatic interpolation can probably be traced back to the prophecy of the Sibyl sung on Christmas Eve. This text probably dates from the second century AD; it was introduced in an apocryphal sermon by St Augustine, which is now included in Matins on Christmas Day.[34] Generally speaking it occurs in the second Nocturne (the third is a very long one containing the genealogy of Christ), and the apocryphal sermon was read during the sixth lesson. When the speaker came to the passage attributed to the Sibyl the tone changed, and the prophecy was announced in a psalmodic formula with two dominants, after which the prophecy itself was read in the form of twenty-seven hexameter verses, the musical form of which never varied – a sign of its great popularity. After the prophecy the sermon continued and led straight into the Respond No. 6.

Apparently this interpolation at a very early date prompted the idea of having a scenic representation in church; the *ordo prophetarum* is nothing else than an extension of these twenty-seven verses. There is evidence of this as early as the ninth century. It is, therefore, not surprising that this practice was extended from Christmas to other festivals; at Easter it was especially solemn and impressive. The *incipit* of the Easter trope is well known; it is the

33. The modern distinction between a monastery of men and a convent of women is not valid for the Middle Ages. 'Conventual' Mass is suitable for a 'convent', i.e. an institution of monks, friars or nuns. Concerning the distinction between parish Mass, conventual Mass and private Mass, see O. Nussbaum, *Kloster, Priestermönch und Privatmesse*, Bonn, 1961.

34. Corbin, 'Sibyllae'.

question put by the angel to the Holy Women, *Quem queritis in sepulchro?*, which occurs in a book of rules for the Benedictines in England, the *Regularis concordia*, as early as the end of the tenth century.[35] From then onwards the idea gained ground and underwent considerable variation and elaboration. The elaborate pieces, suitable for dramatic treatment, are not very early, dating from the thirteenth century (cf. Orleans MS. 201; Tours 927 of the fourteenth century; etc.). Before that we find only tropes for use in processions, either at night (visit to the Tomb) or between Terce and High Mass.

Even in cases where these texts are fairly elaborate they belonged to the liturgy and were not intended as scenic diversions. Convincing proof of this is to be found in a text cited by Coussemaker and too often forgotten.[36] The action described there took place during Matins at the hour of the *Visitatio sepulchri*. Two nuns advanced to the choir and received from the Abbess an order to go to the tomb; they then proceeded in solemn state to this tomb which seems to have been outside the church; they were locked inside the tomb, out of sight and hearing of the congregation. There they carried on their dialogue. They then emerged from the sepulchre carrying the shroud and announced the resurrection of which they exhibited the proof. The 'drama' was then concluded. It had all happened in a place where no one could enter, and can thus hardly be described as 'theatre', however much one might like to think of it as such. It should be regarded only as an extension of the liturgy.

Thus the contents of these pieces were closer to the liturgy than anything else, as can be seen by examining the material collected by Coussemaker. After the interpolated trope the liturgy is resumed. In other words the liturgy itself alternates with tropes (on the liturgical musical theme). The language in the early centuries was Latin; it is only in a few late pieces that one comes across interpolations in the vernacular, e.g. in MS St Quentin 86.[37] The 'dramas' can then be divided into two categories: on the one hand the tropes which could easily be interpolated into the service and, later on, pieces of a more popular nature: the music of these latter was certainly at a remove from the liturgy. Confirmation of this is to be found in the nature of the manuscript collections which contain the 'dramas': the tropes, with all their embellishments, are included in the liturgical collections. But as soon as a piece is more specifically scenic in character (while still performing its liturgical function shown by its attachment to the final *Te Deum*) it will be found in collections which may be religious but which actually are not used in the service proper, (e.g. the Tours MS 927).[38]

35. See K. Young, *Drama*, i, 201 ff. and 582 ff.; Smoldon, 'Easter Sepulchre'.
36. Coussemaker, *Drames*, pp. 340 ff.; taken from St Quentin (Origny-Sainte-Benoite) MS 86.
37. See above, fn. 35.
38. This opinion is the outcome of a year of conferences at the Ecole des Haute-Etudes (Sorbonne); see *Ecole pratique des Hautes-Etudes*, 4me. section, *Annuaire*, 1963 (reports on year 1962–3, p. 173).

Finally, our present knowledge does not permit us to state definitely whether the repertory of liturgical 'dramas' was destined for the monasteries or for the secular churches. What does emerge clearly from the sources is that the 'dramas' (processions or scenic pieces) formed part of the tradition of a particular church from which they were rarely separated; new tropes or scenic elaborations were, as a rule, connected with the same centres.

Liturgical drama probably began to flourish from the beginning of the tenth century onwards. But the more elaborate scenic pieces did not make their appearance until the very end of the eleventh century (cf. the *Sponsus* of the Saint-Martial MS., Paris, Bibl. Nat. 1139)[39] and the fullest repertoire dates from the thirteenth century. Copies were made in the fourteenth century, after which the idea of liturgical drama gave place to the more highly developed 'Mystery' plays which were more attractive, because they were more scenic. But this very theatrical element caused the expulsion of the plays from the Church building itself, and the play moved to the *parvis*. This move to the porch or the courtyard was to prove decisive for the subsequent history of drama.

HYMNS

The liturgical hymn is a strophic poem of a popular type, without refrain, each stanza of which is sung to the same melody. Its proper place was in the Office hours (an exception being the *Veni Creator* which was sung at Easter Mass, LU p. 885). There was only one hymn to each liturgical hour. At Vespers it came after the capitulary prayer; at Complines after the psalms; at Matins after the psalm *Venite*; and at the beginning of the minor Office hours (i.e. Lauds, Prime, Terce, Sext, None). There was generally no hymn for the Office of the Dead, with a few exceptions as in the Office of Arras, edited by Dom Brou and in the Mozarabic service.[40]

The place of the hymn in the liturgy had been fixed by a decree of St Benedict in the fifth century, by which time it already had an earlier history which must be taken into account. The hymn known to the classical pagan world and to primitive Christianity was of a different kind: the term then signified a song of praise addressed to a divinity. Throughout the first centuries of the Christian era three criteria are postulated for a hymn, namely, song, praise and – specifically – praise addressed to divinity.[41] If these three

39. See Chailley, *Saint Martial*, pp. 109–15.

40. Brou, 'Office' stresses the exceptional nature of this collection. The Mozarabic service, too, is characterized by features peculiar to it.

41. This definition is confirmed throughout antiquity. In the Christian world the authority most often quoted is Saint Augustine (354–430); see his *Enarratio in psalmum* LXXII, *Patrologia Lattna XXXVI*, col. *914: hymni laudes sunt Dei cum cantico: hymni cantus sunt continentes laudem Dei. Si sit laus, et non sit Dei, non est hymnus. Si sit laus et Dei laus, et non cantetur, non est hymnus. Oportet ergo ut si sit hymnus habeat haec tria: et laudem et Dei et canticum.*

were not present, then one spoke not of a hymn but of a composition of another sort. Moreover, this ancient form of hymn did not need to be in verse: certain prose acclamations, antedating the Middle Ages, were accepted as hymns as, for example, the *Te Deum* and the *Gloria in excelsis* (known as the hymn of the angels).[42] The hymn, according to the liturgical definition, made its appearance with St Hilary (d. 367), but it is thought that the difficulty of these pieces[43] prevented them from becoming popular. St Ambrose of Milan (*c.* 340–97) first defined the form of the hymn as we know it so that, indeed, for a long time the generic term 'Ambrosian hymns' (*hymni Ambrosiani*) was used to distinguish these hymns from the so-called hymns of ancient times. In its new form the hymn was no longer bound by the three criteria mentioned above; the liturgical hymn could extol the saints and was invariably set in verse form.

The Ambrosian hymn consisted of several stanzas in iambic dimeters (two measures, i.e. four feet of iambics) and was sung to a simple syllabic melody. Four authentic examples are known to us: *Veni redemptor gentium, Jam surgit hora tertia, Deus creator omnium* and *Aeterne rerum conditor.* St Ambrose caused his hymns to be sung in order to sustain the spirit of the faithful on Easter night in AD 387 when the Empress Justina of the Arian sect was laying siege to his Church. There is no doubt that one of the reasons they enjoyed such success at the time was that they had been sung before and were already familiar to the people. Their actual composition, then, probably dates from the beginning of the episcopate of St Ambrose (AD 373), and it is probable that the Bishop-Saint wrote many more than the four well authenticated hymns, although there is no general agreement on this point.[44] But their general introduction into the Roman rite was slow and beset with difficulties. At times all poetry except the Biblical psalms was proscribed, as at the Council of Braga in 563 ('*Nihil poeticae compositum in ecclesia psallatur*'). On the other hand hymns must have been known within the Roman ritual, since St Benedict designated the exact place in the service, which they occupy to this day. But they were adopted only for the monastic rites, and it was gradually that they found their way into secular liturgical books.[45] As a result of this state of affairs there exists considerable diversity between the Benedictine and secular repertoires, and also between the secular repertoires themselves.[46]

42. Cf. also Walafrid Strabo who cites, *c.* AD 840: *ille hymnus quem nato in carne Christo angeli cecinerunt* '*Gloria in excelsis*', *Monumenta Germaniae Historica, Capitularia,* ii, ed. Boretius-Kraus, chapter 26, p. 506.

43. From the *liber hymnorum* of St Hilary only three hymns have survived in the MS of Arezzo, Fraternità di S. Maria vi, 3, ff. 1–15. See W. N. Myers, *The Hymns of Hilary of Poitiers in the Codex Aretinus,* Philadelphia, 1928; also W. Bulst, *Hymni Latini antiquisimi,* Heidelberg, 1956, pp. 31–5.

44. Compare the views expressed in the articles on 'hymne' by Dom Maur Cocheril in Michel, *Encyclopédie de la Musique,* 1958–61, cols. 517–19; on 'Hymnologie' and 'Hymnus' by W. Irtenkauf in *Lexikon für Theologie und Kirche,* 1960, cols. 567–9, 569–73.

45. Mearns, *Hymnaries,* shows how the texts were gradually introduced.

46. See Vogel, *Hymnaire*; Stäblein, *Hymnen.*

One clear proof of the popularity of the hymns and the esteem in which they were held is to be seen in the fact that from the outset they rapidly increased in numbers. There was first of all the repertoire of the Spanish poet Prudentius (d. AD 410), which was followed by a number of compositions attributed, naturally, to eminent authors such as popes, to ensure their wide circulation. And yet very few of these can be ascribed to a particular writer with any certainty. Venantius Fortunatus of Poitiers (d. AD 605) was the recognized author of *Vexilla regis* and *Pange lingua . . . certaminis* (LU p. 575 and 709), while Theodolphus of Orleans (d. AD 821) has left us the *Gloria laus* for Palm Sunday (LU p. 588). Apart from these two authors there are few authenticated examples from early times.

The repertoire greatly increased in the course of the centuries. In the twelfth century Rome itself officially recognized the hymns that were then being sung in all the churches and had been admitted to the service books of these churches for some two centuries past. Obviously the way in which the repertoires were formed was somewhat capricious, so that a systematic historical study becomes a knotty problem. Moreover the texts contained in the various repertoires are numbered not in tens, but in hundreds. The monumental collection *Analecta hymnica medii aevi*, started by G. M. Dreves in 1886, has grown to sixteen volumes and is still incomplete. After the genre had been officially included in the Roman service books production of hymns continued in ever increasing quantities until the seventeenth century, when Jean de Santeul was commissioned by Mgr de Harlay, Archbishop of Paris, to form a complete collection of hymns for inclusion in the Breviary. In spite of the extraordinary bulk of this repertoire it is of musical as well as literary interest.

A study of these hymns is beset with difficulties, mainly because of their profusion, but also because each church formed its own repertoire according to taste, since initially the hymn was not part of the official liturgy. As a rule, the text of each hymn was adapted to several timbres (i.e. melodies serving more than one text), and each timbre, in turn, served a variety of texts. Within a homogeneous tradition this is not surprising, but some of the timbres proved to be so generally useful that they were adapted, somewhat indifferently, to many texts of considerable metrical divergence.[47] Consequently, the tables of contents of hymn texts in individual repertoires varied according to locality, and the same texts were often sung to different melodies. Thus, the differences in the content of these various repertoires are an excellent indication of their place of origin. This is convincingly shown by Stäblein's collection, which draws not on isolated pieces but on a series of

47. Br. Stäblein provides a methodical re-classification of these melodies which makes it possible to check the facts in *Hymnen*. The adaptation was sometimes made with little regard for the structure of the melody. Corbin, 'Portugaises' has shown some extreme examples where sections of the melody are allotted to verses that are either too short or too long, without regard for cadences or modality.

some of the most interesting and most ancient repertoires, together with their melodies.[48]

Finally, it should be mentioned that some of the hymns are provided with one, and even two, refrains (e.g. *Pange lingua ... certaminis*).[49] These are thought to be processional hymns. Ceremonial marches of this kind inside a church or monastery have texts to accompany them only in certain cases (e.g. the processions on the Feast of the Purification, Palm Sunday, Easter Eve and Rogation Days). In general traditional texts are taken for granted, for instance during the daily procession in the cloisters between Terce and conventual High Mass – whether taking place in a community of monks or of canons. It became customary to sing certain hymns on these occasions: the *Salve festa dies*, for example, which was handed down by oral tradition and had a definite march rhythm. These processional hymns appear as a group in a section of Stäblein's collection, where they are assembled for the first time.[50]

THE EASTERN CHURCH [BY DIMITRIJE STEFANOVIĆ]

Byzantine music is the liturgical and ceremonial chant which was sung in unison, unaccompanied, in Greek Orthodox churches from the fourth to the fifteenth centuries.[51] Byzantine historiographers refer also to secular and instrumental music, of which, with the exception of a few folk songs in a Mount Athos manuscript, no trace has come down to us. The oldest versions of Byzantine and Latin psalmodic recitation and melodies go back to a common source, the chant of the Early Christian Age, of the Churches of Jerusalem and Antioch, which derived from the music of the Jewish Synagogue.

Between the earliest document of Christian chant, the fragmentary 'Oxyrhynchus Hymn' written on papyrus at the end of the third century, and the earliest Byzantine musical manuscript with notation from the middle of the tenth century, no other musical document with notation has been preserved. Psalms, Canticles and other hymns were orally transmitted and written down in manuscripts without notation. The structure of the 'Oxyrhynchus Hymn' is built up from a number of melodic formulae, a principle of composition characteristic for the Ambrosian, Gregorian and Byzantine melodies. This fact supports the theory of an unbroken tradition from the music of the Primitive to that of the Byzantine Church.

48. Stäblein's work deals, in turn, first with the contents of one book, then of another belonging to a different region.

49. LU, 709; the complete refrain is sung before the first stanza of the hymn is taken up. After subsequent stanzas the first half of the refrain (*Crux fidelis*) alternates with the second half of the refrain (*Dulce lignum*).

50. Stäblein, *Hymnen*. For processional hymns see pp. 478–500; for the *Salve festa dies*, p. 482.

51. Byzantium, the New Rome or Constantinople, the capital of the Empire of the East, was solemnly inaugurated by Constantine the Great in 330; in 1453 it was taken over by the Turks and the Byzantine Empire ceased to exist. Greece was under Turkish domination until 1821.

Byzantine hymnography is the poetical expression of Orthodox theology. Byzantine poetry and music are intimately linked together: the melodies receive their expression and rhythmical nuances from the text. The earliest and basic form of Byzantine hymnography is the *Troparion*. Originally a short prayer sung after each verse of a psalm, it was later composed in strophic form and is known to have formed part of Matins and Vespers in churches and monasteries in the fifth century. From the sixth century a monostrophic *Troparion* ('Ο μονογενὴς υἱός), attributed to the Emperor Justinian I (527–65) has come down to us and is still sung at the liturgy. The most important group of independent *Troparia* are the *Stichera*, collected in the *Sticherarion* (see pp. 85–6). As a constitutive element, however, a number of *Troparia* make up the two great poetic forms of Byzantine hymnography, the *Kontakion* and the *Kanon*.

The rise of the extended form of the *Kontakion* and its introduction into the liturgy are associated with one of the greatest of Byzantine hymnographers, the sixth-century Romanos. The *Kontakion* is a poetical homily which consists of eighteen to thirty or even more *Troparia*, all structurally alike and composed on the pattern of a model stanza, the *Hirmus*, collected in the *Hirmologion* (see p. 85). The most famous *Kontakion* attributed to Romanos is the *Akathistos Hymn* which consists of twenty-four stanzas, forming an acrostic of the letters of the alphabet.

Towards the end of the seventh century another complex poetical form, the *Kanon*, made up of nine Odes, hymns of praise, modelled on the pattern of a *Hirmos*, was introduced into the Morning Office. The invention of the *Kanon* is ascribed to Andrew of Crete (*c.*660–*c.*740). The first school of *Kanon* writers flourished in the monastery of St Sabas, near the Dead Sea, in the middle of the eighth century. Among the authors of *Kanons* the names of John Damascene (*c.* 675–*c.* 748) and Kosmas of Jerusalem in particular rank high.

At the beginning of the ninth century the Studios monastery in Constantinople became the centre of Byzantine hymnography. This was the time of the Iconoclast controversy.[52] The great representative of the Studios tradition was Theodore Studites (759–826). With other hymn writers Theodore inaugurated a second period of the *Kontakion* and introduced changes in the inner structure of the *Kanon*. While the Odes of the *Kanons* of the other hymn writers of the School of St Sabas are paraphrases of the Canticles, loosely linked together, the Odes of Theodore's Kanons constitute

52. The Iconoclast controversy (726–842) began as a conflict over the popular custom of paying reverence to icons. In 726 the Emperor Leo III ordered the destruction of sacred images. Later the controversy developed into a political struggle: the Isaurian emperors attempted to place the Orthodox Church under the power of the state. The opposition of the monks of the monasteries in Palestine and those of the Studios monastery in Constantinople finally triumphed, icons were reinstated and in 843 the Patriarch of Constantinople Methodius introduced the Feast of Orthodoxy which is celebrated on the First Sunday in Lent.

a unity. A single thought is worked out and varied in all the Odes. The most significant difference between *Kontakion* and *Kanon* lies in the increasing use and greater variety of the music in the latter form.

Authors of the schools of St Sabas and of the Studios, the *Hymnodoi*, composed many hymns which were introduced into the service. About the middle of the eleventh century an authoritative revision of the Office books was made, the addition of new hymns to the repertoire was prohibited, and the standardized liturgical books were put into circulation. Consequently the artistic activity of the monks was concentrated upon the embellishment of the music.

From the twelfth century onwards, especially in the fourteenth century, and even after the fall of the empire in 1453, the originally simple Byzantine melodies were embellished or new ones composed in the melismatic 'kalophonic' style. By using extended coloraturas the musicians, the *Melurgoi*, made the words of the text unrecognizable. Composers who also gave instruction in singing were called *Maistores*. Among them the most famous were Ioannes Glykys, Ioannes Koukouzeles (fourteenth century) and Manuel Chrysaphes (fifteenth century).

After the hymn writing in the east had come to an end there was still some poetical activity in the eleventh century and up to the middle of the twelfth century in the Greek colonies and monasteries in Sicily and southern Italy. In 1004 a Basilian monk, Nilus the Younger, founded a monastery at Grottaferrata, near Rome, which became the centre of Byzantine ecclesiastical life in Italy. The comparative study of the eastern and western rites, texts and melodies (e.g. pieces transmitted in Greek by western manuscripts and Latin pieces translated into Greek) bears witness to the profound cultural and spiritual unity which existed between east and west.

Byzantine music is preserved in manuscripts with different phases of notation from the tenth to the nineteenth centuries. After the fall of Constantinople the way for the introduction of Oriental elements was open – nasal voice production, augmented intervals, accidentals, *glissandi*, irrational, non-tempered intervals. Byzantine music flourished, however, in the island of Crete. But in the sixteenth and seventeenth centuries the art declined as a whole until a revival took place at the end of the seventeenth century which led to a renewed Turkish and Oriental influence.

Neo-Byzantine melodies were composed in the eighteenth and nineteenth centuries. Composers used the existing oral tradition as the basis for their melodies and, in consequence, medieval Byzantine elements, such as melodic formulae and tonal characteristics, can be detected in them.

The most important liturgical books with musical notation include the *Hirmologion* (with hymns called *Hirmi*)[53] and the *Sticherarion* (with some

53. The *Hirmologion, Laura B. 32* from Mount Athos, dated around 950, is the earliest extant Byzantine manuscript with musical, as distinct from ecphonetic notation.

fourteen hundred hymns called *Stichera*). These are divided into several collections: the *Stichera of the Menaia* for the fixed feasts of the twelve months of the ecclesiastical year;[54] the *Stichera of the Triodion* for the movable feasts from before Lent to Holy Saturday; the *Stichera of the Pentekostarion* for the period from Easter Sunday to the Sunday of All Saints; and the *Stichera, including the Antiphons, of the Oktoechos*, for a cycle of eight consecutive Sundays, each in one of the eight modes.

A number of other liturgical hymns is found in books written for the soloist: the *Psaltikon* and the *Kontakion*, as well as those in the choir books called the *Asmatikon*. Liturgical anthologies (*Akoluthiai*, i.e. orders of service) appear from the fourteenth century on. The hymns in the *Hirmologia* and the *Sticheraria* manuscripts are more or less syllabic, while those in the *Psaltikon*, the *Kontakion* and the *Asmatikon* are melismatic. Most of the repertoire in the anthologies is melismatic. Further sub-divisions in the *Sticherarion* comprise: the *Stichera Idiomela*, which consists of hymns with their own melodies; *Stichera Automela*, containing hymns whose melodies serve as models for the *Stichera Prosomoia* (which imitate the melodies of the *Automela*).

There are two systems of notation. The ecphonetic regulates the *cantillation* of the lessons from the Prophets, the Gospel, Acts and Epistles. The texts are grouped in manuscripts called *Lectionaries*, *Prophetologia* and *Evangelia* from the tenth to the end of the thirteenth centuries. The neumatic notation specifies the execution of the melodies of hymns. Both systems derive from the ancient Greek prosodic signs.[55] Some fifteen different ecphonetic signs, in red or vermilion, are placed at the beginning, the end, above, beside or under a group of words, indicating syllables that were to be raised or lowered. As their derivation was prosodic rather than musical they could not in themselves express melody.

The musical signs are set in one line above each syllable. Manuscripts can be classified as containing:

1. the Early Byzantine notation, the so-called Chartres-Coislin,[56] from the tenth to the twelfth centuries;

2. the Middle Byzantine, diastematic notation from the twelfth to the fourteenth centuries;

---

54. The calendar entries in the manuscripts keep the old, Julian style which is thirteen days behind the Gregorian one. The ecclesiastical year starts on 1 September and ends on 31 August. Each of the 365 days of the year commemorates one or more saints and often a feast falls on the same day as well. The liturgical rubrics are regulated by a book called the *Typikon*. Music is provided for almost every day of the ecclesiastical year.

55. The invention of the prosodic signs or accents, is ascribed to the grammarian Aristophanes of Byzantium (*c.* 180 BC). They were introduced in the Hellenic age as a guide for declamation when Greek became the predominant language in the Eastern Mediterranean.

56. Named after two manuscripts; see Wellesz, *Byzantine*, pp. 263, 272.

3. the Late Byzantine, Koukouzelean, from the fourteenth to the nineteenth centuries.[57]

Most of the repertoire of hymns is written down in the Middle Byzantine notation from which transcriptions into the staff notation are published in the *transcripta series* of the *Monumenta musicae Byzantinae*.[58]

The fifteen interval signs of the Middle Byzantine notation are divided into two main groups: the *Somata*, representing 'bodies' which move in steps (ascending and descending seconds); and the *Pneumata*, representing 'spirits' which move in leaps (ascending and descending thirds and fifths). Among the *Somata* there are six different signs for the same interval of an ascending second, each representing a particular way of singing the interval; in fact conveying different nuances of expression, such as normal, emphatic, quick, shortening of the note, hesitant with a restrained and weak intonation, intensified. Other intervals, fourths, sixths etc., are expressed by way of combination. Another sign, the *Ison*, stands for the repetition of a note. *Ison* also denotes the 'drone', the holding note. The initial note of a melody is governed by the modal signature. The system of neumes consists of a chain of interval signs placed above the syllables to be sung. Each neume indicates the interval between itself and the previous one.

In addition to the interval signs there are a number of subsidiary 'great' signs or *Hypostases* which indicate no interval but give an expressive value. The introduction of these innovations is ascribed to the famous *Domestikos* (precentor) Ioannes Koukouzeles (*c.* 1300) and his fellow *Maistores*. Theoretical treatises, known as the *Papadikai*, were in fact elementary text books on music which included a concise introduction to the Late Byzantine notation. Although written in the fifteenth and sixteenth centuries these *Papadikai* helped investigators to discover the meaning of the Middle Byzantine neumes and, consequently, to reconstruct the system of Byzantine music.

Since the Byzantine neumes originated in prosodic signs, their shape more or less imitates the movements of the melody to be produced by the human voice. These are expressed by movements of the hand of the conducting precentor, the method being called *Cheironomia*. The rhythmical relationship among the notes, i.e. their relative duration, was fixed, but there was no division into bars. Phrases were divided by a dot in the manuscripts and

57. In 1821, the final reform by Chrysanthus made it possible for the music to be printed. This reformed, Chrysanthine notation is still in use in the Greek Orthodox Church.

58. The *Monumenta musicae Byzantinae* were founded in Copenhagen in 1931 by Professors Carsten Høeg (d. 1961), H. J. W. Tillyard (d. 1968) and E. J. Wellesz. Some fifty years ago the key for transcribing Byzantine musical signs into modern notation had not yet been discovered. The fundamental works of the founders of the *Monumenta* made possible all future research. About thirty volumes – sponsored by the *Union Académique Internationale* have been published in the four series of the *Monumenta: principale, subsidia, transcripta* and *lectionaria*. Cf. E. Wellesz, 'A Note on the Origins of the *Monumenta Musicae Byzantinae* (1931–71)' In Velimirović, *Eastern Chant*, ii, pp. vii–x.

by a dividing stroke in the published transcriptions. The phrases do not as a rule contain a fixed number of syllables, as the hymns were not composed in metre, but nearly always in rhythmical prose, like the Psalms and Canticles. The unit of time was the quaver, which was not sub-divided in the Middle Byzantine notation. In the Koukouzelean system semiquavers were made use of in new compositions.

The *Echoi* (modes) in Byzantine music should be thought of not merely as scales in the modern sense, but as groups of melodies of a certain type built upon a number of basic formulae which characterize the *Echoi*. There are four authentic and four plagal modes, each being designated by one or more modal signatures indicating to the singer whether he should start on a low or a high note. To help the singer check the correctness of his sung phrase, medial signatures are sometimes found at certain points of the melodies. The tonal system of Byzantine chant is a wholly diatonic one, its central octave having the internal structure of our diatonic octave d–d^1. The central octave consists of a series of eight notes arrived at by combining two groups of four notes each, namely, the tetrachords d–g and a–d^1. The similarity of this system with that of the Gregorian modes is remarkable, and in all like-lihood the Gregorian modes derived from the Byzantine modes (see p. 64). Indeed the four authentic and the four plagal modes of the Byzantine system are based on scales corresponding to the eight Gregorian modes.

Byzantine melody is a sort of mosaic consisting of two kinds of conventional formulae: patterns which are restricted in principle to a single mode or pair of modes; and ornaments and melismas usually attached to fixed points within the tonal system.

The majority of the *Scriptoriae* and libraries where extant manuscripts are kept include the major Greek, Russian, Bulgarian and Serbian mona-steries; among them the Palestinian monastery of St Sabas, the monastery of St Catherine on Mount Sinai, those in Jerusalem, Constantinople and Mount Athos. In addition there is the important Italian monastery of Grottaferrata near Rome which was untroubled by Turkish and other foreign domination and preserves the tradition of Byzantine hymnography up to the present day. Unlike the western tradition, where there are marked differences among certain orders, rites, and kinds of chant, the Orthodox tradition is fairly uniform. It is not surprising therefore to find manuscripts written in any of these *Scriptoriae* containing almost exactly the same melodies.[59]

The study of the Slavonic chants (Russian, Bulgarian and Serbian) and of the influence of Byzantine chant on the liturgical music of the Slavonic countries has been greatly aided by the recent discovery of medieval frag-mentary documents of Serbian and Bulgarian chants.[60]

59. Collections of Byzantine musical manuscripts have been microfilmed and can be ordered from the Library of Congress, Washington DC.

60. An International Board, chaired by E. Koschmieder, was constituted in December 1967.

ERNEST H. SANDERS

3 Polyphony and Secular Monophony: Ninth Century–c. 1300

THE FIRST STAGES OF POLYPHONY[1]

The musical tradition produced by western civilization gradually gave rise to the unique concept of music divorced from its intrinsic ancillary functions; ultimately music no longer needed to serve as an ingredient of processes such as ritual, ceremony, work, dance or recitation of poetry. The evolutionary accumulation of creative genius that yielded such autonomous genres as fugue, sonata and symphony was conditioned by three interrelated factors: (1) musical notation, (2) the exploitation of various simultaneous combinations of more than one sound and (3) the fashioning of discrete, more or less individualized, musical artifacts.

No musical culture other than that of the Christian west – at least to the middle of the twentieth century – is dependent on systematic notation. The

1. This chapter incorporates material from some of Ernest H. Sanders' previous essays, especially 'The Medieval Motet' in *Gattungen der Musik in Einzeldarstellungen: Gedenkschrift Leo Schrade*, vol. 1 (Bern and Munich, 1973), 403–79.

notation that began to appear in Frankish liturgical manuscripts of the ninth century evidently arose in answer to a growing need for a mnemonic tool. Since it functioned only as a reminder of the contours of traditional melodies serving as decorations and intensifications of liturgical texts, its symbols, called neumes, did not indicate pitches with graphic precision. (Notation employing neumes – see chapter 2, pp. 60 and 86 – is called neumatic notation.) But little time elapsed before it was realized that notation had didactic and conceptual potentialities far exceeding the immediate problems of memorization.

The earliest extant documents using notation for purposes other than to facilitate the rendering of chant melodies are the treatise entitled *Musica Enchiriadis* and its companion, the *Scholia Enchiriadis* (late ninth century). In part these two 'hand-books' or 'manuals' of Frankish origin, concern themselves with a particular technique of ornamenting plainchants (*pro ornatu ecclesiasticorum carminum*); for the first time an author describes how to effect the simultaneous conjunction of pitches with a chant melody. The result, an ensemble of separate concordant strands (*concentus concorditer dissonus*), was, according to the author, customarily called *organum*.

It is noteworthy that the first record of this practice appears only about half a century after tropes and sequences had begun to flourish; in fact, references to organal performance occur fairly often in the texts of sequences. Like the latter, *organum* owed its rise and cultivation in the monasteries to the growing medieval impulse towards elaboration.[2] In addition, this particular type of elaboration by means of vertical intervals (*symphonie*) undoubtedly goes back to unrecorded secular practices of north-western Europe.

Just as earlier treatises had classified the melodies of traditional plainchant, the *Musica Enchiriadis* represents the first of many undertakings of *ars musica* to organize, codify and demonstrate a new phenomenon: the simultaneous sounding of more than one musical pitch. Evidently such procedures were no longer completely novel to the learned monastic observers of the time. Of necessity, the author did not employ neumatic notation for this purpose, but the so-called Daseian system of notation, which fixes pitches and intervals precisely and graphically. Neumatic notation is meaningful only in conjunction with text; derived from accentual symbols, it has no inherently musical origin. Unlike Gregorian monophony, however, which is heightened speech, polyphony, that is simultaneity of pitches, is an eminently musical phenomenon; it is based on the detachment of pitch from language and on

2. The medieval tendency towards extension and elaboration has been discussed (see above p. 77) in conjunction with tropes. The term 'sequence' referred to a trope that was substituted for the melisma of an Alleluia chant. Tropes and sequences began to flourish in the early ninth century. In the present chapter references to the troping process usually apply to a general artistic principle and are not restricted to the technical categories of trope or sequence.

the consideration of pitch as a separate entity. Organized polyphony thus requires, for its theoretical demonstration, a rational ordering of the tonal material and a notational system which clearly represents individual pitches.

The human voice as speech medium provides no basis for the conception of a pitch system, since without the intercession of some sort of instrumental model it only projects indeterminate pitches in conjunction with words. The voice, i.e. the vocal chords, can be 'fretted' only by analogy with a stringed instrument provided with frets. (In the earlier Middle Ages a fretted mono-chord was often used for experiments connected with the construction of a scale, and in later centuries the guitar and lute provide instances of fretting.) Thus, while performance and perception of distinctly different pitches need not depend on man-made instruments, systematization of pitches has to be an instrumental function. Significantly, no matter how it was realized in performance, music was generically referred to in the Middle Ages as *musica instrumentalis*.

This notion of an instrumental origin is the basis for the proper conception of polyphony. No medieval writer gives a semantic explanation of the use of the term *organum* for polyphony, thus putting on us the onus of fathoming its meaning. *Organum*, the Latinization of the Greek *organon*, signifies 'tool', 'instrument'. Hence, the early use of the term *organum* as a designation for western polyphony points to its instrumental derivation.[3] *Organum* – tooled, organized music – constitutes the initial adumbration of music as an auto-nomous language and art, whose tendencies were to be increasingly instrumental.

For the most part, the examples of polyphony given in the *Musica Enchiriadis* and the *Scholia Enchiriadis* are still primitive enough to require notation only as a device of explication, but not to help in rehearsal or per-formance. To a pre-existing chant, called *vox principalis*, a new voice is sub-joined (*vox organalis*), which is chained to the original melody at a fixed interval; the *vox organalis* (or organal voice) lies either a fifth or a fourth below the *vox principalis*. Clearly no notation is necessary to sing a chant in this manner; a singer only has to find the appropriate register in order to duplicate the melody.[4] Since this technique of parallel *organum* amounts to the decorative underscoring of a melody with an unvarying interval, it is not surprising that the organal sonority could be reinforced by means of octave duplication of one or both of the parts.

3. Only one author ventures an explanation of the term '*organum*'. Johannes Affligemensis, writing in the early twelfth century, says the use of the term is due to the organ-like sound of early *organum*. Indeed, the beginning of vocal *organum* may well have been stimulated by the practice of accompanying a melody instrumentally with a parallel line or a drone bass.

4. As in the case of the *fauxbourdon* of the fifteenth century, such parallelism does not involve im-provisation, as has often been stated, but, on the contrary, slavish observance of a rigid rule.

Apart from its historic priority the significance of parallel *organum*, at least with respect to its potential evolution, is minimal. Of more importance is a variant of the technique of parallelism (see example 1) which came into being not because of a desire for greater sonorous variety, but in order to eliminate accidental imperfections in the organal interval, since parallelism at the fifth or fourth in a diatonic gamut will at times produce diminished fifths or tritones. The former are obviated in the *Musica Enchiriadis* by the construction of an unusual gamut consisting of interlocking Dorian scales on *G*, *d* and *a* and therefore containing only perfect fifths. Tritones, on the other hand, are avoided by tampering not with normal diatonicism, but with the principle of parallelism.

Example 1. *Musica Enchiriadis*

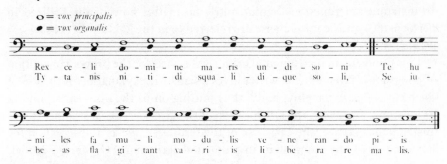

[King of heaven, Lord of the roaring sea,
Of the bright sun, and of the uncouth soil,
Thy humble servants, in worshipping Thee with devout melodies,
Entreat Thee that Thou mayest liberate them from their manifold misfortunes.]

Of all types of motion – parallel, oblique, similar and contrary – only similar motion is not represented. Unisons, seconds, thirds and a fifth occur in addition to the normal fourth. Its greater variety and apparent freedom notwithstanding, the rules for this type of *organum* were still simple enough to allow an *organizator* to add the necessary pitches below those of the *vox principalis* without benefit of notation; choice was minimal. (In one of the medieval treatises the singer-composer who supplied the additional part in *organum* was called the 'organizator'.) Essentially, the *vox organalis* is still a duplication, although with occasional modifications, for instance at cadential points where parallel motion is abandoned.

Not until the early eleventh century do we come upon further evidence of polyphony. Nearly all the sources, theoretical as well as practical, come from France or at least lean on French models. This seems to be so in the case of an English manuscript (Cambridge, Corpus Christi College, 473), which is one of the 'Winchester Tropers', two collections of chants for soloists, including a good many tropes and sequences.[5] Not only is it the earliest liturgical source of *organum*, but the extent of its polyphonic repertoire is unmatched before the emergence of the so-called 'Notre Dame School'. Since the monophonic corpus of the two books reflects monastic liturgical practices of north-central France, it has been assumed that the *organa* may well be modelled on similar French compositions no longer extant.

The polyphony appears in a sizeable section of the Cambridge manuscript, headed '*Incipiunt melliflua organorum modulamina super dulcissima celestia preconia*' ('Here begin the honey-sweet melodies of the *organa* on the delightful heavenly songs of praise') and containing altogether 158 organal voices for 'Kyrie' and 'Gloria' tropes, tracts, sequences, Alleluias, antiphons and responsories. (Fifteen additional organal voices entered subsequently are contemporaneous in style and notation.) In contrast to the examples in the *Musica Enchiriadis*, therefore, the polyphony elaborates solo chants, of which nearly two-thirds belong to the Mass. Thus this is the first document to show that polyphony had become the domain of the soloist, a practice that was to be maintained on the continent to the end of the fourteenth century. Around 1100 it became customary to reserve contrapuntal elaboration within the liturgy for those chants or chant passages apportioned to the cantors; any remaining portions continued to be sung monophonically by the chorus. Logically, *organum* was left to the soloists not only because they were the most highly trained musicians, but also because the performance of a *vox organalis* tended to have some latitude of improvisation.

Attempts to read the Winchester polyphony, all of which serves the liturgy of important feasts, encounter considerable obstacles, not only because of the neumatic notation, but also because the organal voices are collected in a separate section of the manuscript, apart from the chants they decorate. Evidently the style of the Winchester *organa* applies and extends the principles of the second type of *organum* of the *Musica Enchiriadis*. While the organal voice often parallels the *vox principalis* at the lower fourth, it crosses to the fifth above the *cantus firmus* when the latter lies low. In either low or high position it remains stationary where this is contrapuntally desirable and favours contrary or oblique motion to reach the cadential unisons.[6]

The traditional relative position of the two parts is maintained in the *Micrologus* (*c.* 1025) by Guido of Arezzo, who devotes two chapters (18 and 19) to *organum*. His treatise still describes parallel *organum*, in which the organal voice is now restricted exclusively to the lower fourth. He clearly prefers an organal style, however, which, though dominated by the fourth, also admits the major second, major third and – less commonly – the minor third; moreover all types of motion occur in Guido's examples (parallel,

---

5. The other manuscript (Oxford: Bodleian Library, Bodley 775) contains no *organa*.

6. The most recent and authoritative study of the Winchester polyphony is Holschneider's book of 1968.

contrary, similar and oblique). Avoidance of the tritone is no longer given as the reason for the dispensation from parallelism; variety of intervals is desirable for its own sake. There are also a few instances of voice-crossing. What is particularly important is Guido's concern with cadential motion, which in effect sanctions the cadential writing in the Winchester *organa*: the two voices should preferably end on a unison, preceded by contrary or oblique motion. Thus the *Micrologus* reflects, at least by implication, an incipient reorientation from sonorous duplication (parallelism or modified parallelism) to counterpoint (variety of intervals and of motion).

In some of the organal settings of the solo portions of a dozen responsorial chants, which were written on three leaves dating from the second half of the eleventh century (Chartres, Bibliothèque Municipale, 4, 130 and 109), this reorientation is a *fait accompli*. These settings were almost totally destroyed by fire in the Second World War. The transcription of two of these leaves presents problems of notation familiar from the Winchester *organa*, but in MS 109 (*c*.1100) the neumes are written on dry-point four-line staffs. Manuscripts 130 and 109 place the organal part directly above the *vox principalis*, though their relative position in the register depends on the tessitura of the chant melody; voice-crossings are common, especially when a chant occupies the middle of the Gregorian range (e.g. first and eighth modes). Yet the frequency with which the pitches of a chant lie below those of the added part clearly shows that subordinate decoration of the original melody, with its preference for the vertical interval of the fourth, has given way to contrapuntal considerations. The appearance of 'diastematic' notation with its precise indication of pitch robbed plainchant of whatever melodic or ornamental flexibility it may still have possessed. With this precision of a graphic notation, a chant could now be turned into a *cantus firmus* subservient to the composer's creative impulses.

The history of the *cantus firmus* begins in the early years of the twelfth century: it is the six centuries' long and fascinating story of composers' various efforts to bend the chant to their purposes. The processes of composition governing this new approach to the contrapuntal exploitation of chant melodies can be gleaned from the twenty-third chapter of the *De musica*, written in the early twelfth century by Johannes Affligemensis.[7] Evidently the *organizator* subdivided the chant into sections, each being delimited by one word of two or more syllables. (Monosyllables formed a unit with the preceding or the following word.) Since (1) the last note of each unit required a perfect consonance (unison or octave, depending on the position of the appropriate note of the chant), (2) contrary motion was now stipulated as normal and (3) voice-crossings were common, as both parts

---

7. Recent research implies that the author of this treatise was not an Englishman named Johannes Cotto, but a monk in Affligem, near Brussels.

occupied the same range: this counterpoint, though rid of the principle of parallelism, is still fairly predictable and was presumably executed *supra librum*.[8] Each unit tends to begin with a consonance, i.e. unison, octave, fifth or fourth, though the latter necessarily declined as a structural interval in the evolving polyphony of the *cantus firmus*. Intermediate intervals within a section need not be consonant; in fact the appearance of the cadential third between fifth and unison is little less than a contrapuntal inevitability (see example 2).

Example 2. Johannes Affligemensis, *De Musica*

Lau - da - te   do - mi - num   de   ce - lis

[Praise the Lord from the Heavens.]

ORGANUM AND DISCANT

The author of one of the two oldest treatises written in the early twelfth century and concerned exclusively with *organum*[9] (MS Montpellier, Faculté de Médecine, H 384) stated expressly that the construction of an organal voice was largely determined by the final chant note of each section:

One must beware with all care and the greatest caution that the *discantus* have no more notes than the *cantus*. . . . For it is beyond dispute that *discantus* is one thing and *organum* another. Thus, when you wish to ornament the end of a period or section, make sure that you don't all too frequently give the *discantus* excessive melismatic passages, lest in the mistaken belief that you are making a *discantus* you actually construct an *organum* and destroy the *discantus*. . . . Discant and *organum*, however, are considered to differ in this way: while a discant corresponds to its *cantus* with an equal number of notes, which form consonances or unisons with it, an *organum* is joined with its *cantus* not note against note, but with an unlimited multiplicity and a kind of wondrous flexibility.

These sentences place in relief the most substantial achievement initiated by French musicians of the late eleventh century. Apart from the old style, now called *discantus*, a new technique had evolved, allowing the *organizator* to sing melismas over each note of the *vox principalis*; the term *organum* was transferred to the new style. The strictures against the introduction of organal style into discant settings for purposes other than cadential elabora-

8. *Supra librum* is a fourteenth-century term denoting the extemporized rendition of a counterpoint to a chant in a liturgical book.

9. The other document, entitled *Ad organum faciendum* and likewise of French provenance, is preceded in the main source that preserves it (Milan, Biblioteca Ambrosiana, M. 17. sup) by three *organa* in letter notation. There are a few additional minor sources of polyphony prior to the twelfth century.

tion are here formulated with a didactic precision seldom mirrored by the preserved repertoire. (The situation is comparable to the neat division of sixteenth-century counterpoint into a number of species, none of which looms large in the reputable compositions of that time.) While the new style doubtless originated in the desire for cadential ornamentation, in many discant settings of the twelfth century the upper part will have roughly from one to four notes against one in the lower part, apart from terminal melismas (see example 3).

Example 3. British Museum, Add. 36881, fol. 13ᵛ; text of last two stanzas from MS Bib. Nat., fonds lat. 1139, fol. 59ʳ

Fraude nota Adam condoluit
Eva quoque que scelus monuit
Fit commota.

Fit commota planxitque nimium
Que seduxit et se et socium
Adam Eva.

Adam Eva mali convivio
Imposuit longo exilio
Uxor seva.

Uxor seva decepit hominem
Fraude sed fraus per sanctam virginem
Est adempta.

Est adempta plebs diabolica
Ergo plaudat voce magnifica
Plebs redempta.

Plebs redempta plaudat magnifice
Benedicat nato deifice
Ex Maria.

Ex Maria natus est dominus
Cuius regni non erit terminus.
Et *gratias*.

[When the world's first progeny was led astray,
The dwellers in paradise were perturbed at the discovery of this offence.
At the discovery of this offence, Adam grieved greatly,
And Eva also, who counselled the crime, was disturbed.

She was disturbed and lamented much,
Eva, who had led astray both herself and her consort Adam.

Adam, sharing the apple with her,
Was burdened with the long exile by Eva, his wicked wife.

His wicked wife ensnared man with her offence,
But through the holy virgin the burden of this offence has been taken away.

And taken away is the devilish host;
Therefore let the host of the redeemed sing its praises mightily.

Let the host of the redeemed praise mightily
And bless Him whom God caused to be born by Mary.

Mary gave birth to the Lord,
Whose reign shall have no end. Let us give thanks.)

Prima mundi occurs in a manuscript (London, British Museum, Additional 36881) which is the latest of the four sources that are often regarded as a group preserving the so-called St Martial polyphony. (The others are Paris, *Bibliothèque Nationale, fonds latin*, MSS 1139, 3719 and 3549.) Actually none of them can be proved to have originated in the Benedictine abbey of St Martial at Limoges, which acquired several such manuscripts in the early thirteenth century, nor can they be considered a group, though they are linked by a few concordances. Their area of origin is Southern France, and the probable dates of the manuscripts vary considerably (*c.* 1100 for MS 1139, second half of the twelfth century for the London MS). All but the oldest of the sources employ staff notation; in MS 1139 the neumes are carefully placed in relation to a single dry-point guideline which may or may not have a clef. The music, which seems characteristic of the first half of the twelfth century, is about equally divided between monophony and polyphony; most of the seventy-odd *organa* are settings of rhymed, rhythmic poetry, usually strophic, which MS 1139 designates as *versus*.[10] Many of these end with 'Benedicamus Domino', thus revealing their function as substitute tropes[11] for the versicle which, together with the response 'Deo gratias', occurs near the end of all Offices, and was an occasion for particularly florid singing at Vespers, Matins and Lauds. The texts of the majority of the *versus* indicate that they served as elaborations of Office services. Their use for the Mass was less common, while several others were evidently destined for more informal occasions. Apart from the *versus* there are a few polyphonic sequences, tropes, 'Benedicamus' settings etc.

The poetry of the *versus* ranges from the simplest rhymed versification to highly complex structures. The musical designs, which do not necessarily parallel the forms of the poetry, likewise exhibit a great variety – from simple strophic arrangements to continuous musical settings with sophisticated structural relationships. But even the *vox organalis* of as unassuming a song

10. The genre of *versus* originated in the Carolingian era (*c.* 800). A few monophonic settings dating from before the twelfth century have survived, but the notation of most of them is indecipherable.

11. For a discussion of the process of troping, see pp. 77–9 and 90.

as *Prima mundi* reveals a skilful attention to contour, proportion, direction and balanced recurrences that explains the tendency away from note-against-note counterpoint.[12] In spite of its apparent simplicity, *Prima mundi* no longer reflects a procedure that can be extemporized on the basis of rules; this is a fully-fledged composition with complex vertical and horizontal relationships, whose conception and execution by composer and performer are based on a notational system which indicates pitches and intervals un-equivocally. The introduction of clef and staff was the crucial step with which notation began to advance from a descriptive mnemonic device to a prescriptive tool responsive to the creative impulse towards the shaping of polyphonic compositions.

It seems particularly significant that this momentous development should first appear in settings of non-Gregorian material. It is true, of course, that our knowledge of twelfth-century polyphony is hardly extensive enough for confident generalizations; what we know is likely to be no more than the tip of the iceberg. Yet it is tempting to conclude that it was a song repertoire nurtured by indigenous attitudes and conventions which sparked off the striking developments of 'art music' in the twelfth century. In contrast to Christian ritual chant, the *versus* are poetry consisting of phrases defined and related by rhyme and versification. Most of the tunes also contrast with the music of the Office and Proper of the Mass, which ranges between the extremes of chanting on a single reciting note and melismatic jubilation. The *versus* melodies are generally made up of phrases displaying ordered and balanced relationships and recurrences, features they share with the dance; moreover their often four-square phraseology as well as their frequent tendency towards pentatonicism or the major mode (see example 8, p. 102) also seem to point to a secular origin. Evidently songs such as these, with their clarity and plasticity, stimulated composers to further 'organization'. Furthermore a number of circumstances leads us to believe that the impulse towards using simultaneous sounds in music is also rooted in the secular realm.

Refinement and extension of fundamentally simple and palpable elements of balance and ordered correspondence – this was the aim of composers, as shown in the horizontal (melodic) as well as the vertical (contrapuntal) dimensions of much of the St Martial polyphony. The melodic relationships between component phrases of these closed forms are often matched by devices of contrapuntal integration, such as voice exchange (see p. 109) and inversion, which are easily achieved in counterpoint in two equal parts. They occur especially in terminal melismas, where they are often emphasized by sequential repetition (see example 4).

12. Note-against-note counterpoint continued to be cultivated for centuries in many less advanced peripheral localities.

Example 4. Quoted after Treitler, *JAMS* (1964), 37–8

In contrast to discant style, organal compositions are less concerned with lucidity of form, and the generally conjunct style of the melismas often seems reminiscent of responsorial psalmody (see example 5).

Example 5. Bib. Nat., fonds lat. 3719, fol. 70ʳ

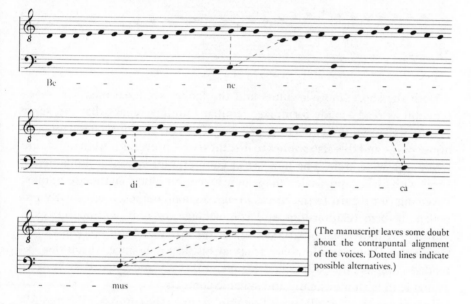

(The manuscript leaves some doubt about the contrapuntal alignment of the voices. Dotted lines indicate possible alternatives.)

It is quite logical, therefore, that of the polyphonic proses[13] in the repertoire the older type produced organal arrangements, while the modern proses with their rhymed, rhythmic and strophic poetry were given more song-like discant settings.

The octave leap in example 5 is one feature showing that, in spite of its conjunct flow, organal style was not intended to be 'neo-Gregorian'. Melismatic *organum* undoubtedly started, and was maintained for a considerable time, as an improvisational practice, spinning exuberant melodic threads from consonance to consonance. By about the middle of the twelfth century,

13. Sequences were often called 'proses'.

however, organal melismas begin to be composed of more clearly defined components, often sequential, thus revealing the influence of a new shaping energy that caused the gradual replacement of improvisation by composition (see example 6).

Example 6. Taken from an *organum* treatise, MS Rome, Biblioteca Vaticana, Ottob. lat. 3025, fol. 48^{r-v}

Both the short 'motivic' units and the longer sectional members often function as ready-made formulae; familiar building blocks that can serve equally well in a number of circumstances. Thus the sectional character of an upper part – and this also applies to discant style – prevents it from unfolding freely in a wide arch. The new art of counterpoint caused a fundamental break with earlier approaches to melodic invention. But even though he must have constant regard to the *cantus firmus*, a good composer was clearly impelled to form relationships and connections not only within, but even beyond the individual progressions. For the articulation of sectional alternation there was considerable variety at his disposal, since within one extended composition (still called *organum*) discant and organal style were available in both melismatic and syllabic contexts.

In a few of the 'Benedicamus Domino' settings the composer ingeniously combined the *cantus firmus* with a trope-like *versus* in the upper part, thus creating a new genre, the troped *organum*. Characteristic of this genre are the frequent terminal assonances of the words of the *cantus firmus* and of those sung simultaneously in the *vox organalis*. The last six verses of the poem, of which example 7 gives the beginning, end in 'o', while the final two verses approximate (and even echo) the word 'Domino' more closely, by ending with 'termino' and 'Domino' respectively.

Another manuscript, dating from about the middle of the twelfth century, preserves twenty-one polyphonic compositions, of which one is a *contra-factum* of a St Martial *versus*. This book, the so-called Codex Calixtinus,[14]

14. Though authentic, this is actually a misleading title, since the compilers fraudulently invoked the authority of Pope Calixtus II (d. 1124) to enhance the prestige of their undertaking.

Example 7. Bib. Nat., fonds lat. 1139, fol. 60ᵛ

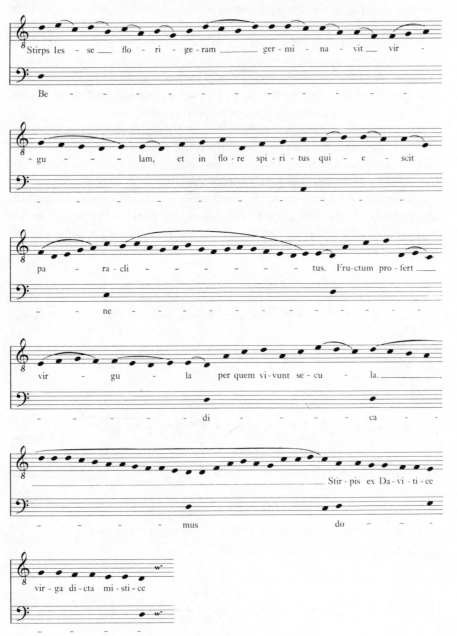

[The tree of Jesse has sprouted a flowered branch,
And in that flower reposes the Holy Ghost, our protector.
The branch brings forth fruit that gives life to the ages.
From this branch of the mystic tree of Jesse . . .]

contains an elaborate musical liturgy for St James in its first part, evidently written in France for the famous monastery Santiago de Compostela in north-western Spain, which, because of its possession of the bones of the apostle, was almost as important a goal for pilgrimages as Rome and Jerusalem. The manuscript, which has been in Compostela since the twelfth century, doubtless owes its existence to a desire to honour a revered institution, located in an area alive with Christian agitation against the Moors, with an elaborate and fitting rite for its patron saint.

Apart from nine *versus*, many of which are 'Benedicamus' substitutes (see also p. 115 below), the polyphonic compositions of the Calixtine manuscript consist of five responsories (solo portions), one sequence, two 'Kyrie' tropes, one Alleluia (solo portions), and three 'Benedicamus' settings. For all but two of the compositions, names of clerics are given as composers, though the authenticity of the ascriptions is dubious. Organal style prevails in the responsories, the Alleluia, and the 'Benedicamus' settings, while a discant, neumatically ornamented,[15] is characteristic of the remaining pieces.

Example 8. Codex Calixtinus, fol. 187ᵛ

Vox   no - stra re - - so - net Ia - co - bi

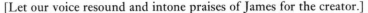

in - to - net lau - des cre - a - to - - - ri.

(The last of the four stanzas ends 'dicamus domino'.)

[Let our voice resound and intone praises of James for the creator.]

Example 9. Codex Calixtinus, fol. 190ʳ

Be - - ne - - di - - ca - mus____

15. A neumatic melody is not syllabic, but is less florid than a melismatic melody. Neumatic melodies are likely to contain between two and five notes per syllable.

In example 8 the interval *b–f* occurs at times between the two parts. Throughout the Middle Ages *b–f* was abstractly conceived as part of a scalar series of fifths (*a–e, b–f, c–g*, etc.). Avoidance of a diminished vertical interval such as *b–f* was seldom specified in the notation, since it became a dilemma only when the composition, which was basically a graphic fixation of a series of concepts, became concrete. Then, in rehearsal, the matter was as a rule 'accidentally' resolved by subjecting one of the ingredients of the false interval to a kind of 'adjectival modification'; presumably, the *b* was usually flattened, though there is evidence that already in the late twelfth century the *f* was sometimes sharpened. Such adjustments of intervals (diminished fifth, diminished octave etc.) came to be known as *musica ficta*.

THE NOTRE DAME SCHOOL

In the history of western civilization the twelfth century plays a remarkable role. Its cultural accomplishments include not only the developments in poetry and music described earlier, but

the complete development of Romanesque art and the rise of Gothic; the full bloom of vernacular poetry, both lyric and epic; and the new learning and new literature in Latin. The century begins with the flourishing age of the cathedral schools and closes with the earliest universities already well established. . . . It starts with only the bare outline of the seven liberal arts and ends in possession of the Roman and canon law, the new Euclid and Ptolemy and the Greek and Arabic physicians, thus making possible a new philosophy and a new science . . . .[16]

Education and learning, formerly the privileges of the monasteries, found a broader base in the cathedral schools. Paris became not only the urban and political centre of France, but, with its Notre Dame Cathedral, begun in 1163, it also assumed the leadership of all learning and therefore of music. And it is in Paris, in the second half of the century, and more specifically at Notre Dame, that we encounter the first composer of western polyphony whose name has come down to us.

LEONIN. 'Master Leoninus was generally known as the best composer of *organa*, who made (*fecit*) the *Magnus Liber organi de gradali et antifonario* (the great book of *organum* for Mass and Offices) for the enhancement of the divine service.' This sentence, taken from a treatise on music written about 1280 by an Englishman known as Anonymus IV,[17] contains all the explicit

16. Charles H. Haskins, *The Renaissance of the Twelfth Century*, Cambridge (Mass.), 1939, pp. 6f.
17. He appears as the fourth of a number of anonymous authors in Edmond de Coussemaker's edition of medieval writers on music, *Scriptorum de musica . . .*, Paris, 1864–76.

information we have about Leonin. We have circumstantial evidence that he must have composed his cycle in the years around 1170 'for the enhancement of the divine service' at Notre Dame. What we do not know is what else he may have composed; the evidence we possess shows him only as a composer who applied polyphony to Gregorian *cantus firmi*, specifically to responsories and 'Benedicamus' chants (Vespers, Matins and Processions), and to Graduals and Alleluias (Mass). Responsories and Alleluias had received festal polyphonic settings since the eleventh century (Winchester, Chartres, Compostela etc.), but to produce a cycle of *organa* for the solo portions of responsorial chants of important feast days throughout the liturgical year was a new and strikingly ambitious notion, foreshadowed only in the Winchester Troper. It clearly indicates that polyphony had achieved a state of equilibrium similar to that represented by Bach's *Orgelbüchlein* or Isaac's *Choralis Constantinus*.

Anonymus IV, as we have seen, tells us that Leonin was regarded as 'the best composer of *organa* ('*optimus organista*'). And indeed organal portions preponderate in the *Magnus Liber*, often with astonishingly long melismas in the upper part, now called *duplum*, decorating single notes of the *cantus firmus* in the lower voice, designated 'tenor' since it truly sustains the upper part.[18] The performance of the tenor with its extraordinarily extended notes may have been aided by the organ – the only instrument, apart from bells, which was liturgically acceptable in the Middle Ages.

Discant style is generally applied to melismatic passages in the chant. It is in the Leoninian discant sections, of which each *organum* usually contains one or two, that a momentous new development becomes clearly apparent for the first time; in discant, writes a theorist, 'at least two notes – it goes without saying, a long one and a short one or their equivalent . . . – must be set over any note of plainchant'. Hence discant gave rise to measured music (*musica mensurata*) by setting against the tenor notes a standard of subdivision that recognized a basic differentiation of long and short – in that order. Long and breve (ratio: 2:1) were the only precisely measurable units of the emerging *musica mensurata*. The primacy of this rhythm is doubtless because, in 'second-species counterpoint',[19] the note which intervenes in the added part between two vertical consonances is often dissonant and therefore recognized as of lesser value. The ligatures,[20] which were the traditional notational symbols for melismatic music, therefore begin to assume mensural meaning. The fact that dissonance is resolved by consonance (rather than the reverse) accounts for the most basic mensural symbol and its interpretation: the binary ligature is read as a unit, with the second of its two

18. The frequently advanced explanation of the term 'tenor' as due to the 'held' notes of the *cantus firmus* seems less convincing.

19. Notes of half the value in the counterpoint against the *cantus firmus*, e.g. minims against semibreves.

20. The term 'neume' went out of fashion around 1200 when, in the new square notation, symbols combining two or more notes came to be known as ligatures.

notes having twice the length of the first.[21] The notational practice that tended to make the last note of a ligature in the upper part coincide with the appropriate note of the lower part (except at beginnings of phrases) goes back to the early twelfth century. What was new was that relationships of duration as well as of pitch could now be shown in notation.

Example 10. W_1, fol. 29 (25)[r]

In comparison with earlier polyphony example 10 shows a greater awareness of phrase structure, cadential correspondences and motivic relationships, rhythmic as well as melodic. In fact in many such discant passages the articulation of the chant melisma in the tenor seems to be determined solely by the melodic design of the *duplum*.

A significant number of discant phrases have a length of four beats. The same preference for a fairly square design of phrases seems to characterize many organal passages as well (see example 10), thus differentiating them from the 'wondrous flexibility' of the St Martial type. This observation is offered with due caution, since the rhythmic notation of organal *dupla*, which lack the contrapuntal and mensural control of the tenor, is often still somewhat inconsistent and imprecise;[22] organal phrases therefore seem melodically and rhythmically less congealed than discant passages. Yet a tendency towards

21. These are generally transcribed as quaver (eighth-note) and crotchet (quarter-note) respectively, with a bracket indicating the original ligature.

22. This inconsistency and imprecision makes attempts at rhythmic readings of pre-Leoninian polyphony even more hazardous and suspect.

a rationally balanced phrase structure in both organal and discant sections is apparent; sometimes such stylistically disparate sections are even joined by related phrases. Nevertheless at this stage of the evolution of mensural music and of its notation, a degree of flexibility approaching improvisation must have been possible as the performer linked the phrases of an organal *duplum* together. In their alternation the contrasting organal and discant passages may be compared to arioso and aria of a later age.

PEROTIN. After his tantalizingly brief reference to Leonin and his epoch-making volume, Anonymus IV continues with a more detailed report about later developments:

> This book [the *Magnus Liber*] was in use until the time of Perotinus Magnus, who shortened it and composed a great many better *clausulae* or *puncta*, because he was *optimus discantor* and better than Leoninus. . . . Moreover, this same Magister Perotinus wrote excellent *Quadrupla* (i.e. compositions for four voices), such as *Viderunt* and *Sederunt*, replete with artful musical turns and figures, as well as a considerable number of very famous *Tripla*, such as *Alleluia Posui adiutorium*, [*Alleluia*] *Nativitas* etc. Besides, he also composed *Conducti* for three voices, e.g. *Salvatoris hodie*; and two-part *Conducti*, such as *Dum sigillum summi patris*, and monophonic *Conducti*, e.g. *Beata viscera* and many more. The book, or rather the books, of Magister Perotinus were in use in the choir of the Church of Our Blessed Virgin in Paris until . . . the present day . . . .

In the Middle Ages there was no copyright, but there was the constant obligation to perfect the craft of music (*ars musica*) and its artifacts in the context of divine worship. Hence there are variant versions for many passages in the *Magnus Liber*. It has often been claimed that Perotin,[23] member of the post-Leoninian generation, shortened the *Magnus Liber* because its chant settings were intolerably long. But liturgical practice had not changed so as to warrant these alterations. Moreover Perotin himself had written a number of polyphonic chant settings whose organal sections are of truly vast proportions. Thus his abbreviations are in tune with the constantly changing concepts of musical style, whose benefit such an excellent work as the *Magnus Liber* was deemed worthy of receiving. There are therefore considerable differences between the three versions of the *Magnus Liber*, preserved together with much other music of the period in the principal Notre Dame manuscripts[24]

23. On circumstantial evidence his dates may be given as approximately 1165–1225.

24. Wolfenbüttel, Herzog August Bibliothek 677; Florence, Biblioteca Laurenziana, Plut. 29 Codex 1; Wolfenbüttel, Herzog August Bibliothek 1206. In the indicated order these manuscripts (W₁, F and W₂) mirror three successive stages of the polyphonic repertory of the so-called Notre Dame School (*c.* 1215, *c.* 1230, *c.* 1245). Other differences between the three versions of the *Magnus liber* are due to the spread of its type of polyphony to other Parisian churches, where variant liturgical conventions produced polyphonic settings of chants not appropriate to Notre Dame.

(two of them housed in Wolfenbüttel and abbreviated as W_1 and W_2 and one in Florence, abbreviated as F).

Fortunately we possess concrete evidence for what seems to have been the beginning of this process of modernization and tightening. The F manuscript contains 155 extremely concise snippets of discant polyphony, most of which were intended to serve as replacement for the long organal passages in the *Magnus Liber*.

Example 11a. F, fol. 178ʳ

Et   fi - li -   -   -   -   -   o.

Example 11b. F, fol. 182ᵛ

Ma   -   -   -   -   -   -   nus.

The rhythm of example 11b is noticeably more spacious and 'measured' than that of examples 10 and 11a and evidently accounts for the doubling of the customary note values in the tenor. Likewise the substitutes which replace Leoninian discant passages nearly always have relatively quiet and disciplined rhythms, contrasting with those of the original passages. There are several *organa* that were largely re-composed in this new manner, replacing the more unruly, barely contained rhythms of Leonin's settings.

The rhythmic style of these more modern *dupla* dominates the extraordinary variety that Anonymus IV admired in the *tripla* and *quadrupla*[25] ('replete with artful musical turns and figures').

To the best of our knowledge it was Perotin who began to cultivate three-part polyphony. The two four-part settings of the Graduals for December 25 and 26 (*Viderunt* and *Sederunt*), with their huge organal sections, represent truly exceptional feats (see example 12 over, the end of the Gradual *Sederunt*).

25. *Tripla* and *quadrupla* respectively denote *organa* for three or four voices as well as the third and fourth voice of such compositions.

Example 12. The end of the Gradual, *Sederunt*, for December 26, by Perotin

— — am.

tu — — am.

[. . . make me well by dint of Thy compassion.]

Careful examination of this excerpt – less than one tenth of the entire setting (respond and verse) – reveals the extraordinary ingenuity with which the phrase content of three homogeneous voices is related within each part and, at times, among two or even all three of them, usually by means of part exchange or varied voice exchange. (This technique of having a group of notes wander from one voice to another is characteristic of Perotin; 'voice exchange' [German: *Stimmtausch*] is the standard English term. For other illustrations see example 4c of this chapter and the melisma of example 5 of chapter 6.1). In a dazzling display of inventiveness Perotin weaves his arsenal of rhythmic and melodic formulae into sections whose sub-division into periods gives both organal and discant passages a novel, dance-like swing. His procedure compels admiration, especially as the two-part framework (i.e. the high-low contrapuntal boundary) rarely exceeds an octave. There are, in fact, octave and unison parallels, as well as parallel fifths, but they are clearly embodied within a drive and direction both melodic and contrapuntal. This pull towards the cadence accounts for many of the dissonant longs,[26] in line with the tradition of passing dissonances existing in discant style ever since the *organum* described by Johannes Affligemensis. The ornamental appoggiatura dissonance, already part of Leonin's vocabulary (as in example 10), is also common. The display of dissonances, as well as the fact that the breve is, with rare exceptions, the shortest value, gives a fair indication of the rather lively tempo which, we must assume, governs this music. This concept is confirmed by thirteenth-century theory, according to which the breve is as short as is compatible with full voice production.

26. Concerning long and breve see p. 104. In modern transcriptions the equivalent of the long is crotchet or dotted crotchet. Concerning the dotted crotchet see below, p. 113, fn. 31.

Yet with all their full sonority, variety and organal monumentality, the *quadrupla*, written in the last years of the twelfth century, remained isolated accomplishments. Even three-part writing declined temporarily, as Perotin, and possibly others, turning to the further development of discant style,[27] began to cultivate a less imposing genre.

Ever since Leonin's time there had been a tendency to divide the tenor notes of discant passages into more or less regular groups. It was almost inevitable that the predilection for *dupla* with balanced phrase designs, which accounts for this practice, would lead to the shaping of more clearly defined groups. The first distinct tenor pattern to emerge is a result of a sharper, 'masculine' delineation of the common feminine group of four longs |♩ ♩ ♩ ♩ ♪|, which becomes |♩ ♩ ♩ ♪ |. Two other patterns appeared almost at the same time: |♩ ♩ ♩ ♪ |♩ ♩ ♪ | and its converse |♩ ♩ ♪ |♩ ♩ ♩ ♪ |.

Perotin's new attitude towards phrase design led not only to the patterning of the tenor but also to the recognition of discant passages as distinct entities. Even some of the substitute abbreviations give the impression that they exist not merely to be inserted somewhere in place of more old-fashioned passages, but that they are in fact miniature pieces of music with a life of their own. But apart from these, hundreds of more or less lengthy discant settings of Gregorian melismas, separated from their original monophonic or potential polyphonic environment, are gathered in three fascicles of MSS W_1 and F, constituting that new species of music which Anonymus IV called *clausula* or *punctum*. According to him, a great many *clausulae* were written by Perotin, who thereby produced the first repertoire of self-contained and independently shaped pieces of music based on Gregorian tenors, i.e. on rhythmically patterned or (less and less often) grouped melismas. There is thus a fundamentally significant difference between *organum* and *clausula*: a liturgical *organum* is not a piece of music, since, no matter how much of a strain the polyphony imposes on the *cantus firmus*, it is the chant as a whole (including the monophonic choral portions) which is the only entity with integrity. The 'music of the future' (thirteenth and fourteenth centuries) evolved from the radical notion of carving a segment out of a chant in order to compose a piece of polyphony with precisely measured ingredients.

The artistic traditions of troping[28] and the medieval interdependence of music and words make it inevitable that poetic texts should have been applied to the vocalized *dupla* of many *clausulae*. They were, as one might say, predestined to be wedded to appropriate verses. The combination of troping and polyphony that had produced troped *organa* was restricted by the Notre Dame School to the *clausula* repertoire; the resulting pieces were called

27. Anonymus IV describes Perotin as *optimus discantor* (best composer of discant), in contrast to Leonin, *optimus organista*.

28. See pp. 90 and 97.

motets.[29] This circumstance helps to explain the nagging ontological enigma of the *clausula*, which might well be formulated in the manner of Bernard de Fontenelle's supposed question to the sonata, *Clausula, que me veux-tu?*

The known facts are these:

1. Certain *clausulae* were originally composed as part of an *organum*;

2. In the F version of the *Magnus Liber*, *clausulae* appear as replacements of or additions to older passages in W_1; several of the replacements are not abbreviations. This substitute use of *clausulae* had begun to decline in the last preserved version of the *Magnus Liber* in W_2.

3. *Clausulae* turn up as motets in F and W_2 as well as many other manuscripts, while there are very few early motets for which no *clausulae* functioning as sources are known.

It may have been necessary to trope pre-existing *clausulae* in order to compose motets, since melismatic discant had brought about the reform of notation, introducing fixed time values. For several decades the thirteenth century possessed no individual symbols with which to express rhythms in music *cum littera* in notation. In these circumstances it seems difficult to imagine the composition or the rehearsing of a motet without the aid of a melismatic model. One must conclude, then, that the *clausulae* were a pivotal phenomenon. Their availability as substitutes, used less and less, points to the past, while their adaptation as motets[30] explains their continued cultivation as well as the otherwise inexplicable multiplicity of *clausulae* built on the same chant melisma. To be sure, a good many of them are not known as motets and were probably not equipped with a text. Yet, on the whole, *clausulae* with patterned tenors doubtless came to be viewed as potential motets.

The following excerpt (example 13) from the *triplum, Alleluia Pascha nostrum*, probably by Perotin, may serve as an example. With the added textual trope for the upper voices it is a motet; without it, a *clausula*.

Example 13. Florence MS (and other sources)

29. For the reasons for this term, see below, pp. 136–7.

30. See p. 141, fn. 63 for references to *motetus* texts in connection with *clausulae*.

gau - di - um per a - zi - mum sit a - ni - mum pa - scha   le - tum,

le - to le - tum est   de - le - tum ex - u - lat ex - i - li - um post

tri - du - um   ces - sat va - cu - um tu - um mors de - cre - tum,

II

am - ple - xa - tur par - vu - lum   dat os - cu - lum dat a - nu - lum pa -

- ter et vi - tu - lum,   o quam dul - ce fer - cu - lum in

a - ra cru - cis tor - ri - dum, a quo flu - it

sa - pi - dum cru - or po - cu - lum no - - strum.

[Our joy is made full; let our Passover be joyful in view of the uncorrupted
soul; death has been snatched from Death, with the passing of three days the
exile is exiled, and vain and empty is thy decree, o Death. The Father embraces
His child and gives him a kiss, a ring, and a calf [cf. Luke 25:20–3]; o how sweet
is the burning hot dish there on the mound of the cross, the dish from which
flows the tasty blood, our drink.]

It is an element of great charm that the musical phraseology of most
clausulae, while carefully planned, exhibits no deadly regularity. The phrases
of *Nostrum* are made up of groups of 4, 8 and 12 longs; and its phrase
structure might be summarized as set out in the following table, where L
stands for long.[31]

> Upper parts: $(8L+12L)+2\times(12L+8L)+3\times4L$
> Tenor: $9\times(4L+4L)$

It will be seen that the tenor (amounting to 18 bars in modern transcription)
contains the equivalent of 72 longs (or dotted crotchets) which are organized
into groups of twice four longs $(4L+4L)$, repeated nine times: $9\times(4L+4L)$.
The 72 longs of the upper voices are organized differently: 20 longs, $(8+12)$,
followed by 40 longs $(2\times(12+8))$, followed by 12 longs (3×4). Such
numerical diagrams, however unfamiliar, serve to emphasize the importance
of proportion in medieval art, whether in music, architecture or some other

---

31. In such formulae the 'long' is considered as containing three breves; binary and ternary longs
came to be called *longae duorum temporum* and *longae trium temporum*; a binary long could not be followed
by another, since all rhythms consist of 'two notes – it goes without saying, a long one and a short
one – or their equivalent'.

discipline.[32] Since the versification fits the musical phrases of the pre-conceived *clausula*, it cannot be regular. Irregularity of verse structure therefore became a hallmark of the thirteenth-century motet; the music, with its varied phrase layout, is the primary measuring tool. Thus the appearance of irregular verses is usually due to the musical structure.

Of course the poetry also has its effect on the music. A decisive result of the adaptation of text to *clausulae* appears in the weight and articulation of individual notes. A comparison of any motet with the ligature notation of the melismatic original shows how the propulsive flow of the melismatic phrases is profoundly affected by the individual declamation of each note. The iambic implications of the binary ligatures, i.e. up-beat, down-beat, are often converted into truly trochaic rhythms by the words.

Finally, *Nostrum* demonstrates another Perotinian innovation. The Gregorian melisma in the tenor is repeated (as indicated by the Roman numerals I and II in bars 1 and 9 of the tenor of example 13) and as a result a rhythmic redistribution of the pitches occurs in the second statement. The purpose of this device is obviously a more expansive superstructure. Tenor repetition, often involving more than two statements as well as rhythmic redistributions, soon developed into a favourite procedure; this is shown by the fact that nearly half the pieces in the *clausula* fascicles of W_1 and F are constructed in that way. A particularly sophisticated example occurs in a re-composition of the Alleluia in *Alleluia Pascha nostrum* of the *Magnus Liber* (example 14).

Example 14. F, fol. 109^v

A further device that begins to make its appearance is the application of two different tenor patterns to two successive statements of one plainchant melisma (see example 15).

32. See also the diagram on p. 120 and the discussion of number as 'the divinely logical principle' on pp. 124–7.

Example 15. W₁, fol. 90 (81)ᵛ

CONDUCTUS AND DOUBLE MOTET. The type of motet, like *Nostrum*, in which two upper voices homorhythmically sing the added text, is commonly referred to in modern commentaries as '*conductus* motet'. The term '*conductus*', common from the time of Leonin to the end of the thirteenth century, first occurs in a Norman-Sicilian manuscript of the first half of the twelfth century; subsequently it appears in the 'Codex Calixtinus' of Compostela and in the Daniel play of the Beauvais manuscript (now in the British Museum), which has been assumed to date from about 1150, though it appears in a manuscript compiled *c.* 1230. Of the four specimens in the Compostela manuscript, where each is labelled *Conductum*, three precede the reading of lessons; they were to be sung, while the reader was being 'conducted' to the lectern.[33] The *conducti* of the Daniel play too had processional or 'walk-on' functions. (The plural of *conductus* is frequently *conducti*, though the alternate plural *conductus* also occurs. The plural of *conductum* is *conducta*.)

Not unlike a good many of the St Martial *versus*, then, the Compostela *conducta* functioned more or less as introductory tropes. For one of them the manuscript indicates that it could be used both as introduction to a lesson and as substitute for a 'Benedicamus'. In fact the *conductus*, originating as a special kind of *versus*, soon replaced the latter as a general term for a monophonic or polyphonic setting of a rhymed, rhythmic and usually strophic Latin poem. Notre Dame *conducti* fulfil a variety of functions: some are paraliturgical, such as substitutes for the 'Benedicamus'; many are devotional songs of a less ecclesiastical character; others are topical, concerned with moral issues, installations of bishops and political events such as accessions of rulers or deaths of important personages. The poetic texts of the *conductus* were never intended as entertainment; they were devotional, homiletic, ceremonial or ancillary to the liturgy.

33. For an English counterpart see chapter 6.1, example 1; the third stanza of the poem reveals its liturgical function.

Conducti make up a large part of the Notre Dame repertoire. Of roughly two hundred polyphonic pieces about 30 per cent are written in three parts. Like the *versus*, the *conductus* does not usually borrow any of its melodic material from chant; the tune is allotted to the lowest voice (tenor), and the text is declaimed homorhythmically, often articulating its structural subdivisions with melismas in discant style. Most frequently, these *caudae* (tails), which are not intrinsic parts of the tune, appear at the end and at the beginning (see example 16).

Example 16. F, fol. 351ʳ⁻ᵛ

Pan - ge me - los   la - cri - mo - sum   la - cri - mans e - le - gi - a,

tem - pus ve - nit plan - ctu - o - sum,   tem - pus   frau - dans gau - di - a,

ad e - clip - sim nox me - ro - ris   ob - li - quat spe - cta - cu - la,

re - gnet do - lor   nam do - lo - ris   cau - sa stat in   spe - cu - - -

- - - - - - - - - - - - - la.

[O weeping elegy, invent a tearful melody; the time of lamentation comes, the time that steals all gladness; the night of grief eclipses all things; let sorrow reign, for the cause of our sorrow dominates everything.]

Pange melos is one of the least pretentious *conducti* in the Notre Dame collection; but even its modest melisma demonstrates how the *caudae* of *conducti* for two voices must have been the proving ground for the polyphony of the novel *organa tripla*.

Most of the polyphonic *conducti* are discant compositions[34] of far more impressive proportions with numerous melismas; many of the elaborate pieces disdain simple strophic settings, clothing the poetry in a musical garment of ever-varying inventiveness. In a number of cases the melismas which intersperse a single piece are so long that the tail seems to be wagging the dog (example 17).

Example 17. End of *conductus, Porta salutis ave*

34. Organal melismas are rare and of very modest length; they may occur at cadence points.

– – ve.

[Hail, because Thou takest away our woe.]

The ingenious melodic interrelationships demonstrated by this example leave the simple device of voice exchange far behind. Both examples prove that 'the *conductus* admits secondary consonances', as we are informed in a treatise written in the 1230s; undoubtedly the author (or reporter) meant the imperfect consonances of the major and minor thirds.

The tradition of the polyphonic *versus* reaches its proudest embodiment in the Notre Dame *conducti*. It is a twelfth-century species which achieves its ultimate, most luxuriant growth in the early decades of the thirteenth century. But as this century progresses, both *organum* and *conductus* yield increasingly to *clausula* and motet with their novel and irresistible challenges for French (i.e. primarily Parisian) composers.

A good number of *clausulae* strike out in a significant and adventurous direction; some of the *duplum* phrases overlap the tenor patterns in such a way as to begin and end over the last and first notes of tenor phrases respectively. While this may seem a modest accomplishment, it must be stressed that there is a small, but significant number of *clausulae* for more than two voices.[35] For the composers of the time the potential complexity of phrase structure in such pieces must have been an exciting challenge. In several *clausulae* they exploit the technique of offset phrasing, while constructing phrases composed only of an even number of beats. An excerpt from *Domino* (a *clausula* from a 'Benedicamus' setting, example 18) demonstrates a further step ahead. Since the upper parts have hocket[36] passages, some of their phrases contain an odd number of beats.

35. There are thirty, of which one is *Mors*, the only *clausula* for four voices, undoubtedly by Perotin.
36. Hocket: the dovetailing of alternating individual notes and rests (or short groups of notes and

Example 18. W₁, fol. 12 (8)ʳ; F, fol. 42ᵛ; W₂, fol. 29ʳ

do -

I

II

- - mino

rests) between two or more voices. The device was often introduced into motets of the thirteenth and fourteenth centuries. Complete pieces written in this manner were also called hockets.

A veritable *chef-d'œuvre* is a short four-part setting of *Sederunt*, composed for the repeat of the respond after the *quadruplum* setting of the verse of the Gradual. The *cantus firmus*, consisting of seven notes, is stated three times in grouped, though unpatterned longs.[37] But since the composer (?Perotin) evidently envisaged a piece making prominent use in various ways of the number 12, the last long of the tenor is extended by a further three beats (or longs), making the total length of the composition 24 rather than 21 longs. This span of time is divided into two sections of 12 each which, in turn, are further sub-divided in various ways by the design of the phrases:

Triplum & Quadruplum	2L+4L+4L+2L	+4×3L
Tenor & Duplum	6L +4L+2L	+5L+4L+3L

It is hardly possible to exploit the numeral 12 in a more tightly organized composition.

Regardless of the degree of its complexity, the device of staggered phrases wreaks havoc with the procedure of turning three-part *clausulae* into *conductus* motets. Any attempt at such a conversion would necessarily entail more or less extensive adjustments in the music. Most *conductus* motets consisted of a *clausula* in two parts to which a new *triplum* was added. It is revealing that of the thirty patterned discant sections and *clausulae* for more than two parts in W_1 and F only four were made over into *conductus* motets. The reason is plain: contrapuntal and structural expertise had begun to transcend the inherent limits of the species.

In the case of many a *conductus* motet appearing in more than one source the various versions of the tenor and *duplum* agree, while those of the *triplum* usually vary. This is a feature that shows up the fundamental cleavage which begins to appear between *conductus* and motet. In the former, the text governs the tenor and all superimposed voices, chaining the parts together. A polyphonic *conductus* is a setting of poetry in which the chief function of the music may be compared to manuscript illumination; the upper parts decorate the tune and, together, they decorate the text. In the syllabic portions the texture is a homogeneous entity consisting of two or three parts. This is why in the *conductus* one so often meets the vertical interval of the third which blends the parts. Even in the *caudae* the parts are not differentiated, but related in character; they are often linked by voice exchange[38] or similar devices.

The motet, on the other hand, lacks the unifying bond of a single text. Both textually and musically, tenor and *duplum* are distinct entities. From

---

37. Modern transcription in Husmann, *Notre Dame*, p. 38, where the three statements are indicated by Roman numerals. The barring and rests in this transcription obscure the inner structure at times.

38. Concerning 'voice exchange', see p. 109.

the beginning the motet aimed at creating an individual profile for each of its parts. Only the earliest motets still show a certain fondness for the interval of the third, and voice exchange is atypical in *conductus* motets; it would, in any case, be possible only over repeated configurations in the tenor. As composers came to grips with the intrinsic problems of motet composition, it was found that three- and four-part construction had to be abandoned. The notion of transforming such *clausulae* as *Domino* into a motet was at first inconceivable, and the *triplum* was dropped. After the initial flourishing of *conductus* motets, the great majority of motets preserved in the earliest sources were for tenor and *duplum* only, as are almost all *clausulae*.

The *triplum* comes into focus as soon as it is animated by a text of its own. The 'double motet' has different texts for *duplum* and *triplum*; it thus extends the principle of individual profiles for the separate parts and represents a concept of marvellous daring.[39] Of the sixty-nine motets preserved in F (the earliest source to transmit a collection of such compositions) only three are double motets. It is all the more astonishing that one of these (see example 19) in combining three parts differentiated not only as to texts but also in the music, already fully realizes the potentiality of the genre. The words of the *duplum* praise the deeds of the dedicated clerics, while the *triplum*, in a tone of uninhibited outrage, castigates the *ypocrite pseudopontifices, ecclesie duri carnifices* (hypocritical pseudo-bishops, vile slayers of the church). The tenor of the composition, which originated as a *clausula* for two parts, proceeds in longs and double longs, the *duplum* in longs and breves, and the newly added *triplum* almost exclusively in breves. Moreover, the parts, like those of most other medieval double motets, are differentiated in their phrase structure: in the *duplum* the composer disposes almost all its phrases in lengths of four or six beats, while the phrase layout of the lively *triplum* is more varied. Its first half[40] corresponds to the first statement of the chant melisma in the tenor, and its numerical design may be indicated by the following table:

$$2 \times 4L + 5L + 2 \times 4L + 1L \quad + 2 \times 2L + 6L + 4L + 3L + 6L \quad + 5 \times 5L$$
$$\text{22 longs} \qquad\qquad\qquad \text{23 longs} \qquad\qquad \text{25 longs}$$

Within these sections of 22, 23 and 25 beats (or longs) the phrases proceed mainly in 4s, 5s and 6s. The design of this motet points to a first-rate musician; there is nothing that argues specifically against Perotin's authorship, though admittedly there is not even indirect evidence that he wrote the *triplum*.

39. Not until Mozart's operatic finales does the simultaneous singing of several texts reappear significantly as a principle of composition.

40. The two tenor statements are indicated by Roman numerals in example 19.

Example 19. F, fols. 411ᵛ–413ʳ

[*Triplum:* The hypocrites, pseudo-bishops, vile slayers of the church – guzzling and gorging they clink their goblets. In tears they sow shrubs, in their 'pulpits' they thunder forth with Jupiter, as judges and punishers they point their fingers at honest supplicants. But two-faced, playing God in their seats, they give before all eyes a godly aura to their stalls, where they lurk individually. They ruminate their gall-filled sting and offer it as honey. In their slippery way they fabricate codices of errors and then don't show their faces. Practitioners of lust and crimes, they diminish the weight of coins . . .

Duplum: Like the stars of the firmament shine the deeds of the prelates; they are the fundament of the sacred foundation, fount of all virtue, path of morality, seemly ornament, clouds trickling honey, winds fructifying earth, field, and vineyard, rooting out worm, thorns, and weed, planting the lily in the hearts of the faithful; they separate the pure grain from the chaff, for things supernal they spurn all that is earthly, . . .

Tenor: And he shall rejoice.]

GOTHIC CONCEPTS. Number as the divinely logical principle activating and sustaining the harmonious cosmos is a medieval view of dogmatic force. Since the basic intervals of music represent a hierarchy of rational and fundamental relationships of number, *musica instrumentalis* (see p. 91) was regarded as the sounding symbol of *musica mundana*, the numerically constituted universe. Music concretely demonstrated numerical order. It was (together with arithmetic, geometry and astronomy) one of the *artes quadriviales* in the context of the seven liberal arts, because 'it is the discipline or science dealing with the numbers . . . that are found in pitches' (Cassiodorus). Moreover, man's harmonious constitution (*musica humana*) attunes him to the ordered system of the principal intervals of music; with its proportions music reconciles all imperfections into harmonious agreement. The medieval view of the symbolic significance of music as *numerus sonorus* was so comprehensive that, according to a writer of the early fourteenth century, 'in a general survey music is seen to embrace nearly everything'.

For the medieval *musicus*, therefore, the proper purpose of music was the realization of numerical relationships in musical sound. This concept is rooted in St Augustine's view that the composer's calling is to fashion works as audible embodiments (*numeri corporales*) of the inaudible essence (*numeri incorporales*). 'Thou hast ordered everything in accordance with measure, number and weight' – that famous sentence from the Book of Wisdom, endlessly quoted as biblical and divine justification for all aspects of medieval man's concern with number, remained an influential maxim in music till the end of the seventeenth century.

Mathematical formulae are embodied in most medieval art; their manifestation occurs in architecture as well as poetry and manuscript illumination. Just as architecture in the Middle Ages was thought of as a visual demonstration of musical proportions, music, i.e. measured discant, was described in architectural terms by the end of the thirteenth century: 'The tenor, however, is that part upon which all others are founded, just as the parts of a house or building are erected on its fundament. It is their yardstick and gives them quantity.' (Johannes de Grocheo, *c*. 1300). 'Hence', said an author writing about thirty years later, 'that part is called tenor, because it sustains and founds measured polyphony.'[41]

This traditional concept of music, based on number, was embodied in the hierarchy of consonant intervals (octaves, fifths etc.). To this Perotin and his generation added another system, also founded on number, which is embodied in both rhythm and the co-ordination of phrases. It was the striking achievement of these men to have evolved a well-planned order of duration as well as of pitch.

The motet is an aural manifestation of numerical musical proportions, not only in the consonant flow of its voices, regulated by good melodic design and proper counterpoint, but also in the measured disposition of its elements and structural members. This is primarily a matter of metaphysics and only

41. Visual evidence of this view of the motet may perhaps be seen in the way its voice parts came to be written in the manuscripts inscribed after about the middle of the thirteenth century: *triplum* either on the left half of a page or on the verso of a folio; *duplum* on the right half of a page or on the recto facing the *triplum*; tenor under both voices at the bottom of the page(s), with the appropriate Gregorian word or words placed like a label below its initial notes. In the earliest manuscripts, such as F and W_2, the parts of a motet are notated successively, often continuing from the recto of a folio to its verso. Thus the motets could not be performed from the book. Evidently the advances of the Franconian era (see below, pp. 139–40) accounted for the new arrangement, since the rhythmically unambiguous Franconian notation of music *cum littera* (see above, p. 111) made sight-reading possible. The growth of this skill, for which some evidence begins to crop up in the early fourteenth century, may therefore be said to be due to the development of the thirteenth-century motet.

consequently of aesthetics. 'To the medieval thinker beauty was not a value independent of others but rather the radiance of truth, the splendour of ontological perfection, and that quality of things which reflects their origin in God.'[42] At its best, the purpose and meaning of the motet is to be an image of the divine order, and its composition is a joyous science.

With the emergence of the *clausula*, *cantus-firmus* polyphony, having become *musica precise mensurata* (Grocheo), was turned away from its subordinate function of ornamentation of a Gregorian chant. The inert *cantus planus* ('plain' or 'even' because it was *ultra mensuram*), became animated by structural thinking that removed it from its proper environment. Since versification, being based on number and proportion, had been regarded as a division of music since Cassiodorus, the conversion of the *clausula* into the motet constituted its full realization.

A well-made motet is a concise form in tonal,[43] temporal and poetic terms; its superstructure (the upper voices), built on the properly placed notes of the *cantus firmus*, is designed to unfold, demonstrate and articulate the fundamental numerical theme given by the tenor. The motet is a polyphony of notes, of texts and of interrelated numbers governing rhythms and phrase structure. As the result of a long and pervasive tradition of number symbolism, numbers carried connotations which, for medieval man, were endowed with divine significance. Numbers were not merely integers but were also capable of sensuous perception. The change from, say, four to six was not so much the addition of two as it was a shift to another sphere: 'The senses delight in things duly proportioned as in something akin to them, for the sense, too, is a kind of ratio, as is every cognitive power.'[44]

Such structures are basically not accompanied songs or duets, 'expressing' the text(s). The role of poetry in a medieval motet is best defined by analogy with the stained-glass windows in a Gothic church. The images in the poetry of the upper part(s) relate to the music in the same way as stained-glass windows (and the events they depict) relate to the building of which they are a part. The music does not accompany, elucidate or intensify; but the poetry illuminates and reflects the structure of the music.

Erwin Panofsky has emphasized *manifestatio* (total elucidation or clarification) as 'the first controlling principle of Early and High Scholasticism' and has defined the three requirements of the classic *Summa* as

(1) totality (sufficient enumeration), (2) arrangement according to a system of homologous parts and parts of parts (sufficient articulation), and (3) distinctness and deductive cogency (sufficient interrelation). ... According to classic High Gothic standards the individual elements, while forming an indiscerptible whole,

---

42. Otto von Simson, *The Gothic Cathedral*, New York, 1964, p. 51.

43. Not, of course, in the commonly accepted sense of tonality.

44. Thomas Aquinas, quoted in Erwin Panofsky, *Gothic Architecture and Scholasticism*, New York, 1958, p. 38.

yet must proclaim their identity by remaining clearly separated from each other
...; and there must be an unequivocal correlation between them.[45]

Like the cathedral, a well-composed motet may be termed a *Summa*;
medieval man moulded music, as *numerus sonorus*, into a composite whole, a
creation symbolizing the transcendental order of *musica mundana*, thus
achieving a quintessential embodiment of the Gothic spirit. The motet's
prestige, for whatever reasons, is shown in the many thirteenth-century
musical manuscripts that are devoted more or less exclusively to it; musical
sources of the fourteenth century, most of which mix the genres, tend to place
the motets at the beginning.

The accomplishments of Perotin display a creative mind of staggering
brilliance. It was he who for the first time wrote polyphony not just for two
voices, but *tripla plurima nobilissima* and even compositions for four voices.
He modernized the *Magnus Liber*; he gave greater strength and precision to
the rhythmic component of music; he invented a new musical genre – the
clausula; he initiated the tradition of presenting *clausula* tenors in rhythmic
patterns, which function as the yardstick for the numerically interrelated
ingredients of fully measured compositions; it was doubtless his thought to
present a chant melisma two or more times in one *clausula* to produce a well-
proportioned piece of music; and we need not shrink from crediting him
with the introduction of new rhythms, with the codification of the modal
system[46] and with many features of its ingenious notation. In addition, both
his melodic style and his counterpoint exhibit great suppleness, *élan* and
energy. And, finally, certain aspects of his style are indicative of resourceful
assimilation of English musical traditions.[47]

The greatness of Perotinus Magnus, as he was called, rests essentially on
qualities he shares with the other outstanding 'classical' masters among
European composers. Like them he fulfilled the crucial functions of focussing
diverse 'national' influences, creating well-organized, large-scale masterpieces. These are, stylistically and formally, the consummate high points of
the period, bequeathing an important artistic heritage pregnant with possibilities for the future. Small wonder that throughout the thirteenth century
and still in the early fourteenth, manuscripts inscribed in France, England,
Spain, Italy and Germany continued to transmit music by Perotin or his immediate successors. His activity in Paris coincided with the erection of Notre
Dame. Both the cathedral and the *œuvre* of Perotin are climactic monuments
of classic Gothic.

45. Panofsky, *Gothic Architecture*, pp. 30, 31. Such terms as 'indiscerptible' (incapable of being
divided into parts) and 'summa' (synthesis, composite whole) become clear in the context of Panofsky's
book.
46. See below, p. 134.
47. See chapter 6.1, p. 275.

SECULAR MONOPHONY

All polyphonic compositions written prior to *c.* 1220 had Latin texts, whether they were elaborations of *cantus firmi* or settings of poems. Polyphony (*ars discantus*) as a particular branch of the quadrivial subject of music, was a clerical art. While musical settings of vernacular poetry go back to the early years of the twelfth century, throughout both the twelfth and the thirteenth centuries such melodies, almost without exception, seem to have been sung monophonically.[48]

The poetic tradition established by the *trobadors* (or *troubadours*) arose *c.* 1100 and was maintained for approximately two centuries. Its beginnings therefore coincide with the appearance of the St Martial *versus*, and both show the simultaneously rising standards of life and art in monastic as well as in feudal society. In fact the geographic area in which the *versus* was culti-vated in the early twelfth century is also largely the homeland of the *trobadors*, i.e. roughly the southern half of France. Provençal, the language of *trobador* poetry, was cultivated as a literary language far to the west and north of Provence. The extraordinary flourishing of this poetic tradition is indicated by the large number of *trobadors* (450) whose names are known to us. About 2600 of their poems are preserved.

Normally this poetry was sung; indeed, one *trobador* compared a poem without melody to a mill without water. While the earliest known *trobadors*, such as Guillaume VII of Poitou (=Guillaume IX of Aquitaine) were mem-bers of the nobility or even of royalty, all strata of society produced poets – the nobility (Bertran de Born), the bourgeoisie (Guiraut de Bornelh), the common people (Bernart de Ventadorn), and the clergy (Peire Cardenal). In fact during its central period the *trobador* tradition was sustained largely by men who could not claim noble birth and who often spent their lives as professional poets and singers, performing their functions as either resident or itinerant entertainers. Many of them employed *joglars* (French: *jongleurs*), who would sing the songs. Often such hired performers would become in-dependent, thus assuming a prominent role in the dissemination of the grow-ing repertoire. Some even advanced into the ranks of creative artists.

The oldest and simplest type of vernacular song in France was the epic *chanson de geste*, a species of French poetry cultivated and disseminated by the *jongleurs*. It consisted of strings of verses sung to the same music in the fashion of a litany; occasional cadences sub-divided the verses into quasi-strophic groups (*laisses*). But the lyric poetry of the *trobadors* was more com-plex, developing into a highly sophisticated variety of topics, poetic forms, melodic styles and musical structures. Topical categories were the *sirventes*

---

48. Even Machaut, the first composer to concentrate on polyphonic settings of French poetry, still wrote some forty monophonic compositions.

(moral, political, educational), *alba* (warning lovers of the approaching morning), *planh* (lament), *tenso* (polemic dialogue), songs of the crusades etc. Most prominent, however, was the *canso*, whose concern with courtly love is central to *trobador* poetry. The parallelism between the adoration of the Virgin Mary and the adoration of the unattainable noble lady is an obvious indication of the interdependence of sacred and secular spheres.

Many other circumstances show the interchange between sacred and secular, Latin and vernacular. While members of the clergy wrote Provençal poetry, vernacular verses turn up in several *versus*, three of them in the oldest St Martial manuscript. The earliest generic term for *trobador* songs was *vers*. As in the *versus*, poetic structure was achieved through the varied co-ordination of the verses by means of rhyme and number of syllables. Often the metrical characteristics are similar, and *contrafacta* are not uncommon.

Many *trobador* melodies are stylistically indebted to sacred models. Especially the earlier songs exhibit Gregorian characteristics, either in their carefully moulded continuity, made up of non-recurrent phrases, or in their quasi-psalmodic declamatory manner (see examples 20 and 21[49]).

Example 20. Bernart de Ventadorn

49. Examples 20, 21 and 22 are based on examples 1, 3 and 7 in Stäblein, *Acta.* (1966). All the examples of secular monophony are strophic songs.

[When I see how joy causes the lark to move its wings and fly towards the sun and how, with pleasure pervading its heart, it forgets itself and plummets down, ah! then I am seized by great envy of everyone whom I see joyful and happy. How strange that my heart does not at once melt with longing!

Example 21.Bernart de Ventadorn

[My love, I know full well that you don't think of me, that I have no greeting, no message, no token of friendship from you. Surely I must be waiting too long, and evidently another is catching what I hunt, since good fortune is not with me in this.]

Others exhibit double-versicle components, like the sequence (*lai*), or in a non-continuous strophic manner like many *versus*, the most usual formal scheme being aab.

In the last quarter of the twelfth century more popular influences began to affect both style and form of much *trobador* music. The melodies often consist of relatively simple, more or less symmetrically balanced phrases which tend to stress the interval of the third. Structures are made up of neatly designed reiterations or recurrences of phrases, and the tendency towards syllabic text setting favours a delivery approaching metrically organized rhythm (see example 22).

Example 22. Guiraut de Bornelh

lan – can vei los ra – mels flo – rir e'lh chan-son pel bo – schat — ge
dels au – ze – letz en – a – mo – ratz e si to m'e - stauc
a – pen – satz ni pres per mal – au – rat — – ge
can vei chans e ver – gens e pratz, eu re – no – vel e m'as-so – latz.

[With all the pain of my tooth I cannot help changing my tune, as the new flowers grow, as I see the branches blossom, and as the woods resound with the song of birds in love; and though I am oppressed with many a concern and sorrow, I feel restored and relieved when I hear the songs and see the gardens and meadows.]

The poetry of the *trobadors* was much admired elsewhere, and in the second half of the twelfth century it led to the appearance of the *trouvères* in northern and north-eastern France (except at the royal court, which showed little interest in the movement). As in the south of France, members of the nobility were prominent at first, but by about 1200 other strata of society began to concern themselves with courtly conventions and to contribute to the growing body of lyric poetry. Some of the outstanding *trouvères* were King Richard the Lionhearted, Moniot d'Arras, Gace Brulé, Thibaut IV de Champagne and Colin Muset. The *jongleurs* were the counterparts of the Provençal *joglars*, and the poetic categories (*serventois, aube, pastourelle, plainte, tenson, chanson, chanson de croisade*, etc.) were mostly modelled on types of *trobador* poetry.

On the whole thirteenth-century melodies are of a relatively simple, popular kind, favouring thirds, triadic elements and sequential patterns. Melismas do not usually occur and the compass does not often exceed an octave. Many tunes favour the major mode.[50] Continuity without the reappearance of phrases or phrase elements is rare in *trouvère* melodies, most of which feature artful repetition, recurrence or variation of structural members. Formal schemes which often occur, such as that of the *lai*, are based on the principle of the double versicle (a a b b c c . . .), or else content themselves with repetition of the initial aab . . . . In *lai* types parallel phrases may be differentiated by *ouvert* and *clos* (first and second) endings (see example 23).

50. Grocheo recognized that secular songs could not be classified according to the church modes.

Example 23. Paris, Bib. de l'Arsenal, 5198, fol. 135^r; Moniot d'Arras

Ce   fu   en mai   au   douz   tens gai   que   la   se - sons est   be - le,
main me   le - vai   io - er   m'a - lai   lez

un   ver-gier, clos   d'es - glan - tier,   o -
u - ne   fon - te - ne - le;   en   vi   dan - cer   un   che - va - lier   et

- i   u - ne   vi - e - le;   la
u - ne   da - moi - se - le.

[It was in May, in that sweet and happy time when the season is beautiful; I rose early and went to play near a fountain. In an orchard, hedged with sweet-brier, I heard a viele; there I saw a knight and a maiden dancing.]

In some cases the double versicles exhibit different beginnings, but identical endings. This feature was exploited in the *estampie* (Latin, *stantipes*), usually an instrumental form of music, consisting of a number of double versicles with identical endings.

A new feature that begins to appear in the course of the thirteenth century is the incorporation of strophic refrains, undoubtedly reflecting popular practice. The term *ballade*, which came to designate a specific type of refrain song, was surely at first just a generic expression for dance songs, in which refrain forms with their leader-chorus tradition were of course peculiarly at home. A variety of such forms existed,[51] and it was only towards the end of the century that three formal types had crystallized and became preferred so exclusively that they are known as *formes fixes*: *ballade*, *rondeau* and *virelai*. In all three types several musical sections are allotted to the soloist, of which the first is repeated. But before discussing musical design it is necessary to explain the convention in the use of small and capital letters designating the sections. Small letters indicate musical components; for instance, ab refer to two musical strains. Capital letters, AB, indicate the same music with the refrain text. The abbreviation abAB, therefore, means two musical strains, the first time with words differing from the refrain text, to be followed by the same music with the refrain text. In the case of several stanzas, the words of ab, therefore, vary from stanza to stanza.

Thus, the musical form of the *ballade* is aab; the refrain occurs at the end of the b strain. The *rondeau* differs from the *ballade* by the inclusion of an

51. They are rare in the *trobador* repertoire, but occur in some of the Notre Dame *conducti*.

internal half-refrain plus a full refrain at the end: aAabAB. More commonly, the form had full refrains acting as a frame (as well as the internal half-refrain), ABaAabAB. The *virelai* has the following design: ABccabAB, the last AB serving as link between stanzas. In the course of the century these song types became so stylized that neither dancing nor the alternation of solo and chorus had to be aspects of their performance.[52].

Further manuscript evidence of secular monophony of the thirteenth century comes to us from Bavaria and Austria, Spain and Italy. The songs of the German *Minnesinger*, who were contemporary with the *trouvères*, are largely derived from the art of the *trobadors*. Many of their songs are adaptations or *contrafacta* of Provençal *cansos* (*chansons*) or of other types of *trobador* and *trouvère* songs; the German *Minne* corresponds to the *amour courtois*. The preferred form, counterpart to the *ballade*, consisted of an *Aufgesang*, made up of two *Stollen* (aa) and an *Abgesang* (b); as in the *ballade*, *Stollen* and *Abgesang* often ended identically. At times the entire *Stollen* would reappear at the end of the *Abgesang*.

If music was written for the poetry of Italian imitators of the *trobadors* (*trovatori*) and of the *dolce stil nuovo* in Italy extolled by Dante, none has survived. There exists, however, a large repertoire of monophonic spiritual songs in Italian[53] known as *laude* (or *laudi*). These songs, mostly characterized by a rather artless style and favouring *virelai* form, were sung by the numerous religious fraternities (*compagnie de' laudesi*) which existed in Italy during the thirteenth and fourteenth centuries. The practice received added impetus from the flagellants, a movement that gained prominence in the 1260s.

Spanish and Portuguese courts had welcomed *trobadors* since at least the year 1200. Their songs, finding sympathetic audiences everywhere, soon stimulated the growth of an indigenous repertoire of *cantigas*. Alfonso x (1230–84) caused manuscript collections of *cantigas* to be compiled, and himself is said to have been the author of an undetermined number of songs. Of the total of more than two thousand poems about 1700 have secular topics (*cantigas de amigo, cantigas de amor* etc.). The music for only six of these is preserved, while all of the 427 sacred songs have survived with their melodies; (402 of these are *cantigas de Sancta María*).[54]

NEW TRENDS IN CLAUSULA AND MOTET

During the remainder of the thirteenth century composition of *organa* and *conducti* gradually decreased, and all significant musical evolution took place within the genres of *clausula* and motet. The three most important develop-

52. The functional aspect of the dance suffers a similar atrophy in the Baroque suite.
53. A few of these have Latin texts. Concerning the *dolce stil nuovo* and the *laude*, see chapter 5.
54. These *cantigas de Sancta Maria* and modern transcriptions of them are discussed in chapter 8.1, p. 377.

ments that occurred still in the first two decades of the century were the loosening of tenor rhythms, the formulation of the system of rhythmic modes and the introduction of the vernacular.

The *clausulae* represented the experimental music of the period, and it was here that the breve was first introduced into the patterned *cantus firmus*. The earliest such patterns seem like diminutions of their predecessors: | ♩ ♪♩ ⁊ |, | ♩ ♪♩ ⁊ | ♩. ♩ ⁊ | and | ♩. ♩ ⁊ | ♩ ♪♩ ⁊ |. *Clausulae* with lively and increasingly varied tenor patterns became more frequent. At the same time musicians soon realized that it was possible to reverse the usual order, i.e. of placing the breve before rather than after the first long of the phrases in any part, e.g. | ♪♩ ♪♩ ♪⁊ |. In the circumstances it became necessary to put the many available rhythms into categories, since the notation of these rhythms required different ways of grouping and interpreting ligatures. The system of rhythmic modes, i.e. rhythmic 'ways', was the result.

1st mode: | ♩ ♪♩ ♪♩ ♪♩ ⁊ | etc.

2nd mode: | ♪♩ ♪♩ ♪♩ ♪⁊ | etc.

3rd mode: | ♩. ♪♩ ♩. ♪♩ ♩. ♪♩ ♩. ⁊⁊ | etc.

4th mode: | ♪♩ ♩. ♪♩ ♩. ♪♩ ♩ ♩. ⁊⁊ | etc. (uncommon)

5th mode: | ♩. ♩. ♩. ♩. ♩. ♩. ♩. ⁊⁊ | etc.[55]

6th mode: | ♫♩ ♫♩ ♫♩ ♪⁊ | etc.

Obviously the interpretation of ligatures in modal notation depends on the context. For instance, according to the mode, there are five different 'ways' of reading ternary ligatures (including the fifth-mode tenor pattern). While modal rhythm is mainly a feature of *clausulae* and motets, some *organa tripla* and a few *conductus caudae* also display the new rhythms.

The rhythmic mode of each part in a composition was invariably consistent. Two parts could be written in differing rhythmic modes, as long as those modes with iambic ingredients (second and third) were not mixed in the same passage with the rhythms of the first mode. Of course just as some Gregorian melodies are difficult to accommodate within the system of classi-

55. Tenor patterns featuring three longs usually made use of ternary ligatures ♩ ♩ ♩ ⁊ .

fication of the melodic modes, the six rhythmic modes are a didactic codification of some astonishingly lively rhythms, the graphic indication of which sometimes puts the system of melismatic notation to a severe test (see example 24).

Example 24. F, fol. 148ʳ

Tanquam

Not until the fourth phrase of the *duplum* of this example does it become apparent that its basic rhythms are those of the second mode.

While these various innovations can reasonably be ascribed to Perotin, the introduction of the vernacular into motet polyphony was a step he may have witnessed, but evidently did not himself cultivate. Just as the polyphonic *musica mensurata* had furnished a reliable musical yardstick with which to measure Latin poetry for the first time, the musical settings of French poems too were now drawn into its orbit. *Musica cum littera*, prior to the motet, could not be measured precisely, whether the text was Latin or French. Syllabic music, monophonic as well as polyphonic, had no symbols of notation denoting fixed rhythmic relationships, since only ligatures and similar configurations could convey rhythms. Grocheo states that, in contrast to monophonic secular song, polyphonic music was specifically referred to as *musica mensurabilis*, *musica mensurata* or *musica precise mensurata*. Examination of the secular repertoire confirms Grocheo: the notation, though diastematically precise (staff notation with clef), was, with few exceptions, ambiguous in regard to rhythm, indicating that the performer did not have precise guidance, as he did in melismatic discant. But, despite indications to the contrary, repeated efforts have been made since the beginning of the twentieth century to impose a rhythmic system on the secular monophony of the twelfth and thirteenth centuries. The almost exclusively predominant theory, for which no concrete evidence exists, associates poetic metre with the system of rhythmic modes, even though the facts are that measured music had its beginnings in melismatic discant, where it was a necessity, and that the modal system cannot have come into being much before *c.* 1210. Moreover, *trobador* and *trouvère* poetry, like the Latin poetry of the time, was not based on systematic metrical arrangements of stressed and unstressed syllables; the only fixed elements of versification were rhyme (with identical accentuation) and the number of syllables. And the application of modal rhythm to songs in which individual syllables are decorated with short melismas is a Procrustean procedure, often obscuring the contour of the melody and the structure of the song. In secular monophony, music, no matter how artful the melodies, functioned as a decoration of the text, and in many cases the performance was doubtless freely declamatory. Modal rhythm implies meanings for the notation that seem appropriate only in a small number of songs.[56] The same caution must be brought to the rhythmic interpretation of the syllabic portion of *conducti*, to which modal rhythm cannot be applied, at least not before it developed in *clausula* and motet. There is no evidence that quantity (i.e. length) was systematically allotted to syllables in music *cum littera* (French or Latin) prior to the motet, which is the sole species to furnish examples to thirteenth-century theorists for the demonstration of the rhythmic modes.

The intrusion of the French language into *cantus firmus* polyphony[57] must have occurred soon after the development of the modal system. It was doubtless the application of French poetic texts to the upper parts of motets that caused the *duplum* to be called *motetus* and in turn gave the genre its name. *Motetus* is a Latinization of the French *mot*, which in the twelfth century was often used to denote a stanza or strophe in French poetry. *Motetus*, at first evidently signifying a *clausula* with French poetry in the upper part or parts, soon came to designate any such pieces, whether the texts were French or Latin.[58]

The advent of the French language and of the rhythms of the second mode seem to have been related phenomena, since the 'iambic' mode is more commonly associated with French than with Latin texts. French motets rapidly

56. The melodic variants of individual songs appearing in several manuscripts often differ so greatly as to indicate that not even the melodic structure of such tunes was regarded as rigidly fixed. That this repertoire, far less authoritative than plainchant, originally depended on oral transmission is also indicated by the relatively small number of notated *trobador* tunes (fewer than 300). Those that were written down were presumably particularly complex or appealing. While many more *trouvère* melodies have survived, they often exist in a number of acceptable variants, to which, moreover, the scribes (applying their professional training with varying degrees of self-consciousness) may well have contributed when they inscribed *chansonniers* for aristocratic collectors.

57. Very few motets with Provençal texts are known.

58. The most comprehensive, though not always the most accurate, source of thirteenth-century motets is MS Montpellier, Bibliothèque de l'Ecole de Médecine, H 196 (*Mo*); the transcriptions by Yvonne Rokseth, *Polyphonies*, are not always reliable. Other important motet manuscripts are Paris, Bibliothèque Nationale, nouvelles acquisitions françaises, 13521, generally referred to as the La Clayette manuscript (Cl), and Bamberg, Staatliche Bibliothek, Lit. 115 (Ba). A large number of motets are preserved in W₂ and Las Huelgas (Hu), both of which also contain other types of polyphony.

became more prominent than Latin, and few of them maintained any obvious verbal relationship with the text of the *cantus firmus*, so characteristic of the tropes. The dwindling topical connection with the chant is particularly well demonstrated by the occasional practice of combining a French *triplum* (*contrafactum* or original) with a Latin *motetus*, thereby adding another element to the individual and distinct character of the upper parts. But even a good many poems in the Latin motets either retain only a topical connection with the text of the *cantus firmus*, while giving up the assonances characteristic of the texts of troped *organa* and *clausulae*, or else depart from the tenor's words and their connotations altogether. Other motets, Latin as well as French, continue to cultivate assonance with the word or syllable that acts as a heading (*incipit*) for the tenor; rather than reflecting liturgical necessity, this device often shows poetic ingenuity and delight in punning, e.g. *Maniere esgarder/Manere*. Latin motets are usually about the Virgin Mary. Less common topics are the occasions of the church year and moral exhortations. The majority of French motet poems deal with love – courtly, urban or pastoral. A few other texts reflect the convivial life of the city (i.e. Paris); the remaining texts are either Marian or hortatory. The earliest motets, such as *Nostrum*, were still closely related to the genre of troped *organa* and may have been used within their appropriate *organa* (in this case the *triplum*, *Alleluia Pascha nostrum*). But there is no question that on gaining musical independence *clausula* and motet (Latin as well as French) soon gave up their connection with church and liturgy and became pieces of clerical and aristo-cratic chamber music, whose patterned Gregorian tenors are likely to have been performed on instruments. In fact before long strong objections were raised against the performance of motets in church. Ecclesiastical authorities considered monophony and subservient polyphony (simple discant) as appropriate ways of rendering Gregorian chants, and these methods of musical adornment of the liturgy continued to be generally favoured throughout the Middle Ages. When viewed in a larger, European context, Notre Dame polyphony was an excessive development.

The enormous vogue of French two-part motets – often, like many French double motets, incorporating refrains from song literature – seems to have been in full swing by the third decade of the century, thus showing the far-reaching secularization of the genre. Their tenors did not favour the tradi-tional slow, steady patterns, but tended to approximate the rhythmic quality of the *motetus*. No other type of motet shows a comparable decline in the old-fashioned tenors without breves; in fact it seems as though for a good part of the century the motet was often on the point of being transformed into another genre, i.e. the polyphonic song (see examples 25a and 25b[59]).

59. *Mo* stands for the Montpellier MS, see p. 136, fn. 58.

Example 25a. Beginning of *Mo*, No. 208

[By no means should anyone repent of love because of the suffering that comes with it; for everyone gets suffering from it . . .]

Example 25b. Beginning of *Mo*, No. 235

[Nevermore shall I remember her who has my heart and will forever have it . . .]

Since a motet could be viewed as a song accompanied by a tenor with the tenor part often exhibiting patterns of a liveliness commensurate with the *motetus* part, it was only one step further to regard the *motetus* part as an unaccompanied song. There are numerous cases of motets appearing in certain sources with their tenors missing or notated in so corrupt and useless a manner as to indicate complete lack of comprehension and sympathy on the part of the scribe. Presumably at the time such *motetus* parts were performed freely, like *trouvère* songs. There is a distinct contrast between the generally correct notation of the tenors of Latin motets in MS W₂ and the carelessly notated tenors of the French motets in the same source. There are even cases of *moteti* which were cut from their polyphonic environment and turned into strophic songs.

It is hardly surprising that these developments tended to erode the integrity of the *cantus firmus*. Changes in structure and pitch in deference to the upper part are by no means uncommon. Motets that accommodate refrains, and motets with upper parts shaped like *rondeaux*, are particularly striking. The tenors often have to be unpatterned or irregularly shaped, and in *rondeau* motets they are bent to fit the form of the *motetus*.

A marginal development destined to remain largely unsuccessful was the attempt to revive four-part writing by combining three separately texted voices over a tenor. In most of these 'triple motets' the *quadruplum* was added to an already existing double motet, generally with dubious contrapuntal success and often (as in the case of many double motets) without any regard for topical correlation of the poems. What had made it possible for Perotin to increase the parts of his counterpoint to four was his frequent use of voice exchange and his recognition of the third as a contrapuntal interval. The result was a relatively chordal sonority. The triple motets, on the other hand, have little in common with the polyphony of *organum* and *conductus*. They did not remain viable as a species for the same reason that the three *conducti* for four voices in MS F were unsuccessful. The syllabic style of the time was characterized by a framework of two parts which rarely exceeded an octave; chords frequently consisted of two notes only (such as F–C or F–C–F). Such a style could hardly accommodate four parts.

FRANCONIAN AND PETRONIAN MOTET

It is in the French double motets that the subsequent phases in the evolution of the species occurred. The very rhythm that had caused the modal system to emerge proved to be the agent of its undoing, since it was the long in the second mode that had a marked tendency toward subdivision (see example 24, p. 135). Moreover, sixth-mode *tripla*, in some of which several of the breves are halved not only melismatically but also syllabically, became quite common. When, in the association of a second-mode *motetus* and a sixth-mode *triplum*, more than half the longs of the *motetus* were dissolved into ornaments, what remained of the code of the modal system made little sense and hardly reflected the actual behaviour of the notes.

As a result of the proliferation of shorter note values and the increasing prolixity of the French texts of the *tripla*, the modal system became unworkable. This state of affairs made the growth of a new system of notation inevitable. The man whose codification of the new developments proved most compelling and durable was Franco of Cologne. Franco's notational system, explained in his *Ars cantus mensurabilis*, dating from the 1270s, gave recognition to the semibreve, three of which equalled a breve, and posited graphic symbols for long (⌐), breve (▪), and semibreve (◆) in music *cum littera*. The semibreve now replaced the breve for a value of short duration, and the

resultant lengthening of the breve further increased the ornamental animation of the *moteti*.[60] The latter do not usually participate in the lively declamation of the *tripla*, though several motets have Franconian rhythms in both
upper voices.

In Franco's system the standard ratio between long and breve was no
longer 2 : 1 (see p. 104) but 3 : 1. A long containing three breves, called *longa
perfecta*, became the unit of measurement, and the time-span filled by a
perfect long or its equivalent was called a perfection. If only two breves took
the place of a perfect long, the second of the two (*brevis altera*) had twice the
value of the first. (This principle of 'alteration' also applied to a pair of semibreves.) On the other hand a perfect long could be made imperfect by a
single breve, which would deprive it of one third of its standard value.
Franco replaced the modal ligature notation with a new system. The length
of individual notes was now precisely delineated and, as a result, the rhythmic
meaning of the components of each ligature also became unequivocal, regardless of any modal context. Naturally these and other reforms were bound
to undermine the system of the rhythmic modes. The mingling of rhythms
stemming from the 'inconsistent' modes 1 and 2 now became possible.
Modal inconsistency, which had formerly occurred only where refrains had
been quoted, was no longer inconceivable, though composers were relatively
slow to avail themselves of the new freedom, and theorists continued to
describe the modal system until the early fourteenth century, albeit more and
more perfunctorily. Only in its strictly ternary organization[61] did the Franconian system continue traditional habits of musical thought. A contemporary theorist still denies the possibility of performing – and therefore
composing – a piece consisting of nothing but imperfect longs. And, in fact,
motets with duple rhythm (i.e. binary subdivision of the long) are exceedingly
rare.

In the style of the Franconian motet[62] the natural, more or less square and
dance-like swing of the modal phrases now gave way to a more complicated
phraseology, whose relatively complex rhythms were defined by the underlying regularity of the neutral measuring units, the beats of the breves. While
a modal phrase in a Notre Dame composition is generally a rhythmically
homogeneous, indivisible whole, a phrase in a Franconian motet could be
described as one where the composer has decided, at his discretion, to include in it a chain of any number of perfections. A new system of measuring

60. In modern transcriptions the long is therefore usually represented by a dotted minim (half-note)
not, as in Notre-Dame music, by a crotchet (quarter-note).

61. The ternary rhythmic organization of thirteenth-century music was originally a matter of the
proportionate valuation of consonance and dissonance (see above, p. 104). The numerous invocations
of the Trinity with which writers of the later thirteenth century justify the perfection of this system
are symbolism after the fact.

62. The term denotes the style in general. Franco's authorship is not established for any specific
composition.

time by mechanical units has begun to impinge on organic time as it had been experienced. Significantly, the appearance of this new style coincided with the invention of the mechanical clock which, beginning with the thirteenth century, gradually displaced the older time-pieces operated by water or sand, and the sundial.

At this period, i.e. after 1250, the Notre Dame repertoire ceased to be both the model and leader in the field of music. With the advent of the new notational system, *clausulae* ceased to be written, the need for their composition having been removed.[63] Chants, other than the traditional Gregorian melismas, began to appear as tenors of motets. Fewer and fewer pieces turn up which are concordances or *contrafacta* of Notre Dame compositions. The enormous international dissemination of the Notre Dame motet repertoire with its endless adaptations (new texts, new *tripla*, etc.) not only shows its popularity in educated circles, but also reveals it as a kind of ready-made proving-ground for the study and practice of motet techniques. Towards the end of the thirteenth century this communal aspect of art-music gave way to a situation where individual compositions were no longer subject to being remodelled. The disappearance of notational ambiguity made each composition into a finished product.

Several different trends manifest themselves in the late thirteenth century. The major achievement of Petrus de Cruce of Amiens (fl. *c.* 1290–1300) was to progress beyond Franco's ternary sub-division of the breve. As many as seven semibreves could take the place of a breve. This proliferation of the semibreve was restricted to the *tripla* of motets; the *moteti* basically continued to exhibit steady modal rhythm (usually first mode), while the tenors as a rule moved in unpatterned longs or double longs. The speed of the lower parts was retarded by the *triplum*, whose increasing sub-division of the breves was more often syllabic than melismatic. Though it has a text, the musical structure of the *motetus* seems often closer to the tenor than to the *triplum*. The latter, by far the most rapid of the three parts, never hockets with the *motetus*, and its register is somewhat higher than that of the other two parts, expanding the framework of the two outer voices to a twelfth. Hence, Petronian motets[64] tend to give the impression of a *triplum* supported by two lower and slower parts. The declamation of the irregular French verses rushing on in headlong fashion is rhythmically and prosodically so capricious that it often seems to approach rhymed prose. In a rather romantic way the music primarily serves the virtuoso manner of declamation. Generally

---

63. Apart from MSS W₁ and F, only the so-called 'St Victor' manuscript, Paris, Bibliothèque Nationale, fonds latin 15139 (StV), contains *clausulae*. For each *clausula* the beginning of an apposite *motetus* text is indicated in the margin. On the other hand, in manuscripts of the late thirteenth century the voices of motets are no longer written successively but are arranged so as to permit performance by reading rather than memorizing.

64. As in the case of the Franconian motet, the term denotes the style in general and is not restricted to the two motets known to have been composed by Petrus de Cruce.

these motets with their shapeless and inconspicuous tenors resist all analytical search for rational phrase structures; the same tendency is already in evidence in many Franconian motets.

There exists, concurrently with the Petronian motet, another major type characterized by the cultivation of French poetry and by favouring a texture of accompanied song. But in contrast to the Petronian style this type had a lively tenor, at times to the point that its patterns are no longer modal but approximate the rhythm of the upper parts. (These traits recall many of the motets for two parts.) Some *cantus firmi* are so closely adapted to the design of the *motetus* as to include semibreves or hocket passages. Furthermore the dissolution of the modal system enabled composers to introduce secular *cantus firmi* (refrain songs, dance tunes, street cries), which invariably retained their original rhythms and shapes.

An additional sub-species was the Latin double motet, which seems to have led an existence mainly apart from the prominent Parisian tradition. As a more or less distinct type it evidently branched off early in the thirteenth century from the Perotinian *conductus* motet; its manuscript distribution indicates that it was cultivated particularly in areas peripheral to central France. On the whole motets of this type exhibit a continuing affinity with the *conductus*. Their texts retain a traditional trope-like relationship with the *cantus firmus* and are, therefore, topically linked to each other. In fact, several cases indicate an attitude that bypassed the *clausula* and points back to the troped *organum*, since these motets elaborate in trope-like fashion Gregorian melodies which usually do not belong to the specialized *clausula* repertoire. A further frequent characteristic is lucidity of form, often delineated by melodic or rhythmic devices and, in a number of cases, by melismatic *caudae*. The simpler compositions exhibit uncomplicated phrase structures, with the upper parts either declaiming their related texts homorhythmically throughout the piece, or presenting syllabic and melismatic passages in alternation. But many apparently peripheral works exhibit a fine concern with elegant phrase structure, often supported by unusual *cantus firmi* that were evidently selected for their concision or because of their patently repetitive design.[65]

Musica precise mensurata, since the early days of the *clausula*, had been patterned music with the design of the phrases in the upper parts depending on the pattern, if not to say module, of the *cantus firmus*. The numerically unstructured polyphonic song, on the other hand, had, ever since the twelfth

---

65. For instance, No. 58 in the Montpellier MS subdivides imaginatively a time-span of 60 longs with 6s, 7s and 8s. The two statements in the tenor are of 30 longs each: $2 \times [5 \times (2+4L)]$. Against these the *motetus* and *triplum* proceed in phrase-lengths emphasizing the numerals 7 and 8:

Triplum	$5 \times 8L + 4L + 2 \times 8L$
Motetus	$6 \times 7L + 2 \times 9L$
Tenor	$2 \times [5 \times (2+4L)]$

century, allotted the composed tune to the tenor. The main melody was not apportioned to the top part; this applied to polyphonic *versus* and Notre Dame *conducti*, and even to the few extant polyphonic *rondeaux*, composed much like *conducti* by Adam de la Halle (d. 1288). But the tendencies manifesting themselves in the disintegrating two-part motet, and the dissolution of the modal system, towards 1300, made it possible for the freely composed song to rise to the surface of the polyphonic complex. The supporting tenor was not shaped in rhythmic patterns or modules, as in the motet, but was conceived as an added accompaniment. In the early fourteenth century monophony more or less ceased to be of artistic significance. While there is no evidence that allows us to date the earliest *ballades* of Machaut before the fifth decade of the fourteenth century, the polyphonic *chanson* seems to have been an established genre in the 1320s.

The re-Latinization of the motet and the increasing rarity of motets with secular tenors go together with this development. As it was now possible to set French lyric poems as songs accompanied by a flexible and commensurate tenor, the vernacular receded from the motet, whose poetry turned away from its concern with *amour courtois* and dealt with topics which had been more common in peripheral motets and *conducti*.[66] Henceforth *chanson* and motet go their separate ways, with the often non-ecclesiastical motet unequivocally committed to the dignity of its essential purpose, as already defined by some of the compositions written in the Perotinian era. Inspired by divine laws, the motet is that species of *musica instrumentalis* which at its best fulfills man's obligation to create audible images of *musica mundana*; as a rule, a fourteenth-century motet is a construction embodying a particular numerical concept. The commanding figure, who evidently recognized these evolutionary tendencies and gave French music of the fourteenth century its decisive orientation was Philippe de Vitry, one of the most significant men of his age. His accomplishments in music and poetry are indicated by the author of the *Seconde rhétorique*, who reports that '*il trouva la manière* (i.e. the new, definitive manner) *des motets et des ballades et des lais et des simples rondeaux*'.

---

66. With its preference for French poetry Machaut's motet production is exceptional.

NANIE BRIDGMAN

4.1 France and Burgundy: 1300–1500

INTRODUCTION

After the brilliant predominance in the artistic domain shown by France during the preceding centuries, the fourteenth century saw the beginning of a retrenchment which the historians of literature and art have not failed to observe. It is true that throughout the western world the disintegration of the Middle Ages brought difficult times, marked by profound changes in social structures, economic conditions and, above all, in man's thinking. With the installation of the papacy at Avignon in 1309 the Roman Catholic Church itself, which had hitherto represented the unshakeable pillar of the medieval world, entered upon a period of turmoil which was to continue until the end of the Great Schism in 1417. Moreover the threat of the Turks, which became still more menacing after the abject defeat of French knight-hood at Nicopolis in 1396, disturbed the security of Christendom, while the fall of Constantinople in 1453 dangerously narrowed the borders of the western world. The history of France was then dominated by the great conflict with England normally referred to as the Hundred Years' War, whose unfortunate episodes were continued on French soil between 1340 and 1475, accelerating the decline of the material and spiritual hegemony of France. This pitiful confrontation with an enemy who sought to impose its domination over the entire country sealed the fate of the prosperity achieved by the last Capetian monarchs, provoking a state of crisis which continued throughout the fourteenth and fifteenth centuries. All this contributed to the widespread feeling of despair: the severe defeats which created the greatest material and moral disarray; the pillaging organized by bands of soldiers often unemployed and transformed by this circumstance into veritable brigands who devastated and massacred; the Black Death which struck France more severely than elsewhere: the *Jacquerie*,[1] the uprising of the peasants exasperated by the nobles who oppressed and did not defend them and a system of taxation that became increasingly burdensome, leading to economic instability.

Then, after the 'rest-cure' gained by the reign of Charles V, dubbed 'the Wise' (1364–80) who drove back the English with the help of Du Guesclin,[2] the accession of the half-wit, Charles VI, gave rise to the bitter rivalry of the houses of Orleans and Burgundy and to the civil war which tore apart the country, dividing it between the Armagnacs and Burgundians. Following the resumption of the Hundred Years' War and the national disaster suffered by the French in the battle of Agincourt (1415), England's new infant king, the son of Henry V, was proclaimed King of France in 1422. The regency was assumed by his uncle, the Duke of Bedford, who occupied Paris. The country, already in a state of complete disintegration, underwent a veritable schism when, in opposition to the 'King of Paris', Henry VI, the dauphin Charles was in turn declared 'King of Bourges'. If one adds to this sombre picture the renewed disasters of the Hundred Years' War, the growing general poverty and the still more profound demoralization, one can under-stand how the character of Joan of Arc has come to achieve a mythical significance in French history. Struggling persistently for the king, she pro-vided the necessary prestige for the coronation of Charles VII at Rheims, as well as contributing to the liberation of French territory. Henceforth the people who had been won over to the cause of their legitimate king actively participated in the struggle, and after the recapture of Paris (1436) they

1. So-called from the jacque or peasant's jerkin; cf. C. W. Previté-Orton, *Shorter Cambridge Medieval History*, 1962, ii, 881.

2. Bertrand Du Guesclin, Constable of France, d. 1380, cf. C. W. Previté-Orton, Shorter Camb. Med. Hist., ii, 884–5.

turned to the recovery of Normandy and Guyenne (the Gascon coastland) (1450-3). The victorious king was then able to order the Mint to strike medals commemorating the expulsion of the English from France. But the difficult task of finding a definitive solution to the centenarian conflict was to fall to Louis XI, after another Anglo-Burgundian alliance had renewed the threat of invasion from two directions. The Duchy of Burgundy had begun its brilliant rise with the marriage of Philip the Bold to Margaret of Flanders (1369) which marked the first step in Burgundian expansion towards the northern countries; an expansion which his successors, thanks to a skilful exploitation of wills and marriages, stretched to such a point that the 'Low Countries', presided over by Philip the Good, represented an independent state and a true European power. The ambition of Charles the Bold led him to break definitively with France and to renew the alliance with the English foe so that he could himself wear a crown. But, paradoxically, this ambition was to prove his downfall, for the cunning Louis XI came to terms with Edward IV, signing the Treaty of Pecquigny (1475) by which the latter renounced all his pretensions to the French crown. The death of Charles the Bold at Nancy in 1477 effectively shattered the dream of a unified kingdom of Burgundy and allowed Louis XI to annex Artois, Boulogne and Picardy, thus marking a great step forward in the territorial unification of France. The final step was achieved by the regent Anne of Beaujeux, daughter of Louis XI, who arranged the marriage of her brother, the future Charles VIII, with Anne of Brittany in 1491, thus securing the allegiance of the hitherto most independent province in the kingdom. Thus, at the end of the Middle Ages, thanks to the authoritarian power exercised by Louis XI who had even succeeded in placing the French church under his power, the country henceforth acquired the appearance of a great centralized monarchy which it was to keep for three centuries.

It would seem natural that in such a troubled country artistic creation should have difficulty in asserting itself. In the literary field, if the Hundred Years' War did not actually mark a complete hiatus, it probably prevented reconstruction at a time when the vast medieval forms were disappearing along with the society that had created them. There were certainly poets who continued the tradition of the preceding centuries, but as their art was still based on the ideals of chivalry and feudal nobility, they were much inferior to their predecessors. These poets no longer had contact with the reality of their time, and not until the advent of Villon is it possible to speak of an authentic expression of contemporary thought. What with the war, the misery and the pillaging, it is not surprising that no great name can be found in French literature to rival that of Dante, Petrarch or Chaucer, even though in his time Alain Chartier was compared with Petrarch and the somewhat faded charm of Christine de Pisan inspired some of Binchois' best *chansons*. Nor is it surprising, since activity was centred at court, that the greatest

French writing of the time should be found in the *Chronicles* of Jean
Froissart who was able to relate events in a precise and sober manner, far
removed from the unbearably artificial tone of lyric poetry. In a France ex-
hausted by struggles, no new cathedrals were built; instead the old edifices
were perfected or finished off in the 'flamboyant' variant of the late Gothic
style, characterized by a profuse decoration which tended to cover over everything and to conceal the architecture's functional elements. There are not
even any great names in painting until Jean Fouquet, and in the fourteenth
century the most active artistic centre was Avignon, where the popes called
upon Simone Martini and where some remarkable works like the famous
anonymous *Pietà* were created.

If great painters and writers were lacking in France at this time, music
enjoyed a better fortune. Free from the doubts that haunted the other arts,
music, by its very essence, offered an escape from the reality of life, which it
did not seek to evoke. Moreover it so happened that the two greatest musicians
of the fourteenth century – Philippe de Vitry and Guillaume Machaut (to be
discussed later) were natives of the unfortunate kingdom. It is fitting that
we should examine, in so far as the surviving documents allow, the conditions
in which music was able to develop, the views that were currently held, the
patrons of the art and its place in society.

The most active artistic centres were clearly under the aegis of the Church
and Court. In the Church, however, polyphonic music and the innovations
attempted by the composers were not always accepted without resistance.
Besides the decretal, *Docta sanctorum patrum*, promulgated by Pope John
XXII (1324–5) against those who disfigured the traditional plainchant by the
introduction of new rhythms, thus ridiculing the act of devotion with an
ostentatious lasciviousness,[3] certain theologians were entirely opposed to the
introduction of art-music in the Church. At the end of the thirteenth century
St Thomas Aquinas set forth such views: '*Ergo cantus non conveniunt divinis
laudibus*'.[4] And Denys le Chartreux, nearly two centuries later, still shows a
certain reluctance to countenance polyphonic settings, since they only serve
to beguile the audience. He recognized the ecstatic character of musical
emotion, but scorned it as '*lascivia animi*'.[5] On the other hand Pierre d'Ailly,
chancellor of the University of Paris (1389–95) and later Bishop of Cambrai,
seems to have realized the benefits of this emotion which derives from the
power of harmony when he writes: '*virtus armoniarum adeo rapit animas
humanas in se, ut eas abstrahat non solum ab aliis passionibus et sollicitudinibus;
sed etiam in se ipsis.*' ('The power of harmony captures human souls so

3. Cf. *NOHM*, iii, 3; Latin text and English translation in the old *Oxford History of Music*, 6 vols.,
1901–5, ii, 89–91; cf. also *MGG*, s.v. Johann xxii.
  4. *Summa theologiae*, pars II/2, quaestio 91, articulus 2; cf. Migne's edn. (1841), col. 706.
  5. J. Huizinga, *The Waning of the Middle Ages*, London, 1924, p. 246.

strongly that it deflects their thoughts not only from other passions and anxieties but even from themselves.')[6]

It is clear that these churchmen regarded music as Christians and moralists, never considering it as an autonomous art whose intrinsic beauty should be appreciated. They only conceded its usefulness in supporting the ardour of piety – which is probably the only reason, far removed from the present-day idea of artistic enjoyment, why certain authors deemed the restricted use of music advisable.

One of these was Philippe de Mézières, counsellor to King Charles v, who, in the rules for the *Chevalerie de la Passion* formulated in 1384, recommended that the divine service be celebrated with the playing of the organ, trumpets and instruments of all kinds which were played during Mass. Mézières rejected the music of his own century, however, and warned against those who followed its fashions.[7] Nevertheless not only at Avignon, in the very entourage of those popes who were so scornful of all innovation, but also at the royal chapel, religious music continued to enrich its polyphonic technique. The tradition that the kings of France were to sponsor musically distinguished chapels was inaugurated by St Louis who, in 1248, founded the *Sainte-Chapelle du Palais* which remained under the direct protection of subsequent monarchs. As early as the fourteenth century the regulations stipulated that the children should learn three or four motets every day.[8] We know that Charles v maintained his chapel 'richly and generously', and the fact that three successive kings (Charles vii, Louis xi and Charles viii) were assured of the services of the great Ockeghem in their chapel at Tours for more than forty years shows the importance accorded by the Court to music in church ceremonies. Charles viii was especially discerning in his choice of musicians, as shown in his insistent demands in April 1492 to Piero di Medici for the return of Alexander Agricola to France, who apparently left the Chapel Royal for Florence without permission: '*Pour ce que nous desirons singulièrement recouvrer en nostre dicte chappelle icellui Alexandre . . .*'.[9]

Besides the service of God, people at Court on the other hand, noblemen and even certain members of the bourgeoisie whose prosperous enterprises had gained them a high social status, could satisfy an ideal inherited from the Middle Ages, courtly love. *L'amour courtois* still constituted the principal source of inspiration for the secular song which, in the fourteenth century, began to gain the place of honour in the history of French music that it was to retain thereafter.

6. J. Gerson, *Opera*, ed. Ellies du Pin, Antwerpiae 1706, i. 538.

7. Paris, Bibliothèque Mazarine, MS 1943, fo. 60–61v⁰, Quoted by N. Jorga, *Philippe de Mézières*, Paris, 1896, p. 457.

8. M. Brenet, *Les Musiciens de la Sainte-Chapelle du Palais*, Paris, 1910, p. 16.

9. Picker, 'Charles viii'.

The musical life at court was evidently dictated by the kings, who did not all have the same degree of leisure or taste for the arts. Among the French sovereigns of the fourteenth century, Charles V was the most notable as a Maecenas, surrounding himself with philosophers and talented artists, a new feature in the history of the French monarchy. This cultivated collector assembled in his palace at the Louvre a veritable museum, and his 'rich library' (which was to provide the basis of the Bibliothèque Nationale) already contained some fifty thousand volumes, if we are to believe Christine de Pisan. The same poetess informs us that the king had numerous musicians to whom he 'listened with pleasure at the end of his meals' ('*oyoit voulentiers à la fin de ses mengiers*').[10]

After Charles V's death the court found a new brilliance when the new king, Charles VI, married Isabel of Bavaria who had a mad craving for dancing and court festivities. Also characteristic of the spirit of the time, inherited from the medieval courtly ideal, was Charles VI's so-called 'Court of Love' founded on 14 February 1401 at Paris in the *Hôtel de Bourgogne* by a few prominent lords and poets with the avowed intention of honouring the fairer sex and cultivating poetry, but probably also intended to distract attention from the terror of the plague. Established firmly enough to survive the disaster of Agincourt, this court brought together all classes of society from the king himself, who was one of its *Grands conservateurs* (Guardians) to small citizens, from powerful bishops to simple clerics. The members celebrated their meetings with a Mass '*à son d'orgues, chant et dechant*' ('with melody and counter-melody, to the sound of the organ'). The names of a number of musicians were found amongst the members.[11] The head of this *Cour d'Amour, le Prince d'Amour*, 'maintained musicians and gallants who could make and sing all kinds of *chansons, ballades, rondeaux, virelais* and other amorous ditties and who could perform melodiously upon instruments'.[12]

ARS NOVA

That the fourteenth century should mark a new order of things for France and in particular for music, was the primary intention of Philippe de Vitry when he gave to one of his musical treatises, compiled at Paris around 1320, the proud title of *ars nova*, a term now used to denote all fourteenth-century music. About the same time, and again at Paris, another theorist, Johannes (Jean) de Muris, took up the same expression, probably under the friendly

10. Ch. de Pisan, *Le Livre des fais et bonnes meurs du sage roy Charles V*, ed. S. Solente, Paris, 1936, i. 44.

11. Piaget, 'Cour'.

12. Guillebert de Metz, *Description de la ville de Paris au XVe siècle*, ed. Le Roux de Lincy, Paris, 1855. (Le Trésor des pièces rares ou inédites) p. 85–6.

influence of Vitry, for one of his works which he entitled *Ars novae musicae*. It seems likely that these terms were justified, since in his *Speculum musicae* the conservative theorist, Jacques (Jacobus) de Liège, opposes the *ars nova* of the modern composers (*moderni*) to the *ars antiqua* of the older generation. In a manuscript at Paris, moreover (Bibliothèque Nationale MS. Latin 7378A) which is a slightly modified version of Vitry's treatise copied in the fourteenth century, the compiler clearly distinguishes between the notation used '*in veteri arte*' ('in the old art') and that used by modern musicians in '*nova arte*'.[13] Moreover, the decretal of Pope John XXII, in which there is also an allusion to the '*novellae scholae*' ('new schools'), provides decisive proof of the introduction of new techniques in the music of the early fourteenth century, which were counter to age-old customs and whose inevitable progress the traditional establishment of the church attempted to check. For the severity of the pontiff's criticism[14] and the precise expression of his rebukes leads one to assume that this evolution – not to say revolution – was not carried out with everyone's blessing. Ordinary Christian folk as well as official authorities were alarmed by this new art which was invading their churches. So much so that, according to one observer, one should consider the *ars nova* as the

movement of the young in revolt who, at the dawn of the fourteenth century, rose up in their College at Paris against the abuses of power and *contested* an obsolete and sclerotic art to discover and impose a musical language which is no longer the prisoner of the sacrosanct pillory of the numerical trinity and the perfection of proportions.[15]

In fact the papal injunctions received little response from composers, and *ars nova* continued to follow its course, not only in France, but also in Italy, as is attested by the quantity and quality of the musical monuments that have survived.

No art can boast of being completely new, and that of the fourteenth century is no exception. But it undeniably represented an innovation in three essential points, which are moreover linked together by the reciprocal relationship of cause and effect: notation, rhythm and harmony, and the various genres. In the case of notation it was Philippe de Vitry's *Ars nova* which sanctioned the new technique by its codification of the available material. In regard to graphic symbols of notation, Vitry introduced, in addition to the existing note values of Franco of Cologne,[16] a new figure, the *minima* (minim) ♩ which was soon to give rise to an even smaller note-value, the *semiminima* (semiminim) ♪, which allowed greater diversification of rhythm. Henceforth the semibreve was the metrical unit (*tactus*) and had

---

13. Cf. Gilles, *Mus. Disc.* (1956), 36, 46; also Gilles, *Mus. Disc.* (1958) 59.
14. See above, p. 148, fn. 3.
15. Clercx, 'Figures'.
16. See chapter 3, p. 104, and p. 140.

a duration approximately equal to that of the *longa* in the thirteenth century. The Franconian system had known only two rhythmical sub-divisions, namely, long into breves (*modus* or mode) and breve into semibreves (*tempus* or time); Vitry now introduced the division of semibreves into minims (*prolatio* or prolation). Moreover, whereas until the end of the thirteenth century only 'perfect' mensuration, which was based on ternary division, was permitted, 'imperfect' mensuration, based on binary division, was now recognized. Although already in the thirteenth century a long note-value could be rendered imperfect by being preceded or followed by a shorter note, only in the *ars nova* did imperfection acquire the same importance as perfection: it was this state of affairs that Jacques of Liège regretted after Vitry had admitted it without discussion, completely abandoning the former superiority of perfection. To clarify things Vitry introduced at the same time the idea of time signatures following simple principles which henceforth designated the following combinations:

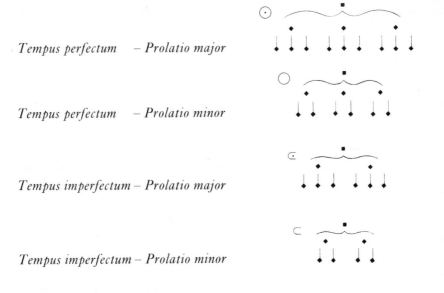

Tempus perfectum   – *Prolatio major*

Tempus perfectum   – *Prolatio minor*

Tempus imperfectum – *Prolatio major*

Tempus imperfectum – *Prolatio minor*

In addition, with the use of the *punctum divisionis* which marks passing imperfection within a predominantly ternary rhythm and of contrasting passages in red notation, which after Vitry have a very precise significance indicating certain changes in note values, it is clear that composers now had at their disposal a fairly complex system with which to notate all the subtleties of the newest and freest rhythms which were to be exploited – sometimes even to excess.

One of the most remarkable contributions of the *ars nova* is seen in the constructional principle which is referred to as 'isorhythm', a process which had hitherto remained very elementary, relying on the use of short rhythmic motives (or *ordines*), comprising only a few notes.[17] Henceforth it is the longer unit, repeated several times to the same rhythmic pattern (the *talea*) which provides the basis for the composition. Sometimes this principle of construction applies to pitch as well as to rhythm. The melodic unit (called *color*) may coincide with the rhythmic unit (*talea*), or the two may overlap. In regard to rhythm, the repetition was sometimes straightforward, at other times the pattern was speeded up (diminution) or slowed down (augmentation). Finally isorhythmic procedure could apply to a single voice, or a few; but in certain instances it affected all the voices. At any rate these subtleties were not perceptible to the average listener and only revealed their secrets to informed musicians; thus this technique, which takes such pains in order to satisfy the intellect, reflects the medieval predilection for a symbolical art addressed only to a restricted group of the initiated, and at the same time constituting the supreme test of the composer's skill. The isorhythmic motet which is the most original form of the *ars nova* was to enjoy an exceptional development and lasting favour for more than a century.

THE MASS

The *ars nova* introduced the first polyphonic settings of the Ordinary of the Mass: in the previous century only the Proper had been elaborated in this way. It seems that with the new supremacy of Avignon over Paris, musicians were to find, in the papal entourage, an environment most favourably inclined towards new settings for the service. Manuscript collections have been preserved which reveal the Avignon repertoire: one, copied around 1360, preserved at the Chapter Library at Ivrea (Italy); the other, dating from the end of the century, preserved at the Cathedral Library of Apt (France). These contain numerous Mass fragments, twenty-five in the Ivrea Codex and forty-five in the Apt Codex, thus showing clearly that musicians setting the Ordinary of the Mass were no longer content merely to improvise on Gregorian themes but composed new polyphonic pieces. This represents a great advance in the field of church music, which leads to the consideration of the five movements of a Mass as a complete cycle.

The first example of a complete musical setting of the Ordinary in a single manuscript unites different pre-existing Mass fragments. Such an example is provided in the case of the so-called Mass of Tournai (*Messe de Tournai*) which is probably the oldest of the rare fourteenth-century Mass-cycles which include the Masses of Toulouse, Barcelona and Besançon. In the case of the last of these however (also sometimes called the Sorbonne Mass), it should be noted that the first 'Agnus', which seems to have been taken from a

17. Concerning the repetition of rhythmic patterns in the earlier motet, see chapter 3, p. 114 and its discussion of the tenor in example 13; cf. also D. Harbinson, 'Isorhythmic Technique in the Early Motet', *ML*, xlvii (1966), 100.

'Sanctus' in the Ivrea Codex, shows the first symptoms of the 'parody' principle, which consists of constructing a Mass on material borrowed from an earlier polyphonic work, a principle which was to survive for several centuries.[18]

These compositions for the Ordinary (both complete cycles and separate movements) can be classified in three groups according to the musical style they adopt: the first is that of the motet, which however generally avoids isorhythm, with the two upper voices singing the same text in elaborate polyphony, while the tenor, which has little melodic character, acts as a harmonic support; the second is the *discantus* (discant) style in which the top voice, which also sings the liturgical text, is prominent, while the two other voices act as a quasi-instrumental accompaniment. Finally, the third type is in the old *conductus* style, with all the voices singing the same text simultaneously without instrumental intervention.[19] An exception must be made for Machaut's Mass, which is on a quite different artistic plane and will be discussed later.

SECULAR MUSIC

The new state of society, which saw the rise of an enterprising bourgeoisie and the loss of the Church's prestige after its unconcealed, shattering quarrels, contributed to another innovation of the fourteenth century: the development of secular music which, towards the end of the thirteenth century in France, had already embraced polyphony with the *rondeaux* of Adam de la Halle, the first monuments of free polyphony in the vernacular. The secular repertoire even held an important place in the music of the papal entourage, as may be seen from the manuscripts emanating from the Avignon court.

Among the poetic forms favoured by the musicians was the old medieval *lai*, which differs from the thirteenth-century type in that it is generally cast in a succession of twelve stanzas, all of which differ in metre, rhyme and melody except the last, which resumes the music of the opening stanza. Each stanza is divided into two sections sung to the same melody. Sometimes these sections are further divided into two sub-sections sung to the same melodic portion. The *lai*, which was normally monophonic, provides a great diversity of style with a melodic line which is sometimes simple and sometimes brilliantly ornamented. The *rondeau* and *virelai* continue in the already established tradition,[20] and the *chanson balladée* (a new designation given to the *virelai* with three stanzas) retains the structure of the thirteenth-century *virelai* with its stanzas interspersed by a refrain which also opens and closes

18. The model on which a parody Mass is based is not a monophonic melody but a polyphonic complex of voices. See Schrade, *Acta* (1955), 13; also Lockwood, 'Parody'.

19. H. Stäblein-Harder, *Critical*.

20. See below, p. 169.

the composition. The *ballade*, whose form had hitherto remained variable, acquired a stricter form at the beginning of the fourteenth century. The usual type now consisted of three stanzas, each consisting of three couplets. This was followed by a refrain agreeing in rhyme and metre with the last line of the stanza. The first and second couplet are sung to the same music (AA′), differentiated by *ouvert* and *clos* endings; the third couplet has different music (B) and is followed by the refrain (R), the total musical design being AA′BR. Isorhythm also appears occasionally in the *ballade*, which, along with the motet, provides the greatest evidence of the innovations of the fourteenth-century art.

A further new development was the canon at the unison, which accumulated a considerable repertoire and was known as the *chace* (*caccia* in Italy). These pieces may depict hunting scenes, but are often animated by a market scene, the imitation of a bird-song or other such picturesque subjects.

Attention should finally be drawn to the hocket,[21] a rhythmic procedure borrowed from the thirteenth-century motet, consisting of rapidly alternating notes and silences (rests) between one part and another which, developed on a large scale, becomes a musical form in its own right. This technique had already aroused the indignation of Pope John XXII, who reproached the disciples of the new school with breaking up the continuity of melody by means of hockets ('*nam melodias hoquetus intersecant*'). In the same way one might also recall the protests of Denys le Chartreux against the '*fractio vocis*' which he compares to artificially curled hair or plaited garments in reflecting only variety and which he condemns as the symbol of a soul which is similarly cracked.[22]

VITRY

The first testimony of the transition to a new art is provided by the curious *Roman de Fauvel* (Paris, Bibliothèque Nationale MS français 146), a violent satire against the Church written by Gervais Du Bus between 1310 and 1314 to which Chaillou de Pestain added a number of poems and pieces of music around 1316. If he did not actually write the 160 musical pieces that are introduced there, he at least showed great discernment in their choice, for it had French and Latin texts in both monophonic and polyphonic settings, the latter whether written in the old *conductus* style of the preceding century or in the new motet form displaying many of the characteristics of the *ars nova*, to the extent that certain of them have been attributed (without definite proof) to Philippe de Vitry. The latter, as has been said, was one of the great figures who dominated musical life in France in the fourteenth century, another being Guillaume de Machaut.

21. See chapter 3, p. 118, fn. 36.
22. Huizinga, *The Waning of the Middle Ages*, p. 246.

Born in Champagne on 31 October 1291, Philippe de Vitry was appointed canon at Clermont-en-Beauvaisis in 1323 and in 1350 became Bishop of Meaux where he died on 9 June 1361. As a statesman, poet and musician he won the admiration of his contemporaries. He was the friend of Petrarch, who addresses him, in two letters that have been preserved, as the best French poet of the time. He was known as the 'Prince of Musicians' or, as Simon Tunstede writes, 'the flower of the whole world (*totius mundi*) of musicians'. Even a century later he is praised, in an anonymous treatise, as the flower and gem of singers.[23] Unfortunately fame did not suffice to preserve his work from destruction, and very little remains for posterity to judge his talent. Although in the *Art de seconde rhétorique* he is hailed as the one who '*trouva la manière des motets et des ballades et des lais et des simples rondeaux*', only about fifteen motets have survived, and only two that actually bear the composer's name, the authenticity of the others being attributed to him on the basis of historical and stylistic criteria. These works are disseminated in numerous manuscripts, the two most important being the aforementioned *Roman de Fauvel*, in which one can assume five motets as being the work of Vitry, and the Ivrea Codex, which contains nine more. In addition seven are also found in the La Tremoille manuscript (from the collection of the Duchess of Tremoille at the Château de Serrant) whose music has unfortunately been lost, although the table of contents survives.[24]

Isorhythm plays an important part in all these motets, and it seems as though Vitry was responsible for the development of this procedure as a unifying structural principle, in which he already uses the resources that are developed later on, such as the diminution of the note-values (double and triple) of an isorhythmic tenor. This composer should, therefore, be considered as the true instigator of the *ars nova*, in that he not only announced its advent in the prophetic title of his treatise, but also applied its innovations in his own works. It is perhaps worthy of note that this *magister in musica*, who played such a determining role in the evolution of music in France, was, in addition, an ardent patriot, engaging his powers to the full during the Hundred Years' War against the traitors of his country, and venting his wrath in caustic invective against the English foe whose total disappearance he so desired, as is seen in his motet, *O creator deus pulcherrimi*, whose tenor and contratenor pronounce these words, in which the allusion is clear: '*Jacet granum oppressum palea – Quam sufflabit Francus ab area*' (The grain lies crushed beneath the straw – May France blow it far away).[25] All the evidence shows Vitry to have been one of the greatest figures of this moment in French history.

23. R. Casimiri, 'Teodono de Caprio ... del sec. XV', *Note d'archivio*, xix (1942), 38–42 and 93–8.
24. Droz, 'Chansonnier', with facsimile.
25. Unfortunately the music of this motet has not survived, see Schrade, *Commentary*, i, 119; also Pognon 'Vitry'.

MACHAUT

Guillaume de Machaut, born around 1300, was, like Vitry, a native of Champagne, highly esteemed both as a poet and musician, who served a number of masters. While he held the post of secretary to the King of Bohemia (John of Luxemburg) he travelled to Poland and Lithuania and stayed at the Court in Prague. After the death of King John at Crécy, he joined the service of the Duke of Berry and later that of Charles, King of Navarre, and finally that of King Charles V himself. After 1337 he settled at Rheims, where he was given a canonry and where he died in 1377. In contrast to the case of Vitry, and despite the inevitable losses (amongst others those of a manuscript listed in 1420 as belonging to the collection of the Dukes of Burgundy), the poetic and musical works of Guillaume de Machaut seem to have survived in their entirety, copied in eight main manuscripts completely devoted to his works. They are all preserved in the Bibliothèque Nationale at Paris: MSS français 1584, 1585, 1586, 9221 and 22545–6 containing the musical compositions and MSS français 843, 881 and 1587 containing only poetry. It is probable that this imposing collection of manuscripts was organized under the direction and according to the instructions of Machaut himself, as is suggested by the note found in the table of MS 1584: 'Here is the order which G. de Machaut wishes to have in his book' (*Vesci l'ordenance que G. de Machau vuet qu'il ait en son livre*'). One should also mention the Vogüé manuscript (now at the Wildenstein Gallery in New York). Moreover, this corpus is completed by thirty-four fragmentary sources, the whole list being included, along with a detailed description of all the manuscripts in Schrade's edition of Machaut's works.[26] Machaut thus appears as the only musician of the Middle Ages whose work has survived in virtually complete form. This work, which embraced all the forms practised at the time, represents the full blossoming of the theories attributed to the *ars nova* and, thanks to the richness of the sources and the greatness of the artist, it occupies what Schrade describes as the 'lion's share' in the history of French fourteenth-century music.

The 142 compositions which constitute the musical works consist of 42 *ballades*, 33 *virelais*, 23 motets, 21 *rondeaux*, 19 *lais*, one Mass, one hocket, one *complainte* and a *chanson royal*. It seems surprising that an ecclesiastic should show such a marked preference for secular music and, in this way, the renowned composer may be said to illustrate one of the characteristics of his time, the tendency towards secularization. It is also surprising that a composer of such importance should still be devoted to monophonic music, which had been rather neglected since the compositions in the *Roman de Fauvel* (second decade of the century). Machaut seems to have been one of the few

26. Schrade, *Commentary*, ii, 7–8, 19–54.

(if not the only one) to practise this type of composition in no less than 17 *lais* and 25 *virelais*, as well as the *complainte* and *chanson royal*, both of which are taken from the *Remède de Fortune*.[27]

It is obvious that the old form of the *lai*, whose distinguished career lasting almost two centuries was gloriously crowned by Machaut, remained an attractive form to the poet on account of the lyricism of its inspiration, which is clearly reflected in titles like the *Lay des dames*, the *Lay mortel*, the *Lay de bonne espérance* or the *Lay de plour* [*pleur*] – all directly derived from the traditional subject-matter of the *trouvères*. Polyphony, however, reclaims its rights in the *Lay de la fonteinne* and the *Lay de confort*, which carry a rubric that they are in canon. The first of these consists of twelve stanzas, of which the odd stanzas are monophonic, alternating with three-part *chace* which form the even stanzas, each employing a different theme. The *Lay de confort* consists of a sequence of twelve canons for three voices. In addition, Richard Hoppin[28] considers *Un Lay de consolation* (which had previously been transcribed monophonically) as a piece for two voices, the melody of the second portion of each stanza providing a counterpoint to the first: the polyphony for two voices thus produced can hardly be the result of chance, although the evidence is entirely internal and not based on any indications in the original source.

The *virelai* (also designated *chanson balladée* or *virelai ballade*) for which Machaut again favoured the monophonic form, reserving two-part polyphony for only eight of his twenty-five pieces, was not to disappear like the *lai*, but, in its polyphonic guise, retained great popularity throughout the century.

In the realm of polyphony Machaut was able to display his genius to the full and here, too, he showed an original turn of mind in his preference for certain genres above others. Thus whereas the motet had been the most esteemed of forms, Machaut reveals a clear predilection for the *ballade*, writing nearly twice as many *ballades* as motets. The form is that of an accompanied song rather than a contrapuntal composition like the motet, and the isorhythmic structure so characteristic of the latter appears in only two parts of a single *ballade*, *S'amours me fait*. It was very probably due to the influence of the motet, however, that he adopted the principle of polytextuality, providing two and even three different texts in certain of his *ballades*. One example is the double *ballade*: *Quant Theseus – Ne quier veoir* in four parts, in which the two upper voices (supported by two instrumental parts) sing two different texts simultaneously, though joining in the same refrain at the end. Unity of musical texture is assured, nevertheless, by numerous thematic affinities between the two *cantus* parts. The two triple

27. The *Remède de Fortune* explains the construction and style of seven lyric forms, illustrating each (such as *lai, rondeau*, etc.) with a single musical example.

28. R. Hoppin, *Mus. Disc.* (1958), 93; with musical transcription.

ballades are written on the same principle: *Sanz cuer m'en vois – Amis dolens – Dame par vous* in which the three texts are sung in canon to the same melody and *De triste cuer – Quant vrais amans – Certes je di* written for three *cantus* parts in a counterpoint of three different melodies.

As for the *rondeau* for which Machaut inherited numerous models among the work of his predecessors, both poets and musicians, he remained faithful to the classical form of the poem, to which he gave the shape of an accompanied song, only the top voice being provided with words. The *rondeau, Ma fin est mon commencement./Et mon commencement ma fin* has acquired a certain celebrity on account of its intricate construction. There are three parts (tenor, *cantus*, *triplum*): the *triplum* sings the entire *cantus* melody (forty bars in Schrade's transcription) in crab canon, while the tenor employs the same method at the half-way mark (bars 21–40 of the tenor are a reversal of its own bars 1–20).

The motet had secular as well as sacred texts. Machaut, in fact, prefers the former, whether in Latin or French, only two of his motets being connected with the liturgy, the rest treating mainly social and political themes. Nearly all his motets (twenty out of twenty-three) have isorhythmic structure in the tenor part with certain isorhythmic elements in the *motetus* and *triplum* parts. These compositions are distinguished by their solid and balanced construction, and although their rhythm is surprisingly conservative, generally adhering to the greater prolation (*prolatio major*) without complicated formulae or syncopation, their musical sensitivity always cleverly conceals the strictness of the carefully calculated structure.[29]

Although Machaut seems to have neglected church music, it is, nevertheless, in this field that he produced the greatest masterpiece of medieval music with his so-called *Messe de Notre Dame*, which offers the first example of a cyclical setting of the Ordinary of the Mass by a single composer. In this work he shows a great variety of styles, the homophonic writing of the old *conductus* in the long sections of the 'Gloria' and 'Credo' contrasting with the contrapuntal motet-style which is applied in all the other sections of the Mass. These latter have an isorhythmic construction based on Gregorian themes, not only in the tenor and contratenor parts but sometimes in the *motetus* and *triplum* parts. (The melodies used are from Mass IV, LU 25, in the 'Kyrie' and from Mass XVII, LU 61, in the 'Sanctus' and 'Agnus'.) The almost consistent use of the minor prolation, which in Machaut's work is always associated with new experiments in complex rhythm, leads one to believe that this Mass belongs to the latter part of his creative period. As well as these technical considerations much could be said about the purely musical qualities of this work, which remains today as one of the greatest monuments of sacred music.

29. Günther, *Mus. Disc.* (1958), 29–36.

Finally, another religious work which merits special mention is the three-part *Hoquetus David* in which the polyphony (very probably intended for instruments) is based on a tenor in long notes, the 'hocket' being shared by the two upper parts. The work is fascinating because of the complicated interplay of broken rhythms. The three-voice parts are named *David triplum – David hoquetus – David tenor*, after the Gregorian melody taken from the alleluia verse *Nativitas . . . ex stirpe David* which the composer chose as a *talea* for his isorhythmic construction.

THE END OF THE MIDDLE AGES

The genius of Guillaume de Machaut did not open any new and fruitful paths and his intimate art, in fact, marks the end of the creative movement of the *ars nova*: after his death in 1377 French music languished. Not that there was any shortage of composers, as may be seen in the Chantilly Codex (Musée Condé, MS 1047) which is the most important source for the latter part of the fourteenth century, and whose contents cover the period between about 1369 and 1390. This source reveals no less than thirty-two names, all imitating their great predecessor. But none of these composers has come down to posterity with any imposing work which can compare with the artistic activity of the Canon of Reims. Besides the Chantilly manuscript, which marks the beginning of a transitional epoch, another manuscript at Oxford (Bodleian Library, Can. Misc. 213, fasc. 5–8), dating from about 1422–8, marks the end of the period during which no French composer appears bold enough to provide any new impetus, all the surviving examples representing the average art of their time. A study of these two manuscripts shows the extent of the triumph of secular over sacred music, the Chantilly Codex containing, for example, only thirteen motets against ninety-nine *chansons*. Although few motets survive, however, they nevertheless remain faithful to the principle of isorhythm in all the voice parts. Moreover, they tend to revert to Latin texts on religious subjects, thus abandoning the tradition of Machaut in favour of that of Vitry. Despite certain important innovations in rhythm, their form remains more conservative than the polyphonic *chanson* from which they differ increasingly and to which they were eventually to yield the supremacy they had enjoyed for two hundred years.

Although there is little information on the numerous composers represented in these manuscripts, their relative chronology may be approximately established by dividing them into two groups: the first comprises musicians of the late fourteenth century who were close to the late contemporaries or immediate successors of Machaut, such as Solage, Trébor, Senleches, Jean Vaillant and d'Andrieu (whose greatest claim to fame is the fact that he set to music the lament of Eustache Deschamps on the death of Machaut). The second group, representing the beginning of the fifteenth century, includes

Tapissier, Carmen and Cesaris (all three mentioned by Martin le Franc in the passage dealing with music from his *Champion des Dames*) and also Baude Cordier and Pierre Fontaine, the last-named in the service of the Duke of Burgundy. Apart from these, other composers represent this later period, such as Richard de Loqueville and Nicholas Grenon, about whom there is some biographical information and who left some significant work, providing the indispensable link in the chain leading to Dufay.

The musicians of the first group, the immediate successors of Machaut, retain the techniques of complex rhythmic notation from the *ars nova*, developing and complicating them to the extreme limits of sophistication. They attempted to surpass their master in his favourite form, the *ballade*, whose length was now doubled and whose refrain was treated quite separately. Moreover its subject matter was no longer the exclusive and anonymous domain of courtly love but now included history, hitherto the special preserve of the motet. The *ballade* thus became an occasional piece, celebrating, for example, a royal marriage (e.g. Trébor's *Passerose de beauté*), the conquests or virtues of a sovereign (e.g. Trébor's *Se Alexandre* and *Se July Cesar*, composed in honour of Gaston Phébus, the same composer's *En seumeillant* for John 1 of Aragon; and Solage's *S'ainsy estoit*, celebrating Jean de Berry). Thus elevated in the hierarchy of forms, the *ballade* adopted a more complex style, with an abundance of rapid coloraturas, showing an extreme refinement. But the art gained nothing as a result.

It was this very excess of complexity which at the end of the century led some composers to seek greater simplicity; such a composer was Hasprois (died around 1428) who wrote short *ballades* in a purely syllabic style that presaged the work of the next generation. Moreover the short and simple form of the *rondeau* gains in favour with musicians like Johannes Cesaris and Baude Cordier whose works are mostly found in the Oxford manuscript and who, in shaking off the rhythmic and notational complexities that were threatening to destroy the polyphonic *chanson*, prepare the way for Dufay and Binchois.

But the greatest effort to achieve simplification was to be made by two composers who spent part of their careers at Cambrai where Dufay underwent his musical education: Richard de Loqueville, the harp-player of the Duc de Bar, whose name appears in 1410 at Cambrai Cathedral where he held the post of 'master of the children' until his death in 1418; and Nicholas Grenon who, before being appointed singing master (*Maistre de chant*) at Cambrai in 1421, had since 1413 been in the service of John the Fearless at the court of Burgundy, where, a decade later, Binchois was to spend the last thirty years of his life. These composers provide evidence of a new spirit in both their secular and sacred music. Although, as Schrade indicates,[30] there

30. Schrade, *Congress Wégimont 1955*, pp. 58–9.

are certain harsh conflicts in their works which still show many of the complexities inherited from the *ars nova*, there are also clear signs of an attempt to escape from them, and it is in this light that they will be considered here. It will suffice to quote, among the five surviving chansons by Loqueville,[31] the *ballade*, *Quant compaignons s'en vont jouer*, a simple composition in which the consistently syllabic melody of the soprano is supported by two lower parts in the style of an instrumental accompaniment. In his motet, devoted to Saint Yves, on the double Latin text, *O flos in divo – Sacris pignoribus dotata* with its syllabic melody, one has the impression of great simplicity which is again found in his Mass fragments (three 'Glorias', one 'Credo' and one 'Sanctus' trope). In the four-part 'Sanctus', however, he attempts a more studied counterpoint which seems to mark the limit of what he managed to achieve in this direction (despite the fact that in one of the 'Glorias' he alternates episodes for two and three parts with a certain degree of skill). The work of Nicholas Grenon goes even further than Loqueville's along the new path so that he 'occupies an advanced position in the new period.'[32] It is not that he broke completely with the past; he still engages in certain subtleties of writing, but he usually succeeds in instilling his style with a great clarity through the simplicity of his melodic line, which is freed from superfluous melismata and whose short phrases are broken up by regular cadences. This tendency can be seen in his *rondeau* in syllabic style, *La plus jolie et la plus belle* or again in his Christmas motet for three voices, *Nova nobis gaudia*, which is based on a single text and whose isorhythm is very much simplified.

DUFAY AND HIS ERA

HIS LIFE AND TIMES. After this transitional era during which the way had been opened towards the future and the ground prepared for more novel productions, it so chanced that there arrived on the scene the very musician capable of achieving this end, Guillaume Dufay. His was a comprehensive genius, showing equal skill in the sacred and secular fields, but it was in the former, and particularly in his settings of the Ordinary of the Mass, that his achievement was most notable. After the supremacy of secular music since the early fourteenth century there was, from the second quarter of the fifteenth century on, a revival of interest in sacred music which was to retain its commanding position for some time. It has been suggested that this evolution was the consequence of a renewed intensity of religious feeling related to the pietism of the Flemish theologians, Ruysbroeck and De Groote, crystallized in the Low Countries by the Brotherhood of Common Life. It does not seem, however, as though France experienced this form of popular

31. Printed in Reaney, *15th Century*, iii.

32. Schrade, 'La Musique de Machaut à Dufay', in Manuel, *Histoire*, i, 883; the two works of Grenon, discussed below, are in Marix, *Bourgogne*.

devotion, the *Devotio moderna*, against which a man like Gerson, for example, showed a certain defiance. For this reason one may perhaps deduce that the new flowering of religious music was due to the fact that the Church had finally accepted the introduction of polyphony into the liturgy and had more-over discovered that this music provided a fitting complement to official ceremonies.

Composers received commissions with greater frequency. 'Free' composi-tion without solicitation (or compensation) was an alien concept to the period: every work was written with the view of fulfilling a precise demand for a particular occasion. At all events, in the case of Dufay whose importance was soon recognized by his contemporaries, it is certain that the preference he seemed to show for religious works was, more than anything else, the result of the numerous commissions he received in that genre. The innovations which he introduced were, however, entirely due to his own genius.

Neither the date nor the place of birth of Guillaume Dufay is known, but it seems likely that he was born between 1390 and 1400 in the northern region of France near the present borders of Belgium, an area then part of the old Low Countries. He may thus be numbered among the many musicians who, for want of a better term, are usually described as Franco-Flemish. The present state of information about his life leaves many gaps in the course of his career. He began his musical education at Cambrai Cathedral, where he is listed among the choristers between 1409 and 1414. His 'Italian period' began around 1420 at Rimini and Pesaro in the service of the Malatesta family for whom he wrote two motets (*Visilissa ergo* and *Apostolo glorioso*) and a *chanson* (*Resveillies vous*) which appear to mark the beginning of his creative activity. In 1428 his name figures for the first time among the singers of the papal choir where he remained until 1433; during these five years he put his talent at the disposal of the Church and of the pope, writing thirty Mass fragments, two *Magnificats*, a cycle of hymns and four great motets more or less connected with ecclesiastical life at Rome. His relations with the court of Savoy began in 1433 and, according to his own testimony, lasted seven years, although it is impossible to specify the actual dates, since in 1435 he resumed his post at the papal chapel where he stayed until 1437. His duties, however, were now centred not at Rome but at Florence and Bologna, where Pope Eugene IV had taken refuge (not returning to Rome until 1443). In 1446 and 1450 he is mentioned among the members of the court of Burgundy, first as a chaplain and later as '*cantor illustrissimus domini Ducis Burgundie*' ('most illustrious singer of our Lord, the Duke of Burgundy'). These men-tions, however, probably refer to an honorary title rather than a real post, for in 1451 his name is again found in the archives of the court of Savoy, re-curring in 1438 and 1455, when he is described as '*conseiller et maistre de la chapelle de Monsegneur*', that is, Duke Louis. From around 1451 Dufay retired to his canonry at Cambrai where he took part in the deliberations of the Cathedral chapter and where he died on 27 November 1474. The honours of every kind that were conferred upon him during his lifetime and the praise bestowed on him after his death, show that his contemporaries thought of him both as a distinguished person and as a great composer.

In conclusion, one perceives certain points in this biography which help to explain Dufay's genius: in the first place, the fact that his early education was undertaken at Cambrai, which at that time was an important centre of religious musical life. Then, his sojourn in Italy at the beginning of his composing career, where he experienced in turn court life at Rimini and ecclesiastical life at Rome, allowed him to assimilate the musical style of that country. Finally, his itinerant musical life provided him with many artistic experiences, while his general culture, unusual for a musician (Dufay was a Bachelor of Canon Law) must have helped to enrich and deepen his natural gifts.

CHANSONS. Although his clerical vows did not prevent Dufay from devoting himself to secular music, he does not reveal the full measure of his talent in this field. Most of his *chansons* seem to date from before 1435, that is to say, from his youth, but this small-scale form offered too restricted a terrain for a composer so eager for new ideas. Nevertheless he does not appear inferior to his contemporaries in any way in this field, and by his striving for vocal equilibrium, associated with the growing feeling for tonal harmony, he opened the way for the late fifteenth-century French *chanson*. Many of the texts are amorous in the tradition of courtly poetry, a smaller proportion celebrate the month of May or the New Year. In formal terms, the *rondeaux*, of which there are fifty-nine, are much more numerous than the *ballades* and *virelais* (fourteen in all). In setting these poems Dufay displays more talent than the texts themselves merit, regenerating the expression of the stereotyped texts by his unparalleled melodic sense. He was thus able to break away from the metrical restrictions of the verse form by skilfully concealing the poetic caesura. This he did by overlapping the vocal parts, thus giving an impression of continuous composition by breaking the poem's monotony with instrumental interludes and, like his predecessor, Loqueville, by using a short instrumental ritornello as a prelude. Not only was he capable of achieving the tender grace and discreet charm which are such prominent features of the refined civilization of fifteenth-century France in pieces like *La Belle se siet* or *Craindre vous veuil*, but also of providing settings such as that of Antoine de Cuise's *rondeau, Les Doleurs dont me sens tel somme*. Here the upper voice is supported by two lower parts which betray their instrumental nature both by their low range and by a remarkable series of leaps in fourths, fifths and even octaves. Equally remarkable is the transformation of the character of the entire piece when it is first performed in $\frac{3}{4}$ time and thereafter in ¾ time, as the composer specifies.[33] But it was an Italian text, Petrarch's *Vergine bella che di sol vestita*, which inspired Dufay's most notable secular piece, to which he gave an unusual degree of continuity through the introduction of numerous instrumental passages which inject variety into this vocal genre and at the same time obscure the seams which separate the component units of the formal pattern.

MOTETS. Not all Dufay's motets can be described as religious music, some of them being occasional pieces of secular character. The texts themselves bear witness to the role played by the composer in the events he was commissioned to celebrate, and many of them include topical references whereby each part (though with different words) expresses some more or less obvious allusion to the event being commemorated – as in the motet *Ecclesie militantis* for five voices, each with a different text. This was composed on the occasion of the election of Pope Eugene IV (the Venetian, Gabriel Condulmer), which took place on 3 March, 1431: in this work the two upper parts celebrate the origin and virtues of the pontiff while the contratenor expresses the hope that the new pope will bring peace and the two tenors sing two *cantus firmi*, the first *Ecce nomen Domini* and the second *Gabriel*. But Dufay did not always require such an intellectual exercise to arouse his inspiration, and the simple *Alma redemptoris mater* in three parts, which he composed at Rome during his service at the papal chapel, has a perfect beauty: the Gregorian melody is unfolded in the *cantus* supported by the transparent and delicate harmonies of the two lower parts.

The motet, whether sacred or secular, provided Dufay with a framework that measured up to his genius, which found its most natural expression in depicting religious feelings or in evoking important events rather than in the conventional utterances of courtly love. From the point of view of musical structure two groups may be clearly distinguished in his motets: the isorhythmic motet, directly derived from the past, and the *cantilena* motet, which marks a decisive step towards the style of the future. Whereas the composers of the *ars nova* had regarded isorhythm as an ideal mould for their music, in the fifteenth century musicians felt that it tended to restrict the free flow of their imagination. In his isorhythmic works, though, Dufay nevertheless managed to construct pieces imbued with lyricism and to achieve the happiest balance between pure construction and the imponderables of feeling – as in the motet *Nuper rosarum flores*, composed for the consecration of Florence Cathedral in 1436, in which the composer's melodic talent and expressive powers reach their apotheosis, providing one of the clearest testimonies of Dufay's genius and of the influence of Italian music

33. Besseler, *Dufay*, vi, pp. x, xii, lxii, 97–8.

on his work. In the *cantilena* motet[34] the composer is freed from all constraint; he is no longer the slave of any form and can unfold his melody in the top part (*superius*) with the other parts providing an accompaniment. Thus in the *Salve regina*[35] the Gregorian melody is exposed in the *superius*, first in its traditional form, then in ornamented paraphrase, beneath which the three lower parts form a solid contrapuntal web with a strong feeling for tonality. This is maintained by the frequent cadences on the dominant. The *Ave regina coelorum*[36] in four parts, which Dufay is said to have asked for on his death-bed and in whose text he had, with this intention, introduced tropes of a highly personal tone (*miserere tui labentis du Fay*) shows a quite different structure, since the liturgical melody with more or less free variations appears in the tenor. The result is a truly polyphonic composition in which each voice plays an equal role.

Among Dufay's religious works one must consider separately those written for regular church services in the narrower sense of the word. In these the composer guards against any studied refinement in constructing simple, three-part pieces clearly intended for liturgical use. Because of this restriction the *Magnificats* and Sequences occupy only a secondary place in his creative work, while the hymns, generally in *fauxbourdon* style (see p. 167, fn. 38 and p. 301), were still being performed in ceremonies at Rome in the sixteenth century.

MASSES. At the time when Dufay was making his appearance on the musical scene the cyclical Mass was not yet in general use, which explains why he himself composed a large number of separate Mass fragments which are nothing more than motets. This also helps to explain why, even in his complete Mass settings, he did not immediately seek the principle of unity which unequivocally links the different parts of the composition into an indivisible whole. Nine Masses by Dufay are known (one of dubious attribution) covering almost the whole of the master's creative career. His early examples were of the *cantilena* type, generally set for three parts, in which the *superius* (as in the motet in the same style) sings the melody over an instrumental accompaniment provided by the lower parts. Later this tended to give way to the Mass based on a single *cantus firmus* in the tenor part, in which the four parts form a free polyphony in essentially vocal style. The Masses *Sine nomine*, *Sancti Jacobi* and *Sancti Antonii Viennensis*, all for three parts, belong to the first group. The first of these would seem to be a

34. The style of secular song (*cantilena*) of the period is usually characterized by a prominent treble part supported by other parts (e.g. tenor and countertenor) which sound like an accompaniment and are of a quasi-instrumental nature, if not actually instrumental. When one encounters such a style in a motet or Mass one speaks of a *cantilena* motet or *cantilena* Mass. (An alternative epithet is 'treble dominated', e.g. treble dominated motet.)

35. *DTO*, vii, 178; cf. LU, 276.

36. Besseler, *Dufay*, v, 124.

free composition, not based on a *cantus firmus*;[37] in its declamation of the text and other procedures it employs a style reminiscent of the composers of the Avignon school of the fourteenth century. This style had probably been introduced into Italy by the Franco-Flemish composer Ciconia of Liège, and Dufay might have made its acquaintance there. The *Missa Sancti Jacobi*, in which Dufay employs as *cantus firmi* Gregorian melodies that receive the most varied treatment in the different movements, owes its particular significance to the fact that the principle of *fauxbourdon*[38] is employed for the first time in its Communion. Although the *Missa Sancti Antonii Viennensis* is also of the *cantilena* type it nevertheless shows Dufay's first steps towards an essentially vocal form of polyphony in which all the parts are of equal importance. It is to this type that the five Masses he wrote after 1430 belong. This second group comprises the Masses *Caput*, *La Mort de Saint Gothard* (recently attributed to Dufay without irrefutable proof), *L'Homme armé*, *Se la face ay pale*, *Ecce ancilla Domini* and *Ave regina coelorum*, all for four voices. The *Missa Caput* is the first cyclic Mass which Dufay based on a single *cantus firmus*. The fact that the latter is taken from the Sarum rite (liturgy of Salisbury) reinforces the hypothesis that Dufay followed this new path under the influence of English music. The *Caput* theme which is sung in the tenor, twice in each of the five movements, first in ternary, then in binary measure, affirms the unity of the cycle; this unity is further stressed by another motive which appears in the upper parts at the beginning of each movement. (Such initial motives, used to bind together Mass movements, are called *motifs de tête* or 'head motives'.) In the next three Masses, *La Mort de Saint Gothard* (assuming it is the work of Dufay), *L'Homme armé* and *Se la face ay pale*, Dufay introduces another innovation in selecting a secular melody as the *cantus firmus*. The Mass *Se la face ay pale*, based on the tenor of one of his own *chansons*, is especially notable for its artistic merit. The *cantus firmus* in the tenor is treated more freely than in the *Caput* Mass, and the harmony produces a strongly tonal effect. As Leo Schrade writes of this work, Dufay 'realizes a grandiose ensemble in which all the parts are governed by the same constructional principle'. The *Missa L'Homme armé*, written between 1450 and 1460, inaugurates a notable tradition, as that *chanson* was used as a *cantus firmus* by so many famous composers after

37. Note, however, that in the MS xix, 145 of the Biblioteca Marciana (Venice), f. 1ᵛ the Kyrie of this Mass includes the words *Salvator noster*.

38. The French term *fauxbourdon* and the English term 'faburden' (probably derived from it) both refer to a musical practice characterized by successions of first inversion (or $\frac{6}{3}$) chords. Whether the English influenced the French, or vice versa, or whether both influenced each other, is a matter of controversy. Both the French and the English uses of $\frac{6}{3}$ chords are discussed in chapter 6.1, as is Dufay's canon (i.e. rule) for producing *fauxbourdon* in the *Missa Sancti Jacobi*. In this instance the *cantus firmus* is in the top part; the bottom part is written out, usually at the sixth below (though occasionally turning to the octave). The third part, in the middle between these two, is not written out, but the 'canon' directs that it is to be performed a fourth below the top part. Obviously, successions of $\frac{6}{3}$ chords are bound to result. See pp. 300–1.

Dufay, extending as far as Carissimi in the seventeenth century. Dufay's version offers many fine examples of free counterpoint which anticipate the works of the younger generation, and, in particular, of Ockeghem, who might well have in turn influenced the old master.

In his last two Masses, composed about 1463, which mark his full creative maturity, Dufay returns to Gregorian melodies from the antiphons *Ecce ancilla Domini* and *Ave regina coelorum*. In the latter especially, all the procedures employed since the *Caput* Mass are brought to their perfection: freedom in the treatment of the *cantus firmus*, a more developed 'head motive' technique extended to the lower parts, as well as counterpoint of considerable craftsmanship and the judicious use of the four voices, sometimes sub-divided into opposing groups of two. It might be said that this Mass, along with the motet Dufay wrote in his old age on the same theme,[39] represents a final apotheosis, crowning the composer's career, although his *opus ultimum* was probably a Requiem Mass which he himself mentions but which unfortunately has not survived.

The richness and variety of the innovations introduced by Dufay in the many forms he adopted, and the principle of clarification with which he unravelled the sterile complexity which had fettered his predecessors, actively contributed towards establishing a new development in music whose course he directed in a decisive manner.

BINCHOIS

Although Dufay was without a peer in the domain of sacred music, in the case of the *chanson* he is often compared to his contemporary Gilles de Binche, called Binchois, born at Mons (Hainault) about 1400. Having served as a trooper (*soudart*) in his youth, Binchois was in the service of the Duke of Suffolk at Paris in 1424 and spent the last thirty years of his life (d. 1460) as the chaplain of Duke Philip the Good of Burgundy. The very fact that Binchois spent most of his career in Burgundy and that his French *chansons* attained such unparalleled perfection has led certain musicologists to apply the epithet 'Burgundian' to the court *chanson*, and sometimes even employ the term 'Burgundian School' for all the musicians of this period. It is true that Burgundy, which had previously been only a French province ruled by a French prince, had gained an increasing autonomy to reach the point, with Charles the Bold, of open confrontation with the French monarchy, and that the cry '*Vive Bourgogne*' (found, for example, in folio 93 verso of Manuscript 1783 of the Vienna National Library, which was copied in 1500) expresses a national consciousness. One should not forget, however, that the musicians of Philip the Good were for the most part reared in French culture

39. If the motet was composed before the Mass, this represents yet another early example of 'parody', see above pp. 153–4; also *NOHM*, iii, 224 and Reese, *Renaissance*, p. 76.

and that their style, particularly that of Dufay and Binchois, was directly descended from the French music of the fourteenth century, albeit enriched by Italian and English experiences. As a result, it is impossible to isolate specifically 'Burgundian' characteristics. At most one might, in acknowledging this expansion and modification of French civilization, speak of the 'Franco-Burgundian' *chanson*, as does Anglès[40] with his '*franco-borgoñesa*', following the term that Huizinga adopts to describe the culture of this period.[41]

In spite of the ecclesiastical post that Binchois occupied at the Burgundian court, he played no decisive role in the evolution of the Mass, leaving no complete setting, but only independent fragments written in the style of the secular *chanson*. In his hymns and the four *Magnificats* he adopts the very simple form of *fauxbourdon*. His motets display greater variety, occasionally showing an understanding of the subtleties of isorhythm but generally preferring the *cantilena* style which was more natural to him. For Binchois was attracted most of all by secular music, and it was through his *chansons* that he earned his reputation as one of the foremost composers of his time. In these *chansons*, all in three parts and most of them inspired by the subject of courtly love, he displays less variety than Dufay, but his delicacy of feeling enabled him to set with greater expression certain poems particularly suited to his style, tinted with tenderness and melancholy, as for example the *rondeau*, *Triste plaisir et douloureuse joye* by Alain Chartier or the *ballade*, *Dueil angoisseux, rage demesurée* by Christine de Pisan.

OCKEGHEM AND HIS TIME

The evolution of the style of sacred music, instigated by Dufay and his generation, was carried a step further by his immediate successor, Johannes Ockeghem, whose early works come from the same period as the old master's years of maturity. Born probably in Hainault around 1420[42] he was a singer at Antwerp Cathedral in 1443–4 and between 1446 and 1448 a chorister in the chapel of Charles de Bourbon at Moulins. Finally, from 1452 until his death in 1495 he was attached to the French chapel where he served in succession, Charles VII, Louis XI and Charles VIII, first as a singer and then as *maistre de chapelle*. He also received the honorary post of treasurer of St Martin of Tours in 1461, one of the most lucrative posts in the kingdom. This uninterrupted stay in France of nearly half a century justifies his inclusion here among the musicians of that country, despite the fact that he was born in the Burgundian province of Hainault and that he received his early musical education at Antwerp. This connection finds added support

40. Anglès, *Católicos*, iii. 19 (i.e. M.M.E., x. 19).
41. Huizinga, *The Waning of the Middle Ages*, p. 227.
42. The precise place and date are unknown; cf. Lesure, *Nord*, p. 173; Reese, *Renaissance*, p. 118.

if one considers that Ockeghem without doubt continued in the tradition of Dufay, who was himself the product of the French *ars nova*.

Ockeghem possessed, among the composers of the fifteenth century, one of the most searching minds, and his work bears witness to his bold originality, his scorn for the facile and the individuality of his style far removed from all Italian influence. He reveals an unusual contrapuntal skill, the most obvious example being his famous *Deo gratias* constructed as a canon for thirty-six voices which acquired a truly legendary reputation in the sixteenth century. Even during his lifetime his feats of ingenuity were famous and kept his memory alive long after his death, even outside the musical world, for in an anonymous poem submitted to the competitors of the Puy at Rouen in 1523 he is compared to God himself. As late as 1552 Rabelais mentions him in the second place in his list of musicians in the Prologue of his fourth book of *Pantagruel*.

Continuing the tradition of his great predecessor Dufay, Ockeghem gave a predominant role to religious music, and only twenty *chansons* survive to testify to his activity as a court musician. The gravity of his nature led him to prefer texts which express melancholy and underline the sobriety of his spacious melodic language. The lament he composed on the death of Binchois, *Mort tu as navré de ton dart*,[43] is a good example of his ability to arouse emotion without any undue complexity of means. His *chansons* reflect the great diversity of his talent: in them one finds simple syllabic declamation in a piece like *Ma Bouche rit* as well as the beautiful melodic themes of *Ma Maistresse* or *D'un autre amer*, the imitative writing of *Petite camusette* or *Fors seulement*, and the canonic intricacies of *Prenez sur moi vostre exemple amoureux*, which constitutes a veritable tour de force.

In his religious work Ockeghem gives first importance to the Mass, of which he has left fifteen, making him one of the greatest masters of this form. Two of them are notable for subtle contrapuntal feats which seem always to have attracted this composer: the *Missa cujusvis toni*, written without clefs, can be sung in any of the four authentic Church modes as long as the correspondingly correct clefs are introduced for each of the four parts. The second work, the *Missa prolationum*, has only the two antecedent voices written out because the two consequent parts derive from them by different time signatures (prolations). The resultant four-part texture is of particular complexity since the two pairs of voices unfold two different canons at the same time. One should not conclude, however, that Ockeghem, preoccupied above all else with intellectual problems, was a purely cerebral composer for whom expression was only a secondary consideration, and thus regard this great artist as merely 'the man of canonic ingenuity'. For although he was a virtuoso in his handling of counterpoint, he never sacrificed beauty for the

43. Marix, *Bourgogne*, p. 83.

sake of technical display, and even when he indulged in one of those experiments whose difficulties and unexpectedness he savoured, he succeeded (though this was not his principal aim) in endowing his pure polyphony with the power to move the listener.[44]

Freely composed like the two above Masses, that is to say, without a pre-existent *cantus firmus*, the *Missa Mi-Mi* (also called *Quarti toni*) which is based on the descending fifth e–a (mi–mi according to Guidonian solmization) outlined in the bass at the beginning of each section of the work, can be considered as one of the most revealing products of Ockeghem's genius and personality. Written in compact polyphony in which each part participates equally, with no marked attempt to underscore any particular passage of the sacred text and free of all 'wordly' elements, this powerful and meditative Mass embodies the profound and grave religious feeling which characterizes Ockeghem's sacred music. This achievement is sometimes explained by the influence on him during his youth of the mystical movement of the Brotherhood of Common Life, which was active in Antwerp at that time. The Masses *Sine nomine* and *Quinti toni* for three parts, also freely composed, are unified by an identical motive at the beginning of each section.

Besides these free Masses, Ockeghem composed nine based on the old *cantus firmus* principle; of these only two are taken from the liturgy – the *Missa Caput* and (*Missa*) *Ecce ancilla Domini* – five being based on secular chansons, either by the composer himself, *Ma Maistresse* and *Fors seulement*; or by others, *Au Travail suis* (Barbingant) and *De plus en plus* (Binchois), the fifth drawing on the famous anonymous *chanson*, *L'Homme armé*. These *cantus firmi* are either reproduced in their entirety in the tenor, as in *L'Homme armé* or, as in the case of *Fors seulement*, the voice parts of the original polyphonic *chanson* are used in all the parts of the Mass according to the parody method which was to be employed so much in the sixteenth century.[45]

Finally mention should be made of the Requiem Mass, notable not only for its exceptional expressive qualities, but also for its historical importance in being the first extant polyphonic Mass for the deceased.

The sacred music of Ockeghem also includes nine motets, among which *Gaude Maria* deserves special attention as the most highly developed and original in its skilful and varied treatment of the plainchant material, the logic of its construction and the modernism of its tonal colour, a work clearly showing the way towards the future. In another motet to the Virgin, *Ave Maria* for four parts, Ockeghem breaks with the framework bequeathed to him by his predecessors, and without using any liturgical tenor achieves a beautiful and entirely personal composition in which all the parts collaborate in erecting a contrapuntal structure which is both compact and 'flamboyant'.

44. Concerning Ockeghem's canon for 36 voices (see above p. 170) as an expression of the song of the angelic choirs, see Lowinsky, 'Ockeghem'.

45. See above, p. 154, fn. 18.

BUSNOIS

While Ockeghem was above all a composer of Church music, his most famous contemporary, Antoine de Busne, or Busnois, was especially renowned for his *chansons*. These two composers were often associated in the minds of their contemporaries, although their talents were so different, and Tinctoris dedicated to them his *Liber de natura et proprietate tonorum*, acknowledging the pair as the most illustrious masters of the time.

Neither the place nor the date of the birth of Busnois is known, nor, indeed, the place of his early musical training. He himself provides the earliest extant biographical information when he refers to himself as a musician attached to Charles, then Count of Charolais and later Duke of Burgundy, into whose service he entered around 1465. He accompanied the same Charles the Bold on his travels and after the Duke's death remained at the Burgundian court until 1482. He died in 1492 at Bruges, where he held the post of *rector cantoriae* at the Church of Saint-Sauveur. Busnois thus spent most of his life in Burgundian circles at the very time when the Duchy was breaking free from French influence and looking to its northern provinces to provide its artists and musicians. The Burgundian court then became a brilliant centre of musical creation, and Busnois was one of the composers who provided distinguished examples of the new style with its extreme refinement, complex rhythmic experiments, bold dissonances, an obvious relish for musical enigmas and a special attention to ornamentation. Busnois' style differed a good deal from that of Ockeghem; it was one which might – in this instance – justify the epithet 'Burgundian'. It was in the same spirit that Busnois, poet as well as musician, conceived his verse, showing a marked predilection for word-play so dear to the so-called *Rhétoriqueurs*, then much in favour at the Burgundian court.

Although Busnois does not show the same scope as Ockeghem in the field of religious music, some of his motets nevertheless provide much evidence of his complex and refined personality. He was fond of surprise effects which capture the listener's attention, and his occasional pedantic humanism led him to seek out the bizarre and the *recherché*. Of his nine motets two are freely composed, five employ Gregorian tenors, and the two most original, *In hydraulis* and *Anthoni usque limina*, use freely-invented themes under the guise of a *cantus firmus*. *In hydraulis* has a curious text with a first part which evokes the musical theories of Pythagoras in a florid language with many Greek words, and a second which is a dithyrambic homage to Ockeghem. Built upon a tenor of three long notes, repeated in *ostinato* manner and probably intended for an instrument, this motet constitutes a good example of musical fashion at the Burgundian court. The *St Anthony* Motet is no less curious – full of rhythmic and contrapuntal subtleties, with a tenor based on a single note, D; it was probably intended to be sounded at various points by a bell, as suggested by Fétis, because of a verbal canon (rule) written in an obscure formula notated on a pennant bearing the design of a bell.

In accordance with the wishes of a young prince keen on festivities and amusements, Busnois provided music to accompany worldly pleasures, and his seventy-seven *chansons* rank among the most successful examples of their kind. The beauty of their melodic line, the subtlety of their rhythms, their sense of harmonic colour and their more consistent use of imitation display the variety and originality of the great composer's gifts. The much abused theme of unrequited love inspired him to write delicate little masterpieces which, although perhaps limited in range, abound in tenderness and gentle intimacy very much in keeping with the general feeling of the poem, if not seeking to underscore individual words. It will suffice to mention, as an example, *Je ne puis vivre*, dedicated to Jacqueline d'Hacqueville, which in the words of Van den Borren[46] reveals an 'impression of rare and delicate beauty'.

There were many other composers besides Busnois at the Burgundian court who distinguished themselves in *chansons* of the same style. Among these Hayne van Ghizeghem, who was also a singer in the service of Charles the Bold, and whose *De tous bien pleine* was one of the most celebrated *chansons* of the time, deserves special mention.

But the end of the fifteenth century also marks the end of what might be called 'French Burgundy'. After the death of Charles the Bold the successors of the Burgundian heritage retained only those northern provinces whose Flemish and Walloon musicians were to give birth to the so-called Franco-Flemish or Netherlandish school. Henceforth these northern musicians would no longer look towards France but towards Italy. In the sixteenth century the gulf widens between the aesthetics of French music proper, and that of Josquin des Prez and his successors. The French reacted against complex polyphony while the foreign schools were to develop with the utmost skill the systematic imitative style, already outlined in the fifteenth century by the composers of the Burgundian court.

46. Borren, *Etudes*, p. 281.

FRANÇOIS LESURE

4.2 France: 1500–1600

INTRODUCTION: CHANSONS

It is rather paradoxical to describe the music of sixteenth-century France by the term 'Renaissance'. While this designation accurately denotes the artistic and humanist movement originating at the court of Francis I, it is not easily applied to the music of that court. Far from deriving its inspiration from ancient or Italian sources, the music appearing in France towards the end of Josquin des Prez' life-time was rooted in more popular traditions and, in any case, represented a reaction against an over-refined technique. For more than two centuries leadership had been exercised by the Low Countries and certain areas of present-day northern France, whose singers and musicians were in demand throughout the courts of Europe and who spread a style of writing which was universally admired and adopted.

Between 1500 and 1520 there was a kind of pause in the course of western music, which, in the secular field, led to the emergence of a distinctly national style in the French *chanson* – a form which hitherto had been of an inter-national character. Up to this time it would be quite arbitrary to speak of specifically 'French music', but from the sixteenth century on such a des-cription becomes increasingly valid, whether in the context of the *chanson*, sacred or instrumental music.

The reign of Louis XII (1498–1515) and the first years of that of Francis I (1515–47) correspond to a period of transition, in which the poetic themes chosen by the musicians were no longer bound by the conventions and complications of the *école des rhétoriqueurs* but subjects which characterize what Molinet[1] described as the '*chanson rurale*': such pieces, which generally employ three voices, were written by Antoine de Févin, Jean Mouton, Mathieu Gascongne and Ninot le Petit. This new type of *chanson*, which contrasts with the more traditional art cultivated at the Brussels Court of Margaret of Austria (with such composers as Pierre de la Rue), flourished especially at the court of Queen Anne of Brittany, who had married Louis XII when he succeeded to the throne. It is probable that Willaert wrote his three-part *chansons* of folk-like character when he was a student of Jean Mouton at Paris around 1515.

With the exception of a few manuscripts most of the 'rustic' *chansons* of this generation appeared in Italy, for there was no music printing in Paris before 1528. Moreover, one can discern stylistic parallels between what was happening at the time in France and in Italy where the *frottola* and other new forms of secular music were making their appearance.[2] On both sides of the Alps established forms, as well as those employing the traditional *cantus firmus* in long-note values, were to all intents and purposes abandoned, and the character of these pieces, with their much stronger tendency towards tonality, became purely vocal.

April 1528 marks the birth of what is now usually called the 'Parisian' *chanson*.[3] The printer Pierre Attaingnant began distributing throughout Europe a new type of secular music which was striking in its simplicity, neatness and clarity. Whether they were anecdotal, courtly or erotic, these pieces all had the same family-likeness and were almost invariably set in four parts: the declamation of the words was syllabic, the musical phrases were moulded on each line and imitations between one voice and another were short.[4] The principal poets who provided the textual material were Mellin de Saint-Gelays and Clément Marot. The latter may even have intended his *chansons* from the very outset for musical setting, for about thirty of them appeared with their musical accompaniment before being published in any purely literary collection issued in his name.[5] The forms which most

---

1. See the discussion of Busnois and Burgundian court life, pp. 172–3, concerning the *rhétoriqueurs*. This literary school was characterized by an excessive concern for patronage, neglect of nature, an insincere cultivation of the themes of courtly love, and great complexity in metrical and verbal devices. One of these *rhétoriqueurs* was the poet-musician Jean Molinet, who wrote the dirge on the death of Ockeghem, composed by Josquin. Concerning Molinet and rhetoric in general, see MacClintock, *Mus. Disc.* (1959), 109.

2. See Haar, *Chanson & Madrigal 1480–1520*.

3. See Lesure, *Anthologie de la Chanson Parisienne*.

4. See Borren, 'Reflexions'.

5. See Rollin, *Marot*.

appealed to composers, however, were stanzas of four or ten lines, preferably in lines of eight or ten syllables. The type which most profited from this evolution was, perhaps, the epigram,[6] a form which, as Joachim Du Bellay later wrote, 'may say nothing of any striking interest in the first nine lines, as long as there is an amusing witticism in the last'.

The most notable musicians of Francis I's reign are Claudin de Sermisy and Clément Janequin, the former being the most typical exponent of the new type of *chanson* in which the music slavishly annotates the text, following its declamation with great precision. As for Janequin, his quick rise to fame was largely due to his vast descriptive pieces like *La Bataille de Marignan* and *Le Chant des oiseaux*, whose success spread throughout Europe. Until about 1545 the Parisian *chanson* was widely propagated in Italy, Germany and the Low Countries, its popularity being based not only on its intrinsic vocal qualities but also on the possibilities it offered to instrumentalists. Its often brilliant and distinct rhythm ideally suited the technique of lutenists, flautists and keyboard players in Italy, who were soon to refer to the *canzon alla francese*.

These characteristics do not imply, however, that the *chanson* of the time of Francis I was devoid of lyricism. Though certainly partial to anecdote, eroticism and *double entendre*, it could also aspire to reflections of love and refined thoughts. Towards the middle of the century the *chanson* was gradually transformed through its contact both with the Italian madrigal and the new poetry. In 1549 Du Bellay dismissed as *episseries* (spiced nothings) the old forms such as *rondeaux*, *virelais* and *chansons* (making an exception of the work of Saint-Gelays), and the poets of the new school extolled the more serious and extended forms like the elegy, epistle and ode. The musicians followed this movement, albeit a few paces behind: Boyvin composed the first musical setting of the sonnet in French,[7] Gardane the first dialogue; and Sandrin wrote a *chanson* in Alexandrines in which the last two stanzas were printed below the musical setting of the first. These are still isolated cases. The important turning-point is the year 1552 with its manifestos of a new style: Pierre Certon's first book of *chansons* in strophic, syllabic and homophonic style, and Pierre de Ronsard's *Amours*, which include a musical supplement providing examples for the singing of several poems to the same music. Henceforth one finds two distinct styles in the *chanson*: one homophonic and strophic which leads to the *air de cour*, the other following the polyphonic tradition.

Ronsard's work affected a whole generation of musicians. In proclaiming that harmony is the fundament of all matter, the poet takes up the thesis of the medieval philosophers for whom music constituted the sum of human

6. See Lesure, 'Marot'.
7. See Lesure, *Anthologie*.

knowledge, a kind of encyclopedia of the 'Great Universe'; in extolling the ethical effects of this art, in attempting to prove that music had always been the distinguishing feature of virtuous men who were 'born aloof from base feelings', he reunited the Platonist ideal with the concept of the innate nobility of music. In so doing he created in France a kind of mystique of the union of poetry and music; thus it is hardly surprising that more than thirty musicians set to music some two hundred of Ronsard's poems in the second half of the sixteenth century. The most successful settings were those of court musicians like Guillaume Costeley, but there are also fine examples from the pen of provincials like Guillaume Boni, Pierre Clereau and Antoine de Bertrand, not to mention Roland de Lassus, resident in Munich, whose first *chanson* was printed at Paris in 1557 and whose triumph was to be so complete that he was soon considered the greatest of French musicians.

In the Parisian salons, in the châteaux of the Ile-de-France, or in the provinces, groups of people met under the auspices of some Maecenas or a music-loving princess, to sing *chansons* to the accompaniment of the lute or to discuss musical topics. In Paris the most famous of these groups met at the home of Catherine de Clermont, Countess of Retz, where musicians such as Costeley and Adrian Le Roy were brought together with poets, among them Tyard, Desportes and Jodelle. In Toulouse the composer Antoine de Bertrand met the poet Robert Garnier at the meetings of the 'Floral Games'. Everything indicates that a mutual esteem and respect existed in these decades between the two groups of artists, who felt that they were renewing a tradition which had been lost since the days of Greek antiquity.

At the same time the gulf between the *chanson* and madrigal was narrowed increasingly. Like the new madrigal, the *chanson* was now written in five rather than four voice-parts; and it too attempted to underscore the expressive sense of certain words by musical figures, a technique now specifically referred to as 'madrigalism'. In this quest for expression the musicians held the trump cards. The grandiose political ambitions of the Valois monarchs were reflected not only in the pomp and pageantry at court but also in its cultural ambitions. Rich rewards were offered to the greatest artists and poets and Charles IX almost succeeded in luring the 'divine' Lassus from Munich into his service. Adrian Le Roy acted as musical counsellor to the king and kept him abreast of novelties. In a letter addressed to Lassus in 1574 Le Roy gives a lively example: he had performed a chromatic madrigal by Nicola Vicentino for Charles IX who replied: 'Orlando would not know how to make this chromatic music.' But the musician immediately presented a new work by Lassus which he had been holding in reserve. 'When the king had heard it,' wrote Le Roy, 'he found it so ravishing that I cannot describe his pleasure.' The way was thus open for an experiment which will be considered here at some length, since it represents the most original endeavours of sixteenth-century French music: the *musique mesurée à l'antique*.

ACADÉMIE DE POÉSIE ET DE MUSIQUE

The history of *musique mesurée* and of the *Académie* of Jean-Antoine de Baïf was, until fairly recently, considered as an almost isolated chapter in the evolution of French music, arising from the endeavour of a few humanists. But in the last fifteen years the work of D. P. Walker and F. Yates has shown that this movement formed an integral part of a general political, philosophic and artistic complex, that it had repercussions in the history of ideas and that it explains the often ambiguous attitude of the different factions at the court of the last Valois monarchs. From a purely musical point of view the originality of Baïf's experiment should not be exaggerated. German humanism, although assuming a somewhat pedagogical character, had already wrestled with the problem, as shown in the musical settings of Horatian odes by Tritonius, Hofhaimer and Senfl. Later, in 1555, in France itself, Claude Goudimel, who worked perhaps on a higher intellectual plane than his fellow French musicians, set to music a collection of Horatian odes in the original Latin; unfortunately no sample of this work has survived. But Baïf probably owed little or nothing to these experiments; what he attempted for the first time was to provide the problem of the union of poetry and music with a complete theoretical and practical solution of great boldness.

In contrast to other artists Baïf had no palpable model to which he could refer. His point of departure was the knowledge that there had existed in ancient times a firm union between poetry and music, and that this union had certain 'effects' which he wished to rediscover. David and Orpheus were singled out for praise on account of their powerful evocation of these effects. The entire direction taken by French humanism was to be dictated by the return to antiquity: in creating an *Académie* Baïf's aim was nothing less than the rebirth of the ancient union. It goes without saying that he and other French humanists were indebted to the Platonic Academy founded in Florence in the fifteenth century and to the musical idea of its leader, the philosopher Marsilio Ficino. The aim of the musicians, influenced by Baïf, among them Costeley and Le Jeune, was to affect the souls of their listeners by specific kinds of music, comparable to the manner in which Dorian or Phrygian music was reported to have impinged upon listeners in ancient days. As if it were necessary to prove the efficacy of these effects in the hands of musicians, certain writers felt the need to recount contemporary exploits, similar to those of Timotheus who, by his singing, manipulated the will of Alexander. The most notable was that of Claude Le Jeune who is said to have stirred a listener profoundly in the course of a performance, but immediately afterwards to have assuaged him by the power of his music. In the final analysis it was the close subjection of music to the text, through the use of chromatic and enharmonic *genera*, which was reputed to possess the secret of acting upon the soul.

Around 1567 Baïf and the musician Thibaut de Courville set to work to endow France with a poetry and music especially conceived to achieve this intimate union in order to recreate these effects. It was the collaboration of these two which provided the basis for the experiment in *musique mesurée à l'antique* and the creation of the *Académie de Poésie et de Musique* which was officially recognized in 1571. As a result, the art of music in general, and especially the French *chanson*, grew to be more highly esteemed by humanists. Strangely enough, what these musicians attempted 'with great study and labour' for vernacular poetry they did not think of applying to religious music, although the metrical structure of the Latin language would have facilitated such a task. The king, Charles IX, is thought to have considered this notion himself – if we are to believe an account dating from 1572, which commands the payment to Baïf of 120 *livres tournois* '*pour faire composer par les compositeurs et musiciens de l'Académie une messe en musique ... commandé par Sa Majesté*'. But no trace of such a work remains to substantiate the commission. To the present author's knowledge, the only extant example of a setting of a liturgical text in the style of *musique mesurée* is a motet published much later by Du Caurroy in his *Preces ecclesiasticae*. It is true however that nearly all the religious music of J. Mauduit (Masses, Vespers, hymns and motets), which would surely have provided striking examples of this procedure, have been lost.

The aims and organization of the *Académie* were more ambitious and revolutionary than those of any other academic institution of the time. Its members were of two kinds: professional musicians, called *musiciens*, who had strictly to obey Baïf and Courville and who, in return, received a salary and were aided in the event of illness; and the audience, called *auditeurs*, who, once accepted, were obliged to pay a subscription. The music performed remained a secret to all but the members; no one was allowed to copy or to communicate the works sung in the course of the concerts; and no new member could be admitted without the consent of the whole assembly.

The very object of this *Académie* was thus to restore 'the measure (*mesure*) and rules of music used by the Greeks and Romans in Ancient times' and to develop further the early attempts at 'measured verse (*vers mesurés*) set to measured music (*musique mesurée*) so far as possible according to the laws of the masters of music of the good and ancient age', in other words, to do so in accordance with classical metre and custom. Even the wisest of the humanists seem to have ignored the fact that syllabic 'quantity' had disappeared from Greek and Latin since the time of the Roman Empire. From the end of the fifteenth century there had been isolated attempts to revive this notion in French poetry. Nevertheless, Baïf was the first to apply the principle in works of a certain amplitude; above all, to associate it with music. His secondary aim was to make the *Académie* 'a school to serve as a nursery, when one day poets and musicians might emerge, instructed and reared in the good art'. The general aims of this programme were realized, though their consequences were not as decisive as their originator had hoped.

Unfortunately we have no details of the concert performances which took place in the secrecy of the *Académie*. Instrumental as well as vocal music was featured, and the academicians went a stage further than Ronsard's friends in the revival of the lyre. In imitation of Italy, and with the co-operation of a Paris instrument-maker, Antoine Potin, they devised a curious instrument with eleven strings, on which Thibaut de Courville (*c.* 1530–81) excelled in virtuosity. In 1572 Courville bore the title of '*Joueur de lyre du Roi*'. It is likely that Lassus, in the course of his sojourn at Paris, was present at one of these meetings to which his friend, Adrian Le Roy, would naturally have thought of bringing him, for in August 1571 Baïf, in a letter to Charles IX, speaks of 'notable people both French and foreign' and in 1576 Lassus published in the press of Le Roy and Ballard *Une Puce*, the first *chanson mesurée* ever to be printed. In his desire to convince the entire artistic world of the value of his theories, Baïf conceived the idea of organizing a meeting of all the musicians in Christendom, with the aim of putting to the test the emotional possibilities of the music of the other composers in comparison with that of the *Académie*.

It has often been said that the death of Charles IX in 1573 was fatal to Baïf's enterprise. Under Henri III the original *Académie* was succeeded by the *Académie du Palais*, so-called because its sessions were held at the Louvre, under the direction of Guy du Faur de Pibrac, the author of moralizing quatrains of little poetic value, which several musicians, including Lassus, strove to set to music. The truth of the matter was that, in the first place, the character of the court had changed significantly after 1573. The spirit of the Counter-Reformation is reflected in the fact that the court *divertissements* were to a large extent replaced by spectacular processions in which the nobility exchanged their ballet costumes for those of penitents. It is interesting that this nobility consisted of more or less the same people as had been present at the court functions under Charles IX. Baïf has described the change which events imposed on him in the choice of his collaborators. When the collaboration with Courville ended he attached himself to the lutenist Jacques du Faur, who left Paris shortly afterwards, to retire to the south. Du Faur was succeeded by Claude Le Jeune (*c.* 1530–1600), the Huguenot composer who belonged to the humanistic entourage of François, duc d'Anjou. Finally, there came Jacques Mauduit (1557–1627) who applied Baïf's principles of *musique mesurée* in the most consistent manner.

BALLET COMIQUE

The 'school to serve as a nursery' provided for by the statutes seems actually to have functioned. In 1576 an *émigré* Italian composer, Fabrice Marin Caietain, mentioned lessons he received from Courville and Lambert de

Beaulieu, the most famous singer of his time, who later collaborated in the composition of the *Ballet comique de la Reine*. Caietain showed his mentors the *chansons* he had composed for his master, the Duke of Lorraine. He wrote: 'Following their warnings and good advice I have corrected most of the mistakes caused by my failure to observe the alternation of long and short notes.'

Baïf had still greater ambitions which are not mentioned in the statutes of the *Académie*. He wished to revive ancient drama, and to restore the role of music in the theatre to its former importance. No doubt choruses were already sung in French tragedies; some of these have been preserved in the form of psalms for Protestant tragedies. Jodelle for his part had even presented a complete entertainment with musical participation, carrying his interest in the problem so far as to apologize (in the prologue of one of his comedies) for the fact that the music separating the acts was a poor imitation of that of the ancients. In all these cases, the music merely consisted of *pièces rapportées*, that is, recurring pieces, or *ritornelli*, which framed the dramatic action without being integrated into it. Baïf on the other hand affirms in a poem published in 1573 that he had a ballet in readiness for which Courville and Le Jeune had composed the music and in which even the dancing was *mesurée*, according to the same principles as the verse. But the performance never took place, and the poet never realized his ultimate plan to unite music and poetry on the stage; moreover, his influence is only indirectly felt in the *Ballet comique de la Reine*, the first conscious union of drama, music and dancing in France, from which the author Baltazarini (alias Beaujoyeux) excluded music which was strictly *mesurée*.

Beaujoyeux was a violinist of Piedmontese origin who did not have such high ideals, although certain contemporary poets compared him to the ancient Greeks. Brantôme describes him as an audacious spirit who had a gift for recounting beautiful tales and one who had 'seen and experienced some fine amorous adventures'. But Beaujoyeux merely considered it a good idea to 'interweave' poetry and music and occasionally to blend them, since 'the Ancients never recited their verses without music and Orpheus never played without verses'.

The *Ballet comique*, which had as its subject the enchantments of Circe, was given as part of the sumptuous festivities presented at the court of Henri III in 1581 on the occasion of the marriage of the King's favourite, the Duke of Joyeuse, with the Queen's half-sister. The *Ballet* was probably the culminating point of a fortnight of daily entertainments which included jousts, banquets, fireworks, combats, tournaments and concerts. The most interesting fact is that the text, the music and even the scenic design have been preserved, whereas for the court *divertissements* of Charles IX's reign one has to rely on little more than a few references in the poetry of Ronsard. The work's only link with the *Académie* is the presence of Beaulieu, the principal composer of the vocal and instrumental music ordered by Beaujoyeux. It would be difficult, in view of the many intrigues of Henri III's entourage, to discover the reasons why Baïf was not involved in the *Ballet comique*. At Henri III's court (1574–89) the tide of favour changed frequently and rapidly. The Queen Mother, Catherine de Medici, saw in these court entertainments a means of temporarily avoiding the disunity of the country's potentates, and in the very subject of Circe an allegory encouraging good will towards the royal family.

CLAUDE LE JEUNE

As might be expected, a good deal of instability existed as well among poets and artists, with religious and political 'factionalism' affecting all spheres. Some stayed within the Catholic tradition, among them Ronsard, Baïf and Desportes; Beaujoyeux married a Protestant, and Le Jeune, who was himself a Protestant, had to flee from Paris during the factional struggles of 1588–90. On the other hand the supporters of the Counter-Reformation also represented a significant faction, and Pibrac even agreed to glorify St Bartholomew's Night in poetic terms. These religious and political parties, disparate as they were, intermingled and made their joint impact at about the same time. The key to the problem may perhaps be found in the entourage of the Duke of Anjou, which at one time included Le Jeune, Beaulieu, Pibrac and Beaujoyeux. There are several signs suggesting the activity here of another *Académie*: in 1578 one of its appointed poets, the obscure Louis Hesteau, celebrated the *enchantements* of Beaujoyeux. But this circle is still little known, although the evidence of its existence serves to show the continuation of the role and first principles of Baïf's *Académie*.

Thus in 1581 the original *Académie de Poésie et de Musique* still retained its vitality and influence at court. Although it may have modified its activity in a direction different from that envisaged by the original statutes and no longer have organized regular meetings, its main protagonists continued to produce works on the same principles. It may seem strange that the works of the *musiciens mesurés* were not published by Le Roy and Ballard, who were always on the look-out for novelties, but in view of the secrecy imposed by the statutes, the appearance of these works in print would understandably have been delayed.

It remains for us to examine briefly the practical effects on music of Baïf's endeavours, the success encountered by the works written in *musique mesurée* and the influence they might have had on the subsequent history of music. Fifteen years after the founding of the *Académie* few 'measured' works had yet been published. Moreover these comprised pieces written only under the influence of the early experiments, not expressly for the *Académie* itself. Examples include *Une Puce j'ay dedans l'oreille*, the famous song sent by

Lassus to his friend Adrian Le Roy in 1576, and the four *chansons mesurées* published in 1583 in the *Premier livre d'airs* by the King's organist, Nicolas de La Grotte, who had collaborated with Le Jeune in the entertainments organized for the marriage of the Duke of Joyeuse; others include those published by the Italian, Fabrice Marin Caietain in 1578. In 1586 twenty-three *chansonettes mesurées* by Baïf himself appeared in a four-part musical setting by the latest of his collaborators, Jacques Mauduit, who followed the strictest principles of metrical music. The result is somewhat monotonous, leaving an impression of austerity which might be intentional. Written in a purely chordal style, these pieces lack any devices which might have concealed the alternation of long and short notes and might have stood in the way of the comprehension of each syllable of the poetry. It was a controversial work, and, although reprinted as a model, it offered insufficient artistic opportunities to musicians. Mauduit's influence was certainly more effective as a choir-master and later, after the death of Baïf in 1589, as a concert organizer and finally as the friend and protector of Claude Le Jeune, whose works he saved from fire during the Huguenot persecutions in 1590.

With Claude Le Jeune we encounter the most important composer to be influenced by the ideas of Baïf's circle. Only a small part of his *chansons* and airs appeared in his lifetime, the remainder being published after 1600 through the efforts of the composer's sister and niece. In quantity they represent an imposing group of works which have not yet been re-edited in their entirety. Most of Le Jeune's pieces employed a chordal idiom, because in each of the four or five voice parts the syllables were required to have the same rhythmic values, thus allowing no real musical development: stanzas and refrain followed one another according to the prescribed and foreseeable pattern. But the composer was able to discover great possibilities for variety within these restrictions. By substituting an ornamental figure of several shorter note values for the required longer note, these expressive arabesques become comparable to a painter's brush stroke which suddenly highlights the colouring. In fact, the most remarkable feature of this music is its rhythm.

Towards the end of the sixteenth century, the hybridization between the air and the strict *chanson mesurée* reaches a point where it often becomes difficult to distinguish between the two forms. The only valid criteria are extra-musical, namely that the lines of the pure *chanson mesurée* are not rhymed and may be scanned according to rules similar to those of classical metre. But henceforth the air aims at the same ideal of syllabic style and precise declamation, so that one can sometimes falter in describing as *airs mesurés* works by Pierre Bonnet, G. Tessier or N. de La Grotte which are, in fact, ordinary airs, written under the more or less conscious influence of Baïf's friends. This perhaps represents not the least of the results of the *Académie* of 1570.

MASS AND MOTET: 1500-1550

The forms of sacred music cultivated in sixteenth-century France were the same as those of the previous century. The cyclic setting of the Ordinary of the Mass remains the rule, although an isolated 'Credo' is still found, recalling the time, a little earlier, when Petrucci published a collection of Mass fragments.[8] The 'Credo' in question is the eight-part setting by Jean Maillard, published by Le Roy and Ballard at Paris in 1557. French Masses were normally scored for four voices but included sections in two, three ('Benedictus') or five voices ('Agnus'). With the increase in the number of Low Masses in the liturgy they were always of the *missa brevis* type, that is to say, there were few melismas and little imitation. These stylistic criteria apply to those sections which have extensive texts ('Gloria', 'Credo') as well as to those where the length of the text does not normally impose restrictions ('Kyrie', 'Agnus'). All these characteristics are in contrast with the Mass in fashion among contemporary composers in the Low Countries (Gombert, Clemens, etc.). After the middle of the century when Goudimel's Masses began to appear, and after the death of Sermisy (d. 1562) and Certon (d. 1572), the Mass tended to become even shorter and still more homophonic. Finally, apart from a few exceptions, they are all parody-Masses, borrowing their material from either motets or *chansons*. The texts of some of the latter are decidedly amorous,[9] a long-established practice which had been condemned by the Council of Paris in 1538 but which nevertheless continued. In the case of a Mass based on Gregorian chant, the composer might use a short, liturgical fragment (e.g. *Veni sponsa* by Jean Leleu) or an almost complete plainsong melody (e.g. *Christus resurgens* by Louis Van Pulaer and *Ave Maria* by Antoine Févin). At all events, in their treatment of the text, French composers, unlike their neighbours, paid only slight attention to a vague idea of Latin accentuation.

While the practice of commissioning musical settings for Low Mass was wide-spread, the motet too enjoyed a considerable vogue, nearly four hundred being published by Attaingnant between 1534 and 1535. Here the composers generally draw on the Gregorian repertoire of psalms, antiphons and sequences. There is no longer anything similar to the *chanson*-motets with Latin tenors by Compère or Agricola, still to be found in Petrucci's earliest publication.[10] The texts of these motets were usually divided into two sections and, by the end of the century, into even more sub-divisions. Four-part texture is a frequent feature in the motet, but less consistently employed than

8. *Fragmenta missarum*, Venice, 1505.
9. Such as the Masses *M'Amie un jour* by Maillard and *O gente brunette* by Marle.
10. Hewitt, *Odhecaton*.

in the Mass; five and even more parts are not uncommon. But the most distinctive feature of the French motet was its treatment of the text: composers attached more importance to the clarity of the verbal text and its comprehension than to the work's purely musical elaboration. This deliberately syllabic style seems to have arisen at the very end of the fifteenth century,[11] simultaneously with a similar transformation in the realm of the *chanson*.

CLAUDIN DE SERMISY

The work of Claudin de Sermisy deserves special mention, since it is remarkably varied. He was the only composer of his generation who has left a Passion as well as Masses, motets, *chansons* (both secular and 'spiritual') without actually favouring any of these forms, either in quantity or quality. Apart from an anonymous Passion published by Attaingnant in 1534, Sermisy's Passion according to St Matthew is the only French polyphonic setting of the century.[12] It is based entirely on a single melodic pattern, that of the Gregorian *turba* and the scoring is for low voices. Those sections representing the crowd consistently employ four voices, while the words of Judas, St Peter or Pilate are sung sometimes by two, sometimes by four voices.

Along with one five-part example (*Quare fremuerunt*) Sermisy wrote thirteen four-part Masses which, for Pirro,[13] 'represented the sum of his achievements'; here he remains faithful to the parody principle even in the Mass *Ad placitum*[14] which, however, claims to be free of all pre-existent melodic material. Only two are based on secular themes (*Voulant honneur* and *O passi sparsi*). Besides plainsong, his models are Josquin, Richafort and Festa, to whom one might add, in the case of the *Missa plurium motectorum*, Gascongne, Conseil and Févin. Sermisy's Requiem Mass, which reveals an absolute respect for the liturgical tradition, should be singled out here. Certain Masses have affinities with the 'northern' tradition of Josquin and his school: examples include *Domine quis habitabit*, *Philomena praevia* and especially *Novem lectionum* with its almost wholly polyphonic writing and angular melodic lines. But as a general rule Claudin de Sermisy leans towards a more homophonic style. Another influence of secular music can be detected in certain rhythmic and melodic formulae, recalling *chansons* and dances.

In the absence of a sufficient number of editions and critical studies it is more difficult to judge Sermisy as a composer of motets – mostly set for four voices but some for three, five and six. Their quality, variety and consistency of style, however, seem to confirm his position as his country's fore-

11. See Brumel's *Ave ancilla* in Hewitt, *Canti B*; and his *Mater patris* in Hewitt, *Odhecaton*.
12. Reese, *Renaissance*, p. 339.
13. Pirro, *Histoire*, p. 319.
14. Meaning 'as it pleases' or 'at the composer's fancy' or 'freely composed'.

most composer of sacred music. Some of these motets were no doubt connected with important events taking place in the *Chapelle royale* as, for example, *Quousque non reveteris pax*, which must date from just before the Peace of Cambrai (1531). Not only are his melodic lines longer and more curved than those of his compatriots, but the contrapuntal imitations are more consistent, and the melismas more frequent, with a tendency to emphasize certain words in the manner of 'madrigalism'. He makes little use of homophony in his motets and, as in his Masses, shows a predilection for opposing two groups of two voices each. In the five-part *Quare fremuerunt*, one of his longest motets, three parts are separated from the ensemble throughout an extended passage in the second part of the work. Several of his motets still approximate the style of the *chanson*, however, as, for example, *Praeparate corda vestra* and *Domine, quis habitabit*. Through their mastery of the art of pleasing proportions, clarity and simplicity, Claudin's motets reveal the most perfectly poised French style; he had discovered a mean between the inheritance of the Josquin era and a world permeated with the Parisian *chanson*.

THE REFORMATION

French sacred music was clearly shaken by the crisis arising from the Reformation. To Calvin's mind melody was only admissible as a vehicle for words; music ought not to draw attention to itself. Instruments were suppressed; hence the destruction of a large number of organs in France during the religious wars. The first attempts to create an original repertoire designed for the new religious cult are found at Strasbourg where, in 1538, a small group sang psalms to German melodies. Calvin was struck by this group's enthusiasm and decided to organize his own Psalter. Having tried to adapt psalms translated by Clément Marot to the Strasbourg melodies, he charged Louis Bourgeois with correcting and extending this work. The latter modified the rhythm, accentuation and certain melodies of the existing repertoire and composed a number of new pieces. Contrary to an opinion still generally held, he made little use of popular tunes but, on the other hand, borrowed a good deal from the Gregorian repertoire. When Marot died, after completing only forty-nine psalms, Calvin entrusted the task to Théodore de Bèze, who completed the translation of the entire Psalter into French verse in 1562. This collection enjoyed considerable circulation, and the singing of psalms by groups of the faithful became the symbol of the reformers' determination in the face of official persecution. The collection aroused a great deal of interest at the French court itself. While Diane de Poitiers enthusiastically sang psalms, official musicians like Arcadelt, Janequin and Certon published four-part settings of texts from the Psalter. However, the most renowned polyphonic settings were those of Claude Goudimel, who also wrote secular songs and works for the Catholic liturgy and who was a victim of the St Bartholomew's Day massacre at Lyon in 1572. Other settings appeared *en forme de motets*, that is, in free polyphonic style; or for a single voice with lute accompaniment, destined not for collective worship but for intimate family performance.

SACRED MUSIC: 1550-1600

The first religious works of Lassus were published by Le Roy and Ballard at Paris in the year 1564, a cardinal date marking the beginning of his almost complete supremacy in this field. The striking success of this composer was felt immediately, and he seems to have eclipsed the activity of the French school. Although the older generation like Certon, Maillard and Marle, together with a few younger musicians like Le Jeune, continued their activity until about 1570, only five or six publications of religious music by French composers appeared between 1570 and 1582, and none at all after that date. It is symptomatic, perhaps, that an edition of three Masses by Sermisy,[15] first published at Paris in 1558, should have been reprinted in 1583. Lassus himself was so concerned in maintaining his French success that in 1571 he entrusted to his friend Le Roy the printing of the first edition of some twenty newly-composed motets (*Moduli quinis vocibus*), and in 1587 confided the manuscript for two masses, *Locutus sum* and *Beatus qui intellegit* which had not been printed previously, to the same publisher. Moreover he did not disdain to take part in the annual *Puy de musique* at Evreux, where his motets carried off the prize in 1575 and 1583.

It would in fact be exaggerated to talk about a decline of the French school. Publishing suffered from the repercussions of the dreadful internal crisis that shook the country. But there was no real break in the traditions of musical instruction. The prize-list of the Evreux *Puy* between 1575 and 1589 offers proof of this: each year the honours were bestowed upon a motet by a Parisian or provincial master and many newcomers made their names there: Du Caurroy (1576), Mauduit (1581), A. Blondet (1583), P. de l'Estocart (1584) and so forth.

As we have seen, some non-Huguenot musicians were not afraid of setting the Psalters of Marot and Bèze or, like Janequin and N. Millot, the Proverbs of Solomon. But once the crisis had passed, the Catholics sought vernacular texts suitable for their own use: thus Pibrac's *Quatrains* were set to music by Boni, Planson, l'Estocart and Lassus himself. These texts, with their simple piety, enjoyed great popularity well into the seventeenth century. Philippe Desportes also provided a new translation of the psalms. The Jesuit, Michael Coyssard, in his *Hymnes sacrez* even published French paraphrases of the

15. Allaire, 'Sermisy'.

'Credo', *Pange lingua*, *Conditor alme*, *Stabat mater* and so forth, which could be sung to the old melodies of the corresponding Latin text. He stood up to his detractors who had criticized him for translating this sacred doctrine into the vernacular, reminding them of the approval his work had received from the chief of the Inquisition at Rome in 1597; at the same time he defended popular hymns and Noëls, the music of Antoine de Bertrand (notably his posthumous *Airs spirituels*) and Desportes' psalms.

Finally, in the early years of the seventeenth century, the dramatic performances generally favoured by the Jesuits invested music with an important role. An example is *Céciliade*, produced in 1606 by N. Soret, into which Abraham Blondet, the *maistre de musique* at Notre Dame, had introduced a large number of choruses in homophonic style. Among the four-part settings are the hymn which Saint Cecilia sings in the blazing cauldron, and Valerian's air. From a dramatic point of view both these pieces would seem to have demanded a setting for solo voice. But the monodic style was still associated with secular use, despite the fact that G. Bataille, D. Caignet and others had set several of Desportes' psalms for a single voice with lute accompaniment.

The traditional settings of Latin texts gradually changed in style, the new manner being fully developed in the work of Formé (b. 1567) and Du Mont (b. 1610). One of the instigators of the new trend was Jacques Mauduit, whose Requiem Mass, sung for the funeral of Ronsard at the Collège de Boncourt in 1586, required instrumental participation. Unfortunately only the opening five-voice *Requiem aeternam* survives. He also introduced instruments in his *grands concerts des Ténèbres* which he organized at the hospital of the Abbey of St Antoine every year during Holy Week.

The Venetian technique of pitting two choral groups against each other (*cori spezzati*) became established in France at the end of the sixteenth century. In connection with the celebrations of the Edict of Nantes and the Peace of Vervins in 1598, a performance took place, at Notre Dame, which may be characterized as an antiphonal dialogue between the musicians of the Royal Chapel and those of the Royal Household. The first notable composer to make extensive use of the double-choir technique was Du Caurroy, master of the Chapel Royal under Henri IV (1589–1610). His *Preces ecclesiasticae* (published 1609) show great variety in scoring; sometimes a single piece, such as *Virgo Dei genitrix*, contains passages for three, four, five and seven parts; the motets for double choir are in five, seven and eight parts. An equally keen sense of sonority is displayed in his five-part *Missa pro defunctis* (composed about 1590) which reflects his contrapuntal skill more successfully than his secular music does. His full and accurate employment of a Gregorian *cantus firmus* in the *Lux aeterna* creates a passage of great eloquence.[16]

16. See Martin, *Du Caurroy*; Launay, 'Motets'.

INSTRUMENTAL MUSIC

Before examining the instrumental music itself it is worth having a look at the situation in the country's instrument-making. Although not officially organized into corporations until 1599, instrument-makers were numerous both at Lyons and Paris early in the century, and there was very active commerce with neighbouring countries. About seventy of them (this figure does not include organ-builders), are known between 1540 and 1610, which is enough to destroy the nineteenth-century legend suggesting Mirecourt in Lorraine as the cradle of the French stringed-instrument manufacture. Certainly violins were imported from Brescia, Cremona and Venice, with lutes from Padua and Nuremberg and cornetts from Venice, and copies of these were made. But the Parisian industry had its own makes of harpsichord, violin and lute, which were produced in large numbers; after the death of Pierre Aubry (1596) about four hundred instruments were found in his shop, and more than six hundred in the premises of Claude Denis who died in 1587. From the middle of the century onwards, the king had his own organ and harpsichord makers.

The public interest in instrumental music is seen in the early publications of Attaingnant, the first music-printer in France, with a series of tablatures, seven of them '*en tablature des orgues, espinettes et manicordions*' ('keyboard tablatures for organ, harpsichord and clavichord') appearing between January and April 1531.

All the arrangements are anonymous. It is possible that the editor called upon the king's organists, Roger Pathie or Antoine Delahaye, or perhaps upon the Notre Dame organists, Jean Regnault and Pierre Mouton. There is no reason, however, why the composer or arranger of these tablatures should be sought at Paris. The most progressive organ-builders were not necessarily found there (Paris was not the most important diocese), but at Rouen, Bordeaux and Dijon as well, and even at Amiens and Reims. It is known that Attaingnant was in touch with different provincial cathedrals, and the Parisian type of organ did not, in fact, predominate in the provinces until around 1600. The instrumental repertoire includes transcriptions of liturgical music (verses, motets) and *chansons*, as well as dances and preludes. In general one can discern greater affinity with the Italian than with German arts, in that the French reject ornamentation as an end in itself, but integrate it into their musical thought. The 'versets' (verses) for both Masses and *Magnificats* are designed to function as instrumental movements, alternating with the choral movements within the same work: the instrumental movements closely respect the *cantus firmus* which generally figures in the tenor or bass. This given melody is surrounded by ornate embellishments and scale fragments. There is greater freedom in the verses of the *Magnificat*, with a few imitative entries and greater rhythmic suppleness. But the most varied pieces are the *Te Deums* in which the Gregorian melody, sometimes fragmented, passes from one voice to another, allowing the organist to display his virtuosity in exploiting the whole range of the keyboard, with rapid passage-work.

In motet transcriptions, the composer, while retaining the structure of the model, linked successive entries by melodic arabesques, which are so continuous that the result approaches a new melody. The preludes published by Attaingnant prove that, in the free forms, the French organists had scope to display their skill in the diversity and intensity of the melodic figuration. The dances have to be set apart, since they were clearly intended for the harpsichord or clavichord. Here we discover the technique of the variation form, notably in the *pavane-gaillarde* pairs and in the groups of three which anticipate the later arrangement of the French suite.

The period between Attaingnant and Titelouze forms a somewhat barren interlude in the history of French keyboard music. A group of nine *chansons*, preserved in one tablature (Munich, MS 2987) dating from around 1550, shows that the French remained faithful to sobriety in ornamentation while moving more boldly in the direction of tonality; an isolated *ricercar* (Upsala, MS 87) is by Nicole Grouzy, the *maistre de musique* at Chartres; two short fantasies, one incomplete, are by the organists of Charles IX, Guillaume Costeley and Nicolas de La Grotte. Thus there is little material to document the evolution which preceded the blossoming forth of a veritable school of mature keyboard music in France in the seventeenth century.

In the first half of the sixteenth century it is the music for lute which seems to have been most subject to foreign influence, as can be seen by the presence, both at Paris and Lyon, of lutenists such as Rippa, Brayssingar, Bakfark, Paladino and Bianchini, and the publication of their works in France. Nor do the three lute players who served at court at the beginning of Francis I's reign appear to be French. At first glance the first two lute tablatures printed by Attaingnant in 1529–30 – preludes in the manner of Francesco da Milano and newly-imported *pavanes-gaillardes* – might be attributed to Italian influences. On the other hand there are certain features characteristic of an indigenous art: *chanson* transcriptions, less ornate in general than those for keyboard, *basses danses* and *branles*. Although this repertoire remains anonymous, the initials of P.B. are found at the beginning of some of the dances. Daniel Heartz has suggested[17] that this might refer to Pierre Blondeau, clerk and later *noteur* (scribe) at Sainte-Chapelle between 1506 and 1532. The hypothesis remains tenuous, since it hardly seems likely that the same man could have later become a mere '*joueur d'instruments*', as suggested by a document of 1550.

Between 1529 and 1551 the Mantuan lutenist Albert de Rippe (Alberto da Rippa) is shown as one of the most brilliant ornaments of the musical establishment at the court of Francis I, both as a composer and a virtuoso who had

17. Heartz, *Attaingnant*, pp. lv-lxii.

played before the pope, the emperor, and King Henry VIII of England. His work was not printed in its entirety during his lifetime; several of his pieces appeared after his death in quite different versions which probably do not faithfully reproduce the originals. Among his pupils was Guillaume Morlaye who, in his collections of music for lute and guitar, gives an important place to the foreign repertoire, which was not only of Italian but also of Spanish and English origin.

From the middle of the century onwards, vocal music continued its evolution under the influence of the madrigal, while lute music assumed a more national character with Adrian Le Roy (c. 1520–98). Music counsellor to King Charles IX and a friend of Lassus, he produced in his triple capacity (as composer, pedagogue and publisher) three books of music for the lute, five for guitar, and two for cittern, all of which are extant. Unfortunately the instruction books for the guitar, lute and mandora have been lost, although that for the lute is preserved in an English translation dating from 1568 and 1574. Whereas in his instruction-books he analyses different ways of transferring, for example, the *chansons* of Lassus to an instrumental idiom, Le Roy's own transcriptions tended to be simple. He preferred the technique of variation to that of ornamentation and sometimes, as in the dances, retained only the *superius* (top part) of the original, making the rhythms of the *chanson* more flexible and showing a predilection for parallel motion. Le Roy also wrote *doubles*[18] – the first of the species in the French repertoire – which are full of rhythmic refinements. His *fantasies* have a clarity and balance which seem to forsake the great polyphonic structures.

The last branch of instrumental music to be considered here is that for the ensemble, referred to in the records of courts and municipalities where composers and performers are often precisely mentioned. From about 1530 court instrumentalists were divided into two groups: those of the *chambre* (chamber) – players of lutes, cornetts, fifes and drums (pipes and tabors) and those of the *écurie* (stable) – violins, shawms, sackbuts and flutes. Under Charles IX the violins passed to the chamber, an indication of the more sophisticated role which was henceforth reserved for them. The majority of these instrumentalists were at the same time leading figures in the old popular community of 'instrument-players' which had its seat at the *Hôpital Saint-Julien-des-ménétriers* (The Hospital of St Julian of the Minstrels) in Paris and from which various bands were recruited which participated in the life of the city in one fashion or another. Some of these occasions tended to be in the nature of public pageantry, such as ceremonial processions for distinguished visitors, princely marriages, jousts and tournaments and festival of guilds and cor-

18. The *double* is a variation (or 'diminution' or 'division') which repeats the original, the *simple*, in unmistakable fashion, though it thinly disguises the *simple* by quicker note values and other devices of ornamentation.

porations; others were in the nature of more private festivities (weddings, banquets and serenades). Gradually the best of these instrumentalists formed the nucleus of what was to become, at the beginning of Louis XIII's reign, the *24 violons du roi*. After 1590 the Italian instrumentalists who had hitherto been attached to the court returned to their homeland, disenchanted by the civil disorders and poor, irregular pay. As a result of this exodus the repertoire of the court and of the municipality tended to be much the same.

The sources of music for instrumental ensemble which have been preserved mostly consist of music for the dance. An exception must be made, though, for a collection by J. Moderne entitled *Musique de joye*, printed by him at Lyon around 1550. This was largely a revised edition of the *Musica nova* published at Venice in 1540 but with the addition of three pieces by musicians who were probably of Lyonnaise origin, N. Benoist, G. Colin and G. Coste. These pieces are the first French examples of the genre of the *ricercare*, a kind of textless instrumental motet written in an imitative style already cultivated in Italy by Willaert (and others) and suitable for instrumental ensemble such as a consort of viols.

But the essence of the repertoire of violinists, oboists (shawm-players), flautists and cornettists was provided by the *danseries* which were to all intents and purposes a speciality of French publishers. In 1529 Attaingnant issued two collections of *gaillardes*, *pavanes* and *basses-danses* for the benefit of amateurs. Then between 1550 and 1564 a wave of publications emerged from the Paris presses, whose composers and arrangers were Claude Gervaise, Etienne du Tertre and Jean d'Estrée. The great majority were *pavanes* and *gaillardes* which might be linked as *couples*, sometimes with a certain thematic unity; *allemandes*, and *branles* (occasionally grouped together as suites). The famous canon of Langres, Thoinot Arbeau, describes the disposition, movements and figurations of some of these dances in his *Orchésographie* of 1589.[19] There are many affinities between these dances and the *chansons* of the Parisian type as described above. Their simplicity and clear-cut structure assured them of a great success throughout Europe, which is reflected in the many transcriptions and copies made by editors like Susato and Phalèse in the Low Countries.

The instrumental art of this last generation of French musicians is represented in *Terpsichore musarum*, a publication edited by the German musician M. Praetorius, and published at Wolfenbüttel in 1612. The three hundred or so pieces in this anthology had been communicated to him by Antoine Emeraud, the French dancing-master of the Duke of Brunswick, and later harmonized in five parts by Praetorius and P. F. Caroubel, a Parisian violinist of Italian origin. Besides a large number of *branles*, the

19. Published in English translation by C. W. Beaumont, with musical transcriptions by P. Warlock, London, 1925. More recent research is incorporated in the translation by J. Sutton, New York, 1967.

most numerous dances are *courantes* and *balletti*. In these latter there may be grouped together *entrées*, *sarabandes*, *courantes* and *gaillardes*, thus giving some idea of the purely instrumental portions of the ballets of Henri IV's court. In this collection one already finds certain harmonic refinements which provide much of the charm of the music of the *24 violons*.

JOHN CALDWELL

4.3 The Low Countries: 1500–1600

INTRODUCTION
THE PERIOD OF JOSQUIN DES PREZ
THE PERIOD OF CLEMENS NON PAPA
THE PERIOD OF ROLAND DE LASSUS
INSTRUMENTAL MUSIC

INTRODUCTION

The influence of the music to be discussed in this chapter extended far beyond the territorial limits suggested by its title.[1] Both by their own travels and by the avidity with which their compositions were seized on by foreign publishers (notably Ottaviano de' Petrucci at Venice), the composers of the Netherlands managed to achieve a truly international reputation. Diverse in nationality themselves, they were united in their cultivation of a polyphonic style of such passionate intensity and technical assurance that it became the model for almost the whole of the known musical world. Paradoxically it was in France herself, in spite of some publications by Attaingnant, that the idiom made the least headway: the clear formal outlines, simple melodic ideas and submission to verbal accentuation in the sacred and secular works of Jannequin, Sermisy and their successors are utterly opposed to the more learned, musically self-sufficient style of the Netherlanders. But in Italy and Germany the conquest was virtually complete.

It must not be supposed that this domination was the result of a sudden efflorescence at the turn of the century. It was, on the contrary, the result of a long series of developments all tending towards the same end. In the late thirteenth and early fourteenth centuries the Liège composer Johannes Ciconia and his compatriots Arnold and Hugo de Lantins travelled to Italy

---

1. See above, pp. 168 and 175.

and profited from contacts with Italian style. At about the same time as these last two, Dufay himself, the native of Cambrai, made the same journey; and it was his own profound personal change of style on his return around 1440 that laid the foundations of the Netherlands manner. This style, based on the interdependence and equality of four voices, was cultivated and intensified by his follower and probable pupil Johannes Ockeghem.

The stage was thus set for the massive achievements of the late fifteenth and sixteenth centuries. This period may be sub-divided into three, each centred around a single composer of outstanding genius: the first around Josquin, the second around Clemens non Papa towards the middle of the century and the third around the highly cosmopolitan figure of Roland de Lassus (equally well known as Orlando di Lasso) during the latter half.

THE PERIOD OF JOSQUIN DES PREZ

Before discussing Josquin himself, a word must be said about Jacob Obrecht, whose dates (?1450–1505) make him virtually a fifteenth-century composer. He has been called a 'real Dutchman',[2] which is true enough as far as modern political divisions are concerned, but has less relevance to the fifteenth-century situation. It is sufficient to state that he was in all probability a native of Bergen-op-Zoom in North Brabant, and for that reason is unlikely to be the 'Jacobus de Ulandia' mentioned in a list of singers of the chapel of Hercules I at Ferrara in 1474. After a short period as choirmaster at Utrecht (c. 1476) his professional career was taken up by various appointments in Bergen-op-Zoom, Bruges and Antwerp, with a year or so at Cambrai cathedral (1484–5). There were also two well-authenticated visits to Ferrara, where he died in 1505. Five of his masses were printed by Petrucci in a single volume in 1504.

Obrecht's style is full of Italian light and grace, coupled with a certain Flemish rigidity. It is also a strange mixture of the modern and the archaic. The Italianate and modern elements are an easily flowing melodic line and a strong sense of harmonic structure, especially at cadential points. Sometimes the easy flow degenerates into an over-facile habit of sequential repetition; but at its best it carries a natural conviction. The rigidity is often created by the use of complex syncopations in small time-values, heard against a strictly metrical beat moving much more slowly. It is also at times the result of a mechanical method of chopping up a *cantus firmus* in ways which contradict the original phrase structure and laying it out in long notes, with long rests between the artificial phrases thus formed, as in the Mass *Si dedero*.[3] This method often obliges the composer to spin out his free material (usually quite

2. Reese, *Renaissance* 186.
3. Facsimile of Tenor in Apel, *Notation* 183. The work is based on a motet by Agricola.

independent of the *cantus firmus*) at greater length than its nature would seem to permit.

Obrecht was perhaps happiest with Masses, where the words did not impose an obligation on the composer to respond in a particular way; the Mass in those days was as universal and as non-committal a mode of expression as the symphony has been in more recent times. Those of Obrecht encompass the entire emotional gamut of his day, from the warmth of *Ave regina caelorum* to the steely brilliance of *Caput*; from the slender texture of the early, three-part *De tous biens plaine* to the massive architecture of *Sub tuum praesidium*. Everywhere (with the possible exception of *Salve diva parens*) there is dependence on existing models, and the net is widely cast: a single plainsong (*Beata viscera, Petrus Apostolus, O quam suavis, Sicut spina rosam, Libentur gloriabor* and *Caput*); more than one plainsong (*de Sancte Martino, Sub tuum praesidium*); monophonic metrical tunes (*Maria zart, L'Homme armé*) and polyphonic sources, sacred or secular (*Fors seulement, De tous biens plaine, Fortuna desperata, Ave regina caelorum, Si dedero* etc.). In *Sub tuum praesidium* the texture increases from three parts in the 'Kyrie' to seven in the 'Agnus', the later movements incorporating the simultaneous quotation of plainsongs which carry their own texts; so that for instance in the 'Agnus' four different texts are heard at the same time.

Most of the Masses based on polyphonic models not only take their tenor as a genuine *cantus firmus*, but also make use of material from the other voices. Even so, Obrecht scarcely approaches a genuine parody technique.[4] In *Ave regina caelorum*, for example, he presents the tenor of Frye's motet (rhythmically altered) as a *cantus firmus* throughout the Mass; Frye's upper part is also quoted in the 'Credo' and 'Benedictus', but only where the *cantus firmus* itself is absent. The *Caput* Mass shows a different kind of dependence: the Gregorian *cantus firmus* is presented in a rhythmic form identical to that in the Masses on the same chant by Dufay and Ockeghem.[5] Obrecht would certainly have come across the former while he was choirmaster at Cambrai, where the 'Kyrie' of Dufay's Mass had been copied as recently as 1463.[6]

The best of Obrecht's motets are those in which the broad structural layout of the Masses is retained, such as *Factor orbis* (for Advent) and *Laudemus*

---

4. The essence of parody lies in the quotation of at least some part of the original polyphonic texture. See Sparks, *Cantus Firmus* 152. Strict parody, in which the whole of the original music was retained and new words substituted, was employed in the Middle Ages and known as *contrafactum*. In Josquin's *Missa Mater Patris*, the model is quoted intact in the third 'Agnus' with two additional parts (see below, p. 200). In general, however, sixteenth-century parody emerged as the product of a tentative and cautious use of polyphonic material, initially with the individual parts used separately and later in combination. Works such as Ockeghem's *Missa Fors seulement* and the Masses of Obrecht mentioned here are the first steps in this direction.

5. Bukofzer, *Studies*, 256–71.

6. Bukofzer, *Studies*, 268, and the reference there given; the conclusion that the entry refers to the entire Mass may, however, be unwarranted. Cf. Reese, *Renaissance* 69.

nunc Dominum (for the dedication of a church).[7] These are each in two sections, triple and duple respectively, and are in five parts. Both have as *cantus firmi* a series of antiphons unified by mode and liturgical origin. The texts of the other parts are a collection of biblical and liturgical quotations, possibly assembled by Obrecht himself. Polytextuality is taken to an extreme in *Factor orbis*, where all five parts have a different text. Also assembled with the motets in Wolf's edition are such items as the *Magnificat* (alternating with plainsong) and the votive antiphons *Alma Redemptoris Mater* and two of the three settings of *Salve Regina*. These last are in three, four and six parts respectively. The three-part setting is full; in the others the odd-numbered verses must be sung in plainsong. The four-part setting survives only in an important manuscript of Segovia Cathedral which has been described by Anglès and which contains nine unpublished motets and many Dutch songs ascribed to Obrecht.[8] *Ave regina caelorum* is a song-motet in which Frye's tenor is transposed from the fifth to the first mode.

Obrecht's *chansons* exhibit a growing independence of the old *formes fixes*: *rondeau*, *virelai* and *ballade*. Of these three, the *rondeau* held its own for the longest time, possibly because its refrain was sung to the whole of its music. The earliest pieces to depart from the *formes fixes* are simply *rondeaux* with only the refrain underlaid; and as late and mature a piece as Josquin's *Faulte d'argent* (to which we shall return) has a text of which the rhyme scheme (abba) is that of a *rondeau quatrain* refrain. In the case of Obrecht, the fact that usually only the *incipit* of the text is given makes the intended form uncertain; some of them indeed may have been designed in the first place as purely instrumental pieces. About two-thirds of the titles are in Flemish, and it is these which illustrate both the use of freer forms and instrumental characteristics. The French pieces tend to be based on polyphonic models, but those with Flemish titles often seem to derive from Dutch folk-tunes. All these features are to be found in his charming *Tsaat een meskin*.[9]

If Josquin des Prez (*c.* 1440[10]–1521) eventually surpassed his great rival it was not merely by virtue of the fact that he outlived him. (There are many variant spellings of his name: the first part appears also as Jusquinus or Jodocus, the second as Pratensis, or des Pres or des Prez. The acrostic of one of his motets suggests des Prez as the preferred spelling. Both in his own time and today he is usually referred to as Josquin.) He was much more in the

---

7. Ed. J. Wolf, *Obrecht* vol. vi, Nos. 2, 5; ed. Smijers-Crevel, *Obrecht*, Motets, ii.

8. *Van Ockeghem tot Sweelinck*, ed. Smijers, contains in its first volume the four-part *Salve Regina*, many of the Dutch songs and the 'Kyries' of three Masses found in this source. The reader is warned that the *Pater noster* (Wolf, No. 14) printed in the first edition of *HAM*, No. 76, is by Willaert, and that the *O vos omnes* which with *O beate Basili* (prima pars) replaces it in the second edition of *HAM* No. 76b, (Wolf No. 18) is by Compère. *Si oblitus fuerit* (Wolf, No. 11) is by Ninot le Petit. Reese, *Renaissance* 190.

9. *HAM*, i, No. 78.

10. See Sartori in *Annales Musicologiques*, iv (1956), 55–83.

direct line of succession from Dufay and Ockeghem than Obrecht. He retains much of Ockeghem's fluidity of style and construction; and while he must have profited to a certain extent from Obrecht's clarity of texture and harmony, he is far removed from the archaic and mechanical elements in the style of the latter. There is a good deal of significance in Reese's remark that 'culturally and in every other sense that matters, he was a Frenchman'. Even more than Obrecht, he profited from visits to Italy, where he could be found at various times between 1459 and 1499. In later life he settled in France and the Netherlands: he was *maistre de chapelle* to Louis XII until the latter's death in 1515, and then canon of St Gudule in Brussels and provost of the cathedral chapter of Notre Dame at Condé, where he died in 1521. Few of his works can be dated with certainty, but the Italian pieces can be assumed to have been written before about 1500, while those of them ascribed to 'Jusquin d'Ascanio' evidently refer to his period in the service of Ascanio Sforza at Milan around 1479. The Mass *Hercules dux Ferrariae* may also refer to his employment by Hercules I around 1499. Petrucci published no fewer than three books of his Masses (in 1502, 1505 and 1514); and the fact that two such obviously mature ones as *Da pacem* and *Pange lingua* were not included even in the third of these may point to a still later date of composition (they were eventually produced by Johannes Ott at Nürnberg in 1539).[11] There is a general sense of progression from complexity of structure to a greater simplicity and reliance on purely musical means of expression.

Josquin's Masses, apart from the few which survive only in manuscript, may conveniently be considered in order of publication. Those of 1502 (*L'Homme armé super voces musicales*, *La sol fa re mi*, *Gaudeamus*, *Fortuna desperata* and *L'Homme armé sexti toni*) already display a mixture of styles: *L'Homme armé super voces musicales* is noticeably more schematic than its companions. Its title refers simply to the fact that the *cantus firmus* is heard on each degree of the hexachord (*vox*) in turn. In spite of this, each movement is made to end on D.

Hercules dux Ferrariae, though first published in 1505, is also rigidly constructed and probably several years older. Its *cantus firmus* is derived from the solmization syllables suggested by the vowels of its title: *re ut re ut re fa mi re*. No greater contrast could be imagined than between it and the *Ave maris stella* from the same collection. Here the plainsong hymn pervades all parts of the texture, as in later paraphrase Masses, although the tenor part can lay some claim to be the *cantus firmus* – bearer-in-chief. The other Masses of 1505 (*Malheur me bat*, *L'Ami Baudichon*, *Una Musque de Buscaya* [*Biscaya*] and *D'ung aultre amer*) are apparently earlier works.

The 1514 collection includes the Mass *Mater Patris*, a fully-fledged parody Mass in that the polyphonic texture of Brumel's motet is itself the

---

11. *Misse tredecim*. A chronology of Josquin's works is attempted by Osthoff in his article in *MGG*.

basis of the composition (the 'Agnus III' simply consists of the three-part motet in full with two added parts); *Faisant regretz*, based on a four-note motive from Frye's *rondeau*, *Tout a par moy*; *Ad fugam*, and *Sine nomine*, both in canon throughout; *Di dadi*, whose proportions are indicated by pictures of dice; and *De beata Virgine*. This last is unified by its choice of *cantus firmi* from a liturgical rather than from a musical point of view. The plainsongs are those of the Ordinary associated with Masses of the Blessed Virgin Mary, including the tropes which were discarded by the Council of Trent. They are 'Kyrie' and 'Gloria IX', 'Credo I' (invariable), 'Sanctus IV' and 'Agnus IV' (Vatican numbering). Although each of these plainsongs is in a different mode, Josquin brings some unity to the scheme by transposing some of the melodies: the tonic of the 'Kyrie' and 'Gloria' together becomes G, that of the 'Sanctus' and 'Agnus' is C.

Turning finally to the two Masses published by Ott, that on *Da pacem* is a *cantus firmus* Mass not consistently ascribed to Josquin in the sources, although its authorship can scarcely be doubted. *Pange lingua*, on the other hand, is of unquestionable authenticity, bearing all the hallmarks of a late work. The plainsong hymn pervades the texture to such an extent that no one voice can be regarded as the bearer of the *cantus firmus*: in other words it is a genuine paraphrase Mass[12] of the kind favoured until late Renaissance times. In a single work he recalls Ockeghem at his most prophetic (compare the tonality of his *Missa Mi-mi* and the setting of *Suscipe deprecationem nostram* in both works) and at the same time reaches forward to the world of Palestrina's *Aeterna Christi munera*.

Much of Josquin's most characteristic work is to be found in his motets. Some of the large-scale tenor-*cantus firmus* motets, such as the early *Huc me sydereo/Plangent eum*, recall Obrecht in the grandeur of their structural layout. The use of more than one text simultaneously is also an archaic feature here. This reappears in the so-called *chanson*-motets, amongst them the noble *Déploration* on the death of Ockeghem (*c*. 1495), where the tenor voice sings the introit *Requiem aeternam* against the French text of the other parts.[13] More appealing, perhaps, are some of the shorter four-part works. Here Josquin's grace and lightness of touch, obtained through his consummate mastery of texture and the ingenious pairing of voices, are readily apparent, as in the familiar *Ave Maria ... virgo serena*, which begins with an imitative paraphrase of the plainsong sequence. *Tu pauper refugium* (the second part of *Magnus es tu*)[14] shows exactly the same loosely articulated con-

---

12. 'Paraphrase Mass': paraphrased (i.e. ornamented) *cantus firmus* in all voices. In the fifteenth century 'paraphrase technique' implies primarily ornamentation of *cantus firmus*, usually in the top part. In the sixteenth century the main criterion is the fact that the *cantus firmus* permeates all voices, whether ornamented or not. See Marshall, *JAMS* (1963) 347.

13. Modern edition in Smijers, *Josquin*, fasc. v (*Secular Works*, ii, 56) and ix (*Motets*, v, 152: without French text.)

14. *HAM*, i, No. 90.

struction, its perfectly-proportioned phrases being linked together in a natural and unobtrusive manner. This last piece also illustrates the mature Josquin's liking for Phrygian tonality.[15]

It is impossible to do justice to Josquin's motets in so short a space, and the same may be said of the *chansons*. They resemble the motets in several respects: their freedom of structure and their expressive content; their preference, in many instances, for more than four parts and for the use of canon; and in the case of the *chanson* motets, as we have seen, the use of plainsong *cantus firmus* and the consequent polytextuality, here involving the use of two languages simultaneously. The five-part *Faulte d'argent*,[16] to take a single example, conceals a continuous canon between the second and fourth voices among the free imitation, while a regular ternary form is superimposed on the four lines of verse of which the text consists. There is also a trend here away from the sentiments of *amour courtois* in the Burgundian tradition towards the satirical and bawdy; a field to be well tilled by Clemens non Papa. The six-part *Petite camusette*, again, with its resemblance to Ockeghem's original, is a *tour de force* of technical skill subordinated to expressive purposes.

Many composers of Netherlandish origin can receive only brief mention in this chapter as their lives were spent largely elsewhere. Heinrich Isaac (b. before 1450), although a native of Brabant, spent most of his mature life in Italy, Germany and Austria. He was in the service of the Medici at Florence and later court composer to the German Emperor Maximilian I at Vienna. Except in the simplest of the Italian carnival songs, however, his art is distinctively Netherlandish in its contrapuntal severity, and nowhere more so than in the *Choralis Constantinus*, a monumental series of settings of the Proper of the Mass, more fully discussed in chapter 7, on German music.

Alexander Agricola (b. ?1446, d. ?1506), apparently a Fleming by birth, is first heard of in Milan in 1472. Although he spent a good deal of time in Italy, he was at Cambrai Cathedral in 1475–6 and in the service of Philip the Handsome of Burgundy from 1500. It was during a trip to Spain with the latter that he apparently died, like his royal master, of a fever. His style, like that of Obrecht, is a strange mixture of archaic and modern: he was much addicted to the *formes fixes* in his numerous *chansons*; but in his Mass *Je ne demande*, published with four others by Petrucci in 1504, he uses a genuine parody technique in the 'Gloria' by quoting simultaneously two parts of Busnois's original *chanson*.

Numerous other Flemish musicians are found (with Agricola) in a list of musicians in the service of Cardinal Galeazzo Maria Sforza at Milan in 1474: Gaspar van Weerbecke (*c*. 1445–after 1514), Johannes Martini (d. after 1499) and Loyset Compère (d. 1518), as well as Josquin himself and many

---

15. Cf. Obrecht's liking for major tonality.
16. *HAM*, i, No. 91.

more. Compère however spent much of his life in St Quentin (possibly his native town), and can also be grouped with a number of composers whose lives were spent mostly in France: Antoine Brumel (d. ? Ferrara, after 1520), Antoine de Févin (d. Blois, *c.* 1512) and Jean Mouton (*c.* 1470–1522). Between them they testify to the continued vitality of Netherlands style even south and east of Paris; the emergence of a national French style, distinct from that of the Netherlands, had hardly yet begun.

Finally, Pierre de la Rue (d. 1518) deserves separate, though brief treatment. He was born in Picardy and died at Courtrai, and indeed spent most of his life in the Netherlands; like Agricola, he was in the service of Philip the Handsome (subsequently in that of his sister, Margaret of Austria) and travelled with him to Spain. Among a large number of Masses, motets and *chansons*, the Requiem stands out as a work of astonishing originality. In it is found, in accentuated form, the problem of range already encountered in Ockeghem; the lowest part occasionally descends to the B flat below the bass stave. While it is clear that the composer intended to exploit the dark sonorities of the lowest vocal registers, a transposition up a fourth (as in the *Das Chorwerk* edition[17]), while far from nullifying such effects, would tend to enhance the deliberate use of a higher *tessitura* in the Offertory, 'Sanctus' and Communion. The vocal style of writing as well as purely liturgical considerations forbid one to think of instrumental help with the lowest voices, and it seems likely that the use of very low clef-combinations implied an upward transposition even in the context of the variable pitch-standards of those days, just as, not so long afterwards, the use of high clef-combinations or *chiavette* were interpreted as an instruction to transpose down.

In spite of the bright vision of a motet like *Lauda anima mea*, the prevailing impression left by the works of Pierre de la Rue is of a sombre, poignant quality. A capacity for solving technical problems in a purely musical way, as exemplified by the use of mensuration canon[18] in the *L'Homme armé* Mass, provides a further link between this, one of the most forward-looking Netherlanders of his day, and the fast-vanishing world of Ockeghem and his generation.

THE PERIOD OF CLEMENS NON PAPA

This period is characterized above all by the development of an entirely indigenous style in France, together with the increasing dominance of the Netherlands style in Germany, Italy and Spain. We are concerned here, of course, only with the spearhead of the developments in the Low Countries themselves. The idiom in the era succeeding the death of Josquin was

17. Blume, *La Rue*.
18. A canon in which a single written part must be read simultaneously in different mensurations. See *HAM*, i, No. 92.

directly dependent on his own mature style: pervading imitation, equality of treatment among the voices and the careful use of dissonance are all to be found. The motet now decisively outweighs the Mass as the favourite form of sacred music; and among the Masses themselves the parody technique is uppermost.

A group of three composers of outstanding importance worked in the Netherlands sufficiently consistently to qualify for treatment here: Clemens, Gombert and Crequillon; many others, such as Verdelot, Willaert and his pupil de Rore, settled permanently in Italy and belong to the musical history of that country; while Jacques Arcadelt (*c*. 1504–after 1567) after an Italian period settled in France from *c*. 1553 and wrote *chansons* and Masses in the French style.

The links between the Josquin and the Clemens periods are provided by such men as Mouton, the teacher of Willaert, Antonius Divitis and Jean Richafort. Divitis (born Louvain *c*. 1475, died ? after 1526) was active in Italy and Spain as well as in the Netherlands. Only a small quantity of his music survives. Richafort (*c*. 1480–1548) is more significant, and many of his thirty-five motets provided models for parody masses. Such works as *Quem dicunt homines* were composed sufficiently early in his career to be the source of Masses by Divitis, Mouton and even Josquin himself. Like Josquin, his *chansons* are in imitative polyphony and often in five or more parts.

The central figure amongst Clemens' older contemporaries is Nicolas Gombert (*c*. 1500–after 1556), a member of the chapel of Charles v from 1526 to *c*.1540. He later settled in Tournai. He is the great early master of the consistently imitative style, and his sacred music achieves a fine balance between technical perfection and depth of expression. A definite break has now occurred with the Josquin manner. The pairing of voices so characteristic of the latter has now completely disappeared, and all the parts are employed almost continuously. Also typical of the new era is the preponderance of some 160 motets over fewer than a dozen Masses.

Already in his first published Mass, *Da pacem* (Attaingnant, 1532), all the characteristics are there. The smoothly-flowing polyphony in all four parts contrasts vividly with the rather archaic *cantus firmus* manner of Josquin's Mass of the same title. Unlike the latter, it is probably a parody Mass, although in this case the polyphonic model has not been identified. All but one of the others are parodies, ranging from the grandeur of the five-part *Media vita* (based on his own six-part motet; it is only in the 'Agnus' of his Mass, however, that Gombert attains six-part texture) to the exquisite *Je suis desheritée*, based on the famous *chanson* attributed to Johannes Lupi (but in later editions of the *chanson* attributed to Pierre Cadeac). Here, of course, there is an approach towards the concision of the French style, but too great a submission is avoided by the occasional drawing-out of the phrases of the original (as at the beginning of the 'Sanctus') and by the ascent from four to six parts in the final 'Agnus'. The only certain exception to the rule that all his Masses are parodies is the six-part *Missa tempore paschali*, probably an early work and based largely on plainsongs for the Ordinary of the Mass. The 'Credo' is in eight parts and the final 'Agnus' in twelve, the latter being based on the Easter antiphon *Et ecce terrae motus* in an old-fashioned long-note presentation. Gombert scarcely avoids congestion amongst the parts in this work; and indeed he is inclined to be rather stiff whenever he writes for more than five voices.

Fine as some of the Masses may be, Gombert's greatest distinction is as a composer of motets. Apart from the *Magnificats* on the eight tones (the even verses are set for four parts, leaving the odd verses to be sung in plainsong), the best of these are based on sombre texts or are in honour of the Virgin. It is not without justification that the beautifully flowing *Super flumina Babylonis* from the first book (1539) has recently been included in an anthology.[19] *Ave sanctissima Maria*, from the same set, breathes a penitential fervour which is entirely suited to the text. A second book of four-part motets was published in 1541, and two books of five-part works appeared in the same years. The six-part works are perhaps less immediately attractive, although one of them (*In illo tempore*) retained favour even as late as the time of Monteverdi, who was to write a Mass based on its themes.

Gombert's *chansons*, which have not yet been published in their entirety, are hardly likely to throw much new light on the composer. The five- and six-part examples published by Susato scarcely differ from the motets in their technique, although he tries to accommodate the lighter mood of some of the texts by means of syllabic setting in shorter note-values. More immediately appealing is a four-part example, *Hors envyeux*, first published by Attaingnant in 1535, where the mood of the text is reflected more accurately.

Jacobus Clemens non Papa represents the continuing Flemish tradition. He may have been born (on the island of Walcheren) as late as 1510. Some publications by Attaingnant may indicate a period in Paris, but he would have returned to the Low Countries by *c.* 1545, where he died *c.* 1557.[20] It is difficult to assess the relative merits of Gombert and Clemens, for in spite of some external similarities they were artists of an essentially different type. Clemens was by far the more boisterous and exuberant of the two, as shown especially in the *chansons*. With his fifteen complete Masses (including a Requiem), more than two hundred motets, fifteen Magnificats and ninety-three secular pieces, he is more prolific (within a shorter life-span) than Gombert in all genres of music, even though the proportions between the genres remain similar; and there are also the *Souterliedekens* (little Psalter songs). Gombert's

19. *HAM*, i, No. 114.
20. See the articles in *MGG*, and in *Musica Disciplina*, 1961 and 1964, all by Bernet Kempers.

consummate musicianship and gravity of style have seemed to many to raise him on a pinnacle above all his contemporaries; but it is possible to see in Clemens the more complete musical personality. The sheer size of Clemens' output has been held to be a disadvantage, but he maintains a remarkably high standard in general, and fecundity is not always a sign of the second-rate.

The Masses can be dealt with briefly. With the exception of the Requiem they are all parodies, both sacred and secular models being used; two (*Ecce quam bonum* and *Pastores quidnam vidistis*) are parodies on his own motets.[21] The Requiem is based on the appropriate plainsongs.

On paper Clemens' motets appear to be depressingly uniform.[22] The appearance however is deceptive, for he covers a wide range of expression from the splendour of *Gaudent in caelis* to the gloom of *Vox in Rama* (both published by Ulhard in 1549). The former is an example of the influence of plainsong in Clemens' work. The text is a Gregorian antiphon (the words differ slightly from those given in the present-day books, however) and the imitative material is quite clearly derived, for the most part, from the chant. More overt statements than this appear to be entirely absent from his output.

The oldest surviving editions of motets by Clemens are contained in four books of *Cantiones Sacrae* printed in Antwerp by Susato in 1546 and 1547. *Pater peccavi*, from the third of these books,[23] may be one of the earliest that survive, being somewhat reminiscent of Josquin in its occasional use of voice-pairing. It also illustrates the 'responsorial' type of motet in its strictest form. The first part is a setting of the respond itself, while the second sets the verse (*Quanti mercenarii*) and the partial repeat of the respond to its original music (from *Fac me sicut unum* to the end). The musical and textual form is therefore ab, cb. There is here no reference to the original plainsong melody. There is no question of such motets having been sung liturgically as responds; they simply take a responsorial form, the text on occasion being drawn from other sources.

The motets of Clemens' fullest maturity are represented in the eight books of *Cantiones ecclesiastici* published by Susato in 1553 and in the four books of *Cantiones sacrae* published by Phalèse at Louvain in the following year. The very essence of his art is to be found in the fifty-four motets for four, five and six voices first printed in these collections. In many of them, as the editor of the complete edition says, 'one feels ushered into the privacy of their author's prayers'. In the very first of them, *Tristitia et anxietas*, the scriptural text is changed so that *oculi nostri*, for instance, becomes *oculi mei*; while the second part, *Sed tu Domine*, is almost entirely personal and non-scriptural. We see

21. The *Missa Misericorde* may be a parody on a *chanson* by himself.
22. Published in Bernet Kempers, *Clemens*, iii, ix, xii–xv.
23. Also printed at Lyons in 1547.

here a rare instance of an 'extreme' key-signature (in this case two flats) in connection with highly emotional texts; an even more celebrated example is the use of three flats in the five-part *Qui consolabatur me*. Such pieces have been cited by Lowinsky in support of a 'secret chromatic art' in the Netherlands motet[24]; but the different editions of *Qui consolabatur me* are not consistent in their use of key-signatures and there is much to be said for the occasional editorial cancellation of flats rather than a wholesale application of *musica ficta* in the attempt to smooth away melodic and harmonic augmented fourths. In spite of Lowinsky's brilliant arguments, the case for a secret chromatic art remains unproven.

Various instances of Clemens' choice of texts, and his juxtapositions of unrelated scriptural texts, have been quoted in order to link the use of a chromatic art with the trials of secret adherents of Protestantism. Certainly texts like that of *Confundantur omnes*[25] lend support to the idea that Clemens regarded himself as belonging to a persecuted minority. Other texts are more truly 'ecclesiastical'; yet others are scarcely sacred, as in the well-known *Musica Dei donum optimi*,[26] an ode in praise of music.

The *Souterliedekens* are 'versified and musically arranged psalms'[27] (and canticles), three-part settings of the melodies printed by Symon Cock of Antwerp in 1540.[28] The vast majority of these melodies are Dutch folksongs, and Clemens' settings match them in simplicity of style. They were printed as the fourth, fifth, sixth and seventh of Susato's *Musyck Boexken* published in 1556 and 1557; ten of the pieces are by Susato himself, which may indicate that Clemens died before the work was quite finished.

The *Magnificats*, like those of Gombert, set only the even-numbered verses; there are two settings each of tones one to seven, and one setting of tone eight.

In his *chansons*, Clemens achieves a subtle fusion of the French and Netherlandish styles. In many of the earlier ones he approaches Jannequin in freshness and lightness of touch, as in *Frisque et gaillard*, published by Attaingnant in 1541. Attaingnant indeed appears sometimes to confuse the two composers, and they collaborated in a setting of Marot's licentious *Blaison du beau et du laid tetin*. The Netherlandish element is more clearly seen in the later pieces for five and more parts: the five-part *La belle Margaritte* contains a canon at the octave throughout; but the style, even in the six-part setting of the same text, remains exquisitely luminous and buoyant. There are, finally, a few Dutch songs and instrumental pieces.

24. Lowinsky, *Chromatic*. See below, p. 208, fn. 30.
25. Bernet Kempers, *Clemens*, xii, 99.
26. Bernet Kempers, *Clemens*, xii, 106.
27. Bernet Kempers, *Clemens*, ii.
28. The tunes have no connection with those of the Calvinist psalter (see pp. 187, 209), which enjoyed such wide distribution throughout Europe.

THE PERIOD OF ROLAND DE LASSUS

Although much of Lassus' art belongs to the musical history of Italy, Germany and France, his Netherlandish origin justifies a brief account at this point. Born at Mons, *c.* 1532, he passed much of his early life in the cities of Naples, Palermo and Rome. Returning to Antwerp in 1555, he moved to Munich in the following year, where he remained until his death in 1594.[29]

Apart from a book of five-part madrigals published in Venice in 1555, Lassus' earliest publications appeared at Antwerp: a collection of four-part madrigals, *villanesche*, *chansons* and motets (Susato, 1555), and a book of five and six-part motets (J. Laet, 1556). After that his music was published all over Europe, and practically everything he printed was reissued many times.

The contents of these two books afford a useful insight into the precocity of the youthful composer and the universality of his appeal. Even the madrigals and *villanesche*, while obviously amongst the very earliest examples of his work which we possess (together with the contents of the Venice book and some *villanelle* in a Rome anthology of 1555), betray an astonishing individuality, as well as being among the earliest to be printed outside Italy. It is in the *chansons* and motets however that we can best examine the spirit of the Netherlands in Lassus. In the former, contrapuntal science is delightfully related to the spirit of the words: Lassus challenges Clemens on his own ground and excels him in the polished refinement of his wit. In his motets, the break with the past is more complete. In the five- and six-part works of the second Antwerp publication in particular, his imaginative response to the content and rhythms of the Latin words recalls the adventurous spirit of the madrigal. Like many of his Netherlandish predecessors he is bold in his choice of texts, many of which, without exactly being profane, are neither specifically sacred. Even among those drawn from the Bible there is a preference for the strongly passionate and dramatic, and their musical treatment, with its angular melodic lines and strongly marked rhythms, provides a perfect counterpart. Thus, early in his career, Lassus prepared for the culmination of the Netherlanders' achievement later in the century.

Lassus was not the only Netherlander of this period who spent much of his life abroad. Giaches de Wert (1535–96) lived almost continuously in Italy from his boyhood onwards and played an important part in the development of the Italian madrigal. Jacobus Kerle (*c.* 1532–91) was born in Ypres, and was in Italy from an early date until 1563. A period of travel (including visits to his native town) ended in 1582, when he became court chaplain to Rudolph 11 at Prague, where he died. His ten *Preces*, published at Venice in 1562, were apparently performed at the openings of sessions of the Council of Trent, and his clear, undemonstrative style had an undeniable

---

29. See chapter 7, p. 361.

influence on Italian composers of church music, including Palestrina himself. Philippe de Monte, longer-lived than any of his contemporaries (1521–1603), provides yet another instance of a composer who spent his earlier life in Italy and his later life in Germany and Bohemia. He visited England as a member of Philip II's choir in 1554–5. His later years were spent at Vienna and Prague (where he died) in the service of the imperial court. Monte's friendship with William Byrd, then aged eleven or twelve, may well have stemmed from his English visit. In 1583 he sent Byrd a copy of his eight-part psalm, *Super flumina Babylonis*, to which the Englishman replied in 1584 with an eight-part *Quomodo cantabimus*. (Monte's setting however does not consist of the first part of the psalm, but of isolated verses in a changed order, including *Quomodo cantabimus*. Byrd's response, while it sets consecutive verses, does not complete the psalm; moreover it is completely different in style, emotional expression being subordinated to the intricacies of canonic writing. Nevertheless it was probably through Monte rather than any other single composer that the Netherlands style made such headway in England.)

Monte's earlier works consist almost entirely of madrigals, of which he eventually published over one thousand examples. Unlike Wert, he was no innovator in this field, being content to combine his solid contrapuntal skill with a moderate amount of chromaticism and word-painting (see chapter 5, p. 240).

Hubert Waelrant (*c.* 1517–95), on the other hand, spent most of his life in his native country, probably bound by his teaching and publishing activities at Antwerp, where he died. He composed settings of French metrical psalms as well as Latin motets, the latter often resorting to picturesque modernisms in the illustration of the words. His Protestant sympathies are very thinly concealed in his choice of texts for these works.[30] A more orthodox point of view is represented by the sacred music of Andries Pevernage (1543–91), choir-master of Antwerp from 1585 until his death.

A final group of Renaissance Netherlanders is represented by Corneille Verdonck (1563–1625), a pupil of Waelrant, and most illustriously by Jan Pieterszoon Sweelinck (1562–1621). Sweelinck's keyboard music is often considered Baroque in conception; but in his vocal music he appears as the last great representative of Renaissance style, and the greatest since Clemens among those who resided mainly in the Low Countries. He lived for most of his life in Amsterdam, where he was organist of the Oude Kerke from 1580 or even earlier. He therefore represents the Protestant tradition, in spite of the publication of a set of five-part *Cantiones sacrae* in 1619. Although these were written *cum basso continuo ad organum* the style is essentially Renaissance, the keyboard being less obviously necessary than in, say, Schütz' *Cantiones Sacrae* of 1625, to which it is parallel in many ways. In spite of the

---

30. See the discussion of *Musica reservata* in connection with Lassus and Adrien Petit Coclico in chapter 7, p. 361. See also Lowinsky, *Chromatic*, passim.

brilliance of such favourites as *Hodie Christus natus est*, the four books of
psalms (1604–21) in the metrical versions of Clément Marot and Théodore
de Bèze are a more durable monument. In every case the traditional Genevan
melodies, arranged or composed by Louis Bourgeois and others, are used.
There is great variety of treatment: sometimes they are used as a simple
cantus firmus, but more frequently they are paraphrased in order to provide
points of imitation. Both techniques may be seen in the second item of the
first book, a magnificent setting of psalm 24. In the first part, the *cantus
firmus* is presented first in the top part of the four, and then, transposed down
a fourth, in the *altus*. In the second section, reduced to three parts, each line
of the tune serves as a separate point of imitation. In the final part the *cantus
firmus* is again stated twice, this time in the bass and tenor respectively, but
at the same pitch. The equally impressive psalm 23 (No. 10 in the same book)
illustrates the increasing of the number of parts from four to six in the three
sections successively. These two psalms set the complete text (*tout au long* in
the phraseology of the succeeding books) while others are strophic: the music
sets only the first stanza of the translation and must be repeated for each successive stanza (not printed in the original or modern editions). The four books
do not retain the biblical order of the psalms, and the curious total of 153 is
attained by some duplications: Psalm 3, for example, occurs as a strophic
setting in Book I and complete in Book III.[31] These two books each conclude
with a non-psalmodic setting: Book I with the *Cantique de Siméon* (*Nunc
dimittis*) and Book III with the *Oraison dominicale* (Our Father). All in all
these splendid works, in from three to eight voices, represent the summit of
Sweelinck's creative achievement.

Sweelinck also wrote secular music to French and Italian words. His work
represents an ideal fusion of madrigalian and *chanson* techniques; as in the
madrigals of Monte, a solid contrapuntal element is allied to an acute feeling
for the sense of the words. This is not so much apparent as one might expect
in the *Rimes françoises et italiennes* (1612), for these, apart from a single four-
part *chanson*, are in two and three parts only and reflect the spirit of the
canzonetta; but in the five-part *chansons* of 1594 he combines Italian clarity
with Flemish science to admirable effect. In the eighteen pieces he ranges
from the freshness of *Jeune beauté* to the gravity of *Regret, soucy et peine*;
the dominant impression however is of elegance and charm.

Sweelinck's music is the brilliant culmination of the native Flemish
tradition of Obrecht and Clemens. But his style also carried within itself the
seeds of its own decay, and Sweelinck (except in his keyboard music) did not
have the vision, as did Monteverdi in Italy and Schütz in Germany, to push
these progressive techniques to their logical conclusion, and so inaugurate a
new idiom in the Low Countries.

31. The other two psalms set twice are 27 and 134.

INSTRUMENTAL MUSIC

Instruments played their part in the musical life of the Netherlands, just as they did elsewhere, although it is still far from clear to what extent they were employed in the vocal music of the period. Internal evidence, such as the presence of sustained *cantus firmi*, rhythmic complexity and so on, point to the use of instruments in the church music of Obrecht and his contemporaries, but with the advent of the style of pervasive imitation under Josquin and Gombert their use in such a context would presumably have declined. In secular vocal music, however, they must have continued to be played, as is made clear by many paintings, such as a charming one depicting the performance of a *chanson* by Clemens.[32] The printed and manuscript copies, however, do not mention instrumental participation, and it is therefore uncertain just how they would have taken part. The one exception to this rule is the existence of *chanson* transcriptions for voice and lute, as in the second part of Phalèse's *Hortus musarum* (1553).

The origins of music for instrumental ensemble are far from clear, but many pieces by Obrecht and others, in which the only words are those of the title, have a distinctly instrumental flavour. The *basse dance* was as popular in the Low Countries as elsewhere[33]: this was a *cantus firmus* dance, the tune being played in long notes against a lively accompaniment, at first improvised and later written down. Its quicker companion, the Italian *saltarello*, was known in France as the *pas de Brabant*, a name which sufficiently indicates its origin. Obrecht's *T'Andernaken* well illustrates this kind of dance. During the first two decades of the sixteenth century, the older type of *basse dance* was gradually superseded by a new kind, known as the *basse dance commune*. This differed from the older type in being without *cantus firmus* and normally in four parts: but it retained the characteristic metrical alternation between ¾ and ⅜ (to use the original note values). It is this kind of *basse dance* that is included in Susato's third *Musyck boexken* of 1551, which also contained a *saltarello, branles, allemandes, pavanes* and *galliards*. The *ricercare* and *canzona* do not appear to have been widely cultivated in the Netherlands.

Solo instrumental music is confined mainly to the lute, consisting mostly of *chanson* and dance arrangements: the fantasias included in the first part of Phalèse's *Hortus musarum* (1552) are by foreigners such as Francesco da Milano and Gintzler. As for keyboard music, it is difficult to find anything of any distinction before Sweelinck. His own work in this field, with its marked Baroque tendencies, falls outside the scope of this chapter.

---

32. Bernet Kempers, *Clemens*, x, frontispiece.

33. An important source containing *basse dance* melodies is at Brussels (MS 9085), available in facsimile and transcription in Ernest Closson, ed., *Le Manuscrit dit de Basses Danses de la Bibliothèque de Bourgogne*. Brussels, 1912. (*Dance* is a Renaissance variant spelling of '*danse*'.)

FEDERICO GHISI

5 Italy: 1300–1600

THE FOURTEENTH CENTURY

DOLCE STIL NUOVO AND ARS NOVA. The love poetry that has come down
to us from the end of the thirteenth century was written to order for special
occasions and sought to imitate the carefree poetry of the troubadours. As a
result of this approach, and in spite of its good craftsmanship, the general
tone of the genre was monotonous. It continued to flourish in Italy for a
long time because of the influence of the Provençal poets, some of whom are
mentioned in the *Divine Comedy*. Dante was the first to distinguish the
secular literary culture of the *dolce stil nuovo* in Italy from the courtly poetry
imported from France. He hoped to re-awaken the national spirit and thus
to create a national art distinct from Provençal poetry, which was written
to be set to music and which held undisputed dominion at the court of Anjou
at Naples.

The language of Dante's poetry is remarkable both for the sweet sounds
of the words themselves and for the natural force of its prosody; but this
does not imply that it was intended to be sung with the delicate support of a

musical instrument. The verses and rhymes have a euphony of their own, and it seems likely that, because of this condition, no written musical tradition for the poetry of Dante has been preserved as testimony of the Florentine music of the period. And yet musical references are frequent in the *De Vulgari Eloquentia* and in the circle of poets belonging to the *dolce stil nuovo*,[1] from Dante to Cavalcanti. In the *canzoniere* of Cino da Pistoia we find lists of the names of professional musicians such as Garzo, Casella, Lippo Paci de' Bardi, Sochetto and Floriano da Rimini, who were in contact with Petrarch and who set to music some of his more popular *canzoni* and *ballate*. Not a single copy of their settings has come down to us. Their music was monodic, and we shall see that the development of monody[2] over the centuries is a characteristic aspect of Italian music, tied, no doubt, to the lack of a polyphonic medieval tradition in the peninsula prior to the fourteenth century. Such was the power of the church and its concentration in the seat of the papacy at Rome that it prevented the establishment of other local monastic centres of religious culture. This was in strong contrast to the flourishing of famous regional schools of polyphony in France, associated with St Martial at Limoges and Notre Dame at Paris. On the other hand the ancient liturgical tradition of the Catholic Church employed the monophonic practice of Gregorian chant, even when it is sung by the choir in unison. One is not surprised, then, to find in the second and third books of the *Divine Comedy* Dante's accurate observation of the liturgical psalmody of the Latin Office as the model for music.

But the rise of the communes made possible the formation of new secular centres of scholastic culture: the universities. It seems likely that, during his youth, Dante was in Bologna, where Guido Guinizelli studied and Cino da Pistoia taught; both were poets of the *dolce stil nuovo* school. Recent discoveries in the archives of the Cathedral of Padua show that the University of Padua was a centre for the teaching of polyphony, since it had the most famous Italian theorists of *cantus mensuratus* on its faculty during the first half of the fourteenth century. In the same way the discovery of new material in the town of Cividale contributes to a greater knowledge of Italian polyphony in the thirteenth century. Fra Salimbene's chronicle relates that this polyphony was limited to the sequence and to the *conductus* in two or three voices and was sung by the Franciscan monks of Pisa, Lucca and Siena.

History is indebted to Johannes Wolf for the discovery of an interesting piece in the Vatican library (MS Lat. 2854) which deals with Dante's circle and Pope Boniface VIII whose reign (1294–1303) is put into perspective by a Tuscan poet and musician in his employ, Bonaiutus de Casentino. The Latin

1. The *dolce stil nuovo*, 'sweet new style', is mentioned in a conversation between Dante and the soul of the poet Bonagiunta, *Divina Commedia*, Purgatorio, canto xxiv.

2. Monody is an expressive melody, whether presented in a single line or music with a homophonic accompaniment.

text is addressed to Master Accursino, Boniface's doctor, and concerns household remedies (*medela*) prescribed for an illness of the pope: '*Hec medela corporalis Fructum det spiritualis Amoris et Gaudii.*' The entire piece is a strophic song for two parts, couched in a formal pattern resembling that of the *ballata*, where the concluding lines of each stanza are sung to the same music as the opening lines, i.e. the refrain.[3] This work is an important musical document from the period central to the strife between the papacy and the rising national monarchy of France (Philip IV, 1285–1314).

In his disapproval and indignation against the corruption and abuses of the papacy, and in his plea for the political unification of Italy, Dante draws on a European tradition – also to be found in the famous *Roman de Fauvel*. This didactic French poem of religious and moral sentiments contains bitter invectives and allegorical references to animals. The musical interpolations in the *Fauvel*,[4] which were written down in the second decade of the fourteenth century, sometimes anticipate, in their daring stylistic procedures, the coming French polyphonic tradition of the succeeding decades, which was to influence the fledgling Italian *ars nova*.

Alongside the art of the troubadours, which was imitated but not assimilated by the Italian minstrels – for they remained far from the medieval teachings of the romances – there existed a native tradition of spiritual lyrics written in the vernacular. This tradition, like that of monophonic chant, was distinctly popular. The *laude* of Jacopone da Todi and of Garzo, preserved in the two famous collections of *laude* at Cortona and Florence, are the only Italian musical documents of the thirteenth century. They were sung in unison by processions of the faithful and by groups of *laude* singers who gathered in the Florentine churches even before the new minstrels of Christ became known in the countryside.[5] Strange as it may seem, the spiritual *lauda*, as sung with devotion by the Florentine populace, was not considered as acceptable, either poetically or musically, in Dante's classification of poetry. This is difficult to comprehend, since this regional heritage of secular monophonic music, based on texts displaying an intensely ascetic love in imitation of Christ's Passion and in solemn celebration of the cult of the Virgin, was born in a climate of profound religious mysticism which flourished from the time of St Francis to that of Dante. Because of the poetic similarities of the *lauda* and the regular *ballata* with a refrain, and because of the fact that both had musical settings which alternated syllabic recitation with melodic ornamentation, these two forms mark the point of confluence between the *dolce stil nuovo* and the developing *ars nova* of the fourteenth century. *Lauda* and

3. For a transcription see *NOHM*, iii, 42; for the pattern of the *ballata*, see p. 219.
4. See chapter 4.1, p. 155.
5. The Confraternity of Orto San Michele was founded during the period in which Dante lived in Florence. Even earlier, the Company of the Blessed Virgin was located in the church of Santa Reparata. For musical examples of the *lauda* of the thirteenth century see *HAM*, i, No. 21.

ballata both share some archaic traits to be expected in species derived from monophonic music.

The history of the fourteenth century in Italy is one of great disorders caused by bloody wars and by domestic feuds between the communes which were governed either by a *signoria* or by a republican government. If on the one hand the divisions of the Roman Church caused grave uneasiness, on the other, the spirit of expansion and of competition on the part of the maritime republics brought about the rebirth of commerce, and with it the affirmation of nationalism and independence. These facts cannot be separated from the revitalization of the vernacular.

Once the chains of medieval scholasticism were broken, all the arts came alive in Italy, and the Renaissance was born. Marvellous examples of architectural perfection were built; the vaults and walls of churches and palaces were covered with splendid frescoes. Music, too, was reborn in that surprising lyric flowering of sound called the Italian *ars nova*, a brilliant achievement of Mediterranean art. The term *ars nova*, so common in modern Italian musicology, derives from the same term used in France. There it describes the new musical technique explained in the theoretical treatises published by Johannes de Muris under the title *Ars Novae Musicae* (1319) and by Philippe de Vitry, under the title *Ars Novae notandi* (1320). The 'new art' constituted a revolution in the field of notation and was adopted by all Italian composers of note. It introduced to music the radically new practice of sub-dividing the rhythm into compound metres in opposition to the rigid schemes of the older French motet, which was still tied to allusions and symbols characteristic of medieval scholasticism.

Once the term *ars nova* is extended to the music of France as well as to that of Italy we perceive within this style two national schools which developed along different paths with increasing force. The style of the French school turned more and more towards refinement in fragmentation and in the breaking up of rhythm for the purpose of technical innovation. This music was later paralleled by flamboyant Gothic architecture. In the work of Italian composers, on the other hand, there was a pronounced striving to safeguard the expressive values of their own tradition, based on the linear quality of the melody, whose monodic character is enlivened by a vocalization full of freedom and fancy.

Italian music asserts itself on a theoretical level with the two treatises of Marchetto da Padova, the *Lucidarium in arte musicae planae* (1317) and the *Pomerium artis musicae mensuratae* (1324). Both these treatises seem old-fashioned, compared with the innovations introduced by the French theorists, and, in spite of the inevitable political dedication to Robert of Anjou, they prove the great importance for Italy of the University of Padua and of the flourishing of *ars nova* polyphony under the Scaligeri (Verona) and the Visconti (Milan). The lack of a scholastic tradition in Italy certainly did not

favour music bound to the rules of theory. Instead, contrapuntal improvisation, as it developed in the give-and-take of musical practice, was preferred,
stressing individuality and independence, as the entire period of the Italian
ars nova bears out. A useful documentation is provided by the treatise *Ars ad
Adiscendum Contrapunctum* by Paolo da Firenze (also known as 'Paulus de
Florentia' and 'Paolo Tenorista'). Antonio da Tempo of Padua wrote another
pertinent treatise in 1332, dedicated to Alberto della Scala, which forms a
compendium of poetic metre and contains many references to the polyphonic
madrigal. Also prominent in Padua were the humanist-educator Vittorino da
Feltre and the musical theorist Prosdocimus de Beldemandis who, in 1412,
criticized his contemporaries for their ignorance of Italian musical tradition
and urged them to use their own fourteenth-century system of notation
instead of following the French system.

FORMS AND COMPOSERS. Consideration of the development of fourteenth-
century poetry as part of a general literary renaissance must also take into
account the music which accompanied the merry singing of groups who
gathered to amuse themselves. One notices in this poetry a certain idyllic and
allegorical quality and, even more, the importance of speech rhythm as a
structural element which greatly assists a setting for voices. This poetry,
then, may be justly considered the ideal example of *poesia per musica*, given
the social life of the time, so well portrayed by Giovanni Boccaccio in the
Decamerone.

The development of the new craft of polyphonic music on the fringe of a
small circle of cultivated people (mostly members of the clergy, whether
organists or scholars) involved the growth of a learned art within the context
of the native popular tradition. This development was characterized by a
preference for newly-created melodies harking back to the medieval *conductus*
(see chapter 3, pp. 115–18). On to this ancient musical form were grafted
melismatic figures which surround the descriptive poetry like a musical
garland – a procedure particularly characteristic of the *madrigale* of the
fourteenth century. The *madrigale* in several stanzas was employed by
numerous masters after they had first experimented with the brisker form
of the one-stanza *ballata*.[6] The aesthetic quality of this music may be summed
up by the subtlety of its technical mastery and by its expressiveness, which
is of a particularly elegiac sweetness.

The metrical structure of the *madrigale* consists of two or three stanzas
of three lines each (tercets). The first stanza is provided with a musical
setting; subsequent stanzas are sung to the same music. A refrain of two lines
usually follows when the singing of the stanzas has been completed. The
music of this refrain (called *ritornello*) differs from that of the stanzas

6. The form of the *ballata* is explained on p. 219.

rhythmically and otherwise.[7] Of the two parts which make up the polyphonic composition, the upper is expressive in character and highly ornamented. The lower part serves as a rhythmic and harmonic support and yet maintains its own character, whether it be vocal or instrumental. As for the etymology of the word *madrigale*, many hypotheses have been proposed. The most acceptable is that which derives from the old Tuscan word *matriale* from *cantus materialis*, that is, a song to be sung for amusement and diversion and certainly not for liturgical purposes. Francesco da Barbarino alludes to the term *matrialis* and, in company with Antonio da Tempo, considers it a rustic poetic form for the people. This kind of poetry which was used early on for the music of the *ars nova* is largely of a narrative nature, containing brief passages of imagery, whether descriptive or picturesque, as well as a certain amount of moralizing allegory.

The chief poets in this genre were Alesso Donati and Franco Sacchetti, whose writings clearly reflect its popular nature. These musical settings, along with other current polyphony, flourished in the northern Veneto especially in the area between the Mincio and the Po, and, according to literary documents around 1340, brightened the court of Mastino della Scala and Alberto della Scala at Verona. The music is preserved in the Codex Vatican Rossi 215 which, although a late copy dating from around 1370, is among the oldest of the *ars nova*. Recently a missing fragment of this codex was found in the Greggiati collection of the library at Ostiglia.

The spread of *ars nova* music took place in the second half of the fourteenth century, and it is to this period that the major sources can be traced. These list numerous anonymous composers, but whereas their names can often be established, it is not so easy to date their works, for biographical information is extremely scarce. The musicians of the Florentine school were for the most part members of the clergy, whose range of activity included not only religious music but also settings of secular verse to music such as madrigals. Among these men we find the name of Giovanni da Cascia,[8] organist at the Florentine Cathedral. According to the chronicle of Filippo Villani, Giovanni da Cascia spent some time at the court of Mastino della Scala at Verona and perhaps also at that of the Visconti at Milan. His choice of texts shows a preference for sensuous love poems, for example, the madrigal *Nel bosco senza foglie*. Giovanni's competitor in Verona was Jacopo da Bologna, a prolific composer as well as author of the theoretical treatise written in the vernacular, *L'arte del biscanto misurato*. From Verona Jacopo went to Milan in the service of Luchino Visconti, as is made clear by two of his encomiastic madrigals. The texts he set to music are full of popular and allegorical themes. The madrigal

7. For examples of the *madrigale* of the fourteenth century see *HAM*, i, Nos. 49, 50, 54.
8. Also called Johannes (or Giovanni) de (or da) Florentia; for his compositions see *HAM*, i, Nos. 50, 51.

Fenice fu and the setting of Petrarch's madrigal, composed during the poet's lifetime, *Non al suo amante più Diana piacque*[9] are typical of his works.

Another competitor at Verona was Master Piero, perhaps a native of Lombardy, who preferred the use of canonic polyphony in a musical and poetic form of a highly individual nature, the *caccia* (plural: *cacce*). The literary form of the *caccia* derives from the descriptive *madrigale* but is more impressionistic in nature and is characterized by great realism. The name of this form indicates both the subject matter, which often describes vivid hunting scenes, and the technique of successive imitation (i.e. 'chasing') of the same melody by the two principal voices. Often a third part is added to serve as an instrumental tenor to accompany the upper voices.[10] The canonic procedure obviously compels repetition of both melodic and rhythmic elements: thus the alternation of cries and of onomatopoeic passages is enhanced by reiteration, and the illustrative power of the music becomes more effective. The metrical structure of the text corresponds closely to the lively rhythm of the music; long melismas and syllabic recitation alternate. In the *caccia*, as in the *madrigale*, there often appears a closing refrain, called *ritornello*, which is sometimes canonic, sometimes not. *Cacce* and canonic *madrigali* form a large portion of the extant work of Master Piero, and his *caccia*, *Con brachi assai*, is especially memorable. The text of this work was also set to music by Giovanni da Cascia. The latter's own *Per larghi prati* offers an apt description of the traditional subject matter: young Amazons, with flowing hair, lie in wait with bows and arrows. Jacopo da Bologna, too, contributed to the development of the *caccia* with his *Per sparverar* and *Oselletto selvaggio*. But the form of the *caccia* soon underwent both literary and musical changes. These hunting scenes were at times replaced by any kind of noisy action. The *caccia* of the papal singer Zaccaria, *Cacciando per gustar*, which describes a market place, includes the vendors' cries. Other examples depict scenes of great confusion, with fires and battles. These latter continued to be popular with Italian composers of the fifteenth century.

Following a brief flourishing of *ars nova* polyphony in northern Italy, Tuscany (and especially the city of Florence) became the centre of Italian musical life in the fourteenth century. In the second half of that century the influence of Florence was felt in surrounding towns such as Pistoia, as well as in Romagna and Umbria (especially the towns of Imola, Rimini and

9. See *HAM*, i, No. 49.

10. For canonic imitation in the French *chace*, see chapter 4.1, p. 155. In the French *chace* imitation applies to all three parts, whereas the independent *tenor* is characteristic of the Italian *caccia*. Concerning canonic imitation in the English 'rota', see chapter 6.1, p. 272. For an edition of the extant music see Marrocco, *Cacce*; further discussion in Handschin, *Mus. Disc.* (1949) 55 & (1951) 65; also Pirrotta, '... origine ... della caccia'. For the insertion of *cacce* into the sacred dramas of the fifteenth and sixteenth centuries, see below, p. 233.

Perugia) and, finally, in southern Italy in the zone between Teramo and Caserta. Love lyrics not only echoed from the crowded piazzas, they also entered the palaces, brightening the parties and banquets given in the spring on the open terraces and in the loggias. The dances, games and pastimes which entertained an elegant bourgeois society in its leisure moments were accompanied by the sounds of such instruments as viols, lutes, pipes, castanets, tambourines and the portative organ.

The poetic origins of love ballads written for one singer only go back to a popular tradition, observed by Boccaccio in 1348 in his *Decamerone*: these are the songs that his charming maidens sing for their own pleasure. As an example of this Tuscan tradition which was so important in the development of fourteenth-century music that it has become known as Florentine *ars nova*, we have the codex compiled in the fifteenth century which belonged to Antonio Squarcialupi, organist to the Medici family. This codex contains more than 150 pieces, which testify to a glorious musical past. It is from this codex that we know the music of Florentine composers who were contemporaries of Giovanni da Cascia, such as the priest Donato da Cascia, Ser Gherardello da Firenze (d. 1364) and Lorenzo Masini. Of the works of Ser Gherardello and Masini two lively *cacce* have been preserved, respectively, *Tosto che l'alba*[11] and *A poste messe*. In addition there are *madrigali* influenced by the northern Veneto and a small number of *ballate* for one voice, based on poems of Sacchetti and Soldanieri. The Florentine, Filippo Villani, writes of a 'Credo' by a certain Bartolo performed in a Florentine church, but no longer extant. We do have fragments of some polyphonic Masses, a 'Gloria' and an 'Agnus Dei' written by Gherardello, a 'Sanctus' by Lorenzo Masini and a 'Benedicamus Domino' by Paolo Tenorista (also known as Paolo da Firenze). All these compositions preserve the stylistic characteristics typical of the French *ars nova* of Machaut.

Instrumental music flourished along with the old tradition of the love ballad. There were plucked instruments (psalteries, harps and lutes), wind instruments (recorders, bagpipes, trumpets), and bowed instruments (rebecs), arranged in orchestral groups much as we observe them today in many fourteenth-century Sienese and Florentine frescoes. In the British Museum (Add. MS 29987) there is a manuscript containing music for Italian dances, such as the *Lamento di Tristano*, based on a set of variations, followed by an after-dance, a *rotta*; and a *saltarello*,[12] a popular dance based on rapid rhythms.

Beginning with Nicolò (or Niccolò) da Perugia, active in Florence between 1360 and 1370, the narrative literary forms of the *madrigale* and the *caccia* are no longer found in the fashionable texts by Sacchetti, and secular musical tradition seems to have veered away from this style. Love poems, couched in the form of the lyrical *ballata*, were now preferred. The form of the Italian

11. See *HAM*, i, No. 52.

12. Both the *Lamento* and the *Saltarello* are reprinted in *HAM*, i, No. 59.

ballata, not to be confused with the French *ballade*, is almost identical with that of the French *virelai*, also called *chanson balladée*.[13] The stanzas of the *ballata* are framed by a refrain called *ripresa*. The stanzas themselves consist of three parts, namely two *piedi* (singular: *piede*) plus a *volta*. Metrically, the *volta* is related to the *ripresa*, and it is sung to the same music. Using capital and small letters for the musical components (as in chapter 3, pp. 132–3), the *ballata* may be summarized as follows:

Text:	*ripresa*	*piede*	*piede*	*volta*	*ripresa*
Music:	A B	c	c	a b	A B

The chief composer of this new polyphonic form was Francesco Landini, the celebrated blind organist, born around 1325. He was a poet, singer and virtuoso, and became famous when, with his portative organ, he entertained the society of Florence at 'Il Paradiso', the country estate of Antonio degli Alberti. Landini was held in the highest esteem by such fellow citizens as Filippo Villani (his biographer), Coluccio Salutati, Sacchetti and Giovanni da Prato. When he died in 1397 he was buried in the church of San Lorenzo, where today one can admire his austere countenance and the famous organ in the relief of his tombstone. He was considered the most celebrated of the Florentine *ars nova* musicians. Landini's works include 140 *ballate* in addition to some *madrigali* and one *caccia*, most of which are to be found in two famous Florentine manuscripts, both written in the early fifteenth century though recording the treasures of Italian music of the fourteenth century.[14] The first is the Squarcialupi Codex of the Biblioteca Laurenziana (Palatino 87), the other the Panciatichi Codex of the Biblioteca Nazionale (Palatino Panciatichiano 26). Landini's great feeling for melodic aptness permeates the rhythmic and harmonic flow of the voices and is particularly effective in endowing his two-part *ballate* with their lyrical nature. His music is technically refined and sophisticated, both in the expressiveness of its vocal melismas in the upper part and for its close following of the meaning of the poetry (which, in some cases, is the composer's own text). A third part is occasionally used as an instrumental contratenor and serves as harmonic support for the composition. The *ballate*, *El mio dolce sospir* and *Gran pianto agli occhi*, with their delicate sonority and lyric expressiveness, can be considered among the most beautiful pieces of Florentine *ars nova*. In one manuscript (Faenza, Codex 117) we have Landini's version of the *ballata* for three voices, *Non avrà mai pietà*, transcribed for a keyboard instrument (perhaps a positive organ). This is one of the oldest pieces of polyphonic instrumental music to survive and contains brilliant passages of rich ornamentation.

In the last part of the fourteenth century there appeared the remarkable personality of one of Landini's followers, the organist and monk Andrea, a

13. See chapter 4.1, p. 154; also chapter 3, pp. 132–3.
14. One *ballata* and one *madrigale* are reprinted in *HAM*, i, Nos. 53–4.

member of the order of the Servants of Mary.[15] He is known through his numerous *ballate* filled with fervent didacticism. A stylistic return to the older form of the *madrigale* is noticeable in the compositions of Paolo da Firenze (see p. 215). For this reason Paolo is thought to be Florentine, but he also worked in Naples and Rome in the service of Cardinal Angelo Acciaiuoli. The work of Fra Bartolino, who probably came to Florence with other exiles from Carrara, establishes musical parallels between the *ars nova* of Florence and that of the northern Veneto. Villani informs us of Fra Bartolino's great fame for the stand he took against the Visconti by means of political and moral allusions in his compositions.

To conclude, the nearly two hundred musical examples we have of the *ars nova* of the fourteenth century are all preserved in manuscripts of a later date. So small a number is hardly adequate for a chronological assessment, particularly since there are no adequate reliable biographical data for any composer except Landini. In part the expressive power of these Italian polyphonic settings of love poetry is based on melismatic figures conceived in terms of vocal ornamentation and in part on contrasting syllabic passages of sharp rhythmic profile which follow the literary text closely. All this is indicative of the spirit of monody which, thanks to the songs of the troubadours and to the sacred *lauda* of the thirteenth century, had taken root quite naturally in the musical character of the nation.

Although this music may seem historically remote, it has an affinity with modern taste for a variety of reasons, among them rhythmic freedom and diatonic boldness. The melodic lines have an individual, yet delicate character of their own, and the total impression is one of gracefulness. Sweetly tempered as the music is, it seems vague at times, as it hovers elegantly between an ardent sensualism and realistic portrayal of man and his world, both kinds of passage usually following the text closely. With so many compositions in the fourteenth century one is aware of a confrontation between the real world and a universe seen through poetic sensitivity. At times the result strikes us as precious, but more often the music appeals by its freshness and novelty. Rhythmic vivacity is one factor, but there is also a melodic quality difficult to define. Perhaps the notion of *dulcedo* (or *dolcezza*) which appears in so many treatises on poetry and music of the period would seem a proper term for it. Certainly, the experimental and intellectual concepts of the fourteenth century and its intimate structures of sound display a surprising similarity with the strivings and timbres of certain recent music.

ASPECTS OF THE LATE ARS NOVA. In the period from the death of Francesco Landini through the first decades of the fifteenth century a revival of *ars nova* took place in southern Italy between Abruzzi and Campania, in

---

15. Often called Andrea dei Servi or Andrea de Florentia; see also p. 223.

spite of the effect of the more up-to-date developments in French music, brought about by the return of the papacy from Avignon to Rome in 1377. The French quest for rhythmic sophistication led to uncertainties in notation and, consequently, to complications in the rhythmic values. This in spite of the works of musicians like Antonello Amarotus Abbas and Filippotto, both from Caserta, and Antonio Zaccaria (or Zachara) da Teramo, whose simple style, notwithstanding the general contemporary imitation of the musical styles of France, is more characteristic of Italian music. The compositions of these three men are preserved in the Lucca-Perugia Codex (Lucca, Arch. di stato, 29), and date from the beginning of the fifteenth century. In Zaccaria Italian *dulcedo* is more prominent than French *subtilitas*. He preferred picturesque texts, drawn from the erudite genre of the fifteenth-century love lyric, texts filled with repetitions of verbal phrases and infested with Latinisms and odd expressions, satanic and cabalistic in tone. Typical is his *ballata*, *Deus deorum Pluto*. Together with Bartolomeo da Bologna he was also an innovator in his use of the parody technique in movements of the Mass derived from his *ballate*, *Fior gentil*, *Rosetta* and many others. (There can be no doubt that his secular compositions formed the basis of these movements in the parody technique. Whether all of the sacred parodies may with certainty be ascribed to Zaccaria remains still to be ascertained.)

There was another group of composers who, at times, displayed a characteristically national style, namely, Corrado da Pistoia, Giovanni da Genova (Johannes de Janua) and, especially, Matteo da Perugia, who was organist in the Cathedral of Milan from 1402 onward in the service of Cardinal Pietro Filargo. Matteo's compositions form a particularly apt illustration: some of them bear the mark of French mannerism while others are more in the Italian tradition, exhibiting a simple and linear melodic style.

To appreciate how great was the foreign influence on Italian music in the development of the late *ars nova* one has only to recall the influx of singers and chapel masters from the north who were brought to Italy after the return of the papacy to Rome. The French style made itself felt especially in the realm of religious music in the Mass and motet. The establishment of this style as an international language was aided by the simultaneous secular employment of Franco-Flemish composers by Italian princes. Representative of these musicians was the famous theorist and composer Johannes Ciconia from the diocese of Liège. Ciconia (b. *c.* 1335) travelled extensively in Italy (1358–67), visiting various cities with Cardinal Gil Albornoz.[16] He returned to his native country, but received a canonical appointment to Padua in 1403 which he held until his death in 1411. His motets are eulogistic in nature. Typical are those addressed to the famous Paduan jurist Francesco Zabarella, who later became Bishop of Florence. Other motets praise the cities of Padua

16. See Clercx, 'Sejour'; Pirrotta, *Mus. Disc.* (1949) 119; *HAM*, i, No. 55.

and Venice. Ciconia made Italy his second home and there came under the influence of the local *ars nova* tradition. So great was this influence that under him the old tradition of the Italian *madrigale* bloomed again in his *Una pantera in compagnia di Marte* (written in honour of the city of Lucca) and that of the *ballata*, in *Con lagreme [lagrime] bagnandome il viso*, a lament for the death, in 1406, of Francesco Novello, ruler of Padua.[17] Ciconia was one representative link in a succession of northerners who left their imprint on the Italian musical scene. The French influence was continued by such emigrés as Jean de Sarto, Jean de Limbourg and Jean Brasart who, in turn, were succeeded by a new generation of musicians and singers from the diocese of Cambrai under the leadership of Dufay. Later composers from across the Alps included Isaac, Josquin and Lassus. For over a quarter of a century these men went to Italy to add to their own mastery of polyphony new stylistic facets which they drew from the local popular tradition.

The continuation of the traditional *lauda*, during the fourteenth century and into the first half of the fifteenth, was another important aspect of *ars nova* music. These spiritual texts were often adapted to secular settings, proof of the effective and widespread intermingling of music and poetry. Religious poetry did not necessarily have its own musical setting and the use of the most famous pieces of secular polyphonic music for religious texts was a frequent practice. Compositions by Giovanni da Cascia, Landini and Nicolò del Proposto da Perugia contributed to these spiritual *contrafacta*. Jacopo da Bologna's *lauda, Nel mio parlar di questa donn' eterna doname Cristo grazia sempiterna* is a single example. It confirms the ease with which *lauda* singers could adapt their sacred texts to the musical taste of the time.

This intermingling of religious and secular art is an old musical practice, to be found from the Middle Ages to the Renaissance, but especially in the *lauda* of the fourteenth and fifteenth centuries. During this period there was no stylistic dichotomy between the two spheres, a condition which becomes clear to anyone who examines either music of the fourteenth century adapted to sacred texts (sacred *contrafacta*) or the *lauda* preserved in sources from the first half of the fifteenth century. Their structure still uses certain stylistic characteristics of the *ars nova*, but vocal ornamentation is much less elaborate in contrast to the expressive individualism so fashionable with all Tuscan composers in the fourteenth century. This fashion was already beginning to wane at the end of the century, however, and was to disappear completely during the succeeding epoch. This tendency towards more simplicity can be seen in numerous pieces in the two Florentine manuscripts mentioned earlier, namely, the Squarcialupi and Panciatichiano Codices. In these compositions two kinds of passages are prominent: those which are syllabic to a

17. The works of Ciconia are discussed in detail in Clercx, *Ciconia*, Vol. i. They are reprinted in Vol. ii as follows: motets for Zabarella, pp. 160, 187; for Padua and Venice pp. 164, 183; *madrigale* and *ballata*, pp. 52, 63.

degree and the more melismatic. In the former, the two parts move at comparable speeds, with occasionally syncopated rhythms. In the latter, the
skeletal points of the melody are broken up into ornamental notes, reminiscent
of the lyrical effusion which one often meets in earlier Italian lyrics. These
various characteristics are already evident in the works of several composers
preserved in the Squarcialupi Codex, notably those of Andrea de Florentia
(often identified with Andrea dei Servi) and of two Augustinian monks,
Egidio and Guglielmo di Francia.[18] Here we find melodic figures sequentially
repeated and also brief imitation between the parts. These techniques are
also used in an anonymous *ballata* fragment, *Amor amaro* (Siena, State
Archives), which is otherwise quite removed from the tradition of secular
music, in its emphasis on the tormented eroticism of a genre of poetry based
on the theme of the *lamento* or the *disperate* sung by a rejected lover. The same
is true of a *ballata* fragment, *Mercé, o morte* (Pistoia, Bibl. Capitolare Duomo),
a dialogue sad in tone and dramatic in the repartee between the two voices.
In many compositions by Antonio Zaccaria (see p. 221) the stylistic development has already veered away from the tradition of Florentine vocal music
of the past. The characteristic chordal handling of the parts, even if the treatment of rhythm is different from the usual polyphonic technique of *ars nova*
music, is proof that in the total structure of the music, harmony is becoming
increasingly important. This tendency continues both in the secular polyphony and the *laude* of the fifteenth century. It is especially evident in the
laude of a Venetian manuscript (Bibl. Marciana IX 145), dating from the first
half of the century. Here there are passages of syncopation and dissonance,
brief melismatic sections and elements remaining from the *ars nova*. These
stylistic ingredients were imposed on the simultaneous and parallel handling
of the parts according to the rules of harmonic counterpoint. A typical instance was the continued use of the *ars nova* cadence, erroneously attributed
to Landini, since it was first used by the French, with its descent from the
tonic to the lower third and its resolution back to the tonic. This standard
formula can also be found in such foreign masters as Dunstable and Dufay
and after *c.* 1450 in the Montecassino Codex and many others.

   The change in musical notation which took place in the course of the
fifteenth century was of great historical importance. In the beginning, various
rhythmic complexities were dealt with by a system of 'colouration', namely,
the distinction between black notes and red notes, which could be either
hollow or full (in some cases only half full). But during the middle of the
century a process of standardization and simplification took place, involving,
among other features, the gradual abandonment of red colouration for black.
Longer note values were indicated by white notes, shorter ones by black
notes, a principle which is after all still in force today. Even so, the transition

18. The works of these three composers are transcribed in Wolf, *Squarcialupi*, p. 335–59 and 319–21.

from one system of notation to another was slow and its timing differed according to locality. As a result the complexities of notation of late *ars nova*, inevitable in a transitional age with many vagaries of taste and complexities in the rhythm of the music itself, contributed to difficulties of transcribing this music for later generations, and both in Italy and France many of the original sources were lost. Important manuscript collections were often neglected and broken up, since their sole commercial value resided in the parchment material on which they were written. These parchments, in fact, were often re-used for binding archival and legal data. This is one of the several reasons for the scarcity of musical documents for the *ars nova*. The fortunate re-discovery of parchment fragments has left us a rare and precious heritage, one which helps to illuminate so important a period in the musical history of the early part of the fifteenth century in Italy.

THE FIFTEENTH CENTURY

OLTREMONTANI[19] AT THE RENAISSANCE COURTS. The continuation of the cultural exchange between the Franco-Flemish region of Flanders, then part of the Duchy of Burgundy, and the courts of the Italian Renaissance was of primary importance in musical development. The steady immigration throughout the fifteenth century of singers and masters of the Franco-Flemish school had an enormous influence on the development of polyphony in Italy. In view of their great technical experience these musicians were paid large sums of money by the Italian princes who were eager patrons of the arts and equally eager to have their own musical chapels, often quarrelling amongst themselves for the best available foreign talent. Consequently music in Italy was subject to a constant exchange between the elaborate polyphonic crafts-manship of the composers from beyond the Alps, the *oltre-montani*, and the simplicity of its own popular tradition, with its characteristic types of vocal melody. The process of stylistic assimilation was mutual, but fruitful above all for the foreign composers who often acquired new tastes and new expressive sensibilities.

Without minimizing the importance of the earlier polyphonic movement under the leadership of the Englishman John Dunstable, the most important name of the century is to be found among the musicians of the school of Cambrai, that of Guillaume Dufay (b. 1390–1400, d. 1474). He resided, as we have seen,[20] at Rimini and Pesaro, at Rome and Florence. Mention has been made of his setting of an Italian text by Petrarch, and of his Latin motet for Florence. Two other motets in honour of that city are *Salve flos Tuscae*

19. *Oltremontani*, literally 'from beyond the mountains', in this case, northern composers from beyond the Alps.

20. See chapter 4.1, concerning his biography, pp. 162–4; his setting of Petrarch, p. 165; his motets for the pope and the consecration of the cathedral of Florence, pp. 165–6.

gentis and *Mirandas parit haec urbs Florentina puellas*, both inspired by the melodic vocal tradition of Florentine *ars nova*.

The example of Dufay's productive stay in Italy was followed by other foreign composers. In the important centre of Milan the court chapel of the Sforzas dispensed patronage to a number of Franco-Flemish and German musicians, among them Gaspar van Weerbecke, who made the journey to Burgundy and Flanders several times between 1472 and 1498 to engage singers for the ducal chapel. The registers at the court boast such names as Josquin des Prez, Loyset Compère, Johannes Martini and Alexander Agricola. The situation at the cathedral was different, for there the chapel consisted of native singers. This was no doubt the result of the appointment of an Italian as *maestro di cappella*, namely, Franchino Gafori[21] who presided over the chapel from 1484 until his death in 1522. The papal court at Rome, on the other hand, vied with the court of Milan as a loadstone and attracted, besides Dufay, Gaspar van Weerbecke and Josquin at certain stages of their careers.

The court of the Dukes of Este at Ferrara was famous for its patronage in music as well as the other arts. Duke Ercole's musical talent was highly praised, as was that of his family, his wife, Eleanor of Aragon, his brother, Cardinal Ippolito, and his children Alfonso and Isabella (who married Francesco Gonzaga). This court attracted many Franco-Flemish musicians, among them Johannes Martini, who transferred there from Milan in 1475, and the great Obrecht, who came for a short period in 1487 from distant Bruges and returned to Ferrara in the service of the Duke in 1504, to die there in the following year. At the court of Urbino Duke Federico da Montefeltro was another great patron of the arts. Between 1444 and 1481 he collected an extensive humanistic library and gathered together the best musicians for his chapel. His love for art then passed on to his son and successor, Guidobaldo, who married Elisabetta Gonzaga of Mantua.

The many-sided personality of the philosopher Marsilio Ficino (1433–99) introduced musical humanism into the neo-platonic conversations of the Florentine Academy at Careggi, near Florence. Ficino's interest in music was not only a philosophical concern that viewed music as the imitation of the harmony of the spheres; he was also an excellent singer and frequently accompanied himself on his lyre. His philosophy stresses the fact that poetry is enhanced by musical accompaniment, for music was a great religious and moral force. Other members of the Academy, which was sponsored by Lorenzo de' Medici, were: the philosopher Pico della Mirandola, also a singer who, with his vast erudition, defended the theories in praise of music; Domenico Benivieni, noted for his improvisation and performance on several instruments; and Angelo Poliziano who, in his attempts to further literary humanism, was able to bring about the supremacy of poetry written in the

21. Or Gafurio or Gafurius; see p. 228 about his musical treatises.

vernacular rather than Latin. There are frequent references to music in his poems, which were based on pastoral and mythological themes, as well as references to the various instruments used by the ancients (bagpipes, lyre, recorder, cymbals). His drama *Orfeo*, performed in Mantua in 1471 for the visit of Galeazzo Sforza and Bona di Savoia, contained various scenes with music. (The score, which is unfortunately lost, has been erroneously attributed to a certain Germi.) Again in Florence, the all-encompassing spirit of Leon Battista Alberti is characteristic of the unity of the arts during the neo-platonic assemblies at Careggi, particularly his emphasis on the fact that music, like architecture, has a planned structure. In addition the Medici court included various *oltremontani* musicians such as Johannes Stockhem (or Stokhem), Pietrapin, Johannes Ghiselin and Alexander Agricola.

Heinrich Isaac, although dubbed *Arrigo Tedesco*[22], can be considered a Florentine by election, since he spent a large part of his career in Florence. He was brought from Flanders by Lorenzo de' Medici (the Magnificent) about 1484, to hold an important position at court, where he followed the local taste for polyphonic music. In addition to the prince's characteristic carnival songs, he set to music Lorenzo's *canzone, Un di lieto giamai non ebbi amor*. Isaac praises his newly adopted country (and particularly the beautiful women of Florence) in the famous *Canzone delle Dee* (*Song of the Goddesses*, first line, *Ne più bella di queste*). With Poliziano he paid homage to the great prince and protector of the arts in his motet, *Quis dabit capiti meo aquam*, a lament written for the funeral of Lorenzo (1492). Isaac's well-known instrumental *canzone, Palle, palle*, was written for the election of his pupil Giovanni de' Medici to the papacy, and to thank the great family he had served for so long. A piece written in memory of Serafino Aquilano (or dall' Aquila), who died in 1500, is dramatically conceived in the dialogue *Morte che fai?*, based on a *strambotto* by the dead poet.[23]

In addition to such centres of patronage as Florence, Milan and Rome, there were many others, from Siena in the north to Naples in the south. But the importance of Rome increased steadily, particularly under the papacy of Sixtus IV, who built the famous chapel that bears his name. It was begun by the most eminent architects, sculptors and painters available. The musicians who worked there, both foreign and Italian, were equally brilliant. They included Weerbecke, de Orto, Josquin, Guglielmo Guarneri and Cristoforo Roselli.

Even Josquin des Prez, like Dufay and Isaac, must be included in the number of foreign musicians who became Italians by choice, after having lived for many years in Italy. Josquin came to Milan in 1459 where he is listed as a singer at the cathedral until 1472. He then joined the chapel of

22. Concerning Isaac's position in the history of German music see chapter 7, pp. 347–8.

23. The works of Isaac's referred to in this paragraph are reprinted in *DTO*, xiv, part i, pp. 44, 40, 45, 98; Bridgman, *Annales Musicologiques* (1953) 263.

Galeazzo Maria Sforza, Duke of Milan. After the duke's death in 1476 he entered the service of his brother, Ascanio Sforza, who became a cardinal in 1484. Altogether he lived in Italy for about half a century. His continued residence is suggested by documented performances of his works at the papal chapel at Rome and at the Este court at Ferrara until 1499. Some time after that Josquin went to France and eventually settled in his native Burgundy, where he died at Condé in 1521 (see chapter 4.3, pp. 198–208).

The technique acquired during his Milanese apprenticeship contributed to the clarification of Josquin's polyphonic writing, saving his works from the extravagances of Flemish counterpoint. In spite of his mastery of polyphonic complexities Josquin always shows a high sensitivity to the intelligibility of the words and the moods expressed by the text. Working in close collaboration with such Italian poet-musicians as Serafino d'Aquilano, mentioned earlier, he was able to clear the way that was to lead to the stylistic formation of the early madrigal by Willaert and Arcadelt. During the Renaissance musicians were usually paid only in their capacities as singers, a practice that applied to composers even as noteworthy as Josquin. In fact in two of his *frottole* (*El grillo è buon cantore* and *In te Domine speravi*),[24] he alluded to the scanty payment made by his employer, Cardinal Ascanio.

An important place must also be given to the theorists teaching at Italian universities. To the traditional ideas of medieval scholasticism they joined those of humanism. But they also contributed to the formation of new ideas about music by means of their debates and discussions. It is a well-known fact of Renaissance history that Italian courtiers included music frequently in their recorded conversations and that, in addition, many resident foreigners reflected on the nature and theory of music. The fame of the Englishman John Hothby won for him a teaching career at San Martino in Lucca, which lasted from 1468 to 1486. During this period he published the two treatises *Calliopea legale* and *Dialogus in arte musica*. Johannes Tinctoris, of Franco-Flemish background, was his equal. He was cantor at the chapel of King Ferdinand in Naples from 1474 to 1495 and was entrusted with the musical education of the king's daughters. The earliest dictionary of music is Tinctoris's *Terminorum musicae diffinitorum*, dedicated to his pupil Beatrice of Aragon. Of his twelve theoretical works only the *Liber de arte contrapuncti* treats the polyphony of the *oltremontani* as a separate current from the characteristically popular Italian music. Among native Italian theorists those at the University of Padua were important, as was Ugolino da Orvieto, who had been dean at the Cathedral of Orvieto and in 1440 became dean at the Cathedral of Ferrara. While his *Declaratio musicae disciplinae* continues in the tradition of Boethius, he distinguishes between musical theory and the performance of music. In so doing he establishes the fundamental rules of

24. *HAM*, i, No. 95b.

counterpoint and applies the problems of *musica ficta* to the performance of music. The doctor and astrologer Giorgio Anselmi (born at Parma before 1386), who taught at several north Italian universities including Parma, discusses in his *De musica* (1434) the chromatic division of the scale.

But at the end of the fifteenth century the new ideas on contemporary music written in the popular style, and therefore typically Italian, began to dominate the older ideas of music coming from the tradition of scholasticism. In the treatises of the Florentine Pietro Aron or Aaron (born around 1480) the distinctions between singers and instrumentalists are established. The changes brought about in the harmonic relationships by the beginnings of chromaticism in the new sixteenth-century madrigal are also made clear. But the publication in 1482 of Bartolomeo Ramos de Pareja's *Musica practica* provoked numerous responses from theorists who did not agree with the revolutionary ideas of this Spaniard who had come from Salamanca to the University of Bologna. The conservative Italian theorists were thoroughly shaken by the extreme, surprisingly modern, ideas of Ramos, especially those concerning the substitution of the octave for the Guidonian hexachord and the use of chromaticism with the sub-division of the diatonic scale into twelve equidistant semitones. While Ramos attacked everyone from Pythagoras to Boethius, and his contemporary Hothby as well, a colleague from Bologna, Nicola Burzio, defended the theorists and composers in his work, *Musices opusculum*. In his turn Ramos was admirably defended in 1491 by one of his students, Giovanni Spataro in *Honesta defensio*. The quarrel even extended to Franchino Gafori who held the chair of music at the University of Milan and was the most famous teacher among the Italian theorists of the time. Not only did he compose pieces of religious polyphony of great originality, in the Franco-Flemish style, but his numerous treatises are important for the way in which they deal with the new musical problems. Gafori aired these problems in *Practica musicae* (1496) in connection with the daring theories developed by Ramos. Here he defended the traditional theories of music, although in other treatises Gafori made no reference to any controversy. In the humanistic circle at the court of Lodovico il Moro, Gafori was able to discuss problems of theory and performance with Leonardo da Vinci, who alluded to them many times both in his discussions of painting and his dream of the unity of the arts. In the same way the Florentine monk, Luca Pacioli, maintained in *De divina proportione* (1498) that according to the laws of the universe music must be placed with the other arts.

SECULAR SONGS AND SACRED CONTRAFACTA. In spite of the religious and courtly tone of the music played in the chapels of Italy as a result of the predominance of northern polyphony, the basic characteristics of the Italian vocal tradition of secular poetry set to music continued to derive from popular forms. The tradition survived, though less obviously, during the second half of the fifteenth century when *ars nova* was on the decline. Very few names emerge from this continuous tradition of Italian secular music which was despised by the masters of polyphony at the chapels. Indeed almost all the composers remain anonymous, and the number of volumes containing their music is small, which may be attributed, among other reasons, to the changes in musical notation. (See p. 224.)

In spite of the paucity of sources for lyrics, it is possible to make a few observations. This music, inspired by popular forms, had its own melodic language and displayed linear clarity within the harmonic texture. It was characterized by a predilection for the solo voice and was, therefore, homophonic; it was also capable of spontaneous and free vocal improvisation, often devised to show off the virtuosity of the performer. Usually the poets themselves composed the music for their verses, but at times it was left to the singer, while the lute provided the customary accompaniment. The numerous historical chronicles of the age recount that improvisation, in singing and in playing, was the custom, rather than performance from written music. This custom, naturally, favoured the extemporaneous creation of music for the poetic texts. Because it was often put together rather rapidly, and because of the difficulty of writing it down, copies were not often made. On the other hand the poets and scribes intent on preserving the poems written in the vernacular did not fail to copy the texts in the various collections of anonymous fifteenth-century poetry. Moreover, the music often sung in the piazzas as entertainment for large gatherings and in the Renaissance courts was not considered a fit subject for scholarly discussion; it enjoyed a momentary vogue and was valued mainly for the pleasure it brought, or as an accompaniment for poetry. One must also remember the considerable expense that was incurred in the lavish illustrations of the religious collections of polyphonic music, made on parchment. That secular music was considered less important was an attitude which may be gathered from various anthologies of polyphonic music, such as two manuscripts at Bologna and one at Venice[25] where we occasionally find bits and pieces of *laude* and *strambotti*, but only in the blank spaces between Mass and Latin motet parts, or in the margins of the manuscripts. The lack, then, of extant music, due to a variety of reasons, was bound to lead to its relative neglect in the history of music.

The evolution of the secular forms of vocal music in the various parts of Italy was gradual, due in part to the transformation of the *ballata* into a more typically Italian form varying from region to region. This development is parallel to that of language and the progression which led to the pre-eminence of the vernacular over the humanistic Latin of the academies. As early as the first half of the fifteenth century the *strambotti* and *canzonette* of Leonardo Giustiniani (1388–1446) lead the way to the work done later by

25. Bologna, Conservatorio G.B.Martini, Q. 15 (*olim* Lic. Mus. 37) Bologna, Bibl. Univ. 2216; Venice, Bibl. Marciana, Ital. ix, 145.

Tuscan poets from Poliziano to Lorenzo the Magnificent. At first Sicily and Naples and later the Veneto and Tuscany were important centres for the cult of popular poetry and for the performance of *strambotti* (see p. 235). It is thus not surprising that Giustiniani, whose poems were written for the people and not for the courts, should stand out from the humanists for his talents as poet and musician. According to Bembo, who himself sang and interpreted Giustiniani's music, the compositions could be used for any poetic text which was rhythmically similar to the original, even religious music such as the *lauda*. It was not until his old age that Giustiniani began to compose religious works, encouraged to do so by his brother, a Venetian patriarch.

In the fifteenth century the dual function of music as a carrier of both secular and religious texts had the result that sometimes the secular music of *strambotti* was used for religious texts, especially for the *laude*, thus giving us a means of locating further examples of the poorly documented repertoire of that century. In its use of secular music the Church preserved the original setting, where polyphonic or monodic, and continued this practice as late as the seventeenth century. We are therefore able to recover popular pieces which would otherwise have been lost, mainly from the period 1450 to 1480. In fact, the first lines of secular poems whose settings had been used for *laude* are often indicated in editions dating from about 1480–1510, along with the instruction that they are to be sung in the manner of *strambotti*; the bottom of the page often carries the rubric *cantasi come gli strambotti*. This transfer of music from one text to another, often called 'parody' or '*contrafactum*' may be studied in such instances as Giustiniani's lyric, *Mercé te chiamo o dolce anima mia*, which also served the *lauda*, *Mercé te chiamo Vergine Maria*. Other material is provided by various versions of early fifteenth-century settings, notably, *Con desiderio vo cercando*, originally sung to a secular tune, *La Vita della sgalera*.[26] In a study of subsequent versions of the same lyric, changes of style are noticeable, particularly a development away from the rhythmic fragmentation and melodic decoration characteristic of the *ars nova* towards a harmonic style more typical of Italian music in the fifteenth century.[27]

Another method of recovering lost Italian popular tunes is to examine the re-workings of these melodies in polyphonic compositions by Franco-Flemish composers at the beginning of the century. The *lauda*, *O diva stella, o vergine Maria*, which derived from a well-known secular lyric by Giustiniani, *O rosa bella, o dolce anima mia*, set to music by Dunstable, Ciconia, and others, is a good example.[28] *O rosa bella* also appears as a *cantus firmus* in several Masses; other popular melodies, having served as models for *laude*, may also be

---

26. For *Mercè te chiamo* and *Con desiderio* see Ghisi, 'Strambotti', pp. 57 ff. and 52 ff.

27. Examples can be found in manuscripts at Bologna, Florence, Madrid, Montecassino, Paris, Perugia etc. See Ghisi, 'Strambotti', pp. 68–78.

28. See Ghisi, 'Strambotti', p. 74; *HAM*, i, No. 61; *NOHM*, iii, 128, 153.

recovered from Masses: *Humil madonna non mi abbandonare*, derived from *Gentil madonna non mi abbandonare*, is used in the Mass *Gentil Madonna*; *Aggio visto il cieco mondo* from *Aggio visto lo mappamundo*, is used in the Mass *Ayo [Aggio] visto*.[29]

In spite of their great contemporary popularity, few examples of the crude dance songs which were sung for the May Day festivals (*Calendimaggio*), as accompaniment for the attendant masquerades, have come down to us. There are two exceptions: *Era di maggio* and *Maggio valente*.[30] Lorenzo the Magnificent tried to raise this popular poetry to an art form by experimenting with various metres and with new and various kinds of music. He wrote his first carnival song around 1480, about *bericuocolai* (pastry vendors), and gave it to Heinrich Isaac, his court musician, to set to music. On the one hand Lorenzo satirized certain traditional pastimes and classes of people (bakers, small shopkeepers, the poor begging for alms); on the other hand he was not averse to extolling the passing pleasures of life, as, for instance, in his *Trionfo di Bacco e d'Arianna*. In addition to Lorenzo there were also his imitators and such contemporary poets as J. da Bientina, Giovanni (called il Giuggiola), G. B. dell' Ottonaio; and, after Lorenzo's death, Giambullari, Lasca and Varchi. Their carnival songs, usually set to music, deal with local figures and the artisans of Florence. They describe the emblems and tools of various craftsmen such as tailors, belt-makers, brick-layers, coopers, painters and other comic or controversial figures. The *Trionfi* and *Carri* were secular masquerades meant to please the eye with their splendour; they dealt with mythological allegories or historical epics. Examples are the triumphs *Dea Minerva*, *Pace* and *Tre Parche*, as well as *Paolo Emilio*, dealing with the trophies of war. One should also mention the grandiose and ornate *Carri* for the *Quattro complessioni* and the *Quattro tempi dell'anno*, created for the glorification of the Medici. During the rule of Piero Soderini (1502–12) tribute was paid to the Medici family, then in exile, by the famous and exceedingly macabre *Carro della morte*, designed by the painter Piero di Cosimo. But with the return to power in 1511 of Lorenzo's sons Giovanni and Giuliano, the Florentines had their carnival once again. The return of the carnival brought with it the return of carnival songs, such as Machiavelli's *Diavoli*, as well as new triumphs. These are described by Vasari in his life of Jacopo Pontormo, and include those of the companies of the *Diamante* and the *Broncone*, the latter devised by the historian Jacopo Nardi and celebrated in the pageant of the *Sette trionfi del secolo d'oro*.

The settings of the early carnival songs maintained the tradition for three parts, as had been done in dance songs. Following the characteristics of local

29. See Ghisi, 'Strambotti', pp. 61 f.; for a comprehensive survey of the *lauda*, including a reprint of over 90 pieces, see Jeppesen, *Laude*.

30. Florence, Bibl. Naz., Cod. Magl. xix, 108.

popular polyphony, these settings were at times serious and slow, at times in a care-free ternary rhythm. Most of the music is the work of the Florentine organist Bartolomeo and of other local composers who have remained anonymous. A few names, however, have come down to us: Isaac's setting of Lorenzo's *bericuocolai* is lost but his *Canzone delle Dee*, in praise of Florence, is extant;[31] Agricola composed Lorenzo's *Canto de' facitori d'olio* for four parts; and Coppinus, previously in the employ of the Sforzas, provided a *Canzona di naviganti* and a *Canzona dei giudei*.

Parodies of the soldiers of fortune employed in the imperial armies enliven many of the carnival songs. The typical soldier was an expert at handling many weapons (lances, halberds), an excellent performer on many instruments (rebecs, trombones) and in addition a care-free toper. He figured as the protagonist of drinking songs (*vinate*) and of the *Todesche* (or *Tedesche*) characterized by rough vernacular texts and a musical similarity to the later *villanelle alla napoletana* (to which genre Lassus was to contribute).

Immediately following Lorenzo's death, democratic monasticism under the leadership of Savonarola reigned in Florence. Epicureanism was replaced by a carnival held in the name of Christ. Corruption was threatened by the sinister strains of the 'Triumph of the Sieve', for the sinners were to be winnowed from the just. During the carnivals of 1497–8 the famous 'Bonfires of Vanity' included the burning of musical instruments and 'books of lascivious music', destruction which only served to increase the gaps in our knowledge of secular music. On the other hand, Savonarola, who aimed at a reform of the lewd and frivolous poetry, unwittingly contributed to the preservation of some songs. Determined as he was to make the *laude spirituali* the songs of the people, he required them to be sung to the melodies of the most famous of Lorenzo's carnival songs and others that were even more lascivious. We have already discussed this procedure of transfer, variously called *travestimento spirituale*, 'sacred parody' or *contrafactum*, and as a result we possess several carnival songs in their original versions. It is this practice which explains how Lorenzo's *lauda*, *O maligno e duro core*, came to be sung to the carnival song of the *Profumieri* and how the *lauda*, *Gesú, mio dolce Gesú*, was sung to the music of the song of the *Spazzacamini*.[32] Similarly, the original music for the song of the *Ferravecchi* and for the song of the *Bardoccio* is extant in the form of religious versions to be found in the *Laude libro primo*, printed by Petrucci in 1508 and preserved in the Biblioteca Colombina at Seville.

The changes in the system of musical notation and in the style of Italian secular polyphony which occurred around the middle of the century were

31. *DTO*, xiv, part i, p. 40; see also Isaac's May Day song, p. 41.
32. S. Razzi, *Libro Primo delle Laudi*, 1563; Florenz, Bibl. Naz. Cod. Magl. xix, 141; Bibl. Naz. Cod. Pan. 26; Bibl. Naz., Cod. Banco Rari 62.

now, for all practical purposes, complete. Music had shifted from an individual art of sophisticated sensitivity, which was characteristic of the period immediately following the *ars nova*, to a regional art of the Renaissance courts where it was adapted to the spiritual needs of the people, as cared for by the church. Once Italian polyphony had shed its archaic dissonances, a simple and linear vocal style emerged which followed the poetic text syllabically. In doing so it displayed a harmonic orientation which pointed forward to the homophony of early opera; it also conformed to practical necessities in that the music was intended to be sung by people out of doors. Moreover, the religious *lauda*, whether polyphonic or monophonic, was also inserted into performances of the *sacra rappresentazione*, the religious drama of the period. Sometimes these musical interludes consisted of polyphonic *laude* composed for sacred texts. But there are also many instances of secular music disguised as *lauda spirituale*. Whatever its origin, the musical punctuations of *laude* in these sacred dramas are far from casual. In the works of Feo Belcari (*Annunciazione, Abramo e Isaaco*) the use of the *lauda* ushers in the climactic finale, intended to induce catharsis, when the gates of Heaven open before the eyes of the enthralled spectators and hymns of rejoicing are sung, such as *Laudate il sommo Dio* and *Chi serve Dio con purità del core*. In the works of Castellano Castellani praises are sung to the apostle in the sacred drama *San Tommaso*; in *Santa Eufrasia, O Maria del ciel regina* is sung; and in *Sant'Onofrio* the angels themselves sing hymns. In *San Giovanni e Paolo*, by Lorenzo the Magnificent, the *lauda* and its intense praise of God is used with great power to arouse the religious fervour of the audience. Some hundred literary texts of such works (standing somewhere between drama, pageant and oratorio) have come down to us, some attributed to specific authors, as in the examples cited above, others anonymous. Not all the instances of musical intervention are occasioned by serious turns in the religious action. There are also light and lively episodes, and at times we come across instrumental and vocal *cacce* filled with the echoes of hunting horns and the barking of dogs as in the *Santa Margherita* and *Santa Uliva*. *Santa Margherita* also contains the secular song *O vaghe montanine pastorelle*, which has been transformed into the *lauda, O vaghe di Gesù, o verginelle*. In *Santa Uliva* there are four symbolic figures dressed in white, barefoot, wearing masks of the dead, who sing *O fallaci desiri, o vani pensieri*. *Santa Uliva* (1525) with its thirteen intermezzi and wealth of musical illustrations is altogether reminiscent of the secular *intermedi* which graced the festivities of the Medici court. Thus the music of the *sacre rappresentazione* is linked to a tradition which extends from Corteccia's music for the wedding festivals of 1539 to that of Corteccia's pupil Luca Bati for an *Esaltazione della croce* of 1589. And with that latter date we are extremely close, both in chronological and stylistic terms, to the birth of opera.

THE SIXTEENTH CENTURY

FROTTOLA AND MADRIGAL. Secular popular music, in the last decades of the fifteenth century, played an important role at the courts of northern Italy. Based on the practice of improvisation, both in regard to the verse and the musical setting, the latter relied to a large extent on standard melodic patterns. Among the cultivated poets who provided texts were Francesco Galeota, Benedetto Gareth (Cariteo), Bernardo Accolti, Francesco Cei and Serafino Aquilano. Besides the improvised lyrical forms there was also the genre of the dance song called *ballo* sometimes performed by voices, sometimes by instruments, and at other times in combinations of both. These *balli* were characterized by an element of lively worldliness and were important in the development of polyphony in the more international form of the *bassadanza*, heavily tinged by the court ceremonies of France and Spain, though sharing in the origins of the Italian tradition. The choreography for these dance pieces was developed at the Aragonese (i.e. Spanish) court at Naples, the Sforza court at Milan and last, but not least, at the French orientated court of Lorenzo the Magnificent, who himself wrote two *bassedanze*, *Venus* and *Lauro*. There are descriptions of the musical dance forms of the period in several treatises: *L'Arte della danza* (1455) by Antonio Cornazano; *De arte saltandi* by Domenico da Piacenza (active at Ferrara), dedicated to Ippolito Sforza; and *De practica seu arte tripudii* (1463) either by Guglielmo Ebreo da Pesaro or Giovanni Ambrogio (perhaps one and the same person). The very few musical sources which have so far come to light contain *balli* for four voices, such as *Partita crudele*, *Tentalora*, *Fortuna d'un gran tempo*, and *Rotibouilli gioioso*.

It is from this period of the regional and popular music of the late fifteenth century that the art of the *frottola* derives. The growth of this form is well documented in literary sources, but we have little of the music, for apparently it was not copied down. When moveable musical type was invented, however, a large enough market developed to make the printing of music economically feasible. Between the years 1504 and 1514 Ottaviano Petrucci published in Venice and in nearby Fossombrone no less than eleven books of *frottole*. These books are collections of the best music that had been written up to that time and contain many pieces not found in the manuscript collections dating from the end of the fifteenth century. Petrucci was soon followed in Rome by Andrea Antico and by other music printers in Venice and Florence. The *frottola* was popular in Milan, Venice, Ferrara and Urbino, but the most important centre was Mantua, because of the great interest in music of Isabella d'Este and her husband Francesco Gonzaga. A new generation of aristocratic poets who wrote for their own amusement was beginning to replace the writers of extemporaneous verses. Typical of these were Niccolò da Coreggio, Veronica Gambara, Vincenzo Calmeta, Antonio Tebaldeo and Panfilo Sasso (or Sassi). At the same time the masters of musical improvisation were being replaced by professional musicians. Most famous at the court of Mantua was Bartolomeo Tromboncino from Verona, who moved to the court of Ferrara in 1513.[33]

Verona also supplied Marchetto Cara (who worked for the Gonzagas as early as 1495), Michele Pesenti, Giovanni Brocco and Antonio Rossetto. Other important musicians were: Filippo and Rossino from Mantua; Niccolò Pifaro, Antonio Stringari and G. B. Zesso from Padua; Francesco D'Ana, organist at St Mark's (1490–1503) and Filippo di Lurano from Venice; Antonio Caprioli from Brescia and Giacomo Fogliano from Modena. The great interest in the *frottola* is reflected in the works of foreign musicians as well: Josquin, Compère and Carpentras have all left examples of this form.

The poetic form of the *barzelletta* or *frottola* (from *frocta*, a miscellany of witty sayings or jokes) derives from the *ballata*, with an opening refrain and stanzas composed of lines of eight syllables. At some point earlier in the fifteenth century there was added to this genre the *strambotto*, a lyric of eight hendecasyllabic lines with the rhyme-scheme ab-ab-ab-cc. Some old-fashioned types of lyric reappear in Petrucci's *Sixth Book of* Frottole (1506) as, for example, *Aime sospiri*. But in the vocal decoration there is no longer any trace of the style of the *ars nova*, rather a free treatment of the vocal line, as frequently encountered in Petrucci's instrumental transcriptions for lute.

In Petrucci's collections of the *frottola* there are diverse types: the *oda*, composed of four verses without a refrain, rhymed abbc-cdde-effg; the *capitolo*, composed of three-line stanzas of hendecasyllabic lines linked together in the rhyme scheme aba-bcb-cdc; the *sonnetto* of long literary tradition and the *canzone* which, because of its great structural and metrical freedom, may be taken as a forerunner of the madrigal. There is an example of the polyphonic *villota*, a form of no fixed metre which ends in nonsense rhymes and often attempts to imitate various instruments (examples: *falilelá*, *tandadera*, *dirindella*, *stronche*) or simply literary assonances based on syllabic repetition at times exactly like musical onomatopoeia. The texts of the *villota* are in Venetian dialect, contain archaic forms, and are often filled with the jargon of thieves and many lascivious puns. The polyphonic *villota* derives from melodies, vocal solos or dances, based on the popular non-learned tradition of the fifteenth century. At the beginning of the sixteenth century these melodies became part and parcel of polyphonic pieces functioning as the tenor part of an imitative texture. Similar to the *frottola* and the *villota* in tone and content are the rather strange *incatenature* (chain songs) or quodlibets which were composed of *incipits* or longer quotations of popular lyrics, using both text and tune of the original. The result is a collection of the best Italian popular art, intended as pure entertainment. Famous among

33. For examples of *frottole*, printed by Petrucci, including some of Tromboncino, see Schwarz, *Petrucci*; also *HAM*, i, No. 95.

these quodlibets is Isaac's *Donna di dentro*, which is combined with the melodies of two *balli*, *Fortuna d'un gran tempo* and *Dammene un poco*.[34] Several others of these chain songs are contained in a manuscript in Florence.[35]

In the eleven books of *frottole* published by Petrucci there is also a group of lyrics which reflect several of the characteristics of Florentine carnival masquerades and triumphs. We find, for example, evocations of various crafts and trades, and cries of street vendors, all punctuated by salacious puns. Typical are the songs of mowers, pilgrims, convicts; chestnut vendors, millet vendors, amazons; and the music for a triumph of fortune (*canto* or *trionfo della fortuna*) written by Tromboncino, Cara and other musicians. The tone of these pieces is much like that of other *frottole*: amorous and moralizing, with word-painting sometimes of a naturalistic kind. Within the musical texture of four vocal parts there is a marked prominence of the soprano part, whose declamation is strictly governed by the rhythm of the text in order to facilitate comprehension of the words. There is also a good deal of decoration in the cadences. In the vocal style, melody appears to be a prime factor and the parts are simple and conceived in linear fashion; yet they show a disposition towards chords and even consecutives, thus producing a homophonic accompaniment. In this way they continue to anticipate the precepts of Florentine monody and, to a certain extent, already realize that ideal which assumed such over-all importance in Italian music at the end of the sixteenth century.

Good instances are provided by the remarkable lyrics of Cara and Tromboncino. The former's *S'io sedo a l'ombra amor* and the latter's *Suspir soavi* are harbingers of the future madrigal. Undoubtedly instruments – recorders, viols, lutes, harps and the cembalo – were employed in the performance of the *frottole*, but were probably restricted to the refrains and the interludes. The accuracy of Baldassare Castiglione's description in the *Book of the Courtier*, concerning the way in which *frottole* were to be sung, accompanied by a lute, is confirmed by Petrucci's editions (1509–11) which were edited by Francesco Bossinensis under the title *Tenori e contrabassi intabulati con sopran in canto figurato*.[36] There are also transcriptions and adaptations of *frottole* for the chamber organ or for the harpsichord, which were printed in Andrea Antico's *Frottole intabulate da sonare organi*, published in Rome in 1517. At the same time lute music was becoming increasingly important, as illustrated by Petrucci's publication at Venice in 1507 of the tablature books of Francesco Spinaccino da Fossombrone and the fourth book of the Milanese lutenist, Giovan Ambrogio Dalza.[37] Their arrangements for the lute of *canzoni francesi* and *frottole* contain passages of counterpoint in augmentation

---

34. *DTO*, xiv, part i, p. 35.
35. Florence, Bib. Naz., MS Magl., xix, 164–7.
36. See Disertori, *Frottole*.
37. For examples of Spinaccino and Dalza, see *HAM*, i, No. 99.

and diminution. These paved the way for the technical virtuosity, free improvisation and variation characteristic of the new musical form of the instrumental *ricercare*. The first *ricercari* for organ are to be found in a collection by Marco Antonio Cavazzoni (also known as Marco Antonio da Bologna; also as d'Urbino), entitled *Ricercari, mottetti, canzoni* (Venice, 1533). Other keyboard examples appear in the work of Jacopo Fogliano from Modena, preserved in a manuscript at Castell'Arquato (Piacenza). Still other examples for lute, with a somewhat more elaborate technique, appear in a manuscript of *c*. 1517 of Vincenzo Capirola of Brescia.[38] In conclusion, the increasingly important role played in musical culture by the popular *frottola* is but one part of that process which endured throughout the sixteenth century and which brought about the rise of the madrigal as the new Italian secular form. The historical importance of this new form extended far beyond Italy itself, and became of general European importance, eventually ending the long preeminence of the northern composers. (Needless to say, the madrigal of the sixteenth century must not be confused with the *madrigale* of the fourteenth century, described on pp. 215–16.)

Literature was to determine the form of the madrigal and its subsequent importance in the history of Italian secular polyphony. The use of freer rhyme schemes constitutes the first distinction between the madrigal and the *frottola*, since the freer the form of the poetry the freer the music setting seems to be; great liberties were often taken in the repetition of verbal phrases. Cardinal Pietro Bembo's fondness for the poetry of Petrarch and the influence he had on his circle of poets and musicians[39] opened the way for the madrigal.

The stanzas of the madrigal derive from the *canzone*. The form was particularly suitable for music because of the great variation possible in the metre and rhyme. With Bernardo Pisano's *Musica sopra le canzoni del Petrarca*, printed by Petrucci in 1520, we have the first encounter between the new musical genre and rather elegant poetic texts.[40] This collection, which shows a clear preference for Petrarch's *Canzoniere*, also contains texts by Boccaccio, Bembo, Cassola, Ariosto, Sannazaro and others. The music however follows closely the new poetic fashion of the serenade commissioned by noblemen for the ladies they were courting and for important ceremonies. The actual musical term appears for the first time in 1530 in a book printed in Rome under the title *Madrigali di diversi musici* (of which a unique copy survives in Seville).[41] But as the literary aspect of the madrigal developed, the form became most important in the closed circles of the academies where artists and amateurs read and listened to each other's work and to the music which

38. For Cavazzoni and Fogliano see Benvenuti, *Cavazzoni*; for the lute pieces, Gombosi, *Capirola*.
39. Mace, *MQ* (1969), 65.
40. Einstein, *Madrigal*, i, 128–35; cf. also D'Accone's edition.
41. Another edition with an expanded title, was printed at Rome on 1 March 1533 [1534, new style]. Of this a copy survives in Munich, see Einstein, *Madrigal*, i, 154.

they had commissioned. The earliest academy dedicated primarily to the study of music was the Accademia Filarmonica at Verona, established in 1543. The concerts, which were performed by professional musicians, were sung *a cappella* and employed a limited number of singers, usually one for each part. Instruments doubled or at times substituted for the voices. (Concerning the use of instruments within the *a cappella* style, see footnote 55, p. 248.) These groups were well suited to the intimate nature of the madrigal. Their *musica reservata*, as it was called, aimed at a full realization of the ideal structural union between words and sounds. Throughout the century the madrigal aspired to this ideal by means of the modern harmonic innovations of chromaticism and by the virtuosity of the vocal style. From this ideal stems the great emphasis placed on certain locutions in the poetic text (reflecting the emotions of pathos, pain or even tragedy) in their endeavour to picture the words in music, as it were. This led to a tendency on the part of composers to over-emphasize the realistic musical expression of verbal concepts of movement by means of intervals, figurations, runs or simple vocal progressions, i.e. ascending-descending; or of space, i.e. high-low. The pictorial aspects of the text were sometimes reflected by ingenious visual effects in the musical notation: this *Augenmusik* (eye-music), as the German musicologists call it, uses such devices as black or white notes to correspond to the emotions expressed. The writing of madrigals became so fashionable that the new elements of this musical style were thoroughly established: the main characteristics were sophisticated and sensitive decorations of the literary text which, at times, tended to be mannered. The average madrigal was not strophic but through-composed (*durchkomponiert*), employing a variety of sonorous structures and sub-divisions into several parts which followed the text closely. The independent treatment of the voices in imitative passages resulted in polyphony which was actually based on the tradition of motet and *chanson*, a relief from the syllabic declamation on a homophonic succession of chords frequently encountered in the early stages of the madrigal as a heritage from the *frottola*.

The art of the madrigal was first practised by a group which included not only the Italian Costanzo Festa, but also such Franco-Flemish composers resident in Italy as Verdelot, Arcadelt, Gero, Berchem and Willaert. Festa won acclaim with his three-part madrigals written in Rome during the time he was in the papal service (1517–45). Philippe Verdelot, who worked in Venice and in Florence, became famous for his eight books of madrigals, some on texts by Bonifazio Dragonetto and Pietro Aretino and one on the famous sonnet by Petrarch, *Quand'amor i begli occhi a terra inclina*. Jacques Arcadelt (*c.* 1505–68) spent some time in Florence and about 1539 is mentioned as a member of the papal chapel in Rome.[42] His *First Book of Madrigals*

42. Festa: see Einstein, *Madrigal*, iii, Nos. 20–1; also *HAM*, i, No. 129. Verdelot: Einstein, Nos. 16–19, 95. Arcadelt: Einstein, Nos. 22–4, 52; also *HAM*, No. 130; also chapter 4.3, p. 203.

(first extant edition 1539) brought him swift fame, particularly the well-known *Il bianco e dolce cigno*. Arcadelt's elegance, the nobility of his sentiments and mastery of the style of the French *chanson*, which he applied to his Italian compositions, all contributed to his eminence in the early tradition of the madrigal. His position is confirmed by the fact that Michelangelo entrusted to him two of his own poems for musical setting, *Io dico che fra noi* and *Deh, dimmi, Amor*, both published in the *Primo Libro*.

Adrian Willaert, the Franco-Flemish composer (born *c.*1490, perhaps at Bruges) was active at Venice from 1527 to 1562.[43] He was greatly influenced by the Petrarchism of Bembo and, as a result, his settings of Petrarch's sonnets (in the anthology *Musica Nova* of 1559) combine the traditional traits of Franco-Flemish polyphony with the Italian style. The music contains harmonic and chromatic innovations and the treatment of the text brings out the pictorial qualities of certain words and phrases. Nicola Vicentino (1511–72) one of Willaert's pupils, was employed by the Este family in Ferrara and Rome and was interested in theoretical experimentation, as shown by his treatise *L'Antica musica ridotta alla moderna pratica*. He is important in the history of the madrigal for his *avant-garde* use of harmonic chromaticism. Cipriano de Rore, born in 1516, perhaps at Antwerp, became one of Willaert's pupils in Venice. He further advanced the ideas of his teacher concerning chromatic alteration and is important for the rhythmic variety of his music and the intense dramatic accents with which he endowed his poetic texts.[44] He set to music the entire *Canzoniere* of Petrarch as well as sentimental poetry by Claudio Tolomei, Giovanni della Casa and Francesco Molza. The complexity and emotional intensity of his madrigals for five voices served as stylistic models for the composers who came after him during the last half of the century. Among these followers, not distinguished for their originality, but nonetheless pleasing for their somewhat academic compositions, were: Giovanni Nasco of Verona and Domenico Ferrabosco (of unknown origin) who wrote a famous madrigal based on Boccaccio's ballad from the *Decamerone*, *Io mi son giovinetta*. Francesco Corteccia (1504–71)[45] showed original talent in his first book of madrigals (published 1547) which contained pieces written for the Medici Family that were sometimes sung as interludes for court presentations of comedies.

Composers of such overall importance as Palestrina and Lassus[46] also composed madrigals which, though of high quality, were not necessarily

---

43. Concerning Willaert's position at St Mark's in Venice and some of his pupils also at St Mark's, namely, Cipriano da Rore, Andrea Gabrieli and Gioseffo Zarlino, see p. 249. See also Einstein, Nos. 31–2, 43.

44. See Einstein, Nos. 45–9; also *HAM*, No. 131.

45. Einstein, Nos. 25–7, 96; McKinley, *Corteccia*; Minor, *Renaissance*.

46. In the following paragraphs madrigals of the best known composers of the century are discussed: Palestrina, Lasso, Monte, Marenzio, Gabrieli, Gesualdo, Monteverdi. These composers are fully dealt with in Einstein's monumental work, and musical examples are readily available in standard anthologies, as well as in editions of the individual composers.

exceptional. As a reaction to the severe censorship concerning religious music brought on by the Council of Trent there arose a desire to express, in secular music, sentiments of a more frivolous kind. Among the champions of this new madrigalian style in Rome were Palestrina, Domenico Ferrabosco and Leonardo Barré. In 1583 a 'noteworthy company of excellent musicians in Rome' published their secular works for fashionable society. The composers included such important papal musicians as Anerio, Nanino and Giovanelli as well as Palestrina. The Counter-Reformation had no effect on the development of the madrigal, in spite of the fact that Palestrina seems to be excusing himself in the preface to his motets based on the *Song of Songs* for having written secular music in a style which he dubbs *alacriore* (more sprightly). Some discretion was used however in the choice of texts to be set to music, although the poetry of Petrarch remained by far the most popular. Palestrina's madrigals follow the earlier tradition, yet temper secular expressiveness with the austerity of the ecclesiastical style. In spite of this he achieved great fame for his setting of *Vestiva i colli*.

The musical education of the young Lassus (also known as Orlando di Lasso, see p. 207) during his long stay in Italy explains the interest of this international composer in the madrigal. Typically Flemish in the breadth and eclectic nature of its style, his music is not without polyphonic complexity, even though his varied use of rhythms and the lively, expressive clarity of his music reveal the influence of light-hearted, popular music. This, as we shall see, is present mainly in his *villanelle*. The last work to be finished before his death, the *Lagrime di San Pietro*, based on Tansillo's text, is directly in line with the severe limits imposed by the Counter-Reformation. Two other Flemish composers, Filippo di Monte and Giaches de Wert, studied music in Italy during their youth. Filippo di Monte (1521–1603) spent about a quarter of a century in such centres as Naples and Rome, after which, in 1568, he entered the service of the Habsburgs at Vienna and Prague, which position he retained until his death. He produced an extraordinary number of madrigals (over a thousand) almost all of excellent quality, which follow the classic form without notable stylistic innovations. Giaches de Wert (*c.* 1536–96), a native of the province of Antwerp, worked at the courts of Mantua and Ferrara. He was one of the first composers to set the poetry of Torquato Tasso to music. He also pioneered a style in which a group of solo voices (such as a *concertino* of three high voices) was joined by two lower voices to form a *tutti* of five voices within the frame-work of a five-part madrigal. The celebrated Tarquinia Molza of Ferrara was a star-performer in these madrigals, in company with two other female virtuoso singers.[47]

In Venice Andrea Gabrieli developed a highly personal style of vocal music. One of its features was the division of the many voices into contrasting

47. Einstein, *Madrigal*, pp. 568–75 and 831–3; *NOHM*, iv, 59–60, 144–7 and 369–70; *HAM*, i, No. 146a. See also chapter 4.3, p. 207.

groups, a technique which was later developed by Andrea's nephew Giovanni.[48] To the list of important madrigalists from Venice and elsewhere should be added the names of Vincenzo Ruffo, Claudio Merulo, Annibale Padovano, Costanza Porta, Marco Antonio Ingegneri, Gioseffo Guami and Luzzasco Luzzaschi. Alessandro Striggio, who worked in Florence with Vincenzo Galilei, contributed to the genre of the *intermedi* (interludes) with madrigals written between 1565 and 1585.

MARENZIO AND MONTEVERDI. The madrigal reached its perfection at the very end of the century, when the role of native Italian composers increased in importance and that of the *transalpini* (a synonym of *oltremontani*) diminished. Perhaps its greatest practitioner was Luca Marenzio (1553–99), who lived in Rome for the major part of his life in the service of Cardinal d'Este and Cardinal Aldobrandini. Jacopo Sannazaro was one of Marenzio's favourite poets, among whose works he especially admired the dialogues from the *Arcadia*. The pastoral inspiration and sensual charm mixed with melancholy, so typical of Sannazaro's work, are reflected in the emotional character of Marenzio's picturesque musical images. Examples are the madrigals *O voi che sospirate* and *O fere stelle*. The charm of the Virgilian eclogue may be found in Petrarch's *Zefiro torna* and in Tasso's *Vezzosi augelli*.

Chromaticism as a means of expression, introduced by Vicentino and de Rore, reached great maturity of harmonic sophistication and dramatic vitality in the music of Carlo Gesualdo. The musical extravagance of this Neapolitan composer is displayed in his constant attempts to express the 'affections' of Tasso's poetry: he uses unexpected chromatic alterations and the resultant modulations add to the sonority of the music to a degree which savours of a distinctly modern style. Fascinating examples are *Io tacerò*, *Mercé grido piangendo*, *Moro lasso* and *Io pur respiro*.

In his first four madrigal books (which included settings of poems by Allegretti, Bembo, Guarini, Bentivoglio, Strozzi, Tasso and others) Claudio Monteverdi remained faithful to tradition, in spite of some harmonic innovations which gave rise to an exchange of polemics with Artusi. A break occurred with the fifth book (1605) where an instrumental *basso continuo* was added to the vocal parts, indicating that the madrigal of the sixteenth century had been transformed in an endeavour to reach a new freedom of expression. Some of the pieces in this book anticipate music for the stage, notably, excerpts from Guarini's *Pastor fido*. Under the guise of a declaration by Monteverdi's brother, the *Scherzi musicali* of 1607 set forth the composer's views on modern music, in reply to Artusi's criticism. Among the musical innovations of the *Scherzi* is the employment of instrumental *ritornelli*. The sixth book (1614) contained more works, related in one way or another,

---

48. Concerning the use of contrasting groups, *cori spezzati*, by Willaert, Andrea and Giovanni Gabrieli, see pp. 249–50.

to the stage. His opera *Arianna* had been an outstanding success at Mantua in 1608, in spite of the sudden death of Caterinuccia Martinelli, who was to have sung the title role. The *pièce de résistance* of the opera then (and at its revival in 1640) was the heroine's famous *Lamento*, which is included in the sixth book in the form of a madrigal for five voices. There is also a memorial to Martinelli entitled *Lagrime d'amante al sepolcro de l'amata*, in addition to arias and duets which further refine the application of recitative style to vocal expressiveness. The elements of the new *stile rappresentativo* are even more pronounced in the seventh book of 1619: settings of poems by Guarini, Chiabrera and Marino; two *lettere amorose* in the Florentine manner; and – most obviously – the setting of *Tirsi e Clori* which, like *Arianna*, boasted a libretto by Rinuccini. (*Tirsi e Clori*, originally a work for the stage involving both song and dance, had been performed in Mantua in 1615 but was first published in this volume.) The eighth book (1638) bears the title *Madrigali guerrieri et amorosi* and, in spite of its seemingly polyphonic nature, it is another affirmation of the new theatrical and choreographic genre created by Monteverdi in connection with the Florentine reform of the musical drama. The famous *Ballo delle ingrate*, composed originally for the celebrations in Mantua in 1608 and based on Rinuccini's text, is published here along with various *Trionfi d'amore*, where victories in battle are cleverly symbolized by vocal and instrumental passages notable for their rapid rhythms (*stile concitato*). These pieces and the pantomimic cantata for the stage, *Combattimento di Tancredi e Clorinda*, based on Tasso's *Gerusalemme Liberata*, also included in this collection, are admirable examples of the *stile concitato*. Their great variety is evidence of Monteverdi's progressive mastery of the madrigal form. The style of these pieces, both polyphonic and homophonic, could not but help to bring about the final realization of opera.

VILLANELLA AND BALLETTO. While the madrigal received its prime impulses, notably its polyphonic structure, from the *oltremontani*, i.e. Franco-Flemish musicians, it nevertheless also absorbed regional Italian influences. Important among these was the Neapolitan *villanella* (or *villanesca*), a simple and popular genre characterized by symmetrical form, a three-part texture and consecutive triads (causing the despised consecutive fifths). If the northern *frottola* preceded the *madrigale*, the southern *villanella* accompanied it throughout the sixteenth century in that the two forms were addressed to the same public, i.e. the academies. The texts of anacreontic poetry tend toward Petrarchism as well as toward the carnival masquerades.

The *villanella* first appeared in print in 1537 at Naples with the *Canzoni villanesche alla napoletana*, containing the work of anonymous authors, and spread to Venice in 1544 with Willaert's *Canzoni villanesche* (for four voices). The first stage of the *villanella* is represented by the work of such Neapolitan composers as Domenico da Nola, G. Tom. di Maio and Leonardo dell'Arpa.

Lassus (who had lived in Naples in his youth) also contributed to the genre, employing more than three voices. He arranged to have some pieces published as early as 1555 (*Madrigali, villanesche* ..., Antwerp), some as late as 1581 (*Villanesche, moresche* ..., Paris). In these compositions, based on dialect texts, Lassus responds with a pungent realism to the poems which are so colourful both in setting and the characters they depict. Later composers continued the process begun by Willaert and Lassus, namely, to increase the number of voices and to expand the range of expression of a genre whose playful vivacity was initially tinged with a provincial flavour. By the latter part of the sixteenth century the number of voices reached as many as six, notably in the works of Giovanni Ferretti (*c.* 1540–*c.* 1605) and Luca Marenzio. The elegance of the humour is reminiscent of Vecchi's madrigal comedies.

The *villanella* had many popular companion forms (*balletto, canzonetta, mascherata, moresca*) among which the *balletto* is particularly important. These dance songs, based on pastoral and allegorical texts, frequently formed part of the vocal and instrumental entertainments of the academies and the courts. Giovanni Giacomo Gastoldi (*c.* 1550–1622) is probably the most widely known composer of such dance songs. His *Balletti* for five voices (Venice, 1591; frequently reprinted) indicate on the title page that they were intended 'for singing, playing and dancing'; and indeed they were destined to become the most influential examples of 'vocal dance music', even reaching Morley and Hassler beyond the Alps. Moreover, Gastoldi's *Balletti* form a unified whole and thus an important forerunner of Vecchi's *Amfiparnaso* and other madrigal comedies by Vecchi and Banchieri, discussed below.[49]

The two genres of *balletto* and *villanella* both belong to a category called *madrigale drammatico*. This term does not signify scenic production of a play but refers to the dialogue form of the *commedia dell'arte* and to the frank and satirical realism of that popular form of drama. In spite of the implicit theatrical nature of the *madrigale drammatico*, linked as it was to the influences of a sentimental if not amorous Arcadia, it was secular chamber polyphony and therefore performed by musicians without a scenic setting. Each character expressed himself through dialogue, whether the text was serious or satirical. The form was certainly not that of Florentine monody, because accompaniment by a *basso continuo* was excluded, although a vocal accompaniment of sorts did occur, as in the imitations of chattering, chirping, etc. As G. B. Doni wrote in his *Trattato de' generi e de' modi della musica*, we find in this genre representations of the so-called humours (comic and otherwise) of various nations (Germans, Moors, Jews, Turks), through the imitation of the sound effects of their languages; and of human types and occupations usually symbolized by masks (whether of carnival or of the *commedia dell'arte*).

49. *HAM*, i, No. 158; Einstein, *Madrigal*, iii, Nos. 77–8. See also Einstein, i, 604, 794, 803.

The composers of humorous madrigals include Alessandro Striggio, who, in 1567, published *Il Cicalamento delle donne al bucato* (The Chatter of the Women at their Washing), a realistic and satiric dialogue; and in 1569 the animated *Gioco di primiera* (Game of Cards). Both these works, combining several single numbers into a cyclical composition, are among the fore-runners of the so-called madrigal comedies by Croce, Vecchi and Banchieri. Giovanni Croce (c. 1557–1609), chapel master of St Mark's in Venice from 1603, produced two such cycles, the *Mascherate piacevoli* (1590) and the *Triaca musicale* (1595), in which characters from the *commedia dell'arte* alternate with picturesque peasants from the Venetian country-side. Both Croce and his contemporary Orazio Vecchi (1550–1605) occasionally employ one of the companion forms of the *balletto*, the *canzonetta*, which repeats its musical sections at the beginning and end (AABBCC or simply AABB). Vecchi, a canon and man of letters as well as a gifted composer, is best known for his madrigal comedies such as the *Amfiparnaso* (1597). In the preface the author describes the work as a *commedia harmonica* for five voices 'to be seen with the mind', for it 'enters through the ear and not through the eye', proof that Vecchi's music was not intended for the theatre. The action is to be found only in the music itself, while in the sentimental and grotesque se-quences there is a perfect correspondence between the various types of sonority and the image which the composer wished to evoke. Vecchi's *Convito musicale* (1597) and the *Veglie di Siena* (1604), containing various styles of contemporary music, ridicule in a witty and playful manner the entertainments offered by the Accademia degli Intronati of Siena.

Adriano Banchieri (1567–1634), an Olivetan monk from Bologna with a wide musical background, was a follower and gifted imitator of Vecchi. The rise of opera and other dramatic music meant that Banchieri, who did not ask for a stage presentation of his compositions, was obliged at least to intro-duce a narrator, whose spoken text preceded each vocal episode. Elsewhere the composer approached more nearly full-fledged theatre by the insertion of brief *intermezzi* in the style of the *mascherata* or other popular forms. The extremely successful madrigal comedies *La Pazzia senile* (1598), *Il Zabaione musicale* (1603), *La Barca di Venezia per Padova* (1605), *Il Festino nella sera del Giovedì grasso* (1608) and *La Saviezza giovenile* (1628), influenced by Monteverdi's style, were built around farcical situations nourished by a sense of fantasy, both capricious and burlesque.

SACRED POLYPHONY. After 1480, native Italian composers, though still under the influence of Franco-Flemish polyphony, introduced a contra-puntal texture of striking simplicity into portions of the liturgy. Notable in this connection are settings of the Passions, which endow the Latin texts with clarity; the expressive *Lamentazioni* for four voices by Tromboncino, pub-lished by Petrucci in 1506, the motets of Francesco d'Ana and the religious music of Franchino Gafori, who wrote numerous motets and *Magnificats* as well as the *Missa de Carneval* and the *Missa Trombetta* for the chapel of the cathedral of Milan.

In Florence the religious polyphonic music of the younger generation, which included Bernardo Pisano and Francesco Corteccia,[50] veered away from the contrapuntal technique of the Franco-Flemish musicians which had been brought to Italy by Heinrich Isaac. The younger masters exhibit a tendency toward harmonic-vertical thinking and seem to avoid elaborate artifice. Bernardo di Benedetto Pagoli, born in Florence in 1490 and better known as Bernardo Pisano, was a defender of this indigenous tradition. A protégé of Cardinal Giovanni de' Medici (later Pope Leo X), he received an appointment to the papal chapel before returning to Florence, where he died in 1548. His *Responsori* for Holy Week helped to bring about at Santa Maria del Fiore, the Cathedral of Florence, the formation of a musical tradition probably influenced by Spanish polyphony through Eleanor of Toledo, wife of Cosimo I. The leader of the movement was Francesco Corteccia. In his two Passions (based on the Gospels according to St John and St Matthew) for four equal voices, and numerous motets, *laude*, hymns and Responsories, Corteccia developed his own style and harmonic structure, rich in expression. The famous archives of the Florentine Cathedral contain not only important manuscripts of the music of Corteccia but also collections of the work of two Florentine chapel masters who served the Grand Dukes between 1585 and 1637, Luca Bati and Marco da Gagliano. The former left behind a manu-script folio (1598) of psalms, *Magnificats* and various Vesper services. Gagliano is represented by Responsories, polychoral Masses and motets composed for various solemn celebrations held in the cathedral.

In Rome the sixteenth century saw the rise of several musical establish-ments in addition to the Sistine Chapel (named after Pope Sixtus IV and consecrated in 1483). Among the most important were the following three: the Julian Chapel at St Peter's (named after the bull of Pope Julius II in 1512) and the chapel of the two great papal churches in Rome, Santa Maria Maggiore (where Palestrina was a choir-boy in 1537) and San Giovanni Laterano (where Lassus was appointed chapel-master in 1553).[51]

Between the years 1545 and 1563 the Roman Church held its great Ecumenical Council at Trent. After much debating a number of important reforms were made. Particular attention was given to religious music, and a revision of the liturgy was thought necessary. In their zeal for reform, the more uncompromising cardinals and even Pope Paul IV wanted to abolish

---

50. The secular music of these two Florentine composers has been discussed above, see pp. 237 and 239. Both the sacred and the secular works of Pisano have been reprinted in D'Accone, *Florentine* [*CMM*, xxxii, i, (1966)]. Concerning Pisano's biography see Einstein, *Madrigal*, pp. 128–35 and D'Accone, *Mus. Disc.* (1963) 115. Concerning Corteccia's sacred music see above, p. 239, fn. 45.

51. *MGG*, article 'Rom', columns 697, 704.

the use of polyphony (or, rather *musica figurata*), proposing a rigid adherence to Gregorian chant in its place. Because of the ever-increasing popularity of the practice of using secular music for religious texts ('parody' Mass) and the failure of choirs to convey clearly the meaning of the words they were singing, the Council, in a session of 1562, decided to forbid the performance of any music corrupted by the 'impurities and obscenities' of the vernacular.

The theory that polyphonic music was saved by Palestrina is no longer tenable, and as a result the reforms in religious music brought about by the Council have been reduced to more modest proportions in current estimation. In effect the highly criticized abuses dealt mainly with Masses based on the secular *chansons* of the Franco-Flemish school, such as *L'Homme armé*, *Je suis desheritée* and *Filomena*. There were ample grounds for the objections recorded by the sixteenth-century cleric Bernardino Cirillo of Aquila, such as, 'Which devil made them put these songs into the Mass?' And yet, these popular sources had themselves been so transformed by contrapuntal techniques that they were often not recognized by the ear of the faithful. Moreover secular words had never been inserted in the text of the liturgy during the singing of the Mass. The dislike for this much licence reflects the reactionary spirit of the church when it was confronted by the natural evolution of secular polyphony. By way of an historical answer a century later, King John IV of Portugal (1604–56) came to the defence of Palestrina and of modern music, attacking the arguments against polyphonic Masses.[52]

This rather late recognition of the modern quality of Palestrina's music would lead one to think that the conservative elements of the Church had waged a campaign against polyphony from the beginning precisely because of the *avant-garde* tone which the modern technique of the Franco-Flemish 'parody' Mass[53] lent to all the major polyphonic compositions of the time. In addition to the substitution of a tenor based on free invention for the tenor *cantus firmus* of long liturgical tradition, the thematic procedure of parody, which involved the complete reworking of musical passages taken from motets, *chansons* and madrigals belonging to other composers, became widespread. But the same reformers who proposed a return to medieval psalmody in order to combat polyphony did not realize that the reform they suggested for a truly inspired religious music had already begun before the Council met, and was reaching its full development through the natural evolution of Palestrina's style. His music, a veritable vault of sound, represents a synthesis of the northern Gothic and the Italian Renaissance traditions. The elaborate techniques found in counterpoint and in the development of vocal texture were taken from northern composers, but the music became much

52. *Respuestas a las dudas que se puiseron a la Missa 'Panis …' del Palestrina* (Lisbon, 1654; Italian translation, Rome 1655).

53. Concerning the tradition of parody Masses see chapter 4.1, p. 154 and chapter 4.3, p. 197. Concerning the Council of Trent: Fellerer, *MQ* (1953) 576; H. Beck, 'Konzil'; Weinmann, *Konzil*.

more alive under the influence of the Mediterranean tradition – the lively fruit of popular homophony. In conclusion, the attempt made by the Roman Church to ostracize polyphony, Franco-Flemish in origin, was more a question of principle and form than of content, and the presumed rescue of polyphony itself came about as a natural development of the works of superb musicians like Palestrina. By re-working forms thought to be already destroyed through frivolity and bad habits, he was able to turn a desert into a lush and fragrant garden.

The actual date of birth of Giovanni Pierluigi of Palestrina (a town near Rome) probably occurred between 1525 and 1526. For seven years, beginning in 1544, he was organist and choir-master of the cathedral of his birthplace. He was summoned tó Rome by Pope Julius III in 1551 as chapel-master of the Julian Chapel at St Peter's and later (January 1555) joined the Sistine Chapel as singer. But after the sudden deaths of Julius III and Marcellus II Palestrina was dismissed by Paul IV from the Sistine Chapel (September 1555) because of his married status, which was not acceptable to clerics. From 1555 until 1560 Palestrina was chapel-master at San Giovanni in Laterano and from 1561 to 1566 at Santa Maria Maggiore. He then taught music at the Roman Seminary (Seminario Romano) and rejoined the Julian Chapel at St Peter's in 1571 as chapel-master, a post he held until his death in 1594. The number of his works published during his lifetime is considerable; he received commissions not only from the clergy but also from the courts of Madrid, Vienna and Mantua. In spite of the fame he attained with his music, which was performed in the papal chapels, the numerous dedications to princes and popes commending to their kindness the protection of the editions of his work remain proof of the fact that he felt a need to defend it against the hostile reformers of the Council. In his first collection of motets, dedicated to the stern cardinal of Carpi, Palestrina claims to have 'used themes noble in origin, such as the Gregorian melodies, in place of the repudiated songs of the people'. In the dedication to King Philip of Spain of the second and third books of Masses, which include the famous *Missa Papae Marcelli* for six voices, Palestrina comments on his own artistic activity which, he says, he has 'developed by means of studied technical skill and perfection, according to the way of singing prescribed by the Church, in a clear and intelligible manner'.[54] The third book of Masses, however, includes *L'Homme armé* for five voices, printed with the title in plain view next to the Mass *De beata Vergine*. It is true that Masses clearly derived from secular models were probably shelved because of their controversial nature, but it is equally true that years later, in order to evade the decrees of the Council, Palestrina had recourse to subterfuge. Following the model of the parodies of *laude*, he concealed the original theme of the Mass *L'Homme armé* by the device of a

---

54. For examples of Palestrina's masses and motets see *HAM*, i, Nos. 140–1. For a discussion of his style and technique, Andrews, *Palestrina* and Jeppesen, *Palestrina*.

general title, that is, *Missa quarta*. Moreover, under the ambiguous title *Missa sine nomine* is hidden a parody of the four-voice *chanson*, *Je suis desheritée*; in the same way the Mass *Primi toni* is inspired by the well-known madrigal by Ferrabosco, *Io mi son giovinetta*. In his last works Palestrina printed other Masses of the same kind which eluded the *non expedit* of the Church and even wrote a 'parody' Mass on one of his own secular madrigals, *Vestiva i colli*.

It must be remembered that this close rapport between the sacred and secular spheres was a constant feature of Renaissance music. Even the motet was not exempt from these reciprocal influences and, in turn, was to contribute to the development of the madrigal. By the close of the sixteenth century the religious madrigal differed from the secular only in that the former was performed in church and the latter at the gatherings of sophisticated society. The imposing edifice of Palestrina's works represented the best response to the objections raised by the Council of Trent. His utilization of secular resources for sacred music commanded universal approbation and contributed to the ultimate restoration of polyphonic music, with all its powers, to the services of the liturgy. This restoration was carried on in Roman Catholic church music by his contemporaries in Venice and Munich, Andrea Gabrieli and Lassus. (It is, of course, equally to be perceived in the fervour of the music for the Reformation, for instance in the work of Huguenot composers from Goudimel to Claude Le Jeune.)

The great Roman school represented by Palestrina also included the names of Giovanni Animuccia, Felice Anerio, Giovanni Maria Nanino, Francesco Soriano and the Spaniard Tomáso Luis de Victoria. The entire production of religious music was dominated by the *a cappella* ideal[55] and followed the polyphonic tradition for the celebration of liturgical ceremonies in the great basilicas. As a manifestation of popular piety and devotion, the Counter-Reformation favoured the creation of new religious confraternities and the re-birth of the ancient spiritual song, the *lauda*. As early as 1517 people gathered in the oratory of Divino Amore to sing and pray, thereby establishing the custom for gatherings of both laymen and clergy. This custom was taken up again by St Filippo Neri in the oratories of San Girolamo della Caritá and of Santa Maria in Vallicella (in Rome) for the purposes of meditation, listening to sermons, and joining together in singing religious songs. The homophonic dress of the *lauda*, taken for the most part from parodies of popular secular songs, was well suited to this end. Its narrative

55. In the nineteenth century scholars believed that this ideal implied a purely vocal performance, without instruments. Modern research has shown, however, that instruments frequently doubled the voices, and by the end of the sixteenth century keyboard instruments frequently assisted in the performance of vocal polyphony. Nevertheless, the ideal was a real one, and the distinctly vocal flavour of the music is apparent in such aspects as choice of intervals, treatment of dissonances, length of notes, etc. See the article 'a cappella' in *MGG* and the conclusions in Jeppesen, *Palestrina*, pp. 288–94.

nature and its dialogue structure, treating events taken from the Old Testament, with choral passages of rather simple arrangement, lent themselves to easy and spontaneous performance. Among those who composed these *laude* were Giovanni Animuccia, Agostino Manni, Giovenale Ancina (who composed the collection *Il Tempio armonico*),[56] Dionisio Isorelli and Palestrina. The dramatic tone later assumed by the musical dialogue of the *lauda* and the introduction of accompanied monody in the style of recitative in a context which originally had been polyphonic, helped, along with Emilio de' Cavalieri's sacred drama, *Rappresentazione di anima e di corpo*, to create the oratorio, a new form of religious music composed for the Italian texts.

As we have seen, the desire for greater comprehension and clarity of the text, unencumbered by intricate polyphony, which was raised at the Council of Trent and subsequently by the leaders of the Counter-Reformation, did not prevent the creation of elaborate masterpieces of religious music by Palestrina and his contemporaries. But a concern with clear enunciation of the text reappeared with great force later in the writings of Vincenzo Galilei and various champions of the genre of opera and *stile recitativo*. The many documents attesting to the rise of opera invariably declared open battle against counterpoint as the cause of obscuring the words. The importance given by the Florentines to the poetic and dramatic message of the text encouraged the rise of recitative in the widest sense and thereby contributed to the spectacular decline of polyphony in the seventeenth century.

INSTRUMENTAL MUSIC. The reputation of Venice as a European musical centre can be said to date from the appointment, in 1527, of Adrian Willaert (*c.* 1490–1562) as chapel-master of St Mark's. Although there was certainly a flourishing musical culture there before his time, Willaert's fame quickly led to Venice becoming a centre of pilgrimage for younger composers who came to seek instruction from him, thus beginning a process which continued up to the time of Monteverdi. The Franco-Flemish contrapuntal techniques formed the basis of Willaert's own style, both in his Masses, which are almost all of the 'parody' type, and in his motets, mostly based on plainsong tenors. It is this style that was soon transmitted to the younger generation of native Italian composers, who (unlike those of Josquin's generation) were by now in a position to absorb and develop such techniques for themselves. In addition to his own infusion of these northern elements into Italian music, Willaert showed his absorption of the Italian style, in both his concern for expressive declamation and his development of *cori spezzati* (divided choirs).

The sub-division of a choir into several groups, usually two or three, which might sing now separately, now jointly, became characteristic of Venetian

56. Published in 1599. Concerning the dramatic elements of the *lauda* in the later sixteenth century, see *NOHM*, iv, 835 and Smither, *Acta* (1969) 186.

poly-choral music. It is to be observed in Willaert's *Salmi spezzati* (divided psalms) of 1550, in which he raised the simple alternation of choirs found in the works of his north Italian predecessors to a more sophisticated level. Due to Willaert's reputation the positions of chapel-master, first organist, and second organist at St Mark's acquired, up to the end of the seventeenth century, a prestige comparable to appointments at Westminster Abbey or St Thomas's at Leipzig.

Among Willaert's pupils were some of the most famous composers of the period, two of them succeeding him at St Mark's as chapel-masters, namely, his fellow Netherlander Rore who was succeeded after his death by the Italian Zarlino.

Andrea Gabrieli (1510/20–86) who became second organist in 1564 must be reckoned as one of the most important composers and pupils of Willaert to succeed to a post at St Mark's. Andrea's place in the cathedral was inherited by his nephew and pupil, Giovanni Gabrieli (1557–1612). Giovanni developed more fully the techniques of the new style of polyphony for voices and instruments which his uncle had introduced in such works as *Sacre canzoni*, in five parts, the *Libro primo delle Messe*, in six parts, the *Canzoni ecclesiastiche*, in four parts and the *Salmi Davidici*, in six parts.

During the first half of the sixteenth century, the lute was the favourite instrument in use in northern Italy and especially in Venice, as testified by the numerous tablatures of madrigals that remain to be sung and played. Among the printed compositions for lute those of Francesco da Milano (1497–1543, nicknamed *il divino*) are remarkable for their depth of feeling. Two of them were published in 1536; one at Venice by Francesco Marcolini and one in Milan by Giovanni Antonio Casteliono. They are often transcriptions of vocal music to Latin, French or Italian texts, for instance the celebrated lute version of Janequin's *chanson*, *La Bataille de Marignan*.[57]

The *ricercare* had already developed as a separate instrumental form and was cultivated by lutenists and organists. Dance music had its development with the *pass' e mezzo* (or *passamezzo*), the *pavana* and, later, the *saltarello* and the *gagliarda*, while the melodies of the *romanesca* and of the *follia* fall into the general scheme of *bassi ostinati*, used for support and harmonic accompaniment. The arrangement of these dances in series is a forerunner of the Baroque suite.

The style of the fantasia and the *ricercare* for lute, rich in free runs and sudden modulations, can be studied in the tablatures of Giovanni Maria da Crema, a skilful musician who sometimes published transcriptions of keyboard works by Giulio Segni da Modena, the organist at St Mark's. Giacomo Gorzanis, a lutenist resident at Trieste, is the author of several anthologies, printed between 1561 and 1571, and also of a remarkable manuscript col-

---

57. Concerning Francesco da Milano see *NOHM*, iv, 690; Manuel, *Histoire*, i, 1227; Ness, *Milano*.

lection (preserved at Munich) which contains twenty-four *passamezzi*, twelve in major and twelve in minor, on the twelve semitones of the octave. This anticipation of the 'well-tempered' cycles of the eighteenth century connects Gorzanis with such theorists of his own epoch as Zarlino, Vicentino and V. Galilei.[58] In 1568 Galilei's *Fronimo* appeared, his own arrangement for the lute of a large repertoire by various authors of madrigals, *canzoni*, *balli*, psalms and *ricercari*. This was followed in the last decades of the century by the publications of dances, fantasias and other works for lute by Gostena, Molinaro, Radino and Terzi.[59] Two important treatises on dancing, both containing lute versions of dance music, should be noted: the *Ballarino* (1581) by Fabritio Caroso and *Le Gratie d'amore* (1602) by Cesare Negri.

Italian organ music also grew in stature during the sixteenth century. It was ushered in by two large collections, composed by Girolamo Cavazzoni and printed in tablature (Venice: *Primo libro* 1542, *Secondo libro* 1543). The collections consisted of freely-composed pieces making use of imitation (*ricercari*); arrangements of secular songs (*canzoni*); and liturgical pieces (sections of hymns, *Magnificats* and Masses). Cavazzoni is remarkable for the freedom with which he treats his *cantus firmus*, whether it be sacred or secular, and the extensive and truly instrumental process of imitation to which he subjects his themes.

The tradition of organ music at the chapel at St Mark's understandably aroused fierce competition for a place at one of the two organs in the Venetian basilica. If many of the tablatures were intended for the limited number of ranks of the positive organ, the instruments in St Mark's offered a larger number of registers, including what is nowadays termed a chorus of principal stops, with ranks extending up to one-foot pitch,[60] creating an exquisite sweetness of sound. Throughout the sixteenth century some of the foremost keyboard composers and virtuosi received appointments as organists at St Mark's. (The Venetian records are rather confusing since the original documents do not always distinguish between the first and the second organist.) Among them were G. Segni (1498–1561) appointed in 1530, J. Buus (1510/20–1564) 1541, G. Parabosco (1520/24–1557) 1551, Annibale Padovano (1527–75) 1552, C. Merulo (1533–1604) 1557, A. Gabrieli (1510/20–86) 1564, G. Gabrieli (1557–1612) 1585, V. Bell'haver (*c*. 1530–87) 1586 and Gioseffo (or Giuseppe) Guami (or Guammi) (*c*. 1540–1611) 1588.[61]

Girolamo Diruta, in *Transilvano*, his treatise on playing the organ and other keyboard instruments (two parts, Venice 1593–1609) included not

---

58. Concerning Crema and Gorzanis, see Manuel, *Histoire*, i, 1239, 1242.

59. For modern editions of lute music by Crema, Galilei, Gostena, Molinaro, Radino, Terzi, see index of composers in the bibliography for this chapter.

60. Jeppesen, *Orgelmusik*, pp. 26 f., 35 ff.; Dalla Libera, *Organi*.

61. For Buus see Sutherland, *MQ* (1945) 448. For the work of the Gabrielis and other Venetians see Torchi, *Arte*, iii. For modern editions of Keyboard works by Cavazzoni, Merulo, Padovano, Parabosco, Segni, see index of composers in the bibliography for this chapter.

only works by composers who were organists at St Mark's (A. Gabrieli, Merulo, Bell'haver), but also valuable instructions both in regard to playing technique and ornamentation. Diruta distinguished clearly between a technique proper to the organ, and one to harpsichord and clavichord. Another author who provided important treatises on the techniques of instruments was Silvestro Ganassi. His *Fontegara* (Venice 1535, facsimile Milan 1945) is a tutor for the recorder; as in the case of *Transilvano* Ganassi's instructions on ornamentation apply also to other instruments. His *Regola Rubertina* (two parts, Venice, 1542–3; facsimile Leipzig, 1924) is a tutor for the viol family, with detailed instructions for fingering and bowing. The compositions which he provides as practice pieces show that even before the middle of the century technical demands must have been high and included extensive double-stopping.[62]

Altogether the instrumental repertoire developed an independent and truly idiomatic style. In the works of such composers as Claudio Merulo and G. Gabrieli, the *ricercare* is no longer reminiscent of the motet (or, indeed, of any other vocal form), but, building on the foundations laid earlier in the century by Cavazzoni and others, it displays liveliness of progression, a sonority often based on doublings at the fifth and a free texture (i.e. rapid changes from sparse to full chords). These characteristics apply to a variety of pieces, whatever their title, and to a variety of media, whether for solo keyboard instruments or ensembles. One encounters such titles as *ricercare*, *canzona* (or *canzone*), *sonata*, *intonazione*, *toccata*. The ensembles are sometimes purely instrumental; at other times double choirs of voices and instruments are employed. Examples of both may be found in Giovanni Gabrieli's *Sacrae symphoniae*, the first part of which was published at Venice in 1597 and the second in 1615. Part 1 includes the famous *Sonata pian e forte*[63]; Part 2 the motet *In ecclesiis*.[64] The sonata is scored for two 'choirs' or groups of instruments, namely, a first choir of a cornett and three trombones and a second choir of a violin and three trombones; a *forte* effect is achieved when the two combine. The motet is scored for two choirs of four voices each plus a third choir of instruments (cornetts, violin and trombones) and a *basso continuo* for organ; when all three choirs combine, as they do in the final Alleluia, the dynamic power is considerable.

Gabrieli's main achievement in his sonatas and *canzone* was to break away from their vocal prototypes by creating groups genuinely instrumental in their attention to timbre. These ensembles were carefully chosen for the effects of resonance, colour and contrast of which they were capable. Cornetts and trombones played an important part, to which violins and lutes were sometimes added. The whole ensemble was often supported by some

62. *HAM*, i, No. 119.
63. *HAM*, i, No. 173; also reprinted Benvenuti, *Gabrieli*, ii, 64.
64. *HAM*, i, No. 157; also reprinted Arnold, G. *Gabrieli*, v, 32.

thorough-bass accompaniment on the organ: either a *basso seguente* (doubling the lowest part) or a *basso continuo*. Thus Gabrieli may be considered the main architect of a truly instrumental style. By reason of his contribution the Venetian School reached its highest point at this time. Foreigners like Heinrich Schütz and Leo Hassler, as well as minor composers, were schooled in it.

The more frequent use of the term *sonata*, the gradual disappearance of the term *canzone* in the course of the seventeenth century, and the stylistic analogies between the two genres make it likely that the former derived from the latter. Whatever the title, the *concertante* character of the upper parts, arranged in two choirs with contrasted dynamics of *piano* and *forte*, and supported by organ and lower-pitched instruments, opens the way to the concerto and anticipates the musical ideas of the Baroque era.

The rise of the orchestra is a major phenomenon in this period. In this connection the instrumental ensembles which performed at Renaissance courts for the presentation of *intermedi* were remarkable both for the sheer number of instruments and the variety of tone colour. The function of these orchestras was to double and thus to strengthen the polyphonic texture of the voices. As early as 1539, on the occasion of the wedding festivities of the Duke of Florence, Corteccia used groups of plucked string instruments and wind instruments. At some points a number of brass instruments (e.g. four cornetts and four trombones) were prescribed; at other times a variety of tone colour was produced by different keyboard instruments (e.g. harpsichords and small organs, employing several registers); on still other occasions a vigorous *tutti* sound is envisaged: *i vari strumenti suonati tutti ad un tempo*.[65] The same is true of the large apparatus of sonorities employed in later *intermezzi*, notably those of 1589 which employed an orchestra of greater dimensions than was prescribed for Monteverdi's *Orfeo*, the score of which is in fact anticipated here. The directions for performance in 1589 specify *organo di pivette* (regal), *violino alla francese* (modern violin), *sopranino di viola* (small viol of very high range) and *viola bastarda* (a small size bass viol suitable for chordal accompaniment). There were also ensembles drawn from families of well-established instruments, specified in the plural, some plucked (lutes, citterns, harps), some bowed (viols, lire) and some blown (trombones).[66]

The relationship between voices and instruments, and the principles of their effective combination, were discussed between 1590 and 1610 in various theoretical treatises on methods of performing the *basso continuo*. These treatises are remarkable in their formulation of principles before the *basso continuo* became the generally established norm and also because they articulate at this early stage the premises essential for the development of opera to come. Here we find a new set of values being established; harmonic-

65. *NOHM*, iv, 788 f.; A. C. Minor, *Renaissance*, pp. 58 f., 104, 229, 349.
66. *NOHM*, iv, 793 f.; D. P. Walker, *Intermèdes*.

vertical thinking, opposition to contrapuntal polyphony, and an anticipation of the dramatic, even theatrical, use of the instruments in the orchestra. In Bottrigari's *Desiderio* (1594) care is taken to distinguish between melody instruments and chordal instruments; and Agazzari's *Del sonare sopra il basso* (1607), with its instructions on how to employ melody instruments above a *basso continuo*, can be classed as among the oldest books on instrumentation.[67] In the *Concerti ecclesiastici* (1595) of Banchieri a *basso continuo* part, with regular bar-lines, is printed under the treble; and in Viadana's *Concerti ecclesiastici* (1602) the title-page boasts that the addition of the *basso continuo* for organ constitutes 'a new and convenient method'. Viadana's important preface is another treatise on the subject,[68] and his distinction between solo and chorus parts is a milestone in the development of the Baroque concerto. At the end of the Renaissance period, as the result of Florentine and other experiments in stage music and opera, a musical revolution had taken place. The results of this revolution were many, the most important being monodic singing in the *stile recitativo*, the use of the *basso continuo* and the carefully specified employment of instruments in the orchestra.

67. Strunk, *Readings*, pp. 424–31.
68. Strunk, *Readings*, pp. 419–23.

ERNEST H. SANDERS

6.1 England: From the Beginnings to c. 1540

EARLY POLYPHONY

Ever since the early years of the twentieth century France has been regarded as the centre of medieval music. Manifestations of a musical tradition elsewhere in Europe have usually been considered as peripheral, a term connoting minor importance and provincial conservatism. Yet how significant a role music in fact played in medieval England is indicated by the large quantity of scraps, flyleaves, paste-downs and detached fragments of polyphonic music of the thirteenth and fourteenth centuries that have been discovered in the last twenty-odd years. It is one of the greatest misfortunes in the history of music that no more or less complete codex of English polyphony prior to the 'Old Hall' manuscript (see pp. 289–96 below) has come down to us. This melancholy fact is the more painful when one realizes that the numerous preserved fragments, many of them transmitting only remnants, show that England has a larger number and a greater variety of sources of medieval polyphony than any other area of Europe. The manuscripts transmitting the music of the period of the first two Tudor kings give evidence of the work of nearly a hundred native composers at a time when the Flemings were monopolizing sacred music elsewhere. When one recalls the terrible devastation of manuscripts during the reign of Henry VIII, attempts at extrapolating the erstwhile wealth of English medieval music seem both staggering and reasonable. In the circumstances it is doubtful whether a fairly comprehensive view of English music in the Middle Ages can ever be obtained. But even the tattered and scattered remains form compelling proof of the vitality and individual profile of English medieval polyphony. The available evidence leaves no doubt that, at least from some time before the middle of the thirteenth century in England, the Middle Ages were an outstanding *saeculum musicum*.[1]

Apart from the Winchester *organa*,[2] collections of polyphonic music composed prior to *c.* 1250 are preserved in two sources only. In neither is the style of the pieces significantly different from contemporaneous stylistic conventions in France. A twelfth-century manuscript at Cambridge (University Library, Ff. 1.17) contains twenty-two monophonic and thirteen polyphonic pieces, most of which are *versus*.[3] (There are two

Example 1. Cambridge, University Library, Ff. 1.17, fol. 4ʳ

Quid adesse? Homo gaude
Presul adest dignus laude
Omnis ordo gratulare
Et suef aleiz
Nam est dignum exultare
Et si m'entendeiz.

Datus tibi sit hic clamor
Nicolae noster amor.
Iam et noster quis sit rector?
Et suef aleiz
Iube domne dicat lector
Et si m'entendeiz.

1. The view that in the fifteenth century 'composers from northern France were the only ones with a solid past and (as it turned out) hope for the immediate future' and that 'whatever [the English] could now give the French they owed it to them, having got it all from France in the first place' is to be found in several publications, among them R.L.Crocker, *A History of Musical Style*, New York, 1966, p. 143.

2. See chapter 3, pp. 92–3.

3. Concerning *versus* and their occurrence in the 'St Martial' repertoire, see chapter 3, p. 97.

[Let us rejoice and celebrate,
Let us venerate Nicholas,
Let us not cease singing his praises, *And walk softly*,
And let us extol him in song, *And thus you'll hear me.*

Why be here? Let everyone be glad,
Our praiseworthy patron protects us,
Let all ranks render thanks, *And walk softly*,
For it is fitting to rejoice, *And thus you'll hear me.*

Let this acclamation resound for Thee,
Nicholas, our loved one.
And who indeed should be our guide and master? *And walk softly*,
Let the reader say, 'Command, Lord, [the granting of Thy blessing]',
  And thus you'll hear me.]

concordances with the 'St Martial' repertoire.) The *versus* (*conductus*), *Exultemus et letemur*, is representative; see example 1.

One of the polyphonic compositions is a troped *organum*, *Amborum sacrum spiramen/ Benedicamus Domino*, which is somewhat more modern and considerably more ingenious than its St Martial counterparts.[4] In contrast to the latter, it applies textually untroped discant style to the melismatic passage of the tenor, while for the remainder the *vox organalis* is made up, in the fashion of a quodlibet, of phrases of various pre-existing tunes with their original Latin (Gregorian or troped) or French texts; each syllable of the *cantus firmus* is made to coincide with the appropriately assonant final syllable of a quotation in the upper part. The manuscript is also noteworthy in that one of its *versus* is the earliest known composition for three voices; though much of its counterpoint seems rather haphazard and not particularly felicitous.

The other source is the famous manuscript now at Wolfenbüttel, and usually abbreviated as W_1.[5] While most of its content consists of music of the Notre Dame school, there are a number of indications that the manu-script was written in England. Not only are there notational features characteristic of thirteenth-century English conventions, but a somewhat later medieval hand has entered a remark on one of its pages that the book belonged to the monastery of St Andrew's in Scotland. (This does not necessarily mean, though, that St Andrew's library was its first repository.) Moreover, W_1 contains a number of thirteenth-century 'Sanctus' and 'Agnus' tropes, five of which are for three parts. These have no counterpart in the other Notre Dame sources, but resemble two 'Sanctus' tropes for three parts in an English fragment (Cambridge, University Library, Ff. 2.29 [d]) which also contains a concordance of one of the Notre Dame *organa tripla*.

4. See chapter 3, p. 100.
5. See chapter 3, p. 106, fn. 24.

In its last (11th) fascicle W₁ transmits an insular collection of forty-seven two-part chant settings for Lady-Masses (i.e. votive Masses of the Virgin). The compositions, probably dating from the 1230s, comprise 'Kyrie' tropes, a 'Gloria' trope, Alleluias, a Tract, Sequences, Offertories, 'Sanctus' tropes, and 'Agnus' tropes, and generally exhibit the discant style of *conducti* and *organa* of *c.* 1200. Apart from relatively modest cadential flourishes, organal style does not occur.[6] A sample of the music is given in example 2, the final double versicle of a setting of the sequence *Laudes Christo decantemus* (a Marian adaptation of *Laudes crucis attolamus*).[7]

Example 2. W₁, fol. 205 (188)ʳ

6. The extant sources indicate that organal composition with the sustained tenor notes typical of the *Magnus liber* and of the Perotinian *tripla* and *quadrupla* seems not to have been favoured by English musicians of the twelfth and thirteenth centuries. Only one such composition is preserved, a setting for three voices of *Alleluia nativitas* (Worcester Cathedral, Additional 68, No. xviii, fols. 1ᵛ–2ʳ), which is not an entirely independent composition, since it incorporates a famous Perotinian *conductus* motet, i.e. a textual trope of one of the discant passages from Perotinus's setting of the same Alleluia.

7. For another example see Frank Ll. Harrison, *Music in Mediaeval Britain*, London 1958, 131.

*MS: Ut

[Tender Jesus, hear us,
Who are gathered here to offer Thy mother's praises,
And after this life transport Thy mother's servants
To the palaces of God, the Father.

And make those whom you wish to serve Thy mother
Not suffer any bitter calamities,
But, rather, when the day of wrath comes,
Grant and bestow eternal joy.
Amen.]

Few medieval songs with English texts have been preserved, and the existing ones nearly all date from the thirteenth century. Evidently there was no native song art in England to compare with the French, Provençal or Spanish productions. A possible reason for this dearth is the prevalence of French cultural influences in early Gothic England. The pervasiveness of French as the literary language was such that it even intruded occasionally into Latin poems set by English medieval composers (see p. 256). The marriage of Henry II and Eleanor of Aquitaine, who was a keen patroness of the *trobadors* and their art, may also have helped to prevent the development of an English art-song repertoire.

A mere handful of English songs has purely secular texts without any religious overtones, while three of the religious songs are English adaptations of the crucifixion sequence *Stabat iuxta Christi crucem*. The preponderance of sacred lyrics can be attributed to the propagandistic zeal of the Franciscan friars, who seem to have inhibited most indications of a rise of English musical lyricism. Nearly all the extant polyphony composed in England before the mid-fifteenth century sets Latin texts and is therefore liturgical or at least clerical. Despite the destruction of manuscripts, the remaining evidence compels the conclusion that England produced few polyphonic settings of English lyrics before the early Tudor period and that *cantus firmus* polyphony was restricted to Latin texts in the upper voices. The notion of dismembering a plainsong so as to obtain a *cantus firmus* for the structural support of a musical superstructure with vernacular texts must have seemed improper to the English,[8] whose concern with liturgical propriety usually caused them to retain the trope-like connection between the texts of the upper voices and the tenor.

8. Only one motet with English poetry has come to light.

The few remaining thirteenth-century settings of English poetry are either monophonic or in two parts. The latter show a striking preference for the interval of the third (untypical elsewhere in Europe before the fifteenth century). In these duets the 'upper' voice tends to occupy the same register as the tenor with consequent frequent crossings of the parts (see examples). (It is the modern custom to call such duets 'gymels', but the term appears only in the fifteenth century, when it means the temporary splitting of one voice into two of equal register.)[9]

Example 3. London, British Museum, Arundel 248, fol. 154[v]

> Je - su Cri - stes mil - de mo - der, stud bi - held hire sone o
> The sone heng the mo - der stud,   and bi - held hire chil - des
>
> ro - de, that he was i - pi - ned on.
> blud,   wu it of hise wun - des ran.

Anonymous IV[10] twice points out that the predilection for the major and minor third is typical of Western England; 'in some regions', he says, 'as for instance England, in the area known as West-country, they are called the best consonances ...'

THE THIRTEENTH CENTURY

FREELY COMPOSED POLYPHONY. In contrast to the twelfth-century compositions, much of the Latin polyphony written in thirteenth-century England[11] no longer shared all its stylistic features with continental repertoires, but absorbed the idiosyncrasies of style prevailing in the isolated specimens of vernacular polyphony, particularly the partiality to the interval of the third.[12] How much Latin duets had in common with two-part settings

9. For a discussion of the term see *NOHM*, ii, 342; for an example from the fifteenth century see *NOHM*, iii, 315.

10. See chapter 3, p. 103.

11. All completely preserved compositions and some significant fragments will be published in Ernest H. Sanders, *English Polyphony in the 13th and Early 14th Centuries*.

12. While the tradition of Pythagorean tuning caused medieval theorists to view the major third as a complex ratio (81:64) and therefore as an inharmonious and dissonant interval, two Englishmen – Theinred of Dover (twelfth century) and Walter Odington (*c*. 1300) – were evidently impelled by the indigenous love of the third to point to the proximity of 81:64 to the far more harmonious ratio 5:4.

of English poetry is well demonstrated by the *conductus* ('Agnus' trope), *Rex eterne glorie*, whose middle section is given in example 4.

Example 4. Cambridge, Gonville and Caius College, 803/807, No. 32ᵣ

Qui   na - tus   es   de - vir - gi - ne

sub hu - ma - na spe — ci - e   mi - se - re - re   mi - se - re — re.

[Thou who art born of the virgin and thus art of mankind, have mercy, have mercy.]

A composer writing counterpoint for two voices of equal range was likely to introduce the device of voice exchange. As long as the *duplum* decorates a given tune, however, the two voices are functionally not equivalent, and voice exchange is therefore not practicable.[13] It is for this reason that this device, much loved by English composers, rarely appears in the syllabic portions of *conducti*, but often enlivens the *caudae* (see example 5).

Example 5. Cambridge, Jesus College, Q.B. 1, Strips 4ᵣ, 7ᵣ, 26ᵣ, 5ᵣ

Hinc   [hinc] vox le - ti - ci - e per - so - nat

qui - a lux ho - di - e   ra - di - at   lux ce - le - bris   te -

13. Concerning the terms 'voice exchange', *conductus* and *cauda*, see chapter 3, pp. 109 and 116. Sometimes voice exchange is feasible between a tune and its counterpoint in successive statements; that is, where pieces employ repetition, strophic or otherwise. Double versicle forms naturally lend themselves to this technique, and there are quite a few sequences and tropes of widely scattered European provenance that prove the international cultivation of this type of composition until the fourteenth century.

[Hence, let the joyful voice resound, because the light shines today, because the treasured light banishes all darkness.]

In the extant polyphonic repertoire of the thirteenth century compositions for two voices are quite rare. Most polyphony was written for three voices, and even four-part counterpoint is a good bit more common than in continental repertoires. Some of the three-part *conducti* seem to have been conceived as duets for equal voices with an added third voice (*triplum*) of similar range. The tenor and *duplum* (second part) form mostly thirds; to these the *triplum* adds thirds and fifths; many such pieces consist of long stretches with a nearly uninterrupted array of 'triads' (see example 6).

Example 6. Oxford, Worcester College, 3.16 (A)*, fol. 1ʳ

-ex - pug - na - bi - li   nos cir - cum · det vir - tus al - tis - si - mi.

[... Thou, aurora of the everlasting king, cause the power of the Highest to surround us with an impregnable wall.]

Soon however such compositions were conceived in three parts from the outset, without the necessity of depending on a two-part foundation. This is clearly demonstrated by the two ways in which English composers applied voice exchange to three-part texture. One procedure was to write triple voice exchange, i.e. to write a melody consisting not of two, but of three phrase elements (a, b, c), all of which can be combined simultaneously, as in example 7, the intermediate *cauda* of the *conductus, Quem trina polluit*. This

Example 7. Durham, University Library, Bamburgh Collection, Select 13, front fly-leaf recto (Concordance: Oxford, Bodleian Library, Lat. Lit. d 20, fol. 35^v)

type of procedure which, as the horizontal projection of a simple harmonic scheme, depends on thirds, fifths and octaves as the three basic intervals, was known as *rondellus*, a term denoting both a particular technique of composition and a complete piece composed in this manner. 'And when what is sung by one may be sung by everybody in turn, such a tune is called *rondellus*, i.e. a rotational melody....' The quoted definition by Odington is preceded one hundred years earlier by a description of Welsh music in the *Descriptio Cambriae*, written by Giraldus Cambrensis in 1198:

When they make music together, they sing their tunes not in unison, as is done elsewhere, but in parts with many [simultaneous] modes and phrases. Therefore, the number of people singing ... is matched by the number of songs and voices in different ranges that the listener hears; yet, they all accord in one consonant and properly constituted composition, marked by the enchanting delight of B flat....[14] This specialty of this race is no product of trained musicians, but was acquired through long-standing popular practice.

The assumption that Giraldus is describing the *rondellus* is strengthened by the probable provenance of those English sources which for the first time transmit pieces exhibiting voice exchange or *rondellus* technique. While they post-date the *Descriptio* by five or more decades, some of them seem to have originated in localities twenty to forty miles east of Wales.

Example 8. Oxford, Bodleian Library, Lat. Lit. d 20, fol. 23[r]

14. See below, p. 270, fn. 21.

Apart from the *rondellus* procedure, voice exchange came to be adapted to three-part texture by restricting it to the two upper voices (ᵇₑ ᵇₑ) and supporting it with a repetitive tenor (a a) (see example 8).

Both devices (*rondellus* and voice exchange) came to be applied to the composition of *musica cum littera* as well as to melismatic passages. Odington, in the passage quoted above, provides an example of *rondellus*[15] which consists of twice three phrase elements. The first half is melismatic, while only one of the three phrases of the second half has text, which is therefore sung successively by each of the three voices. This latter procedure occurs often and is demonstrated by the *rondellus* section of the *conductus, O laudanda virginitas*, which shows a remarkably ingenious combination of *rondellus* and hocket technique (see example 9).

Example 9. Oxford, Bodleian Library, Wood 591, flyleaf 1ᵛ⁻ʳ

---

15. The passage and example are reproduced in facsimile in Wooldridge, *Early English*, i, plate 41; translation and transcription in Wooldridge, *Polyphonic*, i, 319–21.

[In Sinai truth is revealed, and the oil is the proof;
O blessed burial, o royal dignity, having gone through suffering.]

Example 10, from a manuscript in Worcester Cathedral,[16] exemplifies voice exchange between *duplum* and *triplum* over a repetitive tenor in a non-melismatic *conductus* section.

Example 10. Worcester Cathedral Lib., Add. 68, No. XIX, fol. a2ᵛ

[Hail, rose among flowers, giving birth to salvation, hail, Thou who art praised by the saints and bringest salvation to the world.]

16. The fragmentary sources of English thirteenth-century polyphony preserved in the Worcester Cathedral Library were the first to receive attention in modern times, and the anonymous composers therefore came to be referred to as the 'Worcester School'. Though Worcester seems indeed to have been a major centre of polyphonic composition, the original provenance of some of these fragments is not certain. Moreover, a number of concordances exist, of which two seem to have originated at Norwich (example 7) and Meaux Abbey respectively. Yet, it may be of some significance that almost all the concordances are somewhat younger than their 'Worcester' counterparts. The contents of MSS Oxford, Bodleian Library, Lat. lit. d 20, and Worcester Cathedral, Additional 68, have been transcribed, with varying reliability, in Luther A. Dittmer, ed., *The Worcester Fragments*, 1957.

Should the text be declaimed by the two upper voices only, the texture would in effect be that of a *conductus* motet. If such compositions were written, none has been preserved.[17] Several pieces exist, however, in which a poetic text is recited by the two upper voices, which alternate melismatic and syllabic passages over a freely composed and tonally centred tenor laid out repetitively in double versicles. Usually the result of the voice exchange is that each poetic verse is sung by both voices in turn. In example 11 however the text is continuous.

Example 11. Oxford, Bodleian Library, Lat. Lit. d 20, fol. 23[r]

[Thy sweet-flowing remembrance, O Mary, gives me wonderful joy, O Mary, Thou queen . . .]

Example 11 is the continuation of example 8. Voice exchange among the upper parts over the repeated phrase in the tenor (a a) has been described in connection with example 8. Example 11 shows another repeated tenor phrase, or double versicle (d d). The entire scheme of *Dulciflua*, i.e. example 8 plus example 11 plus its continuation, is given below. The letters from 'a' to 'o' each indicate melodic phrases in the three parts. The eight phrases of the verbal text are indicated by numerals attached to the letters of the upper voices. The lowest part, or tenor, has no text. As one would expect, in view

17. Of all the English sources of thirteenth-century polyphony only one (Cambridge, Trinity College, 0.2.1) transmits *conductus* motets, each of which is based on a *cantus firmus* and therefore has no voice exchange. Three of its nine compositions are concordances of motets preserved in Notre Dame manuscripts.

of the double versicle structure of the tenor, the rhyme scheme of the verses sung by the upper voices is paired, i.e. f_1 rhymes with f_2 etc.

triplum:	c	b	f_1	e	i_3	h	l_5	k	o_7	n	Coda
duplum:	b	c	e	f_2	h	i_4	k	l_6	n	o_8	Coda
tenor:	a	a	d	d	g	g	j	j	m	m	Coda

Elements of *conductus*, *rondellus* and motet are intermingled in this composition: the melismatic introduction (over the pair of phrases a a in the tenor) derives from the *conductus*; the simultaneous singing of syllabic phrases (with text) and melismatic phrases (without text) as a result of voice exchange, from the *rondellus*; and a supporting tenor without text from the motet.[18] But in overall texture and construction this composition comes closer to the motet than to the other two genres, and, in fact, pieces like *Dulciflua* were apparently known as motets. More complex designs are not uncommon, as that of the *pes*-motet[19] in a manuscript at Princeton (Garrett 119, fols 3a–4b) whose two upper parts have separate, though related texts and no melismatic passages. Some variants apart, its structure is:

triplum:	c	b	f	e	i	h′	l		b	c	e	f	h	i′	k
duplum:	b	c	e	f	h	i′	k		c	b	f	e	i	h′	l
pes:	a	a	d	d	g	g	j		a	a	d	d	g	g	j

The examples prove that the stylistic distinction between *conductus* and motet was not as rigid in thirteenth-century England as knowledge of the Notre Dame repertoire might lead one to expect. In contrast to the continental *clausula* motet, which strikes one as a primarily musical structure to which a text is attached, an English *pes*-motet gives the impression of providing poetry with a musical setting. Therefore, procedures which in France characterized distinct genres sometimes occur in one and the same composition in England. For instance in two of the compositions in one manuscript (University of Chicago, 654 App.) the freely composed tenor carries a poetic text of its own, while the two upper voices share another text in the fashion of a *conductus* motet; one of the pieces also contains a *rondellus* section, while the other ends with a lengthy passage in which the upper parts, engaging in voice exchange, alternately declaim the text. The role played by the techniques of voice exchange and *rondellus* shows that English predilections account for a much greater stylistic homogeneity in the entire repertoire[20] than is the case in the French polyphony of the time.

18. In many English manuscripts of the time these supporting, word-less tenors, showing internal repetition, are called *pes* (foot; fundament; ground) rather than tenor. In contrast to these freely composed tenors or *pedes* continental motets employ *cantus firmi* derived from Gregorian melismas which lack internal repetition (paired phrases) and are therefore unsuitable to support voice exchange in the upper voices.

19. See above, fn. 18.

20. This observation also applies to the texts; most of the poetry of thirteenth-century English polyphony is Marian.

Not only were the border lines between polyphonic genres far more fluid in England than in France, but several sources make no attempt to keep *conducti*, motets and *rondelli* in separate groups. Since some of the *rondelli* are polytextual, the only unique criterion of a *pes*-motet is that its freely invented lowest voice has no text.

In the preserved English repertoire of the second half of the thirteenth century most of the *rondelli*, and of the *conducti* with voice exchange or *rondellus* sections, and of the *pes*-motets are in the Ionian mode (F major) or at least Mixolydian and F major[21] (see examples 10 and 11 above). In almost every case the combined effect of the three (or four)[22] voices is the constant reinforcement of the *finalis* (tonic). The *pes* of a motet with voice exchange produces variations on a tonic ostinato, with the supertonic, because of its cadential function, holding a place of structural importance second only to that of the tonic (see example 12).

Example 12. Worcester Cathedral Lib., Add. 68, No. XXVIII, fol. b2[v]

In a good many motets the *pes* consists of only one melodic element which is stated more than twice. Here it seems that the double-versicle structure of the *pes* in the case of motets with voice exchange merged with the idea of rhythmic *ostinato*, familiar to English composers from continental motets, to produce melodic *ostinati* or grounds over which the upper voices unfold without voice exchange. For instance the *pes* of the motet whose beginning is given in example 13[23] is stated nine times. There is evidence that such a *pes* was sometimes a well-known tune, e.g. a snatch of a popular song, a refrain,

21. The frequent appearance of a single flat in lieu of a clef in several English sources of the thirteenth century can be adduced in explanation of Giraldus' reference to 'the enchanting delight of B flat' (see above, p. 264), by which he probably meant the English preference for F – Ionian.

22. *Conducti* do not seem to have been written for four voices in medieval England. Motets for four voices generally consist of a *pes* or tenor and three voices with separate texts. In a few cases two upper parts are supported by a pair of textless parts, one of which is usually a filler and may be either un-labelled or designated as *secundus tenor* or *quartus cantus*.

23. The notes for the beginning of the *quadruplum*, which are missing in the source, are reconstructed. The *pes* is closely related to the tenor of the *conductus* passage quoted in example 10, p. 267 above.

Example 13. Worcester Cathedral Lib., Add. 68, No. XXXI^v and No. XXVIII, fol. 1^r

[O how Thou glitterest in glorious light, queen of the tribe of David . . . O how blessed Thou art, Mary, our most gentle Lady . . . O how happy a woman is the fairest virgin, the dearest mother of Christ . . .]

or a dance phrase. Many such *pes*-motets exhibit sophisticated phrase structures of admirable elegance. *Te domine laudat/Te dominum clamat*, for instance (Worcester Cathedral, MS. Add. 68 No. XIII, ff. 1^v–2^r) has a *pes* which consists of four complete statements, followed by one incomplete statement. Each of the complete statements amounts to 30 longs (or beats or measuring units) symmetrically subdivided into 5 units of 6 longs each: $5 \times 6L$.[24] The upper two voices are mostly made up of phrases of 8 longs (at times extended by a short melisma to 10 longs); but a unit of 14 longs occurs once in both *duplum* and *triplum*: these 14 longs may be considered as a double phrase (or the equivalent of 2 phrases). The beginning of the *duplum*, for instance, consists of 5 phrases plus a double phrase, the equivalent of 7 phrases: $10+2 \times (10+8)+14$. Thus, it will be seen from the following table

24. Concerning the importance of proportion and number in medieval phrasing see chapter 3, pp. 113, 120 and 121 where the same abbreviations are used: 10L+8L (or: 10+8) denotes two phrases, one of 10 and one of 8 longs; $2 \times (10+8)$ means twice two phrases or a total of 4 phrases.

that each of the upper voices consists of 16 phrases (namely 14 simple phrases plus a double phrase). These 16 phrases accommodate the 8 couplets of the 2 Latin poems (*Te domine laudat* and *Te dominum clamat*) and are poised against 5 statements of the wordless *pes* in the following scheme:

triplum	2×8	+2×(10+8)		+8	10	+2×(10+8)	+14	10	+8
duplum	10	+2×(10+8)	+14		2×8	+2×(10+8)	+8	8	+10
pes	5×6	+5×6			5×6	+5×6		3×6	

There are two compositions that must be singled out because of the ingenuity with which voice exchange is combined with an *ostinato pes*. One, the motet *Puellare gremium/Purissima mater*, is constructed on a *pes* with two component phrases of unequal length and different modality. Each phrase is treated as a double versicle, and the entire *pes* is stated three times (see example 14). (Since it lies relatively high, the 'bass' notes are often supplied by the *duplum*.) While each of the upper voices has a separate text over the

Example 14. Worcester Cathedral Lib., Add. 68, No. XIII, fol. 4^r

first and third statements of the *pes*, they share the same text in the central portion of the motet. Here voice exchange is employed in which syllabic (or near-syllabic) passages alternate with melismatic wordless passages. This procedure serves to emphasize the central idea of the poem. The phrases of the upper voices group themselves into three large sections. In the *triplum* the total time-space of 114 longs is divided into 34+40+40, in the *duplum* into 40+40+34, over a tenor whose structure consists of 3×4 phrases: $3 \times (2 \times 9L + 2 \times 10L)$.

The other composition to combine the idea of voice exchange with that of a supporting ground is the famous and most widely known piece of English medieval music, the *Sumer Canon* (*c*. 1250)[25] which is one of the two extant *rotae* (rounds) written in thirteenth-century England.[26] The manuscript stipulates that the tune is to be sung as a round by up to four voices, supported by a *pes*. The *pes* itself differs from the norm in that it is for two voices (not one), which enter simultaneously and engage in continuous voice exchange. In other words, the *rota* 'Sumer is icumen in, Lhude sing cuccu', is superimposed upon the *pes* 'Sing cuccu, Sing cuccu nu'. Actually the melody of the *rota* is so constructed that it could be sung as a *rondellus* for three, four, six, eight or twelve voices. (Round and *rondellus* are, of course,

25. London, British Museum, MS Harley 978, f. 11^v. References to earlier literature on the subject will be found in Handschin, *Mus. Disc.* (1949) 55.

26. The other rota is *Munda Maria mater*, a round for three voices without *pes* (Oxford, Bodleian Library, Lat. lit. d 20, fols. 12^r–12^v).

closely related, since the only differences between them are the successive, rather than simultaneous, entrances of the voices in a round and the necessity for ending it arbitrarily.)[27]

Nearly all the compositions discussed so far have a sound which is peculiarly and indubitably English. This quality derives from several factors: in addition to the frequent employment of the major mode, there is the stress on the chords of the tonic and supertonic; the emphasis on triads and, secondarily, $_3^6$ chords (the latter functioning most prominently as penultimate chords at cadence points; there is also a predilection for regular periods, for rhythms with trochaic ingredients (mainly ♩ ♪ ♪♩. ♩ ♪ etc.), and for the rhythm known on the continent as first mode.[28] At the ends of phrases the cadential motion, with subsequent rests, emphasizes the important degrees of the scale, relating these degrees to each other (and to the tonic) in a manner suggestive of the tonal procedures of later centuries. The characteristic English love of chordal sonority accounts for a fair number of effective and convincing compositions for four voices, several of which have a full triad, with the tonic note doubled at the octave, for their final chord.

All these facets of style are quintessentially embodied in the *Sumer Canon*, the earliest extant secular composition[29] that must be called a tonal organism, both melodically and harmonically. Giraldus's description of Welsh music makes it possible to assume that the *Sumer Canon* is a particularly sophisticated sublimation of popular traditions; very probably only pieces of more than common complexity, like the *Sumer Canon*, were written down. Due to freakish luck it was preserved through the centuries to corroborate the existence, at least since the late twelfth century, of a flourishing musical culture that evidently exerted a vital influence on the specifically English evolution of the *conductus* and the motet in the thirteenth century.

That the French were well aware of the special characteristics of English polyphony is borne out by a French double motet, preserved in two con-

27. The *Sumer Canon* presumably ends after the leading voice has sung its part twice.

28. See chapter 3, p. 134. Iambic or related rhythms (second and third modes), which gained only gradual acceptance outside central France, begin to appear in the late thirteenth century, and even in the fourteenth century many English sources still show so decided a preference for trochaic rhythm that, irrespective of Franconian tradition, pairs of semibreves were often written so as to make the first of two notes twice as long as the second. Duple rhythm (i.e. two equal breves taking the place of the long) is as rare as in France and begins to occur only toward the end of the century. (In all probability, therefore, the 'English Dance' printed as No. 40c in *HAM*, i, should not be performed in $_4^3$ time as indicated there, but in $_8^6$ time.)

29. Though the piece has an alternate Latin text, its origin is surely secular. A piece as charming as the *Sumer Canon* and stylistically related to it, even though it does without voice exchange, is the 'bell motet' (*Campanis cum cymbalis/Honoremus dominam*) for two bell-like *pedes* and two texted upper voices (Oxford, Bodleian Library, Mus. c. 60, fol. 85ᵛ). While it begins with a tonic pedal, the last two thirds of the motet, which is as English as change-ringing, exploit the continual alternation of the tonic and supertonic triads, a device which was to remain popular in England for centuries.

tinental manuscripts, which pokes fun at English and Scottish *godaliers* (guzzlers of good ale). This composition, dating from the second quarter of the century, is the only continental *cantus firmus* motet of the time whose upper voices engage in voice exchange, a procedure made possible by the unusual selection of a sequence as tenor. This motet is, therefore, strong evidence for the assumption that the parodied musical practice, abandoned by French composers as a result of the growing prominence of the motet, was known as typically English at least as early as *c.*1225. Moreover, voice exchange and *rondellus* are described only by English theorists. English influence may be responsible for a number of features: the relative frequency of thirds in a number of Notre Dame *conducti*; voice exchange in many *conductus caudae* as well as in many *organa* for more than two voices, composed in Perotin's time; and the preference for a regular structure made up of phrases that are robustly four-square and dance-like. It is noteworthy, for instance, that passages in English compositions also appear with little or no change in Perotinian polyphony. Since the insular manuscripts preserving such compositions (including the *Sumer Canon*) can hardly be dated earlier than the middle of the thirteenth century,[30] it may, of course, be objected that the assumption of English influence on Perotin and his contemporaries is hazardous. It must be said, however, that the fact that the continental manuscripts preserving the music of the Notre Dame School postdate the repertoire by a good many decades has no bearing on the chronology of Notre Dame polyphony; similarly, the many lacunae in the English sources, as well as the probability of the existence of popular polyphony not dependent on notation, justify the acceptance of the circumstantial evidence that such techniques as voice exchange were already common in English music around the turn of the century and that English influence is likely to have had a considerable share in the shaping of the musical style of the second Notre Dame generation.

CANTUS FIRMUS

For most of the thirteenth century the English partiality to homogeneous and tonally unified compositions (with or without voice exchange) seems to have prevented the technique of the continental motet from taking root. In France the matter of tonal unity was of relatively little importance, as is attested by the practice of writing *clausulae* and motets; many of the chant melismas on which they are based are not tonal units. Even a good many of the freely composed continental pieces of the thirteenth and fourteenth

---

30. The attempt made in the 1940s to interpret the rhythm of the *Sumer Canon* (as well as of other English compositions) as binary and to postulate its date of composition as *c.* 1310, is untenable. The document preserving it can be said to date from the 1250s.

centuries lack an unequivocal tonal centre. Moreover, in contrast to the *pes*-motet with its relatively homogeneous texture and sonority, the continental motet characteristically forges unity out of heterogeneous components. While a few insular sources exhibit French influence, *cantus firmus* motets are, on the whole, quite rare. The French tradition of imposing repetitive rhythmic *ostinato* patterns on motet tenors and keeping the upper voices strictly syllabic is evident in relatively few English compositions of the thirteenth century. More often that not, plainsong tenors, many of which contain internal repetitions, are not even identified in the manuscripts; in at least one case the *cantus firmus* is labelled '*pes*', even though the three upper voices, like those of English *cantus firmus* motets generally, trope the text of the chant. There must necessarily be some uncertainty whether the *pedes* of a few of the English thirteenth-century motets are, in fact, freely composed or *cantus firmi*; a dividing line is not always discernible, especially in view of the composers' occasional tampering with the melodic substance of properly labelled Gregorian tenors. Sometimes a *cantus firmus*, particularly if it has some internal repetitions, is shaped so as to resemble a *pes*, as in the Marian double motet on the tenor *In odorem* preserved in Oxford (Bodleian Library, MS, Corpus Christi College, 497), of which a motet in the Montpellier manuscript, usually abbreviated as *Mo*[31] is a *contrafactum*. A comparison of the structure of its tenor[32] with that of the same tenor in a Perotinian motet (*Mo*, No. 95) makes the conceptual difference strikingly apparent (see example 15).

Example 15. *Mo*, Nos. 70 and 95

31. See chapter 3, p. 140, fn. 60.

32. The upper voices of this motet proceed in eight-beat phrases which are neatly staggered, since irregular phrases occur at the beginning, middle and end. At the beginning, for instance, the eight-beat phrases in the *duplum* start two longs later than in the *triplum*:

triplum: 10L+8L+8L+8L   etc.
duplum: 12L+8L+8L+8L   etc.

While thirteenth-century English polyphony included few motets in the French sense, a large number of compositions exist that continue the heritage of the troped *organum*. These, however, discard almost completely the old organal style in the tradition of the eleventh fascicle of W_1 (see p. 258 above). The composers produced, in effect, troped discant settings of Gregorian plainsongs. Of the roughly three dozen compositions, most of them for Lady-Masses or Mary-Masses (the latter sung on the occasion of a Marian feast), a little over half represent the responsorial chant categories selected for polyphonic treatment by the Notre Dame School; all but four are settings of Alleluias. The remainder, like the Winchester *organa* and the settings in the eleventh fascicle of W_1, reflects considerable liturgical inclusiveness: one Introit antiphon, one Offertory, a *Regnum prosula* of the 'Gloria', a *prosa*[33] for a Vespers responsory, part of a tract, three 'Kyries', six 'Sanctus' (two with lengthy tropes) and a trope of the *Sursum corda*.[34] Except for one four-voiced composition, all are for three voices.

The Introit antiphon *Salve sancta parens* (Worcester Cathedral, Additional 68, No. XXXI[r]), the most conservative of these settings, demonstrates how closely this repertoire is tied to far earlier traditions. The *cantus firmus* is disposed almost exclusively in unpatterned ternary longs which, in their

33. It is important to recognize the results of the troping process, whether the category be called trope, sequence or prose. See chapter 2, p. 77, fn. 31, and chapter 3, p. 97, fn. 11, and p. 99, fn. 13. The difference between prose and *prosula* is that in the latter the troping process is restricted to verbal additions. See also R. Steiner, *JAMS* (1969), 367.

34. Not until the early fourteenth century is there any documentary evidence for episcopal permission of the application of polyphony to parts of the ritual for which the French sources provide no polyphonic settings.

irregular phrasing, mirror the chant model quite closely; every word is
followed by a long rest, except that monosyllables, in a manner first described by Johannes Affligemensis,[35] are grouped with the next word. The
phrases of the two upper voices, which are of varying length and irregular
(i.e. not necessarily containing multiples of two longs), are parallel in the
fashion of a *conductus*; both parts have the same verbal trope, which frequently displays assonances with the text of the *cantus firmus*.

Almost all the other settings are more progressive. Each upper part has
its own troped text (at times with intriguing cross-references), and a few of
the tenors exhibit dance-like patterns reminiscent of the *pedes* of some of the
freely composed motets. In such cases the Gregorian chant has in effect been
turned into a secular tune (see example 16).

Example 16. Worcester Cathedral Lib., Add. 68, No. X, fol. 2ᵛ (Setting of 'Kyrie' Ed.
Vat. I)

When the *cantus firmus* itself is not a tonal unit, it is to be expected that
many settings would necessarily lack the palpable tonal cohesiveness of the
free compositions. Yet, the English medieval tendency towards tonal
cohesion was so strong that a good number of chants were changed so as to
yield tonally unified tenors of polyphonic settings. At times the alteration
amounts to no more than one or two notes; in other cases the changes are
more extensive. For instance, the first phrase of the tenor of one of the
'Sanctus' settings is freely invented, allowing the composition to begin with
a tonic dyad (i.e. a chord composed of two pitches such as *f–c–f*, without the
third *a*) and at the same time bestowing the form aba'b on the initial three-
fold invocation (see example 17).

Example 17. Worcester Cathedral Lib., Add. 68, No. XXXV (*Olim* Oxford, Magdalen
College, 100), fol. 3ᵛ

35. See chapter 3, p. 95.

Such manipulations are also demonstrable in five fragmentary Alleluias belonging to a group of over forty Alleluia settings, possibly composed by a cleric named William of Wycombe (or Winchcombe), which make up a cycle of Leoninian scope. The majority of these are listed in the extant table of contents of an unknown manuscript and are totally lost; none is completely preserved, and only one is restorable in its entirety.[36] All these works, regardless of whether or not the *cantus firmus* is tampered with, constitute the most compelling examples of the composer's design to effect a compromise between the chant and a tonally organized polyphonic composition built around it. These Alleluias fall into four sections, the second and fourth of which are settings of the solo portions of the respond and verse. Each is preceded by a free section of varying length. Section 1, generally far longer than section 3, is a polyphonic trope to the respond. In the extant compositions it invariably involves voice exchange (over a *pes*) or *rondellus* technique. One of them is in effect as fine a voice-exchange motet as can be found among the independent pieces composed in this manner; indeed, it evidently came to be detached from its Alleluia, since it turns up as a separate motet in the Montpellier manuscript (*Mo*, No. 339).

The short codas of the first sections clearly reveal their structural function as transitions, namely, to provide a bridge from the end of the first section to the beginning of the setting of the respond. In fact, it seems that harmonic aspects – it may not be too far-fetched to refer to them as modulatory considerations – were to some extent responsible for the particular design of these introductory tropes. Not only do they establish the key, as it were, but whenever the respond of an Alleluia starts with a note other than the tonic (e.g. the *subtonium*[37]) the coda to section 1 effects what might well be called a modulation.

Apart from the fact that sections 1 and 2 are linked harmonically, quite often the *pes* of the first section is plainly related to the *incipit* of the Gregorian respond, with which the tenor begins section 2. The impression of thematic unity is strengthened by the handling of the third section (the prelude trope for the verse), which is in many cases thematically and stylistically related to section 1 and has similar modulatory functions. The evidence inescapably indicates that the design of the whole was governed by a strict concept of tonality.

The setting of the verse necessarily produced the longest of the sections so that section 4 is usually about twice as long as all the others combined. While longs are preponderant in section 2 in the tenor, in section 4 the tenor part often breaks into livelier, though unpatterned, rhythms (longs and breves). Some of the chant melismas are textually troped by one or both of the

---

36. *Alleluia Christo iubilemus*, a setting of the Christmas *Alleluia Dies sanctificatus* (Oxford, Bodleian Library, Rawlinson c. 400*, Fragments 1a, 2a, 3a).

37. The note a full tone below the tonic; the note which is a semitone below is called *subsemitonium*.

upper parts at a time. This practice (by no means consistently applied) is still more respectful of the Gregorian text than was the case in the *Salve sancta parens* (see p. 276), since any verbal trope in the upper parts is always arranged so as to permit the simultaneous declamation of the liturgical syllables by all the voices. The style of passages without textual tropes is a kind of combination of *conductus* and *clausula*, depending on the rhythms of the tenor and on whether any given chant passage is syllabic or melismatic. But Notre Dame terminology is quite inappropriate and misleading, since rigid application of preconceived rhythmic patterns for structural purposes is foreign to this repertoire. This circumstance also forbids the description of passages with added text in the upper parts in terms of motet technique. Even where polytextuality occurs, the impression is that of a diversity carefully restricted to maintain the effect of organic homogeneity.

The flowering of English thirteenth-century polyphony, with all its varieties, is astonishing, especially in view of the lamentably fragmentary state of the sources. An attempt at summarizing the salient characteristics of a large part of the music must include:

    1. musical and verbal interrelation and fusion of the voices;

    2. predilection for the interval of the third;

    3. sonorous scoring (usually within an octave) with relative frequency of triads;

    4. tonal unity in free compositions and in *cantus firmus* settings;

    5. predominance of rhythms with trochaic ingredients;

    6. prominence of regular phrase structure, often with dance-like rhythms.

These features have been adduced to influences from secular music as well as from the *conductus*, which itself may well have sprung from the sphere of secular music. It must be recalled in this context that the original function of the *conductus* was closely related to that of the trope. Thus the English polyphonic repertoire owes its considerable homogeneity to the powerful influence of secular practices, which found an initial outlet in two basically related types, i.e. trope and *conductus*. These circumstances help to explain the rarity of motets in the Notre Dame tradition, which are compositions with one or more added texts over a Gregorian melisma. Detached from their chants such melismas did not invite the verbal elaborations of troping. In England however polyphony retained its organic connection with the liturgy in the tradition of tropes and trope-like compositions.

THE FOURTEENTH CENTURY

During most of the thirteenth century the two outer voices of a polyphonic composition rarely formed an interval larger than the octave. Towards the end of the century this framework, i.e. the distance between the outer voices, expanded and the resultant wider texture accommodated a more frequent appearance of $\frac{6}{3}$ chords. The favourite chord of the thirteenth century in England had been the comparatively static combination of a perfect consonance (the fifth) with the imperfect consonance most popular in England (the third). Now the same evolutionary force expanded the framework and replaced the traditional $\frac{5}{3}$ chord with the more 'progressive' $\frac{6}{3}$ combination. Its characteristic quality of flow and progression, resulting from the absence of the perfect fifth, had been reserved largely for the penultimate chord of cadences.[38]

The so-called $\frac{6}{3}$ chord style originated in *conducti*, i.e. pieces of which the composition was not, as a rule, circumscribed by a *cantus firmus*. The great majority of apparently free compositions of the fourteenth century which, by and large, are tonally unified, like their thirteenth-century antecedents, favour the $\frac{6}{3}$ chord style. In addition to $\frac{8}{5}$ chords (usually at cadences) in this style $\frac{6}{3}$ chords often appear in chains of four or five or, more rarely, in longer chains up to a dozen. A modification of the $\frac{5}{3}$ chord, namely the $\frac{10}{5}$, appears less prominently, especially in the earlier part of the century.[39] While the term '$\frac{6}{3}$ chord style' denotes the most characteristic sonority, it must be remembered that in the majority of these pieces the chordal texture is quite varied and includes a good many more or less extensive passages in which no such parallelism whatever occurs (see examples 18a and b).

Example 18a. London, British Museum, Sloane 1210, fol. 143^{v}

38. The sixth, 'a vile and disgusting dissonance' except as cadential ingredient (Anonymus IV), increasingly came to be treated, like the third, as an imperfect consonance in the fourteenth century.

39. Significantly, the *rondellus* disappeared as a species of composition soon after the octave barrier of the two-part framework was breached decisively.

ip – sam sic al – lo – qui – tur:
vir – go ni – hi – lo – mi – nus.

[A messenger is quite secretly sent by the highest Father to Mary, and he addresses her with these words: 'Hail, Mary, full of grace, the Lord is with Thee, Thou shalt be an illustrious mother, but a virgin nonetheless.']

Example 18b. Cambridge, Gonville and Caius College, 727/334, fol. 199ʳ

Ma – ter Chri – sti no – bi – lis o vir – go Ma –
Ut sic pos – sint vi – ve – re vi – te vi – va

– ri – a tu – is e – sto fa – mu – lis
me – ta qua – ti – nus per – ci – pe – re

mi – se – ra – trix pi – a.
que – ant ce – li le – ta.

[O most excellent Virgin Mary, mother of Christ, bestow Thy pious compassion on Thy servants, so that they may live in order to be able to gain entrance to the land of Heaven at the vivifying end of life.]

Even in the few preserved duets, the counterpoint with its frequent sixths generally seems to imply, or at least allow for, the addition of an inner voice (see example 19).

Example 19. Oxford, Bodleian Lib., Dep. Deeds Ch. Ch. c. 34, D. 6, fol. 1ʳ

Vir - ga   sic - ca   si - ne   ro - re   no - vo   ri - tu

no - vo   mo - re   fru - ctum   pro - tu - lit   cum_____   flo - re

sic   quod   vir - go   pe   -   pe - rit.

[The dry branch in a new way, without moisture, brings forth fruit with flower, because this is how the virgin gave birth.]

One of the lower parts may at times be an adaptation of an already existing tune; more often it is freely composed. But the melodic interest is usually concentrated in the top voice which tends to proceed more smoothly. The survival of this style in the carol of the fifteenth century is not surprising since the carol is, in some ways, related to the *conductus* (see pp. 142–3 and p. 142, fn. 65).

Compositions of this sort, which no longer have *caudae*, began to appear around 1300 and are usually referred to as *cantilenae*.[40] Like *conducti* they are written in score with the Latin text placed under the lowest part.[41] The

40. The frequent occurrence of sixths in *cantilenae* is reported by the English theorist Walter Odington, cited above, p. 264, in connection with *rondellus*. Concerning Odington, who flourished in the early fourteenth century, see the article in *MGG*. Concerning *cantilena* style see p. 166, fn. 34.

41. The last (fragmentary) composition in the so-called Robertsbridge Codex is apparently an ornamented keyboard arrangement of an otherwise unknown *cantilena*. The two musical folios of this manuscript (London, British Museum, Add. 28550), whose main contents are a chronicle of Roberts-bridge Abbey, may be dated *c.* 1325. The music consists of keyboard pieces, viz. three *estampies* (one of them fragmentary), arrangements of two motets composed *c.* 1315 by Philippe de Vitry, and the *cantilena*. (Continental motets also turn up in two fragmentary English motet manuscripts of the four-

music of many of these devotional songs exhibits the double-versicle struc-ture of the sequence.[42] What is especially remarkable about a significant number of these pieces is the comprehensiveness and balanced order with which their phrases define the relationships of various scale degrees to the tonic. As regards sense of tonal direction, structural clarity, chordal richness and musical lyricism, these songs are unmatched by any other medieval repertoire.[43] Many of the melodies are likely to belong to an almost totally submerged tradition of vernacular song, since they have a flavour reminiscent of the few extant English songs.[44] Moreover the lyrics are of the type written in the first half of the fourteenth century by Richard de Ledrede, Franciscan bishop of Kilkenny in Ireland, as *contrafacta* for secular songs, with which his vicars and clerks had been 'defiling their throats', especially during the Christmas and New Year seasons.[45]

After 1300 the expansion of the traditional framework of polyphony beyond an octave created a wider texture in which the parts were less likely to occupy the same range. As a result, voice exchange became rare, but in the several instances where it did occur, the phrases which provided the material for exchange tended to grow longer. Some motets[46] were freely composed, others were based on a *cantus firmus*, among them the five motets discussed below. Two of these are based throughout on a liturgical *cantus firmus*, a *prosa*. In those two motets[47] the result of combining voice exchange in the upper parts with a plainsong *cantus firmus* is that the quality of regular harmonic alternation, of a varied *ostinato*, so characteristic of similar compositions of the thirteenth century, is absent from these later works.

Three other motets have been preserved in which the *cantus firmus* itself has been subjected to voice exchange. The two upper voices of *Salve cleri speculum/Salve iubar presulum*[48] are supported by a *prosa* whose phrases,

---

teenth century; see below, p. 289.) These English settings are the earliest remaining specimens of keyboard music in Europe. The pieces are written for two parts, with a third pitch added here and there for enriched sonority. The arrangements of the vocal compositions display an ornamentally, sometimes rather mechanically, elaborated top voice. In the *estampies* the lower part at times equals the upper in liveliness, often forming extensive parallelism (octaves, sixths or fifths).

42. Some of the *cantilenae* may have been intended 'to be sung at the Lady-Mass in place of the sequence' (Harrison, *Mediaeval*, p. 296).

43. The *cantilena* repertoire is to appear in E. H. Sanders, ed., *English Polyphony of the 14th Century* (in the series 'Polyphonic Music of the 14th Century').

44. Cf. the two-part devotional song *Edi be thu heven quene*, *NOHM*, ii, 342.

45. See John T. Gilbert, 'Archives of the See of Ossory', *Historical Manuscripts Commission*, Report X, App. V, pp. 242 ff; also E. K. Chambers, *English Literature at the Close of the Middle Ages*, 1945, p. 82.

46. Publication of the corpus of motets, composed in fourteenth-century England, ed. F. L. Harrison, is in the planning stage (in the series 'Polyphonic Music of the 14th Century').

47. *O homo considera/O homo de pulvere/Filie Jerusalem*, Oxford, New College 362, fols. 83ᵛ & 90; *Balaam/Balaam/Balaam*, ibid., fol. 86 (*MO* 340–1).

48. Oxford, Bodleian Library, Hatton 81, fols. 45ᵛ and 2.

provided with free textless counterpoints, are repeated and divided among the two lower parts by means of voice exchange, except that the first section is a prelude with freely designed lower parts. Voice exchange is also applied to the two top voices, alternately declaiming the text, which is almost completely troped. The texture, while not exactly like a hocket, reminds the modern listener of the *style brisé* of the French clavecinists. Similarly constructed is a motet, also based on a Gregorian *cantus firmus*, *Ave miles/Ave rex*, preserved at Oxford (*Bodleian Library, E Museo* 7, pp. X–XI). The third motet is based on a tune with a French text serving as tenor, *Triumphat hodie/Trop est fol.*[49] The French *cantus firmus*[50] has the form AA BB AA BB AA, its double versicles are divided between the lower parts (see example 20).

In the two compositions just mentioned (*Salve cleri* and *Ave miles*) based on a Gregorian melody – as also in many fourteenth-century motets without *cantus firmus* – the design was evidently dictated by the structure of the top voice (or top voices), so that the tenor becomes unusually irregular with respect to rhythm and phrasing.

A good many *cantus firmus* motets written in the early fourteenth century show a phrase design which modern scholars call 'isoperiodic'. The term 'isorhythmic' has been discussed in connection with the French *ars nova*, which is of a slightly later period (see pp. 152–3). Note however that in the English isoperiodic motets the phrases are clearly separated from each other

Example 20. Oxford, New College, 362, fol. 85[v] and London, British Museum, Add. 24198, fol. 1[v]

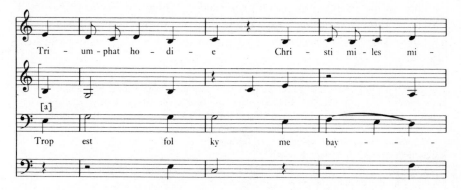

49. Three of the four parts (see example 20) are preserved in two MSS: Oxford, New College 362, fol. 85[v]; London, British Museum, Add. 24198, fol. 1[v]. The fourth has been reconstructed on the basis of voice exchange with the top voice and is therefore enclosed by square brackets in example 20.

50. No continental motet with a secular tenor supports two upper voices with Latin texts. Though English musicians avoided the vernacular in the upper parts of motets, the distinct functional role of motet tenors allowed them to select a French song as *cantus firmus*. The procedure, while piquant, is neither incongruous nor frivolous. The New College and Durham manuscripts (see below, p. 287, fn. 52) contain several such compositions.

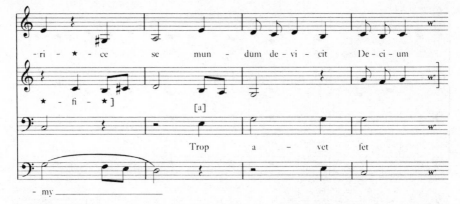

- ri - ★ - ce   se   mun - dum de - vi - cit   De - ci - um

★ - fi - ★]   [a]

Trop   a - vet   fet

- my

[*Triplum:* Today Christ's soldier Lawrence triumphs wondrously, residing among the stars with the saints; and now, crowned with laurels, he rejoices magnificently in Olympus [i.e. Heaven]; marvellously and with great honour the prodigious martyr triumphed over himself, the world, and Decius ...

Lower voices: Too foolish is he who right now gives me his wife to guard, as when night catches us far from people; Lord! Embarrassed by the husband, whose friendship now gives way: 'Too much have you done . . .]

by rests and are usually of the same length. (In isorhythmic organization the phrases are not only of the same length but also consist of the same succession of rhythmic values, e.g.

when a phrase is shaped as follows: 𝅗𝅥. |♩♩ |♩♩ |♩. |♩.. |

an isorhythmic phrase correspondence would be 𝅗𝅥. |♩♩ |♩♩ |♩. |♩.. |

but an isoperiodic phrase correspondence could be either 𝅗𝅥. |♩. |♩. |♩. |♩.. |

or ♩♩♩|♩ ♩|♩♩♩♩|♩. |♩.. |.

In these isoperiodic motets the primary consideration of the artist is the delight in shaping and designing of phrases. Considerations of harmony and tonality, so prominent in English polyphony of the thirteenth century, are secondary, or sometimes non-existent. Another consideration is sophistication in the handling of the phrases: for these are staggered, although of the same length. For instance in one motet preserved at Oxford[51] (*Petrum cephas/Petrus pastor*) three of the parts (tenor, *duplum*, *triplum*; the fourth part is free) display isoperiodic organization in which phrases of 9 longs constantly overlap. The total time-span of 108 longs is organized as follows:

triplum: 12 phrases of 9 longs each;

duplum: a rest of 7 longs is followed by 10 phrases of 9 longs each, plus a final phrase of 11 longs;

tenor: after a rest of 7 longs, and a phrase of 7 longs, 10 phrases of 9 longs each, plus a final phrase of 4 longs.

51. Bodleian Library, E Museo 7, pp. vi–vii.

Contrary to the above example, in other motets the isoperiodic design may affect all four voices. In some cases an isoperiodic design in motets disposes the phrases in such a way that one can perceive isorhythmic structure growing out of it. The motet *Zelo tui langueo/Reor nescia*[52] has a middle voice moving in slow notes and behaving like a tenor; each of its phrases consists of two bars (3 longs plus a rest). The surrounding two parts are made up of phrases of four bars with a dotted minim at the beginning of the second and fourth bars. In the following diagram the beginnings of isorhythm are indicated in the use of musical notation for corresponding rhythmic values; a straight line is used where no such correspondence exists. Square brackets indicate the phrases. The first eight bars, with staggered entries of the three parts, may be summarized as shown in example 21.

Example 21.

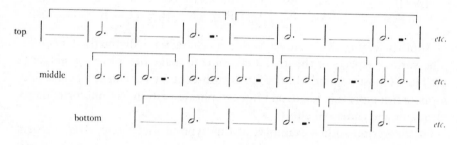

Another notable feature of this motet and several others like it is the placement of the tenor in the middle voice instead of at the bottom. This characteristic will be met again in our discussion of English discant (pp. 289–92).

   Still another type of motet exploits the principle of sectional 'variations' in so consistent a manner as to suggest their designation as 'variation motets'. *Ostinati* and varied *ostinati* which are freely invented (or perhaps borrowed from popular sources) provide the basis for this new type of motet, written during the first half of the fourteenth century, a type that is the successor to the *ostinato pes*-motet of the thirteenth century. The motet *Suspiria merentis/Meroris stimulo* (Cambridge, Gonville and Caius College 543/512, fols. 253ᵛ-254), which combines variation technique and refrain design, may be cited as a composition that (through its alternation of supertonic and tonic) strongly evokes the characteristic harmonic idiom of the preceding century. The tenor of this motet is stated nineteen times and always consists of the same six notes. But the rhythmic guises of these phrases vary, since the

52. London, British Museum, Sloane 1210, fols. 142ᵛ-3. Other similarly constructed motets are: *Quare fremuerunt gentes* in the same source, fols. 140ᵛ-1; *Civitas/Cibus/Cives* and *Rosa/[Regali]/Regalis* in Oxford, New College 362, fols. 86ᵛ-7 and 90ᵛ-1; and *Jesu fili dei/Jhesu fili virginis/Jesu lumen veritatis* in MS Durham, Cathedral Library, C.1.20, fol. 2.

tenor statements (abbreviated in the following diagram as a, b, c, d) appear in four different rhythms:

(a)   (b)

(c)   (d)

These nineteen tenor statements are grouped into nine pairs plus a single statement. Each pair produces two nearly identical phrases with *ouvert* and *clos* endings in each of the two upper voices. The second pair (bb) acts as a refrain section, since it recurs regularly with text and music unchanged. The form may therefore be likened to a rondo and be represented thus:

Upper voices:	ll′	mm′	nn′	mm′	oo′	mm′	pp	mm′	q	mm′
tenor:	aa	bb	aa	bb	cc	bb	dd	bb	d	bb
total design:	A_1	B	A_2	B	C	B	D_1	B	D_2	B

Another feature of the music is that its character is distinctly dance-like. The various aspects of this motet combine to make this piece – a prayer to the Holy Ghost – sound like the fourteenth-century version of a *villanella*:[53] *ostinato* principle (i.e. identical pitches), phrase pattern, refrain form, dance character and cadential effect.

Of the various other examples of this type of motet one, *Mulier magni meriti/Multum viget*,[54] displays the additional device known as sectional acceleration. The tenor melody (stated three times) consists of two nine-measure phrases which, apart from their *ouvert* and *clos* endings, are rhythmically and melodically identical. The two upper parts punctuate the three statements of the tenor with musical refrains over the last three measures of the tenor's second phrase (*clos*). Otherwise the upper parts display no correspondences between the sections. Within each section however there is almost complete correspondence within the two halves, the second being a slightly varied restatement of the first. Both upper voices increase their use of quicker notes[55] progressively from one section to the next so that the last section is the liveliest of the three; in addition the *duplum* and *triplum* rise progressively in pitch.

Several other motets also exploit the principle of sectional acceleration; three of them[56] are relatively early works, dating from the late thirteenth cen-

---

53. The motet (with the first word of the *duplum* misread) is printed in *Acta* (1965) 28–30.
54. Same source as *Suspiria merentis*, Cambridge, Conville and Caius Coll., 543/512, fols. 246ᵛ–7.
55. See the discussion of the Petronian motet, chapter 3, pp. 141–3.
56. The fragmentary setting of the gradual *Benedicta* in MS Oxford, Bodleian Library, Lat. Lit. d 20, fol. 14; the setting of *Alleluia Per te dei genitrix* on fols. 15ᵛ and 16 of the same source; and the fragmentary motet with the *duplum*, *O regina glorie* at Worcester Cathedral, Additional 68, No. XI, fol. 2ʳ.

tury. All of them involve the tenor as well as the upper voices. *O regina glorie* especially is an astonishingly sophisticated specimen, consisting of two sections which are related in the numerical proportion 4:3. In the second section the rhythmic irregularity of the tenor is such that it proves that the proportional arrangement of the composition as a whole is dictated by the upper parts. The most impressive piece of this type, one of the last representatives of voice-exchange technique, is the motet *De sancta Katerina*;[57] an exceptionally expansive work (354 bars) and one of extraordinarily complex design. In each of its five sections the two lower parts, which are freely composed, are in double versicle form, while the upper voices engage in voice exchange. Thus in each of its long sections one of the upper voices sings an entire stanza during the first half of a section, which is taken up by the other upper part during the second half. The sectional acceleration applies to all five sections which, in length, are in the proportions 12:8:4:9:6.[58] The significance of this motet, then, lies in the complexity of its numerical design, introducing techniques of composition which were to become prominent in the age of Dunstable and Dufay. (The motet itself cannot have been composed any later than the first two decades of the fourteenth century, as the evidence of notation and palaeography would suggest.)

The overwhelming majority of the remaining English sources of the fourteenth-century music add nothing to the repertory of motets. Only two sets of flyleaves transmit complete isorhythmic motets approximately of the mid-century, and the contents of both (the rear flyleaves of Oxford, Bodleian Library, E Museo 7 and of Durham, Cathedral Library, C.1.20) are partly made up of continental motets. Thus it would appear that no indigenous English motet techniques were maintained beyond the middle of the century. Yet our knowledge is unfortunately far too fragmentary to permit any definite conclusions.

THE 'OLD HALL' MANUSCRIPT

In addition to *cantilenae* and motets, a third species of polyphonic composition gained increasing prominence in English music of the second half of the fourteenth century. This type is an exclusively English adaptation of an old but persistent international tradition, namely of setting against a *cantus firmus*, often from the repertoire of choral plainsongs, a discant in an upper voice, more or less note against note. Impelled by their love of rich sonority, English composers gave such chant melodies three-part settings

57. The motet appears in three MSS, two of which are in the British Museum: London, British Museum, Additional 40011B, fols. 4^v, 5^v, 6^v, 7^v; ibid., MS Additional 24198, fol. 132; Oxford, Bodleian Library, Bodley 652, fols. 69, I, II^v. Unfortunately the motet is fragmentary in all these MSS; only the third and fifth sections of its five sections can be fully reconstructed.

58. That is to say, the opening three sections accelerate 12:8:4; the concluding two 9:6. There are a few extra longs (bars) in the second section.

in which (a few exceptions apart) the *cantus firmus* is carried by the middle part. Liturgical categories most often set in this manner are the votive antiphon[59] (usually Marian), the 'Sanctus', the 'Agnus', and – occasionally – the 'Credo'.[60] The main source preserving a fairly large number of such compositions dating from the late fourteenth century is the 'Old Hall' manuscript.[61]

A clue to the origin of the custom of surrounding the tenor with two parts (a discant above and a counter or counter-tenor below) may perhaps be furnished by the unusual compositional practices found in many of the settings of the *Spiritus et alme* trope of the 'Gloria', a Marian trope which was a special favourite of late thirteenth and fourteenth-century English composers. The four compositions discussed in this paragraph treat the *cantus firmus* in an unusual manner: it either 'migrates' from the tenor to an upper voice, or is allotted to a middle or a top part. The incompletely preserved four-part setting at Oxford (Bodleian Library, Mus. c. 60, fol. 85), dating from the last third of the thirteenth century, is a superior achievement. One of its sections is made up of a voice-exchange passage over an organal pedal point, while another is a four-part hocket of dazzling skill – the only known specimen of its kind. What is particularly significant is that the *cantus firmus* is treated in an unusually free manner, its pitches being allotted to the tenor only for the beginnings and endings of sections and migrating at times from the lowest part to the one above it. In a setting preserved at the University of Chicago (654 App., fol. 2) it is the top voice which quotes both the text and the highly embellished melody of the chant, while the middle part has a text of its own and the tenor functions as a freely composed support. (It is difficult to determine whether to label this hybrid a motet or a chant setting.) The counterpoint of a third specimen, from *c.* 1300,[62] makes it apparent that the tenor, which has the *cantus firmus*, must have shared its range with the missing *duplum* and generally functioned as the middle part. The lowest notes of the *cantus firmus* were brought into line

59. It must be remembered that motets of this period were not pieces forming an integral part of the liturgy, but might be composed in order to be inserted into the service at certain points. Therefore such pieces as votive antiphons must not be thought of as 'motets'. The votive antiphon 'was the main part of an act of evening devotion, separate from the regular services in choir, which took place in the Lady Chapel or other votive chapel or in the nave, according to its devotional object' (*NOHM*, iii, 307). The daily singing of a votive Marian antiphon, which became a custom in English establishments in the fourteenth and fifteenth centuries, is indicative of the pervading devotional piety of that era.

60. Isolated *cantus-firmus* settings of hymns, *Magnificat*, *Te Deum*, Alleluias and responsory verses also occur in scattered fragments. The polyphonic 'Glorias' were almost always freely composed, often exhibiting stylistic traits typical of the *cantilena*. The tradition can be traced back to the late thirteenth century. Presumably the preference for free settings of the 'Gloria' and also of the 'Credo' is due to the nature of their chants, which are not particularly promising as material for polyphonic elaboration.

61. Old Hall near Ware (Hertfordshire), St Edmund's College. See the editions of Ramsbotham (1933 ff.) and And. Hughes (1969 ff.). See *The Times*, 10 July 1973, p. 2.

62. Oxford, Bodleian Library, Lat. Lit. d 20, fol. 24[v]. It is one of the last specimens of the genre of troped discant, which was evidently a thirteenth-century species.

by transposing them up a fifth, a feature that is shared by a fourth setting, also fragmentary,[63] in which the chant is assigned to the middle part. This fragment is of particular interest, since it exhibits the techniques of para-phrase, migration and partial transposition applied to the *cantus firmus*. But all four settings handle the high *tessitura* of the chant in ways that are otherwise unknown.

A second circumstance that may have helped to make the middle voice the carrier of the *cantus firmus* was the emergence of the sixth as a favoured interval. A composer of motets wishing to combine two parts (largely in parallel sixths) with a *cantus firmus* would certainly find it convenient to drape, as it were, such a duet around the tenor rather than to retain the traditional arrangement of the tenor at the bottom. Several such compo-sitions exist.[64] A related and at the same time perhaps more compelling reason is that the gradual expansion of the overall range of a three-part texture allowed composers to turn more or less tentatively to designing bottom parts with more of a supporting quality than the generally conjunct style of a Gregorian melody could yield. The evidence is rather persuasive. Usually the lowest part of these compositions is the most disjunct of the three, a peculiarity not necessarily due to contrapuntal requirements but to the composer's preference. Whatever the reasons, the plainsong is con-cealed and enveloped.

While all settings of the *Spiritus et alme* trope treat the chant with con-siderable freedom, the other compositions with *cantus firmus* in the middle part generally leave the original melody untouched, except that in most cases it is transposed up a fifth or – much more rarely – a fourth. The reason for this manipulation is shown in the few settings that manage without transposition: either the situation is complicated by extensive crossings of the two lower parts or the entire composition lies unusually low. Instead of transposing the *cantus firmus*, the composer could also make it migrate from one part to another, but by comparison with transposition migration was not often used.

The cases in which the Gregorian melody is apportioned to either the highest or the lowest part (apart from migrant *cantus firmi*) are so rare as to be insignificant. A digression is necessary at this point concerning the notion that in English discant (or descant) for three parts English composers of the fourteenth century placed the Gregorian *cantus firmus* in the bottom part and that the entire style abounded with ⁶₄ chord parallelism. This thesis, widely presented between the 1930s and the 1960s, is based on a cluster of mis-apprehensions. While limited ⁶₄ chord parallelism found its way from the *cantilena* repertoire (see pp. 282–3) into chant settings here and there,

---

63. Oxford, New College 362, fol. 82ᵛ.
64. See above, p. 287.

parallelism was basically inconsistent with the tradition of discant anywhere in Europe and was neither taught nor applied as a system of plainsong elaboration before the second quarter of the fifteenth century (see p. 300). What is characteristic of discant in fourteenth-century England is simply that the Gregorian *cantus firmus* is carried by the middle of three parts. To subsume *cantilenae* under the term discant obliterates an essential distinction evidently taken for granted in the fourteenth and fifteenth centuries. All relevant English treatises of the time consider discant as an elaboration of a plainsong, and discant settings of non-Gregorian songs such as the famous *Angelus ad virginem* are rare.[65]

To resume our discussion of the *cantus firmus* in English discant, the technique of migration originally seems to have been confined to sectional alternation, when a shift in the range of the *cantus firmus* occurred. It becomes a meaningful technical principle in the fourteenth century when the ranges of the constituent parts of many compositions are sufficiently separated to make it appear as a preferable alternative to voice crossings. Clearly, this device could arise only in a musical tradition that, in contrast to French practice, conceived the homogeneous voices of a polyphonic composition from the outset as interdependent parts of an integrated whole. Inevitably, in some compositions of the late fourteenth century, distribution of the notes of the *cantus firmus* throughout all three parts – at times in conjunction with transposition – is no longer a technical expedient but has become a stylistic principle in its own right, serving the composer's design.

The most prominent tradition however is that which allots the *cantus firmus* to the middle part (tenor). In its most severe and least attractive aspect this style is barely more than note-against-note ('first-species') counterpoint. But in most cases at least the top voice was given a somewhat livelier rhythmic and melodic profile; subsequently the bottom part, too, often received more attention from composers. There is no question however that almost always only modest adornments of a strictly functional counterpoint were involved.[66] Both style and liturgical purpose indicate that much of this music was not a polyphony for solo voices but was intended for chorus (two to four voices for each part).[67] The performance of ritual polyphony by balanced choral groups is a corollary of the expansion of the framework of the two outer voices from the interval of a twelfth to two octaves.

65. See E. H. Sanders, 'Cantilena and Discant in 14th Century England', *Mus. Disc.* (1965) 7–52.

66. Because of its prevailingly homorhythmic declamation and musical texture this type of discant composition has often and misleadingly been referred to as '*conductus* setting'.

67. The relative scarcity of polyphonic 'Kyries' may be due to the fact that they were sung with the trope appropriate to a given occasion. They were, therefore, more elaborate, restricted to a specific liturgical event, and more likely to be sung by a soloist.

These circumstances bear witness to the gradually growing importance and musical expertise of the choirs of non-monastic institutions[68] such as collegiate churches, colleges and court chapels (particularly the Chapel Royal),[69] where this repertoire came to be cultivated. Not only festal rituals, which until then had provided the sole occasions for polyphonic elaboration, but even *feriae* (ordinary weekdays) were at times dignified by polyphony, as is indicated by some of the music of the 'Old Hall' manuscript. In due course secular cathedrals and greater monasteries likewise instituted choral polyphony, and by the end of the fifteenth century even parish churches adopted the practice for special occasions.

The 112 extant folios of the 'Old Hall' manuscript (customarily abbreviated as 'OH') contain 147 compositions, most of which are completely preserved. The categories comprise settings of the 'Gloria' (40), of the 'Credo' (35), of the 'Sanctus' (27), of the 'Agnus' (19), of votive antiphons (17), and nine isorhythmic motets. For approximately two-thirds of the pieces a total of twenty-three composers is named, among them Roy Henry (probably Henry IV), to whom one setting each of a 'Gloria' and a 'Sanctus' is attributed. The composers whose names occur most frequently are Byttering, Chirbury, Cooke, Damett, Oliver, Leonel (Power), Pycard, Sturgeon and Typp. By far the most prominent of these is Leonel Power; twenty-one compositions carry his name.[70]

Apart from the 'Winchester Troper', 'OH' is the first sizeable source of medieval English polyphony.[71] Its contents were written in two, possibly three, stages: *c.* 1405–15, *c.* 1415–20, with perhaps a few additions made in the later 1420s. That this manuscript escaped destruction is singularly fortunate, since it affords us a detailed view of the evolution of English liturgical polyphony at a crucial period in the history of western music.

Notwithstanding the apparent rarity of indigenous isorhythmic motets in the fourteenth century, the presence of nine such pieces in 'OH' is a strong indication that cultivation of their own musical traditions did not cause the English to disregard the importance of continental practices. In fact two or three 'OH' compositions are known to be by foreign composers. What is

68. In some cases the voices added to the *cantus firmus* may still have been performed by soloists in the early fifteenth century, but this was merely a passing phase, as choir members became conditioned to the singing of mensural polyphony. What is important is that polyphony was applied to choral chants.

69. The 'Old Hall' manuscript was used at the Chapel Royal.

70. Next to Dunstable (see below, p. 298), who probably was somewhat younger, Leonel (d. 1445) was the most renowned English composer of the time. Damett, the number of whose 'OH' compositions is exceeded only by those of Leonel Power, is named as author of nine works.

71. Seven of the eighteen works preserved in the fragmentary MS London, British Museum, Additional 40011B (probable provenance: Fountains Abbey, Yorkshire) are concordances of 'OH' compositions. A few other fragments also contain 'OH' concordances.

particularly remarkable about this repertoire is that even in the earliest layer of the manuscript, which contains the great majority of the compositions, less than half of the settings are in the traditional discant style for three voices. Among the 'Glorias' and 'Credos' there are a number of pieces which utilize the style and structure of isorhythm. Like the motets they display all the complexities of rhythm and structural proportions characteristic of the continental motet repertoire of the turn of the century. The ritual text, assigned to the upper voices, is taken as the pretext for the selection of an appropriate *cantus firmus*, in accordance with the continental tradition, established in the fourteenth century, of making the selection of a motet tenor dependent on the ability of its text to correspond like a motto to the poetic conceit of the upper parts. The isorhythmic 'Glorias' and 'Credos' of 'OH' show a similar relationship between *cantus firmus* and superstructure. For instance, a 'Gloria', presumed to be by Leonel Power, and a 'Credo' ascribed to him in the manuscript, are respectively based on *Ad Thome memoriam* and *Opem nobis*, two antiphons for the feast of St Thomas of Canterbury; thus these two items of the *Ordinarium Missae* are 'appropriated' for a particular occasion. Non-isorhythmic settings of 'Credos' seldom used a Gregorian *cantus firmus* and settings of 'Glorias' hardly ever. So the idea of basing isorhythmic arrangements of the Ordinary on appropriate Office chants is not as startling as it might seem in comparison with the liturgical propriety of discant settings of chants of the Ordinary.

A few of the 'OH' 'Glorias' and 'Credos' exhibit complex canonic technique in the upper voices, which may point to the composers' acquaintance with the Italians' imitative and canonic ways of writing. The two Englishmen, Byttering and Pycard, were particularly taken with canonic artifice. The latter wrote a 'Gloria' consisting of a double canon over a fifth free part as well as a 'Credo' composed as a three-part mensuration canon (see Chapter 4.3, p. 202) over two free supporting voices. His isorhythmic 'Gloria' (with the *Spiritus et alme* trope) has two upper parts with a high incidence of imitation which seem to be prevented from forming a strict canon only by the exigencies of the *cantus firmus*.[72] These are feats of astonishing virtuosity; no comparable continental compositions exist.

A technique for which no antecedent insular practice is known is that which endows the top voice with a pronounced individual profile, both melodically and rhythmically. In nearly one third of the compositions (excluding the motets) interest is concentrated on the highest part, very much in the manner of the French *chanson*.[73] Unlike the discants, these compositions favour the more modern minor prolation, often with *tempus*

---

72. Pycard also wrote a canonic arrangement of a troped 'Sanctus', in which a free tenor supports three upper voices, which sing the *cantus firmus* (!) in canon.

73. In some cases, especially compositions for four parts, the two upper voices tend towards a non-imitative duet texture.

perfectum (see chapter 4.1 p. 152). Most of them consist of sections with different mensurations, and in several compositions duet sections, some intended for soloists, provide textural change as well as further structural articulation.[74] While a large number of these compositions are freely written, several incorporate the *cantus firmus* either in the tenor or the top part, in which case it is usually transposed up an octave or a fifth; a few compositions exhibit the technique of migrant *cantus firmus*, which maintained itself in England throughout the fifteenth century. In the process of adaptation the chant melody is often subjected to considerable melodic elaboration, with the result that these compositions have the delicate and graceful smoothness of early Burgundian *chansons*, combined with the sonorous quality (prevalence of imperfect consonances) characteristic of the English tradition. Moreover the style reveals a growing avoidance of all dissonances not carefully regulated and prepared. Many of Dunstable's compositions, especially his antiphons, are justly renowned for their imaginative and euphonious *cantus firmus* arrangements. But some highly accomplished specimens by such composers as Oliver, Byttering and Leonel Power can already be found in the old layer of 'OH'; the latest date that can be assigned to them is *c.* 1410. In the later additions to the manuscript the discant and canon techniques are no longer represented, and even the isorhythmic motets begin to adopt the new style, thus initiating a development that was to reach its culmination with Dunstable's motets.

In some of the discant settings of the 'Sanctus' in 'OH' as well as other fragmentary sources of the late fourteenth and early fifteenth centuries, the word *Benedictus* is to be intoned monophonically (and followed by a polyphonic setting of *qui venit in nomine Domini*) comparable to some settings of the 'Gloria', where polyphony starts with the words *Et in terra pax*. Since compositions of the 'Sanctus', without such monophonic interruptions, are on the whole more archaic in style, the intonation of the word *Benedictus* may reflect the gradual beginnings of the practice where even the untroped 'Sanctus', if set polyphonically, would no longer precede the Canon[75] in its entirety. The length of the polyphonic settings caused the choir to divide the 'Sanctus', ending the first half with the first 'Hosanna'; the two parts were separated by the consecration. The concluding 'Hosanna' of a polyphonic 'Sanctus' would, therefore, be in far closer proximity to the 'Agnus Dei' than would be the case if the Ordinary of the Mass were sung in plainsong. It may well be that these musico-liturgical developments caused composers to think of 'Sanctus' and 'Agnus' as a pair and to bracket

74. Two 'Sanctus' compositions, No. 110 by Sturgeon (vol. III, p. 55 and [61] and No. 112 by Leonel (vol. III, p. 66), initiate the growing custom of giving duet settings to *Pleni sunt caeli et terra gloria tua* and *Qui venit in nomine Domini*. (Cf. also ed. Hughes, Nos. 114 and 116.)

75. Concerning the liturgical position of the Canon of the Mass (including the Consecration of the Host) between 'Sanctus' and 'Agnus', see *LU*, pp. 4–6.

them by the same devices of composition. There are at least two probable pairs among the discant settings in 'OH'.[76] In both cases the two items are intended for the same type of liturgical occasion and have identical clefs, the same number of parts, similar modal and cadential features and identical mensurations. A few pairs also occur among the settings in *chanson* style, where the evidence seems still more convincing, since such pieces are stylistically more defined than the discant compositions. In two or three of these cases the pairing involves 'Gloria' and 'Credo'.

It must be remembered in this connection that 'OH' contains a 'Gloria' and a 'Credo' which are isorhythmic and based on two liturgically related chants (see p. 294 above). Just as the two tenors indicate the feast of St Thomas of Canterbury as the occasion for which these pieces were intended, a 'Gloria' and 'Credo' exist, also isorhythmic, which seem to have been written for the Feast of the Blessed Trinity (based respectively on *Tibi laus*, verse of the Trinity antiphon *O beata* and on *Te iure laudant*, another Trinity antiphon).[77] In the latter case the two settings have some similarities in style and technique as well. Though 'OH' no longer furnishes us with evidence, it is a small step from the use of festally related chants to using the same chant as *cantus firmus* for each movement of a 'Gloria'-'Credo' pair. The earliest pair of this sort was composed by Dunstable (d. 1453); both 'Gloria' and 'Credo' are based on the respond *Iesu Christe fili Dei*. The pitches, rhythms and sectional proportions of the tenor are the same in both pieces, though, significantly, isorhythm is otherwise abandoned in favour of a style characteristic of English polyphony of the second quarter of the century, and of Dunstable in particular. This style is characterized by a type of free, triadically melodious, consonant and rhythmically flexible counterpoint.

The various impulses towards musical unification of what one may now begin to refer to as 'Mass movements' soon led to the cyclic unification of the *Ordinarium Missae* by means of basing each of the four movements[78] on one or more statements of the same *cantus firmus* in the manner of Dunstable's 'Gloria'-'Credo' pair.

Use of the same *cantus firmus* is often complemented by other similarities between the movements, such as the sequence of mensurations and the alternation of duets with three-part polyphony. The earliest known '*cantus firmus* Mass' is the *Missa Alma redemptoris mater* by Leonel Power.[79]

---

76. 'Sanctus' No. 92 (ed. Ramsbotham, iii, 7; ed. Hughes, No. 96) and 'Agnus' No. 121 (R. iii, 100; H., No. 125); 'Sanctus' No. 103 (R. iii, 32; H., No. 107) and 'Agnus' No. 127 (R. iii, 122; H., No. 135).

77. The Credo is 'OH' No. 85 (ed. Ramsbotham, ii, 241; ed. Hughes, No. 89); the Gloria is preserved on fol. 9 of the Fountains Abbey MS (see above, p. 293, fn. 71).

78. The Kyrie generally continued to be excluded from polyphony.

79. Two perhaps equally early specimens are the *Missa Rex seculorum*, variously ascribed (in the manuscripts preserving it) to Power and Dunstable, and the *Missa Da gaudiorum premia* by Dunstable, which is only preserved in fragments (including parts of the 'Kyrie').

It ushers in an international tradition continuing for centuries, which is all the more astonishing when one considers that the cyclic Mass imposes musical unity on a group of prayers that are in no way liturgically continuous or unified. It must be stressed that this phenomenon could not have come to pass without the patronage of the growing court chapels and other secular centres of religious observance in England, and the consequent turning from a polyphony of solo voices to choral polyphony. A chapel with a well-trained, fair-sized, and properly balanced choir able to sing sonorous[80] polyphony, with its splendid display of craftsmanship, was a criterion of the prestige to which many aristocratic households aspired, and before long there is evidence of rivalry and envy. In this sense, then, the cyclic *cantus firmus* Mass could be termed a Renaissance phenomenon, since it evidently represents a response to secular rather than sacramental requirements.[81] The effect of the cyclically organized polyphonic Ordinary was to impose on the ritual of the Mass a musical and liturgical order that approximates the modern rondo. The high points of this order derived from the desire to add splendour (if not glamour) to non-monastic religious observances, rather than from any wish for the enhancement of ceremony to satisfy liturgical exigencies.

That English composers were the first to conceive the organization of a *cantus firmus* Mass is indicated not only by the preserved repertoire but also by the fact that a chant used in England, but not on the continent at that time, was used as *cantus firmus* for Mass settings by certain continental composers (*Missa Caput*). Evidently the early decades of the fifteenth century were an age of confluence. On the one hand there was absorption of foreign musical traditions into the 'OH' repertoire, resulting in the adoption of *chanson* style and in the graceful animation of discant style in many Mass sections and votive antiphons. On the other hand English music was largely responsible for the decisive stylistic reorientation taking place in the sacred and secular polyphony of continental composers. Well before adopting the concept of the *cantus firmus*, Burgundian and Franco-Flemish

80. Even though two to four singers sang each part, the result was surely rich and impressive in comparison with the past tradition of solo polyphony, whose roots had been monastic. The rise of balanced choirs with the attendant development of a new repertoire has been described as 'comparable in importance to the rise of the orchestra' and the birth of the symphony (Harrison, *Mediaeval*, p. 45).

81. The flourishing of the cyclic Mass is usually attributed either to religious movements of the time such as the *Devotio Moderna* or to the composers' presumed realization that the unvarying texts of the *Ordinarium Missae* promised for their compositions frequent opportunities for performance. But the first reason holds no water, because the devout pietists had no use for composed Masses; moreover, they were generally hostile to artistic elaboration. The error of the second explanation is that the choice of one *cantus firmus* for all movements of a Mass 'appropriated' the Ordinary for a particular day in the liturgical year. (Admittedly, the choice of a secular *cantus firmus*, coming into use on the continent around the middle of the century, is less conclusive in regard to this argument.) But, in any case, the idea that composers were stimulated by the desire for the longevity of their works seems anachronistic; it took the Age of Enlightenment to put such notions into composers' heads.

composers of the Mass had begun to assimilate influences emanating from English music.[82]

The victory of Agincourt doubtless allowed this trend full rein. As part of the mobile retinue of the king, the Chapel Royal exposed courtly continental audiences to English polyphony. The first specific evidence that English music was widely admired is provided by two German reports on the 'sweet angelic' polyphony performed in 1416 by the singers accompanying the English bishops to the Council of Constance. As the century advanced, English composers came to hold positions in English as well as in other courts on the continent. Dunstable, the most famous English musician of the time, was in the employ of John, Duke of Bedford, who was regent of France from 1422 to 1435. (This explains why most of Dunstable's works survive in continental manuscripts.) Robert Morton was on the payroll of the Burgundian court and other Englishmen of renown, such as Bedingham and Walter Frye, seem to have been active on the continent around the middle of the century. Numerous English works, their composers identified either by name or simply as 'Anglicanus', are preserved in fifteenth-century continental sources.[83] Before it ebbed towards the end of the century, the popularity of English music was such that it predominates in some continental sources.

What made English polyphony so attractive to French ears is indicated in a passing reference to Burgundian music and its genesis in Martin Le Franc's lengthy poem *Le Champion des Dames* (*c.* 1440). In speaking of Dufay and Binchois he comments:

> *Car ilz ont nouvelle pratique*
> *de faire frisque concordance*
> *en haulte et en basse musique*
> *en fainte en pause et en muance*
> *et ont prins de la contenance*
> *angloise et ensuy Dunstable*
> *pour quoy merveilleuse plaisance*
> *rend leur chant joyeux et notable.*

[For theirs is a new practice of writing high and low music in such a manner that with its *musica ficta* (application of accidentals), its phrasing, and melodic design it sounds pleasantly consonant. They have taken on the English way and have followed Dunstable, and their music is so wondrously agreeable that it produces joy and fame.]

The impact of this assimilation of English influences was such that some thirty years later Tinctoris, referring to the same two composers in the

---

82. As to the special case of *fauxbourdon*, see below, p. 301.
83. The richest sources are a group of manuscripts in upper Italy (Trent, Aosta, Modena, Bologna).

preface to his *Proportionale Musices*, still expressed eloquent admiration for the English: 'Thus, it is a fact that in this age the capabilities of our music increased so miraculously that it would seem to be a new art. Of this new art, as I might, in fact, call it, the English, among whom Dunstable stood out as the greatest, are held to be the source and origin.' Sixteenth-century writers still relate Dunstable's pre-eminence as a notable item of information; as late as 1581 Vincenzo Galilei points to him as the fountain-head of Franco-Flemish music.

THE MID-FIFTEENTH CENTURY

In style and technique the English liturgical polyphony, composed during the hundred years after 'OH', continued and developed the heritage bequeathed by Dunstable and his contemporaries. Only three manuscripts and a few fragments remain to instruct us about ecclesiastical polyphony[84] of the middle third of the fifteenth century. Fortunately the preservation of many English compositions in continental sources helps to fill in the picture.

The liturgical portion of the Egerton manuscript (see fn. 84) contains ritual polyphony for Holy Week (except Good Friday); such seasonal specialization is unique in fifteenth-century polyphony. The liturgical categories involved exceed not only the restricted repertoire of the 'OH' manuscript, but also the types of composition preserved in the fragmentary sources of the later fourteenth century. The Egerton settings comprise four processional hymns, parts of four processional antiphons, three Alleluias (solo portions), two Passions (exclusive of the words of the evangelist and of Jesus, which were presumably chanted),[85] one ferial Mass (no 'Gloria' and 'Credo'; the 'Kyrie' is included), one responsory (solo portions), and one litany. The Pepys manuscript[86] is far more inclusive, containing as it does settings of various specimens of nearly all ritual categories for a number of occasions throughout the year. Much of the polyphony in both manuscripts are settings of solo chants. The number of three-part pieces in the Pepys manuscript is about double that of the settings for two parts. There are also five four-part compositions, which reveal the difficulties composers had in

84. For more detailed treatment see the relevant chapters by F. L. Harrison and M. F. Bukofzer in *NOHM*, iii. The three MSS are: London, British Museum, Egerton 3307, written about 1440; Oxford, Bodleian Library, Arch. Selden B. 26, probably written *c.* 1450; Cambridge, Magdalen College, Pepys Library 1236, written *c.* 1460. These three MSS are usually nicknamed 'Egerton', 'Selden', and 'Pepys'. For ecclesiastical music the Selden MS is a minor source, since carols constitute the majority of its compositions; for modern editions of the Pepys and Egerton MSS see bibliography, s.v. Charles and McPeek. The main fragments are at Oxford, (Bodleian Library, Add. C. 87) and Cambridge (Pembroke College, 314).

85. They are the earliest known polyphonic settings of Passion texts.

86. One of the hymn settings (No. 69) is a partial concordance of an Egerton composition.

writing for four voices. Most of the works in the Egerton manuscript are for three voices, at times interspersed with duet sections. Sectional changes in mensuration, common in other sources, are practically non-existent in the Pepys manuscript.

Both sources prefer apportioning the *cantus firmus* to the top voice, often with considerable elaboration.[87] A particularly intriguing example is the setting provided in the Egerton manuscript for the processional hymn *Inventor rutili*, whose five stanzas are given different 'variational' arrangements of the plainsong. While several other compositions dispense with the *cantus firmus*, the melodic and rhythmic design of the upper voice in such cases is not notably different from those incorporating a plain chant. In some compositions the lower parts are hardly less animated in rhythm than the *cantus*.[88] A similar, though more accomplished style, characterizes the fifteen settings of Marian votive antiphons in the Selden manuscript, only two of which accommodate a *cantus firmus*, which is migrant.

The Pepys manuscript offers the first practical evidence of a procedure known as *faburden*. Indications are that the term is an Anglicization of *fauxbourdon*, a technique which continental composers began to use in the later 1420s as a means of adopting the English *cantilena* style with its tuneful top voice and characteristic stretches of $\frac{6}{3}$ chord parallelism. Since the polyphonic Latin *cantilenae* were a foreign genre to French-Burgundian musicians, these composers applied *fauxbourdon* to modest song-like plainchants, e.g. hymns, for which a tradition of transposing the *cantus firmus* an octave and placing it in the top voice of three parts already existed, as in the manuscript preserved in the Chapter Library at Apt in south-eastern France. What was new about *fauxbourdon* in its early strict form was that it produced the English sound in smooth mensural *cantus firmus* settings by means of a canon (rule)[89] which bound an unwritten middle part to the top voice at the lower fourth throughout, while the notated bottom voice followed the given melody at the sixth below, with occasional cadential turns to the octave. The result was a type of *cantus firmus* setting that made $\frac{6}{3}$ chord parallelism a far more mechanically persistent matter than it had been in England. This technique was in turn imported into England around 1430, where it came to be taught as a new and particularly easy type of extemporized or composed discant, which applied *cantilena* sonority to *cantus firmi* by means of a 'canonic' system.[90] An anonymous treatise of *c.* 1450, contained in a collection of discant treatises made by one John

87. The few settings of the *Magnificat* preserved in fragmentary sources also favour this style.

88. The beginnings of this development go back at least to the latest part of 'OH'.

89. It must be remembered that the term 'canon' in this period means 'rule'. The system of rules producing $\frac{6}{3}$ chords is, therefore, a 'canonic' system. What we nowadays call 'canon' was called *caccia* or *chace* or *fuga* up to the sixteenth century. (See p. 280, fn. 38.)

90. Both added voices could be sung alongside the *cantus firmus* with the aid of an ingenious system of imagined transpositions ('sights'), traditionally taught in English treatises on discant.

Wylde, locates the *cantus firmus* in the middle part, thus bringing faburden (*fauxbourdon*) technique into agreement with the English tradition of discant. But before long the English had adopted the prevailing continental custom of transposing the *cantus firmus* up an octave and placing it, gently ornamented at cadence points, in the top part.

Schematic representation of *faburden*, with *cantus firmus* indicated in black notes:
a. *Cantus firmus* in middle voice   b. *Cantus firmus* in top voice

Of course when the *cantus firmus* is in the top voice English tradition is preserved, since in such faburden settings the middle part will sing the *cantus firmus* at the upward transposition of a fifth. Evidently selected verses of hymns, processional psalms, the *Magnificat*, the *Te Deum* and litanies were favoured for faburden arrangement.[91]

To judge by some of the preserved sources, the English often notated only the lowest part, the faburden, of such settings (with the text of the *cantus firmus* written underneath), since obviously the two *cantus firmus* voices could easily fit their parts to that of the singer, the faburdener. This custom, in addition to the often rich ornamentation applied to the upper voices in composed faburden settings, seems to have given rise to increasing neglect of the *cantus firmus*. The faburden settings of the Pepys manuscript afford us insight into the process, which led from the upper parts' decreasing dependence on the plainsong to complete divorce, so that only the faburden would remain as the starting point for a polyphonic composition.[92] It will be remembered that the faburden was originally the counterpoint to the *cantus firmus*. It often moved in parallel sixths to the top voice, but at cadential turns it tended to turn to the octave, either by contrary motion or by leaps. These leaps, and the resultant disjunct motion, may have made faburdens attractive as bass skeletons. Nevertheless the original type of faburden continued to exist side by side with its new offshoot.

A related phenomenon is the use of another category of pre-existing melodies which are enigmatic in more ways than one. In the first place, they do not seem to be plainsongs, and in the second place, they are, for some unknown reason, called 'squares' in the manuscripts. These squares are employed in some Masses (in simple non-festal style) of the late fifteenth

91. A London chronicle of the early sixteenth century describes how 'came the black friars with their cross and every friar a cope, singing the litany with faburden ...; after them came Paul's choir, every priest and clerk had a cope, with all their residentiaries in copes, singing the litany with faburden' (Denis Stevens, *Mus. Disc.* (1955) 110, where the passage is given in its original spelling). Clearly faburden is choral polyphony par excellence.

92. Organ settings of faburdens begin to appear in the second quarter of the sixteenth century. For the liturgical organ repertoire preserved in sixteenth-century English sources, see chapter 6.2, pp. 332–5.

and early sixteenth centuries. A few have been traced back to counters (i.e., counter-tenors, bottom voices, see p. 290) for *cantus firmi* in earlier manuscripts ('OH' and Fountains Abbey). The available evidence indicates that all squares may be counters in older settings of plainsongs or, to put it differently, that squares used as *cantus firmi* were originally counterpoints of Gregorian *cantus firmi.*[93]

THE LATE FIFTEENTH AND EARLY SIXTEENTH CENTURIES

The main categories of polyphonic composition in the late decades of the fifteenth century and the earliest years of the sixteenth seem to have been the festal Mass, the votive antiphon (which was destined to evolve into the anthem in the later years of the sixteenth century) and the *Magnificat*, which, as the most prominent part of the Office, had developed into a large-scale genre in the course of the century. The most extensive of these types, i.e. the festal Mass, is not represented in the source preserving the greatest number of works of the period, the so-called Eton Choirbook (MS Eton College, 178), written between 1490 and 1502. Our knowledge of the large-scale polyphonic Mass by English composers of the late fifteenth century comes solely from isolated fragmentary manuscripts of unknown provenance, such as the Lambeth manuscript (London, Lambeth Palace, 1), datable *c.* 1510, and the Caius manuscript (Cambridge, Gonville and Caius College, 667), which may be dated about 1520. In comparison with the preservation of continental sources, the losses of English manuscripts continue to be very great until the early sixteenth century.

It should be mentioned in passing that the very size of these manuscript sources is clear evidence of the 'growth' of books written for polyphonic choirs. The term 'choirbook' itself implies a book of a size large enough for a dozen or so singers to look on to, while gathered in front of a lectern that supported it. The size of such books increased steadily; the Eton Choirbook measures $23\frac{1}{2}$ in. by 17 in., while the Caius manuscript has the extraordinary dimensions of $28\frac{1}{4}$ in. by 19 in. In the sixteenth century the writing of choirbooks was gradually abandoned in favour of part-books; a development that was furthered by the advent of music printing. Parallel developments are observable on the continent.

The original index of the Eton Choirbook shows that it must have contained at least sixty-seven Marian votive antiphons, twenty-four *Magnificats*, a Passion, and a setting of the Apostles' Creed; about half of the codex is lost. Composers who stand out for quantity as well as quality of their works are John Browne,[94] Richard Davy, Walter Lambe, Robert

93. Isolated cases of sixteenth century keyboard settings of squares have also come to light.

94. John Browne has been described as 'the outstanding figure of the collection and perhaps the greatest English composer between Dunstable and Taverner' (Harrison, *Eton*, X, pp. xvif).

Wylkynson, William Cornysh and Robert Fayrfax. The Eton Choirbook is the first English manuscript to provide a composer's name – there are twenty-five altogether – for each of its compositions. The Caius manuscript contains Masses and *Magnificats*, while the Lambeth manuscript preserves specimens of all three of the major polyphonic categories. The composers primarily represented in the latter two sources are Cornysh, Fayrfax and Nicholas Ludford.[95]

In style and technique, festal Mass and votive antiphon resemble one another so closely that, in effect, the antiphon may be likened to a Mass movement. While earlier settings of antiphons (preserved on the continent) were often freely composed, those written in the second half of the century tended more and more to make use of an extraneous *cantus firmus*,[96] functioning as a core for the increasingly rich counterpoint. Since in such works the selection of a *cantus firmus* is a matter of compositional rather than liturgical motivation, it is probable that the *cantus firmi* of Masses were likewise no longer selected for their liturgical appropriateness but more for their musical fitness.[97] After the middle of the century the tenors of the movements of one Mass were no longer unified by parallel, isorhythmic structure; instead the isomelic principle[98] took hold of the *cantus firmi*. Throughout the century correspondence of length and proportion between movements appear in some of the non-isorhythmic Masses. In more progressive compositions the rhythm of the tenor, which has the *cantus firmus*, is no longer clearly differentiated by old-fashioned long note values from the other parts but, aided by some modest elaboration, approximates them in liveliness. The framework of the two outer parts having been expanded to the interval of three octaves, which is about the maximum for vocal ensembles, British composers satisfied the traditional English love of full sonority by writing consonant counterpoint for large numbers of parts, encompassing a full choral range from bass to boy soprano. Thus, of the ninety-three compositions known to have been assembled in the Eton Choirbook, twenty-two were for four, fifty-two for five, thirteen for six, three for seven and one each for eight, nine and thirteen parts; of the nineteen works in the Lambeth manuscript, sixteen are for five and three for six voices.[99] The duets and larger solo ensembles are, on the whole, very

95. See below, p. 305.

96. Only half of the Eton antiphons are freely composed. A striking case of specific relationship between an antiphon and a Mass is furnished by Frye's *Salve virgo mater* and the four movements of his *Missa Summe Trinitati*, all of which are based on the same *cantus firmus*, its pitches laid out in identical rhythmic arrangements; moreover, all five pieces have the same motto beginning.

97. Musical considerations seem to account for the fact that by the middle of the century, continental composers, evidently following Dufay's example, were basing some of their Masses on secular *cantus firmi*.

98. i.e. same pitches, not same rhythm.

99. Those works preserved in fifteenth-century continental sources that are known or presumed to have been composed by Englishmen rarely exceed three parts.

florid and continue to provide sectional changes of texture (usually without *cantus firmus*); they therefore exhibit many different constellations of voices. Mass movements and major sections of such movements often begin with introductory duets which anticipate increasingly the melodic substance of the *cantus firmus*, thus providing a degree of 'motivic' unification far more intrinsic than the motto beginnings of continental Mass movements of the early fifteenth century.

The florid character of these compositions, with their proliferation of ornate melismatic passages and complex rhythmic detail, accounts for their continental reputation as old-fashioned and somewhat abstruse. While imitation occurs occasionally, especially in the solo sections, it is not yet a major device. The fundamental concept underlying this polyphony is the ornamental elaboration of a structural core (*cantus firmus*) with more and more detail of refinement; it is discant at its most exuberant flowering. It has been pointed out that 'this style has obvious analogies with that of the last period of English Perpendicular architecture'.[100]

Apart from the festal Mass and the votive antiphon, other chant categories, except for the *Magnificat*, are of relatively subordinate importance in English polyphony of the time. (In its liturgical inclusiveness the Pepys manuscript is quite exceptional.) The *Magnificat*, as well as the *cantus firmus* Mass, was organized by way of variation form: quasi-variations were a series of contrapuntal movements built around a tenor. The pitch content of this tenor was not identical for each movement but was substantially similar, since the highly elaborated faburden[101] of the appropriate psalm tone formed the basis for most of the settings. Only the even-numbered verses were set, full sections (or movements) alternating with solo portions, while the remaining verses were chanted or, possibly, faburdened. The same *alternatim* principle also applied to hymn settings,[102] in which the effect of strophic variation is usually more apparent, since the elaborated *cantus firmus* with its relatively song-like quality was traditionally apportioned to the top voice, a procedure which had become more rare in other types of chant setting.

THE FIRST HALF OF THE SIXTEENTH CENTURY

The most prominent English composers of the first half of the sixteenth century can be divided into two groups, according to their active life spans. Three major figures make up the first group: William Cornysh the younger,

---

100. Harrison, in *NOHM*, iii, 303.

101. A 'square' in settings of the first tone; it goes back to the one preserved discant setting of the Magnificat (second half of the fourteenth century).

102. Some of the simpler compositions of the Ordinary of the Mass likewise leave alternate passages of the text to be rendered monophonically.

Robert Fayrfax and Hugh Aston. All died in the early 1520s, but only the first two are still represented in the Eton manuscript, since they were born about twenty years before Aston (b. 1480s).[103] The second group comprises men born in the late fifteenth century. The three most significant composers, who may be said to have been born *c.* 1485–90 and who died around the middle of the sixteenth century, are Nicholas Ludford, Robert Carver (a Scottish composer) and John Taverner. In continuing to display the salient characteristics of the music preserved in the Eton, Lambeth and Caius manuscripts, the polyphony of these six masters and of their lesser or less known contemporaries represents a fairly unified body of music, that further extends traditions reaching back to the generation of Dunstable and Leonel Power.

The versatility of Robert Fayrfax is demonstrated by the novel structural devices that begin to appear in some of his Masses. His *Missa O bone Jesu* uses material from both the beginning and end of his own freely composed setting of the votive antiphon with that text. It is the earliest known example of parody procedure in a Mass by an insular composer, though the technique of parody does not apply to the entire Mass or, indeed, to entire movements.[104] His *Missa Tecum principium* is notable for passages with carefully worked-out imitation, in which the *cantus firmus* does not yet participate. It is therefore an early example of the gradually growing concern with the motivic correlation of the voices which English composers, slowly yielding to Flemish influences, were beginning to evince in the second decade of the sixteenth century. This came about because music by continental composers was copied into English manuscripts, and not only their works, but foreign musicians themselves were imported to be heard at the court of Henry VIII.[105] Thus such members of the Chapel Royal as Cornysh and Fayrfax, in the late years of their lives, began to absorb Italian and Franco-Flemish influences which were to affect English music in subsequent decades. Fayrfax's *Missa Albanus* can be termed an *ostinato* Mass, since its nine-note *cantus firmus* occurs five times in the 'Gloria', seven times in the 'Credo', nine times in the 'Sanctus', and nine times, plus ten final statements in diminution, in the 'Agnus'. Moreover, prior to its last ten appearances, twenty-four statements of the nine-note 'row' are variously presented in

103. Fayrfax is also the first to have some of his works preserved, together with those of later composers, in sixteenth-century part-books, namely, the so-called Forrest-Heather part-books (MSS Oxford, Bodleian Library, Mus. sch. e. 376–81) and the Peterhouse fragments (Cambridge, Peterhouse, 31–2, 40–1).

104. Earlier use of the technique by an English composer active on the continent is demonstrated by the occasional relationships of Walter Frye's *Missa Summe Trinitati* and his votive antiphon *Salve virgo*, see above, p. 303, fn. 96.

105. While his actions were to be largely responsible for our tantalizingly incomplete knowledge of medieval English music, Henry VIII, an excellent musician himself, did much for the music of his time. The choir of the Chapel Royal was the largest and most skilful in England, and several of Henry's foundations had excellent choirs.

inversion, retrograde form or retrograde inversion. In patterned sequences the four permutations of the row are stated six, seven, eight and nine times respectively until the original form returns in the last ten appearances. In a passage of the 'Agnus Dei' five statements are made in each of the five parts in turn. In a somewhat similar manner Hugh Aston makes use of a short phrase from the *Te Deum* twenty-six times at various pitch levels and in different voices throughout his *Missa Te Deum*, except at the opening of each movement. Since only the original form of the plainsong is used, the Mass might be said to contain a series of metamorphoses or variations of a contrapuntal fabric woven around a *cantus firmus*.

Of the second group of composers Carver emerges least clearly, since only seven of his works (five Masses and two votive antiphons) survive. Particularly notable is his *O bone Jesu*, a richly sonorous piece for nineteen parts. His predilection for large ensembles – he also wrote a Mass for ten parts – seems anachronistic, since his contemporaries usually wrote for three to six voices (most commonly for five), and even then a three-part texture generally predominates.

The style of Ludford's large-scale works is similar to that of comparable compositions by Cornysh and Fayrfax. The *cantus firmi* are treated with some freedom and not necessarily restricted to the tenor. Motto beginnings, unrelated to the *cantus firmus*, bestow additional unity on the movements of each of his Masses. The most remarkable of Ludford's works is a cycle of seven Lady-Masses, one for each day of the week from Sunday to Saturday. Though the counterpoint is rather florid, these Masses, which contain settings of Alleluias (solo portions) and of alternate verses of sequences as well as of all five items of the Ordinary, are not large works; all are written for three parts, which alternate with measured monophony, and all are based on 'squares'. These votive Masses of the Virgin are the sole survivors of a genre of liturgical music that must have been quite common, since documentary and other circumstantial evidence indicates that the polyphonic rendition of Lady Masses was widespread in England. Ludford's compositions are thus a specific reminder of the fearfully extensive destruction of musical manuscripts during the reign of Henry VIII.

Taverner's *oeuvre*[106] represents the masterful culmination of the music of the pre-Reformation decades and the long tradition that conditioned it. While the partial parody procedure in his *Missa Mater Christi* is reminiscent of Fayrfax's *Missa O bone Jesu*, his Western-Wynde Mass, which is the earliest known insular Mass on an English secular tune,[107] recalls the

---

106. For a list of his works which shows the growing number of liturgical categories that had become subject to occasional polyphonic elaboration, see Harrison, in *NOHM*, iii, 339.

107. More systematic application of parody procedure than in Taverner's *Missa Mater Christi* is to be found in Tallis' *Missa Salve intemerata*; as to the Mass on 'Western Wynde' Tye and Sheppard also wrote Masses on that *cantus firmus*. No evidence has come to light that any other English secular melody

technique of Aston's *Missa Te Deum*, since each movement consists of nine contrapuntal variations of the *cantus firmus*.

Other tendencies that had begun to appear occasionally around the turn of the century became basic factors of Taverner's most advanced compositions. Especially notable is his cultivation of recurrence and correspondence, either within one voice or throughout the polyphonic fabric. Sequential repetition of clear-cut motives is a common feature, often appearing in compositions that also exhibit 'point-of-imitation' technique. The points are derived from the melodic material of the *cantus firmus* in some of the Masses, such as his *Missa O Michael*, which also contains some strictly canonic passages. In the course of its polyphonic elaboration, the *cantus firmus* becomes thoroughly transformed, being subjected to paraphrase and pervading imitation. This process of transformation was prepared by the growing freedom with which composers had been treating plainchant, thus weakening its original function as backbone of a contrapuntal structure. Thus, the *cantus firmus* lost its distinctive features, became neutralized, as it were, as a rule in the surrounding parts, but often in the tenor as well. The salient feature of this new music is that it is imbued with a homogeneity which is substantial and that its interlocking sections display a striking unity of music and text. This new polyphony is particularly evident in some of the shorter, less elaborate compositions, which also reveal Taverner's cultivation of chordal texture and of antiphonal *concertato* (often involving short text passages alternately tossed from one group of voices to another in successive imitation). Apart from imparting textural colour, both devices, whose adoption again shows continental influence, serve the emphatic delivery of text.

This solicitude for the text, which had originated on the continent, signifies the beginnings of a fundamental break with the past. Printing, humanism and the Reformation were bringing about an individual concern with the word that was reflected in a revolutionary reorientation of composers to the problems of relationships between music and text. After centuries, during which its function had been to decorate a text, to articulate more or less stylized dances and dance-songs or to embody concepts of proportioned numerical structure (to which the text contributed), music was about to enter a new age, in which it was not merely attached to text (or vice versa) but was more integrally bound up with it as an agent of declamation and exegesis. While the new trend concerned itself first with proper declamation, composers soon introduced, at their discretion, devices to interpret the pictorial and affective elements of the text. It is the affective aspect that, paradoxically, was to sustain the gradually developing hegemony

---

was used by English composers of cyclic Masses. Concerning 'Western Wynde', both melody and Masses, cf. *MQ* (1971) 427–43.

of instrumental music, which began to secede from vocal music as the latter became committed to the word. This happened at the very point in time when the expanding framework of the outer parts had reached the natural limits of the choral medium.

SETTINGS OF ENGLISH TEXTS

Evidence of musical settings of English lyric poetry is even scarcer for the fourteenth century than it is for its predecessor. It is true that in manuscripts of the second half of the fourteenth century verbal texts, known as carols, begin to appear. These texts belong to the family of strophic songs and are structurally related to the *virelai* and *ballata*. But no musical settings before the fifteenth century are extant (a few late-comers date from the early 1500s).

The carol was originally an English dance-song. Throughout its history it possessed as one fixed identifying characteristic the presence of a short 'burden' with an invariable text, sung at the beginning and after each stanza. The stanzas often have the rhyme scheme aaab and may end with a refrain. By far the greatest number of carols have sacred subjects, doubtless as a result of the Franciscans' appropriation of this originally secular genre for sacred purposes. Significantly, Latin made considerable inroads into carol poetry, and many of the carols are macaronic,[108] with frequent citations of verses from well-known hymns or antiphons. Others are entirely in Latin and were generally referred to as *cantilenae*, which therefore differ in a number of ways from fourteenth-century *cantilenae*. (*Cantilenae* are especially numerous in the Egerton manuscript.) Since the form of the carol is closely related to that of the processional hymn and since all but one of the major manuscripts preserving polyphonic carols also contain devotional and liturgical polyphony,[109] it may be assumed that many carols with appropriate texts served processional functions, as did many of the *versus* and *conducti* of earlier centuries. Others doubtless had more convivial uses, as might arise on major feasts or other suitable occasions, when 'in view of their devotion to God, His Mother, or any other saint in wintertime a

108. The four verses of the stanzas of one carol (*Novo profusi gaudio*) are successively in Latin, French, English and Latin. Both the burden and the last stanza end with the words *Benedicamus Domino*. It has been suggested, therefore, that this piece and some others with similar endings were intended as troped 'Benedicamus' substitutes and are thus linked historically with the polyphonic *versus* and *conducti* of the twelfth and thirteenth centuries.

109. The liturgical portions of two of them include processional items. The manuscripts are the 'Trinity Roll' (Cambridge, Trinity College, 0.3.58), the Selden manuscript, and the Egerton manuscript, all of which may be said to date from the 1440s, as well as another manuscript preserved in London (British Museum, Additional 5665, known as the 'Ritson manuscript', after the name of its nineteenth-century owner). The carol section of this last MS dates from *c.* 1470, while other compositions were added subsequently (*c.* 1500).

fire is made for the fellows and scholars in the hall, where they may then spend an appropriate amount of time after lunch or dinner performing *cantilenae* or engaging in other proper recreational activities'.[110] Many of the carols and *cantilenae* are, indeed, for use in wintertime, being intended, like a large part of the *versus* and *conductus* repertoires of earlier times, for various occasions of the Christmas and New Year seasons; these were traditionally times of licence, for the suppression of which Bishop Richard de Ledrede had provided his *contrafacta* in the early decades of the fourteenth century.[111] Secular carols, however, often of a moralizing character, were also written, and much of the repertoire must have been sung in courtly households.[112]

Carols were doubtless originally monophonic, and a mere handful of preserved English monophonic carols, as well as occasional unison passages in early two-part pieces, can be taken as evidence of a submerged tradition. Nearly all the hundred-odd carols for which music survives are written, however, either for two parts throughout or for two parts interspersed with three-part sections. These interspersions are sometimes second settings of the burden, sometimes they occur within the stanza and at other times they are more or less varied echo responses. These three-part passages are often marked 'chorus', showing the manner of choral participation characteristic of dance-songs,[113] though polyphonic carols surely were no more danced to than were the movements of a Baroque suite. While neither burden and stanza, nor solo and chorus sections, had to be related, many carols furnish examples of inter-relationships. In musical terms the carols resemble some of the freely composed votive antiphons whose style first emerged in the 'OH' manuscript, particularly those antiphons that were written on a comparatively small scale. But on the whole the carols were more popular in tone, content and technique. The carol makes the impression of a popular genre, sublimated and refined by learning and artistic tradition.

Carols continue to occur in sources that can be assigned to the first third of the sixteenth century, but the rate of their occurrence decreases rapidly: they make up 69 per cent of the secular part of the Ritson manuscript, 37 per cent of the Fayrfax manuscript, and 11 per cent of Henry VIII's manuscript.[114] The poetry has a less spontaneous flavour, and the sacred

110. No. XVII of the Eton College Statutes of 1444, quoted in the original Latin by Harrison, *Annales Musicologiques* (1953), 160. Other establishments had similar statutes. In earlier days some of the *conducti* and motets were surely put to comparable use in religious houses.

111. See above, p. 283.

112. As to the mode of performance, a voice might be doubled or replaced by an instrument. As to courtly households, an account of a royal banquet in 1487 relates that 'the Deane and those of the Kings Chapell ... incontynently [i.e. promptly] after the Kings first course sange a Carall'.

113. That this applied to all carols is indicated by pieces written for two voices throughout that also contain passages marked 'chorus'.

114. Concerning 'Ritson' see above, p. 308, fn. 109; concerning 'Fayrfax' and 'Henry VIII' see below, p. 312, fn. 118.

texts, many of which concern the Passion, tend to exhibit pietistic sentiments. The compositions, generally showing a high level of technique,
display the even-flowing motion of imperfect mensuration, in contrast to
the rhythms (§ or ¾, i.e. ⊏ or O) of the fifteenth century carols. Here, too,
continental fashion transformed insular traditions.

By *c.* 1530 the *forme fixe* of the carol had gone out of fashion, following the
demise of comparable song forms on the continent. Other polyphonic
English songs had, in fact, existed since the early fifteenth century, but were
eclipsed by the carol for decades. The two earliest manuscripts preserving
such songs are in the Douce Collection at Oxford and at Cambridge.[115]
They date from around 1420 and are therefore contemporary with the
latest additions to the 'OH' manuscript. A third source, in the Ashmole
Collection at Oxford,[116] is about twenty years younger, i.e. slightly earlier
than the Selden manuscript (which contains three such songs). A few minor
fragments complete the extant repertoire of the first half of the century.

Both the Douce and Cambridge manuscripts also contain compositions
with French texts, and all three manuscripts (i.e. including Ashmole) show
that the English songs represent attempts of varying expertise to adopt the
stylistic conventions of continental secular polyphony. With the exception
of three three-part pieces (one each in the Cambridge, Ashmole and Selden
manuscripts) all songs are for two parts only. In the two earliest sources
(Douce and Cambridge) one encounters compositions of a relatively
primitive kind, but in the slightly later manuscripts (Ashmole and Selden)
the picture changes: both upper and lower parts have text below the music,
the rhythmic motion of the lower part approximates that of the upper voice,
and imperfect consonances (thirds, tenths and, especially, sixths) predominate, with occasional moderate parallelism.[117] None of the pieces,
however, whether for two or – exceptionally – three parts, displays the
rhythmic and melodic parallelism characteristic of many fourteenth-
century *cantilenae*. Melismas often occur, and final melismas are fairly
extensive and elaborate (see example 22 opposite). The form tends to be
bipartite (ab, aabb, and abb, the latter design being more common than
the others).

English polyphonic songs of the late fifteenth and early sixteenth centuries
are preserved in four manuscripts, all lodged in the British Museum, and

115. Oxford, Bodleian Library, Douce 381 (five English songs) and Cambridge, University Library,
Additional 5943 (ten English songs, one being a concordance of one of the Douce pieces).

116. Oxford, Bodleian Library, Ashmole 191 (seven English songs). The nicknames, 'Douce',
'Cambridge', and 'Ashmole' are self-explanatory. For the MS from the Selden Collection at Oxford
see p. 299, fn. 84.

117. This duet repertoire therefore shows a process of rhythmic and melodic assimilation of the
tenor to the top voice that resembles stylistic developments in the Burgundian *chansons*. Only after the
development of a smooth and integrated duet style did it become possible to extend this new genre of
English polyphonic songs to three parts, i.e. with a contratenor.

Example 22. Oxford, Ashmole 191, fols. 193ᵛ–194ʳ

nicknamed 'Ritson', 'Fayrfax', 'Henry VIII' and 'Appendix 58'.[118] The
first two of these may be dated *c*. 1500, while the third and fourth date
from *c*. 1515 and 1520, respectively. Two-part texture, still represented by
about one-fourth of the songs in the Ritson and Fayrfax manuscripts, has
disappeared entirely from Henry VIII's manuscript; while most of its 109
compositions are for three voices, twenty English songs have four-part
texture, which obtains in only four pieces of the Fayrfax book. The composers in Fayrfax were chiefly in the service of Henry VII, and the book is
thus representative of the music favoured at his court. Likewise, Henry
VIII's manuscript reflects the taste prevailing during the first decades of his
reign.

The fourteen three-part songs in the Ashmole and Ritson manuscripts,[119]
with their elaborate euphonious counterpoint and rather frequent melismas,
resemble the contemporary Burgundian *chanson* repertoire. The songs of
the Fayrfax manuscript continue and extend this tradition.

Each phrase of the words is introduced with a point of musical 'imitation', one
syllable to a note. When all the syllables have been used, the music becomes more
lively; shorter, quicker [melismatic] notes, often in triplets, dance the phrase
along until a cadence is reached. Then the process begins again with the next
phrase.[120]

Gradual adoption of continental features characterizes the culture of the
early Tudor court—in the visual arts, in courtly entertainments and in
music. It is not surprising therefore that works by native composers in such
sources as Henry VIII's manuscript exhibit changes in style that are largely
due to influences from across the Channel. Puzzle canons and their insular
cousins, i.e. rounds, often of great complexity, represent a distinct genre.
But more numerous are the many court-songs in which new attitudes are
revealed by the prevalence of *tempus imperfectum* and the growing prominence of a rhythmically concise chordal style, with the lower parts generally
subordinated to the top part. There is also a growing attention to proper
declamation. In comparison with the earlier repertoire, the style of these
settings, many of which are strophic, is far less ornate; significantly, a good
many of the songs use known tunes.[121]

118. London, British Museum:
1. Additional 5665, 'Ritson', see above, p. 308, fn. 109;
2. Additional 5465, 'Fayrfax';
3. Additional 31922, often called 'Henry VIII', because thirty-three compositions ascribed to him;
4. Royal 'Appendix 58', vocal portion of manuscript.
   119. The one specimen in the Ashmole manuscript is 'Go hert hurt with adversite'.
   120. J. Stevens, *Tudor Court*, p. 16.
   121. J. Stevens, *Tudor Court*, pp. 18, 106, 128. See also J. Stevens, ed., *Henry VIII*. While the per-
centage of strophic songs is relatively low, it is far smaller in earlier collections.

None the less, the Tudor court songs can no more be regarded as evidence of a widespread popular musical culture than the earlier English part-songs. Polyphony was practised by professionals, and even at the royal court the musical mastery of Henry vIII was probably approached by only few aristocratic amateurs. As on the continent, it was in the sixteenth century that the dissemination of part-music and the spread of expertise in its performance was considerably stimulated by the advent of music printing. The first collection of polyphony printed in England appeared in 1530; the *XX Songes*, consisting of carols, songs and instrumental pieces, attest the rise of domestic music in England.

6.2 England: c.1540–1610

LATIN CHURCH MUSIC[1]

The proliferation of musical forms and styles in England after 1540 is especially remarkable in view of the situation before that time. Music in medieval Britain, as Harrison has shown in his classic study, was bound almost exclusively to the Christian liturgy, as set forth in a local usage, the Sarum rite. What was mainly cultivated was, of course, plainchant, but in the larger ecclesiastical establishments certain chants were traditionally replaced by polyphonic settings. The style of these developed greatly over the centuries. But whatever the style or the century, in the main composers set only certain specified liturgical texts, and even in these settings the chant melody was typically preserved in the tenor voice or elsewhere. The late Middle Ages also saw the rise of the votive antiphon, a 'paraliturgical' form whose texts, while not specified, drew from a large stock of standard figures in praise of the Virgin Mary. Apart from this, composers did not choose sacred texts on their own initiative, and if they wrote secular music, little of it has survived. By continental standards, the striking thing about early English music is its restricted scope.

This general situation persisted until past the middle of the sixteenth century. It is true that under the early Tudors a respectable body of secular music comes to light, but it hardly bears comparison to the majestic liturgical polyphony of those times. That this essential repertoire remained very conservative into the last years of Henry VIII's reign appears from one of the few surviving sources of hard evidence, a set of incomplete part-books at

---

1. See Harrison, *Mediaeval* and Harrison's chapters in *NOHM*, iii and iv.

Peterhouse (*c.* 1545).[2] The liturgical forms represented here continue to be limited to the Mass, the *Magnificat* and the votive antiphon; the youngest composers – Thomas Tallis, John Marbeck and Richard Edwards (born *c.* 1523) – rub shoulders with worthies from the turn of the century; and in musical style the newest pieces do not differ greatly from the oldest. Thus the form employed for individual Mass movements, *Magnificats*, and great votive antiphons is as monumental as ever. A large section in *tempus perfectum* is followed by one in *tempus imperfectum*, each sub-divided into straggling segments for full choir (five or six voices) or various semi-choir combinations. The full segments are still sometimes built on a *cantus firmus*, though this is no longer the rule; the rich polyphony, whose exuberant lines Harrison has compared to the arabesque of perpendicular Gothic architecture, still makes little use of systematic imitation in the Netherlandish manner. In England, this manner seems to have made itself felt in more modest compositions, typically for four voices. However, the Peterhouse books include two famous examples of actual Netherlandish writing on a grander scale, the motet *Aspice Domine* by Jaquet of Mantua and a parody Mass *Surrexit pastor bonus* by Johannes Lupi or Lupus Hellinck.[3] These works point to coming developments in English polyphony, and they also mark a trend. In the next half century, English motet manuscripts will regularly include some continental music by such composers as Gombert, Clemens and, especially, Lassus.

Henry VIII was not inclined to doctrinal or liturgical reform, and the dissolution of the monasteries did not affect music too seriously, since these were no longer the main centres of musical activity. The Reformation under Edward VI was quite another matter. The imposition of the two English Prayer Books with their greatly limited rubrics for music; the dissolution of important musical establishments under the Chantries Act; Cranmer's strictures against florid polyphony and the repeated local injunctions against *any* polyphony; the wholesale destruction of organs and liturgical books; the promised abolition of choral foundations – all this must have looked like disaster to English musicians. Although Mary and Elizabeth I headed off actual disaster, Church music never fully recovered. The support for choirs was depleted by inflation and the expropriation of endowments, and organs were rebuilt slowly, if at all. The Chapel Royal flourished, naturally, but to get Westminster Abbey ready for Mary's coronation it was necessary to pay tenpence for 'a pounde of gunpowder to destroye the pigions in the churche' and 'owlde shaftes to shote at the pigions'.[4] Recent research into parish church records of the time has

2. The manuscript is inventoried in Anselm Hughes, *Catalogue of the Manuscripts at Peterhouse, Cambridge*, Cambridge, 1953.

3. L. Lockwood, *ML* (1961) 336.

4. Edward Pine, *The Westminster Abbey Singers*, London, 1953, p. 59.

revealed a very minimal musical life.[5] The self-evident fact is that less music was wanted; the rich forms of Catholic music were never matched by those of the Anglican rite.

Mary's short-lived Roman restoration involved a vigorous musical programme, though it is hard to say how far this extended beyond London. To her reign must be assigned the large Marian votive antiphons of William Mundy (c. 1529–c. 1591) and Robert White (c. 1535–74), who presumably were not old enough to have written them under Henry nor foolish enough to have written them under Elizabeth, as well as some of the larger compositions of Tallis.[6] His brilliant seven-part Mass on the *cantus firmus*, *Puer natus est* has been plausibly interpreted as an abortive compliment to the heir Mary was hoping for around Christmas of 1554.[7] It also appears that Mary's Chapel Royal was directed to prepare a large anthology of polyphonic settings of hymns and responds for the Church year, probably for use at Vespers; later manuscripts[8] preserve an interlocking series of such pieces, mainly by Tallis and John Shepherd (c. 1520–c. 1563; Shepherd appears in Chapel lists from 1553–7). These works are bound to the liturgy as closely as ever, but the particular choice of liturgical forms is relatively new, and so is the style, a straightforward setting of the *cantus firmus* in regular breves, with imitative counterpoint in the other four or five voices. Shepherd laces this style with much rhythmic animation and bold linear designs; Tallis works with short and often rather wooden imitative motives.[9] Some antiphon settings by Tallis, without *cantus firmus*, are also surprisingly rigid in their polyphonic construction. This may indicate lack of ease with the Netherlandish imitative style, as Harrison suggests, but in such works as *O sacrum convivium* and the two settings of *Salvator mundi* the characteristic dense texture and sober pacing seem both personal and controlled.

It is very interesting that Latin Church music continued to exist, and even to flourish, after the accession of Queen Elizabeth. Two developments early in the reign made this possible: the injunction (from the Queen's *Injunctions* of 1559) that an unspecified 'Hymn, or such like song ... in the best sort of melody and musick that may be conveniently devised' might be added to Morning or Evening Prayer, and the promulgation of a Latin Book of Common Prayer for the use of the Chapels Royal, colleges, and public schools. These characteristic gestures of compromise must reflect more than just the personal wishes of Elizabeth, though we should not

5. A. Smith, 'Parish Church', but compare Smith's findings at Ludlow, *ML* (1969) 108.

6. Mundy's church music is printed in Harrison, *Early English*, ii and White's in *Tudor Church Music*, vi.

7. Doe, *Tallis*, p. 21. Doe places the responds of Tallis and Shepherd in the late years of Henry VIII's reign, see *PRMA* (1968–9) 81–95.

8. Principally Christ Church 979–83, which is inventoried in *Mus. Disc.* (1971) 179.

9. Some Shepherd responds have been published in Harrison *Sheppard*. Tallis's Church music appears in *Tudor Church Music*, v.

minimize her interest in music and her personal role in the climate created for music during her reign. The large polyphonic Mass and *Magnificat* were now impossible, but Elizabeth's Chapel Royal services could still feature one massive Latin composition, equal in musical pomp to the votive services she remembered from her father's chapel. Indeed the form and style of the votive antiphon went over directly into the large-scale psalm-motet, which was the important new genre of the 1550s and 1560s.[10] Gradually the form melted down, until a late psalm-motet such as Mundy's *Domine quis habitabit* (Psalm 14) consists of a relentless row of stiff points of imitation *à* 6 lasting through the entire seven verses of the psalm. The later psalm-motets of White, notably his second and third settings of *Domine quis*, experiment with interesting internal repetition schemes; Byrd's later setting of this favourite psalm is a virtuoso exercise in nine-part writing with three basses.[11] White's *Miserere mei Deus* (Psalm 50) employs means of pathetic expression that are rare in English music of this time, the fine settings of *Lamentations* by White, Tallis and Byrd furnishing the only other examples.

William Byrd (1543–1623) came to the Chapel Royal in 1572 from Lincoln. Only three years later, the seventeen *cantiones* or motets that he contributed to a joint publication with Tallis, the *Cantiones quae ab argumento sacrae vocantur* (1575), must have seemed little short of revolutionary on the London musical scene. Next to a few traditional texts set traditionally – a *cantus firmus* respond modelled on a similar work by Robert Parsons, a prayer in the form (but not the style) of an old votive antiphon[12] – there are four respond texts set freely without *cantus firmus*, two freely set hymns and five texts which are completely non-liturgical. The force of this latter innovation must be gauged against the earlier English tradition of setting only specified liturgical or paraliturgical texts, or the more recent tradition of setting whole psalms or block sections of psalms. To take responsibility for the words of a motet implies an appreciation of their individual meaning and actual sonority, over and above their function in the ritual; personal choice of a text goes hand in hand with a more personal musical treatment of it. And the freshness of Byrd's musical style stems as much from his deeper response to the words as from his many novelties of musical technique pure and simple. *O lux, beata Trinitas* sounds brighter than any earlier English music, and *Domine, secundum actum meum noli me iudicare* sounds more despairing. Most of the motets are still very long, but as compared to White or Mundy, Byrd works with a smaller number of points of imitation that are longer in themselves – longer as a result of a new

10. See Kerman, 'Motet', which includes a check-list of psalm-motets.

11. Byrd's complete works, first edited by Fellowes, appear in a revised edition by Dart and others.

12. *Libera me, Domine, de morte aeterna* and the cycle of three pieces beginning with *Tribue, Domine*; see Kerman in forthcoming *Festschrift Westrup*.

concept of contrapuntal development and a new flexibility of contrapuntal technique. His motives, cleaving to the individual words, generally have more profile than those of his predecessors. Byrd shows keen awareness of principles of formal balance among his large points of imitation, and also of the contrasts to be obtained by dropping the imitative style altogether; the most popular number of this print, *Emendemus in melius*, is homophonic all the way through up to an admirably calculated final line in imitation.[13] The intense chromatic inflexion of the lament in the first line (see example 1), to look no further, had never been heard before in English music.

Example 1. Byrd, *Emendemus in Melius*

It is clear that Byrd was the first English composer to understand and penetrate to the heart of the Netherlandish style, rather than simply adopting its surface characteristics. It is also fairly clear where he came to this understanding. Morley testifies to Byrd's friendship with Alfonso Ferrabosco (1543–88), an Italian musician and adventurer who served Queen Elizabeth on and off between 1562 and 1578. 'Master Alfonso' was a prolific and skilful – if not a very imaginative – composer of the Rore circle whose motets and madrigals were very widely copied and admired in England. Each of the Byrd motets named above is directly modelled on a Ferrabosco motet – and in each case Byrd far outstrips his model in depth of musical interest.[14] Byrd's *Cantiones* of 1589–91 take some striking texts from motets by Willaert and Clemens; the ideal, it will be observed, is again that of a relatively early Netherlandish generation. In its density of texture, prolixity of form and fast-moving harmonic rhythm, Byrd's early music sounds archaic compared to that of Palestrina or Lassus.

13. For an analysis of this motet, see Kerman, *MQ* (1963) 431–49.
14. Kerman, *MQ*, p. 448 f, and 'Motet', p. 289 f.

As for Tallis' contributions to the 1575 *Cantiones*, many of them appear to date from the time of Queen Mary. On the other hand, such works as the highly expressive *In ieiunio* and the imaginative *Derelinquat impius* represent a final phase (doubtless now under the influence of Byrd) in a career which quietly epitomizes the far from quiet course of English church music through the reigns of Henry VIII, Edward, Mary and Elizabeth. Tallis' astounding eight-choir, forty-part motet *Spem in alium* must also date from his later years, and mark some extraordinary occasion; Elizabeth's fortieth birthday in 1573 has been plausibly suggested.[15]

In 1589 and 1591 Byrd published two new books of five- and six-part *Cantiones*. Crudenesses of various sorts which are present in the 1575 motets have now been left behind, and the imaginative technical innovations of 1575 are applied with new power, flexibility and expressiveness. Byrd can even be concise when he wishes (which is not often); such works as *Vigilate, Domine non sum dignus*, and the well-known *Laudibus in sanctis* employ dramatic madrigalesque effects. Very few of the texts are liturgical, and among the freely chosen ones it is striking to read so many that refer to oppression, the Babylonian captivity, hopes for freedom, the coming of God and similar topics. Although the case cannot be proved, the present writer has argued that these texts pray, rage and lament on behalf of the Elizabethan Roman Catholic community, of which Byrd was an outspoken member.[16] *Deus venerunt gentes* from Psalm 79, an outcry about martyrs' bodies thrown to the birds and beasts, may well refer to the martyrdom of Father Edmund Campion in 1581; Byrd openly set to music a seditious English poem written about that terrible event. Even innocent Advent texts, such as that to which the following splendid contrapuntal opening[17] is set (see example 2), would have had a special meaning for the recusant community:

Example 2. Byrd, *Domine, praestolamur*

15. By Paul Doe, *Tallis*, p. 41.
16. Kerman, 'Motet', p. 292 f.
17. This opening is analysed by Kerman in *Festschrift Reese*, p. 533 f.

Byrd's three Masses, published half-surreptitiously after 1590, and the two books of *Gradualia* (1605, 1607) are of course explicitly Catholic. The *Gradualia* transmits over a hundred motets, the great majority of which are ordered according to the requirements of the Roman liturgical year; publications of this sort had become popular in Europe in the wake of the Counter-Reformation.[18] As befits a practical collection, the pieces are mostly written for from three to five parts, and they are notably shorter and swifter than the earlier *Cantiones*. What is perhaps most striking here is the breathtaking variety of musical style, and the increasingly direct, simple, profound way in which the music matches the text. 'In sacred words,' Byrd writes in the preface, 'as I have learned by trial, there is such a profound and hidden power that to one thinking upon things divine and diligently and earnestly pondering them, all the fittest numbers occur as if of themselves.' This is a perfect statement of the Renaissance musician's credo, one that bespeaks a very different attitude towards the liturgy from that held by the composers of Henry VIII's time.

A Jesuit missionary who knew Byrd writes in 1605: 'We kept Corpus Christi day with great solemnity and music, and the day of the Octave made

18. Jackman, *MQ* (1963) 17–37.

a solemn procession about a great garden, the house being watched;'[19] the *Gradualia* includes Mass and Office music for Corpus Christi, including the processional hymn. Yet it can hardly be supposed that there were enough undercover services of this kind in England to 'explain' the *Gradualia*. More likely Byrd and his work were treasured as a symbol of the Catholic resistance, and publication was subsidized accordingly. Certainly Byrd appears to have achieved a position in English society matched by no earlier English musician and by few later ones. He already had influential friends at Lincoln; after a few years in London he was granted a monopoly for music printing; he was close to the literary circle around Sidney; he could count on powerful patrons all his life. Byrd was never persecuted for his rather open Catholic activities.

Perhaps the image of Elizabethan England as a 'nest of singing birds' has tended to obscure his real stature. In an age graced by a large company of talented musicians, Byrd occupied a dominant position. This judgement is not made solely on the basis of his great repertoire of Latin Church music, an essentially conservative area which most other composers naturally avoided. There is hardly an area of Elizabethan music to which Byrd did not make fundamental and outstanding contributions.

ENGLISH CHURCH MUSIC[20]

The Reformation created an urgent need for new music, albeit music to stylistic specifications that were as restrictive as the new liturgical categories. Many of the established composers went to work at once. In 1550 Marbeck published *The Book of Common Prayer Noted*, consisting of measured English chant for Morning and Evening Prayer, Communion and the Burial Service; some of the music was simplified from the old Sarum tones, but most of it was newly composed. Though there is some evidence that the daily psalms were chanted in Elizabethan times, the lack of reprints or revisions of Marbeck's book shows that it failed to gain general use. Even before the first Prayer Book of 1549, such composers as Tye, Tallis and Shepherd had written polyphonic – but barely polyphonic – settings of the canticles and some other liturgical texts, as well as anthems. The music had to be very largely syllabic and homophonic in style, and anything more than four parts counts as a distinct rarity. A timorous amount of imitation finds its way into the anthems, which cannot, however, generally be said to bring out the best in their composers.

Many of these Edwardian four-part pieces appear in *Certain Notes to be Sung at the Morning Communion and Evening Prayer* issued by the printer

19. Jackman, *MQ*, p. 35.
20. See Le Huray, *Reformation*; also Le Huray and Daniel, *Sources* (listed, p. 449). A useful anthology edited by Le Huray is Knight's *Treasury of English Church Music*, ii (1545–1650).

John Day in 1565 (after a publishing delay). Music of this kind cannot have attracted wide interest either, for Day's book did not require a second printing, and no other books of anthems or service music appeared until 1614 and 1615. The trade was a little better for publications of four-part psalms – that is, simple settings of metrical psalm tunes. About six books were issued from 1563 to 1621.[21] John Dowland composed such pieces, and so did Tallis; his tunes for the psalm translations by Archbishop Parker, the main figure in ecclesiastical affairs of the 1570s, include 'Tallis' Canon', and also the theme of Vaughan Williams' *Fantasia*. But the best-seller was of course Sternhold and Hopkins' *Whole Book of Psalms*, which reached its definitive version in 1562 and at once went into an endless series of reprints. The tunes, always included as a single line in the prints, derive in part from the Geneva Psalter of 1547. As in Calvinist communities abroad, in England too metrical psalms were evidently very widely sung in services and in private devotions. The Puritans would have no other music, and indeed the extremists would not even have Sternhold and Hopkins; the Psalter brought to America by the Pilgrim Fathers had different tunes to match a newly literal translation of the psalms by Henry Ainsworth.

The most interesting composer of Anglican music in Elizabethan times was a Catholic, William Byrd. With his impressive setting of the Easter Anthem 'Christ rising', published in 1589, Byrd seems to have created an important new genre almost out of whole cloth, the verse anthem, and his songbooks of 1588 and 1589 include many psalms composed in much richer styles than those attempted by his contemporaries. His Great Service, the finest service of the time, probably dates from after the death of Elizabeth, at the time of the beginnings of the High Church movement under Launcelot Andrewes and Laud.[22] Byrd's 1611 songbook includes several more verse anthems and some full anthems that can stand alongside his best Latin motets – 'Retire my soul', 'Arise, Lord into Thy rest', and others – yet these works never found their way into the main corpus of Anglican Church music. Although the foundations for this corpus were laid by such composers as Gibbons, Tomkins, Weelkes and Ward in the first decade of the new century, its real history belongs to a somewhat later period.

SONGS, MADRIGALS AND AYRES

Little would be known of the beginnings of English song in the later Tudor period if the Oxford organist Thomas Mulliner had not copied a few keyboard transcriptions into the anthology that he began compiling around 1550.[23] From this it appears that in the 1540s and 1550s strophic poems

21. See Frost, *Psalm and Hymn Tunes.*
22. See *NOHM*, iv, 466.
23. The *Mulliner Book* is published in *Musica Britannica*, i; see also D. Stevens, *Mulliner Commentary.*

such as those printed later in Tottel's *Miscellany* (1557) were set to simple music of four parts, either in a direct homophonic style (Edwards' 'When griping griefs' – a song remembered in *Romeo and Juliet*) or in a mainly syllabic, half-homophonic, half-imitative style (Edwards' 'In going to my naked bed'). This recalls Edwardian church music, and in fact the music is close enough in style to the humbler French *chansons* of the time. In the 1560s a new genre made its appearance, to which Philip Brett has applied the generic term 'consort song'.[24] These songs are written for a single boy's voice – treble or 'mean' (alto) – and four instruments, presumably viols, which play a brief introduction, an amorphous accompaniment during the verses and brief interludes between them. As to the texts, some wooden strophic poems are found that later appear in *The Paradise of Dainty Devices* (1576 – this, the second of the popular Elizabethan poetic miscellanies, was compiled by Edwards, who had however died in 1566; it is the publisher who says that the poems are 'aptly made to be set to any song in five parts, or song to instrument'). Other texts come from the choirboy plays, the plays that were presented in London by the boys of the Chapels Royal, Westminster and St Paul's. The choirboy 'death songs' – climactic arias lamenting someone's death or the singer's impending suicide – are extremely interesting sports in the evolution of dramatic music, though their function was evidently less dramatic than rhetorical. The existence of this tradition of songs for the stage goes some way to explain the sophisticated use of music in the more famous period of Elizabethan drama.[25]

The origin of this distinctive vocal-instrumental style is obscure, and so is the relation of the older four-part repertoire to the predominantly three-part, tenor-orientated repertoire of Henry VIII's early years. The obscurity will remain unless and until some new sources are providentially recovered. A possible figure of importance in the development of both styles, it may be hazarded, was Philip van Wilder (d. 1552), a Netherlander who rose to a position of considerable influence under Henry and Edward. French *chansons* by Wilder, some of which were printed abroad, circulated widely in English manuscripts and may have provided an impetus for the *chanson*-like songs of the 1540s and 1550s. And as Master of the Children of the Privy Chamber, it is probable that Wilder was directly responsible for dramatic entertainments.[26] One of his motets was adapted to words for a Latin Oedipus play, perhaps the Seneca. To be sure, the named composers of theatrical consort songs belong to a later generation: Robert Parsons of the Chapel Royal (d. 1570) and Richard Farrant (d. 1581), Master of the Children at the Chapel Royal, Windsor, and an associate of the first

24. 'The English Consort Song, 1570–1625'. Brett has published a representative selection of consort songs in *Musica Britannica*, xxii.
25. See Sternfeld, *Shakespearean Tragedy*.
26. See Harold Hillebrand, *The Child Actors*, Urbana (Illinois), 1926, p. 276 f.

Blackfriars' Theatre. Edwards himself was Master of the Chapel Royal from 1561–6.

Byrd composed more consort songs than any other composer, and made the form very much his own. With words adapted to the viol parts, many such songs appeared in Byrd's *Psalms, Sonnets, and Songs of Sadness and Piety* (1588), a popular print which initiated the first active phase in the history of English music publishing. Here the poetry ranges from metrical psalms to sonnets inspired by the 'new poetry' of the 1570s, Sidney and Dyer figuring among the poets, but Byrd obviously felt most at home with strophic poems solemn in sentiment and ponderous in metre. The settings are mainly syllabic, with little word repetition, and all the lines are set at about the same length – indeed the individual lines tend to follow a set overall rhythmic pattern. Example 3 shows a representative example, from Byrd's 1589 songbook.

Example 3. Byrd, 'See those sweet eyes'

(★) the words are adapted by the composer to the viol parts throughout.

As compared with his predecessors, Byrd moulded the melody with new art, and worked out the viol parts in a careful imitative style; he also experimented with duets and choral refrains. Given his preference for sacred and moralistic texts, it will be seen how these developments brought him to the verge of the verse anthem.

Byrd was still writing consort songs, and extremely fine ones, after the turn of the century, though by this time they had become so old-fashioned that he did not include many samples in his songbook of 1611. None the less the importance of the genre may be gauged from the clear traces of it that persist in the lute-ayre, the verse anthem, and – most amusingly – in the pieces called 'cries' which were popular in the early seventeenth century.[27] These are in effect long rambling viol fantasias against which the composers set a 'naturalistic' jumble of calls by hawkers, tradesmen, watchmen, town criers, Thames boatsmen, beggars and so on – a conceit later rediscovered by the composer of *Louise*.

The madrigal, more than any other genre of English music in this period, has to be understood in terms of a foreign tradition, the great tradition of the Italian madrigal. To the Elizabethans, this went without saying. For the historian today who is interested in how musical ideas pass from one milieu to another and take hold, there are few clearer object lessons than the story of the importation, adaptation, naturalization and transformation of the Italian madrigal in England.[28]

Italian madrigals were known here before 1540, but they made their first real effect in the decades after 1570. This was a time of widespread interest in and assimilation of foreign culture, as typified by the remarkable development of poetry in the hands of Sidney and Spenser. The madrigal as a musical form depends on a particular kind of vivid, flexible, swift-moving love poetry; madrigals are inconceivable on texts from Tottel's *Miscellany* or the *Paradise*. But when the 'new poets' of the 1570s translated and adapted Petrarch and the Petrarchists and formed a radically new poetic repertoire on this basis, composers were in a position to do much the same thing with Italian music. For a variety of reasons, madrigals were not published in London until a little later. The main decade of their appearance, the 1590s, coincides with that of the English sonnet sequence, which probably counts as the most extreme product of the Petrarchan literary fashion.

Both the seriousness of English interest in the madrigal and also an instinctive desire to naturalize it are reflected by the first two English madrigal prints, which were anthologies of translated Italian madrigals; in all, five such anthologies were printed between 1588 and 1597. It is significant that a great many poems from the anthologies were later reset by

---

27. Published in *Musica Britannica*, xxii.

28. The music is published in Fellowes' *Madrigal School*; the poems in his *Madrigal Verse*. See Kerman, *Elizabethan Madrigal*.

native composers, who often availed themselves of the music that lay so obviously to hand. The personalities of the anthologists form a pleasant composite symbol for the madrigal movement. Nicholas Yonge was a London lay clerk who met regularly with 'Gentlemen and Merchants of good accompt (as well of this realme as of forreine nations)' to sing Italian madrigals. Thomas Watson was a leading classicist and Petrarchan poet, the author of the first English sonnet sequence, *Hekatompathia* (1582). And the third anthologist was Thomas Morley (1557–*c.* 1603), Gentleman of the Chapel Royal, influential composer and theorist, monopolist of music printing, and the guiding – one is inclined to say, the driving – force of the whole English madrigal development.

The composers most heavily represented in the anthologies are Alfonso Ferrabosco, Marenzio and writers of the light Italian *canzonetta*: Ferretti, Vecchi, Croce and Anerio. The latter group proved to be the most influential in England.[29] Morley excelled in the light madrigal style, though it is only fair to say that his pieces are rather more carefully worked than contemporary *canzonette*, as appears from his popular three-part *Canzonets* (1593) and four-part *Madrigals* (1594). The flexibility of phrase lengths and the rapidly shifting moods of this music, the fluent declamation borrowing from dance rhythms, and the lucid, simple harmonic style in which the facile imitations are couched, must have seemed wonderfully fresh in the world of the consort song. Compare the madrigal 'Love would discharge' (1604) by Thomas Bateson, a close follower of Morley, shown in example 4, with the setting of the same lines by Byrd, cited in the second stanza of example 3 above, p. 326.

Example 4. Bateson, 'Love would discharge'

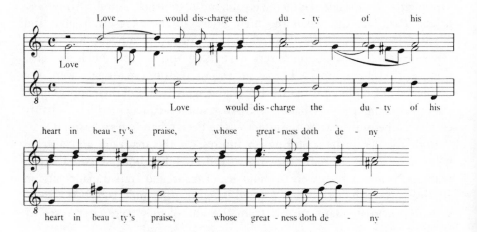

Morley's music follows the words in correct madrigalesque fashion, too, though without the penetration shown by Marenzio in Italy or by Weelkes and Wilbye in England a few years later. Madrigal poems are not strophic; Morley regularly uses the Italian stanza made up of a free mixture of seven- and eleven-syllable lines, the so-called 'madrigal verse' of Baroque operatic recitative. In content, his poems mostly represent the dregs of Petrarchism, trivial conceits of pastoral courtship that might well have appalled Morley's serious-minded teacher, Byrd.

Morley's equally popular next publications take an even lighter stand, though it should be noted that in spite of their titles, the five-part *Balletts* (1595) and the five- and six-part *Canzonets* (1597) also include a few serious madrigals – not always Morley's best work. Many favourite numbers in the *Balletts* and the two-part *Canzonets* (1595), such as 'Sing we and chant it' and 'Miraculous love's wounding', are modelled on specific Italian pieces, sometimes very closely indeed, and quite openly – both sets were issued in London in parallel English and Italian editions! In 1601 Morley edited the most famous of all English madrigal books, *The Triumphs of Oriana*, a set of madrigals in praise of Queen Elizabeth by twenty-three of her devoted subjects, some of whom however had only the vaguest idea as to how madrigals were written. With this brilliant exercise in public relations, Morley unforgettably implanted the idea of an 'English madrigal school'. The *Triumphs* is modelled on the Venetian anthology *Il Trionfo di Dori* – 'Dori' was the bride of a member of a musical academy; Morley's own six-part *Oriana* madrigal is a considerably spruced-up rewriting of the *Dori* madrigal by Giovanni Croce. Planned as a tribute to the ageing queen (possibly for some political purpose), *The Triumphs* also pays warm tribute to Morley and to his success in transmuting the light Italian style into a form that was immediately viable and appealing at home.

All later English madrigalists followed Morley in canzonets and light madrigals. The best of them also composed more serious and monumental madrigals, and although they looked searchingly at Marenzio, here the artistic result was more individual and less Italian. Thomas Weelkes and John Wilbye, composers of very different temperaments, both published their first madrigals at an early age shortly before 1600. Weelkes' first book of *Madrigals* (1597) has its share of uncertainties as well as characteristic audacities and imaginative successes; his *Balletts and Madrigals* (1598) makes a brash effort to outdo Morley's *Balletts* in brilliance; and his magnificent five- and six-part *Madrigals* (1600) reveals the control of a scope, emotion and power that Morley had not attempted. In the virtuoso choral effects of 'Mars in a fury' and 'Like two proud armies', the remarkable chromaticism of 'O care, thou wilt despatch me', and the rapidly changing treatment of the vivid images in 'Thule, the period of cosmography', Weelkes shows an eagerness to pursue the sense of the words that is very

Italian in spirit. At the same time these pieces are tightly constructed from the purely musical point of view, even employing parallel structures; unlike either Marenzio or Monteverdi, Weelkes will not allow word-painting to break his madrigals apart entirely. The same is true of Wilbye, a less robust, more refined imagination, who appears already as a finished master in his *First Set of English Madrigals* (1598). Wilbye sets better poetry than Weelkes (and much better poetry than Morley); while he is no less sensitive to the meaning of his texts than Weelkes, he has in addition a special intuition for the sound of the words, for declamation and cadence. Wilbye can be compared only to Dowland for subtlety of text setting, and indeed there are traces of the idiom of the lute-ayre in a number of his madrigals, such as 'Adieu, sweet Amaryllis' and 'Love me not for comely grace'.

Soon after 1600 taste shifted away from the madrigal and towards the lute-ayre (Morley anticipating the shift by publishing a book of ayres in 1600, and by providing his *Canzonets* of 1597 with a lute part). By 1603 Morley and Fair Oriana were both dead, and the reaction against Petrarchan poetry was broad enough to encompass the music that went with it, as witness Campion's attack on the madrigal aesthetic in his preface to the Rosseter *Ayres* of 1601. Weelkes sank into the routine of a provincial organist and wrote no more serious madrigals, and after 1609 neither did Wilbye, who bettered himself with his employers, the Kytsons of Hengrave Hall, Suffolk, by becoming their steward. Among the later madrigalists John Ward (1613) and Thomas Tomkins (1623) stand out – and Orlando Gibbons' impressive *Madrigals and Motets* (1612) should also be mentioned here, though the pieces it contains are utterly unlike madrigals (or motets). Ward was deeply impressed by Wilbye's *Second Set of Madrigals* (1609), perhaps the finest of all the English madrigal books. He uses the same majestic dimensions that Wilbye is working towards in such madrigals as 'Weep, mine eyes' and 'Draw on, sweet night', and the same distinctive large-scale sequential passages based on pedals. Ward is also notable, and exceptional, in that he takes so many of his texts from the established literature of the day – Sidney, Drayton and Davison's *Poetical Rhapsody*. Although the rise of the madrigal was bound up with a literary movement, English composers never employed a corpus of 'great poetry' for madrigal settings, as the Italians had done with Petrarch, Ariosto and Tasso. This is one reason why the English madrigal development was on the whole lighter in tone than the Italian.

It is interesting to compare the English madrigal development with the slightly later and slightly less extensive lute-ayre.[30] The ayre too had a manifest foreign model, the French *air de cour*; John Dowland (1562–1626), its first and greatest master, spent two formative years in France and many

30. The music is published in Fellowes' *Lutenist Song Writers*; the four-part versions of Dowland's ayres appear in *Musica Britannica*, vi. See D. Poulton, *Dowland*, London, 1972.

more in other foreign countries. Yet where Morley often sounds Italian, Dowland very rarely sounds French. There were of course no anthologies of French airs published in translation prior to Dowland's books, nor could there have been. The case is quite different from that of madrigals. With the words swamped in any case by counterpoint, the literal translations of the madrigal anthologies conveyed the general mood and the point of the various details of word-painting effectively enough, if not perhaps very elegantly. But translations of songs or ayres almost invariably ruin the literary quality of the song poems, and the subtle interrelation of literary and musical values was a central concern of the lute-ayre from its beginnings. Whoever Dowland's anonymous poets were, they rank very high, and he himself had a marvellous ear for the cadence of the English language; the second most famous composer of ayres, Thomas Campion (1567–1620), doubtless did better as a poet than as a musician. Beyond this literary difference between the two developments, there is the difference in personality between the two leading figures. Compared to Morley, Dowland is much more the artist than the entrepreneur, a restless Irish virtuoso buffeted by fortune, and always most admired for his musical studies in melancholia: *Semper Doland semper dolens*. Morley and Dowland symbolize in an almost exaggerated way the gulf between the Elizabethan and the Jacobean *Weltanschauung*. Finally, while one might hesitate to hold up Morley or even Wilbye beside the greatest Italian madrigalists, such as Marenzio or Monteverdi, Dowland far surpasses the contemporary French song writers. Morley could prepare the ground for madrigalists of greater imagination; Dowland was simply followed by lesser men.

His *First Book of Songs or Ayres* (1597) counts as the most successful of all music publications of the period, requiring three reprints in the next sixteen years. The songs are presented with lute accompaniments and also in four-part vocal versions (a procedure followed by other songbooks, some of which add a bass-viol part too); most of the fuller versions were evidently added to make the ayres attractive to madrigal singers and consort players, but there are cases in which the partsong setting appears to have been primary, and it is the lute version that is the makeshift. Dowland's ayres range widely in style, increasingly so in his later songbooks (1600, 1603, 1612). Some ayres are close to folksong or dance – some are simply dances with words adapted, such as 'Can she excuse' set to 'The Earl of Essex's Galliard', and 'Flow my tears', famous all over Europe as the 'Lachrymae Pavane'. Others, more declamatory in inspiration, employ striking leaps and jagged rhythms, though Dowland does not generally approach the style of the 'declamatory song' of the next generation.[31] He adapts features from the old consort song and from the Italian *canzonetta* by way of Morley. He even writes one

31. See Vincent Duckles, *JAMS* (1948, No. 2) 23.

Italian song, a parody (?) of the *nuove musiche* that were beginning to circulate in England; there are duets, masque songs with chorus, songs with treble viol *obbligato*, and *durchkomponiert* songs. Dowland's command of melodic structure is always impressive – the grace with which he moves back and forth through the full vocal range, his subtle feeling for balance, his haunting sequences and the purposeful way in which he stresses melodic goals by harmonic means. There is nothing perfunctory about Dowland's accompaniments, either; they imply a resilient contrapuntal webbing, though it is the lutenist's art to unweave this softly.

Of the later composers, John Danyel, brother of the poet Samuel Danyel, followed Dowland most faithfully in the direction of pathetic expression and intricacy of musical technique. His one songbook of 1606 includes several songs in a determined chromatic style, both in the voice and in the accompaniment. Like the contemporary madrigalists and composers of instrumental music, Danyel seems to have thought of chromaticism as a special feature to be employed intensively in one or two of his compositions and avoided in all his others. The songs of Campion – five books of them – are lighter in style, a fact that Campion explains deliciously: 'The Apothecaries have Bookes of Gold, whose leaves being opened, are so light as that they are subject to be shaken with the least breath, yet rightly handled, they serve both for ornament and use; such are light *Ayres.*'[32] Danyel and several other composers of lute-ayres were connected with the theatre, and it is in the style of the ayre that the play-songs were set, when they were not simply sung to ballad tunes. Indeed if ballad tunes are sung to the lute, they do not sound very different from certain of the simpler lute-ayres.

INSTRUMENTAL MUSIC

The very lively development of instrumental music in sixteenth-century England can be seen to follow the broad outlines that have been drawn for the continental repertoire. Most Renaissance instrumental genres are traceable either to the dance, or to the *ricercare* or fantasia type, based on models from sacred polyphony, or to the *canzona* type, based on the French *chanson*. At certain periods, English music for consorts (mainly viols) seems close in style and form to music for individual instruments (organ, harpsichord, lute). At other periods the two draw apart.

The oldest instrumental repertoire consists of liturgical organ music – antiphons, hymns and a few ordinary and proper Mass items, built on a plainsong *cantus firmus* or a faburden.[33] One type of setting involves loose two- or three-part counterpoint around the *cantus*, perhaps including a free *ostinato* figure; the resulting style can look very much like that of con-

32. From the preface to his *Fourth Book of Ayres, c.* 1617.
33. The repertoire is listed in Caldwell, *Mus. Disc.* (1965) 129.

temporary vocal music. There is for instance a section of a vocal *Magnificat* by Shepherd, *Quia fecit*, transcribed in the Mulliner Organ Book, which would very probably be accepted without question as genuine organ music if the original did not happen to survive. A second type of *cantus firmus* setting is more idiomatic, involving figuration patterns in the treble or bass, sometimes moving quite rapidly and with rhythmic quirks. Neither type reaches a very artistic stage by mid-century. With the exception of the ubiquitous Tallis, the main composers – Alwood, Blitheman, Preston, Redford – do not figure prominently among the known writers of vocal polyphony; it seems clear that the early organist-composers were a somewhat more lowly breed. This is also the impression given in the *Plain and Easy Introduction to Practical Music* of 1597 by Morley, who had recently graduated from the organ bench at St Paul's to the Chapel Royal.

The offertory of one of the votive Masses to the Virgin, *Felix namque*, provided a good occasion for keyboard virtuosity, and this chant was often set. Two enormous settings by Tallis which startlingly prefigure the keyboard technique of John Bull were copied into the Fitzwilliam Virginal Book fifty years after their date of composition – which Fitzwilliam very obligingly records as 1562 and 1564. This shows that *cantus firmus* setting flourished after the plainsong was abandoned; indeed the existence of a large body of plainsong settings independent of the liturgy, both for keyboard and for other instruments, is a peculiarly English phenomenon.[34] Besides *Felix namque* favourite *cantus firmi* were the antiphons *Miserere* and especially *Gloria tibi Trinitas*, of which well over a hundred settings have survived, mostly for viols but also for keyboard and lute. The name they usually bear, *In nomine*, was a minor musicological puzzle until four scholars working independently around 1950 happened upon the answer. It turns out that this freakish repertoire was inspired not merely by a vocal technique, namely *cantus firmus* setting, but by a specific vocal piece, the *In nomine* section from the 'Sanctus' of Taverner's most famous Mass, that based on *Gloria tibi Trinitas* (before 1530). Donington and Dart pointed out that this section is the only one in the Mass that has the *cantus* moving in straightforward regular breves[35] – a style which became general in vocal settings of hymns and responds under Queen Mary. A self-conscious, esoteric and even competitive spirit can be observed among the *In nomine* composers, as among the composers of '*L'Homme armé*' Masses, *Oriana* madrigals, Diabelli variations and the like. A number of the settings refer back to Taverner; an *In nomine* by Byrd improves upon one by Parsons.

As for early English music for a consort of viols, its complexion may be gathered from the title of the most important surviving collection, *A Booke of* In nomines *and other solfaing songs*, B. Mus. Add. MS 31390. The basic

34. Caldwell, *Mus. Disc.*, p. 129.
35. *ML* (1949) 101.

repertoire of this source, consisting of a hundred five- and six-part pieces dating from the 1550s and 1560s or even before, was disseminated widely and in a fairly integral way, as Jeremy Noble has shown.[36] The term 'solfaing' suggests alternative performance in vocalizing, presumably for didactic purposes, and the word 'song', if it is not entirely general in denotation, may acknowledge the fact that half of the pieces are vocal transcriptions. There are native and foreign motets, with or without *cantus firmus*, and especially French *chansons*, mainly by the shadowy Philip van Wilder. In England, as elsewhere, instrumentalists found the *chanson* particularly well suited to their needs. As for the instrumental *In nomines*, they can become extremely elaborate contrapuntal exercises, and a composer like Tye invents all kinds of new tricks for their composition – such as imitative subjects beginning with ten rapid repeated notes, and a metre of 'five minims'. Nothing like this was known in Europe at the time. Even more interesting are a few freely-composed pieces, the first English string fantasias, though they are not usually so named. Parsons' widely-circulated *De la court* and *Lusty gallant*[37] employ interesting echo effects and strong sectionalization, joining motet-like imitative sections and fragments of what sound like galliards within a single large composition. Example 5 shows an excerpt from the former piece.

Byrd's contribution to the instrumental repertoire was not extremely large, but it was telling. After writing a number of *In nomines* and other *cantus firmus* settings, presumably in the 1560s, he turned to free works of striking originality. One fantasia adopts a vocal style, so much so that in

Example 5. Parsons, *De la court*

36. 'Répertoire'. The instrumental music of Tye has been reprinted by Weidner; several *In nomines* are printed by D. Stevens in *Hortus Musicus*, cxxxiv.

37. They appear in Add. 31390; see Noble, 'Répertoire', pp. 97 and 103.

1575 Byrd could turn it into a motet – though the style seems rather to evoke the *chanson*; another fantasia features echoes which are ingeniously manipulated in strict canon throughout (the ultimate model for Sweelinck, perhaps).[38] Byrd wrote a linked pavane and galliard for strings, and other dances or dance fragments are firmly implanted in large-scale fantasias which carry forward the variegated scheme of Parsons. There are also two sets of variations on grounds. Byrd's twenty variations on 'Browning' is one amazing Elizabethan composition, comparable in its isolation and brilliance to Tallis' *Spem in alium* and, it appears, not very much later in date.

Fantasias, dances and variations are the main forms of Elizabethan virginal music, and it is not surprising to find several of Byrd's consort pieces directly transcribed into virginalist sources.[39] In this area, too, Byrd occupies the key position. Perhaps the quality of his virginal music is well enough recognized to make an appreciation unnecessary here, but it may be stressed that much of his large output was already copied into *My Ladye Nevells Booke* by 1591, and that the artistic level of English keyboard music before he came to it was practically non-existent. As has been mentioned, the Mulliner Book anticipates some aspects of Byrd's keyboard style, but no precedent exists for his rich 'idealization' of the pavane and galliard – the first is dated around 1580; the very concept was extraordinary – nor for his very far-reaching development of the theme and variations. Not to burden this essay with more music examples from Byrd, a few variation beginnings are transcribed below from John Bull's Variations on 'Walsingham', a tune also treated by the older composers. In the first excerpt Bull appears to pay homage to an earlier generation, but in the others he launches into a characteristic series of what Burney called 'Bull's Difficulties' (see example 6).

Example 6. Bull, Walsingham

38. Fantasia à 6 (I) in Fellowes-Elliott, *Byrd: Works*, xvii, 48 (equals *Laudate pueri, Byrd: Works*, i, 181) and Fantasia à 5, *Works*, xvii, 19.

39. The main reprints of virginal music are the Fuller Maitland *Fitzwilliam Book*, H. Andrews, *Nevells Booke*, and the keyboard works of Byrd, Farnaby, Gibbons, Bull and Tomkins in *Musica Britannica*.

The justly celebrated *Fitzwilliam Virginal Book* was copied by an imprisoned recusant, Francis Tregian, around 1615. His large, carefully-chosen collection places Byrd and Bull in the context of a lively and adept group of other composers: Giles Farnaby, Peter Phillips, Morley, Gibbons and even Tregian himself. Like all other English anthologies, this one contains foreign music, including some of the early works of Sweelinck, selected with Tregian's usual discrimination. But the implication of this foreign admixture is the opposite of the usual case: here it was the English school that laid the foundations for seventeenth-century keyboard music in Holland, where Bull and Phillips had migrated,[40] and then by way of Sweelinck in Germany.[41] In England, paradoxically enough, keyboard music did not develop – a fact that could be forecast from the Fitzwilliam Book. For it is striking that, except in the matter of keyboard technique, the generations after Byrd added little to his definition of the possibilities of the medium in terms of style and form. Like the Elizabethan madrigal development, indeed, the virginalist development burned brilliantly for a time and

40. On the general question of the foreign travels and sojourns of English musicians, see Dart in *Grove*, ii, 949.

41. See Borren, *Sources of Keyboard* and Curtis, *Sweelinck's Keyboard*.

then burned itself out. The genres that led to significant developments in England were the ayre and the string fantasia. In each case their continuing vitality appears to have depended on dissolving their links with the madrigal on the one hand, and with virginal music on the other.

In the late sixteenth century a new type of string fantasia took a strong hold on England, a type which found no echo among the virginalists.[42] Its main composers were the English sons of Italian musical dynasties, Alfonso Ferrabosco II and Joseph Lupo, and the violinist John Cooper-Coperario, an Englishman – perhaps the first 'Italianated' – who studied in Italy and never dropped his stage name on his return. Most of Coperario's five- and six-part fantasias bear Italian titles, whose significance is not clear. The stylistic allegiance of the new fantasia is to the *canzona*, as appears from the lively, 'instrumental' subjects and the tendency towards sectionalization with brief homophonic interludes. Little of this music is known today, and that which is will probably strike the modern musician as neutral and repetitive. But Coperario and Ferrabosco held important positions at King James's court – Ferrabosco is best known as Ben Jonson's collaborator in court masques – and their instrumental music achieved a great vogue evidenced by dozens of surviving manuscripts. From this repertoire, English chamber music developed in an unbroken line leading to Lawes, Jenkins, Simpson and Purcell.

However the vogue for instrumental music did not extend far enough to make it very attractive to the London music publishing trade. Ferrabosco and Gibbons were able to publish only smaller fantasias, up to three parts, though Anthony Holborne, John Adson and Dowland issued five- and six-part dances. No keyboard music was printed except *Parthenia* (1612–13), a small collection of works by Byrd, Bull and Gibbons. The *Consort Lessons* of Morley (1599) and Rosseter (1607) are collections of light music for the standard 'broken consort' of the time – an incipient trio texture made up of recorder, treble viol, bass viol, lute, cittern and pandora, with the lute often ornamenting the repeated strains by analogy to the virginalist dances. The publishing situation with lute music was somewhat better. Since the lute and cittern enjoyed special popularity among amateurs, there was a demand for instruction books as early as the 1560s. These often include quantities of music, and lute music is preserved in manuscripts continuously from the time of the *Mulliner Book* (which has some cittern pieces added to the end). This repertoire has not been adequately published or studied, but in general terms it would appear to follow the course of keyboard music, excepting, of course, for the liturgical items of the early days.[43]

42. 'Jacobean Consort Music' is reprinted in *Musica Britannica*, ix.

43. See Newton, 'Lute Music' and Lumsden, 'Sources of Lute Music'. Some of the music mentioned in this paragraph has been reprinted: Fellowes, *Gibbons Fantasias*; Warlock, *Dowland Lachrymae*; Dart, *Parthenia*; Beck, *Morley Consort*.

Finally mention should be made of three publications by Thomas Ravens-croft, whose high-flown titles *Pammelia*, *Deuteromelia* and *Melismata* (1609–11) are rather raucously belied by their contents: old freeman's songs, harmon-ized folksongs, catches on blameless texts or bawdy ones, tricky canons on Latin texts, London 'cries', drinking songs, ayres and quasi-madrigals. 'Pittie were it, such Mirth should be *forgotten* of us', says Ravenscroft, and we have him to thank for so unexpectedly brightening a dark corner of English musical history.[44]

POPULAR MUSIC

Yet much has been forgotten beyond recall. If historical surveys of music typically lean hard in the direction of the 'advanced' work of sophisticated composers, one reason is that historians have to work where the sources are, and the music that has survived comprises votive antiphons, motets, services, madrigals, fantasias and the rest. Of course this was not the music that was heard by the population at large, and how widely it was heard, enjoyed or participated in by the wealthier classes is hard to tell. As to elaborate Church music, the evidence suggests that this was performed in only a small number of churches and cathedrals – and, perhaps, in some clandestine chapels maintained by obstinate recusants. As regards elaborate secular music, the number of Elizabethan hearths resounding to domestic music-making has doubtless been exaggerated. In a meticulous archival study of *Musicians in English Society from Elizabeth to Charles I*, Walter Woodfill has published household accounts of several families who spent a lot of petty cash on music, and recent research has brought forward at least two families to match the Kytsons, whose extensive musical establishment is famous in the literature. In 1596 Lord Lumley could inventory 127 (!) musical instruments at Nonesuch, near London;[45] in 1630 Edward Paston of Appleton Hall, Norfolk, a literary-minded but retiring member of a prominent family, could bequeath closets and chests and trunks full of lute-books and part-books which had been specially copied for him and which survive today in the number of about three dozen.[46] (Both Lumley and Paston, by the way, were Catholics and patrons of Byrd.) But as Woodfill insists, the existence of a certain number of devotees does not mean that most or even many Elizabethans were keen musical amateurs or even active supporters of music. The best that can be said is that there was sufficient interest in music to support from five to ten music publications a year out of London, in editions of a few hundred copies, or a thousand at most.

---

44. A facsimile edition of the Ravenscroft books has been issued by M. Shaaber, and most of the music edited by Warlock.
45. Charles W. Warren, *MQ* (1968) 47.
46. Brett, 'E. Paston'.

Examination of music publishing records reveals some surprises.[47] First of all, that London music printing did not start on a regular basis until 1588 is a quite astonishing fact by continental standards, and a damaging one, which does not testify to a flourishing musical culture. To historians of English music, the fifty-odd madrigal prints issued after 1588 may seem like riches, but Marenzio went to twice as many editions on his own, and Philippe de Monte published more madrigals than the entire English madrigal school together. In the first half of the century, when only one or two music prints originated in London, several dozen were specially commissioned abroad for English use and imported; significantly, all were books of plainchant, none of 'advanced' polyphony. The meagre demand for published Anglican music, while Sternhold and Hopkins was reprinted several times yearly, year in year out, has been mentioned above. Metrical psalms, sung without harmony, can probably lay the best claim to being the 'people's music' of this age.

Or this claim might be disputed by the ballad. Over two thousand broadside ballads were registered with the Stationers' Company between 1557 and 1610, and it has been guessed that from three to five times as many were actually published.[48] Only exceptionally do broadsides include music, but they generally recommend a tune – if only 'a pleasant new tune' – for the singing. 'Heart's ease', 'O man in desperation', 'Packington's Pound', 'Fortune my foe' and dozens of others were sung all over England, by all classes, and to all types of poetry. 'Only joy, now here you are' from Sidney's *Astrophel and Stella* was sung to the tune of 'Shall I wrestle in despair', and Marlowe's 'Come live with me, and be my love' to the tune of 'Adieu, my dear'.[49] Some of the melodies originated as descants[50] over grounds, among which are to be found all the standard European favourites. These tunes were diligently intabulated by amateur lutenists into their commonplace books; they were sung and joked about in plays; they formed the basis of the jig and went over to Germany to initiate the *Singspiel*;[51] and as the subject of the virginalists' variation sets, they entered into an 'advanced' musical form that counts as one of the most influential of the day. 'No other country can boast such a wealth of charming sixteenth-century melodies,' a foreign historian has observed, 'and no other country a group of composers who, recognizing the value of this treasure, cultivated and enhanced it.'[52]

As for the waits and municipal musicians who were called upon for civic ceremonies, weddings, 'Church ales', Christmas music at the manor gates,

47. See Steele, *Music Printing*, and A. W. Pollard and G. R. Redgrave, *Short-title Catalogue*.
48. By Simpson, *Broadside Ballad*, p. xi.
49. Pattison, *Music and Poetry*, p. 175 f.
50. Or divisions or variations.
51. See Baskervill, *Elizabethan Jig*.
52. Willi Apel in *NOHM*, iv, 629.

and the rest – Woodfill has assembled a fascinating record of their activities, finances and troubles, but little if anything is known about their music. We can be sure that a surviving twelve-part motet by Edward Blanks,[53] a wait of London, formed no part of his daily repertoire. An examination of the few dozen dances that have been preserved from court masques[54] yields some clues, but these must certainly be regarded as a basis for extrapolation, rather than comparison.

The period from around 1540 to 1610 has long been celebrated as the Golden Age of English music, and there is no cause today for a revisionist view, even though we are now in a position to understand and appreciate the music of other ages too. After the Civil War, music of this period was never entirely allowed to sink into oblivion. While Dunstable and Fayrfax, Lawes and Jenkins had to wait till the twentieth century for rediscovery, this was not true of Tallis, Byrd and Wilbye. The Anglican music was still sung – often from ancient parts – and other music was scored by Dean Aldrich of Christ Church in the seventeenth century, Joseph Alcock of Lichfield in the eighteenth and Joseph Warren in the nineteenth, to mention only some of the better-known names. Burney disdained Elizabethan music, but he certainly knew enough about it; the glee and catch clubs and the Madrigal Society were singing madrigals and four-part ayres and also publishing them. Three complete madrigal sets were actually published in score around 1800 – earlier than any Palestrina, etc., had reappeared – and in 1812 John Stafford Smith was printing excerpts from the Mulliner Book and *Parthenia*. Antiquarian research matured from Oliphant and Rimbault to Arkwright and Squire. By the end of the century, numerous sets of motets and madrigals, a Mass of Tye and a masque by Campion had appeared in large serial musicological editions.

Thus the extremely energetic work of the Rev. E.H. Fellowes, who published the main corpus in the early twentieth century and wrote books about it all, could build upon a considerable tradition. In our own time, scholarship has had mainly to fill in the gaps, and also to place this music in its proper context, both historical and geographical. The context, perhaps, makes the achievements of the English composers seem doubly remarkable – in extent and vigour, considering the restricted scope of medieval English music and the blows it received at the Reformation, and in individuality, considering the pervasive influence all through the period of Netherlandish, Italian and French music. Yet all these factors did not dry up the musical impulse in England or smother its 'native' quality. The complete cessation

53. In Add. 31390; see Noble, 'Répertoire', p. 98.
54. Sabol, *Songs and Dances*.

of the music of the Sarum rite had the effect of breaking a rigidity and making way for the proliferation of new channels of musical invention. Knowledge of continental music provided native composers with a store of sophisticated techniques and attitudes which allowed them to realize their abilities with new power. Both factors, in short, were taken as liberating forces; and it was an age which knew how to make use of its freedom.

WOLFGANG BOETTICHER

7 Germany: 1300–1600

THE FOURTEENTH AND FIFTEENTH CENTURIES

Musical life in the German-speaking countries, in so far as one can speak of a specific local tradition, is largely based on two branches of the same practice: sacred folk-song and liturgical drama. It lies in the very nature of these important realms of music that the decisive contributions are not often associated with individual composers. There are nevertheless one or two individuals whom we encounter as early as the fourteenth century. The so-called 'Monk of Salzburg', probably resident c. 1364–75 in the Benedictine monastery of Salzburg, derived about forty German sacred songs from Latin hymns and sequences.[1] Many of these are to be found in the Mondsee-Vienna *Liederhandschrift* ('Song Manuscript'). The activities of the Swiss poet Heinrich von Lauffenberg (b. 1390, d. 1460 at Strasburg) resulted in

---

1. Concerning sequences and tropes see chapter 2, p. 77, fn. 31.

the creation of sacred *contrafacta*, the melodies of which were not derived from Latin church music but from German secular folk-song. The verbal texts, however, were taken from the Latin liturgy. These 'parodies', which quickly became popular, are of particular interest because in them the poet endeavours to make more even (by comparison with the originals) both the syllabic count and the number of melismatic notes per syllable. Among Lauffenberg's creations one should mention *Ave maris stella, bis grüest ein stern im mer* ('Be thou greeted, star in the sea'), *Kum heil'ger Geist, erfüll min herz* ('Come Holy Ghost and fill my heart' after *Veni sancte spiritus*), *Vern von der Sunne ufegang* ('Far from the rising of the sun', after *A soli ortus cardine*) and *Kum her erlöser volkes schar* ('Come thou saviour of the people', after *Veni redemptor gentium*). Oswald von Wolkenstein (*c.* 1377–1445), an Austrian poet who travelled over the whole of Western Europe, was an important intermediary in the fields of both the sacred *contrafactum* and the French *chanson*. Some hundred and twenty sacred and secular songs by him are extant, among them thirty-six pieces for two and three voices. Finally, mention must be made of the songs of the flagellants, which become important in religious folk-lore by the middle of the fourteenth century. (In Italy, particularly in Umbria, the movement reaches back as far as the middle of the preceding century.) The chronicle of Hugo von Reutlingen (b. 1285, d. *c.* 1360) contains several in musical notation, one of which remained popular for a long time as a processional song in memory of the terrible pestilence of *c.* 1349, *Nu is diu betfart so here* ('Now the pilgrimage has arrived').

The chronicle of Hugo is also a source for the *Minnesinger*, but by and large our main documentation for the works of the *Minnesinger* and their successors, the *Meistersinger*,[2] are the *Liederbücher*, i.e. the song books (or anthologies of song). As will be seen from the following list, these anthologies contain mostly monophonic pieces, though some of the later collections also contain polyphonic settings. The terms *Liederbuch* and *Liederhandschrift* (i.e. manuscript book of songs) are not translated in the following précis. Proceeding from the fourteenth to the fifteenth century, the most important collections are:

1 *Liederhandschrift* of Jena; *c.* 1350; containing 91 melodies;

2 *Liederhandschrift* of Vienna (MS 2701); *c.* 1320–40; containing songs by Frauenlob (*nom de plume* of Heinrich of Meissen, d. 1318 at Mainz), Reinmar of Zweter and 'Master' Alexander;

3 *Liederhandschrift* of Mondsee and Vienna (formerly called Spörl's *Lieder-buch*); *c.* 1400; containing 83 numbered pieces, of which 56 are secular songs;

2. Concerning the music of the aristocratic *Minnesinger*, see chapter 3, p. 133. The activities of their middle-class successors, the *Meistersinger*, were largely carried on by guilds in German cities of the fifteenth and sixteenth centuries and are best known today through Wagner's music drama *Die Meister-singer*.

4 *Liederhandschrift* of Heidelberg; after 1400; written down at the direction of the poet Hugo of Montfort (d. 1423), with some tunes by his page, Burk Mangolt.

5 *Liederbuch* of Hohenfurt (from the local Cistercian monastery); *c.* 1450;

6 *Liederbuch* of Wienhaus (near Celle); *c.* 1460; containing 17 Latin and 36 Low German texts (also 6 texts in which Latin and Low German lines alternate); also containing 15 melodies;

7 *Liederhandschrift* of Colmar (now housed at Munich); *c.* 1460; containing 105 melodies, mostly with sacred texts;

8 *Liederhandschrift* of Donaueschingen; *c.* 1460–80; containing the texts of 39 songs and 21 *Meistersinger* melodies ('töne'), 14 of which are by Frauenlob;

9 *Liederbuch* of Rostock; *c.* 1470–80; as in the case of MS No. 8 the compositions in this MS do not derive from the *Minnesinger*, but from the more middle-class *Meistersinger*; in the present instance this tradition seems to have centred around the University of Rostock; containing 29 pieces of music of one voice and 2 pieces for 2 voices;

10 *Liederbuch* of Anna of Cologne; mostly monophonic songs, the melodies in the character of secular folk song, but the texts sacred, suitable for 'conventual' practice;

11 Lochamer's *Liederbuch* (now housed in Berlin); *c.* 1452 with appendices to 1460; the main source for middle-class German song from the first half of the 15th century; containing, in addition to Latin sacred *contrafacta*, 42 German songs of which 31 are monophonic, 2 for two voices, 6 for three voices;

12 *Liederbuch* of Glogau (also housed in Berlin); *c.* 1480; containing 294 pieces, 158 Latin, 70 German, also a few Italian and Slavonic; by this time most of the pieces are scored for 3 voices; also 61 purely instrumental pieces;

13 Schedel's *Liederbuch* (now housed in Munich); *c.* 1466, with somewhat later appendices; reproduces a repertoire from the middle of the century; the background is primarily middle-class; containing 150 pieces, mostly for three voices, some without text, some French *chansons*, some purely instrumental.

Liturgical dramas were performed from the thirteenth century onwards, usually in front of the church portal, and in the case of the Easter plays vernacular as well as Latin texts were offered. (See the discussion of Easter tropes and Easter plays, chapter 2, pp. 77–9.) But the German Christmas plays are of a later date (St Gall, *c.* 1400). Among other topics presented in German cities after 1300 are the plaint of the Virgin Mary, the fall of Adam and Eve, the fable of the wise and foolish virgins; in the case of female roles they were, at least initially, enacted by clerics.

One of the earliest important sources of German organ music is a collection of 1448 by Adam Ileborgh, rector of Stendal, containing prelude-like movements which specifically postulate the use of pedals. In Conrad Paumann we encounter for the first time a personality with a distinct profile. Paumann (b. Nürnberg 1410, d. Munich 1473) was born blind; at an early age he was appointed organist at St Sebaldus in Nürnberg. From 1451 on he was in the service of the Bavarian Dukes, during which time he undertook several journeys to Italy. Paumann received a knighthood in recognition of his miraculous achievements in spite of his blindness (*il cieco miracoloso*). The three main sources for his music are the *Liederbuch* of Locham (listed above) which includes a section on organ music, the *Fundamentum organisandi*, which may be dated *c.* 1452–5; the so-called Buxheim Organ Book of *c.* 1470; and an anonymous keyboard manuscript of Erlangen of *c.* 1450. In these collections there are instructions for playing and composition for both the beginner and the advanced organist, and the examples concern both the techniques of figuration (or ornamentation) and three-part writing. In a rigorously methodical manner Paumann deals with ascending and descending progressions, parallel and contrary motion, repeated notes (*voces redeuntes*) and concluding formulae (*pausae*). Some of Paumann's specimens are particularly instructive, since they are instrumental versions of the songs found in the *Liederbuch* of Locham. In the Organ Book of Buxheim we also find instructions about the use of the pedals. The majority of the pieces in this collection are in three parts, some even in four. The repertoire is a large one: 256 pieces in all, of which 109 are based on German songs, but there are also instrumental arrangements of quite a few foreign pieces. Of great historic importance is a group of twenty-seven free keyboard movements (i.e. pieces not derived from vocal models) in which chordal sections alternate with those where the *discantus* (melody) is transformed by way of rapid ornamentation. Here we encounter the forerunners of the keyboard and ornamental styles of Arnold Schlick.

THE EARLY SIXTEENTH CENTURY

For the German-speaking countries the style of the sixteenth century is clearly delimited: it is succeeded by a particular style of homophony, usually labelled 'Florentine monody', and is preceded by polyphonic and other practices of Josquin and his slightly older contemporaries. There has been a good deal of controversy about the application of the term 'Renaissance' to German music of this century, at least in its second half. One must grant that the Franco-Flemish and Italian traditions continued actively; at the same time the modifications of these traditions by 'mannerism' are undeniable.[3] Beyond a doubt the invention of music printing by moveable metal type (Petrucci, 1501) was of international consequence, but this new technique seems to have required two decades or more to make itself felt. At the beginning of the century the major German sources were still in

---

3. Such terms as 'Renaissance', derived from *rinascimento* (re-birth) and 'mannerism', derived from *maniera* cannot be fully understood without a study of the visual, literary and musical arts of the period. Even so, these terms have a tendency to become spongeous and rather loosely applied. Broadly and pragmatically speaking it seems safe to use the term 'mannerism' as a chronological label for the late sixteenth century. For a discussion of *maniera* see *ZfMW*, xvi (1934), 3–20, 98–117, 152–70; also *Musikforschung*, xxiv (1971), 245–50, where further literature is cited.

manuscript. Two of these sources are of outstanding importance, namely those at Berlin (formerly Prussian State Library No. 40021) and at Leipzig (University Library No. 1494). The Berlin Codex originally belonged to the Cathedral of Halberstadt and has the rubric *Isaac de manu sua*, establishing the connection with Henricus Isaac (b. before 1450). He was a composer of great stylistic importance for the period, and his position cannot be tied exclusively to a single national tradition, whether it be Franco-Flemish, Italian or German.[4] From 1497 to 1514–15 Isaac lived and worked in German-speaking countries, which won him the appellation *Il Tedesco* or *Germanus*, notwithstanding his Flemish origin. The Leipzig codex was completed in 1504 by Apel, rector of the University, and is perhaps the most significant collection of German music around 1500. Among the composers of its 172 pieces we should mention, besides Isaac: Johannes Aulen, Heinrich Finck, U. Florigal, Adam von Fulda, B.H.(Hartzer?), Rud.H. (Hohenems?), Paulus de Rhoda and Conrad Rupsch. By concordance some of the anonymous pieces can be attributed to other sources, such as the Franco-Flemish composers Obrecht and Weerbecke; indeed foreign names are not absent in this codex (e.g. Verbonnet, Ranlequin del Mol). Of the pieces without text a portion are no doubt intended for organ, or at least, some keyboard instrument. Altogether, the codex consists of twenty-two fascicles. Two composers, A. v. Fulda and H. Finck, are well represented in fascicles 1–4 (forty-seven hymns for the Office, set for three to five voices) and fascicle 13 which contains antiphons as well as an arrangement of the German song *Wär ich ein Falk* ('Would I were a falcon').

ISAAC AND FULDA. Among those represented in the manuscript Isaac is the oldest composer. His main patron was the Emperor Maximilian I, whose court he served at Innsbruck, Vienna, and other residences from 1497 on. We also meet his name at the court of Saxony in addition to that of A. v. Fulda (1497–1500). Isaac's influence on the younger, native German composers extended long beyond his return to Florence in 1514–15. His mastery of 'Netherlandish' counterpoint was probably acquired as a youth in his native country, and his subsequent authority in a variety of national techniques and song repertoires (notably Italian and German) anticipates the universality of Lassus. Well over twenty German songs can safely be attributed to Isaac: twelve courtly, nine of the 'burgher' (middle-class) variety, three sacred. Two have become famous, *Mein Freud allein* and *Innsbruck, ich muss dich lassen* ('My only joy' and 'Innsbruck, I must leave thee'). The second version of the latter song points to the future: the melody is in the discant (treble) rather than the tenor, and the texture of the composition is completely homophonic. Isaac's Masses, some of which were first printed by Petrucci

---

4. See index for references to other chapters.

in Venice in 1506, were also printed, and reprinted, in Germany after his death in 1517, in Nürnberg in 1539 by Formschneider (also by Petreius) and in Wittenberg in 1541 by Rhaw. Isaac's Mass of Songs, *Missa carminum*, includes the *cantus firmi* of German tenor songs[5] and shows the influence of Josquin in the manner in which the melodies of the songs pervade the entire texture, with the technique of imitation affecting all the parts.

Isaac's sacred music was by no means restricted to the Ordinary of the Mass; he was, in fact, the first known composer to devote an entire cycle to the Proper of the Mass. The work was commissioned by the Cathedral of Constance, composed in 1507–9 and published posthumously in three volumes by Formschneider at Nürnberg in 1550–5. The publication was supplemented by a few compositions by Isaac's pupil Ludwig Senfl, under the title *Choralis Constantinus*, in memory of the original commission. Most of the pieces in the cycle are scored for four voices, some based on the local liturgy, i.e. of Constance, some on foreign models. In addition to this imposing cycle of motets, individual motets were circulated in Germany through earlier publications. The effect created by this entire *corpus* of Masses and motets was overwhelming, as illustrated by the treatise *Dodeka-chordon* (1547), in which its author, the Swiss humanist Glareanus, inserts five musical illustrations from Isaac. The repertoire of vernacular German song plainly represented a more humble stratum of music; but here too Isaac's influence was decisive, as shown by the later collections of Forster (1539) and Ott (1544).

Although Isaac was a mature composer when he came to live in the German-speaking countries in 1497, there is no doubt that the work of *Arrigo Tedesco* became integrally related with contemporary and subsequent German history. The Fleming Alexander Agricola, contemporaneous with Isaac, is also referred to in older sources as *de Alemania*, though no documents proving his German origin have been discovered, and there are no *cantus firmi* related to German tenor songs in his Masses or secular songs.[6]

For a native German composer of stature and of consequence for subsequent developments in his country, we must look to Adam von Fulda (b. *c*. 1445 at Fulda, d. 1505 at Wittenberg). From 1490 on he was at the Saxonian Electoral Court of Frederick the Wise at Torgau, and after 1502 he also taught music at the University of Wittenberg. His treatise, *De musica*,[7] written in a Benedictine monastery near Passau, is an important link between the traditional approach of the fifteenth century, the new attitudes of early German Protestantism, and the musical humanism

5. The German tradition of having the melody of a *Lied* (song) in the tenor as *cantus firmus*, surrounded by subsidiary voices, has given rise to the term *tenorlied* (tenor song); this represents the most prominent German tradition from *c*. 1450–1570.

6. For further details see chapter 4.3, p. 201.

7. Reprinted in Gerbert's *Scriptores*, iii.

associated with Luther and some of his contemporaries. Among Fulda's extant works are a Mass in four parts, seven hymns, a few motets and a few German secular songs. Among the latter is *Ach hülff mich layd* ('O, help me in my sorrow'), praised by Glareanus as 'most elegantly composed and most frequently sung over all Germany'. Another indication of the popularity of this composer's songs is that they are included, though anonymously, in an important early collection, the *Liederbuch* of Arndt von Aich, printed *c.* 1520. This anthology of seventy-five anonymous pieces, in four parts, was probably derived from and destined for the repertoire of the court chapel of Bishop Friedrich von Zollern (d. 1506). It also included compositions by the Franco-Flemish Matthaeus Pipelare, as well as Isaac, and two Germans, Hofhaimer and Lapicida.

HOFHAIMER AND FINCK. Paulus Hofhaimer was born in Radstadt(Austria) in 1459 and died in Salzburg in 1537.[8] He came from a family of organists and was possibly a pupil of Lapicida.[9] From 1480 on he was the main pillar of the Imperial Court Chapel at Innsbruck (which later attracted Isaac); he accompanied the chapel on many trips (Frankfurt a.M. 1486, Antwerp 1494). As a famous organist he seems to have been much in demand: at the Saxonian Electoral Court, which also acted as patron to Isaac and Adam v. Fulda; at Passau (1502–6, 1519–21); in the service of the Prince Bishop; perhaps at the Wittelsbach Court in Munich; certainly at Augsburg and after 1524 or earlier at Salzburg Cathedral. Because of his virtuosity he was knighted in 1515. His likeness survives in the works of some of the finest German draughtsmen of the period, including Dürer and Burgkmair, and he was a valued friend of such leading humanists as Celtes, Luscinius, Paracelsus, Pirckheimer and Vachian. So few are the primary sources that we are largely forced to assess Hofhaimer's achievement indirectly, as in anthologies for organ or lute compiled by other musicians. Perhaps his main claim to fame rests on his intelligent and idiomatic improvisation, as illustrated by the ornamentation to be found in keyboard transcriptions of vocal models. He transmitted this art to his pupils and followers, and its practice may be observed in such manuscript anthologies of organ music as those by Hans Buchner (b. 1483 Ravensburg, d. 1538 Constance), Hans Kotter (b. *c.* 1485 Strasburg, d. 1541 Berne), Conrad Brumann (a Hofhaimer pupil, d. 1526 Speyer) and Wolfgang Grefinger (another pupil, b. *c.* 1480 Krems; at the early age of 25 organist at St Stephen's Cathedral, Vienna).

8. In contemporary documents his name is often spelled Hoffhaymer and following his knighthood he became Ritter von Hoffhaymer. Allowance must be made for sixteenth-century German varieties of spelling and for the substitution on the English 'of' for the German 'von' (abbreviated as v.): viz. Adam v. Fulda.

9. In the wake of humanism the latinization of names was frequent: Lapicida for *Steinschneider* (stone-cutter), Melanchthon for *Schwarzerd* (black-earth), Agricola for *Landmann* (peasant) etc.

Hofhaimer's German secular songs are mostly based on courtly texts, partly written by himself. They are remarkable for their lucid, formal disposition and the flexible manner in which the subsidiary parts accompany the main part. These pieces were popular in Germany and abroad: some of them appear in Jan de Lublin's organ anthology (Cracow 1537–48). His settings of Horace's odes, which appeared under the title *Harmoniae poeticae*, were published posthumously at Nürnberg in 1539 (with the assistance of Senfl, who had also aided in posthumous publications of some of Isaac's works). It is a major loss and a curious quirk of fate that no original organ compositions of this famous player and composer are extant.

The dates and details of the life of Erasmus Lapicida are controversial. If we assume the composer to have been a mature man when some of his works were printed by Petrucci in 1503–8, he must have been of considerable age by the time he was published by such German houses as Rhaw in 1538 and Forster in 1539. He died some time after 1545. He is referred to several times in the records of the Heidelberg Court *Kantorei*.[10] It is not surprising, therefore, that Andreas Ornithoparcus, who taught music at Heidelberg and in nearby Mainz praises Lapicida in his *Micrologus* (Leipzig, 1517; translated by John Dowland, London, 1609) as a master '*quorum probata est autoritas*'. Some of his songs were famous, such as *Tandernack*, which was transcribed into lute tablature by Hans Newsidler. In so far as one can assess his song style from the few extant sources, his polyphonic texture was characterized by a nervous criss-cross of voices.

Heinrich Finck (born at Bamberg in *c*. 1445, died at Vienna in 1527) wrote compositions encompassing a great variety of styles. He was very much the universal talent among the native Germans of his generation. The details of his career are well-known from the treatise of his great-nephew Hermann Finck, whose *Musica practica* (first edition, Wittenberg 1536) was often reprinted. When young, Heinrich Finck served as singer in the Cracow chapel, then he studied at the University of Leipzig. His subsequent employments were at the Stuttgart chapel, with Emperor Maximilian, at Salzburg Cathedral, and at a Viennese monastery (Schottenkloster) where he was *regens chori* when he died. His sacred music includes four Masses (in three, four and six parts) and a *Magnificat* in four parts. The style of these polyphonic compositions is somewhat speculative and bears out the verdict of the *Musica practica* that it is 'learned and difficult'. But we encounter a different aspect of Finck's artistic personality when we examine his thirty secular German songs, which were published posthumously at Nürnberg in 1536. Here is a new conception of three-part counterpoint, free and flexible, and far removed from the traditional, stiff *cantus firmus*

---

10. The person in charge of church music is called *Kantor*, and the entire personnel the *Kantorei*. Two centuries later J. S. Bach was *Kantor* (or cantor) of St Thomas, Leipzig.

technique. The web of voices is well balanced, and the moods of the poetry, probably written by the composer, are finely caught in songs of love and farewell.

LATIN ODES. One cannot conclude a discussion of this early generation of German-speaking composers, who were active about a quarter of a century before and after 1500, without mentioning the prevailing tendency towards humanistic imitation of classical antiquity. This tendency became prominent in the sixteenth century. As early as 1494–7 the humanist Conrad Celtes had his students sing Horatian odes set to music by Petrus Tritonius in a simple, chordal style, in four parts. These odes were later published under the title *Melopoiae sive harmoniae* (Augsburg 1507). The simplicity of these settings rested not only on the fact that they were syllabic and that long syllables accompanied long notes while short syllables had short notes, but principally in that all voices moved at the same time to the same rhythmic values; in other words the music was homorhythmic. A similar series of odes was published by Egenolff at Frankfurt in 1532. These German homorhythmic odes with their succession of blocked chords, held together by scansion of the words, form a curious parallel to the simultaneous late flowering of the *frottola*, south of the Alps, which in turn was to influence the *villanesca* which succeeded it.[11] Hofhaimer's pupil Grefinger was responsible for such a collection of odes in 1513, and it is likely that Hofhaimer himself contributed to this genre that was so popular with the humanists. In 1551–2 P. Nigidius of Marburg compiled an extensive anthology which summarized work that had been going on for a quarter of a century, but also included younger composers such as Senfl. Until 1545 or so this type of composition retained the freshness of novelty, though similarly learned collections of odes continued to be published until the early seventeenth century, frequently by schoolmen to offer diversion during the performance of plays at schools. After the middle of the century we encounter several ingenious transformations, such as Lassus' *Sydus ex claro*, but these seem to occur more frequently abroad, notably in the *musique mesurée* of Baïf's academy and, a bit earlier, in the Psalter of Claude Goudimel. Finally, the style of these odes was important in the formation of early Lutheran music.

THE REFORMATION: LUTHER AND WALTER

Martin Luther's writings, pleading reform of ecclesiastical organization and forms of worship, did not fail to grapple with problems of music. The first of these pamphlets appeared about 1520, and as early as 1523 Luther

---

11. For a discussion of *frottola* and *villanesca* see chapter 5, pp. 234–41; for a discussion of the homorhythmic character of *musique mesurée*, about half a century later, see chapter 4.2, pp. 179–81.

wrote two famous hymns, *Ein neues Lied wir heben an* ('Let us sing a new song') and *Nun freut euch, liebe Christen gmein* ('Dear Christian people, all rejoice'). In both of these he made use of the formal and prosodic traditions of the *Meistersinger*. *Ein feste Burg ist unser Gott* ('A mighty fortress is our God'), derived from the 46th psalm, was first printed in the *Gesangbuch* of Klug in 1533. Luther was the author of both text and music of these chorales (Protestant hymns) but it must be remembered that in the sixteenth century authorship was far removed from modern ideas of originality, let alone copyright. Some texts were translations, some adaptations, some new creations. The melodies were often old, fitted to new texts, i.e. *contrafacta*; when they were new they tended to employ existing formulae.[12] Modern scholarship attributes some thirty-six songs to Luther, including the three mentioned above. The majority of these were written by 1524, in which year they were published in a *Cantional* (hymn book) entitled *Geistliches Gesang Büchlein* (*Sacred little song book*). Luther wrote the preface to this *Cantional*. The polyphonic settings, for from three to five voices, were provided by Johann Walter. The first edition of 1524 contained 43 settings, of which 38 were German and 5 Latin; by 1551 the number of Walter's settings had increased to 125, 78 German and 47 Latin. Since it is clear that Walter's *Cantional* of 1524 and its subsequent editions were planned and approved by Luther, two aspects of these books are significant. In the first place they are polyphonic. While other reformers like Zwingli at Zurich and Calvin at Geneva permitted only monophonic music in the service, the older German *Cantionale* expressly perpetuate the Netherlandish heritage. Walter's polyphonic technique is reminiscent of Adam v. Fulda: the *cantus firmus* appears complete, usually in the tenor, surrounded by a texture of secondary parts. This style of choral settings of early Protestant hymns is easy to understand when one considers Luther's high regard for Josquin and Senfl. His preface to Walter's *Cantional* of 1524 defends the existence of music against the young Anabaptists who had argued against all artistic exercise within the service. The contrast between Luther and Thomas Müntzer, a radical in regard to political and ecclesiastical organization, is instructive. Müntzer, in his *Deutsch Evangelisch Messe* of 1524 (German Protestant Mass), maintained the Gregorian intonation and formulae, in spite of translating and adopting the text to the German vernacular. But Luther, in *Wider die himmlischen Propheten* (*Against heavenly prophets*, 1525), demanded that 'text and notes, accent, time and melodic direction (*Weise und Gebärde*) should derive straight from the mother tongue'. Both Luther's chorales and his *Deutsche Messe* (German Mass), first sung at Wittenberg on 29 October 1526, pay eloquent testimony to this creed. Luther made considerable alterations in the musical structure of the Latin mass, notably in the 'tones'

12. See the discussion of *cento* technique in chapter 2, p. 66.

for the lessons, where he chose the eighth mode for epistles and the sixth mode for the gospels.

Johann Walter (born at Kahla in 1496, died at Torgau in 1570) was one of the great cantors of early Protestantism. He began his professional career at the court chapel of Frederick the Wise, the Elector of Saxony. The chapel performed alternately at Torgau, Weimar and Altenburg. (Other composers connected with it had been Adam v. Fulda, Isaac, Hofhaimer and Rupsch, under whom Walter worked.) In 1526 Walter took over the *Schulkantorei* (educational and musical institution) of Torgau which emphasized the two traditions with which he always kept in touch: an urban, middle-class scholarliness (which for centuries remained attached to the teaching of Latin) and the community of a religious brotherhood. Among his major tasks was the composition of a seven-part motet for the inauguration of the renovated chapel attached to Castle Hartenfels near Torgau. In order to pay homage to Luther and the Elector, Walter chose a conservative technique, employing *ostinato* voices. The number of Walter's compositions is considerable; in addition to the six editions of the *Cantional* the following survive in print: a collection of sacred songs for 'mountain men', i.e. miners, *Newe Berckreyen* (1552), a cycle of *Magnificats* (1557) and a few individual songs. Two Passions, twenty-six canons for *Zinken* (cornetts, written for his school in 1542) and various pieces for his Torgau *Kantorei* (where he favoured Josquin and Senfl as well as his own works) remain in manuscript.

RHAW AND SENFL

A representative cross-section of the works of Protestant German composers, *Newe deutsche geistliche gesenge* (*New German sacred songs*) was published in 1544 at Wittenberg by Georg Rhaw (or Rhau, born at Eisfeld in 1488, died at Wittenberg in 1548). Rhaw's activities as printer, publisher and composer proved of considerable importance for the new religious movement. In 1519 he celebrated the famous disputation at Leipzig between Luther and Dr Eck with a *Missa de Sancto Spirito*, in twelve parts, a composition he undertook as part of his duties as cantor at St Thomas'. From *c.* 1523 on Rhaw lived in Wittenberg; his Protestantism had obliged him to leave Leipzig, and in his new abode he was near Luther. His printing shop, founded in 1525, became quickly famous.

Rhaw's combination of musicianship and scholarship is reflected in his publications, many of which have a pedagogic bent. This is true of the anthology of sacred songs just mentioned, which was intended for 'ordinary schools'. It consists of 123 *chorale* motets, i.e. motets based on *chorales*, usually in four parts. The circle from which these works were drawn was that of the leading German composers of the Josquin–Isaac tradition, and with the exception of the somewhat younger Georg Forster (*c.* 1510–87) they belong to the generation born between 1480 and 1500. Some joined the new Protestant movement, others remained Catholics, and in regional terms one encounters a mixture of Saxonian, Austrian, Swiss and other traditions. Nor, indeed, was the collection restricted to Germans. Among the Netherlanders are Stephan Mahu, Lupus Hellinck and Arnold von Bruck (probably of Bruges and not the Austrian town of Bruck). The German composers represented are Martin Agricola (1486–1556), Sixt Dietrich (1490/95–1548), Ulrich Brätel (*c.* 1495–1545), Benedict Ducis (*c.* 1485–1544), Georg Forster, Rhaw himself, Balthasar Resinarius (*c.* 1486–1544), Thomas Stoltzer (1480/85–1526) and Ludwig Senfl (b. Zurich 1490, d. Munich 1543). Clearly Senfl was the leading composer of this group. Other members of some importance included two significant architects of Lutheran church music, Agricola and Dietrich, with whom Rhaw kept in touch (in addition to Luther and Walter). Agricola was cantor in Magdeburg and the author of many treatises, notably the *Kurtz Deutsche Musica* (*Short German Music*, also published by Rhaw in 1528). Both in these and in the motets in the 1544 anthology he aims at simplicity and a native strain. Dietrich grew up as a choir-boy at Constance, where he spent much of his life, but between 1540 and 1548 he paid many visits to Wittenberg, where he was close to Luther's circle. Much of his work appeared in print during his lifetime, a volume of antiphons in 1541 and three volumes of hymns in 1545, both published by Rhaw. Motets and German songs are to be found in anthologies that were published even after his death. His treatment of the main melody is in the German tradition, but his rhythmic structure is highly individual and has been characterized as 'unbalanced and nervous' (Zenck). His use of the *cantus firmus* in the subsidiary parts is notable and so is his avoidance of the more stereotyped motet formulae.

But without doubt Senfl was the star of the circle. He entered the service of Emperor Maximilian in 1496, one year before Isaac whose pupil he became, and he succeeded the older composer in his position at the court chapel, either at Isaac's death in 1517 or even earlier on the occasion of the latter's retirement to Florence. When Emperor Maximilian I died (1519) and his court chapel was dissolved, Senfl eventually moved to Munich where he became *musicus intonator* to Duke William IV in 1523. He remained at the Catholic Wittelsbach court until his death, in spite of several Protestant contacts (notably with Luther in 1530) and thereby became Lassus' most important predecessor in the Catholic south.

Senfl's texture is a dense one, the polyphonic voices are arranged in close layers, in the manner of a German variant of the Netherlandish style, particularly when one considers it as a spiritual neighbour of the orthodox *cantus firmus* treatment of Dietrich. Senfl's work includes seven masses, 240 motets and over 250 German songs. In this last category the composer offers a magnificent summary of all branches of tradition (courtly and folk tunes, aristocratic and middle-class overtones, accents of conviviality and of humanist learning, as well as songs of social criticism). He enlarged the scope of the tenor-song by quick imitative textures and broad memorable statements at beginning and end. This is one of the instances where the homorhythmic style of the humanistic ode settings, mentioned earlier, affected succeeding generations. In his motets Senfl sometimes enlarges the texture from the customary four parts to eight, and occasionally there are even intimations of polychoral writing (*Sancta virgo*). In his part-writing he avoids the rather general melodic style and long curves of Dietrich and other conservative masters and favours motives with a sharp profile, usually quite concise and approaching the style of song. His attention to the cadences and declamation of the words is striking. Often he alternates pairs of voices in a technique reminiscent of Josquin, and the music reflects not only the prosody but also the pictorial suggestions of the verbal text. Angularity is usually smoothed away by a fluctuating harmonic technique which points to the madrigalian procedures of the second half of the century.

Senfl's settings of German songs were probably his most popular compositions, as evidenced by their continuous presence in the printed *Liederbuch* anthologies: E. Öglin, Augsburg, 1512; P. Schöffer, Mainz, 1513–18; J. Ott, Nürnberg, 1534 and 1544; P. Schöffer and M. Apiarius, Strasburg, 1536; H. Finck, Nürnberg, 1536; H. Formschneider, Nürnberg, 1538; G. Forster, 5 vols., Nürnberg, 1539–56; S. Salbinger, Augsburg, 1540; also in the collection *Gassenhawer und Reutterliedlein* (*Songs of the Street and of Horsemen*, Frankfurt a. M., 1535). It is clear that German performance practices favoured Senfl; it is also clear from pictorial sources of the period that instruments often doubled the vocal polyphony (which was still based on the treatment of the song melody as *cantus firmus*). This practice, with its colourful sonorities, was maintained particularly in southern Germany and still receives splendid testimony in Lassus' circle, about 1570–90.

Senfl headed an older German generation, soon to be succeeded by the 'mannerists', the artists of the second half of the century. The treatises of that period reveal that the most important of these works is the *Dodekachordon* (Basle, 1547) of the Swiss scholar Glareanus (1488–1563), who endeavoured to approximate musical theory more closely to actual harmonic practice by extending the system of eight church modes to twelve. He frequently referred to Senfl in his examples. Moreover, Sebald Heyden, the author of a representative teaching aid, several times reprinted, *Musica, id est: Artis canendi* ... (*Music, that is, the art of song*, Nürnberg, 1537), celebrates Senfl as 'the prince of music in all Germany'. Even at the end of the century L. Zacconi, who joined the Munich court chapel under the aged Lassus in 1591, praises Senfl in his *Prattica di musica* (two parts, Venice, 1592–1622) though in the book the practice of ornamentation and other tenets of music teaching are closer to Florentine monody than to Isaac and Senfl.

DUCIS, STOLTZER AND HARTZER

Benedict Ducis was active as a Protestant clergyman in Geislingen and Ulm, and represents the Württemberg region. He composed cycles of the Proper of the Mass, that is to say, antiphons and hymns for the church year, clearly reflecting German, even local liturgical traditions. His methods of construction are less delicate than those of Josquin and his pupils, since he built with larger and rougher blocks, as it were. On the other hand, his texture, sparse and song-like, is not unlike that of Isaac.

Thomas Stoltzer, who was active at the courts of Hungary and Silesia, tended to employ a *cantus firmus* which wanders from voice to voice with carefully controlled artistry. Some 150 pieces are extant, mostly sacred, though not liturgical, and in motet style. But he is also the author of Masses and of a cycle of Introits, covering festal days from Christmas to Easter. Another of his cycles, *Octo tonorum melodiae* for five parts, consists of instrumental pieces arranged according to the eight church modes. Finally, his settings of the psalms, with German texts (1524–6), commissioned by Queen Mary of Hungary, with their free interpretation of the 'affections', must also be considered an anticipation of the practices of Lassus.

Resinarius is a latinized form of Hartzer (or Harzer), and both forms appear in Rhaw's publications. This composer received his musical education as a choirboy in the court chapel of the Emperor Maximilian I and also received instruction from Isaac. He functioned first as Catholic parish priest, later as a Lutheran pastor. Thirty chorale motets appeared in Rhaw's anthology of 1544, and eighty responsories as well as a Passion were also published by Rhaw a year earlier. Resinarius is termed 'one of the great men of the times' in the *Encomium musicae*, a treatise of 1551 by J. Holtheuser. Indeed his music is representative of solid artistry, inspired by the theological circle of Wittenberg, characterized by an easily understood, syllabic diction and a clinging to the authoritative, pre-existing *cantus firmus*. On the other hand various archaisms and a more conventional harmony emphasize the distance between Resinarius and Senfl. Altogether this type of vocal music, prevalent in the second quarter of the century, whether written by composers of the first or the second rank, had a strong influence on the Catholic south (including Lassus). Moreover it transmitted new impulses to the music of the young Protestant movement.

INSTRUMENTAL MUSIC

The first half of the sixteenth century saw a great blossoming of domestic music in Germany, coming in the wake of sociological changes. This development led to an urban musical culture in which craftsmen and patricians, that is to say, the guilds and the middle classes, became decisive participants. As a concomitant the manufacture of musical instruments became important. Nürnberg had supplied trumpets and trombones to Italy as early as the fifteenth century; now these craftsmen were joined by lute and violin builders. Thus there developed an extensive repertoire in tablature notation, i.e. a mode of notation indicating the position of the fingers on the instrument.

German tablatures used a system employing a mixture of numerals and letters, differing from the method used in France (letters only) and Italy (numerals only). This tablature notation lacked the traditional prestige of ordinary notation, but it was practical for domestic performance. The first printed German lute tablature was Sebastian Virdung's *Musica getutscht* (*Music Germanized*, Basle, 1511) and from then on the number of printed and manuscript tablatures grew rapidly. Virdung, a native of the upper Palatinate, was at one time praeceptor of the choirboys in Constance Cathedral. He was thus able to draw on his experience of vocal polyphony, since one of the main functions of these tablatures was to make available for intimate and domestic performance Latin motets and excerpts from the Ordinary of the Mass, Italian madrigals and, particularly after 1540, French *chansons*. Tablatures often provided a theoretical appendix with instruction how to transfer a polyphonic web to an instrumental arrangement. As a result a tradition of pseudo-vocal polyphony grew up with a distinctive German style, craftsman-like and somewhat crude. Among the tablatures published in southern Germany, Switzerland and Austria are those of Arnold Schlick (Mainz 1512; Schlick was also famous as an organist), Hans Judenkünig (Vienna *c.* 1515–19, and another instruction book in 1523), Hans Gerle (Nürnberg 1532, several editions; other publications 1533 and 1552), Othmar Luscinius (Strasburg 1536), Hans Newsidler (Nürnberg 1536; other publications until 1544) and his son Melchior Newsidler (Venice 1566; another collection Strasburg, 1574). Gerle and Newsidler are of particular importance, because their anthologies reflect the international as well as the Germanic repertoire. A somewhat later group of publications of lute music, printed between 1556 and 1592, centred on East Prussia. Many were published in Frankfurt a.d.Oder, whose university stimulated cultural activities. Among them were the collections of B. Drusina (1556), Gregor Krengel (1584) and M. Waissel (1573–92). In the course of the century the repertoires, whether originating in the south or the north, increased in variety, and by the time we approach the year 1600, dances of various nationalities (including Polish dances) appear in the anthologies. One also encounters *ricercari*, fantasias, and toccatas, as well as those dances which later constitute the standard Baroque suite (allemande, courante, sarabande, gigue), not as yet set forth as 'partitas' or 'suites' or 'ordres'. These tablatures were arranged for lutes or other plucked instruments such as guitars or mandoras, later theorbos and chitarrones. The bulk of the

literature (including manuscripts) was considerable. In addition to popular-
izing the motet, Mass and madrigal for a domestic public, it also paved the
way for the rise of a German keyboard style.

Music for keyboard instruments, too, developed quickly. Several
tablatures, some printed, some in manuscript, are extant for the earlier
part of the century, notably those of Hans Buchner, Fridolin Sicher, Conrad
von Speyer and Leonhard Kleber. The German characteristics of this
repertoire reside in the method of 'coloration', that is, ornamentation: the
main notes of the melody are dissolved into rapid figuration of a fantastic
and somewhat unpredictable nature. In the latter half of the century the
texture tends to be more elegant as well as more polyphonic. The influences
of Italian madrigalism (Vecchi, Striggio) and of the later Netherlandish
motet (Lassus) now begin to dominate, whereas dances of the local German
type are less prevalent. The most important printed tablature[13] is that of
Elias Nicolaus Amerbach (*c.* 1530–97), who became organist at St Thomas
in Leipzig in 1561.

NETHERLANDERS IN GERMANY

Altogether, musicians of the Low Countries tended more and more to
provide models of musical technique from 1560 onward. This activity
started in the south but drifted up to and penetrated the north and north-
west of Germany. (After 1580 or so the influence of the Netherlanders was
reinforced by that of Italian composers. Many of these artists became
naturalized.) Important Netherlanders in the service of German-speaking
patrons made contributions to the repertoire of German polyphonic song,
some assimilating the native tone with surprising success. (This situation
applied as much to the southern courts, such as Vienna and Munich, as to
Dresden and Königsberg.) These Netherlanders had many opportunities of
showing their mastery in all genres of music. The court chapels with which
they were associated travelled to give performances on national occasions
such as coronations at Frankfurt or imperial diets at Regensburg. There
were also wedding festivities of dynastic and political importance, which
often prompted the utmost splendour in pageantry as well as music. (Of the
sumptuous wedding between Prince William of Wittelsbach and Renata of
Lorraine, in 1568, we have a most precise and detailed account, including
music.) This group of Netherlandish composers of the late sixteenth century
exhibit their 'mannerism' in the very mixture of their international style
with specific German elements. Without a doubt their leading exponent was

---

13. Published in 1571, with several subsequent editions; other printed tablatures were those of the
Bernhard Schmids, father (1576) and son (1607), Jacob Paix (1583), Johannes Woltz (1617). The most
important manuscript organ tablatures are those of August Nörmiger and Christoph Löffelholtz (both
now housed in Berlin).

Roland de Lassus (or Orlando di Lasso, born at Mons 1532, died at Munich 1594, see p. 207). In spite of the universality of the divine Lassus, the French-Walloon aspects of his Netherlandish heritage, as well as his deliberate assimilation of German elements, are clearly evident. This is not surprising, considering that he was a member of the Bavarian court chapel of the Wittelsbachs from 1556 to his death.

The splendour of Lassus has tended to overshadow his immediate predecessors, those who were active about 1540 to 1565, particularly since no widespread school of successors perpetuated their style. Numerous minor masters set Latin motets and German psalms to music, among them Reusch, Burgstaller and Rabe. There was in the south and south-east a group of composers in touch with Protestantism; among others Stoltzer and Arnold von Bruck,[14] Leonhard Paminger and Matthias Greiter, in addition to a sizeable group of minor humanistic musicians. The Austrian composer Paminger (1495–1567) is the author of an imposing collection of motets in four volumes, published posthumously (1573–80). The Bavarian Greiter (c. 1500–c. 1552) is notable for his German songs, secular and sacred. These were of consequence for a minor group of composers who were associated in one way or another with Heidelberg, among them Georg Forster, a major editor of German song anthologies, and himself a contributor to them. This interim generation is best represented at the Catholic court of Munich by Lassus' predecessor Ludwig Daser (1525–89), who became chapel-master in 1552 but retired in 1559 to make way for his illustrious successor. Later, in 1572, Daser assumed the direction of the Stuttgart chapel. A perusal of the part books of Stuttgart and Munich yields a picture that is fairly typical of the range of works performed by a court chapel. Daser was but one member of a generation who contributed Masses, motets, passions, hymns, litanies and lamentations, as well as motets for secular and political occasions. Works for political events especially were splendidly printed and tended to influence other courts in southern Germany and Austria.

Curiously enough, the compositions of the Netherlanders working in Germany are less closely related stylistically to Lassus' works than those of the native Germans. Mattheus Le Maistre, chapel master at Dresden, who died in 1577, was one of the many Flemish immigrants whose compositions betray his Italian schooling. The *Geistliche und weltliche Geseng* (*Sacred and Secular Songs*, Wittenberg, 1566) for four and five voices hover between the older diction of a Sixt Dietrich and a more modern homophonic manner that was influenced by the *villanella*. Le Maistre's successor at Dresden, the Italian Antonio Scandello (1517–80), already veers towards the new Venetian style. Ivo de Vento, born near Antwerp, probably moved to Munich as a choirboy about 1556, and died there in 1575. Among his printed works are

14. See above, p. 354.

some seventy motets, but his main importance resides in the large number of German songs (over a hundred), in which he draws on the illustrative and suggestive techniques of madrigal and *villanella*. But he did not abandon the polyphonic and, at times, conservative virtues of the older German tradition.

Among the many Netherlandish composers employed in the service of the various Habsburg courts, the most important[15] were Philipp de Monte (1521–1603) and Jacob Regnart (*c*. 1540–99). Monte succeeded Vaet, another Netherlander, as chapel master to the Habsburgs in Vienna and Prague. The prominence of the Italian tradition at these courts in the decades to come is in no small measure due to Monte, since he was one of the most famous, as well as the most prolific, masters of the Italian madrigal, including the *madrigale spirituale*. But whereas Monte influenced the Catholic south in Germany he himself did not participate in the tradition of German music, secular or sacred. On the other hand in the works of Regnart one notices an unmistakeable invasion of Italian homophony with its clear-cut melodic phrases, into the Netherlandish tradition. Regnart trained as a choirboy under Vaet in Vienna. In addition to a St Matthew Passion, 30 masses and 150 motets, he composed a German collection for three voices, *Kurtzweilige Teutsche Lieder nach Art der Neapolitanen oder Welschen Villanellen* (*Amusing German Songs after the manner of Neapolitan Ditties or Italian Villanellas*; 1st edition 1576–9, 2nd edition 1583, several times reprinted). The effect of this publication was widespread, and influenced even an artist of Lassus' stature. It may be said to have started the gradual abandonment of polyphony at the end of the century. The work of Regnart, himself a Franco-Flemish composer, clearly rang the death-knell of the so-called Netherlandish style.

ROLAND DE LASSUS

Lassus owed a great deal to Italian influences. (The Italian form of his name was, in fact, the more widely used, indeed, by the composer himself. On the other hand, English works of reference customarily speak of 'Lassus'.) In his youth Lassus travelled over much of Europe in the train of Ferdinand Gonzaga, a military commander and Viceroy of Sicily. At the age of twenty-one he worked for more than a year at S. Giovanni di Laterano at Rome and before that he had had the opportunity of absorbing the elements of the Neapolitan tradition. It is to this latter source that we probably owe a curiously chromatic work, the *Prophetiae Sibyllarum*, based on a local legend that the caves of Cumae, near Naples, were the seat of the Sibyls. After a short stay at Antwerp Lassus settled at Munich in the autumn of 1556, at the age of twenty-four, and remained at the Wittelsbach court for the rest of his

---

15. Others were Johann de Cleve, Alexander Utendal and Lambert de Sayve.

life, refusing many flattering invitations to other centres, including one to the Protestant court of Dresden to succeed Scandello in 1580. Lassus joined the Munich Chapel as tenor, became its director (*Kapellmeister*) in 1562, and was knighted in 1570. His central contribution is to the Latin motet, distinguished both in quality and in sheer bulk: more than eight hundred pieces are extant, and perhaps half of these were written before 1568.[16] The first cycles of motets published in Germany (1562, 1566) complement the earlier works in that the music follows the text expressively, in a highly individual manner. Themes and motives were chosen with this end in view, and the traditional *cantus firmi* are therefore seldom used. The eloquent, vivid, and at times even vehement musical language is to be found particularly in works employing *ostinato* technique which extended from short motives to broad melodies. In such instances Lassus tended to endow the part that carried the *ostinato* with an emphatic quality which underlines the syllables of the text in almost pedagogic fashion; the entire structure – ostinato and surrounding parts – receives a new depth compared with earlier works. The famous *Penitential Psalms* were the first of many commissions from the Duke of Bavaria (before 1560, though not printed until a quarter of a century later, in 1584). In addition to the published editions, these are transmitted in a magnificent manuscript codex of four volumes, with pictorial illustrations by Hans Muelich and a commentary by the humanist Samuel Quickelberg. This commentary, dating from about 1559, alludes to the concept of *musica reservata* and to Lassus' contribution to it in depicting the affections of the text. The term *musica reservata*, originating in the 1550s, is difficult to define. The consensus of modern scholarship is that this music was 'reserved' for connoisseurs and initiates. It contains unusual modulations in the mannerist style, artfully chiselled counter-voices in the polyphonic texture, a hidden (or, at least, not overt) pictorialism and a high degree of chromaticism. (This last aspect is not to be found in Lassus' *Penitential Psalms*.) Interestingly enough, *Musica reservata* is the title of a collection of motets (Nürnberg, 1552) composed by another Netherlander resident in Germany, Adrian Petit Coclico (1500–63), active at Wittenberg, Frankfurt a.d.Oder, Nürnberg and Copenhagen, and at one time a member of the chapel of Duke Albrecht of East Prussia. Moreover the notions of *musica reservata*, particularly the relationship between the affections of the text and their expression in music, are discussed in Coclico's treatise, *Compendium musices* (also Nürnberg, 1552). In middle age, Lassus, who by this time was master of the French *chanson* and the Italian madrigal, decided to acquire German techniques. He had taken a German wife in 1558, and his extant correspondence with the Bavarian court, polyglot though it was, shows a persistent effort to master the language of his adopted country.

16. Concerning Lassus' sojourn in Antwerp 1555–6 and the motets published at that time see chapter 4.3, p. 207.

Lassus' first volume of German songs appeared in 1567 and consisted mostly of secular pieces in which the traditional *cantus firmus* technique is not so much abandoned as modified by fragmentation and an elegant imitation in the surrounding voices. In the period 1568–73 Lassus stood at the zenith of his fame. His motets extended from small textures to splendid and voluminous sonorities. Stylistically the music tended at times towards the lively characteristics of French *chansons* and German *Lieder*, at other times towards melancholy and pathos. But after 1575 Lassus favoured more and more a reduction of his musical means and greater concentration of expression. In the genre of the *chanson* this may be gleaned from the fact that he set to music, about 1581, the moralizing *Quatrains* of Pybrac in a simple, homophonic style for four voices, influenced, no doubt, by the vogue of *vers mesurés*. The later madrigals, too, avoid courtly love lyrics and deal with the transitoriness of life. About 1575 Lassus paid tribute to the European fashion of the *villanella* and *canzonetta*, imitating their simplicity of texture and strophic structure. A good cross-section of the repertoire of madrigals produced at the Munich court around Lassus is offered in a printed anthology in two volumes, *Musica de' virtuosi della florida capella dell' illustrissimo … duca di Baviera* (Venice, 1569, 1575). It contains compositions of most of Lassus' pupils and collaborators in the court chapel (including a fledgling effort in the second volume by the younger Gabrieli). It is clear that, under the guidance of one of Europe's leading composers, varying talents in various stages of development were given training. As to the sacred works of Lassus' final years, their bulk is considerable and includes many Masses and *Magnificats*, frequently based on the parody technique. Sometimes the models, whether they be motets, *chansons* or madrigals, are Lassus' own, sometimes those of other composers. The transfer from one text to another produces subtle and complex changes of prosody and declamation. Other late works include a *hymnarium*, i.e. a cycle of hymns, and four Passions.[17] Lassus increasingly favoured the preservation of strict liturgical practices, as shown in the three Passions (1575–82) which succeed the St Matthew Passion and the Lessons from the Book of Job (1582), particularly when the latter is compared with the early Lessons from the Antwerp days. The last volume of motets was scored for six voices (*Cantiones Sacrae*, Graz, 1594); it combines anticipations of the Baroque era in the detached treatment of the top voice, with retrospective features, such as a strict, at times even stiff, formal design. In the preface Lassus bewails the excrescences of his youth and states that he aims at a more serious style, fit for the solid approval of a seasoned critic. His last Latin motet was published as an appendix to a cycle of sacred Italian madrigals, the *Lagrime di San Pietro*

17. Of the four Passions only the earlier St Matthew Passion was printed during the composer's lifetime (1575), but all four are now available in modern reprint; the cycle of hymns also remained in manuscript and still awaits a modern edition.

(published posthumously at Munich in 1595); *Vide homo* is scored for seven voices. In it Lassus, without abandoning expressivity, avoids the rich palette of colours of Giovanni Gabrieli or Monteverdi (whose compositions he knew by then). Rather he combines the techniques of motet and madrigal and revives older polyphonic practices. These tendencies, favouring a reduction of means and the preservation of tested and approved styles, is also present in his *Ulenburg Psalter* (Munich, 1588) a setting for three voices of German psalm translations by Caspar Ulenburg. This was probably Lassus' most important contribution to the music of the German Counter-Reformation.

LECHNER AND ECCARD

This late work, because of its German text, was bound to affect Lassus' circle of native pupils, including Protestants. One of the most notable of these was Leonhard Lechner (born *c.* 1553 in the South Tyrol, died 1606 at Stuttgart). Until 1570 Lechner sang under Lassus in the Munich court chapel; in the collection of his motets, about a third of the texts had also been set to music by Lassus. Towards the end of his career Lechner aimed more and more at dramatic eloquence. His *Sprüche von Leben und Tod* (*Sayings of Life and Death*, 1606), which might be termed his Swan Song, probably provides the most important bridge between Lassus and Schütz. What characterizes these settings of short vernacular rhymes is their combination of expressive means derived from the madrigal and the formal elements taken from the motet. A mere decade later Schütz was to attempt similar Italianate experiments in his psalm settings.

Johannes Eccard (born at Mühlhausen in Thuringia 1553, died at Berlin 1611) was Lassus' pupil until 1573. He worked first in southern Germany, where he was employed by the Fuggers in Augsburg (1578); later he moved to north German court chapels: Königsberg in 1580, Berlin in 1608. His excellence lies in his contribution to Protestant German song of which he published several collections, the first in 1574. Eccard's posthumous *Preussische Festlieder* (*Prussian Festive Songs*, two parts, 1642–4) already tend towards the modern homophonic manner. Nevertheless, while the publications of his successors[18] belong, both chronologically and stylistically, to a consideration of the music of the Baroque age, the polyphonic heritage of Lassus may still be perceived in the work of some German composers of the early seventeenth century, among them Melchior Franck, Michael Praetorius and Christoph Demantius. This applies both to their compositions (vocal and instrumental) and to other instrumental pieces which were soon to be organized into orchestral suites.

18. Friedrich Weissensee, *Opus melicum*, 1602; Georg Otto, *Opus musicum*, 1604; Christian Erbach, *Mele sive cantiones sacrae ad modum canzonette*, 1603.

MEILAND AND KERLE

It must also be remembered that during the second half of the sixteenth century the influence of Lassus was enhanced and complemented by other composers who, though resident in Germany, were either born or educated in the Netherlands. Jacob Meiland (1542–77), a German composer, studied in Flanders from about 1560 to 1564, and Jacobus de Kerle (1531/32–1591), a native Netherlander, occupied important positions at Augsburg among others. The three Passions of Meiland (1567–70) antedate those of his senior Lassus and are remarkable in their freedom from the conventional *cantus firmus* technique. His Latin motets and German songs, influenced both by Lassus and by Clemens non Papa, continued to be printed in German anthologies long after his death, for instance, in the *Cygneae Cantiones* (Wittenberg, 1590) and the *Musae Sioniae* (part VIII, Wolfenbüttel 1610). Kerle's international role is well known[19] and is also of particular importance for the German countries, where he worked as a cathedral organist (Augsburg 1568–75) and at the imperial court of the Habsburgs (Vienna and Prague, 1582–91). Some of his scores, among them a secular motet for the wedding of William v of Bavaria and Renata of Lorraine in 1568, have unfortunately been lost. But from the extant works, notably the Masses of his last years, we are able to perceive the qualities by which Kerle established himself. This was a composer who exercised considerable influence, secondary to Lassus but by no means negligible. Like Lassus he had spent the formative years of his career in Italy and had absorbed certain features of the Italian madrigal, such as the expressiveness of the text and the occasional use of homophonic passages for dramatic effect. But it was probably another feature of his works, also shared with the divine Orlando, that proved more fruitful for the future: by reducing his musical means to the barest minimum he contributed to the preservation of the polyphonic tradition which was to be such a distinctive feature of German compositions in the seventeenth and eighteenth centuries.

19. See chapter 4.3, p. 207.

DANIEL DEVOTO

8.1 Spain: From the Beginnings to c. 1450

INTRODUCTION

Our earliest evidence for the existence of music in the Iberian Peninsula comes from two sources: objects discovered by archaeologists which are identifiable as primitive musical instruments, and rock paintings.[1] The former include bull-roarers, bone scrapers, rattles and bone flutes[2] dating from the third millenium BC, while the most famous rock painting is that found at Cogul, near Lérida in Eastern Spain, which shows men and women dancing, belonging to the mesolithic period (8000–2000 BC). During the first millenium BC Spain came under the influence of, first, the Phoenicians, then the Greeks, the Carthaginians, and finally, the Romans. Of these the Greeks and Romans had by far the greatest cultural impact. Numerous vases found at Liria, one of the most important centres of Iberian pottery, show men and women playing musical instruments, notably the *aulos* (both the single and the double kind), the lyre and the *kithara*, the three most

---

1. On this early period see especially Salazar, *España*.
2. For descriptions of the various instruments mentioned in this paragraph see Sachs, *Instruments*.

popular instruments of the Greeks. The Romans, who began to gain control of the whole peninsula after defeating the Carthaginians during the Second Punic War (218–01 BC), were culturally dependent on the Greeks and the only new instrument which they seem to have introduced was the trumpet. Curve-shaped trumpets have been found at Numancia dating from about the second century AD and are also depicted in the famous Osuna reliefs (*c.* 50 BC). The Romans made great use of the organ, whose loud penetrating tone made it especially appropriate for circus entertainments, and although the Iberians did not begin to make their own until about the middle of the fifth century, they were almost certainly using organs long before then.

The Greeks and Romans used instruments almost solely as an accompaniment to singing and dancing, and various writers of the period, such as Silus Italicus (25 or 26–101 AD) in his *De bello punico* and Strabo (born *c.* 63 AD) in his *Geographia* mention the popularity of both these pastimes in Spain, especially among the Galicians, Basques and Asturians. Martial (AD 38–41 to 102 or 103), Pliny the Younger (AD 61–113) and Juvenal (*c.* 60–140), all speak of the *saltatrices* (dancing girls) of Cadiz, who were widely admired and imitated in their day and to whom both Musset and Leo Delibes paid tribute nearly two thousand years later.

During the first two centuries of Roman rule there were repeated tribal uprisings, but after Caesar Augustus had crushed the final resistance (*c.* 43 BC), the peninsula entered a long period of calm and order. It adopted the Latin language and became an important centre of Roman culture, producing great poets and statesmen, such as the two Senecas, Lucan, Martial and Quintilian, and even three emperors, Theodosius the Great, Hadrian and Trajan. The most important event of the period for the future history of Spain was the introduction of Christianity in the first century AD. In spite of the cruel persecution of Christians by certain Roman emperors the faith spread rapidly, and soon after its recognition by Galerius and Constantine the Great in 312, Spain provided Rome with her first pope, St Damasus (*c.* 304–84). She also produced three of the best early Christian poets: Prudentius (*c.* 348–*c.* 405), Juvencus (fl. *c.* 330), and St Pacianus of Barcelona (died between 379 and 392).

The six centuries of Roman rule were brought to an end in 409 by the arrival of the Visigoths (the Western Goths) who soon gained control of the whole peninsula. They had been influenced by the Romans themselves, and although their adherence to the Arian heresy created problems, they did not try to destroy the cultural inheritance of their subjects. The period of greatest political and cultural splendour of the Visigoth Kingdom, which lasted from 562 to 681, also witnessed the flowering of the Spanish liturgy, and may be regarded as one of the finest in the entire history of peninsular music.

MOZARABIC CHANT AND THE
'ETYMOLOGIES' OF ST ISIDORE OF SEVILLE

The music of the Spanish liturgy during the Middle Ages is known rather inappropriately as Mozarabic chant (from *musta rib*, meaning a Christian living under Arab domination. Various scholars have suggested other names, such as Visigothic, Hispanic or Isidorian chant, but none has gained wide acceptance.) In spite of the Mozarabic rite having virtually died out during the eleventh century we now know almost exactly what it was like: this is largely due to the research of several distinguished twentieth-century scholars[3] but we must not overlook the contribution of Cisneros, who tried to reconstruct the rite as early as the end of the fifteenth century. Its origins, like those of the other three great western chants, are obscure, but certain similarities make it possible that all four developed from more or less the same roots.[4]

It is usual to divide the era of the Mozarabic rite into three periods: the Hispano-Roman (from 248, the year of the martyrdom of Saints Fructuosus, Augurius and Eulogius, to 589, the year of the Third Council of Toledo); the Visigothic (from 589 to the Moorish invasion of 711) and the Mozarabic period which ended towards the end of the eleventh century with the suppression of the rite. The earliest surviving manuscripts date from the last period, but two literary works, the *Etymologiae*[5] and the *De ecclesiasticis officiis*[6] by St Isidore of Seville, are contemporaneous with the flowering of the liturgy and tell us much about the music of the time.

St Isidore (*c.* 559–636),[7] one of four children of the governor of Cartagena, all of whom have been canonized, is unquestionably the greatest among a host of scholars and saints of the period remembered for their writings. Practically nothing is known of the saint's life before he became archbishop of Seville on the death of his brother, St Leander. This took place about 600, from which we may conclude that he was born before 560, as forty was the minimum age for the episcopacy. The most important of his many works is the *Originum sive etymologiarum libri XX* usually known as the *Etymologies*, a kind of encyclopaedia or compendium containing all the knowledge of his time. It remained a standard reference book for nearly a thousand years, but towards the end of the nineteenth century an attempt was made to show that it was nothing more than an adaptation of the *Prata*, a lost encyclopaedic work by Suetonius, also drawn upon by St Augustine and Cassiodorus.[8] As

3. See in particular Prado, *Manuel, Rito*; Rojo, *Canto*; Wagner, 'Mozarabische'.
4. See Reese, *Middle Ages*, p. 113.
5. Printed Migne, *Patrologiae*, lxxxii; Lindsay, *Originum*.
6. Printed Migne, *Patrologiae*, lxxxiii, 743 ff.
7. See Fontaine, *Isidore*.
8. See Schmidt, *Quaestiones*.

far as the chapters about music are concerned this certainly does not seem to be the case, and although St Isidore obviously knew both the *Institutiones* of Cassiodorus and the *De musica* and the *Confessiones* of St Augustine, he does not repeat the errors of the former and goes much beyond the latter in mixing scholarly tradition with personal experience. The chapters are short (taking scarcely more than six columns in Migne's *Patrologia Latina*), but their importance and originality were appreciated by medieval scholars who frequently copied them out separately under the title *Sententiae Isidori de musica*.

The first chapter from the *De musica* section (No. 15 of Book III), called *De musica et ejus nomine*, is dependent on Clement of Alexandria and St Augustine. It tells us that the muses, to whom music owes its name, were daughters of Jupiter and Memory and its final sentence '*Nisi enim ab homine memoriae teneantur soni pereunt quia scribi non possunt*' has been much discussed. Fontaine takes it literally, concluding that the most educated man in the Visigothic Kingdom had no knowledge of either the traditional notation of the Greek, such as that described in the *Introduction to Music* by Alypius (*c*. 360 AD) or of the neumatic notation of the Middle Ages. The opinion of musicologists is divided: some doubt the existence of a musical notation of which not a single example remains, whereas others interpret the phrase as indicating only that diastematic notation was not known.

The tendency of medieval theorists towards comprehensiveness rather than selection is illustrated by chapters eighteen and nineteen, which are concerned with the classification of music. In addition to a set of definitions inherited from the Greeks through Cassiodorus which characterized music as 'harmonic', 'rhythmic' or 'metric' St Isidore gives another set derived from St Augustine, using the activity of the performer as its main criterion. According to this second classification music may be 'harmonic', 'organic' or 'rhythmic'; which means produced by the voice, by air passing through a tube, or by the fingers either plucking strings or hitting an instrument. Isidore then discusses each of these classes separately beginning, as one would expect, with singing. This section, together with parts of the *De ecclesiasticis officiis*, clearly benefits from the saint's own musical experience and is therefore especially interesting. It is in this context that he defines *symphonia* or consonance and *diaphonia* or dissonance: his description of the latter (*id est voces discrepantes*) is especially indicative of his practical bias. The definitions of wind instruments are not always what we would expect, as several instruments have changed their names since the seventh century. In his discussion of rhythmic music Isidore gives a list of chordophones as well as of membranophones and idiophones. The short final chapter is more traditional in that it relates to mathematics, with which subject music was associated throughout the Middle Ages. St Isidore's acceptance of this relationship is shown by the plan of Book Three which deals with each of the subjects of the quadrivium in turn: mathematics, geometry, music and astronomy.

The importance of this treatise on music does not lie in the scholarly definitions given at the beginning or in the mathematical speculation at the end, but in what St Isidore tells us of the living music of his age. It is in fact the first theoretical work which owes more to practical music than to the scholarly tradition, and Isidore may be said to bridge the gap between the *musicus* (or theoretician) and the *cantor* (or practical musician). The reputation which the *Etymologies* enjoyed throughout the Middle Ages ensured that the saint's ideas were not forgotten: on the contrary they formed the foundation of a new and more fruitful conception of music.

While St Isidore probably had more influence on the political and liturgical life of Spain than any other of the clergy, several other bishops also played an important role in the formation of the Mozarabic liturgy. St Leander, for example, visited Constantinople early in life, staying at the same house as Gregory the Great, and as we are told that he wrote music (*multa dulci sono composuit*) it is reasonable to assume that at least some of this was liturgical in character. Saragossa, like Seville, could boast of two distinguished brothers, John (d. 631) and St Braulius (d. 651) both of whom were archbishops and who are recorded as having written compositions for the Church. Toledo, the capital and cultural centre of the Visigothic Kingdom produced three great archbishops during this period, St Eugenius (d. 657), St Ildefonsus (d. 667), and St Julian (d. 690), all of whom are known to have contributed to the chant.

The rite remained virtually unchanged during the Mozarabic period. In Catalonia it was replaced by the Roman rite about 800 after the conquest by Charlemagne, but in the rest of Spain it was tolerated until the eleventh century. Papal pressure for uniformity in the Catholic Church was intensified during this century and in 1080 at the Council of Burgos the Mozarabic rite was officially abolished throughout the whole realm. Its replacement was largely effected by monks from Cluny who came to Spain in vast numbers in the second half of the eleventh century. The most important of them was Bernard, who became archbishop of Toledo after its recapture in 1085 by Alfonso VI of Castile. The people of Toledo strongly resisted the change and, as a special concession, six parishes were allowed to keep the ancient chant, but even they seem to have been unable to maintain it for very long, and by the end of the fifteenth century, when Cardinal Francesco Jiménez de Cisneros (1436–1517) tried to revive the rite, the ability to decipher neumes had been lost. Cisneros had the *Missal* published in 1500 and the *Breviary* in 1502. Three *Cantorales* purporting to contain Mozarabic melodies were written at about the same time, probably by order of Cisneros, and although they employ mensural notation it is quite probable that they were based on an earlier manuscript surviving in one of the Mozarabic parishes.[9] Various attempts have been made to restore these melodies to their original state[10] and one must be wary of accepting these reconstructions as authentic. Nearly two hundred years later, Cardinal Francisco Antonio de Lorenzana (1722–1804) published the *Missa Gothica seu Mozarabica* (Los Angeles, 1770) and the *Breviarum Gothicum* (1775), as well as a new edition of Cisneros' *Missal* in the year of his death. These volumes, although inaccurate, have been reprinted in Migne's *Patrologia* (Vols 85 and 86).

Our sources for the Mozarabic liturgy tell us more than those for any other western rite except the Roman.[11] About twenty of the more than two hundred surviving manuscripts have music and they preserve almost the whole cycle of the liturgical year. They were mostly copied at Toledo, San Millán de la Cogolla and Santo Domingo de Silos, but the most important are the Antiphoner of León Cathedral[12] dating from the middle of the tenth century, and the Orational kept at Verona, copied at the end of the seventh or beginning of the eighth century. All these manuscripts are written in neumatic notation and precise pitch is therefore not indicated, but in spite of this, we are able to draw certain conclusions about their contents. The extravagant melismas found in some of them, particularly the Antiphoner of León, show that Mozarabic chant was no less elaborate than the Ambrosian[13] and many pieces show the important part played by the congregation in the Spanish liturgy. About twenty melodies, however, survive in their original form[14] – sixteen antiphons and three responses, all from the Office of the Dead. They are contained in a manuscript from San Millán de la Cogolla (Real Academia de la Historia, MS No. 56) on several pages of which the neumatic notation has been scratched out and replaced by Aquitanian diastematic notation. All the melodies can be made to correspond to modes 1, 2, 3 or possibly 8 of the Gregorian modal system, which suggests that Mozarabic music had a similar system to that of Roman chant.

The only plausible explanation of this change of notation is that the Mozarabic version of the Office of the Dead was still used after the official suppression of the rite. There are other indications that the Spanish chant was not as completely obliterated as is generally supposed: first, the presence of the Mozarabic tones of the Holy Week lamentations in a Gregorian Antiphoner at Silos; secondly, a Spanish Visigothic calendar inserted in a Roman missal of the eleventh century and thirdly, terms belonging to the Mozarabic liturgy in the work of Gonzalo de Berceo, a thirteenth-century poet of northern Spain. These facts prompted Dom Mundó in 1965 to study

9. See Prado, 'Mozarabic', 223.
10. See Rojo, *Canto*, pp. 117–40.
11. For a complete list of these sources, see Rojo, *Canto*, *op. cit.*
12. See Brou, *Antifónario* for a facsimile edition.
13. See *NOHM*, i, 59 ff.
14. Transcribed in Rojo, *Canto*, pp. 66–82.

the dating of the twenty-two manuscripts preserved at Toledo.[15] Paleo-graphical examination showed that one may be assigned to the end of the eleventh century; four should be placed at the turn of the eleventh and twelfth centuries; two can be dated almost exactly, one as 1200, the other between 1192 and 1208; three certainly belong to the thirteenth century and a final manuscript may be placed at the turn of the thirteenth and fourteenth centuries. The copying of manuscripts was a long and costly operation and it is reasonable to assume that it was not done as a useless exercise. Further-more, if twenty melodies were transcribed into diastematic notation to facilitate their performance, there is no reason to believe that others were not transcribed as well: it is simply a question of looking for them. Thus, we see that far from having lost for ever the key to Mozarabic liturgical music, it is quite possible that we are now on the verge of discovering it.

GREGORIAN CHANT

The introduction of Gregorian chant into Spain had extremely important consequences. As in the other European countries, its elaboration by the practice of troping[16] led to the rebirth of western theatrical art, and – even more important – it provided a basis from which polyphony could grow. Catalonia[17] came under French influence first, some 250 years before the rest of Spain, but in a number of ways the musicians of the region maintained their independence. For example, from the tenth to the twelfth century they used a distinctive type of Catalan notation developed by the monks of Ripoll.[18] This Benedictine monastery, which was the centre of the Catalan cultural life throughout the period, enjoyed close relationships with many French houses, among them St Peter of Moissac, St Martial of Limoges, and Fleury. It will be recalled that the two latter played an extremely important part in the history of medieval music, especially in the field of liturgical drama. The school at Ripoll, founded in 888, had a splendid reputation, particularly during the tenth century, and attracted many students from outside Catalonia. Gerbert, a monk of St Gérard of Aurillac who later became Pope Silvester II, was sent there in 967 to complete his education: music was among the subjects he studied and on returning to France in 970 he passed on what he had learned to his countrymen. He seems to have greatly enjoyed his stay because in 985 he still wanted to go back. Besides Gerbert and Abbot Oliva (died c. 1063), a mathematician, musician and poet, however, we know very little about the monks, scarcely more than a few of their names, but the numerous extant manuscripts which were

15. See Mundó, 'Datación'.
16. For a definition of troping, see chapter 2, p. 77, fn. 31.
17. See especially Anglès, *Catalunya*.
18. See Beer, *Handschriften*; Anglès, 'Ripoll', 157.

copied at the monastery testify to their industry. Other important centres of church music were San Cugat del Vallés, Gerona and Tarragona.

In addition to cultivating tropes and sequences, particularly troped epistles,[19] Catalonia made a contribution of its own to the elaboration of the liturgy, namely the *verbeta*. This was a short paraphrase sung on principal feast days after the various nocturns of Matins: it was usually in a simple syllabic style enabling the congregation to sing alternate lines. Liturgical drama also flourished in Catalonia while gaining only limited acceptance in the rest of Spain.[20] It was particularly cultivated at Vich, Ripoll, Seo de Urgel and Gerona, and a twelfth-century manuscript from Vich contains what appears to be the prototype of the so-called 'third stage' Easter Sepulchre Drama.[21] A single scene built around the prophecy of the Sibyl from the *Ordo Prophetarum* seems to have been very popular in Spain.[22] The earliest known example of the tune, which may well be of Mozarabic origin,[23] is preserved in a Spanish manuscript dating from about the middle of the tenth century.[24] The famous *Mystery of Elche*,[25] which survives with Catalan text, probably dates from the beginning of the fourteenth century, but some of the music is much more recent than this.

THE FIRST STAGES OF POLYPHONY

We have already said that polyphony grew from Gregorian chant, but whereas in most European countries it soon achieved a measure of independence, in Spain it remained centred on the ecclesiastical chant right up until the Renaissance. According to Anglès,[26] however, the earliest reference to polyphony is to be found in verse 153 of the *Apotheosis* by Prudentius. In two sixth-century codices this verse contains the words *concentu triplici*, but in another codex dating from the tenth century they have been strangely changed to *concentu duplici*. It is unfortunate that there are no surviving theoretical works which throw light on the early development of peninsular polyphony. Oliva's *Breviarum de Musica*, dating from the second third of the eleventh century, is the earliest which we possess, and there is nothing between this and the *Ars musica* of Juan Gil de Zamora, who flourished in the thirteenth century. The numerous extant copies and translations of works by Arab theorists are no help at all. We possess slightly more information for the twelfth and thirteenth centuries. A man called *Lucas magnus*

19. See Anglès, *Catalunya*, p. 306.
20. See Donovan, *Drama*.
21. See Smolden, *NOHM*, ii, 185.
22. On the *Ordo Prophetarum* see Young, *Drama*, ii, 125 ff.
23. See Corbin, 'Sibyllae'.
24. Some twenty-three versions of the tune are printed in Anglès, *Catalunya*, table opposite p. 294.
25. See Gomez Brufal, *Bibliografia*, for a list of the vast literature about this.
26. See Anglès, 'Culture'.

organista appears in the death-roll of Tarragona Cathedral which was copied in the fifteenth century: he died in 1164 well before *Perotinus magnus organista* had begun his work at Notre Dame in Paris, but we know nothing of his life or work. Two other polyphonists are referred to by name: Petrus Ferrerius (d. 1231), a monk of San Cugat del Vallés, and Bernard of Queizán (d. 1273), precentor of Gerona Cathedral. We also know that King Alfonso x of Castile founded a chair of music at Salamanca in 1254, and Anonymous IV, the theorist to whom we owe our knowledge of Leonin and Perotin, speaks of the existence during the thirteenth century of a polyphonic school at Pamplona.[27]

The first comprehensive work on Spanish polyphonic music was the paper presented by Anglès to the International Congress of Musicology at Vienna in 1927.[28] Since then this same scholar has studied many manuscripts coming from the most important musical centres of the thirteenth and fourteenth centuries: Santiago of Compostela, Toledo, Burgos, Ripoll and Tortosa. In spite of the considerable progress which has been made Anglès' own statement of 1931, that 'the history of polyphonic music in the churches of the peninsula still remains to be explored,' is almost as valid today as it was then.

The oldest extant manuscript containing polyphonic Spanish music is the famous *Codex Calixtinus* or *Liber Sancti Jacobi*,[29] dating from about the middle of the twelfth century; it is a compendium which seems to have been designed to publicize the shrine of St James the Greater at Compostela. In addition to a more or less liturgical part concerned with the saint and his miracles, the book contains the famous poem known as the *Pseudo-Turpin*, and a kind of guide for pilgrims, including a little vocabulary of the Basque language. It seems to have been the work of an unscrupulous monk of Cluny and its attribution to Pope Calixtus II (d. 1124) is as false as that of the *Historia Karoli Magni et Rotholandi* is to the eighth-century archbishop of Reims. The contents of this manuscript are mostly monophonic but include about twenty *organa*, of which one, *Congaudeant catholici*, is regarded by many scholars as being the oldest known three part composition.[30] It is attributed in the manuscript to a certain Magister Albertus, a Parisian, whom we know to have been active between 1147 and 1180.[31] Many other pieces in the collection also appear to be of French origin.

In spite of its initial resistance to the suppression of the Mozarabic rite, Toledo later became one of the greatest schools of Gregorian chant in the

27. See Anglès, 'Cantu'.
28. Printed as Anglès, 'Mehrstimmige'.
29. Whitehill, *Calixtinus*, is a complete edition and Wagner, *Jacobusliturgie* contains all the music. See also *HAM*, i, Nos. 27b, 28b.
30. Transcribed in Gleason, *Examples*, p. 34. See also Reese, *Middle Ages*, p. 268.
31. See Handschin, *Acta* (1932) 5.

whole of Europe. This was largely due to three archbishops, Raymond, Martin Lopez of Pisuerga and the historian, Rodrigo Jiménez de Rada (1208–41), the greatest Toledan archbishop of the Middle Ages. Each of these men greatly increased the size of the cathedral choir. By the middle of the thirteenth century it comprised about a hundred major canons and *racioneros* or beneficiaries, which gives us some idea of the importance and magnificence of the cathedral's music. The most important manuscript of the period is now kept at the Biblioteca Nacional Madrid (No. 20486, sometimes known as the Toledo Codex), and dates from the end of the thirteenth or beginning of the fourteenth century. For a long time it was thought to be a French manuscript because most of the motets and *conducti* it contains are from the Notre Dame School, but it was copied in Spain and also contains Spanish compositions.[32] One of these is the *hochetus*, *In seculum*, which appears to be the oldest known instrumental composition for three parts.[33]

Ripoll and Tortosa were also important centres of religious polyphony, but the most notable collection of part music comes from the convent of Las Huelgas, situated about one kilometre from Burgos. This was founded in 1180 by Alfonso VIII of Castile and his wife Eleonore, and was greatly admired for its magnificence and the high reputation and learning of its nuns throughout the Middle Ages. According to a saying of the time if the pope had wanted to marry he could have chosen none other than the abbess of Las Huelgas. The manuscript, which was discovered there in 1904 by the Benedictines Luciano Serrano and Casiano Rojo, is known as the manuscript of Las Huelgas and was mostly copied towards the end of the first quarter of the fourteenth century.[34] It contains 186 compositions, of which the largest number are for two voices; about fifty are solos, almost as many are for three voices, and one is for four. Apart from a single solfeggio all the pieces are *organa*, sequences, motets or *conducti* (of which one is the only known example of a bitextual *conductus*) and by grouping them according to their characteristics, Anglès was able to trace the development of each type.[35] Of the named composers the one most frequently encountered is Juan Rodriguez, whose name leaves no doubt as to his nationality.

Although many of the compositions contained in Spanish manuscripts are also known from French sources or show undeniable French influence, Spanish documents sometimes fill in gaps in our knowledge of medieval music and also enable us to appreciate the mastery with which peninsular musicians took up foreign innovations and developed them.

The development of the *ars nova* in Spain is much less well-known than that of the *ars antiqua*. The numerous references to music by historians and

32. For a transcription of a three voice *conductus* see Gleason, *Examples*, p. 44.
33. Transcribed in Aubrey, *Motets*, p. 226.
34. It has been published with facsimiles, transcriptions and notes as Anglès, *Huelgas*.
35. For examples of *conducti* see Parrish, *Masterpieces*, No. 11; Gleason, *Examples*, p. 43.

poets hardly compensate for the lack of documents, and what few manuscripts do survive are fragmentary and for the most part have not been made
available in modern editions. Archives of the period, however, show that
music continued to feature prominently in both church and court life. An
especially valuable source of information are the numerous letters written
by King John I of Catalonia and Aragon (1350–96), one of the greatest early
patrons of music.[36] They are mostly to his friends and relations in France
asking for new instruments and performers to play them, but one of them
makes it clear that the king was himself a composer. Court and chancellery
registers also show some light on the practical music of the time; from them,
for example, we learn that in the second half of the fourteenth century the
Chapel Royal at Barcelona was almost entirely dependent for both the
repertoire and its performers on the papal chapel at Avignon.[37] Among the
foreign musicians who worked at the court of John and his successors were
Jacques de Jean Trebor, Gacian Reyneau of Tours, Colinet Forestier and
Jean Martini of Noyen. Secular music by Selesses, Trebor and Reyneau is
preserved in Chantilly, Musée Condé MS 1047,[38] an important *chansonnier*
containing compositions dating from the period between the death of
Machaut (*c.* 1377) and the beginning of Dufay's work.[39]

SECULAR MUSIC

The earliest extant secular music of Spain, and perhaps the earliest in the
whole of Europe, is preserved in a manuscript belonging to the ninth or
tenth century at Madrid (Bib. Nac. 10029). It contains laments or *planctus*,
with Latin texts, on the death of King Chindavinthus in 652 and Queen
Reciberga in 657, of which the words, and perhaps the music too, are by
St Eugenius.[40] Latin songs have also been discovered in other Spanish
manuscripts; they include an epithalamium for a royal wedding which took
place about 910, preserved in a codex at Roda, and a nightingale song contained in another Madrid manuscript (Bib. Nac. 1005).[41] Unfortunately all
these compositions are written in Visigothic neumes and are undecipherable.
Settings of poems by the great Latin poets continued to be popular throughout the Mozarabic period, and we also know of epic songs about the achievements of national heroes, ancestors of the *chansons de geste*.[42]

36. See Pedrell, 'Jean d'Aragon'.
37. See Anglès, 'Avignon'.
38. Contents listed in Wolf, *Notation*, i, 329 ff.
39. Further on foreign musicians who worked in Spain during this period see the following articles by
Anglès, *AfMW* (1959) 5, 'Cantors und Ministrers', 'Cantors i organistes', 'Jacomi', 'Reyneau', 'Spanien'.
For examples of secular music by Trebor and Selesses, see Apel, *French*, and *HAM*, i, No. 47.
40. For further details see Anglès, *Huelgas*, i, 25.
41. See Trend, *Spanish*, p. 50.
42. See chapter 3, p. 128.

In the eleventh century there was a sudden eruption of lyric song in the vernacular; it began in Provence and soon spread all over the continent. The origins of this new but highly developed art have been much disputed.[43] In our day there are two main schools of thought: one believes that it developed from liturgical forms, especially the litany, sequence and hymns, and the other that it was of Arab origin. Gennrich is the principal exponent of the former,[44] and Ribera of the latter.[45] Ribera's theory is based on his discovery of the similarity between the form of the Arab *zajal* and that of the *virelai*. He postulated that the *zajal* was imitated in Spain, from where it spread to Provence and then to the rest of Europe, taking with it a whole repertoire of Arab melody. This theory can at best be regarded as speculative since no Arab melodies are known, but it is actually founded on a false premise, for the forms of the *zajal* and of the *virelai*, though similar, are not identical. The simplest form of the *zajal* is:

A A b b b A (A A) c c c A (A A) etc.

whereas that of the *virelai* is:

A B c c a b A B.

In his basic belief, however, that the courtly poetry of the troubadours was of Arab origin, Ribera may well have been right. In addition to the *zajal* Arab poets and, on their example, Hebrew-Spanish poets, cultivated the *muwashshah*, which had roughly the same form as the *zajal* but repeated the whole of its refrain, not just half of it. Although most of the poem was written in literary Arabic, the final couplets, called the *kharja*, were undecipherable until 1948, when the Arab and Hebrew scholar S. M. Stern realized that these concluding lines were written in the vernacular, i.e. in the Mozarabic dialect.[46] The *kharja* also differed from the rest of the poem in its content; whereas the first part was serious in character, the words of the *kharja* concerned love and were always given to a girl or a woman. It is known that the *muwashshah* was first employed by a poet called Muqaddam or Muhammed from Cabra, near Cordova, who flourished about 900. The first preserved texts date from the eleventh century, which gives these vernacular refrains a priority of about a century over the songs of Guillaume of Aquitaine (1071–1127), the first troubadour of whom we have any record. Many scholars, among them Alonso, Pidal and Spitzer,[47] have accepted Stern's discovery as providing the link between Latin secular song and courtly song in the vernacular.

43. See Jeanroy, *Poésie*, i, 61 ff., for a detailed discussion of the various theories.
44. See, for example, Gennrich, *Formenlehre.*
45. See especially Ribera, *Árabe*, but also Spanke, 'Teoría' which refutes the theory.
46. See Stern, *Chansons.*
47. See Alonso, 'Cancioncillas'; Pidal, 'Cantos'; Spitzer, 'Lyric'.

The earliest surviving repertoire of lyric poetry in Spain is written in the Galician-Portuguese language and would remain outside the history of music but for a discovery made about 1914 by the librarian Pedro Vindel. In an eighteenth-century binding of a much earlier manuscript copy of Cicero's *De officiis*, he found a leaf of parchment dating from the thirteenth century on one side of which were written seven love songs by the Galician troubadour, Martin Codax or Codaz. The poems are also known to us from other sources, but here six of them are provided with their music.[48] They are the only surviving decipherable Spanish love songs of the Middle Ages.

By far the most important collection of medieval Spanish non-liturgical music is that of the *Cantigas de Santa Maria* made by Alfonso x, King of Castile and León from 1252 until his death in 1284.[49] Alfonso was not a particularly successful king in the political field but earned the title of *el sabio* (the learned) by his contributions to science and the arts.[50] The *Cantigas* were copied after 1279 and survive in three manuscripts: one which originates from Toledo but has been kept at Madrid since 1869 and two from Escorial. The most complete is Escorial MS j.b.2, and it is this that provided the basis for the magnificent edition by Anglès.

Alfonso is sometimes called the father of Castilian prose and it is strange that the poems are written in the Galician-Portuguese language. They are in honour of the Virgin Mary, and invite obvious comparison with the *Miracles de Notre Dame* of Gautier de Coinci[51] as well as with the surviving repertoire of the Galician-Portuguese lyric school. Two types of notation are used: the normal modal notation for pieces in ternary rhythm and another which indicates duple time. Some of the songs mix the two and Anglès interprets this as showing that they are rhythmically much freer than had generally been supposed. The majority of the 402 songs are in *virelai* form. Many show strong troubadour or *trouvère* influence whereas others have more in common with Gregorian Chant, particularly the sequence. Some of the melodies were probably centuries old: that for *Madre de Deus, ora pro nobis*, for example, bears a striking resemblance to the Song of the Sibyl, while others have a pronounced Spanish flavour which seems to suggest that they might originally have been folk tunes.[52]

The *Llibre Vermell* (*The Red Book*, so-called because of the colour of its binding) contains ten compositions copied at the end of the fourteenth and beginning of the fifteenth century. It was found in 1806 by P. Villanueva at

48. For transcriptions see Pope, 'Medieval', 18–20, 22–4; Trend, *Spanish*, pp. 213–15; Anglès, *Cantigas*, iii, part ii.

49. Published with facsimile, transcriptions and notes as Anglès, *Cantigas*.

50. See Trend, *Alfonso*.

51. See Reese, *Middle Ages*, p. 216.

52. For single examples from the *Cantigas* see *HAM*, i, No. 22; Parrish, *Masterpieces*, no. 11; Parrish, *Treasury*, no 7; Gleason, *Examples*, p. 22.

Montserrat and was fortunately on loan when all the monastery's archives were destroyed during the Napoleonic Wars. It was returned in 1885 but in the meantime had lost some of the pages originally described by Villanueva. During the fourteenth century the shrine at Montserrat attracted many pilgrims who used to sing and dance in front of the church to refresh themselves. They performed songs written by the monks specifically for this purpose, of which the compositions contained in the *Llibre Vermell* are the only surviving examples.[53] All but one of them are dedicated to the Virgin Mary. The monophonic pieces include *Polorum regina omnium*, whose tune remained popular for two centuries and reappears in Salinas' great treatise, the *De musica libri septem*[54] (Salamanca, 1577) set to the *villancico* text, *Yo me iba, mi madre*.[55] Another of the monophonic songs is the spirited *Los set Gotxs* (*The Seven Joys of Mary*). The polyphonic compositions for two and three voices include three *caças*[56] which are probably the oldest surviving Spanish canons. But perhaps the most interesting piece in the book is another of the monophonic songs *Ad mortem festinamus* (*We hasten towards death*) the oldest known musical version of the Dance of Death.[57]

INSTRUMENTS

With the possible exception of the *hochetus* mentioned above (see p. 374), there is no surviving Spanish instrumental music of the Middle Ages. We are fortunate, however, in possessing a large number of iconographical and literary sources, the collective evidence of which gives us at least some idea of the instruments that might have been used. Perhaps the best of these sources are the miniatures which decorate the manuscripts of the *Cantigas*: they depict about forty different instruments including the lute, both the plucked and struck types of zither (known in Europe as the psaltery and dulcimer respectively), guitar, castanets and transverse flute. The lute, psaltery and dulcimer were introduced into Spain by the Moors and soon spread to the rest of Europe, the lute in particular enjoying wide and lasting favour.[58] In every European language its name is derived from the Arabic word *al' ud*, which means 'flexible stick' and not 'wood' as has been supposed hitherto. The earliest evidence of its presence in the west is probably provided by an ivory dating from 968 which originated at Cordova and is now in the Louvre. A bowed string instrument called *rabáb* in Arabic and *rabé* in Spanish existed from about 1000, as did also the lute.

53. See Ursprung, *ZfMW* (1921) 136; Trend, *Spanish*.

54. For a facsimile edition see Kastner, *Salinas*.

55. See Trend, *ML* (1927) 13.

56. The Spanish form corresponding to the French *chace* and the Italian *caccia* (see p. 217, fn. 10).

57. Of the large literature on the Dance of Death see particularly Whyte, *Dance*.

58. Paradoxically it became rather less popular in Spain than elsewhere, the *vihuela* being generally preferred for aristocratic music and the guitar for popular music.

The first reference to the *qânûn*, the Arabic ancestor of the psaltery, is found in one of the stories of the *Arabian Nights* dating from the tenth century. It probably entered Europe in the next century, preserving its form, oriental decoration and name: *caño* in Spanish, *canon* in French, *kanon* in German and *canale* in corrupt Latin. A smaller variety was called a half *qânûn*: *medio caño*, *micanon*, *metzkanon* or *medicinale*. The dulcimer or struck zither was a Persian and Iraqi instrument of which the Arabic name *santir* is derived from the Greek *psalterion*. The earliest evidence of its presence in Spain is provided by a relief dating from 1184 on the Cathedral of Saint James of Compostela. Two types of guitar are depicted in the miniatures; the *guitarra latina* and the *guitarra morisca*. The former was similar to the modern guitar while the latter was a long-necked instrument developed from the oriental *tanbûr*. The castanets which seem to have been introduced to Europe by Phoenician colonizers were very popular during the Middle Ages and are depicted in several manuscripts besides those of the *Cantigas*. The transverse flute appears to have entered the west by way of Byzantium in about the twelfth century.

An important source of our knowledge of instruments in the fourteenth century are the letters of King John I of Catalonia and Aragon[59] referred to above (see p. 375). In one written in 1394, for example, he points out that he already has a large number of *orguens de coll*, *harpa*, *exaquier*, *rota* and *orguens de peu* and would prefer to receive other instruments. The *orguens de coll* was a small portative organ which was suspended from the neck by a cord, blown by the right hand and played by the left, while the *orguens de peu* was a much larger instrument, standing on the ground, which was played with both hands. The *exaquier*, known in France as *echiquier* and in England as *chekker*, was a stringed keyboard instrument possibly of English origin, while the *rota* was possibly a *cruit* which seems to have been similar in shape to the Greek *kithara*. Among the other instruments which John possessed were the *zelamia* and *bombarde* (shawm and tenor shawm) and the *cornamusa* (bagpipes).[60]

---

59. See Pedrell, 'Jean d'Aragon', and Pedrell, *Organografia*.

60. For further information on the various instruments discussed in this section, see Sachs, *Instruments*; Harrison, *Instruments*; Baines, *Instruments*; Anglès, 'Instrumentalmusik'.

CHRISTOPHER SWAIN AND JACK SAGE

8.2 Spain: c. 1450–1600

FROM *c*. 1450 TO *c*. 1530

CORNAGO. Johannes Cornago, one of the earliest Spanish composers we know of by name, seems to have spent at least part of his life at the Aragonese court of Naples.[1] Under Alfonso V, who ruled from 1442 until 1458, and his son Fernando (1458–94), the court became a centre of cultural life and acquired considerable international prestige. At first its musicians were mostly Spaniards, but as time went on it attracted many foreign musicians, including Tinctoris. Cornago served at the court from 1455 to about 1475 and his compositions seem to have been widely known; they survive not only in MS 871 N at Montecassino, evidently of Neapolitan origin, but also

---

1. See Anglès, *Católicos*, i, 24 (text); Pope, 'Cornago'; Reese, *Renaissance*, p. 576.

in the *Cancionero Musical de Palacio*, the *Cancionero de la Biblioteca Colombina*, the *Pixérécourt Chansonnier* and Trent Codex 88. His largest surviving work, the *Missa de la mappa mundi*, has the words *Ayo (aggio) visto lo mappa mundi* written under the tenor of the 'Gloria' and 'Credo', probably a reference to the map traced at the king's request by Giovanni di Giusto.[2] About a dozen of Cornago's secular pieces with Spanish or Italian words are extant, including seven in Montecassino MS 871 N and three in the *Cancionero Musical de Palacio*. *?Qu'es mi vida? preguntays* is a particularly interesting piece: it appears twice in the Montecassino manuscript, once in a three-part setting and once in four parts with the upper two voices attributed to Cornago and the two lower ones to Oquegan (Ockeghem). The latter version presumably dates from Ockeghem's visit to Spain in 1469–70, while the original was probably written some years earlier at Naples.[3] It has been claimed that Cornago's compositions reveal a definite Spanish character but in fact they appear to differ very little from those of his Franco-Netherlandish and Italian contemporaries.

CHURCH MUSIC. The marriage of Isabella of Castile to Ferdinand of Aragon in 1469 marks the beginning of one of the greatest periods in Spanish history. Ruling jointly in both kingdoms and known as the Catholic Monarchs, Ferdinand (King of Aragon 1479–1516) and Isabella (Queen of Castile 1474–1504) re-established the power of the monarchy and laid the foundations of the greatness that Spain was to achieve in the sixteenth century, both politically and in the arts.[4] Of the many extant manuscripts dating from the period few have been studied in detail, but enough to show that in both sacred and secular music Spanish composers demonstrated a greater degree of independence from the Flemish school than has hitherto been supposed.

Juan de Anchieta (*c.* 1462–1523),[5] a cousin of St Ignatius Loyola and one of the most important musicians of his day, was chaplain and singer to the Catholic Monarchs from 1489 and *maestro de capilla* to the Crown Prince Don Juan from 1495 until the latter's untimely death two years later. The prince was fond of singing and apparently knew how to play several instruments,[6] so we can assume that Anchieta was a skilled performer as well as a composer. After Isabella's death he continued at the court of Joanna and then Ferdinand until 1519, when he was declared too old to reside at court, and retired to Azpeitia, the town of his birth.

The complete list of his works known to date comprises seven motets and hymns, one complete Mass and the first three movements of another, two

2. See Ghisi, 'Strambotti', 61 f.

3. Both versions are printed and discussed in detail in Pope, 'Cornago'.

4. See especially Stevenson, *Columbus*.

5. See Stevenson, *Columbus*, pp. 127 ff.; Coster, 'Anchieta'; Anglès, *Católicos*, i, 6 (text); and Elústiza, *Antología*, pp. xxiii f.

6. See Stevenson, *Columbus*, p. 133; Chase, *Spain*, p. 36.

Magnificats and four secular pieces.[7] There is only one example in Anchieta's surviving church music of his drawing on a secular piece, that is in the 'Agnus' of the *Missa quarti toni* where he quotes *L'Homme armé* transposed to the Phrygian mode, but a lost Mass referred to by Salinas testifies to the fact that he did not avoid the practice. His setting of the *Salve Regina*,[8] a favourite text of Spanish composers, keeps the plainsong for the odd verses and uses polyphony *à* 4 for the even ones (*à* 5 for the last verse), with the chant paraphrased in the top voice. Compared with the compositions of his great foreign contemporaries Anchieta's works are simple, but they do show a certain interest in vocal sonority and rhythm.

The fame and reputation of Francisco de Peñalosa (*c.* 1470–1528)[9] was even greater than that enjoyed by Anchieta. In Cristóbal de Villalón's dialogue *Ingeniosa comparación entre lo antiguo y lo presenté* (1539), he is the first composer cited as worthy to vie with the ancients, even taking precedence over Josquin. Nothing is known of his life until 1498, when he became a singer at the Aragonese court: from 1511 he also held the post of chapel-master to the King's grandson, another Ferdinand, who was later Holy Roman Emperor. He left Spain in 1517, perhaps because of the intensification of Netherlandish influence after the death of Ferdinand, and became a member of the papal chapel in Rome. He returned to his native country in 1525 and died at Seville in 1528. Peñalosa was a particular favourite of both Ferdinand and Pope Leo x (1513–21), and each was active in securing him preferments. Compositions by him survive in some ten manuscripts: they comprise six complete Masses, and parts of three others, about thirty-six motets and hymns, six *Magnificats*, ten completed secular pieces and one incomplete one.[10]

The *Missa Ave Maria*[11] employs several Gregorian chants as *cantus firmi*: the *Ave Maria* in the 'Kyrie', the 'Gloria' of Mass x v, the 'Credo' of Mass i v and part of the *Salve Regina* in the 'Sanctus' and 'Agnus'. Like Anchieta, Peñalosa sometimes confines the borrowed melody to a single voice and sometimes shares it out, but in both cases he makes greater use of imitation. In the 'Gloria' of the *Missa Ave Maria*, for example, the plainsong is in the contratenor throughout transposed from mode 4 to mode 2, and almost every phrase is treated imitatively. Peñalosa was particularly good at combining melodies. In the 'Gloria' of the *Missa Nunca fue pena mayor*[12] based on the famous *villancico* by Wrede (sometimes transcribed 'Urrede'), the

---

7. For examples see Anglès, *Católicos*, i, ii, iii; Elústiza, *Antología*; Stevenson, *Columbus*.

8. Elústiza, *Antología*, pp. 8 ff.

9. See Stevenson, *Columbus*, pp. 145 ff.; Reese, *Renaissance*, pp. 579 f.; Anglès, *Católicos*, i, 7 (text); Elústiza, *Antología*, pp. xxxv ff.

10. For examples see Anglès, *Católicos*, i, ii, iii; Elústiza, *Antología*, Gerber, *Hymnar*; Stevenson, *Columbus*.

11. Anglès, *Católicos*, i, 62.

12. Anglès, *Católicos*, i, 99.

superius has the treble of the secular piece twice in long notes, while the bass has phrases from the 'Gloria' of Mass XV. *Por las sierras*,[13] one of his secular pieces, is a six-part quodlibet in which four *villancico* melodies are sung simultaneously with free outer parts, the bottom part having the words *loquebantur variis linguis magnalia Dei* ('they spoke in various tongues the wonderful works of God'). Peñalosa made little use of such technical feats in his motets, in which his prime concern seems to have been to express the text. The exquisite *Versa est in luctum*[14] shows complete mastery of all those expressive features which were to be the hallmark of sixteenth-century Spanish church music. Compared with Anchieta's style, Peñalosa's is more 'international' in flavour, making greater use of imitation and learned devices.

Church music by about twenty other composers of the period still survives.[15] Juan Ponce (fl. 1510) and Medina (fl. 1479) have each left behind only one sacred composition, and in each case this is a *Salve Regina*. We are scarcely more fortunate with Juan Escribano (d. 1557) and Martín de Rivaflecha or Rivafrecha (d. 1528).[16] The works of Alonso de Alva (or Alba, d. 1504) and Pedro de Escobar (fl. 1507), however, have fared much better and show that both were composers of some stature. Alva's most substantial surviving work is his three-part Mass (Tarazona Cathedral MS 3),[17] with an unusual 'Gloria' in which the two top voices are in canon at the unison throughout. He also composed the 'Agnus' of the *Missa Rex Virginum*, of which Escobar wrote the 'Kyrie', Peñalosa the 'Gloria' and 'Credo' and Pedro Hernándes (=Fernández de Castilleja) the 'Sanctus'. Nearly twenty of his motets and hymns survive in the *Cancionero Musical de Palacio*[18] but only one secular piece.[19]

Pedro de Escobar (fl. 1507) who may well be identical with Pedro de Pôrto[20] appears to have been one of the most popular Spanish composers of his day. His surviving compositions consist of two complete Masses, one of which is a *Missa pro defunctis*, and parts of two others, about twenty motets and hymns and some eighteen secular pieces.[21] 'Agnus III' of his unnamed Mass[22] employs triple canon and even the two free voices make use of imitation. Escobar's most famous motet, *Clamabat autem mulier Chananea*,[23]

13. Anglès, *Católicos*, iii, 75.
14. Printed Stevenson, *Columbus*, p. 159.
15. See Stevenson, *Columbus*, pp. 162 ff.
16. Three motets by Rivaflecha are printed in Elústiza, *Antología*, pp. 23 ff.
17. Anglès, *Católicos*, i, 156.
18. See Gerber, *Hymnar*, for examples.
19. Anglès, *Católicos*, ii, 10, 18, 22, 88, 241; iii, 20, 125, 144, 148, 149, 157, 180.
20. See Stevenson, *Columbus*, pp. 169 ff.
21. For examples see Anglès, *Católicos*, i, ii, iii; Gerber, *Hymnar*; Elústiza, *Antología*.
22. Anglès, *Católicos*, i, 125 ff.
23. Printed Elústiza, *Antología*, p. 33, in a faulty version.

is a masterpiece showing the subjection of technique to an expressive purpose. It is the only peninsular composition to stand beside the works of Josquin, Févin, Willaert and Gombert in Alonso Mudarra's *Tres libros de música en cifra para vihuela*,[24] and a more worthy example of all that was best in music during the reign of Ferdinand and Isabella could hardly have been chosen.

SECULAR MUSIC. A vast amount of secular music dating from the reign of Ferdinand and Isabella survives mostly in five *cancioneros*: one at Seville, usually referred to as the *Cancionero de la Biblioteca Colombina* (CMC),[25] one at Madrid, the so-called *Cancionero Musical de Palacio* (CMP),[26] another at Segovia,[27] another at Barcelona[28] and lastly one at Elvas in Portugal, the so-called *Cancioneiro Musical e Poético da Biblioteca Pública Hortênsia*.[29] MS 7–1–28 at the Biblioteca Colombina was copied at the end of the fifteenth century and is the oldest of the *cancioneros*: it contains some ninety-five pieces, twenty of which are also found in CMP, some with an added voice. Apart from two pieces by Ockeghem and three by Wrede, all the works in CMC seem to be by Spanish composers. Juan de Triana is represented by twenty pieces, Cornago by six, Wrede by three and some eleven other composers by one or two pieces each; the remaining fifty-four compositions are anonymous. Twelve songs have Latin texts, two French and the rest Castilian.[30] The *Cancionero Musical de Palacio* (MS 2.1.5 of the Royal Palace, Madrid), part of which was copied in the fifteenth century and part in the sixteenth, was discovered in 1870 and first published twenty years later. It contains four hundred and fifty-eight pieces, making it the largest Spanish song collection of the century, and this in spite of the fact that fifty-six of its original leaves have been lost. The contents cover at least a fifty-year period; several pieces, *Alburquerque, Alburquerque*[31] for example, are probably re-workings of popular traditional songs dating from before 1450, while others were definitely written well after 1500. Every major Spanish composer of the period is represented: Alonso de Alva, Anchieta, Cornago, Encina, Escobar, Gabriel, Madrid, Medina, Millán, Peñalosa, Ponce, Torre and Triana; as well as a number of foreigners, among them

24. See Pujol, *Mudarra*, p. 79 (music).

25. Published in Haberkamp, *Colombina*; contents listed in Anglès, *Católicos*, i, 103 f.; but see Stevenson, *Columbus*, p. 206 (fn. 34) for corrections.

26. Published in Anglès, *Católicos*, ii, iii; Figueras, *Católicos*, iv, i and ii, contains the texts and a study of them. The first modern edition of CMP was Barbieri, *Cancionero*.

27. Unpublished. Contents listed (with some errors) in Anglès, *Católicos*, i, 104 f.; further on this MS see Anglès, 'Liedkunst'.

28. Unpublished. Contents listed (with some errors) in Anglès, *Católicos*, i, 112 f.

29. Published in Joaquim, *Cancioneiro*.

30. Further on CMC, see Stevenson, *Columbus*, pp. 206–49.

31. Anglès, *Católicos*, i, 131.

Josquin, Wrede, Tromboncino, Fogliano and Robert Morton. Encina heads the numerical list with 62 songs, followed by Millán (23), Gabriel (19), Escobar (18), Torre (15), Ponce (12), Alonso (11), Mondéjar (11) and Peñalosa (10). Over thirty identifiable composers are each represented by fewer than ten pieces, leaving one hundred and seventy-eight songs which are anonymous.[32]

MS 454 of the Biblioteca Central at Barcelona compiled in the last years of the fifteenth century and the first four decades of the sixteenth, besides containing a great deal of sacred music by both Spanish and foreign composers, also includes twenty-six songs with Spanish words. Among the composers represented are Encina, Peñalosa, Lope de Baena and Mondéjar, and three younger men, Morales, Flecha the Elder and Pastrana. The *Cancionero Musical* in Segovia Cathedral, dating from the end of the fifteenth century, originally had two hundred and twenty-eight folios and is principally a collection of Masses, motets and *chansons* by leading Flemish and French composers, Anchieta being the only Spaniard represented. There are about forty Spanish songs at the end of the MS, fourteen of which are also found in CMP. The Portuguese *Cancioneiro* copied early in the sixteenth century contains sixty-five pieces in Spanish or Portuguese, none of which gives any indication of its authorship, though four are essentially the same as compositions in CMP by Encina[33] and three as pieces by Escobar.[34] Although dating from a later period, the so-called *Cancionero de Upsala*[35] should also be discussed at this point. It was printed at Venice in 1556 and contains fifty-four compositions: twelve *à* 2, fourteen *à* 3, twenty-two *à* 4 and six *à* 5, mostly with Castilian texts. Gombert, who visited Spain in his capacity as *maestro di capilla* of the Flemish chapel of Charles v, is the only composer named, and it is possible that the greater amount of imitation in this *cancionero* is due to his influence. Mitjana, the discoverer of the anthology, was of the opinion that this collection comprises works by Spaniards who worked for at least part of their lives in Italy, such as Peñalosa, Escobedo and Morales.[36]

Nearly all the songs in the *Cancioneros* belong to one of two main types, the *romance* or the *villancico*. Throughout the sixteenth century and beyond, a third type has been distinguished, the *canción*, but this is so hard to separate from the *villancico* that it is perhaps best not to regard it as a category on its own. The *romance*, one of the chief forms of medieval poetry, was a long narrative poem, the counterpart of the English ballad. Although

---

32. Further on CMP, see Stevenson, *Columbus*, pp. 249–305.

33. Cf. Joaquim, *Cancioneiro*, pp. 80, 81, 84 and 91, with Anglès, *Católicos*, iii, 54, 53; ii, 193 and iii, 130 respectively.

34. Cf. Joaquim, *Cancioneiro*, pp. 37, 43 and 92 with Anglès, *Católicos*, ii, 229, 243 and iii, 99.

35. See Mitjana, *Cancionero*.

36. See Mitjana, *Cancionero*, p. 47 (text). Querol disagrees with this view.

in the fifteenth century it was more often written in lines of sixteen syllables than in lines of eight syllables, the tunes consisted of four balanced phrases based on eight-syllable lines, the remainder of the poem being sung to the same music; in the musical setting only the even lines rhymed. There are forty-four *romances* in CMP, slightly less than one tenth of the total, and they are mostly by older composers, as the young men had begun to neglect the form in favour of the *villancico*. Both CMC and CMP contain *romances* celebrating Ferdinand's Moorish victories: they include two by Encina, *Una sañosa porfía*, dating from about 1490, and *¿Qu'es de ti, desconsolada?* (c. 1492), two by Torre, *Pascua d'Espiritu Santo* and *Por los campos de los moros*, one by Anchieta, *En memoria d'Alixandre* (c. 1489), and the anonymous *Olvyda tu perdiçión*.[37]

The *villancico* and *canción* can be regarded as Spanish developments of the *virelai* and have the musical form ABBA. The distinction between them is a matter of controversy and some scholars prefer not to make any whatsoever. Others believe that the *canción* was courtly in origin while the *villancico* was based on some kind of popular song. Still others follow Pope and Stevenson and claim that one of the principal differences lies in the verse structure.[38] Both forms consist of a number of stanzas (*copla*) made up of two sections (*mudanza* and *vuelta*) and linked by a refrain (*estribillo*). These scholars maintain that whereas the *canción* always displays symmetry between the metrical and musical schemes, the *villancico* is characterized by asymmetry. For example:

		estribillo		*copla*		
				mudanza		*vuelta*
Symmetrical	Text	a	a	b b		a a
arrangement	Music	A		B B		A
Asymmetrical	Text	a	a	b b		b a
arrangement	Music	A		B B		A

The symmetrical type is most evident in the earlier *cancioneros* and then seems to have been gradually superseded.

In the absence of any clear distinction in the manuscripts the controversy must remain. The original copyist of CMP began by attempting to distinguish between the two, but soon gave up, and the original index dating from about 1525 divides the pieces into only four categories, sacred and secular *villancicos*, *romances* and *estranbotes*.[39] *Villancico* denotes all pieces with Spanish text that were not *romances* and *estranbote* any Italian song.

---

37. See CMP Nos. 126, 74, 136, 150, 126 and CMC No. 52 (fol. 71v) respectively. The CMC example is printed in Stevenson, *Columbus*, p. 247.

38. See Pope, 'Villancico' and Stevenson, *Columbus*, p. 208 f.

39. See Anglès, *Católicos*, ii, 18 ff.

Juan del Encina, who heads the numerical list of composers represented in CMP, was born at Encinas near Salamanca in 1468 or 1469, the son of a shoemaker.[40] He was a chorister at Salamanca Cathedral and a student of the university before joining the household of the Duke of Alba de Tormes about 1490. In 1498 he failed to get a post at Salamanca Cathedral, which may have made him decide to leave for Italy. He enjoyed the patronage of three popes and after holding several preferments *in absentia*, soon after 1520 took up residence as Prior of León, where he died about 1529. Encina himself tells us that most of his works, both poetical and musical, were written between his fourteenth and twenty-fifth years.

One of his duties at Alba was to provide dramatic entertainments, which he called *representaciones* or *eglogas*; he wrote the words, composed the music, probably directed them and at least sometimes acted in them. Some *representaciones* dealt with religious subjects and had their origins firmly in tradition, but others were on secular subjects, and may be regarded as the seeds from which the Spanish lyric theatre grew. Of his fourteen plays all but two end with *villancicos*, some of which survive in CMP and one in the Segovia MS.[41] These songs sometimes show a greater subtlety of expression than is usual in the *villancico*.

In spite of his long association with the church, not a single piece of liturgical music by Encina survives, though he did occasionally set religious verse. Of his sixty-eight poems in CMP, forty deal with love, fifteen have pastoral or rustic subjects, seven are romances, four are humorous songs and four are religious. Some of them are occasional pieces; *Triste España sin ventura*, for example, is probably a lament on the death of Queen Isabella, and *A tal pérdida tan triste* is believed to have been inspired by the death of the Infante Don Juan, Ferdinand and Isabella's only son, in 1497.[42] Of Encina's 62 compositions in CMP, 54 have refrains, 47 of these also display asymmetry between the metrical and musical schemes; 30 are for four voices, 32 for three; pieces in duple time greatly outnumber those in triple time and those in the Dorian and Aeolian modes outnumber those in the Phrygian and Lydian. Homophony is the rule, and although many pieces begin imitatively they do not usually continue so for long.[43]

The pieces by other important composers represented in CMP differ considerably from those of Encina.[44] The songs of Francisco Millán and Gabriel were mostly added to the manuscript after its original completion,

40. See Stevenson, *Columbus*, pp. 253 ff. Chase, *ML* (1939) 420; Chase, *MQ* (1939) 292.
41. For example see CMP Nos. 165, 167 and 174; 'Gran gasajo siento yo', Segovia MS, 198[v].
42. See Nos. 83 and 324 respectively.
43. For single examples of Encina's *villancicos*, see *HAM* i, Nos. 98 a, b, c and Parrish, *Treasury*, p. 94.
44. See Stevenson, *Columbus*, pp. 272 ff.

suggesting that these composers did not form part of the circle at Alba de Tormes. Although all but two of Millán's refrain songs employ the asymmetry characteristic of Encina, they are mostly for three voices, make much greater use of imitation and are never in either the Dorian or Aeolian mode. Gabriel's style also has certain individual traits: he occasionally wrote successions of first inversion chords, for example, whereas neither Encina nor Millán did; Escobar's eighteen pieces, as we would expect, show none of those technical devices that he used in his church music. Francisco de la Torre belonged to an older generation than Encina, and only one of his pieces in CMP displays asymmetry. Juan Ponce on the other hand seems to have been rather younger, and his style is more 'advanced' than Encina's in several ways. He also makes greater use of learned devices than the composers mentioned so far. *Para verme con ventura*, for example, has a mirror canon between the outer voices, and in *La mi sola, Laureola*[45] he treats the four first syllables as a solmization.

Very little is known about Juan de Triana,[46] the chief composer represented in CMC. He held a prebend at Seville Cathedral during 1478, and in 1483 was master of the boys at Toledo Cathedral. All Triana's eighteen surviving compositions are in CMC, two of them being repeated in CMP. They include three examples of the song motet, which was rare during the period. Of his fourteen secular pieces, twelve show agreement of metrical and musical structure. *No consiento ni me plaza* and *Quien vos dio tal señorío* provide good examples of his style.[47]

The anonymous pieces in the collections differ widely. Some seem to be simple arrangements of traditional songs while others are clearly the work of more sophisticated composers. Although it is not typical, one of the most interesting is *A los baños del amor*, which has a four-note solmization *ostinato* in the tenor (*so la mi re = sola m'iré* – I shall go alone).[48]

RAMOS DE PAREJA. The second half of the fifteenth century also saw the publication of an important theoretical work by a Spaniard, the *Musica practica* by Bartolomé Ramos de Pareja (b. *c*. 1440–d. after 1491).[49] After lecturing at Salamanca Ramos lived in Italy at least until 1491, first at Bologna and later at Rome. The *Musica practica* was published at Milan in 1496 and its revolutionary character immediately provoked a great controversy both in Italy and Spain. Among the matters discussed in the

45. Nos. 175 and 343 respectively.
46. See Stevenson, *Columbus*, pp. 208 ff.
47. Both are printed in Stevenson, *Columbus*. See also CMP Nos. 235 and 243.
48. CMP No. 149.
49. See Wolf, *Ramos de Pareja* for a modern edition. Strunk, *Readings* p. 201 ff. contains an excerpt in English.

work were a new solmization system, the nature of certain intervals (notably the major and minor third and the tritone), chromaticism and the construction of a twelve-note scale.[50]

CHARLES V AND PHILIP II. Under Charles V (1516–56) and Philip II (1556–98) Spain became the foremost power in Europe and produced some of the greatest writers, painters and musicians of the late Renaissance. Charles and Philip were both generous patrons of music, but it has been claimed that the latter seems to have favoured Spanish musicians more than his father. Among those who dedicated collections and editions of their works to him were Fuenllana, Pisador, Guerrero and Victoria, as well as La Hèle and Palestrina, and the music section of the new Escorial library was also greatly enriched with manuscripts and prints during his reign. On the other hand Philip frequently censored music that was not strictly devout and acquired a reputation for austerity in the arts generally. Perhaps this in part explains why Spanish publishers showed little interest in printing music during the sixteenth and seventeenth centuries, except for books of songs and pieces for organ and *vihuela*. Nevertheless an impressive corpus of music has survived, either printed and published abroad or in manuscripts, testifying to the fertility of Spanish masters during this period.

Charles V (Charles I of Spain from 1516; Holy Roman Emperor from 1519) had been brought up in the Netherlands, and maintained throughout his life a chapel composed of Flemish chaplains and musicians which accompanied him on all his travels, known in Spain as the *capilla flamenca*. In 1526, however, he established a chapel to be served by Spanish musicians for his wife Isabella of Portugal, which after her death in 1539 was passed on to their children.[51] Under the patronage of the future Philip II, who became regent in 1543, the chapel gained in prestige and importance, and its members accompanied the prince on his many travels. Its musicians at this time included Cabezón, Juan García de Basurto, Pedro de Pastrana and Francisco de Soto. During his long stay in Flanders as Archduke of Burgundy, Philip decided to form a chapel composed of Flemish musicians, and from 1556 when Charles abdicated in his favour, he maintained both chapels. The two co-existed, each upholding its own tradition, until 1636, when they were united to form the Royal Chapel.

It has been suggested that Spanish church music of the sixteenth century is imbued with that same mystical quality sometimes found in such writers as St John of the Cross and St Teresa of Ávila or such painters as El Greco.

50. Further on the *Musica practica*, see Stevenson, *Columbus*, pp. 55–63; Reese, *Renaissance*, pp. 586–7. See also p. 228.
51. See Pope, 'Spanish'.

The suggestion is perhaps valid in isolated cases, certain works of Victoria or Cabezón, for example, but gives a totally misleading impression of the century as a whole. Neither the music of Morales nor Guerrero can reasonably be described as 'mystical', nor even can much of that of Victoria. Throughout the century, in fact, there seems to have been a dual tendency: some composers expressed the text in the most direct intense way possible which often accounts for the mystical quality noticed by some listeners, while others made much more use of technical devices as a means of expression.

MORALES. Cristóbal de Morales (c. 1500–53)[52] was born in Seville and almost certainly came into contact with the three main musicians associated with that town during the early years of the sixteenth century, Pedro Fernández de Castilleja, Pedro de Escobar and Francisco de Peñalosa.[53] In his *Viage de Hierusalem* (1596), Francisco Guerrero calls Castilleja *maestro de los maestros de España* (teacher of the masters of Spain), which has led to the assumption that Morales was one of his pupils, but it is Peñalosa who seems to have influenced him most. From 1526–30 Morales was *maestro de capilla* at Ávila. His whereabouts are then uncertain until 1535, when he was admitted to the papal choir in Rome. He returned briefly to Spain in 1540 and permanently in 1545, taking up the appointment of *maestro* at Toledo in the same year. He resigned in 1547, and it seems that the only other important appointment he held was a similar post at Malaga from 1551 until 1553. Shortly before his death, which occurred some time during September or October 1553, he had applied once again for the post of *maestro* at Toledo.

Morales enjoyed greater fame during his lifetime and for two hundred years after his death than any other sixteenth-century Spanish composer. His works were frequently cited by theorists throughout the sixteenth and seventeenth centuries as models for composers to imitate, and from his death until 1600 they were published at centres as far apart as Alcalá de Henares, Antwerp, Louvain, Mexico, Nürnberg, Paris, Seville and Venice. The Spanish theorist Juan Bermudo, who described Morales as the 'light of Spain' in his *Declaración de Instrumentos* (1555),[54] also referred to him as being foreign because of his great technical mastery and the delight he took in using learned devices. This mastery of technique, combined with the expressive sensibility characteristic of Spanish composers, makes Morales one of the greatest masters of the sixteenth century.

52. See Stevenson, *Cathedral*, pp. 3 ff.; *JAMS* (1953) 3; Anglès, 'Morales y Guerrero'; Trend, *ML* (1925) 19; Mitjana, *Estudios.*

53. On Escobar and Peñalosa, see pp. 384–5 and 383–4 respectively, and on Castilleja, see Stevenson, *Columbus*, pp. 176 f.

54. See Kastner, *Bermudo*, and p. 408.

Morales' twenty-two surviving Masses,[55] sixteen of which were published at Rome in 1544, clearly show the extent to which he was influenced by the Netherlandish tradition. All but two of them are based on pre-existent material, either sacred or secular, but in only three cases is this Spanish in origin. The *Missa Tristezas me matan à* 5 and *Decilde al caballero à* 4, which were both early works, are based on Castilian melodies, and the *Missa Caça* owes its inspiration to Mateo Flecha the Elder's *ensalada à* 5, *La Caça*, itself derived from pre-existent material (Barcelona: Bibl. Cent. MS 588/2 fol. 48v).[56] In both the *Missae*, *Tristezas me matan* and *Decilde al caballero* there are movements in *cantus firmus* style, in which the tenor has not only the melody but also the words of the song. Bitextuality is very common in Morales' works, but usually both texts are in Latin. 'Agnus I' of the *Missa Tristezas* illustrates another favourite practice of Morales especially common in his motets, namely the use of an *ostinato*; here a seven-note figure from the song is repeated ten times in *altus* 11. The 'Hosanna' and 'Benedictus' of *Decilde al caballero* both employ canon, a technique Morales used a great deal in his Masses. The *Missa Caça* is a parody Mass making great use of imitation. Morales did not include these three Masses nor his two solmization Masses, the *Hexachord Mass* and the *Missa Cortilla* (*Missa super fa re ut fa sol la*) in his 1544 publication.

A further three Masses are based on secular French tunes, two – one *à* 4 and one *à* 5 – on *L'Homme armé*, and one *à* 6 on the *superius* of Charles V's favourite *chanson*, *Mille regretz* by Josquin. The four-part *L'Homme armé* is in old-fashioned *cantus firmus* style while the five-part version is a paraphrase Mass. In the *Missa Mille regretz*, Josquin's melody is in the *superius* throughout. Alternative more elaborate versions of the 'Sanctus', 'Benedictus' and 'Agnus' of the Mass are extant in the Roman MS Cappella Sistina 17.[57]

Morales' six Masses based on plainsong themes include two called *De Beata Virgine*, one *à* 4 and the other *à* 5. The latter is unusual in that the 'Credo' is based on the *Ave Maria* antiphon, the melody being stated five times in long notes in the tenor. The four-part *Missa Ave Maria* itself illustrates bitextuality in the 'Sanctus' and 'Agnus III', two extra voices being added for this last movement, which presents the *cantus firmus* in canon. The *Missa Ave maris stella à* 5 employs canon throughout, except in sections for only two or three voices. The *Missa Tu es vas electionis* is a straightforward *cantus firmus* mass, but the *Missa pro defunctis*, which includes the Proper but no 'Gloria' or 'Credo', stands apart from the rest of Morales' Masses in that it is homophonic and austere in style.

55. Printed Anglès, *Morales*, i, iii, vi; see Stevenson, *Cathedral*, pp. 45 ff.; Fox, 'Morales'.

56. Anglès, *Morales*, vii, 83, 58 and 1 respectively. See also Trend, *ML* (1925) 19. A *chanson* setting by Gombert of *Decilde al caballero* is in Mitjana, *Cancionero*, 125 ff.

57. Printed Anglès, Morales, vi, 121.

Seven of Morales' Masses are parodies after motets by Franco-Nether-landish composers: *Benedicta es coelorum Regina à* 4, *Gaude Barbara à* 4 and the five-part *Quaeramus cum pastoribus* are based on motets by Mouton; *Aspice Domine à* 4, *Quem dicunt homines* and *Si bona suscepimus à* 6 on motets by Gombert, Richafort and Verdelot respectively, and *Vulnerasti cor meum à* 4 on an anonymous motet first published by Petrucci in his *Motetti de la Corona* (Venice, 1514).[58] Not content with a thorough reworking of his model in the 'Credo' of two of his Masses, *Vulnerasti cor meum* and *Si bona suscepimus*, he states the Gregorian 'Credo' in mensuralized form in the *altus* and *bassus* I respectively, while the other voices continue with material from the motet. Peñalosa had done something similar in his *Missa Nunca fue pena mayor*,[59] but Morales quotes the Gregorian melody much more literally. This concern for preserving the exact shape of a borrowed melody is characteristic of Morales.[60]

Morales' surviving motets and hymn settings number about ninety,[61] of which more than half were published during his lifetime, chiefly in two collections issued at Venice in 1543 and 1546 respectively. In Spain they frequently appeared in intabulated versions, in the collections of Valder-rábano and Fuenllana, for example, but not in part-books. Morales set texts for every season of the Church's year, but whatever the mood or subject of the words he found an appropriate way to express it. One of his favourite devices was that of the expressive *ostinato*. In the six-part *Jubilate Deo omnis terra*,[62] written for the peace celebrations at Nice in 1538 and one of his earliest datable pieces, tenor I repeats the word *Gaudeamus* eighteen times to a six-note *ostinato* figure taken from the Gregorian introit *Gaudeamus omnes*. The second *altus* part in the six-part *Veni domine et noli tardare* repeats the words and music of the opening phrase five times in each half of the motet, a tone lower on each occasion; while in the five-part *Tu es Petrus*, *cantus* II has its opening phrase twenty times, beginning alternately on G and D.[63] But the most famous example is in the Ash Wednesday motet *Emendemus in melius*[64] when the tenor sings the words 'Remember, man, thou art dust and to dust thou shalt return' six times to the plainsong melody.

Morales' Marian motets include three settings of *Regina coeli laetare* (*à* 4, *à* 5 and *à* 6), and two of the *Salve Regina*, one polyphonic throughout and the other only partly so. The four-part setting of *Regina coeli laetare*,

---

58. All seven models are printed Anglès, *Morales*, iii and vi.

59. See p. 383.

60. Further on Morales' parody technique see Stevenson, *Cathedral*, pp. 77 ff.

61. Anglès, *Morales*, ii and v contain 50; the remainder are to appear in vols. viii and x as yet (1971) unpublished. Stevenson in *Grove*, v, 883–5 and *Die Musik in Geschichte und Gegenwart*, ix, 557–60 also attributes 14 anonymous motets in the collections of 1543 and 1546 to Morales.

62. Anglès, *Morales*, ii, 184.

63. See Anglès, *Morales*, v, 146 and ii, 149 respectively.

64. Printed in *HAM*, i, No. 128.

an *Ave Maria à* 5 and a setting of the hymn stanza *Salva nos stella*[65] all employ canon, and these works together with the *Missa Ave maris stella* suggest that Morales particularly wanted to lavish his technical skill on Marian texts. But perhaps his greatest technical feat is the canon in his setting of the hymn stanza *Solemnis urgebat dies* (Toledo Codex 25 fol. 62–3); the *cantus* repeats the notes of the *altus* but omits the rests. The canon symbolizes the 'rolling up of the world like a scroll on the day of judgement'.[66]

The most celebrated of Morales' works during his own century were the sixteen[67] *Magnificats* (Venice, 1545),[68] eight with the odd- and eight with the even-numbered verses set polyphonically in each of the eight tones. Five settings had been published by Scotto in 1542, and from then until the end of the century Morales' *Magnificats* were reprinted both singly and in groups many more times than his Masses or motets and also many more times than the *Magnificats* of any other European composer.[69] The basic texture is *à* 4, but there are some fourteen soloistic trios and two duos; and the *sicut erat* verse is always set *à* 6, usually with a canon based on the *cantus firmus.* Palestrina added extra voice parts to some of the verses.[70] The only one of Morales' larger-scale works to be published posthumously was the set of lamentations[71] (Venice, 1564, simultaneously by Gardano and Rampazetto). They are in a highly expressive homophonic style, but did not enjoy wide favour.

Morales seems to have written very little secular music: three Spanish pieces and one Italian madrigal are all that are definitely known to be his. Two other pieces sometimes ascribed to him are of doubtful authenticity. Although many features of his style are similar to those of his great Flemish contemporaries, in other ways his works reveal a composer of considerable originality. The work of Morales represents one of the peaks of the Golden Age and may be regarded as an important link between that of the generation of Josquin on the one hand and of Palestrina and Lassus on the other.

GUERRERO. A true evaluation of the music of Francisco Guerrero cannot be made until more of his works are available in modern reprints[72] and have been properly studied.[73] But when these conditions are fulfilled it seems likely that he will be seen to be almost the equal of Morales and Victoria.

65. Anglès, *Morales*, v, 135; ii, 75; and v, 101 respectively.

66. Further on this hymn see Stevenson, *Cathedral*, p. 106.

67. But see Stevenson, *Cathedral*, p. 83.

68. Anglès, *Morales*, iv. See also Parrish, *Treasury*, pp. 108 ff.

69. See Illing, *Magnificat-Komposition*, pp. 6 ff.

70. They can be seen in Anglès' edition. See Anglès, 'Magnificat'.

71. Not yet reprinted. It will be contained in vol. ix of the complete edition.

72. A complete edition is in progress under the editorship of Querol and García, but so far only two volumes have appeared.

73. The best study of Guerrero is in Stevenson, *Cathedral*, pp. 135 ff.; See also Mitjana, *Guerrero*; Anglès, 'Morales y Guerrero'; Trend, *Grove*, iii, 837 ff.

Born in 1528 at Seville, Guerrero was first taught by his brother, himself a composer of some distinction.[74] He became a singer at Seville Cathedral in 1542 under Fernández de Castilleja, and also studied under Morales, presumably on the latter's return to Spain in 1545. He was *maestro de capilla* at Jaen from 1546–9, but then returned to Seville and remained there until he died. In 1551 he was promised the post of *maestro* on Castilleja's death, but this did not occur until more than twenty years later. Guerrero visited Lisbon in 1566, Rome in 1582 and the Holy Land in 1588–9. He published an account of the last trip under the title *Viage de Hierusalem*, which enjoyed considerable popularity and was reprinted in both the seventeenth and eighteenth centuries.

Although Guerrero spent most of his life in Spain, his works were widely published and known abroad during his lifetime. Nine collections were issued under his personal supervision; these comprise two books of Masses (Paris 1566 and Rome 1582), four books of motets (Seville 1555; Venice 1570; Venice 1589; Venice 1597), a book of *Magnificats* (Louvain 1563), a *Liber vesperarum* (Rome 1584) and the *Canciones y villanescas espirituales* (Venice 1589). Other publications containing his music include two issued at Nürnberg (1591 and 1600), the *vihuela* tablatures of Fuenllana (1554) and Daza (1576), and Victoria's *Motecta festorum totius anni* (1585). Among the works surviving only in manuscript are a set of four Passions, one according to each of the evangelists.[75] Eighteen Masses by Guerrero are extant,[76] slightly fewer than the number left by Morales and Victoria, but his total of about one hundred and fifteen motets is considerably higher than that of the older composer and more than twice that of the younger. Victoria paid tribute to Guerrero by including two of his motets in his own *Motecta festorum totius anni* (1585) and also by basing his *Missa Simile est regnum coelorum* (1576) on Guerrero's four-voiced motet (1570) of that name. Others who published parody Masses based on his work include Géry de Ghersem (1598), Alonso Lobo (1602), Juan Esquivel (1608) and Duarte Lobo (1621).

Half of the eighteen Masses were published in the first book (1566), eight in the second (1582) and the remaining one in the motet collection of 1597.[77] Eleven are *à* 4, six *à* 5 and one *à* 6; unlike Victoria and Palestrina, Guerrero wrote no polychoral works. Two draw on secular models, the *Missa Dormendo un giorno* (1566) on Verdelot's madrigal *Dormend' un giorn' a Bai*, and the *Missa Della batalla escoutez* (1582) on Jannequin's *Bataille de Marignan*.

74. See Stevenson, *Cathedral*, p. 315, fn. 13 for biographical details. Two of his motets are printed in Elústiza, *Antología*, pp. 80 and 83.

75. See Anglès, 'Colombina', 33, but also Reese, *Renaissance*, p. 596.

76. An incomplete *Missa L'Homme Armé* reputed to exist at the Monasterio de Santa Clara at Ávila (see Trend in *Grove*, iii, 838 and Anglès, *NOHM*, iv, 390 for example) has not been found by Stevenson. See Stevenson, *Cathedral*, pp. 186–7.

77. Only two are available in reprints: the *Missa Beata Mater* (1566) *à* 4 in Bal y Gay, *Tesoro*, and the *Missa Puer qui natus* ... (1582) in Bordes, *Anthologie*, Messes, II, 159 ff.

About half the remainder are based on plainsong and the rest on motets. Those drawing on Gregorian chants include two *De Beata Virgine* Masses, and two *Requiems*. The 1566 *De Beata Virgine* Mass contains tropes in the 'Kyrie' and 'Gloria', whereas the 1582 version does not, perhaps as a result of the recommendations of the Council of Trent. In his two *Requiems* Guerrero, like Morales before him, alternates plainsong with polyphony in which the chant is in the top voice. The second version includes several movements not usually set polyphonically.

Among Guerrero's parody Masses on sacred models are *Congratulamini mihi* on Guillaume Le Heurteur's five-part motet of that name,[78] *Inter vestibulum* and *Sancta et immaculata*, both based on motets by Morales.[79] The chief characteristic of his parody technique, derived from Morales, is compression: very often he bases an entire movement or section on one or two motives, 'Kyrie I' of the *Missa Sancta et immaculata*, for example;[80] and even when he invents a motive of his own, he always makes sure it will fit with one of the models. He never actually quotes the whole polyphonic complex of his models, and it has been suggested recently[81] that 'permutation Mass' would be a better name for his works of this type.

Morales and Victoria both employed bitextuality in their Masses, but neither to the same extent as Guerrero. It occurs, for example, in the 'Benedictus' of the *Missa Sancta et immaculata*, in the 'Sanctus' and 'Osanna' of *Beata Mater*, as well as in the *Missa De Beata Virgine* from the *Liber primus*, and also in the 'Kyrie', 'Sanctus' and 'Agnus' of the *Missa Ecce sacerdos magnus* from the *Liber secundus*. Although bitextual Masses were rather old-fashioned by 1582, they remained popular in Spain until the beginning of the seventeenth century. Another device inherited from Morales was that of the unifying *ostinato*. Examples occur in the 'Sanctus' of *Sancta et immaculata* and *In te Domine speravi*, and in 'Agnus I' of *Congratulamini mihi* and *Della batalla escoutez*. In the 'Osanna' of the *Missa Beata Mater*, *ostinato* is combined with bitextuality: the *altus* sings an *ostinato* figure four times to the words *Beata Mater*. The 'Agnus' of the *Missa Simile est regnum* has an example of *ostinato* used with a symbolic purpose: the tenor sings a seven-note figure which is then repeated backwards with the words *Vado et venio ad vos* ('I go away and I am coming to you') written above, suggesting an association with Whit Sunday.[82] Several of Guerrero's Masses contain masterly canons, especially in the 'Agnus'; the final movement of the four-part *Missa Inter vestibulum*[83] for example, is

78. Printed Smyers, *Attaingnant*, iii, 104.
79. Anglès, *Morales*, ii, 24 and 17 respectively.
80. Printed in Stevenson, *Cathedral*, p. 197.
81. See Stevenson, *Cathedral*, p. 199.
82. See Stevenson, *Cathedral*, p. 190.
83. Printed in Stevenson, *Cathedral*, pp. 191 ff.

à 6 and employs a three-part canon, while still quoting the source-motet in the three other parts. In the *Missa Beata Mater* not only the final 'Agnus' (which is *à* 5) but also the 'Credo' is in canon.

It is on a few well-known motets by Guerrero that his reputation as *El cantor de Maria* and as a tuneful composer lacking in character and real expressive power has been largely based. This reputation is an unjust one. In the first place, more than three-fifths of his motets have nothing whatever to do with Marian subjects, and in the second place, the great majority of them are more than merely melodious and graceful. They do indeed demonstrate that same mastery of counterpoint evident in his Masses.

Guerrero makes more use of canon in his motets than either Morales or Victoria. His first collection of 1555, for example, opens with eight motets *à* 5, the first in canon at the unison, the next at the second and so on through to the *octavo*. In each case the canon is used to express the idea of following, returning or sending, and in certain ones the interval is also suggested by the text. In *Ambulans Jesu*, for example, the canon is at the second because Jesus saw 'two' brothers, and in *Et post dies sex* it is at the sixth. Another setting in this collection, the *Pater noster à* 8, also published in the *Liber primus missarum*, is composed of four canonic pairs, and can be regarded as one of his greatest technical feats. Sometimes, as in *Ave Virgo sanctissima*,[84] the canon is so skilfully handled as to be almost unnoticeable. This famous motet was published three times during Guerrero's lifetime, in the collections of 1566, 1570 and 1597. Although it does not employ the plainsong melody which is associated with the text, at the words *maris stella* and *salve*, motives from the *Ave maris stella* and the *Salve Regina* respectively are quoted.

Guerrero made much less of *ostinato* in his motets than in his Masses. One of the few examples is *Veni Domine et noli tardare à* 5, which had already been set *à* 6 by Morales with a similar *ostinato* figure. In his use of madrigalesque symbolism he anticipates Victoria: in several motets, for instance, he changes the metre from duple to triple to illustrate the text, or employs all black notes to represent night or death. In the later collections there is a greater concern for expressiveness, perhaps because of the influence of the madrigal: it manifests itself, for example, in the intense *O Domine Jesu Christe* (1589). Guerrero was equally capable of writing in a brilliant and joyful style, as is illustrated by *Pastores loquebantur*, one of his two motets published by Victoria in his *Motecta festorum totius anni* of 1585.[85] The 1563 collection contains one *Magnificat* setting on each of the eight tones with even verses set polyphonically, mostly *à* 4. They do not differ significantly in style from those of Morales.

84. Printed Elústiza, *Antología*, pp. 89 ff. and elsewhere.

85. Printed Pedrell, *Victoria*, i, 142. Additional motets by Guerrero are contained in Elústiza, *Antología* and Rubio, *Antología*. See also *HAM*, i, No. 149.

Neither Morales nor Victoria produced any settings of Spanish words to equal those of Guerrero contained in his *Canciones y villanescas espirituales* of 1589.[86] The word *villanesca* was sometimes equated with *villancico* in the sixteenth century, especially if the poem or the music was regarded as Italianate in character, but its use was far from consistent. Guerrero's collection contains sixty-one songs: thirty-three *à* 5, twenty *à* 4 and eight *à* 3, in that order. In the prologue, which was written by Miguel de Figuera, we are told that a number of the pieces were secular in origin, and that only the words were changed. Twenty of these secular originals have been traced, and in all but two cases the words have been altered to a greater or lesser extent.[87] The music is very similar although there are a number of rhythmic changes, and a great many accidentals implied in the earlier version have been added. These rhythmic changes are interesting in that they provide a rare illustration of how a sixteenth-century composer matched music to words. Figuera tells us also that the songs were composed at the beginning of Guerrero's career, and certainly the only piece that has been dated so far cannot have been composed later than 1554.

The collection is well ordered: each of the three groups (that is, of pieces *à* 5, *à* 4 and *à* 3) is further sub-divided into songs without refrains and songs with refrains. Pieces of the first group are through-composed and rarely contain any kind of repetition, while those of the second are all *da capo* or *dal segno villancicos*. Stylistically the types are different too. Songs of the first type often contain changes of emotion or viewpoint, and correspondingly bold harmony, while the others tend to maintain one mood throughout. Again, it is common for the whole or part of a song of the second type to employ triple metre, while those of the first are all in duple time. The stanza proper is usually scored for fewer voices than the refrain and is sometimes a solo. The most common modes are pure or transposed Ionian or Dorian, though others, especially the Phrygian, are used from time to time to express particularly strong emotions.

Guerrero's *Canciones y villanescas espirituales* contains some of the finest settings of Spanish vernacular texts by any sixteenth-century Spanish composer, and its contents were widely imitated by his successors.

VICTORIA. Tomás Luis de Victoria (born at Ávila in *c.* 1548, died at Madrid in 1611)[88] became a choirboy at Ávila Cathedral about 1558 and served under three choirmasters, Gerónimo de Espinar, Bernadino de

86. Printed Querol and García, *Guerrero*, i and ii.
87. Six of these secular originals have been published in Querol, *Cancionero*. Compare Nos. 34, 36, 38, 40, 42 and 54 in the *Canciones y villanescas espirituales* with Nos. 79, 44, 90 and 59 in the Medinaceli songbook.
88. See especially Stevenson, *Cathedral*, pp. 345 ff.; Casimiri, 'Vittoria', Pedrell, *Victoria*, Collet, *Victoria*.

Ribera and Juan Navarro. He may also have come into contact with Antonio Cabezón, who was a frequent visitor to the town, and Escobedo. In 1565 he entered the Jesuit Collegium Germanicum, a seminary founded at Rome in 1552 by St Ignatius de Loyola, primarily to train missionaries to combat Lutheranism. Nearby was the Roman seminary founded in 1564 by Pope Pius v: Palestrina was its *maestro di capilla* while his sons were being educated there from 1566 to 1571, and in view of the close relationship that existed between the two colleges it is probable that Victoria came under his direct influence. From 1569 to 1574 Victoria was *cantor y sonador del órgano* at the Aragonese church of S. Maria di Monserrato,[89] and from 1573 he also sang occasionally at the other Spanish church in Rome, S Giacomo degli Spagnoli. In 1571 he became a teacher at the German seminary, and in the same year or soon after took over Palestrina's old post at the Collegium Romanum. The two colleges were reorganized by Gregory xiii in 1573 as separate institutions, Victoria becoming *maestro* of the German college. He took orders in 1575 and left the seminary in 1578 for the position of chaplain at the church of S Girolamo della Carità, where he enjoyed daily contact with St Philip Neri. In the dedication of his *Missarum libri duo* (1583) addressed to Philip ii, Victoria writes that he is weary as a result of devoting himself so whole-heartedly to composition, and proposes to return to Spain to lead a quiet, priestly life. The precise date of his return is not known, but it was certainly not later than 1587, in which year he was already serving as chaplain to the widowed Empress María, who was living in retirement with her daughter, the Infanta Margaret, at the Monasterio de las Descalzas de Santa Clara at Madrid. He also served as *maestro* of the convent's choir of boys and men until the Empress died in 1603, and as organist from 1604 until his death.

Most of Victoria's publications were issued in Italy. They comprise three books of motets (Venice, 1572; Rome, 1583 and 1585), a set of *Magnificats* (Rome, 1581), a collection of hymns (Rome, 1583), an Office for Holy Week (Rome, 1585), a *Requiem* (Madrid, 1605), one book of Masses (Rome, 1592), and two miscellaneous collections (Venice, 1576; Madrid, 1600), the first including five Masses, the second, four. Besides the Offices for the Dead (1605) and for Holy Week (1585) and a Litany of the Blessed Virgin, his works comprise twenty Masses, about forty-five motets, some thirty-four hymns, sixteen *Magnificats* for four voices and two polychoral ones, ten Marian antiphons, three sequences and seven psalms.[90] A *Missa Dominicalis* and the hymn *Jesu dulcis memoria* included in Pedrell's complete edition are

---

89. He would almost certainly have trained the choir as well.

90. There are two complete editions of Victoria's works, Pedrell, *Victoria*, which contains a number of errors, and Anglès, *Victoria*, as yet incomplete. See also Rubio, *Antología*, ii. On Victoria's music, see especially Stevenson, *Cathedral*, pp. 373 ff.; May, *Kompositionstechnik*; Reese, *Renaissance*, pp. 600 ff.; Wagner, *Messe*, i, 42 ff.; Leichtentritt, *Motette*, pp. 372 ff.

spurious. Victoria wrote no secular music, and even the total of his sacred compositions is small compared to that of Palestrina, but if he did not rival him in quantity, he certainly equalled him in quality.

To a large extent Victoria's reputation both during his lifetime and since has rested upon the *Motecta*, published in 1572 when he was only twenty-four years old. It contained nearly thirty motets, including such celebrated examples as *O quam gloriosum*, *O magnum mysterium*, *Vere languores nostros* and *O vos omnes*. The remainder were mostly published in the collections of 1576, 1583 and 1585 while he was still under forty, and the comparatively early date of nearly all his motets perhaps explains why so many (over half) are for four voices while only two are for eight.

Victoria was a deeply sensitive man, and his greatness as a composer lies in his ability to translate his response to words into music. Although commanding a superb mastery of technique, he always chose the simplest means of expression that would suit his purpose, and only used learned devices when they were suggested by the text. Some of his most poignant motets indeed are among the simplest: *Vere languores nostros* and *O vos omnes*, for example.[91] In the interest of expressiveness he sometimes used intervals such as the ascending diminished fourth and the ascending major sixth, which were avoided by Palestrina, and also made great use of word-painting and other madrigalian devices. Very few of Victoria's motets make even a passing reference to plainsong, but in one, *Iste Sanctus*,[92] a Gregorian chant is used symbolically. The double canon which runs throughout *Trahe me post te*[93] also has an obvious symbolical significance.

In his hymns Victoria, like Guerrero, set the even verses, while Palestrina set the odd ones. He differs from both of them, however, in that he never goes beyond four parts and never concludes with a canonic stanza. The Office for Holy Week is also mainly *à* 4, with a reduction to three voices in the eighteen responsories. It includes simple but effective settings of the *turba* passages from the Passions of Saints Matthew and John.

Victoria's psalm settings are all polychoral: *Laetatus sum* (1583) is for three choirs; the rest for two. Two were published in 1576, three in 1583 and one each in 1585 and 1600. As in all Victoria's polychoral works chorus I is accompanied by organ, but choruses II and III were apparently left unaccompanied. Very little reference is made to the Gregorian psalm tones. His Marian antiphons comprise four settings of *Salve Regina* (1572 *à* 6, 1576 *à* 5, 1576 *à* 8 and 1581 *à* 8) and two of *Alma Redemptoris Mater* (1572 *à* 5, 1581 *à* 8) and *Regina coeli* (1572 *à* 5, 1576 *à* 8). He tends to quote the Gregorian chant in inner parts in the 1572 versions and in the top voice in the later settings. The six-part *Salve Regina* pays tribute to Morales in that

91. Pedrell, *Victoria*, i, 24 and 27 and Anglès, *Victoria*, ii, 14 and 17 respectively.
92. Pedrell, *Victoria*, i, 43; Anglès, *Victoria*, iv, 26.
93. Pedrell, *Victoria*, i, 140.

it employs an *ostinato* figure. Victoria's other polychoral works consist of three sequence settings, *Lauda Sion* (1585), *Veni Sancte Spiritus* (1600) and *Victimae Paschali* (1600), and two *Magnificats*, one for two choirs, the other for three, both published in 1600.[94] All twelve verses are set polyphonically, whereas in the earlier set of sixteen *à* 4, published complete in 1581, half are set on the odd- and half only the even-numbered verses. They contain a considerable variety of scoring: one of the central verses is usually *à* 3, whereas the last is often *à* 5 or *à* 6 and includes a canon.

Of Victoria's twenty Masses, *Ave maris stella*, *De Beata Virgine* and the two *Requiems* draw on the customary plainsong melodies; the *Missa Quarti toni* appears to be freely composed; *Simile est regnum coelorum*, *Gaudeamus* and *Surge propera* are based on motets by Guerrero, Morales, and Palestrina respectively; the *Missa Pro Victoria* on Jannequin's *La Bataille de Marignan* and the remaining eleven Masses on compositions by Victoria himself. There are fifteen parody Masses, four paraphrase and one that appears to be freely composed; seven are *à* 4, four *à* 5, four *à* 6, three *à* 8, one *à* 9 and one *à* 12.

In no other branch of composition can we study Victoria's development as well as in the Masses. Leaving aside the 1605 *Requiem*, we can see that, unlike Palestrina, Victoria followed the progressive trends of his day. His 1576 collection contains two four-part Masses, while his 1600 one has none for fewer than eight voices; eight Masses published before 1600 conclude with a canonic 'Agnus', but not one in the 1600 publication does: bitextuality appears in the *Missae Ave maris stella* and *Gaudeamus*,[95] but not thereafter. Another way in which Victoria advanced was in his choice of modes: in the first three books, Dorian or Hypodorian predominate, whereas in the last book all four masses are in F major. Triple metre, which was not used at all in the early Masses, such as *Ave maris stella* and *Dum complerentur*,[96] is very common in the polychoral Masses. Another important difference is one of length: the *Missa Dum complerentur* has 657 bars, while twelve of the later Masses have fewer than 500. The chief reason for this is the gradual trend towards homophony; in the *Missa Pro Victoria*,[97] for example, he actually uses fewer imitative points than Jannequin. In the polychoral masses there is an occasional suggestion of *parlando*. His treatment of source-material changed considerably too: whereas in the early Masses he normally began each movement with the opening of his model, in the later Masses he sometimes chose to make use of subsequent sections of his source. There is also a greater quantity of purely free writing in the later examples. In one respect,

94. These works are all printed in Pedrell, *Victoria*, as follows: Hymns, v, 1–108; Office for Holy Week, v, 111–200; Psalms, vii, 1–67; Marian antiphons, vii, 68–130; Sequences, vii, 135–50; Magnificats, iii, 81–106.

95. Printed Pedrell, *Victoria*, ii, 1 ff., iv, 1 ff. and Anglès, *Victoria*, i, 1 ff., i, 99 ff. respectively.

96. Pedrell, *Victoria*, iv, 29 ff.; Anglès, *Victoria*, iii, 87 ff.

97. Pedrell, *Victoria*, vi, 26 ff.

however, Victoria did not change: he always based his parody Masses on compositions with joyful texts. The later Masses may lack the mystical quality of his earlier works, but they are imbued with the same spirit of love and of trust in God which is characteristic of all his music.

SOME MINOR CHURCH COMPOSERS. Besides Morales, Guerrero and Victoria there were of course a great many lesser Spanish composers of church music during the sixteenth century. They include Bartolomé de Escobedo (b. 1510, d. 1563), Pedro de Pastrana (d. after 1559), Juan Navarro (*c.* 1530–80), Rodrigo de Ceballos (or Zaballos), Fernando de las Infantas (1534–1608), Juan Ginés Pérez (1548–1612), Sebastián de Vivanco (*c.* 1550–1622), Alonso Lobo (1555–1617), Juan Esquivel de Barahona (fl. 1608), and Juan Pujol (d. 1626). Escobedo joined Morales at the papal chapel in 1536 and remained there until 1554, when he became *maestro de capilla* at Segovia, but otherwise most of these men spent their working lives in Spain. Infantas and Navarro managed to get collections of their work published at Venice and Rome respectively and some, among them Esquivel, Vivanco and Lobo, at Salamanca or Madrid, but others such as Ceballos and Pérez were less fortunate and their compositions remained in manuscript form. Except in number and quality the works of these men differ little from those of their greater contemporaries.[98]

SECULAR POLYPHONY. Secular polyphony in Spain continued to flourish alongside church music throughout the century. Both the *villancico* and the madrigal were cultivated, though the latter was not adopted in Spain as thoroughly as it was in England. Juan Vásquez however was an outstanding master of both forms, and enjoys the distinction of having had his secular compositions published, a rare honour in mid-sixteenth-century Spain.[99] The *Villancicos i Canciones . . . a 3 y a 4* was issued at Osuna in 1551 and the *Recopilación de sonetos y villancicos a 4 y a 5* at Seville in 1560, both in part books.[100] His works show a great mastery of the Italian madrigal technique with their frequent changes of texture and mood and are fully worthy to stand beside those of his Italian contemporaries. The first seven pieces in the *Recopilación* may be taken as representative. Some are simple *villancicos* after the manner of CMP, whereas others are considerably developed and seem closer to the freer form of the madrigal. The refrain now often occurs only at the beginning and end and even then the second appearance is frequently varied, sometimes quite extensively. Several of Vásquez's *villancicos*, in accordance with the practice of the time, seem to draw on

---

98. Further see Stevenson, *Cathedral*. Compositions by several of them may be found in Elústiza, *Antología*; Rubio, *Antología*.

99. For details of his life, see Anglès, *Vásquez*, p. 9 ff. (text) and Reese, *Renaissance*, p. 612.

100. The *Recopilación* is reprinted complete in Anglès, *Vásquez*. See especially Russell, *Villancicos*.

pre-existent material, presumably folk-song. *Dizen a mí*, for example, appears in both the *Recopilación* and the *Cancionero de Upsala* with the same words and the same basic melody, but the two compositions are in other ways so different that they must be independent.[101] The popularity of Vásquez is attested by the number of times his pieces were transcribed by the *vihuelistas*.

Joan Brudieu although born in France spent most of his life in Catalonia and should be mentioned here. A collection of sixteen of his madrigals was issued in part books at Barcelona in 1585, dedicated to the Duke of Savoy.[102] Five have Catalan words and the rest Castilian. Pedro Alberch Vila's madrigal collection of 1561 contained settings of texts in Spanish, Catalan, Italian and French, but unfortunately only the *altus* part survives, so we are unable to form much impression of the music.[103] Mateo Flecha the elder (*c.* 1481–*c.* 1533) and his nephew Mateo Flecha the younger (*c.* 1520–1604) are chiefly remembered for a publication issued at Prague in 1581 entitled *Las Ensaladas de Flecha*.[104] Several of the *ensaladas* are found in tablature in Fuenllana's *Orphenica lyra* (1554) and others survive in manuscripts at the Biblioteca Central in Barcelona. The *ensalada* was a kind of medley or potpourri based on a textual quodlibet with dramatic, amusing or satirical words. Musically the pieces resemble Jannequin's programme *chansons*.

Other Spanish composers who had collections of madrigals devoted solely to them include Valenzuela, Raval and Rimonte, all of whom spent much of their lives abroad. A great many others are represented in a variety of miscellaneous collections which include MSS 13230 and 13231 in the Medinaceli Library at Madrid,[105] the *Cancionero* of Turin, the *Romances y letras de a tres vozes*, manuscripts in the Biblioteca Nacional in Madrid and the *Cancionero* of the scribe Claudio de Sablonara.[106]

THE VIHUELISTAS. Our knowledge of instrumental music before 1500 is largely confined to the names of instruments and performers.[107] Two instruments especially appear to have grown in popularity during the fifteenth century: the organ[108] and the *vihuela de mano*. The name *vihuela* was used for bowed and plucked instruments of both Spanish and foreign type during the fifteenth and sixteenth centuries but with the addition of

101. Compare Mitjana, *Cancioniero*, p. 130 with Anglès, *Vásquez*, p. 118.

102. Reprinted in Pedrell, *Brudieu*.

103. For two keyboard pieces by him see Anglès, *Carlos V*, pp. 43, 45.

104. See Anglès, *Flecha*. Further on the *ensaladas*, see *NOHM*, iv, 407–8; Reese, *Renaissance*, pp. 615–16.

105. The contents of MS 13230 have been reprinted in Querol, *Cancionero*.

106. Reprinted in Aroca, *Cancionero*. Further on secular polyphony in Spain see Reese, *Renaissance*, pp. 612–17.

107. See p. 379.

108. See Anglès, 'Orgelmusik' and 'Cantores i organistes'.

de mano; *de arco* or *de Flandes* had a more specific meaning. The *vihuela de mano* was similar to the *guitarra* in shape, but had six courses and was tuned like the lute; *vihuela de arco* denoted the viol family and *vihuela de Flandes*, the lute.[109]

The success of the *vihuela de mano* is attested by the number of books for it that were published – some seven out of a total of only seventeen musical publications for the whole century.[110] The earliest of them was Luis Milán's *Libro de música de vihuela de mano intitulado El Maestro*, published at Valencia in 1536; it was followed by Luis de Narváez's *Los Seys libros del Delphín de música* (Valladolid, 1538), Alonso de Mudarra's *Tres libros de música* (Seville, 1546), Enrique Enriquez de Valderrábano's *Libro de música de vihuela intitulado Silva de Sirenas* (Valladolid, 1547),[111] Diego Pisador's *Libro de música de vihuela* (Salamanca, 1552), Miguel de Fuenllana's *Orphenica lyra* (Seville, 1554)[112] and Estéban Daza's *El Parnasso* (Valladolid, 1576).[113]

The volumes contain a wide variety of music, some for *vihuela* alone, the rest for voice and *vihuela*. The first group contains *fantasías*, *tientos*, variations, dances and intabulations of Masses, motets or secular music, and the second, *romances*, *villancicos*, *sonetos*, *canciones* and a few pieces with Latin words. All the collections contain *fantasías*; the forty examples by Milán consist mostly of chords, sometimes enlivened by scale passages, whereas those by Narváez are much more contrapuntal. Later composers hovered between these two extremes: Pisador left examples of both types, whereas Valderrábano in his original *fantasías* achieved a sort of compromise. Fuenllana, like Valderrábano, may have based some of his *fantasías* on vocal pieces. The *tiento* was a short improvisatory piece: there are four examples by Milán,[114] but it was not extensively cultivated by later composers. The four sets of variations called *diferencias* contained in Narváez's *Delphín de música* are among the first published examples of the type. They comprise two on sacred themes, *O gloriosa Domina* and *Sacris solemniis*,[115] and two on the famous Spanish popular melodies, *Conde claros* and *Guárdame las vacas*.[116] The first two are examples of the sectional variation, and the

109. See Salazar, 'Laúd'; Ward, *Vihuela*; 'Lute'; Pujol, *Narváez*, pp. 7–9 (text).

110. See Ward, *Mus. Disc.* (1952) 106.

111. These four volumes have been reprinted: Schrade, *Milán* (another recent edition is Jacobs, *Milán*; see also *HAM*, i, No. 121; Schering, *Geschichte* No. 96); Pujol, *Narváez* (see also *HAM*, i, No. 122); Pujol, *Mudarra*; Pujol, *Valderrábano*.

112. See Riemann, 'Lautenwerk' and Pedrell, *Catàlech*, for a list and description of contents. See also *HAM*, i, No. 123; Schering, *Geschichte*, p. 114; Heartz, *MQ* (1963) 62.

113. Morphy, *Luthistes* contains several excerpts from each of the books and there are also a number of smaller anthologies including Bal y Gay, *Romances* and Villalba Muñoz, *Canciones*. Unfortunately none of the transcriptions is wholly reliable. See also Apel, *Musik*, ii, 12 ff.

114. One of them printed *HAM*, i, No. 121.

115. Pujol, *Narváez*, pp. 41 and 51 respectively. See also *HAM*, i, No. 122.

116. Pujol, *Narváez*, pp. 82 and 85 respectively. See also Apel, *Musik*, ii, 14.

second two of the continuous variation or ground. All the late *vihuelistas* wrote variations on *Conde claros* and *Guárdame las vacas*, Valderrábano as many as 123 on the former.[117] The few dances in the collection are mostly *pavanes*, sometimes with variations: two examples, one by Valderrábano, the other by Pisador, are of particular interest on account of the similarity of their basses to the *folia* bass.[118] Milán is the only composer not to include intabulations in his collection. Narváez and Mudarra include relatively few, but they form the bulk of the publications of Valderrábano, Fuenllana and Pisador. The precise notation of the tablature provides an important clue to the application of *musica ficta* in the vocal original.[119]

The songs of the *vihuelistas* represent the largest surviving corpus of sixteenth-century accompanied song. They continue the homophonic tendencies present in the *frottola*, which had gone underground in Italy after its decline, finally to emerge triumphant at the turn of the century. Many of the Spanish songs consist of a vocal part almost entirely in long notes, though some of these were meant to be discreetly ornamented against a pseudo-polyphonic or, less usually, a chordal or figurative accompaniment. The *vihuela* tablature often includes the vocal line (sometimes distinguished by red ink) but whether the player actually doubled that line is a matter of some controversy.[120] Many songs offer examples of variation technique. Sometimes the first statement is easy for the *vihuela*, giving the voice an opportunity for embellishment, whereas in the second version it is the *vihuela* to which the ornamentation is assigned.[121] More extensive and masterly variations are to be found among those which Narváez wrote on various *villancico* melodies,[122] whereas other songs in the collections provide good examples of internal variation.[123] There are of course many other aspects of this repertoire beside the variation technique which deserve study.[124] It should be remembered, however, that some of the manuals were 'teach yourself' books and not primarily compiled as repositories of enduring works of art.

Mudarra, in his collection of 1546, included six pieces for four-course guitar; and Fuenllana, in 1554, several for both the four- and the five-course

117. Pujol, *Valderrábano*, pp. 75 ff.

118. Further on the *folia* bass see chapter 5, p. 250. The Valderrábano *pavane* is printed Pujol, *Valderrábano*, p. 65.

119. See Fox, 'Accidentals' and Ward, *JAMS* (1952) 88.

120. For a discussion of this see *NOHM*, iv, 128 ff.

121. For an example see Schrade, *Milán*, 1967 edn., pp. 145–55, 345–59 (1927 edn., pp. 72–7, 172–9); Jacobs, *Milán*, pp. 109–23, 254–72.

122. See Pujol, *Narváez*, pp. 61–76; *NOHM*, iv, 138 f.

123. For instance, Pujol, *Mudarra*, p. 119, bars 1–8, 35–42, 50–5.

124. See Pujol, *Mudarra*, pp. 84–119; Pujol, *Narváez*, 58–61, 76–82, Pujol, *Valderrábano*, pp. 4–53; Schrade, *Milán*, 1967 edn. pp. 155–75, 359–78 (1927 edn. pp. 77–87, 179–89); Jacobs, *Milán*, pp. 124–46, 273–92.

instrument.[125] The latter, the so-called Spanish guitar, rapidly gained in popularity and in time completely supplanted the *vihuela*.

KEYBOARD MUSIC. Apart from a few manuscripts, only two printed collections of sixteenth-century Spanish organ music survive: the *Libro de Cifra Nueva para tecla, harpa y vihuela* (Alcalá de Henares, 1557), edited by Luis Venegas de Henestrosa,[126] and the *Obras de Música para Tecla Harpa y Vihuela de Antonio de Cabezón* (Madrid, 1578) published by Hernando de Cabezón and devoted almost entirely to the compositions of his father.[127] The word *tecla* means 'keyboard', and it is probable that the collections were intended for performance on the harpsichord as well as on the organ, harp and *vihuela*. Both employ the same tablature which, unlike the *vihuela* tablature, is unique to Spain;[128] Henestrosa's collection comprises 138 compositions, of which twenty-eight are *tientos*, twenty-three *himnos*, twenty *fabordones* and nineteen *fantasías de vihuela*. The remaining forty-eight pieces include *canciones*, *romances*, *salmos*, motets and *villancicos*. In addition to straightforward intabulations, there are several varied or decorated versions known as *glosas* (the Spanish term for glosses).[129] The nineteen *fantasías* and two *fabordones de vihuela* which are without ascription in Henestrosa's collection, are taken from the *vihuela* tablatures of Mudarra, Narváez and Valderrábano,[130] with one exception. This is a *fantasía* by Francesco da Milano, first published in his *Terzo libro* at Venice in 1547. Some of Henestrosa's transcriptions are fairly faithful, but others omit sections or odd bars of the original, and a few even combine material from two different pieces. He also altered compositions originally intended for the keyboard, which makes it impossible to be certain of any of his texts. The collection does however contain works by leading keyboard composers of the day such as Francisco Pérez Palero, Pedro Alberch Vila and Pedro de Soto, of whom we would otherwise know very little, and it must be regarded as one of the most important sources of the period.

Nearly forty pieces in Henestrosa's collection are attributed to Antonio, who we may be certain is none other than Antonio de Cabezón: in MS 242 at Coimbra University, indeed, several of them actually bear the full ascription.[131] Born in 1510 at Matajudios near Burgos, Cabezón[132] became blind while still a child. In 1521 his family moved to Palencia, and Antonio probably studied music there with the cathedral organist until 1526, in

125. See Koczirz, *AfMW* (1922) 241.
126. Reprinted in Anglès, *Carlos V*. Excerpts in Pedrell, *Antologia*.
127. Anglès, *Cabezón*. Excerpts in Kastner, *Cabezón*, and Apel, *Musik*, ii, 17 ff.
128. See Kinkeldey, *Orgel*, pp. 20 ff.; Apel, *Notation*, pp. 47 ff.
129. See Anglès, *Carlos V*, pp. 170 ff.
130. See Ward, *Mus. Disc.* (1952) 111 f.
131. See Kastner, 'Manuscritos'.
132. See Kastner, *Cabezón*.

which year he was appointed organist, and clavichordist to the Empress Isabella. During frequent visits with the court to Valladolid, Cabezón came into contact with Tomás de Santa María and Narváez, and after his marriage, which took place about 1538, he lived in the same parish as St Teresa and Victoria at Ávila. The Empress died in 1539, but Cabezón continued in the service of the royal children until 1548, when he became exclusively Philip's organist. He accompanied Philip on his travels between 1548 and 1556, and must have met a great many important foreign musicians. About 1560 he moved to Madrid, where he died in 1566.

Cabezón was one of the finest and most influential keyboard composers of the sixteenth century. As early as 1539 Cristóbal de Villalón wrote that he achieved 'perfection in music', and recently some scholars have compared his music with that of Bach. His works comprise twenty-nine *tientos*, thirty-two hymns, nine settings of the 'Kyrie', three sets of versets, nine sets of variations, numerous *glosas* of both sacred and secular compositions and a variety of other pieces.[133] The *tiento*, like its Italian counterpart the *ricercare*,[134] had its origin in the motet, and consists of a series of overlapping points of imitation. Its themes are usually related, though not in an immediately obvious way.

Particularly fine examples of Cabezón's *tientos* are No. XLIV in Henestrosa's collection and the *Fuga al contrario* in the *Obras*.[135] A few *tientos* are more lively in character with sprightly themes, dotted rhythms, triplets and passages of figuration; perhaps the best example of this type is the *Tiento del primer tono*.[136] Cabezón's mastery of counterpoint is equally evident in his hymn settings, which include several of *Ave maris stella* and *Pange lingua*. Two of the latter are based on Wrede's setting: one follows the original fairly closely, the other more freely.[137] The three sets of versets comprise two for the psalmody and one for the *Magnificat*;[138] the former have four versions for each tone and the latter six or seven. They were used for the even verses in alternation to the plainsong verses sung by the choir. The nine sets of 'Kyries' for organ comprise one in each of the eight tones and one *Rex virginum* set.[139] Cabezón's nine sets of continuous variations include three on *Guárdame las vacas* and three which use the *folia* bass;[140] *La Dama le demanda* and two called *Pavana italiana*, the second of which

133. For an index of pieces in Henestrosa's collection see Anglès, *Carlos V* pp. vi–viii and of those in the *Obras*, see Anglès, *Cabezón*, i, 29–31.

134. See chapter 4.1, pp. 237 and 250.

135. Anglès: *Carlos V*, pp. 54 ff. and *Cabezón*, ii, 90 ff. or Schering, *Geschichte*, p. 113, respectively. Howell, *MQ* (1964) 18 contains a detailed analysis of the former.

136. Anglès, *Cabezón*, ii, 78.

137. Compare Anglès, *Cabezón*, ii, 119 and 47 respectively with Gerber, *Hymnar*, p. 117.

138. Anglès, *Cabezón*, i, 31 ff., i, 48 ff. and ii, 7 ff. respectively.

139. Anglès, *Cabezón*, ii, 40 ff. and i, 18 ff. respectively.

140. All six are printed in Anglès, *Cabezón*, iii.

uses the same melody as *La Dama le demanda*.[141] Together with some of the
pavanes in the *vihuela* tablature, they are among the earliest compositions
to use the *folia* bass.

TREATISES. A considerable amount of instrumental music is preserved in
three treatises of the period, those of Diego Ortiz, Juan Bermudo and
Tomás de Santa Maria. Ortiz's *Tratado de glosa sobre clausulas* (Rome
1553)[142] consists almost entirely of musical examples and gives us some idea
of the richness of the repertoire for the bowed *vihuela*. The first book deals
with the ornamentation of cadential phrases in polyphonic music and the
second with three types of piece accompanied by the harpsichord: *ricercari*,
arrangements of madrigals or *chansons*, and variations above either sacred
or secular *bassi ostinati*. Among the *ostinati* which Ortiz uses are the *passamezzo antico*, the *passamezzo moderno*, the *romanesca* and the *folia*. The art
of adding an elaborate fifth part for *vihuela* to a *chanson* enjoyed a brief
flowering and then died, but the *ricercare* and variation survived Ortiz by
more than a century.

   The art of improvisation is discussed even more thoroughly in Santa
Maria's *Arte de Tañer fantasía assí para tecla como para vihuela* ... (Valladolid, 1565)[143] which deals with instrumental technique in general and with
that of the keyboard and *vihuela* in particular. The text is amply illustrated
with examples, some of which are by Santa María himself. They include
short fugal compositions in each of the church modes, in which two subjects
are treated in succession suggesting embryonic *ricercari*. Bermudo's
Declaración de instrumentos musicales (Osuna, 1549, enlarged edition
1555)[144] is a highly comprehensive book dealing with every aspect of learning
an instrument, and includes a number of musical examples which show him
to have been a composer of individuality.[145] He also discusses keyboard
tablature and recommends a system in which each of the notes is numbered
beginning at one with the lowest. Each part has its own line on which the
numbers are written. A similar but simpler system in which the notes of the
diatonic scale are numbered one to seven, and the octave shown by a variety
of modifications of the digits, was used by Henestrosa and Cabezón.[146]

   141. The first *Pavana Italiana* has the same tune as one known in Elizabethan England as 'The
Spanish Pavan'.
   142. Reprinted Schneider, *Ortiz*.
   143. See Froidebise, *Santa Maria*.
   144. See Froidebise, *Bermudo*.
   145. See Stevenson, *Bermudo*, for discussion of various important aspects of Bermudo's contribution
to our knowledge of sixteenth-century music.
   146. See Kinkeldey, *Orgel*, pp. 20 ff.; Apel, *Notation*, pp. 47 ff. On Spanish keyboard music in general
see Jacobs, *Interpretación*.

There are two other important Spanish theoretical works of the period, the *De musica libri septem* (Salamanca, 1577)[147] by Francisco Salinas (1513–90) and *El Melopeo y Maestro* (*The Art of Music and Instructor*) (Naples, 1613)[148] by the Italian Domenico Pietro Cerone (born at Bergamo in 1566). Salinas, who was blind from infancy, spent over twenty years in Italy, returned to Spain in 1561 and took up the chair of music at Salamanca, his old university, in 1566, remaining in this post for twenty-one years. The *De musica* is mostly based on Zarlino, but has a particularly interesting final section in which he illustrates his theories on rhythm and metre by reference to folk song.[149] Cerone joined the chapel of Philip II in 1592 and continued to serve under Philip II until 1608, when he was transferred to the Chapel Royal at Naples. *El Melopeo*, which was written in Spanish, besides having several excellent sections on the art of composition, contains some interesting opinions on the musical life of the period, including a strong criticism of Spanish patronage of music.

147. Kastner, *Salinas* is a facsimile edition.
148. See Strunk, *Readings*, pp. 263 ff. for an excerpt in English.
149. See further Trend, *ML* (1927) 13.

GERALD ABRAHAM

9 The Slav Countries: From the Beginnings to 1600

INTRODUCTION

We know extremely little about the music of the Slavs before their conversion to Christianity. Presumably the Slavonic '*kitharas*' and 'eight-
stringed lutes' mentioned in Byzantine and Arabic sources were what the
Slavs themselves called *gusli* (at that period a vague word). They had *bubnï*
(drums or tambourines), long pipes (perhaps like the large Bulgarian *kaval*
which still survives), horns and other instruments. We know that music
played a part in their religious ceremonies and that they celebrated the deeds
of their ancestors with games and songs. As much might be said of any
people in their state of culture; and, while it is true that references to pagan
rites survived in the words of folk-songs until the nineteenth century, this
tells us how the songs originated but not what they were like twelve centuries earlier. Even after Christianization we at first know little about the
music of the Slavs, but the manner of their Christianization was to have the
most far-reaching consequences for their musical development. It proceeded in the first place from Byzantium when, in 863, Michael III des-
patched the missionary brothers Cyril and Methodius to Rostislav of
Moravia, armed with the Slavonic alphabet invented by Cyril; they collided
with Roman priests from Germany and suffered various vicissitudes, but for

a short period the use of a vernacular Slavonic liturgy was actually agreed to by the pope. Yet Rome triumphed in the end. The Hungarian invasion of the 890s, which not merely destroyed the Moravian Empire but cut the Central European Slavs completely off from their southern brethren, ensured the ultimate death of any traces of Eastern Orthodoxy; the Czechs, Moravians and Slovaks were destined to be Catholics using the Roman liturgy and alphabet, and when in 966 Boleslav I married his daughter to the Polish Prince Mieszko I it was to Catholicism that the Poles were converted. Similarly the southern Slavs near the Adriatic, the Slovenes and Croats, came under the influence of the west. On the other hand the Slavonic liturgy and alphabet had been planted in Bulgaria by the disciples of Cyril and Methodius during the latter part of the ninth century and, most important of all, when in 989 Kievan Russia had Christianity forced upon it by Vladimir the Great (who next forced it on Novgorod) it was Orthodox Christianity, soon spelled out in Cyrillic not Greek letters. The bisection was complete.

MEDIEVAL RUSSIA

Despite the persistent claims of modern Russian scholars that the beginnings of Russian church music were indigenous, it is increasingly clear (as might have been expected) that Kievan Russia acquired Byzantine music with the Byzantine liturgy. The liturgy was soon translated into Bulgarian-Slavonic and no doubt the music also began to take its own course, if for no other reason than that the notation was ekphonetic[1] and therefore open to licence in interpretation. Although we cannot transcribe the early Russian *znamenny raspev* (sign chant) and are only beginning to decipher Old Byzantine notation, scholars have long detected similarities between the Russian 'hook' notation of the twelfth century and the slightly earlier Byzantine '*Coislin*' neumes. Even the quite different *kondakarnaya notatsiya*, in which the Russian *kontakion* manuscripts of the twelfth century are notated, has recently been shown to have Greek affinities. Similar neume-shapes probably, but by no means certainly, indicate similar sound patterns, and the key to early Russian notation lies in comparative study with Greek sources.[2] The music so tantalizingly preserved in this as yet only partly broken cipher consists of the *kontakia*, *stichera*, *heirmoi* and so on of the Orthodox rite, and the classification into eight *glasï* corresponds exactly to the Greek *echoi*.

   The Kievan state broke up through internal pressures and finally disappeared in the early thirteenth century, when practically all Russia passed

---

1. Concerning these prosodic marks, see the chapter on Byzantine music.

2. See Velimirović, *Early Slavic*, particularly his summing-up, pp. 124–7. His main Slavic text is a *Hirmologion* in the Serbian monastery of Khilendar on Mount Athos, but Kievan Russia had plenty of contacts with Athos.

under the 'Tatar yoke' for two centuries – another factor which contributed to her cultural isolation and the intense conservatism of her church music – as the Bulgars and Serbs soon afterwards, and for a much longer period, submitted to the domination of the Turks. Only the oligarchic republic of Novgorod escaped the Tatar scourge, and it was at Novgorod, the cultural heir of Kiev, that the two most important manifestations of secular music in medieval Russia flourished most freely: the *bïlinï* or epic chants, the nature of whose music we may guess from the fragments orally transmitted down to the nineteenth century – each narrative chanted to a short phrase, half-melodic, half-recitative, endlessly repeated – finally published in the folk-song collections of Rimsky-Korsakov and others; and the songs and instrumental music of the *skomorokhi*, the close equivalents of the Western *jongleurs* and *Gaukler*. There had been *skomorokhi* at the Kievan court and an eleventh-century chronicler tells us that they performed before Svyatoslav II, 'some bringing forth the sounds of *gusli*, others singing organal sounds' (*or'gan'ï'ya glasï poyushche*), though what he meant by 'organal' it is impossible to say. Instruments, however, were not only forbidden in church, but in general regarded as things of the Devil so far as the clergy were concerned. The principal performers on them, the *skomorokhi*, flourished mainly among the lower orders, at not too priest-ridden courts, or in a 'free' city such as Novgorod. In Novgorod they were recognized as respectable members of society and achieved something resembling the guilds of Western Europe. Even more important than the *skomorokh* culture in Novgorod was the influence of its ecclesiastical song-school, famous as early as the twelfth century though its outstanding alumni were produced in the late sixteenth, when the cultural supremacy had long passed to Moscow.

The Muscovite princes, who now assumed the title of tsar – Ivan III, Vasily III and Ivan IV (the Terrible) – did everything possible to enhance the glory of their capital. Numerous *skomorokhi* were brought from Novgorod; Pskov and Novgorod were robbed of famous bells, Novgorod of its best singers. Ivan III or his successor established a court chapel of thirty to thirty-five 'singing clerks', the origin of the later imperial chapel, and it was the brother-in-law of Ivan III who in 1490 brought to Moscow the organist Giovanni Salvatore, an Augustinian monk – not, of course, to take part in church services. But before long church music did take a step forward, the step toward primitive polyphony which the west had taken five centuries earlier. The monophonic *znamenny* chant itself had become richer in ornamentation; the 'hooks' were modified in form and other varieties of notation had appeared: the so-called 'road',[3] '*Kazan*' and '*demestvenny*' (festive, court music) signs. The notation still consists of unheighted neumes, though much of the music can now be read partly by collation with

---

3. In early Russian polyphony the middle voice, the *cantus firmus*, is called the *put* (road, way, course).

later manuscripts and Alexander Mezenets' 'alphabet' of the signs ('*Azbuka znamennovo peniya*') compiled in 1668, partly with the aid of the red 'cinnabar marks' indicating pitch and manner of performance introduced by the Novgorod master Ivan Shaydurov towards the end of the sixteenth century. Another famous Novgorod singer of a rather earlier generation, Vasily Rogov, is credited with the introduction of a more elaborate form of *demestvenny* music: *troestrochnoe penie*, 'three-line singing'. But for a long time the three parts were written in three lines of carefully aligned neumes *in campo aperto*. Many years were to pass before Russia acquired the stave.

THE WESTERN SLAVS IN THE MIDDLE AGES

The music of the Western Slavs, the Czechs, Slovaks and Poles, and the Catholic southern Slavs developed quite differently, on the same lines as that of western Christendom in general, though with a considerable time-lag. Before the real impact of western culture made itself felt, their music seems to have been very like that of the Russians; we read of similar instruments, similar ritual use of music, and similar pagan survivals in secular folksong. The arrival of Catholic plainsong among the Czechs and Poles in the eleventh and twelfth centuries is attested by a number of manuscripts: the eleventh-century Proprium in the National Museum at Prague, the *Pontificale* of the bishops of Cracow, the *Missale plenarium* in the chapter library at Gniezno, the Missal in the Monastery Library at Vyšší Brod, all from the twelfth century. The earliest Slovak sources, at Kremnica, date from the same period. The neumes are generally of the St Gall type, though the Slovak examples show certain peculiarities indicating that the manuscripts are of local origin, and after the gradual introduction of diastematic notation during the thirteenth century the Czechs developed peculiar rhomboid forms of neume in the fourteenth.[4] Native elements naturally penetrated the actual substance of plainsong by way of trope and sequence, as in the sequences *Hac festa die tota gratuletur Polonia* (in Wrocław University Library I F 417: early fourteenth century)[5] and *Dulce melos* (in the Sequencer of Arnošt z Pardubic, in the Prague Metropolitan Chapter Library, 1363).[6] We even know the name of the composer of *Dulce melos* – Domaslaus – and that of a still earlier Pole, Wincenty z Kielc, who wrote the words and melodies of the hymns in a 'History of St Stanislaus' of 1255.[7] Liturgical drama sprang from Easter tropes, just as in the west, at the end of the twelfth century.

---

4. The evolution of the Czech rhomboid neumes is illustrated in three plates in Racek, *Středověká hudba*.

5. Feicht, *Staropolska*, p. 3.

6. Pohanka, *Dějiny*, no. 6.

7. See Feicht, *Staropolska*, p. 3, for the hymn *O beate Stanislae*.

Dynastic changes and the foundation of universities at Prague and Cracow strengthened contacts with the west, giving new impulses to national cultures but leading ultimately to divergences between Czech and Polish music. German colonists had been settling in Bohemian and Moravian towns, and Minnesänger had appeared at the Prague Court, notably Frauenlob and, later, Heinrich von Mügeln; a manuscript of *c.* 1410 includes a Czech paraphrase from the *Song of Songs*, *Otep myrrhy*, which is musically indebted to two of Frauenlob's *leiche*. (The German term *leich* is the equivalent of the French *lai*, see p. 131.) But the accession of John of Luxemburg introduced French influences as well and led to the appearance in Prague of Guillaume de Machaut, the king's secretary (1327–9), though Machaut's supposed visit to the Cracow court in 1364 is now believed to be a work of his imagination. When John's son, Charles, became emperor he both encouraged Czech culture and made Prague one of the most important European capitals. The accession of the Jagiełło dynasty in 1386 established a hardly less brilliant court at Cracow. Vernacular words were now set to music and two famous religious songs (both related to the 'Kyrie eleison') made their appearance towards the end of the fourteenth century: the Czech *Hospodine, pomiluj ny* (earliest MS of words only, 1380; earliest MS with music, 1397) and the Polish *Bogurodzica* (first mentioned 1381; earliest MS, *c.* 1407).[8] Both became patriotic symbols of the highest importance. And whereas Polish and Czech polyphony had hitherto not advanced beyond the simplest *organum*, mostly in parallel fifths,[9] at the beginning of the fifteenth century both had reached the *ars nova* stage (see examples 1a and b).[10]

Example 1a. *Flos florum/Ach du getruys blut*, Prague MS

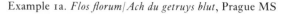

[Flower of flowers among lilies/Ah, thou faithful blood]

8. The musical MSS are respectively Prague, University Library, III D 17 (facs. in Racek, *Středověká hudba*) and Cracow, Bibl. Jagiell. 1619 (facs. in Jachimecki, *Muzyka polska*, i/1, p. 10).

9. See Feicht, *Staropolska*, p. 7 (facs. in *MGG*, x, col. 1391), and Pohanka, *Dějiny*, no. 10.

10. (a) Prague, University Library, V H 31, f. 86b; facs. in Nejedlý, *Dějiny*, i. 219; complete transcription in Pohanka, *Dějiny*, no. 12; (b) Poznan, Library of the University Institute of Musicology; complete transcription (differing from that given here) in Feicht, *Staropolska*, p. 8. Further transcriptions of Czech polyphony from this period, in MS c.l.m. 243 in the Széchenyi National Library, Budapest, are printed in Mužík, *Studie*, pp. 30–40.

Example 1b. *Et in terra pax*, Poznan MS

But at this point the musical histories of the two peoples began to take different courses. With the defeat of the Teutonic Order at Grunwald in 1410, the Polish kingdom entered a period of greater stability in which the arts flourished. On the other hand the burning of Hus in 1415 plunged Bohemia into a series of wars first against Catholic 'Crusaders' and then between moderate and extreme Hussite factions; and while the Hussite movement produced a great corpus of vernacular religious song, it was monophonic song. The Hussites rejected polyphony as a 'frivolous assault on the ears and empty pastime'. It was only in the reigns of George of Poděbrad (1458–61) and the two Jagellon kings of Bohemia that more sophisticated Czech music began to flourish again.

The contrast appears most sharply if we compare the two most important Czech and Polish manuscripts of the first half of the fifteenth century: the so-called 'Jistebnický kancionál' of *c.* 1420 (Prague, National Museum, II C 7) and a Polish manuscript of *c.* 1440, now in the National Library at Warsaw (Kra 52). The Jistebnice songbook does contain a few examples of primitive two-part polyphony[11] and one or two Latin or partly Latin tropes or hymns,[12] even portions of the Mass, but the great bulk of it consists of monophonic Hussite songs, of both the Prague moderates and the Taborite extremists,[13] including the famous *Ktož jsú boží bojovníci* in its earliest form. (The variant used by Smetana in *Mà Vlast* and *Libuše*, Dvořák in his *Hussite Overture* and Janáček in *Mr Brouček's Excursions* was published more than a hundred years later.) These Hussite songs, some of them certainly of earlier origin, religious, bellicose, polemic, are often bold and beautiful in melodic line and their influence is perceptible not only in the songs of the Bohemian Brethren and later Czech music generally but in Lutheran chorales and even Catholic songs. A typical example is the song shown in example 2, probably by the Taborite warrior-priest Jan Čapek,

11. Pohanka, *Dějiny*, nos. 29 and 33–6.
12. Pohanka, *Dějiny*, nos. 23, 32 and 36.
13. Pohanka, *Dějiny*, nos. 27–8, 30, 37–9, 41–2 and 44–6.

to be sung by a multitude 'waiting with bread and wine in the manner of Melchizedek' to greet a victorious army.

Example 2. *Dietky, v hromadu*, Prague MS

The Polish manuscript of some twenty years later is of a totally different nature. Here we have two- and three-part polyphonic pieces, some anonymous but identified as Polish by their texts (e.g. *Cracovia civitas*)[14] and eight by a named composer, Mikołaj z Radomia,[15] side by side with the work of such contemporary western composers as Ciconia, Engardus, Grossim and 'Zacharia'. Mikołaj is thus the earliest Slav polyphonist known to us by name and the earliest Slav composer whom we can firmly associate with a corpus of work. He was probably the *Nicolaus clavicembalista reginae Poloniae* mentioned in 1422 and his panegyric motet, *Hystorigraphi acie*, can be dated 1426; it is stylistically related to, and artistically comparable with, the western pieces in the same manuscript. His other compositions, all in three parts, consist of: two 'Gloria' and 'Credo' pairs with text in all three parts (one of the 'Glorias' has a Marian trope); another 'Gloria' with texted *discantus* and instrumental tenor and countertenor, and a still inaccessible 'Credo'; a similar *Magnificat* with passages in *fauxbourdon* (e.g. at *Ex exsultavit* where the contratenor is derived from the *discantus*, *per bordunum quem incipe in quinta*); and a textless piece which is certainly not the earliest piece of Slavonic instrumental music to be written down, since the Czechs can point to some dance-tunes in a manuscript of *c.* 1396,[16] but the earliest known piece of Slavonic concerted instrumental music (see example 3).

After Mikołaj z Radomia, Polish music seems to have suffered a decline during the rest of the century. Only one little piece from the mid-century, a three-part song to St Stanislas,[17] is worth mentioning, not for its artistic value, which is slight, but for the fact that it is the earliest polyphonic piece with Polish words and the earliest Polish song-setting on a tenor *cantus firmus*. A few pieces from the latter part of the century, all more or less in

14. Three pieces in Szweykowski, *Cracow*, pp. 1–9.

15. Four pieces in Szweykowski, *Cracow*, pp. 10–28; two in Feicht, *Staropolska*, pp. 11–27 (facs. of the 'Credo' in *MGG*, x, pl. 83); textless piece in Jachimecki, *Muzyka polska*, partial facs. p. 69, partial transcription, pp. 72–3. These account for all Mikołaj's compositions in Warsaw, Kra 52, and nearly all his known works.

16. Pohanka, *Dějiny*, no. 13.

17. Szweykowski, *Cracow*, p. 29; facs. in Szweykowski, *Z dziejów*, i, facing p. 65.

Example 3. Warsaw MS

simple note-against-note counterpoint,[18] complete the tale. It was perhaps the poverty of native talent that led King John Albert, *c.* 1492, to invite to his court the German Heinrich Finck, who apparently had sung in the Cracow court chapel as a youth, and who now remained there until 1506.

The position in Bohemia was very similar. The *kancionál* literature flourished, particularly after the emergence of the Bohemian Brethren, the heirs of the Hussites, and one particularly important manuscript was compiled *c.* 1505 for Jan Franus, a leading citizen of Hradec Králové. This so–called *Franusův kancionál*[19] contains both monophonic and polyphonic pieces, not all of them Czech in origin; most of the polyphonic pieces are as simple as the contemporary Polish ones but two are more interesting: a three-part setting of the old Hussite song *Otče, Bože všemohúcí* with the melody as tenor *cantus firmus*, and a gay little three-part song *O Regina, lux divina* which makes use of imitation and has for its tenor *cantus firmus* the tune of a secular dance-song.

POLAND IN THE SIXTEENTH CENTURY

The modest beginnings of sixteenth-century Polish polyphony are to be found in the compositions of Jerzy Liban (1464–after 1546), whose treatise *De musica laudibus oratio*, indebted to Gafuri, was published at Cracow in 1540, and Sebastian z Felsztyna (*c.* 1480–*c.* 1544), whose treatise *Opusculum musices* first appeared in 1515. Liban's only surviving musical work,

18. Examples in Feicht, *Staropolska*, pp. 29–33.

19. Examples of polyphony in Pohanka, *Dějiny*, nos. 55–9; facsimiles in *Miscellanea Musicologica*, xix (Prague, 1966), 214–15; 218–19; 222–3.

based on the melody of an antiphon to St Stanislas,[20] dates from 1501 and is written in simple note-against-note style like the pieces mentioned above, some of which may well be his, but is in four parts – an innovation in Polish music. But four-part writing is the norm in Sebastian's works,[21] which are however more fluid in texture though without imitation, and not without occasional fifths and octaves.

A much more important composer than either of these was Mikołaj z Kraków, but, ironically, although he wrote both religious and secular vocal music as well as keyboard preludes and dances, we know his vocal compositions only through keyboard transcriptions – practically all in the famous organ tablature of Jan z Lublina (compiled 1537–48), where they appear beside music by Heinrich Finck, Josquin, Janequin, Sermisy, Senfl, Verdelot, Cavazzoni and other western masters,[22] though one or two are preserved in the tablature of the Monastery of the Holy Spirit at Cracow,[23] of the same period. Mikołaj's compositions, identifiable generally by the initials 'N(icolaus) C(racoviensis), are shapely and attractive. The dances are simple and lively, the preludes coherent. The best of his secular songs, *Aleć nade mną Wenus* (Yet Venus is above me), suggests the influence of the French *chanson* and the transcriptions of his church music also remind one of the Attaingnant publications: for instance the motet *Date sinceram moerentibus* (see example 4).[24]

Example 4. Polish tablature

20. Szweykowski, *Cracow*, p. 30.

21. Examples in Szweykowski, *Cracow*, p. 32, and Feicht, *Staropolska*, p. 36.

22. The tablature is published complete in facs. in *Monumenta Polonia*, series B, i. Transcriptions of 36 dances from the tablature in Chybiński, *Wydawnictwo*, xx; more transcriptions, including pieces by Mikołaj (some, however, in preposterous orchestral arrangements) in Chomiński-Lissa, *Renaissance*, others in Szweykowski, *Cracow*. The vocal works by Mikołaj printed in score in Chomiński-Lissa, *Renaissance*, Szweykowski, *Cracow*, and Feicht, *Staropolska*, are reconstructed from the organ tablature. See John R. White, 'The Tablature of Johannes of Lublin', *Mus. Disc.*, xvii (1963), 137–62.

23. Transcriptions of *preambula* by Mikołaj and seven anonymous pieces in Szweykowski, *Cracow*, pp. 41–2 and 53–9; reconstruction of Mikołaj's antiphon *Sub tuum praesidium* in Feicht, *Staropolska*, p. 49.

24. Szweykowski, *Cracow*, p. 301.

The mid-century was marked not only by the compilation of these two notable tablatures but by Sigismund I's foundation of the chapel of the Rorantists at Cracow in 1543, generally regarded as a turning-point in the history of Polish music. The Rorantists and the king's private chapel between them sang a very large repertoire of French, Italian and Flemish music by the greatest contemporary masters; and native composers were encouraged as well, though the king soon lost the best of them, the young Wacław z Szamotul (c. 1526–c. 1560) who entered his service in 1547 but left it in 1555 for that of the Wojewoda of Lithuania, the Calvinist Mikołaj Radziwiłł, at Vilna. A great deal of Wacław's music, including an eight-part Mass, has disappeared; of his *Lamentations* (Cracow, 1553) only the tenor part has survived. However, we have two psalm-motets published by Montanus and Neuber in two of their collections (Nürnberg, 1554 and 1564)[25] and a third motet transcribed for organ in the so-called 'little Warsaw tablature',[26] and these are enough to show his mastery of the contemporary fully imitative *a cappella* style. His four-part Polish religious songs and settings of psalm-translations[27] are much simpler, in only lightly decorated note-against-note style. The surviving work of two rather younger composers is almost entirely in these two last fields: Cyprian Bazylik (c. 1535–after 1600) and Mikołaj Gomółka (c. 1535–after 1591). Bazylik, composer, poet, translator and later even publisher, was also at one time in the service of the king and of the Calvinist 'Black' Radziwiłł; Gomółka was for a time *fistulator* (piper, flautist) in the royal chapel and later in the service of various nobles. Bazylik wrote some monophonic hymns, but the important part of his work consists of polyphonic hymns and Polish psalms, all in four parts in more or less decorated note-against-note style (Cracow, 1556 and 1558).[28] Gomółka's setting of the complete Psalter in Polish, *Melodie na psałterz polski* (Cracow, 1580),[29] is more varied, though seldom very elaborate in style, but by no means grammatically faultless; some of his *cantus firmi* are Lutheran chorales, some are borrowed from the *kancionály* of the Bohemian Brethren, some adapted from plainsong; sometimes he puts them in the highest part, as in the later Calvinist psalters of the west, sometimes in the tenor, as in this adaptation of the melody of *Ein' feste Burg* to Psalm 125 (see example 5).[30]

The outstanding Catholic composers of the latter half of the century were Marcin Leopolita (c. 1540–c. 1589), for a time *compositor cantus* to Sigismund

25. One in both Chomiński-Lissa, *Renaissance*, and Chybiński, *Wydawnictwo*, ix, the other in Szweykowski, *Cracow*, p. 64.

26. Reconstruction (a third higher) in Feicht, *Staropolska*, p. 61; facs. of tablature in Jachimecki, *Muzyka polska*, p. 116.

27. All published in Chybiński, *Wydawnictwo*, xxviii.

28. Complete in Chybiński, *Wydawnictwo*, xxxiv.

29. Complete in Chybiński, *Wydawnictwo*, xlvii–xlix.

30. Chybiński, *Wydawnictwo*, xlix, 21.

Example 5. *Ktokolwiek* (Psalm CXXV), Gomółka's *Melodie*

[They that trust in the Lord shall be as Mount Zion.]

II Augustus, and Tomasz Szadek (*c.* 1550–after 1611), who, after serving in the royal chapel and then that of the Rorantists, spent the last thirty years of his life as a simple *vicarius* in the Cathedral at Cracow. Of the three Masses Leopolita is known to have written, only one – a five-part *Missa paschalis* based on four Polish or German Easter songs – survives[31] and three of his motets are preserved only in organ tablature.[32] Two Masses by Szadek are known: *Dies est laetitiae*,[33] a *cantus firmus* Mass for men's voices only (since it was composed for the Rorantists in 1578) and a *missa parodia* on Créquillon's *chanson, Puis ne me peult venir* (or, as he spells it, *Pisneme*) (1580).[34] And behind Leopolita and Szadek stand the more shadowy figures of Krzysztof Borek, whose *Te Deum laudamus* Mass[35] is well worthy to stand beside their work, Walentyn Gawara[36] and Marcin Paligon.[37] Altogether this little corpus of late-sixteenth century Polish church music compares very favourably with all but the outstanding masterpieces of the contemporary west.

In another field, that of lute music, the Poles compare even more favourably. Neither Bakfark nor Diomedes Cato was a Pole, though both have been claimed for Poland, but the intensive cultivation of the lute at the Cracow court during the first half of the century attracted eminent foreign composer-players.[38] Bakfark was there at various times between 1549 and 1566, and his *Liber ... harmoniarum musicarum*, dedicated to Sigismund II Augustus, was published by Łazarz Andrysowicz (Cracow, 1565). Diomedes was a

31. Chybiński, *Wydawnictwo*, xxxv.

32. 'Mihi autem' is printed in Feicht, *Staropolska*, p. 65, with vocal reconstruction above it; reconstructions of *Cibavit eos* and *Resurgente Christo* in Szweykowski, *Cracow*, pp. 89 and 92.

33. Chybiński, *Wydawnictwo*, xxxiii.

34. 'Kyrie' in *Oxford History of Music* (Oxford, 1905), ii, 302, and in Chomiński-Lissa, *Renaissance*, p. 258.

35. Feicht, *Staropolska*, p. 71. Szweykowski, *Cracow*, prints only the 'Kyrie', but also the 'Sanctus' of another Mass by Borek, p. 97.

36. Five-part motet, *Per merita Sancti Adalberti*, Szweykowski, *Cracow*, p. 106.

37. Five-part motet, *Rorate caeli*, Feicht, *Staropolska*, p. 88.

38. On the historically less important Bohemian lutenists, Czech and German, see Emil Vogl, 'Lautenisten der böhmischen Spätrenaissance', *Die Musikforschung*, xviii (1965), 281–90.

later immigrant, of about 1590. But there were two outstanding natives:
Jakub Reys (Jakub Polak/Jacques Pollonois) (*c.* 1545–*c.* 1605),[39] who spent
the latter part of his life at the French court – perhaps for religious reasons,
since he left Poland on the accession of the bigoted Catholic Sigismund III
in 1587, and Wojciech Długoraj (*c.* 1557–*c.* 1619),[40] who emigrated to
Germany at about the same time. Their compositions – preludes, fantasias,
dances (often styled *chorea polonica*), song transcriptions – are all instrumental, but another lutenist, Krzysztof Klabon, *Kapellmeister* to Sigismund
III, published six four-part *Piesni Kalliopy Slowienskiey* (Songs of the
Slavonic Calliope, Cracow, 1588) which look uncommonly like versions of
lute airs and have actually been republished as such.[41]

It was under Klabon, at the end of the century, that Sigismund III moved
his chapel from Cracow to Warsaw, his new capital, and thus put an end to
a chapter in Polish musical history.

BOHEMIA IN THE SIXTEENTH CENTURY

The surviving Czech music from the earliest part of the sixteenth century
appears to consist mainly of Hussite hymns in fairly primitive polyphony,
more or less in the style of those in the already mentioned *Franusův kancionál*. There is some rather more florid writing in a Utraquist Gradual of
1512 from Kolín (Prague, National Museum, XIII A 2).[42] But if we bear in
mind that the *Speciálník Královéhradecký*, a manuscript usually dated
c. 1550, was compiled by at least ten scribes and probably covers a repertoire
of the entire first half of the century – mainly Latin but partly Czech polyphony (Mass-cycles and movements, motets in older and newer styles, in
black and white notation respectively,[43] polyphonic songs and some instrumental pieces,[44] including two by Barbigant and Jean Touront) – the picture
is somewhat altered. In particular there are five three-part pieces with
Czech texts which are written in a more modern imitative style, with old
Czech songs as *cantus firmi* which also provide the openings of the other,
more florid parts.[45] The one based on the famous hymn to St Wenceslas is
typical (see example 6).

39. All his compositions were originally published in the west; they are reprinted practically complete
in Chybiński, *Wydawnictwo*, xxii.

40. Works mostly published by Besard (Cologne, 1603); a fantasia, finale, and five *villanelle* in
Chybiński, *Wydawnictwo*, xxiii (2nd edn., 1964, should be consulted). Nine pieces from the *Lautenbuch
des Albert Dlugorai* (Leipzig, Stadtbibliothek, II. 6.15) in Szweykowski, *Cracow*, p. 130 ff.

41. Szweykowski, *Cracow*, p. 110 ff.

42. See the *Credo* in Snížková, *Ceská*, p. 21.

43. Pohanka, *Dějiny*, nos. 60–2 and 65–6; facs. of motet *O altissime* in *Miscellanea Musicologica*, xix
(Prague, 1966), 224–5.

44. Pohanka, *Dějiny*, no. 67, with imitations of a cackling hen.

45. Pohanka, *Dějiny*, nos. 62–4, and Snížková, *Česká*, pp. 32 and 34; facs. in Snížková, *Česká*, p. 10.

Example 6. *Náš milý svatý Václave* (hymn), Czech MS

[Our dear St Wenceslas]

The only piece with the *cantus firmus* in the descant is ascribed to Gontrášek, a composer of whom nothing is known, but the others are technically so similar that they may be confidently ascribed to him, though one is more ambitious and opens with a harmonic exordium before the imitative music. The *Speciálník* gives us tantalizing glimpses of other Czech composers; Motyčka, Plihal, Klička may or may not be composers' names but Thomek, who is credited with a 'Credo' and 'Sanctus', and a *Jubilamina*, certainly is. Western composers are plentifully represented: Basiron, Alexander Agricola, Weerbecke, Tinctoris, Verbonnet, Isaac and others.

Dynastic changes affected music in Bohemia as in Poland. The Habsburg kings, from 1526 onward, were either heirs to the imperial crown or emperors themselves who either neglected Prague or filled it with foreign musicians. Ferdinand I founded a court chapel at Prague in 1564 but manned it with Netherlanders and Viennese, and then moved it to Innsbruck two years later. Rudolf II (1576–1612) on the other hand loved Prague and music and collected around him such outstanding foreigners as Philippe de Monte, Regnart, Kerle, Luython, and – claimed as a Slovene, though he hardly has a place in the history of Slavonic music – 'Jacobus Handl, *Gallus vocatus, Carniolanus*'. But native talent had room to flourish in the provinces, if not in the capital, writing Czech motets and devotional songs for the Protestants side by side with Masses and Office settings. From the number of composers whose names we know, a few stand out. Jan Trojan

Turnovský (*c.* 1550–after 1595)[46] and Jiří Rychnovský (*c.* 1545–*c.* 1616)[47] usually set Czech texts to polyphony that varies from the extremely simple to the very florid, while Jan Simonides (Montanus) (d. 1587) and Pavel Spongopeus (Jistebnický) (*c.* 1550–1619), both associated with the Catholic stronghold of Kutná Hora, ventured on eight-part writing. Perhaps the best of all, and certainly the most remarkable man, was the Catholic nobleman Kryštof Harant z Polžic (1564–1621), humanist, traveller, soldier, imperial courtier and very well trained musician,[48] who joined the patriotic party on the outbreak of the Thirty Years War and paid the penalty with his life after the Battle of the White Mountain which ended an era in Czech history. His handful of compositions[49] include a six-part Latin motet written in Jerusalem in 1598, a five-part German motet, *Maria Kron*, and a five-part *missa parodia* on Marenzio's *Dolorosi martir*.

THE SOUTHERN SLAVS

Nothing illustrates more dramatically the cultural division of the Southern Slavs by religion than the musical history of the Croats and Slovenes on the one hand and the Serbs and Bulgars on the other. The lands conquered by the Habsburgs or the Venetian Republic could produce such composers as Handl-Gallus or the lutenist Franciscus Bossinensis who merge into the European scene, and whom we surmise to have been respectively Slovene and Croat only because they have told us that they came from Carniola or Bosnia. The Turkish conquest had little effect at first, since Catholic and Orthodox (and Bogomil and Protestant) continued their own practices. It was the religious barrier that was the real dividing factor. The Serbs and Bulgars had their own folk-music and instruments and sang the liturgy in their own dialects of Church Slavonic; doubtless they developed their own dialects of Byzantine chant; but the earliest documentary evidence of genuine Serbian chant dates from the mid-fifteenth century and the neumes are not yet heighted, while that for the *bolgarsky rospev* is later still, though the neumes are diastematic.

---

46. Czech motets and hymns in Snížková, *Česká*, pp. 57–63; and in Pohanka, *Dějiny*, no. 74. Pohanka, *Dějiny*, no. 73, is a 'Kyrie' from a Mass on a Czech song-tune, attributed to him on no very firm grounds.

47. Czech motet, Pohanka, *Dějiny*, no. 75; Latin motet and Hussite Latin tropes from a mass tentatively attributed to him in Snížková, *Česká*, pp. 50–3, and a Czech motet in his style in Snížková, *Česká*, p. 69.

48. See Rudolf Quoika, 'Christoph Harant von Polschitz und seine Zeit', *Die Musikforschung*, vii (1954), 414–29.

49. Published complete by Jiří Berkovec (Prague, 1956); excerpts from Mass in Pohanka, *Dějiny*, no. 76, and *NOHM*, iv, 310.

ROBERT STEVENSON

10 The Western Hemisphere: From the Beginnings to 1600

MEXICAN INSTRUMENTS

POLYPHONY: MEXICO AND GUATEMALA

ANDEAN INSTRUMENTS

FERNÁNDEZ HIDALGO

PÉREZ MATERANO'S LIBRO DE CANTO

BRAZIL

MEXICAN INSTRUMENTS

If the quality of the archaeological instruments unearthed by Mayanists and other area experts on Jaina island (off the Yucatán coast), at various sites in the states of Veracruz and Tabasco and at Teotihuacán (in the Valley of Mexico) provides the historian with sufficient evidence, the 'golden age' of Mesoamerican music antedated Cortés' entry by at least eight hundred years. (The term Mesoamerican is used here to refer to the central area of the Americas, principally Mexico.) Exquisitely moulded multiple flutes that obligatorily sound three- and four-note chords were already a commonplace in the Totonac area before the *Musica enchiriadis*. Totonac and Olmec instrument makers knew how to fashion 'goiter' flutes sounding like oboes after the air column was deflected through an oscillating chamber at the neck. The secrets of instrument manufacture lost after the Aztecs overran Mexico included single-mouthpiece, double flutes producing vibrato sounds.

Just as the Romans abandoned Greek musical subtleties, so also the Aztecs (who founded their capital in 1325) opted for ruder instruments than their Teotihuacán predecessors in the Valley of Mexico – preferring virile percussion to retreating flute and *ocarina*. Accounts dating from the first years after Cortés' invasion, the evidence of a few painted codices that survive, and examination of museum instruments permit the following

generalizations concerning Aztec musical life in 1521, the year in which
Cortés took Tenochtitlan. Among them, music had no independent life of
its own apart from religious and cult observances. Since imperfectly performed rituals offended rather than appeased Huitzilopochtli and his other
no less sanguinary fellow deities, the *teponaztli-* or *huehuetl-*player who
missed a beat or otherwise erred was immediately withdrawn from playing
ensembles to be then and there executed. When poured into the hollow
interior of the two-keyed teponaztli, blood gushing from the opened chests
of sacrificial victims was thought to endow the minor or major third or
perfect fourth sounded by the two keys with 'new life'.

In the *calmécac* – under great duress – fledgling players memorized
complex rhythmic patterns while singers mastered lengthy texts. Just as in
the Second Temple a Levitical guild dominated the music, so also among
the Aztecs a professionalized caste controlled the music incidental to the
severe acts of prayer and penance scheduled every three or four hours
throughout the day and night at the principal shrines. For such a ceremony
as the sacrifice of the Adonis meeting his doom after a pampered year of
pleasure and sexual excess, penitential flutes pitched in piccolo range were
chosen to accompany his ascent to the obsidian knife. At a transvestite
ceremony honouring the Young Corn Mother, a special type of xylophone
with resonators had to be played by women.

Because musicians served as the Aztecs' annalists, they enjoyed considerable social prestige, immunity from taxation, and other privileges – which
they wished to maintain even after switching from their old faith to the new,
implanted by such remarkable friars as Charles v's relative Pedro de Gante
(1480?–1572), the linguist Bernardino de Sahagún (1500?–90) and the
observant ethnologist Diego Durán (1537–88). To bait Christian instruction,
the Náhuatl (Aztec language) texts throughout Sahagún's *Psalmodia
Christiana* (Mexico City, 1583) were fitted to indigenous tunes.

POLYPHONY: MEXICO AND GUATEMALA

Native composers aping Gregorian chant and Spanish polyphony quickly
arose at such centres as Tlaxcala, Oaxaca and Mexico City. Although the
earliest still extant polyphony by such a Mexican Indian composer crops up
in a manuscript dated 1599, a school of sixteenth-century indigenous
musicians can be documented from *Cantares en idioma mexicano*, the manuscript of which was published in facsimile by Antonio Peñafiel in 1904–6.
The most important colonial composer of pure Indian blood in Mexico,
Juan Matías, served from *c.* 1655 to 1667 as *maestro de capilla* in Oaxaca
Cathedral, whence his music spread as far afield as Guatemala (manuscript
polychoral music by Matías could be seen in 1966 at the Seminario Conciliar
Library, Guatemala City). But Toribio de Motolinía (1490?–1565) vouched

for an Indian composer of Tlaxcala 'who had composed unaided a whole [polyphonic] Mass' as early as 1541 and Gerónimo de Mendieta (1525–1604) writing a generation later could boast of Indian-composed Masses, *villancicos* and other liturgical music in four parts that had been 'adjudged superior works of art when shown Spanish masters of composition'.

Among the Spanish-born 'masters of composition' who trained native Indians, the first whose music survives was the Extremaduran Hernando Franco (1532–85) who started as a choir-boy in Segovia Cathedral. In 1575, after several years at Antigua Guatemala, Franco transferred to the Mexico City Cathedral during the next decade bringing choral and instrumental forces to a pitch that competed advantageously with the homeland cathedral in which he was trained. Guatemala, Puebla and Mexico City Cathedrals preserve his music. His *chefs-d'oeuvre*, a cycle of odd- and even-verse *Magnificats*, have recently (1965) been edited by Steven Barwick from a manuscript copied for Mexico City Cathedral in 1611.

After Franco, the next important composer at Antigua Guatemala – Gaspar Fernandes – can be first traced as a cathedral singer at Évora in the 1590s. Beginning as organist at Guatemala Cathedral in 1599, he moved thence to Puebla Cathedral as organist-choirmaster in 1606, dying there in 1629. Particularly fecund in *villancicos*, Fernandes bequeathed the earliest *guineos*, *negros*, and other African-influenced pieces that have reached us from colonial times.[1] Fernandes also composed *villancicos* to Tlaxcalteca texts. He clearly differentiates the musical styles of his African and Mexican Indian pieces, however.

Two sixteenth-century, pure-blooded Guatemalan Indians whose music survives bore the Spanish-sounding names of Francisco de León and Tomás Pascual.[2] At Mexico City, Juan de Lienas may also have been Indian. His works were edited by Jesús Bal y Gay in 1952 from a codex formerly in the Museo Colonial del Carmen, Villa Obregón, D.F. These include a fine *Missa super fa re ut fa sol la*, à 5 modelled on the unique Mass by Melchor Robledo surviving in the Sistine Chapel collection (Codex 22, fols. 21ᵛ–42). A *Salve Regina*, à 5 by Lienas (fl. 1620–40) recorded in 1965 by the Roger Wagner Chorale now rates as one of the most frequently sung masterpieces of colonial Mexican polyphony.

ANDEAN INSTRUMENTS

In contrast with Mesoamerica, the Andean high culture area included tribes like the Chimú, the Mochica and the Chibcha, whose metallurgy permitted the construction of bells, metal pan-pipes, silver, bronze and

1. Stevenson, *MQ* (1968) 475 traces the highly important African influence not only in Fernandes's repertoire but also in colonial music elsewhere in the Americas.

2. Various *villancicos* by Pascual were printed for the first time in Stevenson, *MQ* (1964) 241.

copper trumpets and golden drums. The mania for size inspired the Inca rulers to send balsa rafts as far afield as Panama in quest of conch shells large enough for royal war trumpets. Eight drums, eight dancers, eight singers, or four of each, were considered ideal at Inca feasts and ceremonies. The colour vermilion was also felt to endow their instruments with extra-musical powers. The melodic intervals in the Inca *haylli* (song of praise) consisted of thirds, major and minor, major seconds, perfect fourths and fifths – thus yielding readily to the kind of European harmonization given a pre-Hispanic *haylli* by the Cuzco Cathedral chapel master, Juan de Fuentes, at Corpus Christi of 1551 or 1552. After dressing up eight *mestizo* choirboys in Inca costume and placing a plough in the hand of each, he had them sing the strophes. According to Garcilaso de la Vega's eyewitness *Commentarios reales* (Lisbon: Pedro Crasbeeck, 1609, folio 101ᵛ, col. 2): 'At each refrain, the whole adult choir joined in, to the great content of the Spaniards and the supreme delight of the Indians.'

Whether highland Inca melody strayed beyond pentaphony remains a moot point. But the coastal Nazcas flourishing along the Pacific before AD 1000 were already choosing for a favourite instrument 13- or 14-tube panpipes sounding microtonal intervals, usually between the upper tubes. Often such clay panpipes were moulded in twins, or with one instrument duplicating the other an octave higher. In general, all Inca and pre-Inca instruments, whether *antaras* (panpipes), *qquepas* (trumpets), *quenaquenas* or *pincollos* (end blown flutes, notched) inhabited female voice ranges. Spanish explorers reported a taste for high falsetto singing among Andean males as well. The high-pitched *antara*, with its excessive breath demands, peculiarly suited the Andean indigenes – whose thoracic capacity, expanded by the excessive altitudes in which they lived, surpasses that of any other New World aborigines.

Men blew *antaras*, *pincollos* and *quenquenas*, but women played hand drums – sexual symbolism decreeing vertical flutes suitable for men, but the recessed hand drum appropriate for women. Court music differed radically from plebeian, and only at Cuzco were feasts enlivened with *antara* ensembles or were *pincollo* players gathered on an outside stone platform (called *pingollonapata*), where proper acoustical surroundings enabled the *coya* (Inca queen) to indulge her aesthetic taste. Obviously the kind of refined court music heard at Cuzco was the most fragile and least apt to endure after the Inca royal line ceased. Present-day attempts at piecing together pre-Hispanic upper-class music from the fragments of indigenous melody or instruments found nowadays in out-of-the-way jungles overlook the vital differences in social strata that were noted in both Mexico and Peru by the earliest European commentators on New World music.

Even after the conquest, differences in social strata continued to make themselves felt, but in a different way. The first Indian-descended music directors in South American cathedrals were sons of native princesses, for instance, and not of jungle tribeswomen. In what are now Colombia and Ecuador, the mixing of Spanish and Indian blood gave the cathedrals of Bogotá and Quito their first chapel masters, Gonzalo García Zorro and Diego Lobato in 1575 and 1574 respectively. Lobato's mother had been consort to Atahuallpa, the last Inca ruler, while García Zorro's had been an Indian princess at Tunja. Both claimed Spanish captains for their fathers.

FERNÁNDEZ HIDALGO

Easily the most important composer in sixteenth-century South America, Gutierre Fernández Hidalgo (*c*. 1553–*c*. 1620), directed the music successively at the cathedrals of Bogotá (1584–6), Quito (1588–90), Cuzco and La Plata (Sucre), Bolivia (1597–1620). A wealth of *Magnificats* and other Vespers music by him, still extant in colonial manuscripts at Bogotá in 1967, attest his consummate contrapuntal skill and his lofty ambition to compete with both Francisco Guerrero and Victoria. The musical archive at Bogotá which contains Guerrero's 1582 Masses, Victoria's 1572 *Salve à 6* and Morales' *Magnificats* in manuscript, the Cuzco archive with Philippe Rogier's 1598 Masses (bound with Monte's *Missa ad modulum Benedicta es sex vocum*), and the La Plata (Sucre) archive with Morales and Rogier imprints – they all testify to the discrimination of this remarkable composer, who died with the unfulfilled ambition of seeing five books of his works published: Masses, *Magnificats*, Hymns, Holy Week music and motets. Although only his fourth-tone *Magnificat* had been recorded in 1966, a better selection of his music would place him in the company of all but the two or three most select Spanish composers of his age.

PÉREZ MATERANO'S LIBRO DE CANTO

The first music-theory text composed on American soil – Juan Pérez Materano's *Libro de canto de órgano y canto llano* – also takes pride of place as the first book of any kind known to have been written in what is now Colombia. On 17 June 1559, twenty-two years after reaching Cartagena, Pérez Materano obtained his royal ten-year printing privilege. Where was it to have been printed? At Mexico City Giovanni Paoli, a printer of Brescian origin, had published in 1556 an Augustinian *Ordinarium* that ranks as the first music book published in the Americas. Pérez Materano's royal privilege[3] specifically granted him the right to publish his treatise on 'polyphony and plainchant anywhere in the New World'. But in the 1560s such a privilege can only have meant Mexico City. In the former Aztec capital at least

---

3. Readily available for study in the monthly *Boletín Cultural y Bibliográfico*, iv (1961), 1181–2.

fourteen music books were to be published between 1556 and 1604, the two that appeared in 1584 and 1589 running to 300 and 329 folios each.

Perhaps the strongest sixteenth-century testimonial to Pérez Materano's theoretical knowledge turns up in part 3, canto 1, strophe 30 of Juan de Castellanos's *Varones ilustres de Indias*, published in 1589 – thirty years after Pérez Materano's printing privilege. Castellanos there calls Pérez Materano 'as learned as Josquin des Prez'. Even though overdrawn, the comparison does prove how highly regarded Josquin then was in South America. As late as 1737 the *Triunfos del Santo Oficio Peruano* published at Lima by Pedro José Bermúdez de la Torre still invokes Josquin as the fountainhead of music.

BRAZIL

Brazil attracted a more varied group of settlers before 1650 than the usual Spanish colony. True, the Jewish Luis de Carvajal sang Psalm 137 with harp accompaniment in Pachuca, Mexico, on 27 October 1594. But in the forepart of the next century Recife, Brazil, boasted in Ieosua Velosino the first regularly employed *chazzan* in New World annals. Among the French who tried settling in the Rio de Janeiro region around 1557, Jean de Léry placed all future ethnologists in his debt by collecting *in situ* several melodies of the cannibal Tupinambás, publishing them at Geneva in 1585 and 1586, and later editions of his travel classic *Histoire d'un Voyage*. In the twentieth century Heitor Villa-Lobos immortalized the two melodies published on pages 128 and 219 of the 1586 edition when he incorporated them in the first of his *Trois Poèmes indiens* (*chant et orchestre*, Rio de Janeiro, 1926). The word *maraca* is Tupinambá, and reached Europe via Hans Staden's *True History* of his captivity among them (1554). Part II, chapter 22 of his *Warhaftig Historia* (Marburg: Andres Kolben, 1557) describes at length the use to which the anthropophagous Tupinambás put their maracas.

The earliest extant 'Brazilian' Mass, found in an Arouca (Portugal) manuscript, discloses itself as a parody *à 4* of *O gram senhora*.[4] The list of the maestros at the first capital of colonial Brazil – Baía (Bahia de Todos los Santos) – begins with Bartholomeu Pires, chapel master of Baía cathedral 1565–86. *O Instituto* (a Coimbra University periodical) serialized in several 1910 issues Sousa Viterbo's *A ordem de Christo e a musica religiosa nos nossos dominios ultramarinos*, a monograph that still today remains the richest single collection of documents bearing on early Brazilian cathedral music.

4. Fragments of this were published for the first time in Robert Stevenson, 'Some Portuguese Sources for Early Brazilian Music History', *Yearbook of the Inter-American Institute for Musical Research*, iv (1968), 1–43.

PHILIP L. MILLER

Discography

In most cases the numbers given are from American and English catalogues and are frequently the same in both countries. When they differ, as in the recording of Giovanni Gabrieli on p. 434, American or English labels are indicated by the abbreviations (US) or (Eng), as follows:

Columbia (US) MS 7071, CBS (Eng) SBRG 72663

When available in American catalogues only this is indicated by the same abbreviation, e.g., Decca (US) or London (US). Other abbreviations such as c-t for countertenor or ob for oboe are self-explanatory. It is usually a simple matter to ascertain additional details from such widely used periodicals as the English quarterly *Gramophone Classical Record Catalogue* and the American *Schwann Long Playing Record Catalogue* and similar publications. Though records are often issued in stereo only, some of the older listings are available only in mono. Where stereo and mono numbers differ, the stereo is given first.

RECORD LABELS

Angel
Argo
AS – Anthologie Sonore
Bach Guild
Cambridge
CBS
Chant du Monde
Columbia
Crossroads
Decca (US)

DGG – Deutsche Grammophon
EA – Expériences Anonymes
EMS
Haydn Society
Heliodor
HMV
London (US)
Lyrachord
MAB – Musica Antiqua Bohemica
Musica Sacra
Nonesuch

Odyssey
Oiseau Lyre
Oryx
RCA Victor
SPA
Telefunken
Turnabout
Vanguard
Vox
Westminster

Introduction: Ancient Greece (Chapter 1.1)

History of Music in Sound: Vol. 1, *Ancient and Oriental Music: First Delphic Hymn; Epitaph of Seikilos.* HMV HLP 1–2; RCA LM 6057.

The Early Christian Period (Chapter 2)

History of Music in Sound: Vol. 2, *Early Medieval Music up to 1300:* Byzantine Music; Pre-Gregorian Music; Gregorian Music; Liturgical Drama. HMV HLP 3–4; RCA LM 6015.

Gregorian Chant: *Easter Sunday Mass.* Monks of Benedictine Abbey, Beuron: Pfaff. DGG ARC 3090 (APM 14106).

Masterpieces of Music before 1750: Record 1, *Gregorian Chant to the 16th Century.* Haydn Society HSL 2071 (W.W.Norton).

The Play of Daniel. N.Y. Pro Musica: Greenberg. Decca (US) 79402.

The Play of Herod. N.Y. Pro Musica: Greenberg. Decca (US) 7187.

Polyphony and Secular Monophony: ninth century–c. 1300 (Chapter 3)

ANTHOLOGIES

History of Music in Sound: Vol. 2, *Early Medieval Music up to 1300:* Bernart de Ventadorn; Gace Brulé; Adam de la Halle; Thibault de Navarre; Guiot de Dijon; Frauenlob; Early Polyphony; Dance Tunes. HMV HLP 3–4; RCA LM 6015.

Ars Antiqua: Organum; Motets; *Conductus* and other Early Polyphony; Leonin; Perotin. Munich Capella Antiqua: Ruhland. Telefunken SAWT 9530–1.

Music of the Middle Ages: Vol. 1, *Troubadour and Trouvère Songs:* Guiraut Riquier; Arnault Daniel; Bernart de Ventadorn; Gautier d'Espinal; Gace Brulé. Oberlin, c-t; Barab, viol. EA 0012. Vol. 2, *Twelfth Century:* Leonin; Perotin. Oberlin, c-t; Bressler, t; Barab, viol. EA 0021.

Music of the Twelfth and Thirteenth Centuries: Leonin; Alfonso el Sabio (Alfonso x); Perotin; Neidhardt von Reuenthal; Bernart de Ventadorn; Moniot d'Arras; Adam de la Halle. Brussels Pro Musica Antiqua: Cape. EMS 201.

Secular Music: Pierekins de la Coupele; Moniot d'Arras; Adam de la Halle (*Robin et Marion*); Meister Alexander. Early Music Studio. Telefunken S-9504.

Troubadour Songs of the Thirteenth Century: Peire Vidal; Guiraut de Bornelh; Bernart de Ventadorn; Raimbaut de Vaqueiras; Beatritz de Dia. Early Music Studio: Binkley. Telefunken SAWT 9567.

INDIVIDUAL COMPOSERS

ALFONSO EL SABIO (ALFONSO X)
Cantigas de Santa Maria. N.Y. Pro Musica: Greenberg. Decca (US) 79416.

PEROTIN
Notre Dame Organa. Deller Consort. Bach Guild 5045.

France and Burgundy: 1300–1500 (Chapter 4.1)

ANTHOLOGIES

History of Music in Sound: Vol. 3, *Ars Nova and the Renaissance:* Machaut; Dufay; Binchois; Ockeghem; La Rue; Compère. HMV HLP 5–7; RCA LM 6016.

Masterpieces of Music before 1750: Record 1, *Gregorian Chant to the 16th Century:* Machaut; Dufay; Binchois. Haydn Society HSL 2071 (W. W. Norton).

Music at the Burgundian Court: Binchois; Lantins; Dufay; Ockeghem; Morton. Brussels Pro Musica Antiqua: Cape. Bach Guild 634.

INDIVIDUAL COMPOSERS

ANON
Missa Tournai: Motets. Munich Capella Antiqua: Ruhland. Telefunken S 9517.

BINCHOIS, GILLES
Music of Gilles Binchois. Pro Musica Antiqua: Cape. Bach Guild 364.

BUSNOIS, ANTOINE
Chansons. Nonesuch Consort: Rifkin. Nonesuch 71247.

DUFAY, GUILLAUME
Missa L'Homme armé. Berkeley Singers: Gilchrist. Lyrachord 7150. *Mass: Se la face ay pale.* Vienna Chamber Ch; Vienna Musica Antiqua: Gillesberger. Bach Guild 70653.

LA RUE, PIERRE DE
Requiem; Motets; Laments. Munich Capella Antiqua: Ruhland. Telefunken SAWT 9471; AWT 9471.

MACHAUT, GUILLAUME DE
Mass: Notre Dame. Ambrosian Singers; Vienna Renaissance Players: McCarthy. Nonesuch H 71184.

OCKEGHEM (OKEGHEM), JOANNES
Mass: Mi-Mi; Mass and Chanson: Fors seulement. Lipsiensis Capella: Knothe. DGG ARC 198406.

TINCTORIS, JOHANNES
Missa Trium vocum. Blanchard Ens. Nonesuch 71043.

VITRY (VITRI), PHILIPPE DE
Motets. Munich Capella Antiqua: Ruhland. Telefunken S 9517.

France: 1500–1600 (Chapter 4.2)
The Low Countries: 1500–1600 (Chapter 4.3)

ANTHOLOGIES

History of Music in Sound: Vol. 3, *Ars Nova and the Renaissance:* Josquin des Prez; Obrecht. HMV HLP 5–7; RCA 6016. Vol. 4, *The Age of Humanism (1540–1630):* Costeley; Sermisy; Passereau;

Monte; Lassus; Willaert; Sweelinck.
HMV HLP 8–10; RCA LM 6029.
Masterpieces of Music before 1750: Record
1, *Gregorian Chant to the 16th Century:*
Josquin des Prez; Obrecht. Haydn Society
HSL 2071 (W. W. Norton).
Music at the Burgundian Court: Obrecht.
Brussels Pro Musica Antiqua: Cape. Bach
Guild 634.
Music for the Lute: Attaignant; Besard.
Gerwig, lute. RCA VICS 1362.
Organ Recital: Sweelinck; Clemens non
Papa; Willaert; Attaignant; Sermisy;
Macque. Talsma, org. DGG ARC 198445.
Renaissance Music: Brubier; Moderne;
Willaert; Gascogne; Sermisy; Jachet de
Mantua; Appenzeller; Courtois; Barbion;
Clemens non Papa; Lassus. Munich
Capella Antiqua: Ruhland. Telefunken
SAWT 9561–62.
Sixteenth-Century Vocal Works: Arcadelt;
Passereau; Le Jeune; Costeley; Janequin;
Lassus. Petits Chanteurs de Mont-Royal.
Oryx EXP 36.

INDIVIDUAL COMPOSERS

ARCADELT, JACOB
Masses in 3 to 7 parts; Secular Music.
Capella Cordine: Planchart. Lyrachord
7199.
CRECQUILLON, THOMAS
Motets. Blanchard Vocal Ens. Nonesuch
71051.
GOMBERT, NICOLAS
Mass: Je suis desheritée. Blanchard Vocal
Ens. Nonesuch 71051.
ISAAC, HEINRICH
Missa Carminum. Niedersächsischer Sing-
kreis: Träder. Nonesuch 71084.
JANEQUIN, CLEMENT
Chansons. Montreal Bach Ch: Little. Vox
500710.
JOSQUIN DES PREZ
Mass: L'Homme armé; Motets; *Chansons.*
Prague Madrigal Singers; Vienna Musica
Antiqua: Venhoda. Crossroads 22160094.
Motets. Munich Capella Antiqua; Ruh-
land. Telefunken S 9480. Motets; *Instru-
mental pieces.* N.Y. Pro Musica; Green-
berg. Decca (US) 79410.
LASSUS, ROLAND DE
Madrigals. N.Y. Pro Musica: Greenberg.
Decca (US) 79424. *Masses: Bell' Amfitrit
altera; In die tribulationis.* Prague Madrigal
Singers: Venhoda. Bach Guild 70651; 651.

LE JEUNE, CLAUDE
Chansons. Kreder Ens. Nonesuch 71001.
MONTE, PHILIPPE DE
Madrigals. Prague Madrigal Ch: Venhoda.
Bach Guild 70 655. *Missa secunda sine
nomine.* St Rombouts Ch: Vijverman.
Musica Sacra AMS 5; AM 5.
OBRECHT, JACOB
Mass: Sub tuum praesidium. Lipsiensis
Capella: Knothe. DGG ARC 198406.
Vienna Chamber Ch; Vienna Musica
Antiqua: Gillesberger. Bach Guild 70653;
653.
SWEELINCK, JAN PIETERSZOON
Variations; Toccatas; Fantasias. Leon-
hardt, org & hpschd. Cambridge CRS 1508.
WILLAERT, ADRIAN
Madrigals; Motets; *Ricercari.* Ambrosian
Singers: Stevens. Odyssey 32160202.

Italy: 1300–1600 (Chapter 5)

ANTHOLOGIES

History of Music in Sound: Vol. 4, *The
Age of Humanism:* Demophon; Marenzio;
Luzzaschi; G. Gabrieli; A. Gabrieli. HMV
HLP 8–10; RCA LM 6029.
The Art of Ornamentation and Embellish-
ment in the Renaissance and Baroque:
Archilei; Rore; Merulo; Layolle. Bach
Guild 70697–98; 697–98.
A Florentine Festival: Monteverdi;
Marenzio; Malvezzi; Cavalieri; Trom-
boncino; Nola; Cara; Festa. Musica
Reservata: Beckett. Argo 2RG 602.
Masterpieces of Music before 1750: Record
1: Landini; A. Gabrieli. Record 2: Pales-
trina; Marenzio. Haydn Society HSL
2071–72 (W. W. Norton).
Medieval English Carols and Italian
Dances. N.Y. Pro Musica: Greenberg.
Decca (US) DL 79418.
Storia della Musica Italiana: Vol. 1, Record
1, *Ars Nova:* Jacobus de Bonania;
Giovanni da Cascia; Landini; Trom-
boncino; Marco Cara; Donati; Stefano
Felis; Antiquis; Fanello; A. Gabrieli;
Palestrina; Vecchi. Record 2, *Polyphonia
Profana del 1400 e 1500:* Vecchi; Cop-
pinus; Corteccia; Dalza; Crema; Trom-
boncino; Francesco di Milano; Galilei;
Negri; Caroso; Cavazzoni; A. Gabrieli;
Merulo; G. Gabrieli; Luzzaschi; Rossi;
Ingegnieri; Ferrabosco; Francesco d'Ana;
Monteverdi; Palestrina. Record 6, *La*

Polyphonia Sacra dei Maestri di Scuola Romana: Nanini; Anerio; Francesco Soriano; G.Gabrieli; Croce. Record 7, *Il Madrigale:* Marenzio; Gesualdo; Vecchi; Croce; Banchieri; A.Gabrieli; Striggio; Monteverdi. RCA (Ital) LM 40 000.

INDIVIDUAL COMPOSERS

ANERIO, GIOVANNI FRANCESCO
Missa pro defunctis. Carmelite Ch: Malcolm. Oiseau Lyre 60042. *Viveen felice; Conversione di S. Paolo.* Münster/Westfalen Kirchenmusikschule Ch: Ewerhart. Turnabout 34172.

BANCHIERI, ADRIANO
Festino. Ital. Nuovo Madrigaletto: Giani. Turnabout 34067. *La Pazzia senile.* Marenzio Sestetto: Saraceni. Heliodor S 25060.

GABRIELI, ANDREA
Sacred Music; Ricercar. Ambrosian Singers; Brass Ens: Stevens. Angel S 36443.

GABRIELI, GIOVANNI
Music for Multiple Choirs, Brass and Organ. Biggs, org; Gregg Smith Singers; Texas Boys Choir; Edward Tarr Brass Ens: Negri. Columbia (US) MS 7071; CBS (Eng) SBRG 72663. Canzoni; Motets. Ambrosian Singers; Brass & String Ens: Stevens. Angel S 36443.

GESUALDO, CARLO
Madrigals. Ens: Craft. Odyssey 32160107.

LANDINI, FRANCESCO
Madrigals; *Cacce; Ballate;* etc. Zurich Ancient Instrumental Ens. Odyssey 32160178.

MARENZIO, LUCA
Madrigals. Luca Marenzio Ens: Saraceni. Everest 3179.

PALESTRINA, GIOVANNI PIERLUIGI DA
Missa Papae Marcelli; Motets. Regensburg Cathedral Ch: Schrems. DGG ARC 19182 (73182). *Missa Papae Marcelli.* Wagner Chorale: Wagner. Angel S 36022.

VECCHI, ORAZIO
Il Convito Musicale: Madrigals. Ital. Nuovo Madrigaletto: Giani. Turnabout 34067.

England: from the Beginnings to *c.*1540 (Chapter 6.1)

ANTHOLOGIES

History of Music in Sound: Vol. 5, *Ars Nova and the Renaissance:* Dunstable; Davy; Fayrfax; Taverner; Redford. HMV HLP 5–7; RCA LM 6013.

Die englische Motette im goldenen Zeitalter: Tallis; Taverner; Tye. St John's College Ch: Guest. Musica Sacra AMS 37–STE.

English Keyboard Music: *Tudor Age to Restoration:* Redford; Tallis. Wolfe, hpschd. EA 0013.

In Nomines: Tye; Taverner. In Nomine Players. Bach Guild 576.

Medieval English Carols and Italian Dances. N.Y. Pro Musica: Greenberg. Decca (US) DL 79418.

Music of the Middle Ages: Vol. 5, *English Medieval Songs:* St Godric Songs. Oberlin, c–t; Barab, viol. EA 0029. Vol. 4, *English Polyphony of the XIIIth and Early XIVth Centuries:* Anon. Oberlin, c–t; Bressler, t; Barab, viol; Blackman, viol. EA 0024. Vol. 6, *XIVth and Early XVth Century English Polyphony:* Cooke; Damett; Power; Sturgeon. Oberlin, c–t; Bressler, t; Myers, b; Wolfe, org. EA 0031.

Religious Music, *c.* 1400: Forest; Power; Dunstable. Capella Antiqua Munich: Ruhland. Telefunken SAWT 9505; AWT 9505.

To Entertain a King: *Music for Henry VIII:* Cornyshe; Barbireau; Henry VIII; Richafort; Purcell Consort of Voices: Burgess; Musica Reservata: Morrow. Argo ZRG 566; RG 566.

Treasury of English Church Music: Vol. 1: Queldryk; Excetre; Damett; Dunstable; Frye; Cornyshe. Ambrosian Singers: Stevens. HMV CSD 3504.

INDIVIDUAL COMPOSERS

DAVY, RICHARD
Passion according to St Matthew. Partridge, t; Keyte, bs; Burgess, c–t; Purcell Consort of Voices; All Saints Ch; Burgess. Argo ZRG 558; RG 558.

DUNSTABLE, JOHN
Sacred and Secular Music. Ambrosian Singers: Stevens. EA 36.

TALLIS, THOMAS
Cantiones sacrae in 5 and 6 voices. *Cantores in Ecclesia:* Howard. Oiseau Lyre S311–13. *Lamentations of Jeremiah;* Church Music. King's College Ch: Willcocks. Argo ZRG 5479, 5436; RG 5479, 5436.

TAVERNER, JOHN
Mass: The Western Wind; Kyrie (Le Roy). King's College Ch: Willcocks. Argo ZRG 5316; RG 5316.

England: *c*. 1540–1610 (Chapter 6.2)

ANTHOLOGIES

History of Music in Sound: Vol. 4, *The Age of Humanism (1540–1630)*: Wilbye; Greaves; Weelkes; Morley; Tallis; Byrd; Gibbons; Dowland; Coperario; Bull; Farnaby. HMV HLP 8–10; RCA LM 6029.

The Art of Ornamentation and Embellishment in the Renaissance and Baroque: Parsons. Bach Guild 70697–98; 697–98.

The Consort of Music: Allison; Bull; Byrd; Dowland; Gibbons; Morley; Peerson. The Consort Players and Singers: Beck. Columbia (US) KL 5627.

Early English Keyboard Music: White; Blitheman; Bull; Johnson; Hooper; Farnaby; Byrd; Tomkins. Dart, hpschd. Oiseau Lyre OLS 114–18.

Elizabethan and Jacobean Ayres, Madrigals and Dances: Morley; Dowland; Byrd; Hume; Gibbons; Coperario; Jones; Farmer; Campian. N.Y. Pro Musica: Greenberg. Decca (US) 79406.

Die englische Motette im goldenen Zeitalter: Blitheman; Byrd; Dering; Phillips. St John's College Ch: Guest. Musica Sacra AMS 37-STE.

English Lute Music: R. Johnson; J. Johnson; Cutting; Dowland; Morley; Rosseter; Bulman; Batchelor; Holborne. Bream, lute. RCA Victor (Eng) SB 2150; RB 16281.

English Madrigal School: Vol. 1: Morley; Weelkes; Vautor; Edwards; Bartlett; Bennet; Wilbye; Ward. Vol. 2: Wilbye; R. Johnson; Weelkes; Edwards; Tallis; Shepherd. Deller Consort. Bach Guild 553–54.

An Evening of Elizabethan Verse and Music: Weelkes; Jones; Wilbye; Ferrabosco; Morley; Kirbye; Dowland; Gibbons; Ward; Tomkins. N.Y. Pro Musica: Greenberg; Auden, reader. Odyssey 32160171.

In Nomines: Bull; Tomkins; R. White. In Nomine Players. Bach Guild 576.

Lo, Country Sport: Tomkins; Weelkes; Breton; East; Young; Farnaby; Cavendish; Lodge; Campian. Purcell Consort of Voices. Burgess; Elizabethan Consort of Viols; Tyler, lute. Argo ZRG658.

Lute Songs: Dowland; Rosseter; Morley; Ford; Pilkington; Campian. Pears, t;

Bream, lute. London (US) 25896; 5896; Decca (Eng) SXL 9191; LXT 5567.

Masters of English Keyboard Music: Vol. 1, *Four Centuries of Music for Organ, Harpsichord and Clavichord:* Preston; White; Blitheman; Tallis; Gibbons; Newman; Bull; R. Johnson; Hooper; Farnaby. Vol. 2, *William Byrd and Thomas Tomkins.* Vol. 3, *John Bull and Matthew Locke.* Vol. 4, *Orlando Gibbons and Giles Farnaby.* Dart, org, hpschd, clav. Oiseau Lyre OL 50075–76; 50130–31.

Music of the Waits: Parsons; Bassano; Farnaby; Brade; Adson. Various artists: Smithers. Argo ZRG 646.

The Royal Brass Music of King James 1: Simpson; Harding; Holborne; Leetherland; Guy; Bassano; Farnaby; Johnson; Coperario; Ferrabosco; Doring; Lupo. Ens: Dart. Oiseau Lyre OL 60019.

Treasury of English Church Music: Vol. 2: Marbeck; Tallis; Morley; Byrd; Parsons; Weelkes; Dering; Child; Philips; Tomkins; Mundy; Gibbons; Farrant. Westminster Abbey Ch: Guest. HMV CSD 3536.

INDIVIDUAL COMPOSERS

BULL, JOHN
Keyboard Music. Dart, hpsch. Oiseau Lyre S 255.

BYRD, WILLIAM
Cantiones sacrae in 5 and 6 voices. Cantores in Ecclesia: Howard. Oiseau Lyre S 311–13. Masses, 3, 4, 5 Parts. King's College Ch: Willcocks. Argo ZRG 5362, 5226; RG 362, 226. *Music for Voices and Viols.* Oberlin, c-t; Barab, viol; Blackman, viol. EA 37.

CAMPIAN, THOMAS
Philip Rosseter's Book of Ayres, Part 1. Soames, t; Gerwig, lute; Koch, viol. DGG ARC 3004 (14501).

DERING, RICHARD
Cantiones sacrae. Peterborough Cath. Ch. Argo (5) 318.

DOWLAND, JOHN
Ayres. Von Ramm, m-s; Burgess, c-t; Rogers, t; Klein, b; Binkley, lute; Early Music Studio. DGG ARC 73245 (198345). Ayres. Soames, t; Gerwig, lute; Koch, viol. DGG ARC 3004 (14501). Oberlin, c-t; Iadone, lute. EA 0034.

MORLEY, THOMAS
Canzonets; Madrigals. Ambrosian Singers:

Stevens. Harpsichord Lessons. Aveling, hpschd. DGG ARC 73209 (198309). Ayres. Soames, t; Gerwig, lute; Hoch, viol. DGG ARC 3004 (14501). Madrigals. Deller Consort. Vanguard S 157.

TOMKINS, THOMAS
Consort Music. In Nomine Players: Stevens. Oryx 720. Vocal Music. Ambrosian Singers: Stevens. Oryx 719.

WEELKES, THOMAS
Church Music. St John's College Ch: Guest. Argo ZRG 5237; RG 237.

WILBYE, JOHN
Madrigals. Deller Consort. Vanguard S 157.

Germany: 1300–1600 (Chapter 7)

ANTHOLOGIES

History of Music in Sound: Vol. 3, *Ars Nova and the Renaissance:* Paumann; Buchner. HMV HLP 5–7; RCA LM 6016.
Anthologie de la Musique Chorale Allemande: Les Maîtres de la Renaissance: Isaac; Lemlin; Scandello; Hassler; Fink; Schein; Lassus. Radio-Berlin Ch; Koch. Chant du Monde LDZ-Q 8199.
The Art of Ornamentation and Embellishment in the Renaissance and Baroque: Hofhaimer. Bach Guild 70697–98; 697–98.
German Songs of the Middle Ages and the Renaissance: Isaac; Walther von der Vogelweide; Schlick; Folz; Senfl; Walther; Sachs; Albert. Cuénod, t; Leeb, lute. Westminster XWN 18848.
Organ Recital: Isaac; Susato. Talsma, org. DGG ARC 198445.
Renaissance Music: Isaac; Zwingli. Munich Capella Antiqua: Ruhland. Telefunken SAWT 9561–2.
Songs of the Renaissance (Germany and Austria): Lassus; Hassler; Senfl; Scandello; Franck; Fink; Lemlin; Othmayer; Praetorius; Lechner; Eccard; Vulpius; Friderici. Vienna Academy Ch: Gillesberger. SPA 58.
Weltliche Zwiegesänge aus Georg Rhaws Bicinia Gallica: Stahl; Stoltzer; Voit. Kinderchor Bender. DGG ARC 3072 (14003).

INDIVIDUAL COMPOSERS

DEMANTIUS, CHRISTOPH
Deutsche Passion nach Johannes; Weissagung des Leidens und Sterbens Jesu Christi aus dem 53. Kapitel des Propheten Esajae zu

6 Stimmen. NC.R.V. Vocal Ens: Voorberg. Nonesuch (7) 1138. *Weissagung* ... Spandauer Kantorei: Behrmann. Turnabout TV 34175.

HASSLER, HANS LEO
Lustgarten neuer teutscher Gesäng, Balletti, Gailliarden und Intraden a 4–8. Lipsiensis Capella: Knothe. DGG ARC 2533041. *Neue teutsche Gesäng.* Berlin Motet Ch: Arndt. DGG ARC 3075 (14010).

ISAAC, HEINRICH
Missa Carminum. Hannover Norddeutsche Singkreis: Träder. Nonesuch 71084.

LECHNER, LEONHARD
Gesellige Zeit: Weltliche Chorgesänge. Berlin Motet Ch: Arndt. DGG ARC 3075 (14010). *Das Leiden unsers Herrn Jesu Christi.* Spandauer Kantorei: Behrmann. Turnabout 34175.

SACHS, HANS
Weisen. Bruckner-Rüggeberg, t; Aue, b. (with *Locheimer Liederbuch:* 14 Songs and Pieces) DGG ARC 73222 (198322).

SCHLICK, ARNOLT
Organ Music. Froidebise, org. Nonesuch 71051.

SENFL, LUDWIG
Magnificat; Motets; Lieder. Munich Capella Antiqua: Ruhland. Telefunken SAWR 9431; AWT 9431. *Missa Paschalis;* Lieder. N.Y. Pro Musica: Greenberg. Decca (US) 79420.

WIDMANN, ERASMUS
Dances; Gailliards. (with Praetorius: *Terpsichore;* Schein: *Banchetto Musicale*) Terpsichore Collegium. DGG ARC 73153 (198166).

WOLKENSTEIN, OSWALD VON
Lieder. (with *Glogauer Liederbuch:* Songs) Various Groups. DGG ARC 3033 (14512).

Spain: from the Beginning to *c.* 1450 (Chapter 8.1)
Spain: *c.* 1450–1600 (Chapter 8.2)

ANTHOLOGIES

History of Music in Sound: Vol. 3, *Ars Nova and the Renaissance:* De la Torre. HMV HLP 5–7; RCA LM 6016.
Llibre Vermell motets. Early Music Studio. Telefunken S 9504.

INDIVIDUAL COMPOSERS

ALFONSO EL SABIO (ALFONSO X)
Cantigas de Santa Maria. Oberlin, c-t;

Iadone, lute. EA 23.

CABEZON, ANTONIO DE
Obras de Musica. Froidebise, org. None-such 71016. Rilling, org. Turnabout 34097.

CORRERA DE ARAUJO, FRANCISCO
Facultad orgánica. Rilling, org. Turnabout 34097.

MORALES, CRISTOBAL DE
Magnificat septimi toni; Lamentabatur Jacob; Motets. Blanchard Ens. Nonesuch 71016. Motets. Ambrosian Consort and Singers: Stevens. Dover 7271.

VICTORIA, TOMÁS LUIS DE ·
Motets. Wagner Chorale: Wagner. Angel S 36022.

The Slav Countries:
from the Beginnings to 1600 (Chapter 9)

ANTHOLOGIES

Anthologie Sonore: Vol. 2, Record 5, *16th Century Vocal Music of Russia, Poland, Spain and England:* Szamotulski; Gomolka; Zielenski; Russian Liturgical Chants. Motet and Madrigal Ch: Opienski. AS 10.

Musica Antiqua Bohemica: The Oldest Monuments of Czech Music: Homophonic song from *Hospodine pomiluj ny'* to *Jistebnický kancionál;* Specimens of liturgical drama and two homophonic instrumental pieces. MAB 21. The oldest Czech polyphony: Polyphonic pieces from Prague University Library VH 11, the *Franusúv kancionál,* the *Speciálník kralovéhradecký* (including the setting of '*Náš milý Svatý Václave,* probably by Gontrášek). MAB 22. *Missa super Dolorosi Martir* (Harant z Polžic). MAB 24. *Ráčil pamět' zústaviti';* (Turnovský); '*Vsemohúcí Stvoriteli'* and eight other pieces

from the *Benešovsky Kancionál, Rychnovský Decantabat populus,* two of Vodnaňsky's Odes, the anonymous *Kyrie 'Dunaj, voda hluboká,* etc. MAB 28.

Muzyka polskiego odrodzenia ('Muza' Polskie Nagrania). Pieces from Jan Lublin's Tablature (including Mikołaj z Krakowa's *Ave Jerachia*) and two courants for lute by Jakub Polak. Rutkowski, org; Wysocka-Ohlewska, hpschd. L 0109. Mikołaj z Krakowska's part-song *Aleć nade mna Wenus* and the anonymous *Oczy me mile,* reconstructed from Jan Lublin's tablature; Anonymous part-songs from the Zamoyski and Pulawski *Kancjonals.* Polish Radio Ch: Kolaczkowski. L 0110. Anonymous lament from the *Zamojski Kancjonal: In te Domine speravi* and *Juž sie zmiercha* by Wacław z Szamotul; *Benedictus* from Marcin Leopolita's *Missa Paschalis; Kyrie* by Tomasz Szadek; three Psalms by Gomolka; Bazylik's *Z ochotnym sercem.* Men's and Boy's Ch of State Philharmonic, Poznan: Stuligrosz. L 0111.

INDIVIDUAL COMPOSERS

GALLUS, JACOBUS (HANDL)
Opus Musicum Harmonarium. Prague Madrigal Ch: Venhoda. Bach Guild 70655.

The Western Hemisphere:
from the Beginnings to 1600
(Chapter 10)

Salve Regina: Lienas (Juan Hernández) (*Salve Regina; Magnificat quarti toni*); Hidalgo (*Magnificat septimi toni; Gloria and Sicut erat; Hijos de Eva tributarios Tomás de Herrea*). Roger Wagner Chorale: Wagner. Angel S-36008.

PETER WARD JONES

Bibliography

INTRODUCTION

There is a separate bibliography for each chapter, listing, as well as books and articles, editions of the music itself. The following is a list of bibliographical abbreviations used throughout this book, including footnotes and chapter bibliographies:

Acta: *Acta Musicologica*
AfMF: *Archiv für Musikforschung*
AfMW: *Archiv für Musikwissenschaft*
CMM: *Corpus Mensurabilis Musicae*
Congress: see bibliography, section on Congresses (p. 441)
DDT: *Denkmäler deutscher Tonkunst*
DTB: *Denkmäler der Tonkunst in Bayern*
DTO: *Denkmäler der Tonkunst in Österreich*
Festschrift: see bibliography, section on *Festschriften* (pp. 441–2)
Grove: *Grove's Dictionary of Music*
HAM: *Historical Anthology of Music*
JAMS: *Journal of the American Musicological Society*
LU: *Liber Usualis*
MGG: *Musik in Geschichte und Gegenwart*

ML: Music and Letters
MQ: Musical Quarterly
Mus. Disc: Musica Disciplina
NOHM: New Oxford History of Music
PRMA: Proceedings of the Royal Musical Association
SIMG: Sammelbände der internationalen Musikgesellschaft
ZfMW: Zeitschrift für Musikwissenschaft

All the titles listed in the chapter bibliographies occur as well in the general alphabetical bibliography at the end of this volume (pp. 453–86), together with other items useful for further study. This general bibliography of about a thousand items lists titles in full, e.g. Einstein, A., *The Italian Madrigal*, 3 vols., Princeton, 1949, whereas chapter bibliographies, footnotes, etc. use abbreviated titles which are self-explanatory, i.e. Einstein, *Madrigal*. (If one key-word is not sufficient to identify a title, more words are added. In the case of authors of the same last name, initials are given.) Again, in chapter bibliographies, footnotes, etc., periodical articles are abbreviated and distinguished from books in that titles are given in quotation marks rather than italics. For example: Lesure, *Renaissance* is an abbreviated book title, but Lesure, 'Facture' refers to an article in the periodical *Galpin Society Journal*, listed fully in the alphabetical bibliography under Lesure. When the periodical happens to be a major serial that is listed in our abbreviations (e.g. *ML*, *MQ*, etc.) it seemed most convenient to refer to the periodical itself. As an instance, Einstein, A., 'The Elizabethan Madrigal and "Musica Transalpina"', *ML*, xxv (1944), 66–77 would be abbreviated to *ML* (1944) 66, without mention of the name of the author or title of the article.

Some of the items listed in the alphabetical bibliography are to be found in major research libraries only. For this reason chapter bibliographies and the general bibliography are preceded by a brief discussion of reference tools under the headings of Dictionaries, Periodicals, Congresses, *Festschriften*, Histories, Treatises, General books, and musical sources. Obviously, Dictionaries, Histories, General books and Musical sources are the most frequently used tools. And it goes without saying that those published in a single volume are most readily available in smaller libraries and most easily purchased.

DICTIONARIES

English, American

Baker's Biographical Dictionary of Musicians, rev. N.Slonimsky, 5th ed., New York, 1958; suppls., 1965 and 1971 [good bibliographies].
Everyman's Dictionary of Music, rev. Sir Jack Westrup, 5th edn., London, 1971.
Grove's Dictionary of Music, ed. E.Blom, 5th edn., 9 vols., London, 1954; suppl. vol., 1961.
Harvard Dictionary of Music, Willi Apel, 2nd edn., Cambridge (Mass.), 1969 [dictionary of musical terms; good bibliographies].

French

Dictionnaire de la musique (Bordas), ed. M.Honegger, Paris, 1970 ff. [2 vols., biographical, published 1970; vol. iii, musical terms, in preparation].
Encyclopédie de la musique (Fasquelle), ed. F.Michel, F.Lesure and V.Fedorov, 3 vols., Paris, 1958–61.

German

Die Musik in Geschichte und Gegenwart, ed. F.Blume, 14 vols., Kassel, 1949–68; suppl. fascicles, 1969 ff. [good bibliographies].
Riemann Musik Lexikon, edd. W.Gurlett

and H.H.Eggebrecht, 12th edn., Mainz, 1959 ff. [3 vols. on biography, one on terms; further vols. in preparation].

Italian

La Musica (UTET), ed. G.M.Gatti and A.Basso, Turin, 1966–71 [4 vols., *Enciclopedia storica*, 1966; 2 vols., *Dizionario*, 1968–71; good bibliographies].

Spanish

Diccionario de la música Labor, ed. J.Pena, H.Anglès and M.Querol, 2 vols., Barcelona, 1954.

PERIODICALS

The main periodicals and yearbooks listed below are referred to also in the list of abbreviations at the beginning of this bibliography:

Acta Musicologica, Leipzig, 1928/9–1935; Copenhagen, 1936–53; Basle, 1954 ff.
Archiv für Musikforschung, Leipzig, 1936–43.
Archiv für Musikwissenschaft, Leipzig, 1918/19–26; Trossingen, 1952–61; Wiesbaden, 1962 ff.
Journal of the American Musicological Society, Boston, 1948 ff.
Music and Letters, London, 1920 ff.
Musica Disciplina, Cambridge (Mass.), 1946; Rome, 1948 ff. (Originally published as *Journal of Renaissance and Baroque Music*).
Musical Quarterly, New York, 1915 ff.
Proceedings of the Royal Musical Association, London, 1874 ff.
Sammelbände der internationalen Musikgesellschaft, Leipzig, 1899/1900–1913/14.
Zeitschrift für Musikwissenschaft, Leipzig, 1918/19–1935.

In addition, the following are useful as reference sources for periodical articles:

Music Index, Detroit, 1950 ff. [for the years 1949–66].
Répertoire international de la littérature musicale (RILM), 1967 ff.
Bibliographie des Musikschrifttums, ed. W.Schmieder, *et al*, 1954 ff. [for the years

1950 ff; organized by periods such as Middle Ages, Renaissance and Baroque, etc.]

See also the cumulative indexes provided by individual periodicals, as in the case of *ML, MQ, Mus. Disc.*, and *PRMA*.

CONGRESSES

The publications listed under this heading are all accounts of conferences, whether entitled Proceedings, *Kongressbericht, Colloque* etc. Short reference during the course of this volume is by place and date, e.g. *Congress Basel 1924*. If the main subject of a congress is not music, the subject is usually added in the short reference, e.g. *Congress Oxford 1966, Byzantine*.

1924: Basel – Musikwissenschaftlicher Kongress – Leipzig, 1925.
1927: Vienna – Beethoven Zentenarfeier, Internationaler musikhistorischer Congress – Vienna, 1927.
1935: Florence – *Papirologia*, Atti del IV° congresso internazionale de – Milan, 1936.
1949: Basel – Internationale Gesellschaft für Musikwissenschaft – Basel, 1949.
1952: Utrecht – Internationale Gesellschaft für Musikwissenschaft – Amsterdam, 1953.
1954: Palermo – Atti del congresso ... musica mediterranea – Palermo, 1959.
1955: Wégimont – *Ars Nova:* Colloques de l'Université de Liège – Paris, 1959.
1956: Hamburg – Gesellschaft für Musikforschung – Kassel, 1957.
1956: Vienna – Internationaler musikwissenschaftlicher Kongress – Graz, 1958.
1958: Cologne – 7. Internationaler musikwissenschaftlicher Kongress – Kassel, 1959.
1962: Kassel – Gesellschaft für Musikforschung – Kassel, 1963.
1966: Oxford – *Byzantine* Studies, Proceedings of the XIIIth International Congress of – London, 1967.

FESTSCHRIFTEN

The publications listed under this heading are all volumes in honour of a scholar, whether entitled Essays in Honour, Birthday Offering, *Festschrift*, etc. They are arranged according to the name of the person honoured. See W. Gerboth, 'Index of *Festscriften* and some similar Publications', *Festschrift Reese*, pp. 183–307, and Gerboth's more recent *Index to Musical Festschriften*, New York, 1969. Short reference during the course of this volume is merely by name, e.g. *Festschrift Reese*.

Adler, Guido, 75th birthday, Vienna, 1930.
Albrecht, Hans, In memoriam, Kassel, 1962.
Anglès, Higinio, Miscelánea, 2 vols., Barcelona, 1958–61.
Barblan, Guglielmo, 60th birthday, Florence, 1966.
Besseler, Heinrich, 60th birthday, Leipzig, 1961.
Blume, Friedrich, 70th birthday, Kassel, 1963.
Crozet, René, 70th birthday, 2 vols., Paris, 1966.
Engel, Hans, 70th birthday, Kassel, 1964.
Fellerer, Karl Gustav, 60th birthday, Regensburg, 1962.
Handschin, Jacques, In memoriam, Strasburg, 1962.
Hoboken, Anthony van, 75th birthday, Mainz, 1962.
Jeppesen, Knud, 70th birthday, Copenhagen, 1962.
Johner, Dominicus, *Der kultische Gesang*, Cologne, 1950.
Kroyer, Theodor, 60th birthday, Regensburg, 1933.
Osthoff, Helmut, 65th birthday, Tutzing, 1961.
Plamenac, Dragan, 70th birthday, Pittsburgh, 1969.
Reese, Gustave, *Aspects of Medieval and Renaissance Music*, New York, 1966.
Riemann, Hugo, 60th birthday, Leipzig, 1909.
Rubió i Lluch, Homenatge, Barcelona, 1937.
Schenk, Erich, 60th birthday, Graz, 1962.
Schering, Arnold, 60th birthday, Berlin, 1937.
Scheurleer, D. F., 70th birthday, The Hague, 1925.
Schmidt-Görg, J., 60th birthday, Bonn, 1957.
Schneider, Max, 80th birthday, Leipzig, 1955.
Waesberghe, Joseph Smits van, *Organicae*

Voces, Amsterdam, 1963.
Wagner, Peter, 60th birthday, Leipzig, 1926.
Wellesz, Egon, 80th birthday, Oxford, 1966.
Wiora, Walter, 60th birthday, Kassel, 1967.

HISTORIES

Adler, Guido, ed., *Handbuch der Musikgeschichte*, 2nd edn., 2 vols., Berlin, 1930.
Besseler, Heinrich, *Die Musik des Mittelalters und der Renaissance*, Potsdam, 1931.
Grout, Donald J., *A History of Western Music*, New York, 1960.
Láng, Paul Henry, *Music in Western Civilisation*, New York, 1941 (London, 1942; re-issued 1963).
Manuel, Roland Alexis, ed., *Histoire de la musique* (Encyclopédie de la Pléiade), 2 vols., Paris, 1960–3.
New Oxford History of Music, i–iv, London, 1954–68.
Reese, Gustave, *Music in the Middle Ages*, New York, 1940.
—, *Music in the Renaissance*, New York, 1954 (rev. edn. 1959).
Seay, Albert, *Music in the Medieval World* (Prentice Hall History of Music Series), Englewood Cliffs (N.J.), 1965. (Another volume in the same series, devoted to the Renaissance period, by H. M. Brown, is in preparation.)

TREATISES

Corpus Scriptorum de Musica (American Institute of Musicology), Rome, 1950 ff. Series includes, in vol. v, *Notitia del valore delle note del canto misurato*, ed. A. Carapetyan, 1957.
Coussemaker, E.-H. de, *Scriptorum de musica medii aevi nova series*, 4 vols., Paris, 1864–76 (repr. 1931 and 1963).
Gerbert, Martin, *Scriptores ecclesiastici de musica sacra*, 3 vols., St Blaise, 1784 (repr. 1931 and 1963).
Migne, J.P., *Patrologiae cursus completus*, Series Latina, 221 vols., Paris, 1844–65.
Musical Theorists in Translation, Brooklyn (N.Y.), 1959 ff. Series includes, in vol. viii, *Ad organum faciendum ...*, ed. J. Huff, 1969.
Musicological Studies and Documents (American Institute of Musicology),

Rome, 1951 ff. [23 vols. have appeared up to 1970].

GENERAL BOOKS
(not listed in chapter bibliographies)

Apel, W., *Geschichte der Orgel- und Klaviermusik bis 1700*, Kassel, 1967.
Apel, W., *The Notation of Polyphonic Music, 900–1600*, 5th edn., Cambridge (Mass.), 1953.
Baines, A., *European and American Musical Instruments*, London, 1966.
Harrison, F. L., and Rimmer, J., *European Musical Instruments*, London, 1964.
Lavignac, A., and Laurencie, L. de la, edd., *Encyclopédie de la musique* .... Partie I, 5 vols., Partie II, 6 vols., Paris, 1913–31.
Leichtentritt, Hugo, *Geschichte der Motette*, Leipzig, 1908.
Nelson, R. U., *The Technique of Variation*, Berkeley, 1948.
Parrish, C., *The Notation of Medieval Music*, New York, 1957.
Sachs, Curt, *The History of Musical Instruments*, New York, 1940.
Schaeffner, André, *Origines des Instruments de Musique*, Paris, 1936.
Strunk, Oliver, *Source Readings in Music History*, New York, 1950.
Wagner, Peter, *Geschichte der Messe, 1. Teil: bis 1600*, Leipzig, 1913.
Wolf, J., *Geschichte der Mensural-Notation von 1250–1460*, 3 vols., Leipzig, 1904 [reviewed by F. Ludwig, *SIMG*, vi (1905), 597].

MUSICAL SOURCES

The following general sources will be found in the chapter bibliographies under the names of individual composers, and in the alphabetical list under the names of individual editors. Several of these items are referred to also in the list of abbreviations at the beginning of the bibliography.

Anthologies

Apel, Willi, ed., *Musik aus früher Zeit*, 2 vols., Mainz, 1934.
Davison, A. T., and Apel, W., edd., *Historical Anthology of Music*, 2 vols., Cambridge (Mass.), 1947–50.
Gleason, H., ed., *Examples of Music before 1400*, New York, 1941.
Parrish, Carl, ed., *A Treasury of Early Music*, London, 1959.
Parrish, C., and Ohl, J. F., edd., *Masterpieces of Music before 1750*, London, 1952.
Schering, A., ed., *Geschichte der Musik in Beispielen*, Leipzig, 1931.

Collections

Bordes, C., et al, edd., *Anthologie des maîtres religieux primitifs*, Paris, 1893–5.
Corpus of Early Keyboard Music (American Institute of Musicology), Rome, 1963 ff.
Corpus Mensurabilis Musicae (American Institute of Musicology), Rome, 1948 ff.
Denkmäler der Tonkunst in Bayern, Leipzig, 1900–31.
Denkmäler der Tonkunst in Österreich, Vienna, 1894 ff.
Denkmäler deutscher Tonkunst, Leipzig, 1892–1931.
Musicological Studies and Documents (American Institute of Musicology), Rome, 1951 ff.
Publikationen älterer ... Musikwerke, ed. R. Eitner, 29 vols., Leipzig, 1873–1905.

CHAPTER BIBLIOGRAPHIES

**Introduction: Ancient Greece
(Chapter 1)**

Abert: *Ethos;* Anderson: *Ethos; Aristoxenus:* see edd. by Macran, Rios, Wehrli, Westphal; Bataille: 'Notations'; Düring: *Ptolemaios,* 'Terminology'; Emmanuel: 'Grèce'; Gombosi: *Tonarten;* Grande: *Espressione;* 'Frammento'; Higgins: 'Lute-players'; Hunger: 'Musikfragmente'; Husmann; *Grundlagen;* Jan: *Musici;* Laloy: *Aristoxène;* Landels: 'Agora', 'Brauron'; Lippman: *JAMS* (1963) 3, *Thought, MQ* (1963) 188; Lobel: *Oxyrhynchus;* Longman: 'Papyrus'; Macran: *Aristoxenes;* Marrou: *Education,* 'Melographia', *Augustin;* Martin: *Documents;* Mountford: 'Papyri', 'Scales', 'Fragment'; *Oxyrhynchus:* see Lobel; Page: *Alcman;* Pearl: 'Michigan'; Pickard-Cambridge: *Festivals;* Pöhlmann: *Musikfragmente;* Potiron: 'Notations'; Rios:

Aristoxenes; Sachs: *ZfMW* (1924/25) 1, (1923/24) 289; Schlesinger: *Aulos;* Turner: 'Papyri'; Vetter: 'Musik'; Vogel: *Enharmonik;* Wegner: *Musikleben;* Wehrli: *Aristoxenus;* Westphal: *Aristoxenus;* Winnington-Ingram: 'Aristoxenus', *Mode,* 'Tuning', 'Scale'.

The Early Christian Period (Chapter 2)

Gregorian chant

GENERAL REFERENCE WORKS

Anglès: *NOHM,* ii.58, 91; Apel: *Gregorian;* Bryden-Hughes: *Index;* Corbin: 'Chrétien', *Eglise;* Ferretti: *Estetica, Esthétique;* Froger: 'Chants'; Jungmann: *Missarum; Liber Usualis* [abbreviated LU]; *Paléographie Musicale;* E.Werner: *Bridge.*

OTHER PUBLICATIONS

Baroffio: 'Offertorien'; Bosse: *Untersuchung;* Burne: 'Mass Cycles'; Claire: 'Evolution'; Corbin: 'Cantillation'; Frere: *Sarisburiense;* F.Haberl: 'Choralcredo', 'Gradualien'; Hesbert: *Sextuplex,* 'Offertoire'; Holman: *JAMS* (1963) 36; Homan: 'Cadence', *JAMS* (1964) 66; Hucke: *AfMW* (1956) 285; Huglo: 'Gloria', 'Credo', 'Kyrie', 'Tonaire'; Husmann: 'Alleluia'; McKinnon: 'Polemic';˙ Melnicki: *Kyrie;* Ott: *Offertoriale;* Rönnau: *Tropen;* Schmidt: 'Tractus'; Schrade: 'Cycle'; Steiner: *JAMS* (1966) 162; Thannabaur: *Sanctus;* Wellesz: 'Alleluia'.

Liturgical drama

GENERAL REFERENCE WORKS

Corbin: 'Teatro'; Coussemaker: *Drames;* Lipphardt: 'Dramen'; Stratman: *Drama;* K.Young: *Drama.*

OTHER PUBLICATIONS

Most relevant publications since 1957 are noted in an annual feature by J.Smits van Waesberghe, entitled 'Das gegenwärtige Geschichtsbild der mittelalterlichen Musik', in *Kirchenmusikalisches Jahrbuch.* In addition the following will be found useful: Anderson: *Drama;* Arco Avalle-Monterosso: *Sponsus;* Brandel: 'Drama';

Chailley: *Saint Martial;* Corbin: 'Sibyllae'; Davis: *Non-Cycle;* Guiette: 'Réflexions'; Harbage: *Annals;* Hardison: *Rite;* Jodogne: 'Theatre'; McShane: *Drama;* R.Meier: 'Osterspiel'; Michael: 'Bühne'; Pellegrini: 'Dante'; Smoldon: *MQ* (1965) 507, *ML* (1946) 1; Sticca: 'Passion'; Vey: *Theater;* Wagenaar: 'Planctus'; W.Werner: *Osterspiele.*

Hymns

COLLECTIONS WITHOUT MUSIC

Chevalier: *Repertorium;* Dreves: *Analecta.*

COLLECTIONS WITH MUSIC

Moberg: *Hymnen;* Stäblein: *Hymnen.*

OTHER PUBLICATIONS

Bernard-Atkinson: *Irish;* C.Blume: *Hymnar;* Brou-Wilmart: 'Office'; Corbin: 'Portugaises'; Lipphardt: 'Hymnenstudien'; Mearns: *Hymnaries;* Moragas: 'Himnes'; Stäblein: 'Hymnusmelodie'; Vogel: 'Hymnaire'; Warren: *Bangor.*

Supplement

The following recent books will also be found useful: Dolan, D.M., *Le Drame liturgique de Pâques en Normandie et en Angleterre au moyen âge.* Dissertation, Poitiers, Centre d'Études médiévales, 1972 (in the press); Huglo, M., *Les Tonaires, inventaire, analyse, comparaison* (Publications de la Société Française de Musicologie, IIIeme série, vol. 2), Paris, 1971.

The Eastern Church

In addition to the works listed in Velimirović, *Eastern Chant,* i. pp. xiii–xvi, the following should be consulted:

BYZANTINE CHANT

Huglo: 'Byzance';
Strunk: *MQ* (1942), *Specimina* (*Pars principalis* contains 187 facsimiles from 45 MSS, 10th to 13th century; *Pars suppletoria* contains an introduction), 'Byzantine';
Velimirović: *Eastern Chant,* ii, pp. 1–4.
Wellesz: *Byzantine, Elements.*

MODERN GREEK CHANT
Dragoumis: 'Survival';

BYZANTINE HYMNS
Follieri: *Initia* (identification of hymn incipits).

SLAVIC CHANT
Palikarova: *Byzantine;* Velimirović: *Early Slavic,* 'Slavic Countries', 'Kirchen-slavische'.

Supplement

In addition to the above, the following books and articles published during the last five years will be of use: *Anfänge der slavischen Musik*, Bratislava, 1966; Floros, C., *Universale Neumenkunde*, 3 vols., Kassel, 1970; Levy, K., 'The Italian Neophytes' Chant', *JAMS*, xxiii (1970), 181–227; Huglo, M., 'Les Chants de la Missa Greca de Saint-Denis', in *Festschrift Wellesz*, pp. 74–83; *Musica Antiqua Europae Oorientalis*, Warsaw, 1966 (i); Bydgoszcz, 1969 (ii), 1972 (iii); Veli-mirović, M., 'Present Status of Research in Byzantine Music', *Acta*, xliii (1971), 1–20.

**Polyphony and Secular Monophony:
ninth century–*c*. 1300 (Chapter 3)**

SOURCES

Anglès: *Huelgas;* Aubry: *Motets, Arsenal;* Auda: *Motets;* Baxter: *Wolfenbüttel₁;* J.B. Beck: *Cangé, Roi;* Dittmer: *Wolfenbüttel₂, Firenze;* Gennrich: *Clayette;* Husmann: *Notre Dame;* Knapp: *Conductus;* Liuzzi, *Lauda;* Prado: *Jacobi;* Reckow, *Anonymous IV:* Rokseth: *Polyphonies;* Thurston: *St Victor;* Wagner: *Jakobusliturgie;* Waite: *Polyphony;* Wilkins: *Adam.*

BOOKS AND ARTICLES

Aarburg: *AfMW* (1958) 20, 'Minnesang'; Apel: 'St Martial', *JAMS* (1954) 121; Besseler: *AfMW* (1925) 167; Birkner; *AfMW* (1961) 183; Bukofzer: 'Conductus'; Dahlhaus: 'Organum'; Eggebrecht: 'Ars', *AfMW* (1961) 73; Ellinwood: *MQ* (1941) 165; Ficker: 'Klangformen'; Fuller, *JAMS*

(1971) 169; Geering: *Organa*, 'Retrospek-tive'; Gennrich: *Troubadours, Formenlehre,* 'Rondeaux'; Georgiades: *AfMW* (1957) 223; Göllner: *Mehrstimmigkeit;* Handschin: *ZfMW* (1929) 1, *Acta* (1952) 113, *Musikgeschichte,* 'Motette'; F.L.Harrison: *Acta* (1965) 35; Holschneider: *Winchester;* Hüschen: 'Artes'; Husmann: *AfMW* (1962) 1, *JAMS* (1963) 176, *MQ* (1963) 311; Karp: *Acta* (1967) 144; Kuhlmann: *Motetten;* Ludwig: 'Geistliche', *Repertorium;* Machabey: 'Winchester'; Reaney: *Manuscripts;* Reichert: 'Wechselbezie-hungen'; Rokseth: 'Polyphonie'; Sanders: *JAMS* (1964) 261, 'Perotin'; G.Schmidt: 'St Martial'; H.Schmidt: *ZfMW* (1931/2) 129; Schrade: 'Political'; N.E.Smith: *JAMS* (1966) 328; Spanke: 'St Martial'; Stäblein: 'St Martial', *Acta* (1966) 27; Steiner: *MQ* (1966), 56; Tischler: *Acta* (1959) 86, *Acta* (1956) 87; Treitler: *JAMS* (1964) 29; Vanderwerf: 'Trouvères', 'Recitative', 'Chansons'; G.Vecchi: 'Monodia', 'Uffici'; Waite: *JAMS* (1961) 147; Zaminer: *Traktat.*

Supplement

In addition to the above, the following books published during the last five years will be of use: Arlt, W., *Ein Festoffizium des Mittelalters aus Beauvais in seiner liturgischen und musikalischen Bedeutung*, 2 vols., Cologne, 1970; Eggebrecht, H.H., and Zaminer, F., *Ad Organum Faciendum* (Neue Studien zur Musikwissenschaft, iii); Flotzinger, R., *Der Discantussatz im Magnus Liber and seiner Nachfolge* (Wiener musikwissenschaftliche Beiträge, viii), Vienna, 1969; Lütolf, M., *Die mehrstimmigen Ordinarium Missae-Sätze vom ausgehenden 11. bis zur Wende des 13. zum 14. Jahrhundert*, 2 vols., Bern, 1970; Stenzl, J., *Die vierzig Clausulae der Handschrift Paris Bibliothèque Nationale 15139*, Bern and Stuttgart, 1970.

**France and Burgundy: 1300–1500
(Chapter 4.1)**

Major composers will be found under the names of the following editors: Binchois: s.v. Gurlitt, Rehm; Busnois: s.v. Boer;

Dufay: s.v. Besseler; Grenon: s.v. Marix; Lescurel: s.v. Wilkins; Loqueville: s.v. Reaney; Machaut: s.v. Schrade, Van, G. de; Ockeghem: s.v. Plamenac; Vitry: s.v. Schrade.

SOURCES

Apel: *French Music, French Compositions;* Besseler: *Dufay;* Boer: *Anthonius;* Borren: *Tornacensis;* DTO: vii, xi, xix, xxvii, xxxi, xl; Droz: *Poètes; Chansonniers;* Günther: *Motets;* Gurlitt: *Binchois;* Hoppin: *Cypriot;* Marix: *Bourgogne;* Plamenac: *Okeghem;* Reaney: *15th Century;* Rehm: *Binchois;* Schrade: *Polyphonic;* Stäblein-Harder: *Mass;* Van: *Messe;* Wilkins: *Lescurel, Reina I, Reina II.*

BOOKS AND ARTICLES

Besseler: *AfMW* (1952) 159, (1958) 1, 'Grundsätzliches' [*Schenk*], 'Grundsätzliches' [*Musikforschung*], *Bourdon;* Bockholdt: *Dufay;* Borren: *Dufay, Etudes;* Clercx: 'Figures'; *Congress Wégimont 1955;* Coville: 'Vitry'; Dannemann: *Musiktradition;* Droz: 'Chansonnier'; Gilles: *Mus. Disc.* (1956) 35, (1958) 59; Günther: *Mus. Disc.* (1958) 27; Hamm: *Dufay;* Hoppin: *Mus. Disc.* (1958) 93; Lesure: *Nord;* Levarie: *Machaut;* Krenek: *Ockeghem;* Lockwood: 'Parody'; Machabey: *Machaut;* Marix: *Histoire;* Piaget: 'Cour'; Picker: 'Charles VIII'; Pognon: 'Vitry'; Reaney: *Mus. Disc.* (1952) 33, (1953) 129, (1959) 25, *Acta* (1955) 40; Schrade, *Acta* (1955) 13, *MQ* (1956) 330, *Commentary;* Seay: *Mediaeval;* Stäblein-Harder: *Critical;* S. J. M. Williams: 'Machaut'.

France: 1500–1600 (Chapter 4.2)

Major composers will be found under the names of the following editors: Arcadelt: s.v. Helm, Seay; Beaulaigue: s.v. Auda; Brumel: s.v. Expert (Maitres); Bertrand: s.v. Expert (Monuments); Bonnet: s.v. Expert (Florilège); Certon: s.v. Expert (Monuments), Agnel; Costeley: s.v. Expert (Maitres), (Florilège); Du Caurroy: s.v. Expert (Maitres), Martin, Bonfils; Févin: s.v. Expert (Maitres); Goudimel: s.v.

Expert (Maitres), (Monuments); Janequin: s.v. Expert (Maitres), (Florilège), Merritt; La Rue: s.v. Expert (Maitres); Lassus: s.v. Expert (Maitres) (Florilège); Le Blanc: s.v. Expert (Monuments); Le Jeune: s.v. Expert (Maitres) (Monuments) (Florilège), Walker, D.P., Sanvoisin; Le Roy: s.v. Morcourt; L'Estocart: s.v. Expert (Monuments); Lupi: s.v. Albrecht, H.; Mauduit: s.v. Expert (Maitres) (Florilège); Morlaye: s.v. Morcourt; Mouton: s.v. Expert (Maitres); Passereau: s.v. Dottin; Planson: s.v. Verchaly; Regnart: s.v. Expert (Maitres); Sermisy: s.v. Allaire.

SOURCES (other than the single editions of individual composers listed above)

Bonfils: *Chansons;* Brown: *Theatrical;* Cauchie: *Chansons;* Eitner: *Chansons;* Expert: *Fleur, Florilège, Maitres, Monuments;* Giraud: *Fleur, Chansons;* Heartz: *Preludes;* Hewitt: *Odhecaton, Canti B;* Lesure: *Anthologie;* Mairy: *Chansons;* Maldeghem: *Trésor;* Pidoux: *Psautier;* Smijers: *Motets.*

BIBLIOGRAPHICAL BOOKS AND ARTICLES

Cauchie: 'Recueils'; Frissard: 'Chardavoine'; Heartz: *Printer;* Lesure: 'Du Chemin'; 'Chansons Janequin', *Le Roy,* 'Marot'; Rollin: *Marot;* Thibault: 'Haye', *Ronsard;* Verchaly: 'Chardavoine', 'Desportes'.

GENERAL BOOKS AND ARTICLES

Allaire: 'Sermisy'; Bartha: *ZfMW* (1930–1) 507; Bernstein: 'Gervaise'; Borren: 'Réflexions'; Brenet: *Musique;* Brown: *Theater;* Cauchie: 'Clereau'; Dottin: 'Marot'; Droz: 'La Grotte'; Haar: *Chanson;* Hertzmann: 'Chanson'; Jacquot: *Poésie;* Launay: 'Motets'; Lesure: 'Facture', 'Janequin Recherches', *NOHM,* iv. 237, 'Orchestres', 'Paladino', *Renaissance;* Levy: 'Costeley', 'Susanna'; MacClintock: *Mus. Disc.* (1959) 109; Masson: 'Humanisme'; Pidoux: 'Psaumes'; Pirro: *Histoire;* Saulnier: 'Phinot'; Silliman: 'Responce'; Walker: 'Humanism', *Mus. Disc.* (1946) 91, (1950) 163; Yates: *Academies.*

The Low Countries: 1500–1600 (Chapter 4.3)

SOURCES

Major composers will be found under the names of the following editors; also, where indicated, in *HAM*. Agricola: s.v. Lerner; Brumel: s.v. Carapetyan; Clemens non Papa: s.v. Bernet Kempers, *HAM;* Compère: s.v. Finscher, Hewitt (*Odhecaton*), Blume (*Josquin; Weltliche Lieder*), *HAM;* Ghiselin: s.v. Gottwald; Gombert: s.v. Schmidt-Görg, *HAM;* Isaac: see chapter 7; Josquin: s.v. Smijers, Blume, H. Osthoff; Kerle: s.v. Ursprung; La Rue: s.v. Blume, Lenaerts, *HAM* [see also Section I, Music in France]; Lassus: see chapter 7; Martini: s.v. Gerber; Monte: s.v. Borren, *HAM;* Mouton: s.v. Minor; Obrecht: s.v. J. Wolf, Smijers-Crevel, *HAM;* Pipelare: s.v. Cross; Sweelinck: s.v. Seiffert (1894–1901), Seiffert and Sigtenhorst Meyer (1943 ff.), Leonhardt and Annegarn and Noske (1968); Vaet: s.v. E. H. Meyer; Wert: s.v. MacClintock, *HAM*.

BOOKS AND ARTICLES

Apel: *Notation;* Bernet Kempers: *Mus. Disc.* (1954) 173, (1961) 187, (1964) 85; Bötticher: *Lasso;* Bukofzer: *Studies;* Crevel: *Coclico;* Croll: *Mus. Disc.* (1952) 67; Cross: *Mus. Disc.* (1963) 97; Finscher: 'Compère'; Gombosi: *Obrecht;* Gottwald: *Mus. Disc.* (1961) 105; Kahmann, *Mus. Disc.* (1950) 153, (1951) 143; Lowinsky: *Chromatic;* MacClintock: *Mus. Disc.* (1956) 106; Marshall; *JAMS* (1963), 347; Meier: *Mus. Disc.* (1956) 67; H. Osthoff, *Josquin;* Sparks: *Cantus Firmus;* Van der Straeten: *Pays-Bas*.

Italy: 1300–1600 (Chapter 5)

SOURCES

Major composers will be found under the names of the following editors: Anerio: s.v. Petti; Arcadelt: s.v. Helm, Seay; Asola: s.v. Della Ragione, Fouse; Bossinensis: s.v. Disertori; Cavazzoni: s.v. Benvenuti, Mischiati; Ciconia: s.v. Clercx; Cima: s.v. Rayner; Corteccia: s.v. Haydon, McKinley; Crema: s.v. Gullino; Facoli: s.v. Apel; Festa: s.v. Main; Fogliano: s.v. Benvenuti (Cavazzoni); Gabrieli, A.: Alessi, s.v. Arnold, Benvenuti; Gabrieli, G.: s.v. Arnold, Benvenuti; Galilei, V.: s.v. Fano; Gastoldi: s.v. Hermann; Gesualdo: s.v. Pizzetti, Weismann; Gostena: s.v. Gullino; Jacopo da Bologna: s.v. Marrocco, Schrade; Landini: s.v. Ellinwood, Schrade; Luzzaschi: s.v. Cavicchi; Mainerio: s.v. Schuler; Marenzio: s.v. Arnold, Einstein, Engel, Mompellio; Merulo: s.v. Bastian, Disertori, Dalla Libera; Milano: s.v. Ness; Molinaro: s.v. Gullino; Monte: s.v. Borren; Monteverdi: s.v. Malipiero; Padovano: s.v. Speer; Palestrina: s.v. Espagne, Casimiri; Parabosco: s.v. Bussi; Pisano: s.v. D'Accone; Porta: s.v. Cisilino, Snow; Radino: s.v. Gullino, Ellingworth; Rore: s.v. Meier, Smith; Segni: s.v. Benvenuti (Cavazzoni); Silva: s.v. Kirsch; Terzi: s.v. Caffagni; Vecchi: s.v. Rüegge, Martin, W., Somma; Verdelot: s.v. Bragard; Viadana: s.v. Gallico, Scharnagl; Vicentino: s.v. Kaufmann; Wert: s.v. MacClintock; Willaert: s.v. Zenck; Zarlino: s.v. Flury (1961).

Sources other than the single editions of individual composers listed above: Apel: *Antegnata;* Bonfantini: *Rappresentazione;* Carapetyan: 'Faenza', *Notitia;* Carducci: Cacce; Casimiri: *Monumenta;* Cesari: *Frottole;* D'Accone: *Florentine;* Einstein: *Canzoni, Madrigal;* Hertzmann: *Willaert;* Jeppesen: *Italia, Laude;* Kastner: *Versetten;* Lefkoff: *Lute;* Liuzzi: *Lauda;* Lowinsky: *Medici;* MacClintock: *Bottegari;* Marrocco: *Cacce* (1961); Masson: *Chants;* Meier: *Arcadelt, Nasco;* A. C. Minor: *Renaissance;* Newman: *Dances;* Pirrotta: *Fourteenth Century;* Schmitz: *Figuralpassionen;* Schwarz: *Petrucci;* Slim: *Musica nova;* Stainer: *Dufay;* Torchi: *Arte;* Van: *Monuments;* Vergili: *Madrigalisti;* Walker: *Intermèdes;* Westphal: *Karnevalslieder;* Wiora: *Willaert;* Wolf: *Squarcialupi*.

TREATISES AND CHRONICLES

Elders: *Aaron;* Fano: *Galilei: Dialogo;* Miller: *Glarean;* Peter: *Ganassi;* Schneider: *Ganassi;* Vicentino: *Musica;* Wesselofsky: *Paradiso;* Zarlino: *Dimostrationi; Istitutioni; Sopplimenti*.

BOOKS AND ARTICLES

Alessi: *JAMS* (1952) 187; Andrews: *Palestrina*; Arnold: *PRMA* (1955–6) 47, *ML* (1950) 341, *ML* (1959) 4, *Mus. Disc.* (1961) 200, *Acta* (1965) 62, *Marenzio* (1965); Barblan: 'Rognoni'; Becherini: 'Poesia'; H. Beck: 'Konzil'; Bedbrook: *Middle Ages*; Bonaccorsi: *Lucca*; Borren: 'L'ars nova'; Bridgman: 'Fêtes', *Vie*, 'Braidense'; Brown: *Instrumental*; Burns: *JAMS* (1959) 133; Bussi: *Umanità*; Carapetyan: 'Musica Nova'; Cellesi: 'Documenti'; Clercx: 'Ciconia'; Corsi: 'Madrigali inediti', 'Madrigali e ballate'; D'Accone: *JAMS* (1961) 307, *Mus. Disc.* (1963) 115, *Mus. Disc.* (1966) 151, 'Coppini'; Dahlhaus: 'Gesualdos'; Dardo: 'Crema', 'Liuto'; Disertori: 'Evolution'; Ducrot: 'Cappella'; Einstein: *Madrigal*; Engel: *Marenzio ... Vita*; Fellerer: *Orgel, Palestrina, MQ* (1953) 576; Ferand: 'Motetti'; Ferracci: *Palestrina*; Fischer: 'Chronologie ... du Trecento', 'Influence', 'Jacobo', *Paolo*, 'Répartition', *Studien*, 'Trecentofragment', *Mus. Disc.* (1957) 38, *Acta* (1958) 179–99, *AfMW* (1959 87, *MQ* (1961) 41, *Mus. Disc.* (1963) 75, *Mus. Disc.* (1966) 31; Flury: *Zarlino* (1962); Frotscher: *Orgelspiel*; Gallico: *Cancioniere, Isabella, MQ* (1962) 68; Ghisi: *Canti*, 'Canzoni', 'Lauda', 'Persistance', 'Perugia'; Ghislanzoni: 'Formes'; Goldine: *Acta* (1962) 142; Haar: *Chanson, JAMS* (1965) 22, *Mus. Disc.* (1966) 95; Hagopian: *Ars Nova*; Harran: *JAMS* (1969) 27, *MQ* (1969) 521; Haydon: 'Kerle', *JAMS* (1959) 105; Hilmar, 'Ergänzungen'; Horsley: *JAMS* (1959) 118; Jeppesen, 'Kirchenmusik', *Orgelmusik, Palestrina*, 'Tanzbuch', *Acta* (1950) 36; Johnson: *JAMS* (1953) 227; Kämper: 'Instrumentalduo'; Kaufmann: *Life ... of Vicentino*; Kenton: Gabrieli; Kinkeldey: *Orgel*; Kirsch: 'Silva'; Kniseley: *Soriano*; Körte: *Laute*; Kroyer: *Chromatik*; Kunze: *Instrumentalmusik*; Lerner: *MQ* (1964) 44; Lockwood: 'Accidentals', *MQ* (1957) 342; Lowinsky: *Tonality*; Lunelli: *Arte*; MacClintock: 'Light', *Wert ... Life*; Mace: *MQ* (1969) 65; Marrocco: 'Cacce' (1951), *Acta* (1959) 32, *Acta* (1967) 84; Martinez: *Trecento*; Massera: *Mano*; Meyer-Baer: 'Dante'; C. A. Miller: *Mus. Disc.* (1961) 156; Newman: 'Fallamero'; Nuten:

Madrigali; W. Osthoff: *Theatergesang*; Palisca: *MQ* (1960) 344; Pease: *Mus. Disc.* (1968) 231; Pirrotta: 'Chronologia', 'Sonetti', 'Stil', *Mus. Disc.* (1949) 119, *Mus. Disc.* (1955) 57, *JAMS* (1966) 127; Plamenac: 'Antico', 'Light', *JAMS* (1951) 179, *JAMS* (1955) 165; Pope: 'Montecassino'; Reaney: *Mus. Disc.* (1958) 67, *Mus. Disc.* (1960) 33; Redlich: *Monteverdi*; Rubsamen: 'Festa', *Sources*; Rüegge: *Geistliche*; Sartori: *Petrucci, Strumentale*; (1958) 45; Slim: *JAMS* (1962) 35, *Mus. Disc.* (1964) 63, *Mus. Disc.* (1965) 109; Smither: *Acta* (1969) 186; Southern: *Acta* (1963) 114; D. Stevens: 'Verified', *MQ* (1961) 315, *MQ* (1967) 161; Strom: 'Mehrstimmigkeit'; Tadlock: *JAMS* (1958) 29; Tagmann: *Mantua*; Torchi: *Strumentale*; Vogel: *Vocalmusik*; Wasielewski: *Instrumentalmusik*; Weinmann: *Konzil*; Wilkins: *Mus. Disc.* (1963) 57; Winterfeld: *Gabrieli*; Young: *Mus. Disc.* (1962–3).

England: from the Beginnings to *c.* 1540 (Chapter 6.1)

SOURCES

Major composers will be found under the names of the following editors: Carver: s.v. D. Stevens; Dunstable: s.v. Bukofzer; Fayrfax: s.v. E. B. Warren; Ludford: s.v. Bergsagel.

Sources other than the single editions of individual composers listed above: Apel: *Keyboard*; Charles: *Pepys*; Dittmer: *Worcester*; Harrison: *Eton*; And Hughes-Bent: *Old Hall*; Ans Hughes: *Worcester*; McPeek: *Egerton*; Myers: *Music*; Pearce: *Songs*; Ramsbotham: *Old Hall*; Stainer: *Bodleian*; J. Stevens: *Carols, Henry VIII*; Wooldridge: *Early English*.

BOOKS AND ARTICLES

H. K. Andrews-Dart: *ML* (1958) 1; Apfel: 'England', *Satztechnik, Acta* (1961) 47; Baillie: *Acta* (1960) 178, *MQ* (1958) 196, *PRMA* (1956–7) 15; Baillie-Oboussier: *ML* (1954) 19; M. Bent: *JAMS* (1968) 137, *PRMA* (1967–8) 19; Bergsagel: *ML* (1963) 240, *Mus. Disc.* (1960) 105, *Mus. Disc.*

(1962) 35; Bukofzer: *Mediaeval, MQ* (1954) 29; Caldwell: *Mus. Disc.* (1965) 129; Charles: *Mus. Disc.* (1962) 57; Dittmer: *Mus. Disc.* (1957) 5, *Mus. Disc.* (1954) 19; Elliott, *ML* (1960) 349; Georgiades: *Diskanttraktate;* Greene: *Carol;* Hamm: *ML* (1960) 211; *Mus. Disc.* (1968) 47; Handschin: 'Monument', *Mus. Disc.* (1949) 55; Harrison: 'Eton', *Mediaeval,* 'Sarum', *Mus. Disc.* (1962) 11, *Mus. Disc.* (1967) 67; And. Hughes: 'Pairs', *JAMS* (1966) 352; And. Hughes-M.Bent, *Musc. Disc.* (1967) 97; Ans. Hughes: *Mus. Disc.* (1952) 83; Kenney: *MQ* (1959); Kovarik: *JAMS* (1968) 21; Sanders: *Acta* (1965) 19, *AfMW* (1967) 24, *JAMS* (1962) 249, *Mus. Disc.* (1965) 7; G.Schmidt: *AfMW* (1958) 230; Schofield: 'Sumer', *MQ* (1946) 509; D.Stevens: *ML* (1958) 148, *MQ* (1955) 26, *Mus. Disc.* (1955) 105, *Mus. Disc.* (1959) 155; J.Stevens: *Court, ML* (1951) 29; Trowell: *Mus. Disc.* (1959) 43; Trumble: 'Faburden'; E.B.Warren: *Mus. Disc.* (1957) 134, *Mus.Disc.* (1958) 145, *Mus.Disc.* (1961) 112; W.Young: *Mus. Disc.* (1962) 115.

England: *c.* 1540–1610 (Chapter 6.2)

Major composers and theorists will be found under the names of the following editors and collections: Bull: s.v. *Musica Britannica;* Byrd: s.v. Andrews (Hilda), Fellowes, *Musica Britannica;* Campion: s.v. Arkwright (*Old English*); Daman: s.v. Arkwright (*Old English*); Dering: s.v. *Musica Britannica;* Dowland: s.v. *Musica Britannica,* Warlock; Farnaby: s.v. *Musica Britannica;* Ferrabosco: s.v. Arkwright (*Old English*); Gibbons: s.v. Fellowes, Harrison (*Early English*), *Musica Britannica;* Jenkins: s.v. *Musica Britannica;* Kirbye: s.v. Arkwright (*Old English*); Leighton: s.v. Harrison (*Early English*); Milton: s.v. Arkwright (*Old English*); Morley: s.v. S.Beck, Harman; Munday: s.v. Harrison (*Early English*); Philips: s.v. *Musica Britannica;* Ravenscroft: s.v. Shaaber, Warlock; Shepherd [or Sheppard]: s.v. Harrison; Tomkins: s.v. Harrison (*Early English*), *Musica Britannica;* Tye: s.v. Weidner; Weelkes: s.v. *Musica Britannica;* White: s.v. Arkwright (*Old English*); Wilbye: s.v. Arkwright (*Old English*).

Sources other than the single editions of individual composers, listed above: Dart: *Parthenia;* Fellowes: *Lutenist, Madrigal School;* Frost: *Psalm Tunes;* Fuller-Maitland: *Fitzwilliam;* Harrison: *Early English;* Hunt: *Cranmer;* Knight: *Treasury; Musica Britannica;* Rimbault: *Antiquarian;* Sabol: *Songs;* Simpson: *Broadside;* D.Stevens: *In nomine; Tudor Church Music.*

BOOKS AND ARTICLES

H.K.Andrews: *Byrd;* Arnold: *ML* (1954) 309; Baskervill: *Jig;* Borren: *Sources;* Boyd: *Elizabethan;* Brett: 'Paston': *PRMA* (1961–62) 73; Caldwell: *Mus. Disc.* (1965) 129; Clulow: *ML* (1966) 1; Curtis: *Sweelinck;* Dart: *Grove,* ii 949; Doe: *Tallis;* Donington-Dart: *ML* (1949) 101; Dowling: 'Dowland'; Duckles: *JAMS* (1948, No. 2) 23; Einstein: *ML* (1944) 66; Fellowes: *Cathedral, Madrigal Verse;* Frere: 'Edwardine'; Jacquot: *Instrumentale;* Jackman: *MQ* (1963) 17; Kerman: 'Byrd', *Madrigal,* 'Motet', *MQ* (1963) 431; Le Huray: *Reformation;* Lockwood: *ML* (1961) 336; Lumsden: 'Lute'; Newton: *PRMA* (1938–9) 63; Noble: 'Répertoire'; Osborne: *Whythorne;* Pattison: *Poetry;* Reese: *JAMS* (1949) 7; Schofield-Dart: *ML* (1951) 205; A.Smith: 'Parish Church', *ML* (1968) 108; Steele: *Earliest;* Sternfeld: *Shakespearean;* D.Stevens: 'Chanson', *Mulliner Commentary, Tomkins;* Ward: *JAMS* (1957) 151, *JAMS* (1967) 28; C.W.Warren: *MQ* (1968) 47; Woodfill: *Musicians.*

Supplement

In addition to the above the following recent books and articles will be found useful: Bray, Roger, 'The Part-Books Oxford, Christ Church, MSS. 979–983: An Index and Commentary', *Mus. Disc.,* xxv (1971), 179–97; Doe, Paul, 'Latin Polyphony under Henry VIII', *PRMA,* xcv (1968–9), 81–95; Daniel, Ralph T., and Le Huray, Peter, *The Sources of English Church Music, 1549–1660* (Early English Church Music, Supplementary volume 1), London, 1972; Poulton, Diana, *John Dowland,* London, 1972.

Germany: 1300–1500 (Chapter 7)

SOURCES

Major *Liederbücher* (Song Collections) will be found under the names of the following editors and authors: Anna of Cologne: s.v. Salmen-Koepp; Buxheim: s.v. Wallner (2 edns.), *HAM* (no. 84); Colmar: s.v. Runge, Eberth; Donaueschingen: s.v. Runge (*Colmar*); Glogau: s.v. Ringmann-Kapper, *HAM* (nos. 82–3); Heidelberg: s.v. Runge (*Montfort*), Jammers (*Montfort*); Hohenfurth: s.v. Bäumker; Jena: s.v. Holz, Müller; Lochamer: s.v. Ameln, F. W. Arnold, Petzsch, *HAM* (no. 81); Mondsee-Wiener: s.v. Mayer-Pietsch; Rostock: s.v. Ranke, Thierfelder; Schedel: s.v. Rosenberg; Vienna: see 'Wien'; Wien: s.v. Rietsch; Wienhäuser: s.v. Sievers.

Individual Composers will be found under the names of the following editors and authors (see also Gennrich's anthology, *Troubadours … Minne-and Meistersinger*): Frauenlob: s.v. Rietsch; Hugo von Reutlingen: s.v. Runge (*Colmar*, Eberth (*Kolmar*); Ileborgh: s.v. Most; *HAM* (no. 84); Lauffenberg; s.v. Boehme; 'Monk of Salzburg': s.v. Mayer-Rietsch; Paumann: s.v. Ameln, F. W. Arnold, *HAM* (no. 81); Wolkenstein: s.v. Koller-Schatz.

BOOKS AND ARTICLES

A. A. Abert: 'Nachleben'; Besseler: 'Lochamer'; Husmann: 'Kolmar'; Irtenkauf: 'Ergänzungen', 'Marienklage'; Jammers: *ZfMW* (1924–5) 265; Lipphardt: 'Marienklagen', *Osterspiele;* Michael: *Prozessionsspiele;* H. Osthoff: *AfMW* (1942) 65; Petzsch: 'Lochamer'; Rosenberg: *ZfMW* (1931–2) 67; Salmen: *Erbe;* Schnoor: *ZfMW* (1921–2) 1; Schrade: *Überlieferung;* Schubiger: *Spicilegien;* E. A. Schuler: *Osterfeiern;* Sievers: *Osterspiele;* Southern: *Buxheim;* Ursprung: *AfMW* (1922) 413; Wagner: 'Osterspiel'; Zitzmann: *Kolmar;* Zöbeley: *Buxheim.*

Germany: 1500–1600 (Chapter 7)

SOURCES

Works by major composers will be found under the names of the editors of single composers; in this particular chapter they are frequently scattered among composite editions (anthologies). Reference should be made to the following editors of single composers or anthologies:

A. Agricola: [Cf. chapter on Low Countries, pp. 201, 447; in addition to Lerner's complete edition see also:] Gombosi, *Obrecht;* Hewitt, *Odhecaton;* Maldeghem; Wolf, *Isaac,* xiv, 163, 205; Wolf, *Obrecht,* iii, 55; Schering, *Beispiele,* no. 53.
M. Agricola: s.v. Eitner; Funck; Wolf, *Rhau.*
Brätel: s.v. Eitner, 'Deutsches Lied'; Moser, *Egenolff;* Wolf, *Rhau.*
Dietrich: s.v. Albrecht (H.)-Moser; Eitner, 'Deutsches Lied'; Gudewill; Miller, *Glarean* (see also Bohn); Wolf, *Rhau;* Zenck, *Hymnen.*
Dressler: s.v. Eitner-Halm; Engelke; Ruetz; Schoeberlein.
Ducis: s.v. Eitner, *Forster 1540;* Gudewill, *Forster 1539;* Wolf, *Rhau.*
Eccard: s.v. Eitner; Schoeberlein; Teschner.
Finck: s.v. Eitner, *Finck, Forster;* Gerber, *Apel, Finck, Rhau, Zwölf Hymnen;* Hasse; Hoffmann-Erbrecht; Moser-Piersig; Nowak; *HAM,* no. 80.
Fulda: s.v. Gerber, *Apel;* Schering, *Studien.*
Harzer: see 'Resinarius'.
Hofhaimer: s.v. Bernoulli; Eitner-Maier; Gudewill; Harms; Koczirz; Liliencron, 'Horazischen'; Merian, *Tanz;* Moser, *Hofhaimer;* Moser-Heitmann; Nowak; *HAM,* nos. 87–88.
Isaac: s.v. Beczeny; Birtner; Cuyler, *Choralis, Masses;* Eitner, *Ott;* Fano; Gudewill; Hewitt, *Odhecaton;* Heyden; Just; Lipphardt; Merian, *Tanz;* Webern; Wolf; Schering, *Beispiele,* nos. 55–56; *HAM,* nos. 87–88.
Kerle: s.v. Bordes; Maldeghem; Ursprung; *HAM,* 148.
Köler: s.v. Ameln, *Handbuch,* ii, i; Göhler; Hoffmann-Erbrecht.

Lapicida: s.v. Gudewill; Lenaerts; Moser, *Hofhaimer;* Nowak.

Lasso, R.: s.v. Lipphardt.

Lassus, R. de: [In addition to the comprehensive editions of Haberl-Sandberger and Boetticher-Hermelinck, see also:] s.v. Bäuerle; Therstappen; Schering, *Beispiele,* nos. 125–7; *HAM,* nos. 143–5.

Lechner: s.v. Ameln, *Lechner, Handbuch* (i. 2–4; ii, 1; iii, 1); Ameln-Lipphardt, *Lechner-Hohelied,   Lechner-Johannes;* Lipphardt.

Luther: s.v. O.Albrecht-Moser; Schering, *Beispiele,* 77.

Meiland: s.v. Commer; H.Meyer; Schoeberlein.

Othmayr: s.v. Albrecht; Piersig.

Resinarius: s.v. H.Albrecht-Moser; Blume-Schulze; Gerber, *Rhau;* Wolf, *Rhau.*

Senfl: s.v. H.Albrecht-Moser; Eitner, *Forster, Ott;* Geering; Gerber, *Rhau;* Gerstenberg; Gudewill; Kroyer; Miller, Glarean (see also Bohn); Moser-Piersig; Wolf, *Rhau;* Schering, *Beispiele,* nos. 76 & 84–6; *HAM,* nos. 109–10.

Stoltzer: s.v. Albrecht; Albrecht-Gombosi; Eitner, *Ott;* Engel, *Kugelmann;* Gerber, *Rhau;* Gombosi, *Octo tonorum, 37. Psalm;* Gudewill; Hoffmann-Erbrecht, *Ostermesse, Werke;* Nowak; Wolf, *Rhau; HAM,* No. 108.

Walter: s.v. Ameln, *Handbuch,* i, 2–4, ii, 1, iii, 2; Ehmann, *Spielstücke;* Gurlitt; Kade; Schröder-Schneider; Schering, *Beispiele,* Nos. 80–81, *HAM,* No. 111.

SOURCES

Additional collections, as well as anthologies useful for composers other than those listed above will be found under the following editors: H.Albrecht-Moser; Ameln, *Handbuch;* Bäumker; Boehme; Commer; Heilfurth; Lenaerts; Miller, *Glareanus* (see also Bohn); Merian, *Tanz;* Moser-Fedtke; Moser-Heitmann; Moser-Piersig; Maldeghem; Reimann; Schoeberlein; Tintori-Monterosso.

BOOKS AND ARTICLES

Aber: *Pflege;* Anton: *Luther;* Bartha: *Ducis;* Baumann: *Lied;* Becker-Glauch: *Bedeutung;* Birtner: *AfMW* (1942) 40;

Blaschke: 'Isaac'; Blume, F.: *Kirchenmusik;* Boetticher: *Lasso ... Zeit, Wirkungskreis,* 'Lasso Studies'; Crevel: *Coclico;* Cuyler: *JAMS* (1950) 3; Ehmann: *Fulda;* Federhofer: *Mus. Disc.* (1955) 167, 'Lapicida', 'Monodie'; Frotscher: *Orgelspiel;* Gerber: 'Apel', *Sebaldus;* Gerhardt: *Walter;* Gombosi: *Obrecht;* Gurlitt: 'Walter'; Haas: *AfMW* (1922) 24; Huber 'Doppelmeister'; Kade: *Passionskomposition, SIMG* (1913–14) 535; Kendall: *Acta* (1939) 136; Kretzschmar: 'Luther'; Liliencron: 'Chorgesänge', 'Horazischen'; Lipphardt: *Proprium;* Lowinsky: *Chromatic;* Merian: *Kotter, AfMW* (1920) 22, *Tanz;* Moser: *AfMW* (1920) 337; *Hofhaimer;* Nedden: *ZfMW* (1932–3) 24; Nettl: *Luther;* Niemöller: *AfMW* (1958) 41; Nowak: 'Gesellschaftslied'; H.Osthoff: *ZfMW* (1931–2) 221, *Niederländer;* Paesler: 'Fundamentbuch'; Palisca: *Acta* (1959) 133; Petzsch: 'Weiterdichten'; Pietzsch: *AfMW* (1942) 90; Riemann: 'Apel'; Sandberger: 'Lasso'; Schweiger: *ZfMW* (1931–2) 363; Seidel: *Senfl;* Senn: *Innsbruck;* Smallman: *Passion;* Squire: *SIMG* (1911–12) 264; Sternfeld: 'Reformation'; Wagner: *Messe;* Wallner: *Steinätzkunst;* Werra: 'Buchner'; Wessely: 'Hofhaimeriana', 'Lapicida'; Wolff: 'Tranoscius'; Zenck: *Dietrich,* 'Deutschland'.

Spain: from the Beginnings to *c.* 1450 (Chapter 8.1)

SOURCES

Anglès: *Cantigas, Huelgas;* Brou: *Antifonario;* Whitehill: *Calixtinus;* Wagner: *Jacobusliturgie.*

BOOKS AND ARTICLES

Alonso: 'Cancioncillas'; Anglès: *AfMW* (1959) 5, 'Avignon', 'Cantors i organistes', 'Cantors und Ministrers', 'Cantu', *Catalunya,* 'Culture', 'Instrumentalmusik', 'Jacomi', 'Mehrstimmige', 'Reyneau', 'Ripoll', 'Spanien'; Beer: *Handschriften;* Donovan: *Drama;* Fontaine: *Isidore;* Gomez Brufal: *Bibliografía;* Handschin: *Acta* (1932) 5; Jeanroy: *Poésie;* Lindsay: *Originum;* Mundo: 'Datación'; Pedrell:

'Jean d'Aragon'; Pidal: 'Cantos'; Prado: *Manuel*, 'Mozarabic', *Rito;* Randel: *Responsorial;* Ribera: *Árabe;* Rojo: *Canto;* Salazar: *España;* C. Schmidt: *Quaestiones;* Spanke: 'Teoría'; Spitzer: 'Lyric'; Stern: *Chansons;* Trend: *Alfonso, ML* (1927) 13, *Spanish;* Ursprung: *ZfMW* (1921) 136; Wagner: 'Mozarabische'; Whyte: *Dance.*

Spain: *c.* 1450–1600 (Chapter 8.2)

Major composers and theorists will be found under the names of the following editors: Bermudo: s.v. Froidebise; Brudieu: s.v. Pedrell; Cabezón: s.v. Anglès, Kastner; Flecha: s.v. Anglès; Guerrero: s.v. Querol; Morales: s.v. Anglès; Mudarra: s.v. Pujol; Milán: s.v. Jacobs, Schrade; Narváez: s.v. Pujol; Ortiz: s.v. Schneider; Ramos de Pareja: s.v. Wolf; Salinas: s.v. Kastner; Santa María: s.v. Froidebise; Valderrábano: s.v. Pujol; Vásquez: s.v. Anglés; Victoria: s.v. Anglés, Pedrell.

Sources other than the single editions of individual composers listed above: Anglés: *Carlos V, Católicos;* Aroca: *Cancionero;* Bal y Gay: *Romances;* Barbieri: *Cancionero;* Elústiza: *Antología;* Figueras: *Católicos;* Gerber: *Hymnar;* Haberkamp: *Colombina;* Joaquim: *Cancioneiro;* Mitjana: *Cancionero;* Morphy: *Luthistes;* Pedrell: *Antología;* Querol: *Cancionero;* Rubio: *Antología;* Villalba Muñoz: *Canciones.*

BOOKS AND ARTICLES

Anglès: 'Colombina', 'Liedkunst', 'Magnificat', 'Morales y Guerrero', 'Orgelmusik'; Casimiri: 'Dominicalis', 'Vittoria'; Chase: 'Guitar', *ML* (1939) 420, *MQ* (1939) 292, *Spain;* Collet: *Victoria;* Coster: 'Anchieta'; Fox: 'Accidentals', 'Morales'; Heartz: *MQ* (1963) 59; Hill: *SIMG* (1913) 487; Howell: *MQ* (1964) 18; Illing: *Magnificat;* Jacobs: *Interpretación;* Kastner: *Cabezón,* 'Manuscritos'; Koczirz: *AfMW* (1922) 241; May: *Kompositionstechnik;* Mitjana: *Estudios, Guerrero;* Pedrell: *Catàlech, Victoria Abulense;* Pope: 'Cornago', 'Montecassino', 'Spanish', 'Villancico'; Riemann: 'Lautenwerk'; Rubio: 'Plasencia'; Russell: 'Villancicos'; Salazar: 'Laúd'; Stevenson: *Bermudo, Cathedral, Columbus, JAMS*

(1953) 3; Trend: *Milán, ML* (1925) 19; Ward: *JAMS* (1952) 88, 'Lute', *Mus. Disc.* (1952) 105, 'Vihuela'.

The Slav Countries: from the Beginnings to 1600 (Chapter 9)

SOURCES

Chomiński-Lissa: *Renaissance;* Chybiński and others: *Wydawnictwo;* Feicht: *Staropolska; Monumenta … Polonia;* Pohanka: *Dějiny;* Snížková: *Česká;* Szweykowski: *Cracow.*

BOOKS

Belyaev: *Drevnerusskaya;* Belza: *Istoriya cheshskoy, Istoriya polskoy;* Černušák: *Slovník;* Černý: *Soupis;* Chomiński: *Słownik;* Chybiński: *Słownik;* Findeizen: *Ocherki;* Jachimecki: *Historja, Muzyka na dworze, Muzyka polska, Tabulatura, Wpływy włoskie;* Keldysh: *Istoriya;* Lissa: *Antiqua;* Mokrý: *Anfänge;* Mužík: *Studie;* Nejedly: *Dějiny;* Palikarova: *Byzantine;* Petrov: *Ochertsi;* Racek: *Česká hudba, Středověká hudba;* Szweykowski: *Z dziejów;* Tumanina: *Istoriya;* Velimirović: *Early Slavic.*

The Western Hemisphere: from the Beginnings to 1600 (Chapter 10)

Baratta: *Cuzcatlán;* Barwick: *Franco;* Castillo: *Música;* Catalyne: 'Music'; Harcourt: *Musique;* Martí: *Instrumentos;* Mead: 'Inca'; Mendoza: *Panorama;* Sas: 'Vida'; Stevenson: *MQ* (1968) 475, *JAMS* (1962) 292, *Colonial Peru,* 'Columbia', *MQ* (1964) 241, *Aztec, Mexico, Peru: Aboriginal,* 'Quito'.

Supplement

In addition to the above the following articles will be found useful: Barwick, Steven, 'A Recently Discovered *Miserere* of Fernando Franco', *Yearbook for Inter-American Musical Research,* vi (1970), 77–89; Stevenson, Robert, 'Ancient Peruvian Instruments', *Galpin Society Journal,* xii (1959), 17–43.

GENERAL ALPHABETICAL
BIBLIOGRAPHY

Aarburg, Ursula, 'Ein Beispiel zur mittelalterlichen Kompositionstechnik ...', *AfMW*, xv (1958), 20–40.

Aarburg, Ursula, 'Melodien zum frühen deutschen Minnesang', *Zeitschrift für deutsches Altertum*, lxxxvii (1956/57), 24–45.

Aber, A., *Die Pflege der Musik unter den Wettinern*, Leipzig, 1921.

Abert, A.A., 'Das Nachleben des Minnesangs im liturgischen Spiel', *Die Musikforschung*, i (1948), 95–105.

Abert, H., *Die Lehre vom Ethos in der griechischen Musik*, Leipzig, 1899. [Reprinted Wiesbaden, 1968].

Adler, Guido, ed., *Handbuch der Musikgeschichte*, 2nd edn., 2 vols., Berlin, 1930. [Reprinted Tutzing, 1961].

Agnel, A., ed., *P. Certon: Chansons polyphoniques ... Livre I*, Paris, 1967.

Albrecht, H., ed., *Lupi: Zehn weltliche Lieder* (Das Chorwerk, xv), Wolfenbüttel, 1929.

Albrecht, H., ed., *Othmayr: Ausgewählte Werke*, 2 vols. (Erbe deutscher Musik, ser. i. vols. xvi and xxvi), Leipzig & Frankfurt, 1941 and 1956.

Albrecht, H., ed., *Stoltzer: Ausgewählte Werke* (Erbe deutscher Musik, ser. i, xxii), Leipzig, 1942. [see also s.v. Hoffmann-Erbrecht]

Albrecht, H. and Gombosi, O., edd., *Stoltzer: Lateinische Hymnen und Psalmen* (*DDT*, lxv), Leipzig, 1931.

Albrecht, H. and Moser, H.J. (and others), edd., *Rhau: Musikdrucke aus den Jahren 1538 bis 1545*, Kassel, 1955 ff. [6 vols. published up to 1970, i–v and vii; i–ii Resinarius, vii Dietrich].

Albrecht, O. and Moser, H.J. (and others), edd., *Luther: Werke*, vol. xxxv, Weimar, 1923 [the entire edition, so-called 'Weimarer Ausgabe', Weimar, 1883 ff].

Alessi, G. d', ed., *A.Gabrieli: Musiche di chiesa ... del 1587* (I classici musicali italiani, v), Milano, 1942.

Alessi, G. d', 'Precursors of Adriano Willaert in the Practice of *Coro Spezzato*', *JAMS*, v (1952), 187–210.

Allaire, G.G., 'Les messes de Claude de Sermisy (c. 1490–1562)', *Revue de Musicologie*, liii (1967), 28–40.

Allaire, G. and Cazeaux, I., edd., *Sermisy:*

Opera Omnia (*CMM*, lii), Rome, 1970 ff. [One vol. published by 1971].

Alonso, Dámaso, 'Cancionillas de "amigo" mozárabes (Primavera temprana de la lirica europea)', *Revista de Filologia Española*, 1949, 297 ff.

Ameln, K., ed., *Lechner: Werke*, Kassel, 1954 ff. [nine vols. published up to 1970: i–v, vii–ix, xii].

Ameln, K., ed., *Locheimer Liederbuch und Fundamentum organisandi des Conrad Paumann* [facs.], Berlin, 1925.

Ameln, K. and Lipphardt, W., edd., *Lechner: Hohelied Salomonis*, Kassel, 1928.

Ameln, K. and Lipphardt, W., edd., *Lechner: Johannespassion*, Augsburg, 1926.

Ameln, K. and Mahrenholz, C. (and others), edd., *Handbuch der deutschen evangelischen Kirchenmusik*, Göttingen, 1932 ff.

Anderson, M.D., *Drama and Imagery in English mediaeval Churches*, Cambridge, 1963.

Anderson, W.D., *Ethos and Education in Greek Music*, Boston, 1967.

Andrews, H.K., *An Introduction to the Technique of Palestrina*, London, 1958.

Andrews, H.K., *The Technique of Byrd's Vocal Polyphony*, London, 1966.

Andrews, H.K. and Dart, Thurston, 'Fourteenth-Century Polyphony in a Fountains Abbey Manuscript Book'. *ML*, xxxix (1958), 1–12.

Andrews, Hilda, ed., *William Byrd: My Lady Nevells Booke*, London, 1926 (Reprinted New York, 1955).

Anglès, H., ed., *Antonio de Cabezón: Obras de Música para Tecla, Arpa y Vihuela* (Monumentos de la música española, xxvii–xxix), 3 vols., Barcelona, 1966.

Anglès, H., 'Els cantors i organistes francoflamenco i alemanys a Catalunya el segles XIV–XVI', in *Festschrift Scheurleer*, pp. 49–62.

Anglès, H., 'Cantors und Ministrers in den Diensten der Könige von Katalonien-Aragonien im 14 Jhdt.', in *Kongress Basel 1924*, pp. 56–66.

Anglès, H., ed., *El Codex Musical de las Huelgas*, 3 vols., Barcelona, 1931.

Anglès, H., 'Cristobal de Morales y Francisco Guerrero', *Annuario musical*, ix (1954), 56–79.

Anglès, H., 'De cantu organico: Tratado de un autor catalán del siglo XIV', *Annuario Musical*, xiii (1958), 3–24.

Anglès, H., 'Early Spanish musical culture and Cardinal Cisneros' Hymnal of 1515', in *Festschrift Reese*, pp. 3–16.

Anglès, H., 'Gacian Reyneau am Königshof zu Barcelona in der Zeit von 139 ... bis 1429', in *Festschrift Adler*, pp. 64–70.

Anglès, H., 'Gregorian Chant', in *NOHM*, ii, 91–127.

Anglès, H., 'Die Instrumentalmusik bis zum 16. Jahrhundert in Spanien', in *Festschrift Jeppesen*, pp. 143–64.

Anglès, H., ed., *Juan Vasquez: Recopilación de Sonetos y Villancicos a quattro y a cinco, 1560*, (Monumentos de la música española iv), Barcelona, 1946.

Anglès, H., 'Latin Chant before Saint Gregory', in *NOHM*, ii, 58–91.

Anglès, H., ed., *Mateo Flecha, Las Ensaladas*, Barcelona, 1955.

Anglès, H., 'Die mehrstimmige Musik in Spanien vor dem 15. Jahrhunderts', in *Congress Vienna 1927*, pp. 158–63.

Anglès, H., ed., *Morales: Opera Omnia* (Monumentos de la música española, xi, xiii, xv, xvii, xx, xxi, xxiv), 7 vols., Barcelona, 1952 ff. [xi: 1952, xiii: 1953, xv: 1954, xvii: 1956, xx: 1959, xxi: 1962, xxiv: 1964.]

Anglès, H., 'El músic Jacomi al servei de Joan I, Martin I durant els anys 1372–1404', in *Festschrift Rubió i Lluch*, i, 613–25.

Anglès, H., *La música a Catalunya fins al segle XIII*, Barcelona, 1935.

Anglès, H., 'La musica conservada en la Biblioteca Colombina y la Catedral de Sevilla', *Annuario musical*, ii (1947), 3–39.

Anglès, H., ed., *La Música de las Cantigas de Santa Maria del Rey Alfonso el Sabio*, 3 vols., Barcelona, 1943–64.

Anglès, H., ed., *La Música en la Corte de Carlo V. Con la transcripción del 'Libro de Cifra Nueva para tecla, harpa y vihuela' de Luys Venegas de Henestrosa (1557)*. (Monumentos de la música española, ii.), Barcelona, 1944.

Anglès, H., ed., *La Música de las Cantigas los Reyes Católicos* (Monumentos de la música española, i, v, x), 3 vols., Madrid-Barcelona, 1941–51. [See also Figueras].

Anglès, H., 'La música sagrada [de la Capilla Pontifica de Avignon] en la Capilla real Aragonese', *Annuario musical*, xii (1957), 35–44.

Anglès, H., 'Musikalische Beziehungen zwischen Deutschland und Spanien in der Zeit vom 5. bis 14. Jahrhundert', *AfMW*, xvi (1959), 5–20.

Anglès, H., 'La Musique aux Xe et XIe Siècles: L'Ecole de Ripoll', in *La Catalogne à l'Epoque Romane*, Paris, 1932, pp. 157–79.

Anglès, H., 'Orgelmusik der Schola Hispanica', in *Festschrift Wagner*, pp. 11–26.

Anglès, H., 'Palestrina y los "Magnificat" de Morales', *Annuario musical*, viii (1953), 153–66.

Anglès, H., 'Spanien in der Musikgeschichte des 15. Jahrhunderts', in *Festschrift für Joh. Vincke*, 2 vols., Madrid, 1963, i. 321–56.

Anglès, H., 'Die spanische Liedkunst im 15. und am Anfang des 16. Jahrhunderts', *Festschrift Kroyer*, pp. 62–68.

Anglès, H., ed., *Victoria: Opera Omnia* (Monumentos de la música española xxv, xxvi, xxx, xxxi), 4 vols., Rome 1965 ff. [i: 1965, ii: 1965, iii: 1967, iv: 1968.]

Anton, K., *Luther und die Musik*, 2nd edn., Leipzig, 1928.

Apel, W., ed., *L'Antegnata Intavolatura de Ricercari d'Organo*, 1608, (Corpus of Early Keyboard Music, 9), Rome, 1965.

Apel, Willi, 'Bemerkungen zu den Organa von St Martial', in *Festschrift Anglès*, i, 61.

Apel, W., ed., *French Secular Compositions of the Fourteenth Century* (*CMM*, liii), Rome, 1970 ff. [2 vols. published by 1972].

Apel, W., ed., *French Secular Music of the Late XIVth Century*, Cambridge (Mass.), 1950.

Apel, W., *Geschichte der Orgel- und Klaviermusik bis 1700*, Kassel, 1967.

Apel, Willi, *Gregorian Chant*, Bloomington (Indiana), 1958.

Apel, Willi, ed., *Keyboard Music of the Fourteenth and Fifteenth Centuries (Corpus of Early Keyboard Music*, i) Rome, 1963.

Apel, W., ed., *Marco Facoli: Collected Works*, (Corpus of Early Keyboard Music, ii), Rome, 1963.

Apel, W., ed., *Musik aus früher Zeit*, 2 vols., Mainz, 1934.

Apel, W., *The Notation of Polyphonic Music, 900–1600*, 5th ed., Cambridge (Mass.), 1953.

Apel, Willi, 'Rondeaux, Virelais, and Ballades in French 13th Century Song', *JAMS*, vii (1954), 121–30.

Apfel, Ernst, 'England und der Kontinent in der Musik des späten Mittelalters', *Musikforschung*, xiv (1961), 276–89.

Apfel, Ernst, *Studien zur Satztechnik der mittelalterlichen englischen Musik*, 2 vols., Heidelberg, 1959.

Apfel, Ernst, 'Über einige Zusammenhänge zwischen Text und Musik im Mittelalter, besonders in England', *Acta*, xxxiii (1961), 47–54.

Arco Avalle, S.d' and Monterosso, R., (edd.) *Sponsus Dramma delle vergini prudenti e delle vergini stolte*, Milan, Naples, 1965.

Aristoxenus, see editions by Macran, Rios, Wehrli, Westphal.

Arkwright, G.P.E., ed., *The Old English Edition*, 25 vols., London, 1889–1902. i, Campion, Masque … Lord Hayes, 1889; xi–xii, Ferrabosco, Madrigals from Musica Transalpina, 1894; xxi, Anthems and Motets by White, Kirbye, Wilbye, Daman, 1898; xxii, Milton, Six Anthems, 1900.

Arnold, D., ed., *Andrea Gabrieli. Drei Motetten*, (Chorwerk, xcvii), Wolfenbüttel, 1965.

Arnold, D., 'Ceremonial Music in Venice at the Time of the Gabrielis', *PRMA*, lxxxii (1955–56), 47–59.

Arnold, Denis, 'Croce and the Italian Madrigal', *ML*, xxxv (1954), 309–19.

Arnold, D., ed., *Giovanni Gabrieli: Opera Omnia*, (*CMM*, xii), Rome, 1956 ff. [5 vols. published by 1971].

Arnold, D., ed., *Luca Marenzio: Giovane Donna* (Penn State Music Series, 13), University Park, 1966.

Arnold, D., *Marenzio*, London, 1965.

Arnold, D., 'Music at a Venetian Confraternity in the Renaissance', *Acta*, xxxvii (1965), 62–72.

Arnold, D., '"Seconda Pratica": a Background to Monteverdi's Madrigals', *ML*, xxxviii (1957), 341–52.

Arnold, D., 'The Significance of "Cori spezzati"', *ML*, xl (1959), 4–14.

Arnold, D., 'Towards a Biography of Giovanni Gabrieli', *Mus. Disc.*, xv (1961), 200–07.

Arnold, F.W. and Bellermann, H., edd., *Das Locheimer Liederbuch nebst der Ars organisandi von Conrad Paumann* (Jahr-

bücher für musikalische Wissenschaft, ii), Leipzig, 1867.

Aroca, D.J., ed., *Cancionero musical y poetico del siglo XVII recogido por Claudio de la Sablonara*, Madrid, 1916.

Aubry, Pierre, ed., *Cent Motets du XIIIᵉ Siècle*, 3 vols., Paris, 1908.

Aubry, Pierre, ed., *Le Chansonnier de l'Arsenal*, Paris, 1909.

Auda, A., ed., *B. Beaulaigue, poète et musicien prodige*, Brussels, 1958.

Auda, Antoine, ed., *Les Motets Wallons*, 2 vols., Brussels, [1953].

Baillie, Hugh, 'A London Guild of Musicians, 1460–1530', *PRMA*, lxxxiii (1956–7), 15–28.

Baillie, Hugh, 'Nicholas Ludford (c. 1465–c. 1557)', *MQ*, xliv (1958), 196–208.

Baillie, Hugh, 'Squares', *Acta*, xxxii (1960), 178–93.

Baillie, Hugh, and Oboussier, Philippe, 'The York Masses', *ML*, xxxv (1954), 19–30.

Baines, A., *European and American Musical Instruments*, London, 1966.

Bal y Gay, J., ed., *Romances y villancicos españoles del siglo XVI*, Mexico, 1939.

Bal y Gay, J., ed., *Tesoro de la musica polifonica en Mexico*, 2 vols., Mexico, 1952–60.

Baratta, María de, *Cuzcatlán típico. Ensayo sobre etnofonia de El Salvador*, San Salvador, n.d. (1951?).

Barbieri, J.A., ed., *Cancionero Musical de los siglos XV y XVI*, Madrid, 1890.

Barblan, G., 'I "Rognoni" Musicisti milanesi tra il 1500 e il 1600', in *Festschrift Hoboken*, 19–28.

Baroffio, Giacomo, 'Die Offertorien der Ambrosianischen Kirche', *Die Musikforschung*, xviii (1965), 422–3.

Baroni, M., ed., *Cavalieri: Rappresentazione di anima e di corpo*, Bologna, 1967. [See also: Mantica].

Bartha, D., *Benedict Ducis und Appenzeller*, Wolfenbüttel, 1930.

Bartha, D., 'Probleme der Chansongeschichte im 16. Jahrhundert', *ZfMW*, xiii (1930–1), 507–30.

Barwick, Steven, ed., *The Franco Codex of the Cathedral of Mexico. Transcription and Commentary*, Carbondale, Illinois, 1965.

Baskervill, Charles R., *The Elizabethan Jig and Related Song Dramas*, Chicago, 1929, reprinted New York, 1965.

Bastian, J., ed., *Merulo: Sacred Works* (*CMM*, li), Rome, 1970 ff. [2 vols. published by 1972].

Bataille, A., 'Remarque sur les deux Notations mélodiques de l'ancienne Musique grecque', *Recherches de Papyrologie*, i (1961), 5–20.

Bäuerle, H., ed., *Lasso: Septem Psalmi Poenitentiales*, Leipzig, 1906.

Baumann, O.A., *Das deutsche Lied und seine Bearbeitungen in den frühen Orgeltabulatura*, Kassel, 1934.

Bäumker, W., ed., *Ein deutsches geistliches Liederbuch*. . . ., Leipzig, 1895.

Baxter, J.H., ed., *An old St. Andrews Music Book* [Wolfenbüttel₁], London, 1931.

Becezny, E. and Rabl, W., edd., *Isaac, Choralis Constantinus, I* (*DTO*, v, part i), Vienna, 1898.

Becherini, B., 'Poesia e musica in Italia al primi del XV secolo', in *Congress Wégimont 1955*, pp. 239–59.

Beck, H., 'Das Konzil von Trent und die Probleme der Kirchenmusik', *Kirchenmusikalisches Jahrbuch*, xlviii (1964), 108–17.

Beck, Jean B., ed., *Le Chansonnier Cangé*, 2 vols., Paris, 1927.

Beck, Jean B., ed., *Le Manuscrit du Roi*, 2 vols., Philadelphia, 1938.

Beck, Jean B., ed., *Die Melodien der Troubadours*, Strassburg, 1908.

Beck, Sydney, ed., *Morley: First Book of Consort Lessons*, New York, 1959.

Becker-Glauch, I., *Die Bedeutung der Musik für die Dresdener Hoffeste* (Musikwissenschaftliche Arbeiten, vi), Kassel, 1951.

Bedbrook, G.S., *Keyboard Music from the Middle Ages to the Beginnings of the Baroque*, London, 1949.

Beer, R., *Die Handschriften des Klosters Santa Maria de Ripoll*, Vienna, 1907–08.

Belyaev, Viktor, *Drevnerusskaya muzykalnaya pismennost*, Moscow, 1962.

Belza, Igor, *Istoriya cheshskoy muzykalnoy kultury*, i, Moscow, 1959.

Belza, Igor, *Istoriya polskoy muzykalnoy kultury*, i, Moscow, 1954.

Bent, Margaret, 'New and Little-known Fragments of English Medieval Polyphony', *JAMS*, xxi (1968), 137–56.

Bent, Margaret, 'Sources of the Old Hall Music', *PRMA*, xciv (1967/8), 19–35.

Benvenuti, G., ed., *Andrea e Giovanni Gabrieli e la musica strumentale in San Marco*, (Instituzioni e monumenti dell' arte musicale italiana, i–ii), Milan, 1931–2.

Benvenuti, G., ed., *M.A.Cavazzoni: Ricercari, Motetti, Canzoni; J. Fogliano & J.Segni: Ricercari e Ricercate* (I Classici Musicali Italiani, i), Milan, 1941.

Bergsagel, John D., 'The Date and Provenance of the Forrest-Heyther Collection of Tudor Masses', *ML*, xliv (1963), 240–48.

Bergsagel, John D., 'An Introduction to Ludford,' *Mus. Disc.*, xiv (1960), 105–30.

Bergsagel, John D., ed., *Nicholas Ludford: Collected Works* (*CMM*, xxvii), i, Rome, 1963.

Bergsagel, John D., 'On the Performance of Ludford's *Alternatim* Masses', *Mus. Disc.*, xvi (1962), 35–55.

Bernard, J.H. and Atkinson, R., (edd.), *The Irish Liber Hymnorum* (Henry Bradshaw Society) London, 1898.

Bernet Kempers, K.Ph., 'Bibliography of the Sacred Works of Jacobus Clemens non Papa', *Mus. Disc.*, xviii (1964), pp. 85–150.

Bernet Kempers, K.Ph., ed., *Clemens non Papa: Opera Omnia* (*CMM*, iv), 19 vols., Rome, 1951–72.

Bernet Kempers, K.Ph., 'A Composition by Clemens non Papa in a 16th-century Painting', *Mus. Disc.*, viii (1954), 173–5 (2 photographs).

Bernet Kempers, K.Ph., 'Jacobus Clemens non Papa's Chansons in their Chronological Order', *Mus. Disc.*, xv (1961), 187–97.

Bernoulli, E. and Moser, H.J., edd., *Das Liederbuch des Arnt von Aich* (*Köln um 1510*), Kassel, 1930.

Bernstein, L.F., 'C. Gervaise as chanson composer', in *JAMS*, xviii (1965), 359–81.

Besseler, H., *Bourdon und Fauxbourdon*, Leipzig, 1950.

Besseler, H., 'Dufay in Rom', *AfMW*, xv (1958), 1–19.

Besseler, H. and Van, G. de, edd., *Dufay: Opera Omnia* (*CMM*, i), 6 vols., Rome, 1947–66.

Besseler, H., 'Grundsätzliches zur Ubertragung von Mensuralmusik', *Musikforschung*, xvii (1964), 287–8 [Dufay].

Besseler, H., 'Grundsätzliches zur Ubertragung von Mensuralmusik', in *Festschrift Schenk*, pp. 31–8 [Dufay].

Besseler, H., 'Das Lochamer Liederbuch aus Nürnberg', *Die Musikforschung*, i

(1948), 220–5.

Besseler, H., *Die Musik des Mittelalters und der Renaissance*, Potsdam, 1931.

Besseler, H., 'Neue Dokumente zum Leben ... Dufays', *AfMW*, ix (1952), 159–76.

Besseler, H., 'Studien zur Musik des Mittelalters', *AfMW*, vii (1925), 167, and viii (1926), 137.

Birkner, Günter, 'Motetus und Motette', *AfMW*, xviii (1961), 183–94.

Birtner, H., 'Sieben Messen von L. Senfl', *AfMW*, vii (1942), 40–54.

Birtner, H., and Staehelin, M., edd., *Isaac: Messen* (Musikalische Denkmäler, vii), Mainz, n.d. [pref. 1968].

Blaschke, P., 'Heinrich Isaacs Choralis Constantinus', *Kirchenmusikalisches Jahrbuch*, xxvi (1931), 32–50.

Blume, Clemens, S. J., *Unsere liturgischen Lieder, das Hymnar der altchristliche Kirche*, Ratisbon, 1932.

Blume, F., *Die evangelische Kirchenmusik*, Potsdam, 1931 [rev. enlarged as: *Geschichte der evangelischen Kirchenmusik*, Kassel, 1965]

Blume, F., ed., [Editions of several works of] *Josquin: Missa Pange lingua, 4 Motetten, Missa Da pacem, 3 Evangelien-Motetten, 3 Psalmen, Missa De Beata Virgine* (Chorwerk, i, xviii, xx, xxiii, xxxiii, xlii), Wolfenbüttel, 1930–51.

Blume, F., ed., [*Josquin and others*]: *Weltliche Lieder* (Chorwerk, iii), Wolfenbüttel, 1930 [Josquin, Compère, Pipelare, La Rue].

Blume, F., ed., *La Rue: Requiem und Motette 'Delicta Juventutis'* (Chorwerk, xi), Wolfenbüttel, 1931.

Blume, F. and Schulze, W., edd., *Resinarius* [or Harzer]: *Summa Passionis s. Johannem* (Chorwerk, xlvii), Wolfenbüttel, 1937.

Bockholdt, R., *Die frühen Messenkompositionen von G. Dufay*, Tutzing, 1960.

Boer, C. L. W., *Het Anthonius-motet van Anthonius Busnois*, Amsterdam, 1940 [with facs. and transcr.].

Boetticher, W., *Aus Orlando di Lassos Wirkungskreis* ... (Veröffentlichungen der Gesellschaft für Bayerische Musikgeschichte, i), Kassel, 1963.

Boetticher, W., 'New Lasso Studies', in *Festschrift Reese*, pp. 17–26.

Boetticher, W., *Orlando di Lasso und seine Zeit*, Kassel, 1958.

Boetticher, W. and Fischer, K. v. and

Hermelinck, K. (and others), edd., *Lasso: Sämtliche Werke: Neue Reihe*, Kassel, 1956 ff [10 vols. published up to 1970].

Böhme, F. M., ed., *Altdeutsches Liederbuch*, 3rd edn., Leipzig, 1925.

Bohn, P., ed., *Glareanus: Dodecachordon*, 3 parts (Eitner, *Publikationen*, xvi), Leipzig, 1888–90.

Bonaccorsi, A., *Maestri di Lucca: I Guami e altri musicisti* (Historiae Musicae Cultores Biblioteca, xxi), Florence, 1967.

Bonfantini, M., ed., *Le sacre rappresentazione italiane*, Milan, 1942.

Bonfils, G., ed., *Chansons françaises pour orgue (1550)*, Paris, 1968.

Bonfils, G., ed., *Du Caurroy: Fantaisies à 3–6 parties*, Paris, 1967.

Bordes, C., and others, edd., *Anthologie des maîtres religieux primitifs*, 6 vols., Paris, 1893–5.

Borren, Ch. van den, 'L'Ars Nova', in *Congress Wégimont 1955*, pp. 17–26.

Borren, Ch. van den, *Dufay*, Brussels, 1925.

Borren, Ch. van den, *Etudes sur le XVe siècle musical*, Antwerp, 1941.

Borren, Ch. van den, ed., *Missa Tornacensis* (*CMM*, xiii), Rome, 1957.

Borren, Ch. van den, 'Quelques réflexions à propos du style syntaxique', *Revue Belge de musicologie*, i (1946–7), 14–20.

Borren, Ch. van den, *Sources of Keyboard Music in England*, London, 1913.

Borren, Ch. van den, and Nuffel, J. van, and Doorslaer, G. van, edd., *Monte: Collected Works* [incomplete], 31 vols., Bruges, 1927–39.

Bosse, Detlev, *Untersuchung einstimmiger mittelalterlicher Melodien zum 'Gloria in Excelsis Deo'* (Inaugural Dissertation), Erlangen, 1954.

Boyd, Morrison C., *Elizabethan Music and Musical Criticism*, Philadelphia, 1940, rev. and corr. Philadelphia, 1967.

Bragard, A. M., ed., *Verdelot: Opera Omnia* (*CMM*, xxviii), Rome, 1966 ff. [2 vols. published by 1972].

Brandel, Rose, 'Some unifying devices in the religious music drama of the Middle Ages' in *Festschrift Reese*, pp. 40–55.

Brenet, M., *Musique et Musiciens de la vieille France*, Paris, 1911 [contains: 'Essai sur les origines de la musique descriptive', pp. 83 ff.].

Brett, Philip, 'Edward Paston (1550–1630)

... his musical collection', *Transactions of the Cambridge Bibliographical Society*, iv, part i (1964), 51–69.

Brett, Ph., 'The English Consort Song, 1570–1625', *PRMA*, lxxxviii (1961–2), 73–88.

Bridgman, N., 'Fêtes italiennes de plein air au Quattrocento', in *Festschrift Albrecht*, pp. 34–38.

Bridgman, N., 'Un Manuscript Italien ... à la Bibliothèque nationale', *Annales Musicologiques*, i (1953), 177–267.

Bridgman, N., 'Un Manuscrit milanais (Biblioteca Nazionale Braidense Cod. AD. XIV.49)', *Rivista italiana della musicologia*, i (1966), 237–41.

Bridgman, N., *La vie musicale au quattrocento et jusqu'à la naissance du madrigal (1400–1530)*, Paris, 1964.

Brou, L. and Vives, J., edd., *Antifónario visigótico mozárabe de la catedral de León* (Monumenta, Hispaniae Sacra, v), 2 vols., Madrid, 1953–9.

Brou, Dom Louis and Wilmart, Dom Andre, 'Un office monastique pour le 2 Novembre dans le Nord de la France au XIᵉ siècle', *Sacris Erudiri*, v (1953), 247–330.

Brown, H.M., *Instrumental Music Printed Before 1600; A Bibliography*, Cambridge, Mass., 1965.

Brown, H.M., *Music in the French secular theater, 1400–1550*, Cambridge (Mass.), 1963.

Brown, H.M., ed., *Theatrical Chansons of the 15th and Early 16th Centuries*, Cambridge (Mass.), 1963.

Bryden, J.R. and Hughes, D.G., *An Index of Gregorian Chant*, 2 vols., Cambridge (Mass.), 1970.

Bukofzer, Manfred F., 'Interrelations between Conductus and Clausula', *Annales Musicologiques*, i (1953), 65–103.

Bukofzer, Manfred F., 'John Dunstable: a Quincentenary Report', *MQ*, xl (1954), 29–49.

Bukofzer, Manfred F., ed., *John Dunstable: Complete Works* (Musica Britannica, viii), London, 1953 [rev. 1970].

Bukofzer, Manfred F., *Studies in Medieval and Renaissance Music*, New York, 1950.

Burne, Martin Joseph, 'The Mass Cycles in early Graduals ...', unpub. diss. New York University, 1956.

Burns, J.A., 'Antonio Valente, Neapolitan Keyboard Primitive', *JAMS*, xii (1959), 133–43.

Bussi, F., ed., *Gerolamo Parabosco. Composizioni a due, tre, quattro, cinque e sei voci*, Piacenza, 1961.

Bussi, F., *Umanità e arte di Gerolamo Parabosco Madrigalista, Organista e Poligrafo*, Piacenza, 1961.

Caffagni, M. and Vecchi, G., edd., *G.A. Terzi, Intavolatura di liuto, Venice, 1593–99*, Bergamo, 1964.

Caldwell, John, 'Keyboard Plainsong Settings in England, 1500–1660', *Mus. Disc.*, xix (1965), 129–53.

Carapetyan, A., ed., 'The Codex Faenza, Biblioteca Comunale, 117 [Fa]', Facs. ed., *Mus. Disc.*, xiii (1959), 79–107; xiv (1960), 65–104; xv (1961), 63–104. Also published separately as *An Early Fifteenth-Century Italian Source of Keyboard Music, The Codex Faenza, Biblioteca Comunale, 117*, (Musicological Studies and Documents, 10), Rome, 1961.

Carapetyna, A., 'The *Musica Nova* of Adriano Willaert', *Journal of Renaissance and Baroque Music [Mus. Disc.]*, i (1946–7), 200–21.

Carapetyan, A., ed., *Notitia del valore delle note del canto misurato*, (Corpus Scriptorum de Musica, v), Rome, 1957.

Carapetyan, A. and Hudson, B., edd., *Brumel: Opera Omnia (CMM, v)*, Rome, 1951 ff. [4 vols. published by 1971].

Carducci, G., ed., *Cacce in rime dei secoli xiv e xv*, Bologna, 1896.

Casimiri, Raffaele, 'Una Missa Dominicalis falsamente attribuita a Tommaso Ludovico de Victoria', *Note d'archivo*, x (1933), 185–8.

Casimiri, Raffaele, 'Il Vittoria: nuovi documenti per una biografia sincera di Tommaso Ludovico de Victoria', *Note d'archivo*, xi (1934), 111–97.

Casimiri, R. and Dagnino, E., edd., *Monumenta Polyphoniae Italicae*, 2 vols., Rome, 1930–7.

Casimiri, R., Virgili, L., Jeppesen, K., and Bianchi, L., edd., *Giovanni Pierluigi da Palestrina: Le opere complete*, Rome 1939 ff.

Castillo, Jesus, *La Música Maya-Quiché (región guaternalteca)*, Quetzaltenango, 1941.

Catalyne, Alice Ray, 'Music of the 16th to 18th Centuries in the Cathedral of Puebla',

Yearbook of the Inter-American Institute for Musical Research, ii (1966), 75–90.

Cauchie, M.: 'Les deux plus anciens recueils de chansons polyphoniques imprimés en France', *Revue de Musicologie*, viii (1924), 72–6.

Cauchie, M., 'Les chansons à 3 voix de P. Clereau', *Revue de musicologie*, xi (1927), 77–91.

Cauchie, M., ed., *Quinze chansons françaises dy XVIᵉ à 4 et 5 v.*, Paris, 1926.

Cavicchi, A., ed., *Luzzasco Luzzaschi, Madrigali per cantare e sonare a uno, due e tre soprani (1601)*, Brescia, 1965.

Cellisi, L., 'Documenti per la storia musicale di Firenze', *Rivista musicale italiana*, xxxiv (1927), 579–602, xxxv (1928), 553–82.

Černušák, Gracian, and others, edd., *Československý hudebni slovník*, 2 vols., Prague, 1963–5.

Černý, Jaromír, *Soupis hudebních rukopisů musea v Hradci Králové* (Miscellanea musicologica, xix), Prague, 1966.

Cesari, G., Monterosso, R., and Disertori, B., edd., *Le frottole nell' edizione principe di Ottaviano Petrucci*, i, (Libri I, II, e III), Cremona, 1954.

Chailley, J., *L'Ecole musicale de Saint-Martial de Limoges*, Paris, 1960.

Charles, Sydney R., ed., *The Music of the Pepys MS. 1236* (*CMM*, xl), Rome, 1967.

Charles, Sydney R., 'The Provenance and Date of the Pepys Ms. 1236', *Mus. Disc.*, xvi (1962), 57–71.

Chase, G., 'Guitar and Vihuela: A Clarification', *Bulletin of the American Musicological Society*, No. 6 (1942), 13–14.

Chase, G., 'Juan del Encina, Poet and Musician', *ML*, xx (1939), 420–30.

Chase, G., *The Music of Spain*, New York, 1941.

Chase, G., 'Origins of the Lyric Theater in Spain', *MQ*, xxv (1939), 292–305.

Chevalier, Ulysse, (ed.), *Repertorium hymnologicum*, 6 vols., Louvain, 1892. [A catalogue of chants, hymns, proses, tropes and sequences, giving *incipits*, origins, usual attributions and numerous sources.]

Chomiński, Józef, ed., *Słownik muzyków polskich*, 2 vols., Cracow, 1964 and 1967.

Chomiński, Józef and Lissa, Zofia, edd., *Music of the Polish Renaissance* [English edn.], Cracow, 1955.

Chybiński, Adolf, *Słownik muzyków dawnej Polski do r. 1800*, Cracow, 1949.

Chybiński, A., and others, edd., *Wydawnictwo Dawnej Muzyki Polskiej*, Warsaw and Cracow, 1928 ff.

Cisilino, S., ed., *Costanzo Porta: Opera Omnia*, Padua, 1964 ff.

Claire, Dom Jean, 'L'évolution modale dans les répertoires occidentaux', *Revue Grégorienne*, xl (1962), 196–211; 229–45; xli (1963), 8–29, 49–62, 77–102, 127–51.

Clercx, Suzanne, 'Figures de proue de musique française', in *Les Nuits de Septembre: Festival de musique de Liège* [programme], Liège, 1968.

Clercx, S., *Johannes Ciconia*, 2 vols., Brussels, 1960.

Clercx, S., 'Le premier sejour de J. Ciconia en Italie (1358–67)', in *Congress Palermo 1954*, pp. 223–7.

Clulow, Peter, 'Publication Dates for Byrd's Latin Masses', *ML*, xlvii (1966), 1–9.

Collet, Henri, *Victoria*, Paris, 1914.

Commer, F., ed., *Musica Sacra*, 28 vols., Berlin and Regensburg, 1839–87. [vols. xix, xx (1878–9) contain motets by Meiland.]

Congress Wégimont 1955: L'Ars Nova (Congrès et Colloques de l'Université de Liège), Paris, 1959.

Corbin, Solange, 'La cantillation des rituel chrétiens', *Revue de Musicologie*, xlvii, (1961), 3–36.

Corbin, Solange, 'Le Cantus Sibyllae, origines et premiers textes', *Revue de Musicologie* (July, 1952), 1–10.

Corbin, Solange, *L'Eglise à la conquête de sa musique*, Paris, 1960.

Corbin, Solange, 'Fêtes portugaises: commémoraison de la victoire chrétienne de 1340 (Rio-Salado)', *Bulletin hispanique* (1948), 205–18.

Corbin, Solange, 'La musique dans le monde chrétien', in Manuel, *Histoire*, i, 621–82.

Corbin, Solange, 'Teatro religioso' in Gatti, *Musica: Enciclopedia storica*, iv, 621–7.

Corsi, G., 'Madrigali e ballate inedite del Trecento', *Belfagor*, xiv (1959), 329–40.

Corsi, G., 'Madrigali inediti del Trecento', *Belfagor*, xiv (1959), 72–82.

Coster, A., 'Juan de Anchieta et la famille de Loyole', *Revue hispanique*, lxxix (1930), 1.

Coussemaker, Edmond-Henri de, *Drames liturgiques du moyen age*, Rennes and Paris, 1860.

Coussemaker, Edmond-Henri, de, *Scrip-*

torum de musica medii aevi nova series, 4 vols., Paris, 1864–76. [reprinted 1931 and 1963].

Coville, A., 'P. de Vitry, Notes biographiques', *Romania*, lix (1933).

Crevel, M. van, *Adrianus Petit Coclico*, The Hague, 1940. [See also: Zenck, H., *AfMF* (1942) 170–4].

Croll, G., 'Gaspar van Weerbeke, An Outline of his Life and Works', *Mus. Disc.*, vi (1952), 67–81.

Cross, R., 'The Life and Works of Matthaeus Pipelare', *Mus. Disc.* xvii (1963), 97–114.

Cross, R., ed., *Pipelare: Opera Omnia* (*CMM*, xxxiv), 3 vols., Rome, 1966–7.

Curtis, Alan, *Sweelinck's Keyboard Music: A Study of English Elements in Dutch ... Compositions*, London, 1968.

Cuyler, L.E., ed., *Isaac: Choralis Constantinus, III*, Ann Arbor (Mich.), 1950.

Cuyler, L.E., ed., *Isaac: Five Polyphonic Masses*, Ann Arbor (Mich.), 1956.

Cuyler, L.E., 'The Sequences of Isaac's Choralis Constantinus', *JAMS*, iii (1950), 3–16.

D'Accone, F.A., 'Alessandro Coppini and Bartolomeo degli Organi – two Florentine composers of the Renaissance', *Analecta musicologica*, iv (1967), 38–76.

D'Accone, F.A., 'Bernardo Pisano, an Introduction to his Life and Works', *Mus. Disc.*, xvii (1963), 115–35.

D'Accone, F.A., 'The Intavolatura di M.A. Aiolli', *Mus. Disc.*, xx (1966), 151–74.

D'Accone, F.A., ed., *Music of the Florentine Renaissance*, (*CMM*, xxxii), Rome, 1966 ff. i. Pisano (1966); ii: Coppini, Bartolomeo, Seragli (1967); iii–iv: Layolle (1969).

D'Accone, F.A., 'The Singers of San Giovanni in Florence during the 15th Century', *JAMS*, xiv (1961), 307–58.

Dahlhaus, C., 'Zur chromatischen Technik Carlo Gesualdos', *Analecta musicologica*, iv (1967), 77–96.

Dahlhaus, Carl, 'Zur Theorie des Organums im 12. Jahrhundert', *Kirchenmusikalisches Jahrbuch*, xlviii (1964). 27–32.

Dalla Libera, S., *L'Arte degli organi a Venezia* (Fondazione Cini, Civiltà Veneziana, Studi xiii), Venice, 1962.

Dalla Libera, S., ed., *C. Merulo: Toccate per organo*, 3 vols., Milan, 1958–9.

Dannemann, E., *Die spätgotische Musiktradition in Frankreich und Burgund ...*, Strassburg, 1936.

Dardo, G., 'Considerazioni sull'opera di Giovan Maria da Crema liutista del Cinquecento', in *Festschrift Barblan*, pp. 61–77.

Dardo, G., 'Contributo alla storia del Liuto in Italia: Johannes Maria Alanus e Giovanni Maria da Crema', *Quaderni della Rassegna musicale*, iii (1965), 143–57.

Dart, T., 'English Musicians Abroad (ca. 1575–ca. 1625)' in *Grove*, ii, 949–51.

Dart, T., ed., *Parthenia or The First Music ever Printed for the Virginals*, London, 1960.

Davis, N., ed., *Non-Cycle Plays and Fragments* (Early English Text Society, Suppl. Text No. 1), London, 1970 [pp. 124–33: F.Ll.Harrison, 'Notes on the Music in the Shrewsbury Liturgical Plays'].

Davison, A.T., and Apel, W., edd., *Historical Anthology of Music*, 2 vols., Cambridge (Mass.), 1947–50.

Della Ragione, F., ed., *G.M.Asola. Dieci laudi sacre a 3 voci*, Padua, 1962.

Denkmäler der Tonkunst in Österreich, Vienna, 1894 ff.

Disertori, B., ed., *Le frottole per canto e liuto intabulate da Franciscus Bossinensis*, (Istituzioni e monumenti dell'arte musicale italiana, Nuova serie, 3), Milan, 1964.

Disertori, B., ed., *C.Merulo: Sei Canzoni da sonar a 4*, Milan, 1950.

Disertori, B., 'Remarques sur l'évolution du luth en Italie au XVe siècle et au XVIe', in Jacquot, *Luth*, pp. 19–24.

Dittmer, Luther A., 'The Dating and the Notation of the Worcester Fragments', *Mus. Disc.*, xi (1957), 5–11.

Dittmer, Luther A., 'An English Discantum Volumen', *Mus. Disc.*, viii (1954), 19–58.

Dittmer, Luther, ed., *Firenze, Biblioteca mediceo-laurenziana, Pluteo 29, I* (Publications of Mediaeval Musical Manuscripts, 10–11), 2 vols., Brooklyn, 1966–7.

Dittmer, Luther, ed., *Wolfenbüttel 1099 (1206)* (Publications of Mediaeval Musical Manuscripts, 2), Brooklyn, 1960.

Dittmer, Luther A., ed., *The Worcester Fragments* (Musicological Studies and Documents, ii), Rome, 1957.

Doe, P., *Tallis*, London, 1968.

Donington, R. and Dart, T., 'The Origin of the In Nomine', *ML*, xxx (1949), 101–06.

Donovan, Richard B., *The Liturgical Drama in Medieval Spain*, Toronto, 1958.

Dottin, G., 'Aspects littéraires de la chanson "musicale" à l'époque de Marot', *Revue des Sciences Humaines*, N.S., fasc. 116 (1964), 425–32 [Université de Lilles, Faculté des Lettres et Sciences Humaines].

Dottin, G., ed., *Passereau: Opera Omnia* (*CMM*, xlvi), Rome, 1967.

Dowling, Margaret, 'The Printing of John Dowland's *Second Booke of Songs or Ayres*', The Library, 4th series, xii (1931–2), 365–80.

Dragoumis, M.Ph., 'The Survival of Byzantine Chant in the Monophonic Music of the Modern Greek Church', in Velimirović, *Eastern Chant*, i, 9–36.

Dreimüller, K., 'Die Musik im geistlichen Spiel des späten deutschen Mittelalters', *Kirchenmusikalisches Jahrbuch*, xxxiv (1950), 27–34.

Dreves, Guido-Maria, S.J., (ed.) *Analecta hymnica medii aevi*, 55 vols., Leipzig, 1886–1922. [Volumes concerned with hymns are 2, 4, 11, 12, 14, 16, 17, 19, 22, 23, 27, 43, 48, 50, 51, 55.].

Droz, E., 'Les chansons de N. de La Grotte', *Revue de musicologie*, xi (1927), 133–41.

Droz, E. and Thibault, G., 'Un chansonnier de Philippe le Bon', *Revue de musicologie*, x (1926), 1–8.

Droz, E., Rokseth, Y. and Thibault, G., edd., *Trois chansonniers français du XVe siècle*, Paris, 1927.

Droz, E. and Thibault, G., edd., *Poètes et musiciens du XVe siècle*, Paris, 1924.

Duckles, V., 'The Gamble Manuscript as a Source of *Continuo* Song in England', *JAMS*, i, No. 2 (1948), 23–40.

Ducrot, A., 'Histoire de la Cappella Giulia au XVIe siècle depuis sa fondation par Jules II (1513) jusqu'à sa restauration par Grégoire XIII (1578)', *Mélanges d'archéologie et d'histoire*, (1963), 179–240, 467–599.

Düring, I., *Ptolemaios und Porphyios über die Musik*, Göteborg, 1934.

Düring, I., 'Studies in Musical Terminology in Fifth-Century Literature', *Eranos*, xliii (1945), 176–97.

Eberth, F., *Die Minne-und Meistergesangweisen der Kolmarer Liederhandschrift*, Detmold, 1935.

Eggebrecht, Hans H., 'Ars musica', *Die Sammlung*, xii (1957), 306.

Eggebrecht, Hans W., 'Musik als Tonsprache', *AfMW*, xviii (1961), 73–100.

Ehmann, W., *Adam von Fulda* (Neue Deutsche Forschungen, Abteilung Musikwissenschaft, ii), Berlin, 1936.

Ehmann, W., ed., *Spielstücke für die Blockflöte*, Kassel, 1930. [contains: *Walter: Fugen auf die 8 tonos*].

Einstein, A., ed., *Canzoni Sonetti Strambotti e Frottole, Libro Terio (Andrea Antico, 1517)* (Smith College Music Archives, iv), Northampton, Mass., 1941.

Einstein, A., 'The Elizabethan Madrigal and "Musica Transalpina"', *ML*, xxv (1944), 66–77.

Einstein, A., *The Italian Madrigal*, 3 vols., Princeton, 1949 [reprinted 1971].

Einstein, A., ed., *Luca Marenzio, Sämtliche Werke* [5 part madrigals, books 1–6], (Publikationen älterer Musik, iv/1, vi), Leipzig, 1929–31.

Eitner, R., 'Das … deutsche Lied … (mit Beispielen), *Monatshefte für Musikgeschichte*, xxv–xxvi (1893–4), 149–204 and 1–135 [Brätel 29–33, Dietrich 123–30].

Eitner, R., ed., *Eccard: Neue … Lieder … 1589* (Eitner, *Publikationen*, xxi), Leipzig, 1897.

Eitner, R., ed., *Forster: … Liedlein* [1540] (Eitner, *Publikationen*, xxix), Leipzig, 1905.

Eitner, R., ed., *Heinrich und Hermann Finck: Ausgewählte Kompositionen* (Eitner, *Publikationen*, viii), Leipzig, 1879.

Eitner, R., ed., *M. Agricola: Musica instrumentalis deutsch* (Eitner, *Publikationen*, xx), Leipzig, 1896.

Eitner, R., ed., *Publikationen älterer … Musikwerke*, 29 vols., Leipzig, 1873–1905.

Eitner, R., ed., *60 Chansons zu vier Stimmen* (Eitner, *Publikationen*, xxiii), Leipzig, 1899.

Eitner, R. and Erk, L. and Kade, O., edd., *Otts … Liederbuch … 1544* (Eitner, *Publikationen*, i–iv), Leipzig, 1873–6.

Eitner, R. and Halm, A., edd., *Dressler: XVII Cantiones Sacrae … 1565* (Eitner, *Publikationen*, xxiv), Leipzig, 1900.

Eitner, R. and Maier, J.J., edd., *Oeglin: Liederbuch* (Eitner, *Publikationen*, ix), Leipzig, 1880.

Eitrem, S., Amundsen, L., Winnington-Ingram, R.P., 'Fragments of unknown Greek tragic texts with musical notation',

Symbolae Osloenses, fasc. xxxi (1955), 1–87.

Elders, W., ed., *Pietro Aaron. Trattato della natura et cognitione di tutti gli tvoni di canto figvrato (Venice, 1525)*, Utrecht, 1966.

Ellingworth, Susan, ed., *G. M. Radino: Il primo libro di balli d'arpicordo [1592]* (Corpus of Early Keyboard Music, xxxiii), Rome, 1968.

Ellinwood, Leonard, 'The Conductus', *MQ*, xxvii (1941), 165–204.

Ellinwood, L., *The works of Francesco Landini*, Cambridge, Mass., 1945.

Elliott, Kenneth, 'The Carver Choir-Book', *ML*, xli (1960), 349.

Elústiza, D. J. B. de and G. C. Hernandez, edd., *Antologia musical ... Polifonia Vocal Siglos xv y xvi*, Barcelona, 1933.

Emmanuel, M., 'Grèce', in Lavignac, *Encyclopédie*, Iʳᵉ partie, i, 377–540.

Engel, H., ed., *Kugelmann: Concentus novi, 1540* (Erbe deutscher Musik, Sonderreihe, ii), Kassel, 1955.

Engel, H., *Luca Marenzio. La vita, le opere*, Florence, 1956.

Engel, H., ed., *Marenzio, Villanellen*, Kassel, 1928.

Engelke, B., ed., *Dressler: Praecepta Musicae Poeticae* in *Geschichtsblätter ...* il/l (Magdeburg, 1914–15), 213–50.

Espagne, F., Haberl, F. X., and others, edd., *Giovanni Pierluigi da Palestrina: Werke*, 33 vols., Leipzig, 1862–1907.

Expert, H., ed., *La fleur des musiciens de P. de Ronsard*, Paris, 1923.

Expert, H., ed., *Florilège du concert vocal de la Renaissance*, 8 fasc., Paris, 1928–9.
i, iii: Janequin; ii: Lassus; iv: Costeley; v: Bonnet; vi: Le Jeune; vii: Maudit; viii: Duos (Sermisy, Peletier, Le Heurteur, Gardane).

Expert, H., ed., *Les maîtres musiciens de la Renaissance française*, 23 vols., Paris, 1894–1908.
v: 31 chansons (Attaingnant 1529); vii: Janequin; iii, xviii, xix: Costeley; i: Lassus; x: Mauduit; xii, xiii, xiv, xvi: le Jeune; xvii: Du Caurroy; xxiii: Danseries; ii, iv, vi: Goudimel; xv: Regnart; viii, ix: Brumel, La Rue, Fevin et Mouton.

Expert, H., ed., *Les monuments de la musique française au temps de la Renaissance*, 10 vols., Paris, 1924–9. i: Le Jeune; ii, viii: Certon; iii: Le Blanc; iv–vii: de Bertrand; ix: Goudimel; x: de L'Estocart.

Fano, C., ed., *V. Galilei, Camerata Fiorentina* (Istituzioni e monumenti dell'arte musicale italiana, iv), Milan, 1934.

Fano, F., ed., *V. Galilei: Dialogo della musica antica et moderna* [facsimile], Rome, 1934.

Fano, F., ed., *Isaac: [4] Messe* (Archivum musices ... mediolanense, x), Milan, 1962.

Federhofer, H., 'Biographische Beiträge zu Erasmus Lapicida und Stephen Mahu', *Die Musikforschung*, v (1952), 37–46.

Federhofer, H., 'Graz Court Musicians and their Contribution to the "Parnassus musicus Ferdinandaeus" (1615)', *Mus. Disc.*, ix (1955), 167–244.

Federhofer, H., 'Monodie und "musica reservata"', *Deutsches Jahrbuch der Musikwissenschaft*, ii (1957), 30–36.

Feicht, Hieronim, ed., *Muzyka staropolska*, Cracow, 1966.

Fellerer, K. G., 'Church Music and the Council of Trent', *MQ*, xxxix (1953), 576–94.

Fellerer, K. G., *Orgel und Orgelmusik, ihre Geschichte*, Augsburg, 1929.

Fellerer, K. G., *Palestrina*, Ratisbon, 1930, revised and enlarged edn., Düsseldorf, 1960.

Fellowes, Edmund, H., *English Cathedral Music*, London, 1941 (rev. J. A. Westrup, 1969).

Fellowes, Edmund H., ed., *The English Madrigal School*, 36 vols., London, 1913–24, [Revised by T. Dart and others as *The English Madrigalists*, 1958 ff.]

Fellowes, Edmund H., *English Madrigal Verse*, Oxford, 1920 (rev. F. W. Sternfeld and D. Greer, 1967).

Fellowes, Edmund H., *English School of Lutenist Song Writers*, Series I: Vols. 1–16, Series II: Vols. 1–16, London, 1920–32. [Revised and continued by T. Dart and others as *English Lute Songs*, 1959 ff.].

Fellowes, Edmund H., ed., *Gibbons: Nine Fantasias of Three Parts*, London, 1925.

Fellowes, Edmund H., *William Byrd: Collected Works*, 20 vols., London, 1937–50. [Revised by T. Dart and others, London, 1962 ff.].

Ferand, E. T., 'Die Motetti, Madrigali, et Canzoni Francese ... Diminuti ... des Giovanni Bassano (1591), in *Festschrift Osthoff 1961*, pp. 75–101.

Ferracci, E., *Il Palestrina: Documenti di vita: Problemi e prospettive d'arte* (Collana di studi palestriniani, 1), Rome, 1960.

Ferretti, Dom Paolo, *Esthétique grégorienne, ou Traité des formes du chant grégorien*, vol. i, tr. from the Italian by Dom A. Agaesse, Tournai, 1938.

Ferretti, Dom Paolo, *Estetica gregoriana ossia Trattato delle forme musicali del Canto Gregoriano*, vol. i, Rome, 1934.

Ficker, Rudolf, 'Primäre Klangformen', *Jahrbuch der Musikbibliothek Peters*, xxxvi (1929), 21.

Figueras, J., ed., *La Música en la Corte de los Reyes Católicos* (Monumentos de la música española, xiv, parts i and ii), Barcelona, 1965.

Findeizen, Nikolay, *Ocherki po istorii muzyki v Rossii*, 2 vols., Moscow and Leningrad, 1928–9.

Finscher, L., ed., *Compère: Opera Omnia* (*CMM*, xv), Rome, 1958 ff. [5 vols. published by 1972].

Finscher, L., ed., *Gafurius: Collected Musical Works* (*CMM*, x), 2 vols., Rome, 1955–60.

Finscher, L., 'Loyset Compère and his Works', 4 articles in *Mus. Disc.*, xii (1958), 105–43; xiii (1959), 123–54; xiv (1960), 135–57; xvi (1962), 93–113.

Fischer, K. von, 'A propos de la répartition du texte et le nombre de voix dans les oeuvres italiennes du Trecento', in *Congress Wégimont 1955*, pp. 232–8.

Fischer, K. von, 'Chronologie des manuscrits du Trecento' in *Congress Wégimont 1955*, pp. 131–6.

Fischer, K. von, 'Drei unbekannte Werke von Jacobo de Bologna und Bartolino da Padua?', in *Festschrift Anglès*, i, 265–81.

Fischer, K. von, 'L'influence française sur la notation des manuscrits du Trecento' in *Congress Wégimont 1955*, 27–34.

Fischer, K. von, 'The manuscript Paris, Bibl. Nat., Nouv. Acq. Frç. 6771 (Codex Reina = PR)', *Mus. Disc.*, xi (1957), 38–78.

Fischer, K. von, 'Ein neues Trecento-fragment', in *Festschrift Wiora*, pp. 264–8.

Fischer, K. von, 'On the Technique, origin, and evolution of Italian trecento music', *MQ*, xlvii (1961), 41–57.

Fischer, K. von, *Paolo da Firenze und der Squarcialupi-Kodex*, Bologna, 1969.

Fischer, K. von, 'Reply to N. E. Wilkins' Article on the Reina Codex', *Mus. Disc.*, xvii (1963), 75–77.

Fischer, K. von, *Studien zur italienischen*

Musik des Trecento und frühen Quattrocento, Berne, 1956.

Fischer, K. von, 'Trecentomusik – Trecentoprobleme', *Acta*, xxx (1958), 179–99.

Fischer, K. von, 'Ein Versuch zur Chronologie von Landinis Werken', *Mus. Disc.*, xx (1966), 31–46.

Fischer, K. von, 'Zur Entwicklung der italienischen Trecento-Notation', *AfMW*, xvi (1959), 87–99.

Flury, R., *Gioseffo Zarlino als Komponist*, Winterthur, 1962.

Flury, R., ed., *Gioseffo Zarlino: Drei Motteten und ein geistliches Madrigal* (Das Chorwerk, lxxvii), Wolfenbüttel, 1961.

Follieri, H., *Initia Hymnorum Ecclesiae Graecae* (Studi e Testi, 211–15 bis), 6 vols., Rome, 1960–6.

Fontaine, Jacques, *Isidore de Seville et la culture classique dans l'Espagne visigothique*, 2 vols., Paris, 1959.

Fouse, D.M., ed., *Giammateo Asola, Sixteen Liturgical Works* (Recent Researches in the Music of the Renaissance, 1), New Haven, 1964.

Fox, C.W., 'Accidentals in Vihuela Tablatures', *Bulletin of the American Musicological Society*, No. 4 (1938), 22.

Fox, C.W., 'The Masses of Cristobal Morales', *Bulletin of the American Musicological Society*, No. 5 (1941), 16.

Frere, Walter Howard, *Antiphonale Sarisburiense. A reproduction in facsimile*, 2 vols., London, 1901–25.

Frere, W.H., 'Edwardine Vernacular Services', in *W. H. Frere: A Collection of His Papers* (Alduin Club Collections, xxxv), London, 1940, pp. 5–21.

Frissard, C., 'A propos d'un recueil de chansons de J. Chardavoine', *Revue de Musicologie*, xxx (1948), 58–75.

Froger, Dom Jacques, 'Les chants de la messe au VIIIe et IXe siècles', *Revue Grégorienne* (1947), 161–71, 218–28; (1948), 56–62, 98–107.

Froidebise, Pierre, ed., *Juan Bermudo: Oeuvres d'orgue (1555)* (Orgue et Liturgie, xlvii), Paris, 1960.

Froidebise, Pierre, ed., *Tomás de Santa Maria: Arte d' tañer fantasia (1565)* (Orgue et Liturgie, xlix), Paris, 1961.

Frost, Maurice, ed., *English and Scottish Psalm and Hymn Tunes*, London, 1953.

Frotscher, G., *Geschichte des Orgelspiels und*

der Orgelkomposition, 2 vols., Berlin, 2nd edn., 1959 [1st edn. 1935].

Fuller Maitland, J. A. and Squire, W. B., edd., *Fitzwilliam Virginal Book*, 2 vols., London, 1894–9. [Reprinted New York, 1949; also 1964].

Funck, H., ed., M. Agricola: *Instrumentische Gesänge*, Wolfenbüttel, 1933.

Galilei, Vincenzo: *Dialogo della musica antica e della moderna*, Florence, 1581. [Facsimile edn., Rome, 1934].

Gallico, C., *Un cancioniere musicale italiano del cinquecento*, Bologna, Conservatorio di Musica 'G. B. Martini' Ms. Q. 21 (Historiae musicae cultores Bibliotheca, 13), Florence, 1961.

Gallico, C., *Un libro di poesie per musica dell' epoca d'Isabella d'Este*, Mantova, 1961.

Gallico, C., 'Newly discovered documents concerning Monteverdi', *MQ*, xlviii (1962), 68–72.

Gallico, C., ed., *Opere di Lodovico Viadana*. (Monumenti Musicali Mantovani I), Kassel, 1964 ff.

Gatti, V. M. and Basso, A., edd., *La Musica*, Parte prima Enciclopedia Storica, 4 vols.; Parte seconda: Dizionario, 2 vols., Turin, 1966–71.

Geering, Arnold, *Die Organa und mehrstimmigen Conductus in dan Handschriften des deutschen Sprachgebietes ...*, Bern, 1952.

Geering, Arnold, 'Retrospektive mehrstimmige Musik ...' in *Festschrift Anglès*, i, 307.

Geering, A. and Ursprung, O. and Löhrer, E. (and others), edd., *Senfl: Sämtliche Werke*, Basel (also Wolfenbüttel and Zurich), 1936 ff. [9 vols. published up to 1971, first 4 vols. identical with Erbe deutscher Musik, ser. i; v, x, xii, xv].

Gennrich, Friedrich, *Grundriss einer Formenlehre des mittelalterlichen Liedes*, Halle, 1932.

Gennrich, Friedrich, *Der musikalische Nachlass der Troubadours* (Summa Musicae Medii Aevi, iii & iv), Darmstadt, 1958–60.

Gennrich, Friedrich, 'Rondeaux, Virelais und Balladen ...', *Gesellschaft für romanische Literatur*, xliii (1921) & xlvii (1927).

Gennrich, Friedrich, ed. (tr. R. G. Dennis), *Troubadours, Trouvères, Minne- and Meistersinger* (Anthology of Music), Cologne, 1960.

Georgiades, Thrasybulos, *Englische Diskanttraktate aus der ersten Hälfte des 15. Jahrhunderts*, Munich, 1937.

Georiades, Thrasybulos, 'Sprache, Musik, schriftliche Musikdarstellung', *AfMW*, xiv (1957), 223–9.

Gerber, R., ed., *Finck: Hymnen* (Chorwerk, ix), Wolfenbüttel, 1930.

Gerber, R., 'Die Hymnen des Apelschen Kodex', in *Festschrift Schering*, pp. 76–89.

Gerber, R., ed., *Johannes Martini: 3 geistliche Gesänge* (Chorwerk, xlvi), Wolfenbüttel, 1937.

Gerber, R., ed., *Mensuralkodex ... N. Apel (Ms. 1494 ... Univ. Leipzig)* (Erbe deutscher Musik, ser. i, xxxii & xxxiii), Kassel, 1956 & 1960.

Gerber, Rudolf, ed., *Rhau: Sacrorum hymnorum Liber Primus*, (Erbe deutscher Musik, ser. i, xxi & xxv), Leipzig, 1942–3.

Gerber, R., *Die Sebaldus-Kompositionen der Berliner Handschrift 40021*, (Musikwissenschaftliche Arbeiten, xxi), Kassel, 1965.

Gerber, R., ed., *Spanisches Hymnar um 1500* (Chorwerk, lx), Wolfenbüttel, 1957.

Gerber, R., ed., *Zwölf Hymnen* [Fulda, Finck, Hartzer, etc.] (Chorwerk, xxxii), Wolfenbüttel, n.d. [1934].

Gerbert, Martin, *Scriptores ecclesiastici de musica sacra*, 3 vols., St. Blaise, 1784. [reprinted 1931 and 1963].

Gerhardt, C., *Die Torgauer Walter-Handschriften* (Musikwissenschaftliche Arbeiten, iv), Kassel, 1949.

Gerstenberg, W., ed., *Senfl: Zwei Marien-Motetten ...* (Chorwerk, lxii), Wolfenbüttel, 1957.

Ghisi, F., 'Alcune Canzoni a Ballo del primo Cinquecento', in *Festschrift Engel*, pp. 125–33.

Ghisi, F., 'Gli aspetti musicale della lauda fra il XIV e il XV secolo, prima metà', in *Festschrift Jeppesen*, pp. 51–57.

Ghisi, F.; *I canti carnascialesci nelle fonti musicali del XV e XVI secoli*, Florence, 1937.

Ghisi, F., 'Italian Ars Nova music. The Perugia and Pistoia fragments of the Lucca musical codex', *Journal of Renaissance and Baroque Music* [*Mus. Disc.*], i (1946–7), 173–91.

Ghisi, F., 'La Persistance du sentiment monodique et l'évolution de la polyphonie italienne du XIVe au XVe siècle', in

Congress Wégimont *1955*, pp. 217–31.

Ghisi, F., 'Strambotti e laude nel travestimento spirituale ...', *Collectanea Historiae Musicae*, i (1953), 45–78.

Ghislanzoni, A., 'Les Formes littéraires et musicales italiennes au commencement du XIVe siècle', in *Congress Wégimont 1955*, pp. 149–63.

Gilles, A., 'Un témoignage inédit de l'enseignement de P. de Vitry', *Mus. Disc.*, x (1956), 35–54.

Gilles, A. and Reaney, G., 'A new source for ... P. de Vitry', *Mus. Disc.*, xii (1958), 59–66.

Giraud, Y., ed., *La fleur des chansons rustiques de la Renaissance française*, Paris, 1965.

Giraud, Y., ed., *Vingt chansons de la Renaissance française*, Paris, 1965.

Gleason, Harold, ed., *Examples of Music before 1400*, New York, 1941.

Göhler, G., ed., *Köler: Zehn Psalmen Davids* [Nos. 4, 9], 2 vols., Leipzig, 1900 and 1901.

Goldine, N., 'Fra Bartolino de Padova, musicien de cour', *Acta*, xxxiv (1962), 142–55.

Göllner, Theodor, *Formen früher Mehrstimmigkeit* ... (Münchner Veröffentlichungen zur Musikgeschichte, vi), Tutzing, 1961.

Gombosi, O., ed., *Capriola Lute Book*, (Société de Musique d'Autrefois), Neuilly-sur-Seine, 1955.

Gombosi, O., *Jacob Obrecht*, Leipzig, 1925 [with 31 pieces by various composers from the period 1460–1510].

Gombosi, O., ed., *Stoltzer: 37. Psalm* (Chorwerk, vi), Wolfenbüttel, 1930.

Gombosi, O., ed., *Stoltzer: Octo tonorum melodiae*, Mainz, 1933.

Gombosi, O., *Tonarten und Stimmungen der antiken Musik*, Copenhagen, 1939.

Gomez Brufal, Salvador and Juan, *Bibliografía de Elche*, Alicante, 1957.

Gottwald, C., ed., *Ghiselin: Opera Omnia* (CMM, xxiii), 3 vols., Rome, 1961–8.

Gottwald, C., 'Johannes Ghiselin – Janne Verbonnet. Some traces of his life', *Mus. Disc.*, xv (1961), 105–11.

Grande, C. del, *Espressione musicale dei poeti greci*, Naples, 1932.

Grande, C. del, 'Nuovo frammento di musica greca in un papiro del museo di Cairo', in *Congress Florence 1935 Papirologia*, pp. 369–82.

Greene, Richard L., *The Early English Carol*, London, 1935.

Greene, Richard L., 'Two Medieval Musical Manuscripts ...', *JAMS*, vii (1954), 1–34.

Grout, D. J., *A History of Western Music*, New York, 1960.

Grove's Dictionary of Music, ed. E. Blom, 5th edn., 9 vols., London, 1954. Suppl. vol., ed. D. Stevens, 1961.

Gudewill, K. and Heiske, W., edd., *Forster: ... Liedlein (1539)* (Erbe deutscher Musik, ser. i, xx), Berlin, 1942.

Guiette, Robert, 'Reflexions sur le drame liturgique' in *Festschrift Crozet*, i. 197–202.

Gullino, G., ed., *G. B. della Gostena, Intavolatura di liuto, Venice, 1599*, Florence, 1949.

Gullino, G., ed., *G. M. Radino, Intavolatura di balli d'arpicordo, Venice, 1592*, Florence, 1949.

Gullino, G., ed., *Joan Maria da Crema: Intavolatura di Liuto*, Florence, 1955.

Gullino, G., ed., *S. Molinaro, Intavolatura di Liuto, Venice, 1599*, Florence, 1940.

Günther, U., 'The 14th Century Motet and its Development', *Mus. Disc.*, xii (1958), 27–58.

Günther, U., ed., *The Motets of the MSS Chantilly ... and Modena* (CMM, xxxix), Rome, 1965.

Gurlitt, W., 'Johannes Walter und die Musik der Reformationszeit', *Luther-Jahrbuch*, xv (1933), 1–112.

Gurlitt, W., ed., *Walter: Lob und Preis der löblichen Kunst Musica*, Kassel, 1938.

Haar, J., ed., *Chanson and Madrigal: 1480–1530*, Cambridge (Mass.), 1964.

Haar, J., 'The "Note Nere" Madrigal', *JAMS*, xviii (1965), 22–41.

Haar, J., 'Pace non trovo: A study in literary and musical parody', *Mus. Disc.*, xx (1966), 95–149.

Haas, R., 'Zu Walters Choralpassion nach Matthäus', *AfMW*, iv (1922), 24–47.

Haberkamp, G., ed., *Die Weltliche Vokalmusik in Spanien um 1500: der 'Cancionero musical de Colombina' von Sevilla* (Münchener Veröffentlichungen zur Musikgeschichte, xii), Tutzing, 1968.

Haberl, F., 'Das Choralcredo im vierten Modus in seiner unterschiedlichen Gestalt' in *Festschrift Johner*, pp. 28–33.

Haberl, F., 'Die Gradualien des dritten Modus und ihre musikalische Struktur',

Anuario Musical, xvi (1961), 3–25.

Haberl, F. X. and Sandberger, A., edd., *Lasso: Sämtliche Werke*, 21 vols., Leipzig, 1894–1927 [The Latin motets of *Magnum Opus Musicum*, 1604, in the odd vols. This edn. is supplemented by a 'Neue Reihe' (new series) of Lasso's Works, see Boetticher].

Hagopian, V. L., *Italian Ars Nova Music: A Bibliographic Guide to Modern Editions and Related Literature*, Berkeley and Los Angeles, 1964.

Hamm, Charles, 'A Catalogue of Anonymous English Music in Fifteenth-Century Continental Manuscripts,' *Mus. Disc.*, xxii (1968), 47–76.

Hamm, C. E., *A Chronology of the Works of G. Dufay*, Princeton, 1964.

Hamm, Charles, 'A Group of Anonymous English Pieces in Trent 87,' *ML*, xli (1960), 211–15.

Handschin, Jacques, 'A Monument of English Mediaeval Polyphony,' *The Musical Times*, lxxiii (1932), 510–13, and lxxiv (1933), 697–704.

Handschin, Jacques, *Musikgeschichte im Überblick*, Luzern, 1948.

Handschin, Jacques, 'The Summer Canon and Its Background', *Mus. Disc.*, iii (1949), 55–94; v (1951), 65–113.

Handschin, Jacques, 'Über den Ursprung der Motette', in *Congress Basel 1924*, p. 189.

Handschin, Jacques, 'Über Estampie und Sequenz', *ZfMW*, xii (1929), 1–20; xiii (1930), 113–32.

Handschin, Jacques, 'Zur Frage der Conductus-Rhythmik', *Acta*, xxiv (1952), 113–30.

Handschin, Jacques, 'Zur Geschichte von Notre-Dame', *Acta*, iv (1932), 5–17, 49–55.

Harbage, A. and Schoenbaum, S., *Annals of English Drama, 975–1000*, London, 1964.

Harcourt, Raoul d', and Harcourt, Marguerite d', *La musique des Incas et ses survivances*, Paris, 1925.

Harding, R. E. M., ed., *G. M. Radino, Intavolatura di balli par sonare di liuto, Venice, 1592*, Cambridge, Mass., 1949.

Hardison, O. B., *Christian Rite and Christian Drama in the Middle Ages*, Baltimore, 1965.

Harman, R. A., ed., *Morley: Plaine and Easie Introduction to Practicall Musicke*, London, 1952.

Harms, G., ed., Schlick: *Tabulaturen . . . [1512]*, Hamburg, 1924 (2nd edn. 1937).

Harran, D., '"Mannerism" in the Cinquecento Madrigal', *MQ*, lv (1969), 521–44.

Harran, D., 'Verse Types in the Early Madrigal', *JAMS*, xxii (1969), 27–53.

Harrison, F. Ll., 'Ars Nova in England: A New Source', *Mus. Disc.*, xxi (1967), 67–85.

Harrison, F. Ll., 'Benedicamus, Conductus, Carol: a Newly Discovered Source', *Acta* xxxvii (1965), 35–48.

Harrison, F. Ll., ed., *Early English Church Music*, London 1963 ff.

i, Early Tudor Masses, ed. J. D. Bergsagel, 1963; ii, Mundy, Latin antiphons and psalms, ed. F. L. Harrison, 1963; iii, Gibbons, Verse Anthems, ed. D. Wulstan, 1964; iv, Early Tudor Magnificats, I, ed. P. Doe, 1964; v, Tomkins, Musica Deo Sacra, I, ed. B. W. G. Rose, 1965; vi, Early Tudor Organ Music, I, ed. J. Caldwell, 1966; vii, Ramsey, I, English Sacred Music, ed. E. Thompson, 1967; viii, 15th Cent. Liturgical Music, I, ed. A. Hughes, 1968; ix, Tomkins, Musica Deo Sacra, II, ed. B. W. G. Rose, 1968; x, Early Tudor Organ Music, II, ed. D. Stevens, 1969; xi, Leighton, . . . Lamentations of a Sorrowful Soul, ed. C. Hill, 1970.

Harrison, F. Ll., 'The Eton Choirbook', *Annales Musicologiques*, l (1953), 151–75.

Harrison, F. Ll., ed., *The Eton Choir Book*, 3 vols. (Musica Britannica, x–xii), London, 1956–8.

Harrison, F. Ll., 'Faburden in Practice', *Mus. Disc.*, xvi (1962), 11–34.

Harrison, F. Ll., 'Music for the Sarum Rite', *Annales Musicologiques*, vi, (1958–63), 99–144.

Harrison, F. Ll., *Music in Medieval Britain*, London, 1958.

Harrison, F. Ll., ed., *Sheppard: Sechs Responsorien* (Das Chorwerk, lxxxiv), Wolfenbüttel, 1960.

Harrison, F. Ll. and Rimmer, J., *European musical instruments*, London, 1964.

Hasse, Karl, ed., Finck: *Missa in Summis* (Chorwerk, xxi), Wolfenbüttel, n.d. [1932].

Haydon, G., ed., *Francesco Corteccia: Hinnario secondo l'uso della chiesa romana et fiorentina*, Cincinnati, 1958–60.

Haydon, G., 'The Hymns of Costanzo Festa. A Style Study', *JAMS*, xii (1959), 105–17.

Haydon, G., 'The Hymns of Jacobus de Kerle', in *Festschrift Reese*, 336–58.

Heartz, D., ed., *Attaingnant: Preludes, Chansons and Dances for Lute*, Neuilly, 1964.

Heartz, D., *Pierre Attaingnant, Royal Printer of Music*, Berkeley, 1969.

Heartz, D., 'A Spanish "Masque of Cupid"', *MQ*, xlix (1963), 59–74.

Heilfurth, G., *Das Bergmannslied*, Kassel, 1954.

Helm, E.B., ed., *The Chansons of J. Arcadelt* (Smith College Music Archives, v), Northampton (Mass.), 1942.

Hermann, W., ed., *Gastoldis Balletti a tre voci*, 3 vols., Berlin, 1927.

Hertzmann, E., ed., *Adrian Willaert und andere Meister, Volkstümliche italienische Lieder* (Das Chorwerk, viii), Wolfenbüttel, 1930.

Hertzmann, E., 'Trends in the development of the Chanson in the early XVIth century', in *Papers of the American Musicological Society, 1940*, New York, 1946.

Hesbert, Dom R.J., *Antiphonale missarum sextuplex*, Brussels, 1935.

Hesbert, Dom R.J., 'Un antique offertoire de la Pentecôte "Factus est repente"', in *Festschrift Waesberghe*, pp. 59–69.

Hewitt, H., ed., *[Petrucci:] Harmonice Musices Odhecaton A [Venice, 1501]*, Cambridge (Mass.), 1942.

Hewitt, H., ed., *Petrucci: Canti B ... Venice, 1502* (Monuments of Renaissance Music), Chicago, 1967.

Heyden, R., ed., *Isaac: Missa Carminum* (Chorwerk, vii), 2nd edn., Wolfenbüttel, 1950.

Higgins, R.A. and Winnington-Ingram, R.P., 'Lute-players in Greek art', *Journal of Hellenic Studies*, lxxxv (1965), 62–71.

Hill, A.G., 'Medieval Organs in Spain', *SIMG*, xiv (1913), 487.

Hilmar, E., 'Ergänzungen zu Emil Vogels "Bibliothek der gedruckten weltlichen Vocalmusik Italiens, aus den Jahren 1500–1700"', *Analecta musicologica*, iv (1967), 154–206.

Hoffmann-Erbrecht, L., ed., *Finck: Ausgewählte Werke, I* (Erbe deutscher Musik, lvii), Frankfurt, 1962.

Hoffmann-Erbrecht, L., ed., *Köler: 3 Deutsche Psalmen* (Chorwerk, lxxi), Wolfenbüttel, 1960.

Hoffmann-Erbrecht, L., ed., *Stoltzer: Ausgewählte Werke, 2. Teil* (Erbe deutscher Musik, ser. i, lxvi), Frankfurt, 1969.

Hoffmann-Erbrecht, L., ed., *Stoltzer: Ostermesse* (Chorwerk, lxxiv), Wolfenbüttel, 1958.

Holman, Hans Jorgen, 'Melismatic Tropes in Responsories for Matins', *JAMS*, xvi (1963), 36–46.

Holschneider, Andreas, *Die Organa von Winchester*, Hildesheim, 1968.

Holz, G., Saran, F. and Bernoulli, E., edd., *Die Jenaer Liederhandschrift*, 2 vols., Leipzig, 1901.

Homan, Frederick Warren, 'Cadence in Gregorian Chant', unpub. diss., Indiana University, 1961.

Homan, Frederick Warren, 'Final and internal cadential patterns in Gregorian Chant', *JAMS*, xvii (1964), 66–77.

Hoppin, R.H., ed., *The Cypriot-French Repertory of the MS Torino ... (CMM, xxi)*, 4 vols., Rome, 1960–3.

Hoppin, R.H., 'An unrecognized polyphonic lai of Machaut', *Mus. Disc.*, xii (1958), 93–104.

Horsley, I., 'The 16th-Century Variation. A New Historical Survey', *JAMS*, xii (1959), 118–32.

Howell, A.C., Jr., 'Cabezón: An Essay in Structural Analysis', *MQ*, 1 (1964), 18.

Huber, K., 'Die Doppelmeister des 16. Jahrhunderts', in *Festschrift Sandberger*, pp. 170–88.

Hucke, Helmut, 'Die gregorianische Gradualweise des 2. Tons und ihre ambrosianischen Parallelen', *AfMW* xiii (1956), 285–314.

Huff, J., ed., *Ad organum faciendum ...* (Musical Theorists in Translation, viii), Brooklyn (N.Y.), 1969.

Hughes, Andrew, 'Mass Pairs in the Old Hall and Other English Manuscripts', *Revue Belge de Musicologie*, xix (1965), 15–27.

Hughes, Andrew, 'Mensural Polyphony for Choir in 15th-Century England', *JAMS*, xix (1966), 352–69.

Hughes, Andrew, and Bent, Margaret, 'The Old Hall Manuscript – A Re-appraisal and an Inventory', *Mus. Disc.*, xxi (1967), 97–147.

Hughes, Andrew and Bent, Margaret, edd., *The Old Hall Manuscript* (*CMM*, xlvi), Rome, 1969 ff. 3 vols. published by 1972.

Hughes, Anselm, 'An Introduction to Fayrfax', *Mus. Disc.*, vi (1952), 83–104.

Hughes, Anselm, ed., *Worcester Medieval Harmony* (Plainsong and Mediaeval Music Society), Burnham and London, 1928.

Huglo, Michel, 'La mélodie grecque du "Gloria in Excelsis" et son utilisation dans le Gloria XIV', *Revue Grégorienne*, xxix (1950), 30–40.

Huglo, Michel, 'Origine de la mélodie du Credo "authentique" de la Vaticane', *Revue Grégorienne*, xxx (1951), 68–78.

Huglo, Michel, 'Origine et diffusion des Kyrie' in *Revue Grégorienne*, xxxvii (1958), 85–88.

Huglo, M., 'Relations musicales entre Byzance et l'Occident' in *Congress Oxford 1966, Byzantine*, pp. 267–80.

Huglo, Michel, 'Un tonaire du graduel de la fin du VIIIe siècle' in *Revue Grégorienne*, xxxi (1952), 176–86, 224–31.

Hunger, H. and Pöhlmann, E., 'Neue griechische Musikfragmente aus ptolemäischer Zeit in der Papyrussamlung der Österreichischen Nationalbibliothek', *Wiener Studien*, lxxv (1962), 51–78.

Hunt, J.E., ed., *Cranmer's First Litany, 1544, and Merbecke's Book of Common Prayer Noted, 1550*, London, 1939.

Hüschen, Heinrich, 'Die Musik in den artes liberales', in *Congress Hamburg 1956*, p. 117.

Husmann, Heinrich, 'Das Alleluia multifarie', in *Festschrift Schneider*, pp. 17–23.

Husmann, H., 'Aufbau und Entstehung des cod. germ. 4997 (Kolmarer Liederhandschrift)', *Deutsche Vierteljahrsschrift für Literaturwissenschaft*, xxxiv (1960), 189–243.

Husmann, Heinrich, 'Deklamation und Akzent in der Vertonung mittellateinischer Dichtung', *AfMW*, xix/xx (1962–3), 1–8.

Husmann, Heinrich, *Die Drei- und Vierstimmigen Notre-Dame-Organa* (Publikationen älterer Musik, xi), Leipzig, 1940.

Husmann, Heinrich, 'The Enlargement of the Magnus Liber Organi', *JAMS*, xvi (1963), 176–203.

Husmann, H., *Grundlagen der antiken und orientalischen Musikkultur*, Berlin, 1961.

Husmann, Heinrich, 'The Origin and Destination of the Magnus Liber Organi, *MQ*, xlix (1963), 311–30.

Husmann, Heinrich, ed., *Tropen- und Sequenzenhandschriften* (Répertoire Internationale des Sources Musicales, vol. B v[1]), München-Duisberg, 1964.

Illing, Carl Heinz, *Zur Technik der Magnificat-Komposition des 16.Jh.*, Wolfenbüttel, 1936.

Irtenkauf, W., 'Einige Ergänzungen zu den lateinischen Liedern des Wienhäuser Liederbuchs', *Die Musikforschung*, x (1957), 217–25.

Irtenkauf, W. and Eggers, H., 'Die Donaueschinger Marienklage ...', *Carinthia I*, cxlviii (1958), 359–82.

Jachimecki, Zdzisław, *Historja muzyki polskiej w zarysie*, Warsaw and Cracow, 1920.

Jachimecki, Zdzisław, *Muzyka na dworze Władyslawa Jagiełły*, Cracow, 1916.

Jachimecki, Zdzisław, *Muzyka polska w rozwoju historycznym*, I, Cracow, 1948.

Jachimecki, Zdzisław, *Tabulatura organowa z bibl. klasztoru Św. Ducha w Krakowie z roku 1548*, Cracow, 1913.

Jachimecki, Zdzisław, *Wpływy włoskie w muzyce polskiej* I, Cracow, 1911.

Jackman, James, L., 'Liturgical Aspects of Byrd's *Gradualia*', *MQ*, xlix (1963), 17–37.

Jacobs, Ch., *La Interpretación de la Musica Española del Siglo XVI para Instrumentos de Teclado*, Madrid, 1959.

Jacobs, C., ed., *Milán: El Maestro*, University Park (Penn.), 1971.

Jacquot, J., ed., *Le luth et sa musique*, Paris, 1958.

Jacquot, J., ed., *Musique et poésie au XVIe siècle*, Paris, 1954.

Jacquot, J., ed., *La Musique instrumentale de la Renaissance*, Paris, 1955.

Jammers, E., 'Hugo von Montforts Liederhandschrift,' *Ruperto-Carola: Mitteilungen ... der Universität Heidelberg*, Jahrgang ix (1957), vol. xxi, 58–64.

Jammers, E., 'Untersuchungen über die Rhythmik und Melodik der Melodien der Jenaer Liederhandschrift', *ZfMW*, vii (1924–25), 265–304.

Jan, C. von, ed., *Musici Scriptores Graeci* (Biblioteca Teubneriana), Leipzig, 1895. *Supplementum* of musical fragments, Leipzig, 1899.

Jeanroy, Alfred, *La Poésie Lyrique des Troubadors*, Toulouse-Paris, 1934.

Jeppesen, K., 'Ein altvenezianisches Tanzbuch', in *Festschrift Fellerer*, 245-63.

Jeppesen, K., ed., *Italia Sacra Musica*, 3 vols., Copenhagen, 1962.

Jeppesen, K., *Die italienische Orgelmusik am Anfang des Cinquecento*, 2nd rev. edn., 2 vols., Copenhagen, 1960.

Jeppesen, K., *Die mehrstimmige italienische Laude um 1500*, Leipzig, 1935.

Jeppesen, K., *Der Palestrinastil und die Dissonanz*, Leipzig, 1925, 2nd English edn., rev., *The Style of Palestrina and the Dissonance*, Copenhagen and London, 1946.

Jeppesen, K., 'The Recently Discovered Mantova Masses of Palestrina', *Acta*, xxii (1950), 36-47.

Jeppesen, K., 'Über italienische Kirchenmusik in der ersten Hälfte des 16. Jahrhunderts', *Studia musicologica*, iii (1962), 149-60.

Joaquim, M., ed., *O Cancionero Musical e Poético da Biblioteca Públia Hortênsia*, Coimbra, 1940.

Jodogne, Omer, 'Recherches sur les débuts du théâtre religieux en France', in *Cahiers de civilisation médiévale*, (1965), 1-24.

Johnson, A.H., 'The Masses of Cipriano de Rore', *JAMS*, vi (1953), 227-39.

Jungmann, J.A., *Missarum solemnia, explication génétique de la messe romaine* (Théologie, Etudes ... Faculté de Théologie de Lyon, xix), 3 vols., Paris, 1956. [German original: *Missarum solemnia*, 5th edn., 2 vols., Vienna, 1962] [English tr.: *Mass of the Roman Rite*, 2 vols., New York, 1951-55].

Just, M., ed., *Isaac: Introiten* (Chorwerk, lxxxi), Wolfenbüttel, 1960.

Just, M., ed., *Isaac: 4 Marienmotetten* (Chorwerk, c), Wolfenbüttel, 1965.

Kade, O., *Die ältere Passionskomposition bis zum Jahre 1631*, Gütersloh, 1893.

Kade, O., ed., *Walter: Geystliche gesangk Buchleyn* [Wittemberg, 1524] (Eitner, *Publikationen*, vii), Leipzig, 1878.

Kade, R., 'Antonius Scandellus (1517-1580)', *SIMG*, xv (1913-14), 535-65.

Kahmann, B., 'Antoine de Fevin', 2 articles in *Mus. Disc.*, iv (1950), 153-62; v (1951), 143-55.

Kämper, D., 'Das Lehr- und Instrumentalduo um 1500 in Italien', *Die Musikforschung*, xviii (1965), 242-53.

Karp, Theodore, 'St. Martial and Santiago de Compostella', *Acta*, xxxix (1967), 144-60.

Kastner, M.S., ed., *Altitalienische Versetten für Orgel oder andere Tasteninstrumente*, Mainz, 1957.

Kastner, M.S., *Antonio de Cabezón*, Barcelona, 1952.

Kastner, M.S., 'Los manuscritos musicales ns. 48 y 242 de la Biblioteca General de la Universidad de Coimbra', *Annuario Musical*, v (1950), 78-96.

Kastner, M.S., ed., *Obras de Música para Tecla, Arpa y Vihuela de Antonio de Cabezón*, Mainz, 1951. [excerpts].

Kastner, M.S., ed., *Salinas: De Musica*, Kassel and Basel, 1958.

Kaufmann, H.W., *The Life and Works of Nicolo Vicentino (1511-c. 1576)*, (Musicological Studies and Documents, 11), Rome, 1966.

Kaufmann, H.W., ed., *Nicola Vicentino: Collected Works*, (*CMM* xxvi), Rome, 1963.

Keldysh, Yury, *Istoriya russkoy muzyki*, Moscow and Leningrad, 1948.

Kendall, R., 'Notes on A. Schlick', *Acta*, xi (1939), 136-43.

Kenney, Sylvia, W., '"English Discant" and Discant in England', *MQ*, xlv (1959), 26-48.

Kenton, E., *Life and Works of Giovanni Gabrieli*, (Musicological Studies and Documents, 16), Rome, 1967.

Kerman, Joseph, 'Byrd, Tallis, and the Art of Imitation' in *Festschrift Reese*, pp. 519-37.

Kerman, Joseph, 'Byrd's Motets: Chronology and Canon', *JAMS*, xiv (1961), 359-82.

Kerman, Joseph, *The Elizabethan Madrigal*, New York, 1962.

Kerman, Joseph, 'The Elizabethan Motet: A Study of texts for Music', *Studies in the Renaissance*, ix (1962), 273-308.

Kerman, Joseph, 'On W. Byrd's *Emendemus in melius*', *MQ*, xlix (1963), 431-49.

Kinkeldey, O., *Orgel und Klavier in der Musik des 16. Jahrhunderts*, Leipzig, 1910: reprinted Hildesheim, 1967.

Kirsch, W., 'Andreas da Silva, ein Meister aus der ersten Hälfte des 16. Jahrhunderts', *Analecta musicologica*, ii (1965), 6-23.

Kirsch, W., ed., *Andreas de* [or: *da*] *Silva: Opera Omnia* (*CMM*, xlix), Rome, 1970 ff.

[2 vols. published by 1972].

Kirsh, W., *Die Quellen der mehrstrimmingen Magnificat – und Te Deum – Vertonungen bis zur Mitte des 16. Jahrhunderts*, Tutzing, 1966.

Knapp, Janet, ed., *Thirty-five Conductus*, New Haven, 1965.

Knight, Gerald H. and Reed, William L., edd., *The Treasury of English Church Music*, 5 vols., London, 1965. i, 1100–1545, ed. D.Stevens; ii, 1545–1650, ed. P.Le Huray.

Kniseley, S.P., *The Masses of Franceso Soriano*, Gainesville (Florida), 1967.

Koczirz, A., 'Die Gitarrekompositionen in Miguel de Fuenllana's Orphenica lyra', *AfMW*, iv (1922), 241–61.

Koczirz, A., ed., *Österreichische Lautenmusik* (*DTO*, v. 37), Vienna, 1911.

Koller, O. and Schatz, J., edd., *Oswald von Wolkenstein: Geistliche und weltliche Lieder* (*DTO*, ix, part i), Vienna, 1902.

Körte, O., *Laute und Lautenmusik bis zur Mitte des 16. Jahrhunderts*, Leipzig, 1901, reprinted Farnborough, 1968.

Kovarik, Edward, 'A Newly-Discovered Dunstable Fragment', *JAMS*, xxi (1968), 21–33.

Krenek, E., *J. Ockeghem*, New York, 1953.

Kretzschmar, H., 'Luther und die Musik', *Jahrbuch der Musikbibliothek Peters*, xxiv (1917), 39–44.

Kroyer, T., *Die Anfänge der Chromatik im italienischen Madrigal des XVI. Jahrhunderts* (1535–1560), Leipzig, 1902, reprinted Farnborough, 1968.

Kroyer, T., ed., *Senfl: Magnificat, Motetten* (*DTB*, iii, part ii), Leipzig, 1903.

Kuhlmann, Georg, *Die zweistimmigen französischen Motetten ...*, 2 vols., Würzburg, 1938.

Kunze, S., *Die Instrumentalmusik Giovanni Gabrielis*, 2 vols., Tutzing, 1963.

Laloy, L., *Aristoxène de Tarente et la musique d'antiquité*, Paris, 1904.

Landels, J.G., 'The Brauron Aulos', *Annual of the British School at Athens*, no. 58 (1963), 116–19.

Landels, J.G., 'Fragments of Auloi found in the Athenian Agora', *Hesperia*, xxxiii (1964), 392–400.

Láng, P.H., *Music in Western Civilization*, New York, 1941.

Launay, D., 'Les motets à double choeur en France', *Revue de Musicologie*, xxxix–xl (1957), 173–95.

Lavignac, A. and Laurencie, L. de la, edd., *Encyclopédie de la musique ...*; Partie I, 5 vols.; Partie II, 6 vols.; Paris, 1913–31. [Partial index by Robert Bruce, *Music Library Association Notes*, ser. I, 1936].

Lefkoff, G., ed., *Five Sixteenth Century Venetian Lute Books*, Washington, D.C., 1960.

Le Huray, Peter, *Music and the Reformation in England*, London, 1967.

Leichentritt, H., *Geschichte der Motette*, Leipzig, 1908. [Reprinted Hildesheim, 1967].

Lenaerts, R.B., ed., *Het Nederlands polifonies lied in de zestiende eeuw*, Malines and Amsterdam, 1933.

Lenaerts, R.B. and Robijns, J., edd., *Pierre de la Rue, Drei Missen* (Monumenta Musicae Belgicae, viii), Berchem-Antwerp, 1960.

Leonhart, G. and Annegarn, A. and Noske, F., edd., *Sweelinck: Opera Omnia*, vol. I, fasc. 1–3, *Keyboard Works*, revised edn., Amsterdam, 1968.

Lerner, E.R., ed., *Agricola: Opera Omnia* (*CMM*, xxii) 5 vols., Rome, 1961–70.

Lerner, E.R., 'The Polyphonic Magnificat in 15th-Century Italy', *MQ*, 1 (1964), 44–58.

Lesure, F., ed., *Anthologie de la chanson parisienne au XVIe siècle*, Monaco, 1953.

Lesure, F., 'Autour de C.Marot et de ses musiciens', *Revue de Musicologie*, xxxiii (1951), 109–19.

Lesure, F., 'Les chansons à trois voix de C.Janequin', *Revue de Musicologie*, xliii–xliv (1959), 193–8.

Lesure, F., 'La facture instrumentale à Paris au XVIe siècle', *Galpin Society Journal*, vii (1954), 11–52.

Lesure, F., 'France in the 16th Century', in *NOHM*, iv, 237–53.

Lesure, F., 'Janequin. Recherches su sa vie et son oeuvre', *Mus. Disc.*, V (1951), 157–93.

Lesure, F., *Musicians and poets of the French Renaissance*, New York, 1955.

Lesure, F., 'Les orchestres populaires à Paris vers la fin du XVIe siècle', *Revue de Musicologie*, xxxvi (1954), 39–54.

Lesure, F., ed., *La Renaissance dans les provinces du Nord*, Paris, 1956.

Lesure, F. and de Morcourt, R., 'G.P.

Paladino et son Premier Livre de Luth', *Revue de Musicologie*, xli–xlii (1958), 170–83.

Lesure, F. and Thibault, G., *Bibliographie des éditions publiées par A. Le Roy et R. Ballard*, Paris, 1955.

Lesure, F. and Thibault, G., 'Bibliographie des éditions musicales publiées par N. Du Chemin', *Annales Musicologiques*, I (1953), 269–73.

Levarie, S., *G. de Machaut*, New York, 1954.

Levy, K. J., 'Costeley's chromatic Chanson', *Annales Musicologiques*, iii (1955), 213–63.

Levy, K. J., 'Susanne un jour. The history of a 16th century Chanson', *Annales Musicologiques*, i (1953), 375–408.

Liber Usualis Missae et Officii pro Dominicis et Festis cum Cantu Gregoriano, Edn. No. 801, Tournai, cop. 1934. [All page references apply equally to the copyright 1961 edn.]

Liliencron, R. von, 'Die Chorgesänge des lateinisch-deutschen Schuldramas im XVI. Jahrhunderts', *Vierteljahrsschrift für Musikwissenschaft*, vi (1890), 309–387.

Liliencron, R. von, 'Die Horazischen Metren in deutschen Kompositionen des 16. Jahrhunderts', *Vierteljahrsschrift für Musikwissenschaft*, iii (1887), 26–91.

Lindsay, W. M., ed., *Originum sive etymologiarum libri XX*, Oxford, 1911.

Lipphardt, W., *Die Geschichte des mehrstimmigen Proprium Missae*, Heidelberg, 1950.

Lipphardt, W., ed., *Isaac: Officium Epiphaniae Domini*, Kassel, 1948.

Lipphardt, W., ed., *Lechner: Deutsche Sprüche von Leben und Tod*, Kassel, 1929.

Lipphardt, Walther, 'Liturgische Dramen des Mittelalters', in *MGG*, viii (1960), cols. 1012–44.

Lipphardt, W., ed., *O. & R. Lasso: Teutsche Psalmen ... mit dreyen Stimmen* [1588], Kassel, 1952.

Lipphardt, Walther, 'Rhythmisch-metrische Hymnenstudien', *Jahrbuch für Liturgiewissenschaft*, xiv (1938), 172–96.

Lipphardt, W., 'Studien zu den Marienklagen', *Beiträge zur Geschichte der deutschen Sprache und Literatur*, lviii (1934), 390–444.

Lipphardt, W., *Die Weisen der Osterspiele des 12. und 13. Jahrhunderts*, Kassel, 1948.

Lippman, E. A., 'Hellenic Conceptions of Harmony', *JAMS*, xvi (1963), 3–35.

Lippman, E. A., *Musical Thought in Ancient Greece*, New York, 1964.

Lippmann, E. A., 'The Sources and Development of the Ethical View of Music in Ancient Greece', *MQ*, xlix (1963), 188–209.

Lissa, Zofia, ed., *Musica Antiqua Europae Orientalis*, Warsaw, 1966.

Liuzzi, Fernando, ed., *La lauda e i primordi della melodia italiana*, 2 vols., Rome, 1935.

Lobel, E., Turner, E. G., Winnington-Ingram, R. P., edd., *Oxyrhynchus Papyri*, part xxv, London, 1959, pp. 113–22.

Lockwood, L., 'A Continental Mass and Motet in a Tudor Manuscript', *ML*, xlii (1961), 336–47.

Lockwood, L., 'A dispute on accidentals in sixteenth-century Rome', *Analecta Musicologica*, ii (1965), 24–40.

Lockwood, L., 'On "Parody" as term and concept', in *Festschrift Reese*, pp. 560–75.

Lockwood, L. H., 'Vincenzo Ruffo and Musical Reform after the Council of Trent', *MQ* xliii (1957), 342–71.

Longman, G. A., 'The musical Papyrus: Euripides *Orestes* 332–40', *Classical Quarterly*, new series, xii (1962), 61–66.

Lowinsky, E. E., ed., *The Medici Codex of 1518*, (Monuments of Renaissance Music, 3–5), Chicago and London, 1968.

Lowinsky, E. E., 'Ockeghem's Canon for 36 Voices', in *Festschrift Plamenac*, pp. 155–80.

Lowinsky, E. E., *Secret Chromatic Art in the Netherlands Motet*, New York, 1946.

Lowinsky, E. E., *Tonality and Atonality in Sixteenth-Century Music*, Berkeley and Los Angeles, 1961.

Ludwig, Friedrich, 'Die geistliche, nicht-liturgische, weltliche einstimmige und die mehrstimmige Musik des Mittelalters ...', in Adler, *Handbuch*, i, 157.

Ludwig, F., 'Geschichte der Mensural-Notation' von 1250–1460', *SIMG*, vi (1905), 597 [review of Wolf, *Mensural-Notation*].

Ludwig, F., *Repertorium organorum recentioris et motetorum vetustissimi stili*. Bd. 1 Abt. 1, Halle, 1910; 2nd. edn., ed. L. A. Dittmer (Institute of Mediaeval Music, Musicological Studies, vii), New York, 1964; Bd. 1, Abt. 2 [photographic reprint of page proofs, together with] *Die Quellen der Motetten ältesten Stils* [photographic reprint from *AfMW*] ed. F. Gennrich (Summa musicae medii aevi, vii), Langen bei Frankfurt, 1961; Bd. 2, *Catalogue raisonné der Quellen*, ed. L. A. Dittmer (Institute of Mediaeval Music, Musicological Studies, xvii), New York, 1971.

Lumsden, David, 'The Sources of English Lute Music (1540–1620)', *Galpin Society Journal*, vi (1953), 14–22.

Lunelli, R., *L'arte organaria del Rinascimento in Roma*, Florence, 1958.

MacClintock, C., ed., *The Bottegari Lutebook* (The Wellesley Edition, no. 8), Wellesley, Mass., 1965.

MacClintock, C., *Giaches de Wert (1535–1596); Life and Works*, (Musicological Studies and Documents, 17), Rome, 1966.

MacClintock, C., 'Molinet, Music and Mediaeval Rhetoric', *Mus. Disc.*, xiii (1959), 109–21.

MacClintock, C., 'New Light on Giaches de Wert', in *Festschrift Reese*, pp. 595–602.

MacClintock, C., 'Some notes on the Secular Music of Giaches de Wert', *Mus. Disc.*, x (1956), 106–41.

MacClintock, C. and Bernstein, M., edd., *Wert: Opera Omnia* (*CMM*, xxiv), Rome, 1961 ff. [12 vols. published by 1972].

McKinley, A., ed., *Francesco Corteccia: Eleven Works to Latin Texts*, Madison (Wis.): A-R Editions, 1969.

McKinnon, James, 'The meaning of the patristic polemic against musical instruments', *Current Musicology*, (Spring 1965), 69–82.

McPeek, Gwynn S., ed., *The British Museum MS Egerton 3307*, London, 1963.

McShane, Margaret Mary, *The Music of the mediaeval liturgical Drama*, (Diss. of Cath. Univ. of America, 1961), Ann Arbor, 1962.

Mace, D. T., 'Pietro Bembo and the Literary Origins of the Italian Madrigal', *MQ*, lv (1969), 65–86.

Machabey, A., *G. de Machaut*, 2 vols., Paris, 1955.

Machabey, 'Remarques sur le Winchester Troper', in *Festschrift Besseler*, p. 67.

Macran, H., ed., *Harmonics of Aristoxenus* [Text, English translation and commentary], Oxford, 1902.

Main, A., ed., *Costanzo Festa: Opera Omnia*, (*CMM*, xxv), 2 vols., Rome, 1962–8.

Mairy, A., Laurencie, L. de La and Thibault, G., edd., *Chansons au luth et airs de Cour francais du XVIe siècle*, Paris, 1934.

Maldeghem, R. van, ed., *Trésor musical* (Series I: *Musique profane*, 29 vols.; Series II: *Musique sacrée*, 29 vols.), Brussels, 1865–93. [reprinted in 6 vols., Vaduz, 1965].

Malipiero, G. F., ed., *Tutte le opere di Claudio Monteverdi*, Vienna, 1926–42; reprinted 1967–8.

Mantica, F., ed., *Cavalieri: Rappresentazione di anima e di corpo*, Rome, 1912. [See also Baroni].

Manuel, Roland Alexis, ed., *Histoire de la Musique* (Encyclopédie de la Pléiade), 2 vols., Paris, 1960–3.

Marix, J., *Histoire de la musique . . . à la cour de Bourgogne sous le règne de Philippe le Bon*, Strasbourg, 1939.

Marix, J., ed., *Les musiciens de la cour de Bourgogne au XVe siècle: messes, motets, chansons*, Monaco, 1937.

Marrocco, W. T., 'The Ballata – a metamorphic form', *Acta*, xxxi (1959), 32–37.

Marrocco, W. T., ed., *Fourteenth-century Italian Cacce*, 2nd edn., Cambridge, Mass., 1961.

Marrocco, W. T., 'The 14th-century Italian Cacce', *Speculum*, xxvi (1951), 449–57.

Marrocco, W. T., ed., *The Music of Jacopo da Bologna*, Berkeley and Los Angeles, 1954.

Marrocco, W. T., 'The newly discovered Ostiglia Pages of the Vatican Rossi Codex 215; The earliest Italian Ostinato', *Acta*, xxxix (1967), 84–91.

Marrou, H.: *Histoire de l'éducation dans l'antiquité*, Paris, 2nd edn., 1950.

Marrou, H., 'Μελογραεία', *L'antiquité classique*, xv (1946), 289–96.

Marrou, H. I., *St. Augustin et la fin de la culture antique*, 2 parts, Paris, 1938, 1949.

Marshall, Robert L., 'The Paraphrase Technique of Palestrina in his masses based on hymns', *JAMS*, xvi (1963), 347–72.

Martí, Samuel, *Instrumentos musicales precortesianos*, Mexico, 1954.

Martin, E., *Trois Documents de musique grecque*, Paris, 1953.

Martin, E. and Burald, J., edd., *Du Caurroy: Missa pro defunctis*, Paris, 1951.

Martin, William, ed., *Vecchi: Convito musicale* (Capolavori ... del sec. XVI, viii), Rome, 1966.

Martinez, M.L., *Die Musik des frühen Trecento*, (Münchner Veröffentlichungen zur Musikgeschichte, 9), Tutzing, 1963.

Massera, G., *La 'Mano musicale perfetta' di Francesco de Brugis dalle Prefazioni ai Corali di L.A.Giunta*, (Historiae Musicae Cultores Biblioteca, xviii), Florence, 1963.

Masson, P.M., ed., *Chants de carnaval florentins*, Paris, 1913.

Masson, P.M., 'L'humanisme musical en France au XVIᵉ siècle', *Mercure Musical et Bulletin Français de la S. I. M.*, iii (1907), 333–66 and 677–718.

May, Hans von, *Die Kompositionstechnik T.L. de Victorias*, Bern, 1943.

Mayer, F.A. and Rietsch, H., 'Die Mondsee-Wiener Liederhandschrift und der Mönch von Salzburg', *Acta Germanica*, iii–iv (1894–5), 332–490 and 1–409.

Mead, Charles W., 'The Musical Instruments of the Inca', *Anthropological Papers of the American Museum of Natural History*, xv (1924), 313–47.

Mearns, James, *Early Latin Hymnaries: An index of hymns in Hymnaries before 1100 with Appendix from later sources*, Cambridge, 1913.

Meier, B., ed., *Cipriano di Rore: Opera omnia*, (*CMM*, xiv), Rome, 1959 ff. [6 vols. published by 1972].

Meier, B., ed., *Giovan Nasco und andere Meister, Fünf (Petrarca) Madrigale* (Chorwerk, lxxxviii), Wolfenbüttel, 1962.

Meier, B., ed., *Jakob Arcadelt und andere Meister, Sechs italienische Madrigale*, (Das Chorwerk, lviii), Wolfenbüttel, 1956.

Meier, B., 'The Musica Reservata of Adrianus Petit Coclico and its relationship to Josquin', *Mus. Disc.*, x (1956), 67–105.

Meier, Rudolf, 'Das Innsbrucker Osterspiel. Das Osterspiel von Muri', in *Mittelhochdeutsche und Neuhochdeutsche* (Stuttgart, 1964).

Melnicki, Margareta, *Das Einstimmige Kyrie des lateinischen Mittelalters*, Erlangen, 1954.

Mendoza, Vicente T., *Panorama de la música tradicional de México* (Instituto de Investigaciones Estéticas, Universidad Nacional Autónoma de México, Estudios y fuentes del arte en México, vii), Mexico, 1956.

Merian, W., 'Drei Handschriften aus der Frühzeit des Klavierspiels', *AfMW*, ii (1920), 22–47.

Merian, W., *Die Tabulaturen des Organisten Hans Kotter*, Leipzig, 1916.

Merian, W., *Der Tanz in den deutschen Tabulaturbüchern*, Leipzig, 1927. [Reprinted Hildesheim, 1967].

Merritt, A.T. and Lesure, F., edd., *Janequin: Chansons polyphoniques*, 5 vols., Monaco, 1965–8.

Meyer, E.H., ed., *Vaet: 6 Motetten* (Chorwerk, ii), Wolfenbüttel, 1929.

Meyer, H., ed., *Meiland: Lieder und Gesänge*, Augsburg, 1927.

Meyer, L.S., ed., *Music, Cantelenas, Songs ...*, London, 1906.

Meyer-Baer, K., *Music of the Spheres and the Dance of Death*, Princeton, N.J., 1970.

Meyer-Baer, K., 'Music in Dante's Divina Commedia', in *Festschrift Reese*, 614–27.

Michael, W.F., 'Frühformen der deutschen Bühne' in *Schriften der Gesellsch. für Theatergesch.*, lxii (Berlin, 1963), 62.

Michael, W.F., *Die geistlichen Prozessionsspiele in Deutschland*, Baltimore, 1947.

Michel, F., Lesure, F. and Fedorov, V., edd. *Encyclopédie de la Musique*, 3 vols., Paris: Fasquelle, 1958–61.

Migne, J.P., *Patrologiae cursus completus*, Series Latina, 221 vols., Paris, 1844–65.

Miller, C.A., 'The *Dodecachordon*: Its Origins and Influence on Renaissance Musical Thought', *Mus. Disc.*, xv (1961), 156–66.

Miller, C.A., ed., *Heinrich Glarean, Dodecachordon. Translation, Transcription and Commentary*, (Musicological Studies and Documents, 6), 2 vols., Rome, 1965.

Minor, A., ed., *Mouton: Opera Omnia* (*CMM*, xliii), Vol. i, Rome, 1967.

Minor, A.C. and Mitchell, B., *A Renaissance Entertainment: Festivities for the Marriage of Cosimo I, Duke of Florence, in 1539*, Columbia (Missouri), 1968.

Mischiati, O., ed., *G. Cavazzoni: Orgelwerke*, 2 vols., Mainz, 1959–60.

Mitjana, R., *Estudios sobre algunos músicos españoles del siglo XVI*, Madrid, 1918.

Mitjana, R., *Francesco Guerrero: estudio crítico-biográfico*, Madrid, 1922.

Mitjana, R., Bal y Gay, J. and Pope, I., edd., *Cancionero de Upsala*, Mexico, 1944.

Moberg, Carl-Allan, (ed.), *Die liturgischen Hymnen in Schweden* ... vol. i, Quellen und Texte. Text- und Melodieregister, Copenhagen, 1947.

Mokrý, Ladislav, ed., *Anfänge der slavischen Musik*, Bratislava, 1966.

Mompellio, F., ed., *L. Marenzio, Madrigali a 5 e 6 v.*, Milan, 1953.

Monumenta Musicae in Polonia, Warsaw, 1964 ff.

Moragas, Dom B., 'Transcripcio musical de dos himnes' in *Festschrift Anglès*, ii, 591–8.

Morcourt, R. de, ed., *Morlaye: Psaumes de ... Certon réduits pour chant et luth*, Paris, 1957.

Morcourt, R. de, Jansen, P. and Souris, A., edd., *A. Le Roy: Psaumes; Fantasies et danses; Fantaisies, motets et chansons*, 3 vols., Paris, 1960–2.

Morphy, G., ed., *Les Luthistes espagnols du XVIᵉ siècle*, 2 vols., Leipzig, 1902.

Moser, H.J., ed., *Egenolff: Gassenhawerlin (1535)*, Augsburg, 1927.

Moser, H.J., *Paul Hofhaimer*, Berlin, 1929. [with additions in *ZfMW*, XV (1932–3), 127–38] [Contains edn. of Hofhaimer's complete works.]

Moser, H.J., 'Der Zerbster Luther-Fund', *AfMW*, ii (1920), 337–55.

Moser, H.J. and Fedke, T., edd., *Choralbearbeitungen und freie Orgelstücke* ..., 2 vols., Kassel, 1954–5.

Moser, H.J. and Heitmann, F., edd., *Frühmeister deutscher Orgelkunst*, Leipzig, 1930.

Moser, H.J. and Piersig, F., edd., *Carmina: Ausgewählte Instrumentalsätze [Finck, Isaac, Senfl]* (Nagels Musik-Archiv, liii), Hanover, 1929.

Most, G., ed., *Die Orgeltabulatur von 1448 des Adam Ileborgh aus Stendal* [includes facs.], Stendal, 1954. [reviewed *Musikforschung*, ix (1956), 91–3].

Mountford, J.F., 'Greek music in the Papyri and Inscriptions' and 'Greek music: the Cairo musical fragment', in J.U.Powell and E.A.Barber, edd., *New Chapters in the History of Greek Literature*, 2nd series, Oxford, 1929, 146–83, and 3rd series, Oxford, 1933, 260–1.

Mountford, J.F., 'The Musical Scales of Plato's Republic', *Classical Quarterly*, xvii (1923), 125–36.

Mountford, J.F., 'A new fragment of Greek music in Cairo', *Journal of Hellenic Studies*, li (1931), 91–100.

Müller, K.K., ed., *Jenaer Liederhandschrift* [facs.] Jena, 1896.

Mundó, Anscari M., 'La datación de los códices litúrgicos visigóticos toledanos', *Hispania Sacra*, xviii (1965), 1–25.

Musica Britannica [various edd.], London, 1951 ff.
i, Mulliner Book, ed. D.Stevens, 1951 [rev. 1954]; ii, Locke: Cupid and Death, ed. E.Dent, 1951 [rev. 1965]; iv, Mediaeval Carols, ed., J.Stevens, 1952 [rev. 1958]; v, Tomkins, Keyboard Music, ed. S.Tuttle, 1955 [rev. 1964]; vi, Dowland, Ayres for 4 Voices, edd. T.Dart & N.Fortune, 1953 [rev. 1963]; viii, Dunstable, Works, ed. M.Bukofzer, 1953 [rev. 1970]; ix, Jacobean Consort Music, ed. T.Dart and W.Coates, 1955 [rev. 1968]; x–xii, Eton Choir Book, 3 vols., ed. F.Ll.Harrison, 1956–61; xiv, Bull: Keyboard Music, I, ed. J.Steele and F. Cameron, 1960 [rev. 1967]; xv, Music of Scotland 1500–1700, ed. K.Elliott, 1957, rev. 1964; xviii, Music at the Court of Henry VIII, ed. J.Stevens, 1962 [rev. 1969]; xix, Bull: Keyboard Music, II, ed. T.Dart, 1963; xx, Gibbons: Keyboard Music, ed. G.Hendrie, 1962, rev. 1967; xxii, Consort Songs, ed. P.Brett, 1967; xxiii, Weelkes, Collected Anthems, edd. D.Brown, W. Collins, P.Le Huray, 1966; xxiv, Farnaby, Keyboard Music, ed. R.Marlowe, 1965; xxv, Dering, Secular Vocal Music, ed. P.Platt, 1969; xxvi, Jenkins, Consort Music, ed. A.Ashbee, 1969; xxvii, Byrd: Keyboard Music, I, ed. A.Brown, 1969; xxviii, Byrd: Keyboard Music, II, ed. A.Brown, 1971; xxix, Philips: Madrigals, ed. J.Steele, 1970.

Musik in Geschichte und Gegenwart, Die, ed. F.Blume, 14 vols., Kassel, 1949–68. Suppl. fascicles, 1969 ff.

Mužík, František, ed., *Studie a materiály k dějinám starší české hudby*, Prague, 1965.

Nedden, O. zur, 'Zur Geschichte der Musik am Hofe Kaiser Maximilians I', *ZfMW*, xv (1932–33), 24–32.

Nejedlý, Zdeněk, *Dějiny husitského zpěvu*, 6 vols., Prague, 1954–6.

Nelson, R.U., *The Technique of Variation*, Berkeley, 1948.

Ness, Arthur J., ed., *The Lute Music of Francesco Canova da Milano (1497–1543)*

(Harvard Publications in Music, iii–iv), 2 vols. bound in 1, Cambridge (Mass.), 1970.

Nettl, P., *Luther and Music*, Philadelphia, 1948.

New Oxford History of Music, vols. i–iv, London, 1954–68.

Newman, J., 'A Gentleman's Lute Book: The Tablature of Gabriello Fallamero', *Current Musicology*, Fall 1965, 175–90.

Newman, J., ed., *Sixteenth-Century Italian Dances, from British Museum Royal Appendix MS. 59–62*, University Park and London, 1966.

Newton, Richard, 'English Lute Music of the Golden Age', *PRMA*, lxv (1938–39), 63–90.

Niemöller, K.W., 'Othmar Luscinius, Musiker und Humanist', *AfMW*, xv (1958), 41–59.

Noble, Jeremy, 'Le Répertoire instrumental anglais, 1550–1585', in Jacquot, *Instrumentale*, pp. 91–114.

Nowak, L., ed. [and A. Koczirz and A. Pfalz], *Das deutsche Gesellschaftslied ... 1480–1550* (*DTO*, vol. 72), Vienna, 1930.

Nowak, L., 'Das deutsche Gesellschaftslied in Österreich von 1480 bis 1550', *Studien zur Musikwissenschaft*, xvii (1930), 21–52.

Nuten, P., *De 'Madrigali spirituali' van Filip de Monte, 1521–1603*, Brussels, 1958.

Osborn, J.M., ed., *Thomas Whythorne: Autobiography*, Oxford, 1961; modern spelling ed., London, 1962.

Osthoff, H., 'Deutsche Liedweisen und Wechselgesänge im mittelalterlichen Drama', *AfMF*, vii (1942), 65–81.

Osthoff, H., ed., *Josquin [and others]: 8 Lied- und Choral-Motetten* (Chorwerk, xxx), Wolfenbüttel, 1934 [Josquin, Le Maistre, Holländer, Utendal, Ivo de Vento, Regnart].

Osthoff, H., *Josquin Desprez*, 2 vols., Tutzing, 1962–5.

Osthoff, H., *Die Niederländer und das deutsche Lied* (Neue Deutsche Forschungen, vii), Berlin, 1938.

Osthoff, H., 'Zu Isaacs und Senfls deutschen Liedern', *ZfMW*, xiv (1931–32), 221–3.

Osthoff, W., *Theatergesang und Darstellende Musik in der italienischen Renaissance. (15. und 16. Jahrhundert)*, (Münchner Veröffentlichungen zur Musikgeschichte, 14), 2 vols., Tutzing, 1969.

Ott, Carolus, *Offertoriale sive versus offer-torium*, Tournai, 1935.

Oxyrhynchus Papyri, see Lobel, E.

Paesler, C., 'Fundamentbuch von Hans von Constanz', *Vierteljahrsschrift für Musikwissenschaft*, v (1889), 1–192.

Page, D.L., *Alcman: The Partheneion*, Oxford, 1951.

Paléographie Musicale: Les principaux manuscrits de chant en fac-similés phototypiques; Series I, 18 vols.; Series II, 3 vols.; Tournai, Solesmes, 1889–1969.

Palikarova, Verdeil R., *La Musique byzantine chez les Bulgares et les Russes*, Copenhagen, 1953.

Palisca, C., 'A Clarification of "Musica Reservata" in Jean Taisnier's "Astrologiae" (1559)', *Acta*, xxxi (1959), 133–161.

Palisca, C.V., 'Vicenzo Galilei and some Links between "Pseudo-Monody" and Monody', *MQ*, xlvi (1960), 344–60.

Parrish, C., *The Notation of Mediaeval Music*, New York, 1957.

Parrish, Carl, ed., *A Treasury of Early Music*, London, 1959.

Parrish, C., and Ohl, J.F., edd., *Masterpieces of Music before 1750*, London, 1952.

Pattison, Bruce, *Music and Poetry of the English Renaissance*, London, 1948, (2nd edn., 1970).

Pearce, C.W., ed., *A Collection of Songs and Madrigals*, London, 1891.

Pearl, O.M. and Winnington-Ingram, R.P., 'A Michigan Papyrus with Musical Notation', *Journal of Egyptian Archaeology*, li (1965), 179–95.

Pease, E., 'A Re-examination of the Caccia Found in Bologna, Civico Museo, Codex Q 16', *Mus. Disc.*, xxii (1968), 231–4.

Pedrell, F., ed., *Antología de organistas clásicos españoles*, 2 vols., Madrid, 1908.

Pedrell, F., *Catàlech de la Biblioteca Músical de la Diputació de Barcelona*, 2 vols., Barcelona, 1908, 1909.

Pedrell, F., *Emporio científico e histórico de organografía musical antigua española*, Barcelona, 1901.

Pedrell, F., 'Jean I d'Aragon, compositeur de musique', in *Festschrift Riemann*, pp. 229–40.

Pedrell, Felipe, *Tomás de Victoria Abulense*, Valencia, 1918.

Pedrell, F., ed., *Victoria: Opera Omnia*, 8 vols., Leipzig, 1902–13. [Reprint: Ridgewood, New Jersey, 1965–6].

Pedrell, F. and Anglès, H., edd., *Joan*

Brudieu: Els Madrigals i la Missa de Difunts, Barcelona, 1921.

Pellegrini, Silvio, 'Dante e la "Passione" di Montecassino', *Belfagor*, xvii (1962), 299–313.

Peter, H., ed., *Ganassi: Fontegara* (Eng. tr. D. Swainson), Berlin and London, 1969.

Petrov, Stoyan, *Ochertsi po istoriya na b''lgarskata muzikalna kultura*, Sofia, 1959.

Petti, A. G., ed., *Giovanni Francesco Anerio. Missa pro defunctis cum sequentia et responsorio Libera me*, London, 1966.

Petzsch, C., *Das Lochamer-Liederbuch: Studien* (Münchener Texte und Untersuchungen zur deutschen Literatur des Mittelalters, xix), Munich, 1967.

Petzsch, C., 'Weiterdichten und Umformen ... des Lochamer Liederbuches', *Jahrbuch für Volksliedforschung*, x (1965), 1–28.

Piaget, A., 'La cour amoureuse dite de Charles VI', *Romania*, xx (1891), 417 and xxi (1892), 597.

Pickard-Cambridge, A. W., *The Dramatic Festivals of Athens*, Oxford, 1953.

Picker, M., 'A Letter of Charles VIII ... concerning A. Agricola', in *Festschrift Reese*, pp. 665–72.

Pidal, R. Minéndez, 'Cantos romanicos andalusiés continuardores de una lirica latina vulgar', *Bolétin de la Réal Academia Espanola* (1951), 187 ff.

Pidoux, P., 'Les psaumes d'A. de Mornable, G. Morlaye et P. Certon, Etude comparative', *Annales musicologiques*, V (1957), 179–98.

Pidoux, P., ed., *Le psautier huguenot du XVIe siècle*, 2 vols., Basel, 1962.

Piersig, F., ed., *Othmayr: Reutterische und Jegerische Liedlein*, 2 vols., Wolfenbüttel, 1928 & 1933.

Pietzsch, G., 'Zur Pflege der Musik an den deutschen Universitäten ... des 16. Jahrhunderts', *AfMW*, vii (1942), 90–110, 154–69.

Pirro, A., *Histoire de la musique de la fin du XIVe siècle à la fin du XVIe*, Paris, 1940.

Pirrotta, N., 'Ars Nova e Stil Novo', *Rivista italiana della musicologia*, i (1966), 3–9.

Pirrotta, N., 'Chronologia e denominazione dell'Ars Nova italiana', in *Congress Wégimont 1955*, pp. 94–109.

Pirrotta, N., 'Due sonetti musicali del secolo XIV', in *Festschrift Anglès*, ii, 651–62.

Pirrotta, N., 'Marchettus de Padua and the Italian Ars Nova', *Mus. Disc.*, ix (1955), 57–71.

Pirrotta, N., 'Music and Cultural Tendencies in 15th-Century Italy', *JAMS*, xix (1966), 127–61.

Pirrotta, N., ed., *Music of Fourteenth Century Italy*, (*CMM* viii, 1–5), Rome, 1954–64.

Pirrotta, N., 'Per l'origine e la storia della caccia', *Rivista Musicale Italiana*, xlviii (1946), 305–23.

Pirrotta, N. and Li Gotti, E., 'Il codice di Lucca', *Mus. Disc.*, iii (1949), 119–38; iv (1950), 111–52; v (1951), 115–42.

Pizzetti, I., ed., *Gesualdo da Venosa, Madrigali*, (I classici della musica italiana, xiv), Milan, 1919.

Plamenac, D., 'Another Paduan Fragment of Trecento Music', *JAMS*, viii (1955), 165–81.

Plamenac, D., 'Keyboard Music of the 14th Century in Codex Faenza 117', *JAMS*, iv (1951), 179–201.

Plamenac, D., 'New Light on Codex Faenza 117', in *Congress Utrecht 1952*, pp. 310–26.

Plamenac, D., ed., *Ockeghem: Collected Works*, 2nd corr. edn., New York, 1959–66. [1st edn. 1927–47].

Plamenac, D., 'The Recently Discovered Complete Copy of A. Antico's *Frottole intabulate* (1517)', in *Festschrift Reese*, 683–92.

Pognon, E., '... P. de Vitry et ses amis', *Humanisme et Renaissance*, vi (1939), 49–50.

Pohanka, Jaroslav, *Dějiny české hudby v příkladech*, Prague, 1958.

Pöhlmann, E., *Griechische Musikfragmente. Ein Weg zur altgriechischen Musik*, Nürnberg, 1960.

Pope, I., 'Mediaeval Latin Background of the Thirteenth-Century Galician Lyric', *Speculum*, ix (1934), 3–25.

Pope, I., 'Musical and Metrical Form of the Villancico', *Annales musicologiques*, ii (1954), 189–214.

Pope, I., 'The musical manuscript Montecassino N 879', *Anuario musical*, xix (1964), 123–53.

Pope, I., 'The secular compositions of Johannes Cornago', in *Festschrift Anglès*, ii, 689.

Pope, I., 'The "Spanish Chapel" of Philip

II', *Renaissance News*, v (1952), 1–5 and 34–8.

Potiron, H., 'Les Notations d'Aristide Quintilien et les harmonies dites Platoniciennes', *Revue de Musicologie*, xlvii (1961), 157–76.

Prado, Germán, *Historia del rito mozárabe y toledane*, Santo Domingo de Silos, 1928.

Prado, Germán, ed., *Liber Sancti Jacobi*, 3 vols., Santiago de Compostela, 1944.

Prado, Germán, *Manuel de liturgia hispano-visigótica o mozárabe*, Madrid, 1927.

Prado, Germán, 'Mozarabic Melodies', *Speculum*, iii (1928), 218–38.

Pujol, E., ed., Alonso Mudarra: *Tres libros de musica en cifra para vihuela (1546)* (Monumentos de la música española, vii), Barcelona, 1949.

Pujol, E., ed., *Enrique Enriquez de Valderrábano: Libro de música de vihuela intitulado Silva de Sirenas* (Monumentos de la música española, xxii, xxiii), 2 vols., Barcelona, 1965.

Pujol, E., ed., *Luys de Narváez: Los seys libros del Delphin de música de cifra para tañer vihuela (1538)* (Monumentos de la música española, iii), Barcelona, 1945.

Querol Gavaldá, M., ed., *Cancionero musical de la Casa de Medinaceli* (Monumentos de la música española, viii, ix), 2 vols., Barcelona, 1949, 1950.

Querol Gavaldá, M. and V. Garcia, edd., *Francisco Guerrero: Opera Omnia* (Monumento de la música española, xvi, xix), 2 vols., Barcelona, 1955 ff. [xvi: 1955, xix: 1957].

Racek, Jan, *Česká hudba*, Prague, 1958.

Racek, Jan, *Středověká hudba (se zvláštním zřetelem k české hudbě gotické)*, Brno, 1946.

Ramsbotham, A., Collins, H.B., and Hughes, Dom Anselm, edd., *The Old Hall Manuscript*, 3 vols., London, 1933–8. [See also Hughes, Andrew].

Randel, D.M., *The Responsorial Psalm Tones for the Mozarabic Office* (Princeton Studies in Music, iii), Princeton, 1969.

Ranke, F. and Müller-Blattau, J., *Das Rostocker Liederbuch nach den Fragmenten der Handschrift*, Halle, 1927.

Rayner, Clare G., ed., *Cima: Partito de ricercari & canzoni alla francese* [1606] (Corpus of Early Keyboard Music, xx), Rome, 1969.

Reaney, G., 'The Ballades, Rondeaux and Virelais of ... Machaut ...', *Acta*, xxvii (1955), 40–58.

Reaney, G., 'Chronology of the Ballades, Rondeaux and Virelais ... by G. de Machaut', *Mus. Disc.*, vi (1952), 33–8.

Reaney, G., ed., *Early Fifteenth Century Music* (*CMM*, xi), 4 vols., Rome, 1955–69.

Reaney, G., 'Fourteenth Century Harmony and ... Machaut', *Mus. Disc.*, vii (1953), 129–46.

Reaney, G., 'The manuscript London, British Museum, Additional 29987 (*Lo*)', *Mus. Disc.*, xii (1958), 67–91.

Reaney, G., 'The Manuscript Paris, Bibliothèque Nationale, Fonds Italien 568, (*Pit*)', *Mus. Disc.*, xiv (1960), 33–63.

Reaney, Gilbert, *Manuscripts of Polyphonic Music* (Repertoire Internationale des Sources Musicales, vol. B IV$^{1-2}$), München-Duisburg, 1965–9.

Reaney, G., 'The poetic form of Machaut's Musical Works', *Mus. Disc.*, viii (1959), 25–41.

Reckow, Fritz, *Der Musiktraktat des Anonymus 4* (Beihefte zum *AfMW*, iv–v), 2 vols., Wiesbaden, 1967.

Redlich, H.F., *Claudio Monteverdi: Life and Works*, tr. Kathleen Dale, London, 1952.

Reese, Gustave, *Music in the Middle Ages*, New York, 1940.

Reese, Gustave, *Music in the Renaissance*, New York, 1954 (rev. edn., 1959).

Reese, Gustave, 'The Origin of the English "In Nomine"', *JAMS*, ii (1949), 7–22.

Rehm, W., ed., *Die Chansons von G. Binchois* (Musikalische Denkmäler, ii), Mainz, 1957.

Reichert, Georg, 'Wechselbeziehungen zwischen musikalischer und textlicher Struktur in der Motette des 13. Jahrhunderts', in *Festschrift Handschin*, p. 151.

Reimann, M., ed., *Die Lüneburger Orgeltabulature KN 208^1* (Erbe deutscher Musik, ser. i, xxxvi), Frankfurt, 1957.

Ribera Tarragó, Julián, *La Música árabe y su influencia en la española*, Madrid, 1927.

Riemann, H., 'Das Lautenwerk des Miguel Fuenllana', *Monatshefte für Musikgeschichte*, xxvii (1895), 81–91.

Riemann, H., 'Der Mensuralkodex des Magisters Apel', *Kirchenmusikalisches Jahrbuch*, xii (1897), 1–23.

Rietsch, H., ed., *Gesänge von Frauenlob,*

Reinmar von Zweter und Alexander (*DTO*, xx, part ii), Vienna, 1913.

Rimbault, E. F. and others, edd., *Musical Antiquarian Society, Publications of*, 19 vols., London, 1840–48.

xi, The Whole Book of Psalms ... Published by Thomas Este, ed. Rimbault; xiv, A Collection of Anthems [M. Este, T. Ford, Weelkes, Bateson], ed. Rimbault.

Ringmann, H. and Klapper, J., edd., *Das Glogauer Liederbuch*, 2 vols. (Erbe deutscher Musik, ser. i, vols. iv and vii), Kassel, 1936 and 1937.

Rios, R. da, ed., *Aristoxenus: Elementa Harmonica* [Text, Italian translation and commentary], 2 vols., Rome, 1954.

Rojo, Cassiano and Prado, Germán, *El Canto Mozárabe*, Barcelona, 1929.

Rokseth, Yvonne, ed., *Polyphonies du XIIIᵉ siècle*, 4 vols., Paris, 1935–48.

Rokseth, Yvonne, 'La polyphonie Parisienne du treizième siècle', *Les Cahiers techniques de l'art*, I, fasc. 2 (1947), 33.

Roland-Manuel, *see* Manuel.

Rollin, J., *Les chansons de C. Marot*, Paris, 1951.

Rönnau, Klaus, *Die Tropen zum 'Gloria in excelsis Deo'*, Wiesbaden, 1967.

Rosenberg, H., ed., *Das Schedelsche Liederbuch*, Kassel, 1933.

Rosenberg, H., 'Übertragungen einiger bisher nicht aufgelöster Melodiennotierungen des Lochamer Liederbuchs', *ZfMW*, xiv (1931–2), 67–88.

Rubio, J., ed., *Antologia polifónica sacra*, 2 vols., Madrid, 1956.

Rubio, J., 'El archivo de música de la Catedral de Plasencia', *Annuario musical*, v (1950), 147–68.

Rubsamen, W., *Literary Sources of Secular Music in Italy*, Berkeley, 1943.

Rubsamen, W. H., 'Sebastian Festa and the Early Madrigal', in *Congress Kassel 1962*, pp. 122–6.

Rüegge, R., ed., *Orazio Vecchi, Missa in Resurrectione Domini*, (Chorwerk, cviii), Wolfenbüttel, n.d.

Rüegge, R., *Orazio Vecchis geistliche Werke*, Bern, 1967.

Ruelle, Charles Emile, *Collections des auteurs grecs relatifs à la musique*, Paris, 1895.

Ruëtz, M., ed., *Dressler: Fünf Motetten* (Chorwerk, xxviii), Wolfenbüttel, 1934.

Runge, P., ed., *H. von Montfort: Lieder,*

mit den Melodien des B. Mangolt, Leipzig, 1906.

Runge, P., *Die Sangesweisen der Colmarer Handschrift und die Liederhandshrift Donaueschingen*, Leipzig, 1896.

Russell, E. A., 'Villancicos and Other Secular Polyphonic Music of Juan Vásquez: a Courtly Tradition in Spain's Siglo d'Oro', Dissertation, Univ. of Southern California, 1970.

Sabol, A., ed., *Songs and Dances for the Stuart Masque*, Providence (R.I.), 1959.

Sachs, C., 'Die griechische Gesangsnotenschrift', *ZfMW*, vii (1924–5), 1–5.

Sachs, C., 'Die griechische Instrumentalnotenschrift', *ZfMW*, vi (1923–4), 289–301.

Sachs, Curt, *The History of Musical Instruments*, New York, 1940.

Salazar, A., 'El Laúd, la Vihuela y la Guitarra (Notas)', *Nuestra Música*, i (1946), 228.

Salazar, Adolfo, *La música de España*, Buenos Aires, 1953.

Salmen, W., *Das Erbe des ostdeutschen Volkgesanges*, Würzburg, 1956.

Salmen, W. and Koepp, J., edd., *Liederbuch der Anna von Köln* (Denkmäler Rheinischer Musik, iv), Cologne, 1954.

Sandberger, A., *Beiträge zur Geschichte der bayerischen Hofkapelle unter Orlando di Lasso*, I, III, Leipzig, 1894, 1895. [Vol. ii never published].

Sanders, Ernest H., 'Cantilena and Discant in 14th-Century England', *Mus. Disc.*, xix (1965), 7–52.

Sanders, Ernest H., 'Duple Rhythm and Alternate Third Mode in 13th-Century Polyphony', *JAMS*, xv (1962), 249–91.

Sanders, Ernest H., 'Peripheral Polyphony of the 13th Century', *JAMS*, xvii (1964), 261–87.

Sanders, Ernest H., 'The Question of Perotin's Oeuvre and Dates', in *Festschrift Wiora*, pp. 241–9.

Sanders, Ernest H., 'Die Rolle der englischen Mehrstimmigkeit des Mittelalters ...', *AfMW*, xxiv (1967), 24–53.

Sanders, Ernest, H., 'Tonal Aspects of 13th-Century English Polyphony', *Acta*, xxxvii (1965), 19–34.

Sanvoisin, M., ed., *Le Jeune: Missa ad placitum* (Le Pupitre), Paris, 1967.

Sartori, C., *Bibliografia della musica*

strumentale italiana, 2 vols., Florence, 1952–68.

Sartori, C., *Bibliografia delle opere musicali stampate da O. Petrucci*, Florence, 1948.

Sartori, Claudio, 'Nuove conclusive aggiunte alla "Bibliografia" del Petrucci', *Collectanea Historiae Musicae*, I (1953), 175–210.

Sas, Andrés, 'La vida musical en la catedral de Lima durante la colonia', *Revista Musicale Chilena*, xvi (1962), 8–53.

Saulnier, V. L., 'D. Phinot et D. Lupi, Musiciens de C. Marot et des marotiques', *Revue de Musicologie*, xliii–xliv (1959), 61–80.

Schaeffner, André, *Origines des Instruments de Musique*, Paris, 1936.

Scharnagl, A., ed., *Ludovico Grossi da Viadana Missa Pro Defunctis*, (Musica Divina, 19), Regensburg, 1966.

Schering, A., ed., *Geschichte der Musik in Beispielen*, Leipzig, 1931.

Schering, A., *Studien zur Musikgeschichte der Frührenaissance*, Leipzig, 1914. [Appendix, no. 3: Fulda].

Schlager, K., ed., *Alleluia-Melodien (I) – bis 1100* (Monumenta monodica medii aevi, vii), Kassel, 1968.

Schlesinger, K., *The Greek Aulos*, London, 1939.

Schmid, E. F., ed., *Lechner: Lieder aus Newe Teutsche Lieder (1582)*, Augsburg, 1926.

Schmidt, Carolus, *Quaestiones de musicis scriptoribus Romanis, inprinis de Cassiodoro et Isidoro*, Darmstadt, 1899.

Schmidt, Günther, 'Strukturprobleme der Mehrstimmigkeit im Repertoire von St. Martial', *Musikforschung*, xv (1962), 11–39.

Schmidt, Günther, 'Zur Frage des Cantus firmus im 14. und beginnenden 15. Jahrhundert', *AfMW*, xv (1958), 230–50.

Schmidt, H., 'Die Tractus des zweiten Tones in gregorianischer und stadtrömischer Überlieferung', in *Festschrift Schmidt-Görg*, pp. 283–302.

Schmidt, H., 'Zur Melodiebildung Leonins und Perotins', *ZfMW*, xiv (1931–2), 129–34.

Schmidt-Görg, J., ed., *Gombert: Opera Omnia (CMM, vi)*, 10 vols., Rome, 1951–70.

Schmitz, A., ed., *Oberitalienische Figuralpassionen des 16. Jahrhunderts, (*Musikalische Denkmäler, 1), Mainz, 1955.

Schmitz, A., 'Zur motettischen Passion des 16. Jahrhunderts', *AfMW*, xvi (1959), 232–45.

Schneider, Max, ed., *Diego Ortiz: Tratado de glosas ... (Rome, 1553)*, Kassel, 1913.

Schneider, Max, ed., *Ganassi: Regola Rubertina* (facsimile) 2 vols., Leipzig, 1924.

Schneider, Marius, *Geschichte der Mehrstimmigkeit*, 2 vols., Berlin, 1934–5 [Reprinted Tutzing, 1969].

Schnoor, H., 'Das Buxheimer Orgelbuch', *ZfMW*, iv (1921–22), 1–10.

Schoeberlein, L. F. and Riegel, F., edd., *Schatz des liturgischen Chor- und Gemeindegesanges*, 3 vols., Göttingen, 1865–72 [52 songs by Eccard, 11 by Dressler].

Schofield, B., 'The Provenance and Date of "Sumer Is Icumen In"', *Music Review*, ix (1948), 81–6.

Schofield, B., and Bukofzer, Manfred, F., 'A Newly Discovered Fifteenth-Century Manuscript...', *MQ*, xxxii (1946), 509–36 and xxxiii (1947), 38–51.

Schofield, B. and Dart, T., 'Tregian's Anthology', *ML* xxxii (1951), 205–16.

Schrade, L., *Commentary* to Vols. i–iv of *Polyphonic Music*, 3 vols., Monaco, 1956–8. i: covering Vol. I; ii: covering Vols. II–III; iii: covering Vol. IV.

Schrade, Leo, 'The Cycle of the Ordinarium Missae' in *Festschrift Handschin*, pp. 87–96.

Schrade, Leo, 'A Fourteenth Century Parody Mass', *Acta*, xxvii (1955), 13–39.

Schrade, L., ed., *Luis Milan: Libro de música de vihuela de mano* (Publikationen älterer Musik, ii), Leipzig, 1927 (Reprinted 1967).

Schrade, L., *Monteverdi, Creator of Modern Music*, New York, 1950.

Schrade, Leo, 'P. de Vitry, some new discoveries', *MQ*, xlii (1956), 330–54.

Schrade, Leo, 'Political Compositions in French Music...', *Annales Musicologiques*, i (1953), 9–63.

Schrade, L., *Die handschriftliche Überlieferung der ältesten Instrumentalmusik*, Lahr, 1931. [2nd edn. Tutzing, 1968].

Schrade, L., Harrison, F. L. and Marrocco, W. T., edd., *Polyphonic Music of the Fourteenth Century*, 6 vols., Monaco, 1956–68.

i, ed. Schrade: Roman de Fauvel, Vitry, French Cycles; ii, ed. Schrade: Machaut

(Lais, Motets 1–16, etc.); iii, ed. Schrade: Machaut (Motets 17–24, Mass, Hoquet, Ballades, Rondeaux, Virelais); iv, ed. Schrade: Landini; v, ed. Harrison: Motets of French Provenance; vi, ed. Marrocco: Piero, Giovanni da Firenze, Jacopo da Bologna.

Schröder, O. and Schneider, M. (and others), edd., *Walter: Werke*, Kassel, 1953 ff. [vols. i, ii, iii, v, vi published up to 1970].

Schubiger, A., *Musikalische Spicilegien über das liturgische Drama* (Eitner, *Publikationen*, v), Leipzig, 1876.

Schuler, E. A., *Die Musik der Osterfeiern, Osterspiele und Passionen des Mittelalters, I*, Kassel, 1950.

Schuler, M., ed., *Giorgio Mainerio. Il primo libro de balli (Venedig 1578)*, (Musikalische Denkmäler, 5), Mainz, 1961.

Schwarz, R., ed., *Ottaviano Petrucci: Frottole I und IV*, Leipzig, 1935.

Schweiger, H., 'Archivalische Notizen zur Hofkantorei Maximilians I', *ZfMW*, xiv (1931–2), 363–74.

Seay, A., ed., *Arcadelt: Opera Omnia* (*CMM*, xxxi), Rome, 1965 ff. i: Masses; iii–vi: Madrigals; vii–ix: Chansons; x: Motets.

Seay, A., 'The 15th-Century Cappella at Santa Maria del Fiore in Florence', *JAMS*, xi (1958), 45–55.

Seay, Albert, *Music in the Medieval World* (Prentice Hall History of Music Series), Englewood Cliffs (N.J.), 1965.

Seidel, Wilhelm, *Die Lieder Ludwig Senfls* (Neue Heidelberger Studien zur Musikwissenschaft, ii), Bern, 1969.

Seiffert, M., ed., *Sweelinck: Werken*, 10 vols., Hague/Leipzig, 1894–1901.

Seiffert, M. and Sigtenhorst Meyer, B. van den, edd., *Sweelinck: Opera Omnia, Editio Altera*, Amsterdam, 1943 ff.

Senn, W., *Musik und Theater am Hof zu Innsbruck*, Innsbruck, 1954.

Shaaber, M. A. and Leach, E., edd., Ravenscroft: *Pammelia, Deuteromelia, Melismata*, Philadelphia, 1961.

Sievers, H., *Die lateinischen liturgischen Osterspiele der Stiftskirche St. Blasien zu Braunschweig* (Kieler Beiträge zur Musikwissenschaft, ii), Berlin, 1936.

Sievers, H., ed., *Das Wienhäuser Liederbuch* [facs. & transcr.], 2 vols., Wolfenbüttel, 1954.

Silliman, A. C., '"Responce" and "Replique" in Chansons published by T. Susato', *Revue Belge de Musicologie*, xvi (1962), 30–42.

Simpson, Claude M., ed., *The British Broadside Ballad and its Music*, New Brunswick (N.J.), 1966.

Slim, H. C., 'Francesco da Milano: a Bio-Bibliographical Study', *Mus. Disc.*, xviii (1964), 63–84; xix (1965), 109–28.

Slim, H. C., 'Keyboard Music at Castell' Arquato by an Early Madrigalist', *JAMS*, xv (1962), 35–47.

Slim, H. C., ed., *Musica nova, Venice 1540*, (Monuments of Renaissance Music, i), Chicago, 1965.

Smallman, B., *The Background of Passion Music*, London, 1957; 2nd edn., New York, 1970.

Smijers, A., ed., *Josquin: Collected Works*, Amsterdam, 1921–65 [in 53 fascicles, subdivided into 3 series, namely, Masses, Motets and Secular Works; fasc. V may also be referred to as Secular Works, ii].

Smijers, A. and Crevel, M. van, edd., *Obrecht: Opera Omnia* [new edn.], Amsterdam, 1957 ff. [in progress].

Smijers, A. and Merritt, A. T., edd., *Motets parus chez Attaingnant*, 14 vols., Monaco, 1934–64.

Smith, Alan, 'Elizabethan Church Music at Ludlow', *ML*, xlix (1968), 108–21.

Smith, Alan, 'Parish Church Musicians in England ... (1558–1603)', *Royal Musical Association Research Chronicle*, iv (1964), 42–92.

Smith, G. P., ed., *The Madrigals of Cipriano de Rore for 3 and 4 voices*, (Smith College Music Archives, vi), Northampton, Mass., 1943.

Smith, Norman E., 'Tenor Repetition in the Notre Dame Organa', *JAMS*, xix (1966), 329–51.

Smither, H. E., 'Narrative and Dramatic Elements in the Laude Filippine, 1563–1600', *Acta*, xli (1969), 186–99.

Smits Van Waesberghe, J., Fischer, P., Maas, C., edd., *The Theory of Music from the Carolingian Era up to 1400*, 2 vols. (Répertoire Internationale des Sources Musicales, vol. B III^{1,2}), München-Duisberg, 1961–8.

Smoldon, W. L., 'The Easter Sepulchre Drama', *ML*, xxvii (1946), 1–17.

Smoldon, W.L., 'Liturgical Drama', in *NOHM*, ii, 175–219.

Smoldon, William L., 'Mediaeval lyrical Drama and the Latin Chant', *MQ*, li (1965), 507–17.

Snížková, Jitka, ed., *Česká polyfonní tvorba*, Prague, 1958.

Snow, R.J., ed., *Costanzo Porta: Musica in introitus missarum*, 2 vols., Cincinnati, 1958–61.

Somma, B., ed., *Vecchi: Le veglie di Siena* and *Vecchi: Amfiparnaso* (Capolavori ... del sec. XVI, ii and v), Rome, 1940 and 1953.

Southern, E., *The Buxheim Organ Book* (Institute of Mediaeval Music, Musicological Studies, vi), Brooklyn, N.Y., 1963.

Southern, E., 'Some Keyboard Basse Dances of the Fifteenth Century', *Acta*, xxxv (1963), 114–24.

Spanke, Hans, 'St. Martialstudien', *Zeitschrift für französische Sprache und Literatur*, liv (1931), 282 & 385.

Spanke, Hans, 'La teoriá árábe sobre el origin de la lírica románica', *Annuario Musical*, i (1946), 5–18.

Sparks, E.H., *Cantus Firmus in Mass and Motet*, Berkeley (Cal.), 1963.

Speer, Klaus, ed., *Padovano: Toccate e Ricercari* [1604] (Corpus of Early Keyboard Music, xxxiv), Rome, 1969.

Spitzer, L., 'The Mozarabic Lyric and Theodor Frings', Theories', *Comparative Literature*, iv (1952), 1–22.

Squire, W.Barclay, 'Who was "Benedictus"?', *SIMG*, xiii (1911–12), 264–71.

Stäblein, Bruno, (ed.), *Hymnen (I) – Die mittelalterlichen Hymnenmelodien des Abendlandes* (Monumenta monodica medii aevi, i), Kassel, 1956.

Stäblein, Bruno, 'Eine Hymnusemelodie als Vorlage einer provenzalisches Alba' in *Festschrift Anglès*, ii, 889–94.

Stäblein, Bruno, 'Modale Rhythmen im Saint-Martial-Repertoire?', in *Festschrift Blume*, p. 340.

Stäblein, Bruno, 'Zur Stilistik der Troubadour-Melodien', *Acta*, xxxviii (1966), 27–46.

Stäblein-Harder, H., ed., *Fourteenth Century Mass Music in France* (CMM, xxix), Rome, 1962.

Stäblein-Harder, H., *Fourteenth century mass music in France: Critical Text* (Musicological Studies and Documents, vii), Rome, 1962.

Stainer, Sir John, ed., *Early Bodleian Music*, 3 vols. London, 1901 [Reprinted 1967].

Stainer, Sir John, J.F.R., and C., edd., *Dufay and his Contemporaries*, London, 1898.

Steele, Robert, *The Earliest English Music Printing*, London, 1903 (Reprinted London, 1965).

Steiner, Ruth, 'The Prosulae of the MS Paris ...', *JAMS*, xxii (1969), 367–93.

Steiner, Ruth, 'Some Monophonic Latin Songs Composed Around 1200', *MQ*, lii, (1966), 56–70.

Steiner, Ruth, 'Some questions about the Gregorian offertories and their verses', *JAMS*, xix (1966), 162–81.

Stern, S.M., *Les Chansons Mozarabes*, Palermo, 1953; 2nd edn., Oxford, 1964.

Sternfeld, F.W., *Music in Shakespearean Tragedy*, London, 1963; rev. edn., 1967.

Sternfeld, F.W., 'Music in the Schools of the Reformation', *Mus. Disc.*, ii (1948), 99–122.

Stevens, Denis, ed., *Carver: Collected Works* (CMM, xvi), vol. i, Rome, 1959.

Stevens, D., 'La chanson anglaise avant l'école madrigaliste', in Jacquot, *Poésie*, pp. 121–7.

Stevens, D., ed., *In nomine: Altenglische Kammermusik zu 4 und 5 Stimmen* (Hortus Musicus, cxxxiv), Kassel, 1956.

Stevens, D., 'Madrigali guerrieri et amorosi: A Reappraisal for the Quatercentenary', *MQ*, liii (1967), 161–87.

Stevens, D., 'The Manuscript Edinburgh, National Library of Scotland, Adv. Ms. 5.1.15', *Mus. Disc.*, xiii (1959), 155–67.

Stevens, D., 'Monteverdi's "Vespers" Verified', *Musical Times*, cii (1961), 422.

Stevens, D., *The Mulliner Book: A Commentary*, London, 1952.

Stevens, D., 'Processional Psalms in Faburden', *Mus. Disc.*, ix (1955), 105–10.

Stevens, D., 'A Recently Discovered English Source of the 14th Century', *MQ*, xli (1955), 26–40.

Stevens, D., 'The Second Fountains Fragment: A Postscript', *ML*, xxxix (1958), 148–53.

Stevens, D., *T. Tomkins*, London, 1957.

Stevens, D., 'Where are the Vespers of

Yesteryear? [Claudio Monteverdi]', *MQ*, xlvii (1961), 315–50.

Stevens, John, ed., *Medieval Carols* (Musica Britannica, iv), London, 1952 [Revised 1958] Reviewed by Bukofzer, Manfred F., in *JAMS*, vii (1954), 163–82.

Stevens, John, *Music and Poetry in the Early Tudor Court*, London, 1961.

Stevens, John, ed., *Music at the Court of Henry VIII* (Musica Britannica, xviii), London, 1962.

Stevens, John, 'Rounds and Canons from an Early Tudor Song-book', *ML*, xxxii (1951), 29–37.

Stevenson, Robert, 'The Afro-American Musical Legacy to 1800', *MQ*, liv (1968), 475–502.

Stevenson, Robert, 'The Bogota Music Archive', *JAMS*, xv (1962), 292–315.

Stevenson, Robert, *Cathedral Music in Colonial Peru*, Lima, 1959.

Stevenson, Robert, 'Colonial Music in Colombia', *The Americas: A Quarterly Review of Inter-American Cultural History*, xix (1962), 121–36.

Stevenson, Robert, 'Cristobal de Morales (ca. 1500–53). A Fourth Centenary Biography', *JAMS*, vi (1953), 3–42.

Stevenson, Robert, 'European Music in 16th-Century Guatemala', *MQ*, l (1964), 241–52.

Stevenson, Robert, *Juan Bermudo*, The Hague, 1960.

Stevenson, Robert, *Music in Aztec and Inca Territory*, Berkeley and Los Angeles, 1968.

Stevenson, Robert, *Music in Mexico: a Historical Survey*, New York, 1952.

Stevenson, Robert, 'Music in Quito: Four Centuries', *Hispanic American Historical Review*, xliii (1963), 247–66.

Stevenson, Robert, *The Music of Peru: Aboriginal and Viceroyal Epochs*, Washington, D.C., 1960.

Stevenson, Robert, *Spanish Cathedral Music in the Golden Age*, Berkeley and Los Angeles, 1961.

Stevenson, Robert, *Spanish Music in the Age of Columbus*, The Hague, 1960.

Sticca, Sandro, 'A Note on Latin Passion Plays', *Italica*, xli (1964), 430–3.

Straeten: see Van der Straeten

Stratman, C.J., *Bibliography of the Mediaeval Drama*, Berkeley (Calif.), 1954.

Strom, R., 'Neue Quellen zur liturgischen Mehrstimmigkeit des Mittelalters in Italien', *Rivista italiana della musicologia*, i (1966), 77–87.

Strunk, Oliver, 'Byzantine Music in the Light of Recent Research and Publication' in *Congress Oxford 1966, Byzantine*, pp. 245–54.

Strunk, Oliver, *Source Readings in Music History*, New York, 1950.

Strunk, Oliver, *Specimina Notationum Antiquiorum* (Monumenta Musicae Byzantinae, sér. principale, vol. vii) Copenhagen, 1967.

Strunk, Oliver, 'The Tonal System of Byzantine Music', *MQ*, xxviii, (1942), 190–204.

Subirá, José, *Historia de la música española e hispanoamericana*, Barcelona, 1953.

Sutherland, G., 'The Ricercari of J.Buus', *MQ*, xxxi (1945), 448–63.

Szweykowski, Zygmunt, ed., *Music in Old Cracow*, Cracow, 1964.

Szweykowski, Zygmunt, ed., *Z dziejów polskiej kultury muzycznej*, I, Cracow, 1958.

Tadlock, R.J., 'Alessandro Striggio, Madrigalist', *JAMS*, xi (1958), 29–40.

Tagmann, P.M., *Archivalische Studien zur Musikpflege am Dom von Mantua (1500–1627)*, Bern, 1967.

Teschner, G.W., ed., *Eccard* [Several editions of Eccard's songs, published at Leipzig and Magdeburg between 1858 and 1870].

Thannabaur, Peter Joseph, *Das einstimmige Sanctus der römischen Messe in der handschriftliche Überlieferung des XI. bis XVI Jhdt.* Erlangen, 1962.

Therstappen, H.J., ed. [several works of Lasso, some of them published in the series *Das Chorwerk*, Wolfenbüttel, Berlin, and Kassel, 1929 ff.: *Prophetiae Sibyllarum*, vol. xlviii (1937), *Lagrime di San Pietro*, vols. xxxiv, xxxvii, xli (1935–6), *Sacrae Lectiones*, Berlin (n.d. {1948})].

Thibault, G., 'Un ms. de chansons françaises à la Bibliothèque Royale de la Haye' in *Festschrift Scheurleer*, pp. 347–58.

Thibault, G. and Perceau, L., *Bibliographie des chansons de P.de Ronsard mises en musique au XVIe siècle*, Paris, 1941.

Thierfelder, A. and Claussen, B., edd., *Rostocker Nieder-Deutsches Liederbuch …*, Rostock, 1919.

Thurston, Ethel, ed., *The Music in the St.*

Victor Manuscript, Paris Lat. 15139 (Pontifical Institute of Mediaeval Studies and Texts, v), Toronto, 1959.

Tintori, G. and Monterosso, R., edd., *Sacre Rappresentazioni ... [MS 201] ... Orléans* (Instituta et Monumenta, ser. 1, vol. ii), Cremona, 1958.

Tischler, Hans, 'The Evolution of Form in the Earliest Motets', *Acta*, xxxi (1959), 86–90.

Tischler, Hans, 'The Evolution of the Harmonic Style in the Notre-Dame Motet', *Acta*, xxviii (1956), 87–95.

Torchi, L., *L'arte musicale in Italia*, 7 vols., Milan, 1897–1907.

Torchi, L., *La musica strumentale in Italia nei secoli XVI, XVII e XVIII*, Turin, 1901.

Treitler, Leo, 'The Polyphony of St. Martial', *JAMS*, xvii (1964), 29–42.

Trend, J.B., *Alfonso the Sage and other Spanish Essays*, London, 1926.

Trend, J.B., 'Cristóbal Morales', *ML*, vi (1925), 19–34.

Trend, J.B., *Luis Milan and the Vihuelistas*, London, 1925.

Trend, J.B., *The Music of Spanish History to 1600*, London, 1926.

Trend, J.B., 'Salinas: a sixteenth century collector of folk songs', *ML*, viii (1927), 13–24.

Trowell, Brian, 'Faburden and Fauxbourdon', *Mus. Disc.*, xiii (1959), 43–78.

Trumble, Ernest, 'Authentic and Spurious Faburden', *Revue Belge de Musicologie*, xiv (1960), 3–29.

Tudor Church Music, edd. P.C.Buck, A.Ramsbotham, E.H.Fellowes and others, 10 vols., London 1922–9 [Taverner, Byrd, Gibbons, White, Tallis, Tomkins, Aston, Marbeck, Parsley].

Tumanina, N.V., ed., *Istoriya russkoy muzyki*, I, Moscow, 1957.

Turner, E.G., 'Two unrecognised Ptolemaic papyri', *Journal of Hellenic Studies*, lxxvi (1956), 95–8.

Ursprung, O., ed., *Kerle: Werke I* (*DTB*, xxvi), Leipzig, 1926 [contains *Preces Speciales*].

Ursprung, Otto, 'Spanisch-katalanische Liedkunst der 14. Jahrhunderts', *ZfMW*, iv (1921), 136–60.

Ursprung, O., 'Vier Studien zur Geschichte des deutschen Liedes', *AfMW*, iv (1922), 413–19; v (1923), 11–30 and 316–26; vi (1924), 262–323.

Van, G. de, ed., *G.de Machaut: La Messe de Notre Dame* (*CMM*, ii), Rome, 1949.

Van, G. de, ed., *Les Monuments de l'Ars Nova. Fascicle 1. Morceaux liturgiques 1. Oeuvres italiennes*, Paris, 1938.

Van den Borren: s.v. Borren.

Van der Straeten, E., *La musique aux Pay-Bas avant le XIXᵉ siècle*, 8 vols. Brussels, 1867–8. (reprinted, intr. E.Lowinsky, New York, 1969).

Vander Werf, Hendrik, 'Deklamatorischer Rhythmus in den Chansons der Trouvères', *Musikforschung*, xx (1967), 122–44.

Vander Werf, Hendrik, 'Recitative Melodies in Trouvère Chansons', in *Festschrift Wiora*, p. 231.

Vander Werf, Hendrik, 'The Trouvère Chansons as Creations of a Notationless Musical Culture', *Current Musicology*, i (1965), 61–8.

Vecchi, Giuseppe, 'Tra monodia e polifonia', *Collectanea Historia Musicae*, ii (1957), 447–64.

Vecchi, Giuseppe, 'Uffici Drammatici Padovani', *Biblioteca dell' "Archivum Romanum"*, Series I, vol. xli (1954).

Velimirović, M., *Byzantine Elements in Early Slavic Chant* (Monumenta Musicae Byzantinae, ser. subsidia, iv), 2 vols., Copenhagen, 1960.

Velimirović, M., 'The Influence of the Byzantine Chant on the Music of the Slavic Countries' in *Congress Oxford 1966, Byzantine*, pp. 119–40.

Velimirović, M., 'Stand der Forschung über kirchenslavische Musik', in *Zeitschrift für slavische Philologie*, xxxi (1963), 321–30.

Velimirović, M., ed., *Studies in Eastern Chant*, vol. i, London, 1966; ii, London, 1971.

Verchaly, A., 'Desportes et la musique', *Annales Musicologiques*, II (1954), 271–345.

Verchaly, A., ed., *Planson: Airs (1587)*, Paris, 1966.

Verchaly, A., 'Le recueil authentique des chansons de J.Chardavoine', *Revue de Musicologie*, xlix (1963), 203–19.

Vergili, L., ed., *Madrigalisti italiani*, i ff, Rome, 1952 ff.

Vetter, W., 'Musik', in Pauly and Wissowa, edd., *Real-Encyclopädie der classischen Altertumswissenschaft*, Stuttgart, 1893 ff.

Vey, Rudolph, *Christliches Theater in Mittelalter & Neuzeit*, Zurich, 1960.

Vicentino, N., *L'antica musica, ridotto alla moderna prattica*, Rome, 1555. Facs. ed. E.E.Lowinsky (Documenta musicologica, 17), Basel, 1959.

Villalba Muñoz, Luis de., ed., *Diez canciones españoles de los siglos XV y XVI*, Madrid, n.d. [ca. 1914].

Vogel, Cyrille, 'L'Hymnaire de Murbach contenu dans le manuscrit Junius 25 (Oxford, Bodleian Library 5137), un témoin du cursus bénédictin ou cursus occidental ancien', *Archives de l'Eglise d'Alsace*, ix (1958), 1–42.

Vogel, E., *Bibliothek der gedruckten weltlichen Vocalmusik Italiens aus den Jahren 1500–1700*, 2 vols., Berlin, 1892: reprint revised by A.Einstein, Hildesheim, 1962. [See also: Hilmar].

Vogel, M., *Die Enharmonik der Griechen*, 2 vols., Düsseldorf, 1963.

Wagenaar-Nolthenius, Hélène, 'Der "Planctus Judei" und der Gesang jüdischer Märtyrer in Blois anno 1171' in *Festschrift Crozet*, ii, 881–7.

Wagner, Peter, *Die Gesänge des Jacobusliturgie zu Santiago de Compostela*, Freiburg im Breisgau, 1931.

Wagner, Peter, *Geschichte der Messe, 1. Teil: bis 1600*, Leipzig, 1913. [Reprinted Hildesheim, 1963].

Wagner, Peter, 'Der mozarabische Kirchengesang und seine Überlieferung', *Spanische Forschungen der Görresgesellschaft*, first series, i (1928), 102–41.

Wagner, P., 'Rheinisches Osterspiel in einer Handschrift des 17. Jahrhunderts', *Zeitschrift für deutsches Altertum*, lvi (1918) (Neue Folge, xliv), 100–8.

Wagner, Peter, *Ursprung und Entwicklung der liturgischen Gesangformen*, 1st edn.: Freiburg, 1895; 2nd edn.: 1901 [transl. *Origin and Development of the Liturgical Chant*, London, 1907]; 3rd edn.: 1911 [reprinted 1962].

Waite, William G., 'The Abbreviation of the Magnus Liber', *JAMS*, xiv (1961), 147–58.

Waite, William G., ed., *The Rhythm of Twelfth-Century Polyphony*, New Haven, 1954.
    Reviewed by Bukofzer, Manfred F., in *Notes*, xii (1955), 232–6.

Walker, D.P., 'The Aims of Baïf's Académie…' *Mus. Disc.*, i (1946), 91–100.

Walker, D.P., ed., *Les Fêtes … Florence 1589 … Intermèdes de la Pellegrina*, Paris, 1963.

Walker, D.P., ed., *Le Jeune: Airs (1608)*, 3 vols., Rome, 1951–9.

Walker, D.P., 'Musical Humanism in the 16th and Early 17th Centuries', *Music Review*, ii (1941), 1–13, 111–21, 220–7, 288–308; iii (1942), 55–71 [German tr.: *Der musikalische Humanismus*, Kassel, 1949].

Walker, D.P., 'Some Aspects and Problems of *musique mesurée à l'antique*', *Mus. Disc.*, iv (1950), 163–86.

Wallner, B.A., ed., *Das Buxheimer Orgelbuch* [facs. and commentary] (Documenta Musicologica, ser. ii, vol. i), Kassel, 1955.

Wallner, B.A., ed., *Das Buxheimer Orgelbuch* [transcr. and commentary] (Erbe deutscher Musik, ser. i, vols. xxxvii–xxxix), Kassel, 1958–9.

Wallner, B.A., *Musikalische Denkmäler der Steinatzkunst …*, Munich, 1912.

Ward, J.M., 'Apropos *The British Broadside Ballad and its Music*', *JAMS*, xx (1967), 28–86.

Ward, J.M., 'The Editorial Methods of Venegas de Henestrosa', *Mus. Disc.*, vi (1952), 105–13.

Ward, J.M., 'The Lute in 16th Century Spain', *The Guitar Review*, ix (1949), 26–8.

Ward, J.M., 'Music for *A Handefull of pleasant delites*', *JAMS*, x (1957), 151–80.

Ward, J.M., 'The Use of Borrowed Material in 16th century Instrumental Music', *JAMS*, v (1952), 88–98.

Ward, J.M., 'The *vihuela de mano* and its music 1536–76', Dissertation, New York, 1953.

Warlock, P., ed., *Dowland: Lachrymae*, London, 1927.

Warlock, P., ed., *Ravenscroft: Pammelia and other Rounds*, London, 1928.

Warren, Charles W., 'Music at Nonesuch', *MQ*, liv (1968), 47–57.

Warren, Edwin B., 'Life and Works of Robert Fayrfax', *Mus. Disc.*, xi (1957), 134–52.

Warren, Edwin B., 'The Masses of Robert Fayrfax', *Mus. Disc.*, xii (1958), 145–76.

Warren, Edwin B., ed., *Robert Fairfax:*

Collected Works (*CMM*, xvii), 3 vols., Rome, 1959–66.

Warren, Edwin B., 'Robert Fayrfax: Motets and Settings of the Magnificat', *Mus. Disc.*, xv (1961), 112–43.

Warren, F.E., *The Antiphonary of Bangor*, 2 vols. (Henry Bradshaw Society Nos. 4 and 10), London, 1893 and 1895.

Wasielewski, J.W. von, *Geschichte der Instrumentalmusik im 16. Jahrhundert*, Berlin, 1878.

Webern, A. v., ed., *Isaac: Choralis Constantinus, II* (*DTO*, xvi, part i), Vienna, 1909.

Wegner, M., *Das Musikleben der Griechen*, Berlin, 1949.

Wehrli, F., ed., *Aristoxenus* [Additional fragments; text and German commentary; in vol. ii of *Die Schule des Aristoteles*], Basle, 1945.

Weidner, Robert W., ed., *C.Tye: Instrumental Music* (Recent Researches in the music of the Renaissance, iii), New Haven, 1967.

Weinmann, Karl, *Das Konzil von Trient und die Kirchenmusik*, Leipzig, 1919.

Weismann, W., and Watkins, G.E., edd., *Gesualdo di Venosa, Madrigale*, i–vi, Leipzig and Hamburg, 1957–62.

Wellesz, Egon, *Eastern Elements in Western Chant*, (Monumenta Musicae Byzantinae, Ser. subsidia, ii), Oxford, 1947; 2nd rev. printing, Copenhagen, 1967.

Wellesz, Egon, 'Gregory the Great's letter on the Alleluia', *Annales Musicologiques*, ii (1954), 7–26.

Wellesz, Egon, *A History of Byzantine Music and Hymnography*, 2nd edn., Oxford, 1961.

Werner, Eric, *The Sacred Bridge, The Interdependence of Liturgy and Music in Synagogue and Church*, New York, 1959.

Werner, W., *Studien zu den Passions – und Osterspielen des deutschen Mittelalters in ihrem Uebergang vom Latein zur Volksprache*, Berlin, 1963.

Werra, E.von, 'Johann Buchner', *Kirchenmusikalisches Jahrbuch*, x (1895), 88–92.

Wesselofsky, A., ed., *Il Paradiso degli Alberti: ritrovi e ragionamenti del 1389 romanzo di Giovanni da Prato*, 3 vols., Bologna, 1867.

Wesseley, O., 'Neue Hofhaimeriana', *Anzeiger der Österreichische Akademie der Wissenschaften (Phil.-hist. Klasse)*, xcii (1955), 201–8.

Wessely, O., 'Neue Beiträge zur Lebensgeschichte von Erasmus Lapicida', *Kirchenmusikalisches Jahrbuch*, xli (1957), 16–19.

Westphal, K., ed., *Karnevalslieder der Renaissance*, (Chorwerk, xliii), Wolfenbüttel, 1936.

Westphal, R., ed., *Aristoxenos*. I, Commentary, Leipzig, 1883; II, Text, Leipzig, 1893.

Whitehill, Walter Muir and Prado, Germán, edd., *Liber Sancti Jacobi: Codex Calixtinus*, 3 vols., Santiago de Compostela, 1944.

Whyte, Florence, *The Dance of Death in Spain and Catalonia*, Baltimore, 1931.

Wilkins, N., 'The Codex Reina. A revised description (Paris, Bibl. Nat., ms. n.a.fr. 6771)', *Mus. Disc.*, xvii (1963), 57–73.

Wilkins, N., ed., *A 14th Century Repertory from Codex Reina* (*CMM*, xxxvi), Rome, 1966.

Wilkins, N., ed., *A 15th Century Repertory from Codex Reina* (*CMM*, xxxvii), Rome, 1966.

Wilkins, N., ed., *Lyric Works of Adam de la Hale* [Halle] (*CMM*, xliv), Rome, 1967.

Wilkins, N., ed., *Works of Jehan de Lescurel* (*CMM*, xxx), Rome, 1966.

Williams, S.J.M., 'The Music of G.de Machaut' (unpubl. diss., Yale, 1952), Ann Arbor, 1966 (microfilm).

Winnington-Ingram, R.P., 'Aristoxenus and the Intervals of Greek Music', *Classical Quarterly*, xxvi (1932), 195–208.

Winnington-Ingram, R.P., *Mode in Ancient Greek Music*, Cambridge, 1936.

Winnington-Ingram, R.P., 'The Pentatonic Tuning of the Greek Lyre: a theory examined', *Classical Quarterly, new series*, vi (1956), 169–86.

Winnington-Ingram, R.P., 'The Spondeion Scale', *Classical Quarterly*, xxii (1928), 83–91.

Winterfeld, C. von, *Johannes Gabrieli und seine Zeitalter*, 3 vols., Berlin, 1834. [Reprinted Hildesheim, 1965].

Wiora, W., ed., *Adrian Willaert und andere Meister, Italienische Madrigale*, (Chorwerk, v), Wolfenbüttel, 1930.

Wolf, J., *Geschichte der Mensural-Notation von 1250–1460*, 3 vols., Leipzig, 1904.

Wolf, J., ed., *Isaac: Weltliche Werke* (*DTO*,

xiv, part i, pp. 1–206 and xvi, part i, pp. 203–42), Vienna, 1907 and 1909.

Wolf, J., ed., *Musica practica B. Rami de Pareia* (Publikationen der Intern. Musikges., Beiheft ii), Leipzig, 1901.

Wolf, J., ed., *Obrecht: Collected Works*, 30 fascicles in 7 vols., Amsterdam/Leipzig, 1912–21 [reprinted in 7 vols., Farnborough, Hants., 1968].

Wolf, J., ed., *Rhau: Geistliche Gesänge (1544)* (*DDT*, xxxiv), Leipzig, 1908.

Wolf, J., ed., *Der Squarcialupi-Codex Pal. 87 der Biblioteca Laurenziana in Florenz*, Lippstadt, 1955.

Wolff, H.C., 'Die geistlichen Oden des Georg Tranoscius und die Odenkompositionen des Humanismus', *Die Musikforschung*, vi (1953), 300–13 and vii (1954), 39–53.

Woodfill, Walter L., *Musicians in English Society (from Elizabeth to Charles I)*, Princeton, 1953. (Reprinted New York, 1969).

Wooldridge, H.E., ed., *Early English Harmony*, 2 vols., London, 1897 and 1913.

Wooldridge, H.E., *The Polyphonic Period* (Oxford History of Music, i–ii), 2 vols., Oxford, 1901–5.

Yates, F., *The French Academies of the 16th Century*, London , 1947.

Young, Karl, *The Drama of the Mediaeval Church*, 2 vols., Oxford, 1933.

Young, William, 'Keyboard Music to 1600', *Mus. Disc.*, xvi (1962), 115–50; xvii (1963), 163–93.

Zaminer, Frieder, *Der Vatikanische Organum-Traktat (Ottob. lat. 3025)*, (Münchner Veröffentlichungen zur Musikgeschichte, ii), Tutzing, 1959.

Zarlino, G., *Dimostrationi harmoniche* [Venice, 1571], facs. edn., New York, 1965, and Ridgewood (N.J.), 1966.

Zarlino, G., *Le Istitutioni harmoniche* [Venice, 1558], facs. edn., New York, 1966. [3rd edn., Venice, 1573], facs. edn., Ridgewood (N.J.), 1966.

Zarlino, G., *Sopplimenti musicali* [Venice, 1588], facs. edn., Ridgewood, (N.J.), 1966.

Zenck, H., ed., *Dietrich: Hymnen [1545]* (Erbe deutscher Musik, ser. 1, xxiii), Leipzig, 1942. [2nd enl. edn., rev. W. Gurlitt, St. Louis, 1960].

Zenck, H., 'Die Musik in Deutschland von 1450 bis 1550', in *Numerus und Affectus*, ed. Gerstenberg, Kassel, 1959.

Zenck, H., *Sixtus Dietrich*, Leipzig, 1928.

Zenck, H. and Gerstenberg, W., edd., *Adriano Willaert: Opera omnia*, (*CMM*, iii), Rome, 1950 ff. [8 vols. published by 1972].

Zitzman, R., *Die Melodien der Kolmarer Liederhandschrift*, Würzburg, 1944.

Zöbeley, H.R., *Die Musik des Buxheimer Orgelbuchs* (Münchener Veröffentlichungen zur Musikgeschichte, x), Tutzing, 1964.

Supplement

Bank, J.A., *Tactus, Tempo and Notation in Mensural Music from the 13th to the 17th Century*, Amsterdam, 1972.

Caldwell, J.A., *English Keyboard Music before the Nineteenth Century*, Oxford, 1973.

Chiesa, R., ed., *Francesco da Milano: Opere complete per liuto*, 2 vols., Milan, 1971.

Jackson, P. and Nugent, C., edd., *Jachet of Mantua: Opera Omnia* (*CMM*, liv), Rome, 1971 ff. [1 vol. published by 1972].

Lincoln, H.B., ed., *The Madrigal Collection 'L'Amorosa Ero', Brescia, 1588*, New York, 1968.

Vaccaro, J-M., ed., *Oeuvres d'Albert de Rippe*, vol. 1, Paris, 1972.

Vander Werf, H., *The Chansons of the Troubadours and Trouvères*, Utrecht, 1972.

Wagner, L.J., ed., *George de La Hèle: Collected Works* (*CMM*, lvi), Rome, 1972.

Index

The index appears in two sections. Index I (pp. 488–506) deals with names and titles: persons, places, incipits of chants, madrigals, motets, songs, etc. Index II (pp. 506–24) deals with subjects and categories. There are the obvious musical topics, such as Chant, Chords, Homophony, Motet, *Organum*, Polyphony, Song, etc. There are also general historical categories such as Academies, Catholic, Censorship, Chapel, Court, Humanism, Protestant (with separate entries for Huguenot and Hussite).

In a few exceptional cases the border line between Index I and II is delicate. The reformer Jan Hus appears in I, but the Hussite movement in II.

The two largest categories in Index II are concerned with Manuscripts and Masses. Manuscripts are entered in Index II by the town in which they are located and consulted. For further information the reader is referred to the indispensable reference work in the field, *RISM* (*Répertoire international des sources musicales*). Seven volumes (by 1972), dedicated to manuscripts have appeared in three series: B III, Theory of Music, 2 vols.; B IV, Polyphonic Music, 4 vols.; and B V, Tropes and Sequences, 1 vol. In series B IV will be found, for example, full descriptions of the Squarcialupi Codex of Florence (vol. iv, pp. 755–832) or of the Franus Kancionál at Hradec Králové (vol. iii, pp. 141–63). The present index will assist the student by liberal cross-references to nicknames (Fitzwilliam, Franus, Squarcialupi), also to former names of towns (Breslau, see Wroclaw).

Masses are entered in Index II under three categories:

1. Mass (all aspects apart from individual polyphonic settings of Mass Fragments and Mass Settings);
2. Mass Fragments and Sections, polyphonic (individual compositions of Kyries or of related pairs, such as Gloria-Credo);
3. Mass Settings, polyphonic (individual compositions arranged by title).

Requiem Masses, polyphonic, are separately entered in Index II, pp. 520–1. See also Reese, *Renaissance*, p. 1006.

Apart from Manuscripts, Masses and Requiems, all musical incipits, titles and names of towns are entered in Index I.

Asterisks indicate the presence of music examples; the '*n*' refers to footnotes (i.e. 115*, 283*n*).

Caserta, 218, 221
Cassiodorus, 124, 126, 367–8
Casteliono, G.A., 250
Castellani, Castellano, 233
Castellanos, Juan de, 430
Castiglione, B., 236
Castile, 392
Castilleja, Pedro Fernández de, see Hernándes
Catalonia, 369, 371–2
Catherine de Clermont, 178
Cavalcanti, 212
Cavalieri, Emilio de', 249
Cavazzoni, Girolamo, 251
Cavazzoni, Marco Antonio (or Marco Antonio da Bologna or d'Urbino), 237, 252, 419
Ceballos (or Zaballos), Rodrigo de, 402
Ceciliade (A. Blondet), 189
Ce fu en mai (Moniot d'Arras), 132*
Celtes, Conrad, 349, 351
Cerone, Domenico Pietro, 409
Certain Notes, see Mornyng and Evenyng
Certon, Pierre, 177, 185, 187–8
Cesaris, Johannes, 161
Chaillou de Pestain, 155
Champagne (France), 156–7
Champion des Dames (Le Franc), 161, 298
Chansons (Sweelinck), 209
(Le) Chant des oiseaux (Janequin), 177
Charlemagne, 75
Charles I, Bohemia (= Charles IV, Emperor), 415
Charles V, Emperor, 192, 203, 386, 390, 392, 426
Charles V, France (1364–80), 146, 149–50, 157
Charles VI, France (1380–1422), 146, 150
Charles VII, France (1422–61), 146, 149, 169
Charles VIII, France (1483–98), 146, 149, 169
Charles IX, France (1560–74), 146, 178, 180–2, 191–2
Charles the Bold (Burgundy, earlier Charolais), 147, 168, 172–3
Chartier, Alain, 147, 169
Chartres Polyphony, 104, 191; see also Index II, s.v. Manuscripts
Chartres-Coislin, see Index II, s.v. Notation (c)
Chaucer, 147
Chinda(s)vinthus, King, Visigoths, 375
Chirbury, R., 293
Choralis Constantinus (Isaac), 104, 348
Christ rising (Byrd), 324
Christine de Pisan, 147, 150, 169
Chrysaphes, Manuel, 85
Il Cicalamento delle donne (Striggio), 244
Ciconia, Johannes, 167, 195, 221–2, 230, 417
Cino da Pistoia, 212
Circe, 182–3
Cirillo of Aquila, 246

Cisneros, Francesco Jiménez de, 367, 369–70
Cividale, 212
Clamabat autem . . . (Escobar), 384–5
Clamaverunt, 72
Clemens, Jacobus, non Papa, 185, 195, 201–10, 316, 319, 364
Clement of Alexandria, 368
Clereau, Pierre, 178
Clermont-en-Beauvais, 156
Cleve, Johann de, 360n
Cluny, 369
Coclico, Adrian Petit, 361
Codax (Codaz), Martin, 377
Cogul, 365
Coinci, Gautier de, 377
Colin Muset, 131
Colin, G., 193
Combattimento di Tancredi e Clorinda (Monteverdi), 242
Compendium musices (Coclico), 361
Compère, L., 185, 201–2, 225, 235
Compostela, Santiago de, 104, 373, 379; see also Index II, s.v. Manuscripts
Con brachi assai (Master Piero), 217
Con lagreme (lagrime) bagnandome . . . (Ciconia), 222n
Concerti ecclesiastici
  Banchieri, 254
  Viadana, 254
Condé, 199, 227
Conde claros
  404 (tune)
  Narváez, 404
  Valderrábano, 405
Conditor alme (paraphrase Coyssard), 189
Confundantur omnes (Clemens), 206
Congaudeant catholici (Albertus), 373
Conortz, aras say (Ventadorn), 130*
Conseil, Jean, 186
Consort Lessons
  Morley (1599), 337
  Rosseter (1607), 337
Constance, 348–9, 354, 357
Constance, Council of, 298
Constantine, Emperor, 65, 366
Constantinople, 29, 84–5, 88, 146, 369
Cooke (of Old Hall), 293
Cooper, see Coperario
Copenhagen, 361
Coperario (Cooper), John, 337
Coppinus, Alexander, 232
Cordier, Baude, 161
Cordova, 378
Cornago, Johannes, 381–2, 385
Cornazano, Antonio, 234
Cornysh, William (junior), 303–6
Corrado da Pistoia, 221
Corteccia, F., 233, 239, 245, 253
Cortés, H., 425–6
Cortona, 213
Coste, G., 193

INDEX II